POEMS FOR THE MILLENNIUM

The publisher gratefully acknowledges the support of the Leslie Scalapino Memorial Fund for Poetry, which was established by generous contributions to the University of California Press Foundation by Thomas J. White and the Leslie Scalapino–O Books Fund.

POEMS
for the MILLENNIUM

The University of California
Book of North African Literature

Volume Four

Edited with commentaries by
Pierre Joris
and
Habib Tengour

University of California Press
Berkeley   Los Angeles   London

NATIONAL ENDOWMENT FOR THE ARTS This project is supported in part by an award from the National Endowment for the Arts.

University of California Press, one of the most distinguished university presses in the United States, enriches lives around the world by advancing scholarship in the humanities, social sciences, and natural sciences. Its activities are supported by the UC Press Foundation and by philanthropic contributions from individuals and institutions. For more information, visit www.ucpress.edu.

University of California Press
Berkeley and Los Angeles, California

University of California Press, Ltd.
London, England

For credits, please see page 745. For figure credits, please see page 756.

Library of Congress Cataloging-in-Publication Data

Poems for the millennium, volume four : the University of California book of North African literature / edited with commentaries by Pierre Joris and Habib Tengour.
    p.   cm. — (Poems for the millennium ; 4)
   Includes bibliographical references and index.
   ISBN 978-0-520-26913-2 (cloth) — ISBN 978-0-520-27385-6 (pbk.)
   1. North African literature. I. Joris, Pierre. II. Tengour, Habib.
   PL8014.N652P64 2012
   808.8'9961—dc23   2012024995

Manufactured in the United States of America

21 20 19 18 17 16 15 14 13 12
10 9 8 7 6 5 4 3 2 1

The paper used in this publication meets the minimum requirements of ANSI/NISO Z39.48–1992 (R 2002) (*Permanence of Paper*).

*To those poets of the Maghreb and the Arab worlds
who stood up against the prohibitions.*

CONTENTS

A BOOK OF WRITING

FOURTH DIWAN
Resistance and Road to Independence

THANKS AND ACKNOWLEDGMENTS

As is the custom, we will thank those individuals who have helped us with the labor of this book and are closest to us toward the end of this note. But to start with, we want to acknowledge the push of what we would like to call the extreme contemporariness of history, as the edge of cultural and political events—in this case those of the so-called Arab Spring—coincided with and energized the final year of the redaction of this assemblage. In no small way are those events a vindication of a project that has been in the works for more than a decade now—with at least one of its aims being an assertion of the cultural importance of the Arabo-Berber heritage for the world. So our admiration and thanks go to all those in Tunisia and Libya, but also in Egypt and beyond, who have decided to take to the streets and reawaken the open-minded and pluralistic spirit that once animated the world of al-Andalus and the Maghreb. Upmost in our minds as we worked on this project were those Maghrebian poets, writers, and artists who suffered torture, imprisonment, and, all too often, death at the hands of repressive state systems, both colonial and postcolonial. We remember and thank all of them. May the names of two assassinated Algerian poets who were our personal friends—Youcef Sebti and Tahar Djaout—stand in for all of those courageous fighters for freedom and justice too numerous to name.

It is impossible to list in extenso all the Maghrebian, European, and American poets, writers, and scholars who contributed advice and counsel during the long decade it took to bring the idea of this book to fruition. But among those who functioned as continuous advisers, we give special thanks to the poets Mohammed Bennis, Abdellatif Laâbi, Khaled Mattawa, and Abdelwahab Meddeb. Marilyn Hacker and Madeleine Campbell have been wise advisers and excellent translators. Joseph Mulligan has done amazing gathering and translating from the Spanish for the Western Sahara section, and beyond. In Paris, Éditions de la Différence has graciously given us permission to use the work of many of its Maghrebian authors—*shukran!* More than thanks—as without his unstinting help and hard work as both gatherer and translator (especially of the melhun materials) this would be a different and much diminished book—are due to the Algerian poet and scholar Abdelfetah Chenni, who by right could be named the third coeditor. We also want to express our thanks and gratitude to poet, translator and scholar Peter Cockelbergh, who assisted throughout the process of this book with advice and translation help, and whose proofreading skills came to our rescue in that final proverbial nick of time. On this side of the ocean, we are deeply grateful to the other cofounder of the *Poems for the Millennium* series, Jerome Rothenberg, whose continuous support and advice have been invaluable, and to Charles Bernstein, whose enthusiasm for and defense of this project have been beyond the call of duty.

Institutional help has also played its role in advancing the cause of the book, and we thank the Ministère de la Culture of Luxembourg, which enabled several research trips to Algeria and Morocco. More locally we are grateful to the National Endowment for the Arts for its support and to the Leslie Scalapino Memorial Fund for Poetry, which was established by generous contributions to the University of California Press Foundation by Thomas J. White and the Leslie Scalapino–O Books Fund. Our team at University of California Press, led by Rachel Berchten, has been unstinting in its efforts to ensure a healthy natural birth to this oversize brainchild of ours. Of course the two editors could not have completed this task if Nicole Peyrafitte, son Miles Joris-Peyrafitte, and daughter Hind Tengour didn't have their backs during the often difficult—though always exhilarating—nomadic wanderings that the gathering and shaping of this volume demanded.

INTRODUCTION

This book has been incubating in our minds for a quarter century now, and we have been gathering material for even longer—with the aim of assembling and contextualizing a wide range of writing from North Africa previously unavailable in the English-speaking world. The result is, we believe, a rich if obviously not full dossier of primary materials of interest not only to scholars of world literature, specialists in the fields of Arab and Berber studies, but also to a general audience and to contemporary readers and practitioners of poetry who, to deturn a Frank O'Hara line, want "to see what the poets in North Africa are doing these days." It is a project meant as a contribution to the ongoing reassessment of both the literary and cultural studies fields in our global, postcolonial age. Its documentary and trans-genre orientation means that it not only features major authors and literary touchstones but also provides a first look at a wide range of popular cultural genres, from ancient riddles, pictographs, and magic formulas to contemporary popular tales and songs, and is also in part a work of ethnopoetics. Drawing on primary resources that remain little known and difficult of access, and informed by the latest scholarship, this gathering of texts illuminates the distinctively internationalist spirit typified by North African culture through its many permutations.

A combination of traditional and experimental literary texts and ethnopoetic material, this fourth volume in the ongoing *Poems for the Millennium* series of anthologies is a natural progression from its predecessors. Jerome Rothenberg and Pierre Joris edited the first two volumes, which present worldwide experimental poetries of the twentieth century. Volume 3, as a historical "prequel," covers the new and experimental poetries of nineteenth-century Romanticism worldwide. This volume—which we have at times half-jokingly thought of as a "sidequel," for its southerly departure from Europe and North America, the series's main focus—is conceptually linked to volume 3 in its attempt to present the historical processes that led to the most innovative contemporary work. And the first two, core volumes in fact include—although in a minimal manner, of necessity—a few of the Maghrebian authors who are revolutionizing writing in their countries today. Those books also show the importance of oral literature in contemporary experimentation, a theme deepened and broadened in the volume at hand.

Throughout the years of work on this book, our shorthand working title was "Diwan Ifrikiya," which has the advantage of being brief and concise, though the disadvantage of being slightly obscure compared to the longer, less elegant, but more explicit appellation *Book of North African Literature.* "Diwan Ifrikiya"—as we refer to it throughout this introduction—combines the well-known Arabic word for "a gathering, a collection or anthology" of poems, *diwan,* with one of the earliest names of (at least part of) the region that this book covers. *Ifrikiya* is an Arabization of the Latin word *Africa*— which the Romans took from the Egyptians, who spoke of "the land of the Ifri," referring to the original inhabitants of North Africa. The Romans called these people Berbers, but they call themselves the Amazigh, and even today tribal names—such as Beni Ifren—in their language, Tamazight, include words derived from *ifri.*

"Diwan Ifrikiya" is thus an anthology of the various and varied written and oral literatures of North Africa, the region known as the Maghreb, traditionally described as situated between the Siwa Oasis to the east (in fact, inside the borders of Egypt) and the Atlantic Ocean to the west, spanning the modern nation-states of Libya, Tunisia, Algeria, and Morocco—as well as the desert space of the Sahara. Given the nomadic habits of the Tuareg tribes, the larger Maghreb can include parts of Mali, Niger, and Chad, plus Mauritania, to the great desert's southwest, famous for its manuscript collections. (The spread of the various Amazigh peoples is also describable in terms of their basic food, namely the breadth and limits of the use of rolled barley and wheat flour, or couscous.) We have also included the extremely rich and influential Arab-Berber and Jewish literary culture of al-Andalus, which flourished in Spain between the ninth and fifteenth centuries. This culture was intimately linked to North Africa throughout its existence and even after its final disappearance following the *Reconquista,* given that a great part of Spain's Muslim and Jewish population fled toward the south then, seeking refuge in North Africa.

The time span of "Diwan Ifrikiya" reaches from the earliest inscriptions—prehistoric rock drawings in the Tassili and Hoggar regions in the southern Sahara; the first Berber pictograms—to the work of the current generation of postindependence and diasporic writers. Such a chronology takes in diverse cultures, including Amazigh, Phoenician, Jewish, Roman,

Vandal, Arab, Ottoman, and French constituents. It also covers a range of literary genres: although concentrating on oral and written poetry and narratives, especially those which invent new or renew preexisting literary traditions, our gathering also draws on historical and geographical treatises, philosophical and esoteric traditions and genres, song lyrics, current prose experiments in the novel and short story, and so forth.

From a wider or outside perspective, the overall chronological arrangement makes perceptible the crucial importance of this region in the development of Western culture, adding hitherto little-known or unknown historical data while showing how the Maghreb's present-day postcolonial achievements are major contributions to global world culture. In ancient times, the Maghreb was seen as the Roman Empire's breadbasket—we hope this book shows that at the intellectual and artistic levels this has remained so ever since. To be candid: North Africa is a region whose cultural achievements—including their impact on and importance for Western culture—have been not only passively neglected but often actively "disappeared" or written out of the record. This is true for the majority of this area's autochthonous writers and thinkers, even those few whose achievements have been recognized north of the Mediterranean—often because they became diaspora figures working in Europe. A few examples may suffice: Augustine is certainly considered a major church father, but his North African roots, if not totally obscured, are given little credit. Apuleius, the author of one of the first prose narratives that prefigure our novel, is known as a Latin or late Roman writer, not a Maghrebian. It is also interesting to note in this context that the last poet whose mother tongue was Latin was a Carthaginian, and that by an odd circumstance the first nonoral poet in our chronology, Callimachus—whose forebears immigrated to Cyrenaica (Libya), possibly from the Greek island of Thera, where the first ruler of the Battiad Dynasty came from—wrote in Greek.

We know that during the heyday of Arab-Islamic culture, and more specifically between 1100 and 1300 C.E., scribes and thinkers first safeguarded, then translated and transmitted to the Europeans, much of the Greek philosophy and science that we pride ourselves on as the roots of Western civilization. Many lived and worked in al-Andalus, that thriving center of culture on European shores—a place where a millennium ago Arabs, Jews, and Christians learned to live together in productive peace. Yet the core figures of this period of Arab culture, such as Ibn Khaldun, Ibn Battuta, and Al-Hasan Ibn Muhammad al-Wazzan al-Fasi—whom we know as Leo Africanus—if not unknown, are seriously marginalized in the West. Lip service may be paid to, say, Ibn Khaldun, as the father of sociology, or a French author of Lebanese origin may write a successful novel based on the figure of Leo Africanus, but the actual texts of these writers, thinkers, and mapmakers are rarely available to the Anglophone world—or are available only to specialists or, again, without much context with which to read and appreciate them.

Even if Arab culture went into a long sleep and the high-cultural productions of the Maghreb often became mere imitations of the classical Mashreqi (Near Eastern) models—and thus less creatively innovative—during the centuries between the fall of al-Andalus to the Spanish Christians and the conquest of North Africa by the colonial powers, there was much cultural activity then. This is especially true for the autochthonous Berber cultures which, despite having been Arabized (at least to the degree of accepting Islam, in many instances in a modified, maraboutic form), kept alive vital modes of popular oral literature, for example Berber tales and stories, plus elaborations and updated versions of the Arab-Berber epic of the Banu Hillal confederation. European anthropologists gathered much of this ethnopoetic material in the nineteenth and early twentieth century, but it has since faded from view, we surmise both from a lack of interest shown by the old colonizers and from a justifiable and understandable unease among Maghrebians toward this material so often labeled "primitive" or "preliterary" by those who recorded it. Besides which, the current Maghrebian societies are too busy trying to invent their own contemporaneity and to modernize themselves to have much time or desire to invest their limited resources in reassessing their remote pasts. If this anthology helps to dispel some of this unease or even incites other researchers and writers to look deeper into these hidden and buried histories, it will have accomplished one of its main goals.

The longtime neglect of such a major cultural area is part of a wider, now well-documented, Eurocentrism; permit us to cite an example germane to the project at hand. In the early days of Modernism, Ezra Pound spent time and energy establishing the roots of European lyric poetry, which he located in the French/Occitan troubadour tradition, a lineage that has become canonical over the past century. Open your *American Heritage Dictionary,* and you'll see that it gives the Latin *tropare* as the root of *troubadour*—an etymology that on closer inspection, however, turns out to be reconstructed, presumed, and unattested (i.e., marked with an asterisk). In fact, the field of romance philology has done everything in its power to negate any traces of a non-European origin of—or even strong foreign influence on—European lyric poetry. And yet it has been known since at least 1928, via the work of the Spanish linguist Julián Ribera, that the obvious root of *troubadour* is the Arabic *tarab,* "to sing," specifically to sing a musical poetry that produces an exalted state. (One could also link this ecstatic sense of tarab to Federico García Lorca's *duende*.) Pound, like nearly all other European and American writers and researchers, was looking for European origins—though in his

1913 essay on the troubadours he had a vague inkling that something else was going on, as far as the tunes of the troubadours' *canzos* are concerned: "They are perhaps a little Oriental in feeling, and it is likely that the spirit of Sufism is not wholly absent from their content." It is that kind of belittling and, in the final analysis, deeply denigrating attitude that "Diwan Ifrikiya" addresses and, we hope, redresses somewhat.

This anthology is organized into five approximately chronological diwans, inside which the authors appear in chronological order. Reading through them, one can get a sense of temporal progression and thus of the changes brought by history. The First Diwan, subtitled "A Book of In-Betweens: Al-Andalus, Sicily, the Maghreb," starts with an early, anonymous muwash-shaha—that lyrical poetic form invented in al-Andalus which moved Arabic poetry away from the imitation of classical qasida models going back to pre-Islamic forms. After a wide presentation of Arab and Jewish poets who made al-Andalus so incredible and possibly unique, the diwan ends with Ibn Zamrak's wonderful description of the Alhambra.

The next diwan, "Al Adab: The Invention of Prose," presents a range of materials—from literary criticism through Ibn Khaldun's writings (the ur-texts of what will become sociology) to historical, literary, and cultural doc-uments—that will give the reader a sense of the breadth and width of this pulsating and formative civilization. The Third Diwan, "The Long Sleep and the Slow Awakening," moves us from the end of the fifteenth century (and thus the end of al-Andalus, which can be dated to the final victory of the Spanish Reconquista, in 1492) to the end of the nineteenth, a period during which Arab culture—both in its cradle, the Middle East, and in its Western extension, the Maghreb (in fact, in Arabic *Maghreb* means "West," in both a geographical and a deeper cultural, even mystical, sense)—fell prey to what is usually called decadence, at the political, social, and cultural levels. For the Maghreb, however, even these centuries held creative excite-ment: it was then that one of the great poetic forms of North Africa, the *mel-hun,* came into its own by revitalizing its classical roots through both formal and linguistic innovations, including the use of the Maghrebian vernacular. The innovations and final grandeur of these poems, song lyrics really, are difficult to bring across in translation; suffice it to say that the poems have stood the test of time and still represent the core repertoire of the great mel-hun singers.

The Fourth Diwan, "Resistance and Road to Independence," covers about one hundred years: from the mid-nineteenth (the aftermath of the French colonization of Algeria) to the mid-twentieth century, that moment when the people of the Maghreb begin to demand—and fight for—sovereignty. The shock of colonization may at first have numbed these populations, but in the twentieth century they produced a literature of resistance while on what we have called the long road to independence. A specifically national or nationalist thought also emerged then, as a range of differences—between, before all, Tunisia, Algeria, and Morocco—rose to the surface and began to be theorized. Emblematic of this period are the diwan's two framing figures: Emir Abd El Kader, born in Mascara in 1808, the great nomad warrior who gathered the tribes to fight the French, was a superb writer and poet, a Sufi mystic, and a follower of Ibn Arabi's thought, who died in exile in Damascus; and Henri Kréa, the French-Algerian poet who fought for Algeria's independence and died in Paris in 2000. An amazing span—with other amazing figures, such as Abu al-Qasim al-Shabi, Frantz Fanon, and Kateb Yacine, whose work includes some of the first great classics of modern Maghrebian literature.

A double diwan concludes the book: although it covers only the past sixty or so years, its size demanded the split into two sections. We have divided it according to geography, grouping the two northeastern Maghreb countries (Libya and Tunisia) with the two relatively small countries in the southwest of our area, namely, Mauritania and Western Sahara, while keeping Algeria and Morocco for part 2. The writers in this diwan are those who came of age at the moment of independence and the two to three generations since then. This diwan's size and literary achievement show that the great richness that characterized early Maghrebian culture, even if buried for a time by the "decadence" of one of its foundational cultures and then by the strictures of European colonial impositions, has burst to the fore again—with a vengeance. This richness brings to mind the days of multicultural al-Andalus, even if today we would call it multinational or hybrid or cross-border. For instance, the youngest poet in the last—the Morocco—section of the book, Omar Berrada, sets his work presented here in the company of the three international figures whom he honors: the late-nineteenth-century French avant-gardist Alfred Jarry, the twentieth-century North American performance poet bpNichol, and the great Sufi poet and mystic Ibn Arabi (1165–1240), whom we will meet on several occasions throughout "Diwan Ifrikiya."

The diwans are interrupted, leavened, given breathing room—however you experience it—by a series of smaller sections, four "Books" and three "Oral Traditions," whose roles are multiple: filling in detail, giving context, or foregrounding specific areas. Thus "A Book of Multiple Beginnings" precedes the First Diwan, taking the reader from an early Berber inscription (see p. 10) to a prehistoric rock painting in the southern Sahara's Tassili and Hoggar region (see p. 12) through the first centuries of recorded literary output. The Phoenician, Greek, and Roman writings from this period include some of the world-class achievements of Maghrebian culture.

Creation myths and tales of origin logically open this section. This puts the autochthonous Berber peoples rightfully at the start of the Maghrebian adventure while also foregrounding a tradition—the oral tradition—that has consistently produced major literary achievements over several millennia. This tradition is so ample and important that we had to create three independent sections ("Oral Traditions 1–3") dispersed throughout the anthology to try to do justice to its richness—which persists today, as the third of the sections, presenting contemporary oral work, shows. The distribution of these sections also reflects the fact that many of this anthology's contemporary writers source and resource themselves in that oral tradition's imaginary—one could go so far as to consider it the Maghrebian collective unconscious.

The other books concentrate on the poetry of the Sufi mystics ("A Book of Mystics"), on the very specific poetics of Arabic calligraphy ("A Book of Writing")—a core sense-making, meditative, and aesthetic dimension of Arab culture—and, finally, on a few diasporic writers ("A Book of Exiles"), both those who have left North Africa for whatever reason but feel themselves Maghrebian despite their exilic position and those who have come and stayed, deciding to become Maghrebian or return to lost roots. Ironically, this smallest of subsections could be the largest: the diasporic or exilic dimension is one of the main characteristics of Maghrebian literature, given that the majority of its authors live and write on two or more shores.

Although it may seem counterintuitive for "A Book of Exiles" to include such writers as Hélène Cixous and Jacques Derrida, who are seen as essentially French (even if some of their work points to—and their late work indeed insists more and more on—the importance of their Maghrebian roots), their contributions here deal exactly with exile from the Maghreb and the related question of choice of language (see, for example, Derrida's essay *The Monolingualism of the Other,* which is a response to and an elaboration of the Moroccan poet and thinker Abdelkebir Khatibi's writings on this problem). Their work also helps to contextualize the problems of the surrounding obviously Maghrebian contemporary writers, who faced both the necessity of actual exile and the difficult decision of which language to write in. Although their mother tongue was usually one of several Berber languages or a *darija* (dialectal) variation of Arabic, more often than not they forwent these in favor of either the old colonial language, namely, French, or classical Arabic (which some Berbers, including even the great Algerian writer Kateb Yacine, consider as much of a colonial/imperial imposition as French).

Writing in French invariably connects the author with the old colonial metropole—no matter if he or she lives in the Maghreb or in self-imposed or forced exile elsewhere—as that's where the major publishing houses are (only recently have independent houses emerged in the Maghreb). Writing in Arabic means dealing with small local publishers and getting caught up in all the political and censorship problems this has meant for most of the time since independence, or trying to publish in Lebanon or Egypt, the major Mashreqi publishing centers. The latter is also fraught with problems, as Maghrebian and Mashreqian cultures do not necessarily coexist easily. But no matter if they publish in Paris or Beirut, these writers have little chance of being translated into and published in English. The little interest and financial support our cultural institutions and publishers have been able to garner for translations from French and Arabic have been squarely devoted to Parisian, Beiruti, and Cairene authors. Even greater are the difficulties of those Maghrebian authors who chose to write in Berber—though Morocco and Algeria have each recently declared it an official national language—or use the ancient tifinagh alphabet, as does the Tuareg poet Hawad, who now lives in southern France. It is therefore also an aim of this gathering to provide a space for the mixing and mingling (at least in English) of writers who in their own countries and in other (usually country- or language-specific) anthologies have to exist in a kind of de facto cultural apartheid.

Many if not most of the texts are appearing for the first time in English translation, while others are retranslations into contemporary American English of older Englished versions. The genres and the original languages—Tamazight (Berber), Greek, Latin, Arabic, and French—are manifold. Obviously a work of this order cannot be the work of one or even two persons. If we are the "author-editors" and, for some part, the translators of this anthology, we are fully aware of our limits: although between us we do have English, Latin, French, and Arabic, we do not know all the ages, all the languages, all the cultures that have contributed to this gathering. Our role has been threefold: (1) as the principal gatherers and arrangers of materials worked on by many other scholars, writers, and translators, (2) as the creators of the specific shape this book has taken (although here we owe a debt to Jerome Rothenberg, the collaborator with one of us on the first two volumes in the *Poems for the Millennium* series), and (3) as the purveyors of a range of translations done singly or in collaboration whenever no translations could be found, as well as of most of the contextual materials, such as prologues and commentaries, given to make more tangible and understandable the textual productions—poems, narratives, mystical visions, travel writings—of an area of the world not necessarily familiar to the general reader. To keep the volume from being overlong and to maintain focus on the texts themselves, we have not provided an individual commentary for every author although in many cases further information is included in the prologues. We do know the Maghreb well: Habib Tengour is Algerian, was born and raised in Algeria, taught at the University of Constantine for many years, and, though now based in Paris, returns to his home country and other Maghrebian countries a number of times a year. Pierre Joris also taught for three years in the 1970s at the University of Constantine (where he and Tengour met) and has since returned regularly to this book's three core countries: Morocco, Algeria, and Tunisia.

It is our contention that "Diwan Ifrikiya" is especially important today, at a moment in history when the West's, especially the United States', convulsive engagement with Arab culture is in such a disastrous deadlock. Paradoxically, the United States is publishing more books on Arab countries, regimes, economics, and politics than ever before, though nearly all of them concentrate on the negative and paranoia-creating aspects of "Islamic terrorism" and do their best to claim noncivilization status for the region they cover (by suggesting, for instance, that it suffers from a combination of "primitive," bloodthirsty religion and misuse of modern Euro-American technologies) or are written from similarly dismissive perspectives. Such works do not permit the reader to understand what deeply animates these populations, in truth so near to us yet always pushed back and occulted. A book concerned with Maghrebian cultural achievements, in fields such as literature and philosophy, allows us to share in this universe, which is part of ours, no matter how deeply repressed. Knowledge of the Maghreb is, we believe, essential in a world where a nomadic mind-set is crucial for understanding (or inventing) the new century—especially if we do not want to repeat some of the deadliest errors of the last.

It is a marvelous coincidence that although we first thought of this book a quarter century ago, we actually gathered and wrote it exactly when Tunisia and Libya saw the start of a revolution, called the Arab Spring, that is still going and may be the shape-shifter that will determine the outcome of this century. We hope that through its polyvalent view of the region's cultural achievements, our book will help to further a deeper understanding of this strategic part of the world.

Pierre Joris
Habib Tengour
New York / Paris
Spring 2011

A BOOK OF MULTIPLE BEGINNINGS

Prehistoric rock painting, southern Sahara Tassili region. From Henri Llote, Vers d'autres Tassilis *(Paris: Arthaud, 1976).*

PROLOGUE

(1) Human traces in North Africa go back to more than 40,000 years B.C.E. But our knowledge of them is limited to a specific area: the region of Gafsa in west-central Tunisia, with ramifications toward the high plains between Constantine and Sétif in Algeria, and areas of the Sahara and ancient Cyrenaica—modern Libya. In this region snail farms and a stone and bone industry were found, indicating that from about 8000 until 4000 B.C.E., the human inhabitants seem to have been rather sedentary: they lived on snails, plants, and wild fruit while also hunting mammals and birds. They had clearly discovered the concept and practice of art, as shown by the Capsian tools, worked ostrich eggs, and burned and incised stones found in the quarries of el-Mekta, Tunisia, and preserved in the Gafsa Museum. The Capsian cultures (named for the town of Gafsa, which in Roman times was known as Capsa) probably came into being later than those of the Sahara and the Sudan, which had evolved a Neolithic culture including ceramics by the end of the seventh millennium B.C.E.

At the core of the Capsian Neolithic a range of differentiations appears, with each region showing its own characteristics. The definitive desertification of the Sahara marked this long Neolithic (lasting from circa 6000 to circa 3000), creating in its wake a separation between two worlds, one of which would be forced to turn toward the sea. We know little about the evolution of North Africa in the second millennium B.C.E. Numerous megalithic monuments, difficult to date with any accuracy, are disseminated throughout the region around Constantine. They do, however, suggest Mediterranean influences. The introduction of the horse—which will make the reputation of the Numidians in their confrontation with the Romans—also dates from this period.

It is via the Mediterranean that North Africa entered history with a capital *H:* the world of writing, of traditions diffused over many centuries, and of archeology, which reveals the ancient presence of the Phoenicians and the Greeks, from the most eastern parts of what is today Libya to the Pillars of Hercules. When Elissa (a.k.a. Dido), sister to the king of Tyre, founded Carthage in 814 B.C.E., the region was peopled by Berbers. The ancient Greeks called the territory between the Egyptian border and the Pillars of Hercules, including the Saharan zones, *Libya,* picking up on the Egyptian name "land of the Libu." Homer has Menelaus travel through Libya on his way home, and according to the poet it was a land of great riches, where lambs have horns as soon as they are born, ewes lamb three times a year, and no shepherd ever goes short of milk, meat, or cheese. He called the inhabitants of this paradisiacal land the *Lotophagi,* the Lotus-eaters. But it is Herodotus who has left us the most accurate description of the ancient Libyan populations: he is the first to clearly establish a distinction between the nomadic and the sedentary populations. Some of the names he cites have survived, such as those of the Atlantes (together with the famous legend of Atlantis), the Auses (Oasians), and, most important, the Maxyes. After the Roman conquest, *Libyan* will no longer be the name of all the Berber peoples, but only one of them.

With the Roman invasion of Africa, "Libya" is divided into four regions: Libo-Phoenicia, Numidia, Mauritania, and Getulia, the Saharan backcountry. Knowledge of the Berber peoples gets more precise during the period of Roman colonization, when Roman historians record several traditions concerning the autochthonous populations. The name *Mazyes* (per Kektaios) or *Maxyes* (per Herodotus) is Latinized as *Mazaces* or *Mazax* and applied to Caesarean Mauritania, though by the third century B.C.E. several peoples carried this label. The variations on the name probably derive from an original Berber denomination, as up to today the Berbers call themselves Imazighen or Amazigh, meaning "free man." The question of whether they are an autochthonous population or arrived in that part of the world as a result of migrations is still sometimes hotly debated.

In *De Bello Jugurthino* (The Jugurthine War), the Roman historian Sallust relates the settlement of North Africa according to Punic books attributed to the Numidian king Hiempsal II. To sum up Sallust, this supposedly happened in three stages. Libyans and Getulians formed the original settlement. Persians and Medes from Hercules's army in Spain invaded, finally amalgamating via intermarriage. The mix of Persians and Getulians produced the Numidians, while that of Medes and Libyans resulted in the Moors. Finally came the Phoenicians, who colonized the shores and founded a number of cities.

The Berbers emerged from "obscurity" only in the third century B.C.E., when the Numidian and Moorish kingdoms got involved in the wars between Rome and Carthage along the whole perimeter of the eastern Mediterranean. Previously Carthage had played an essential role in the region's development by spreading its customs and adapting them to local circumstances. Punic, for example, was used by literate Berbers and survived the demise of the city of Carthage, flourishing side by side with the Berber languages for a long time. It is interesting to note that despite the existence of an alphabet of their own, literate Berbers have mostly used the language of the other (Punic, Greek, and Latin, then Arabic and later French) in their writings. After Carthage created several commercial centers along the coast of Africa, its rivalry with the Greeks transformed the habitat, the culture, and the religious life of this region, primarily from the fourth century B.C.E. on. Roman domination, which eventually stretched across all of North Africa, combined with the Carthaginian civilization's influence (more or less profound depending on Carthage's relation to each city) and the different levels of development of the various Berber populations to create the originality and the diversity of the North African space. And this was the result despite the unity that could not but emerge from the centralizing power of Rome—felt in, for instance, the Hellenistic and Roman culture dispensed in schools, be they in Carthage, Cirta, Caesaria, or smaller cities such as Madaurus, where Apuleius was born.

The economic weight of the African provinces also gave them a certain cultural leverage. The Berbers were talented practitioners of Latin letters: Apuleius's *Metamorphoses*, a.k.a. *The Golden Ass*, remains important to this day, standing as one of the great early prose works foreshadowing the development of such literary forms as the novel. But it is before all in the domain of religious thought, with the spreading of Christianity, that North Africa and specifically Numidia was to make a capital contribution. Tertullian (155–222 C.E.) was the first major Christian author and the first Maghrebi writer of religious matter in Latin. He opened the way to a wide literary tradition then developed by Cyprian of Carthage (d. 258), Arnobius (d. 330), Lactantius (250–325), Optatus of Milevis (d. 387), and Dracontius (c. 455–c. 505), whom some claim as possibly the last poet whose mother tongue was Latin. And then there is of course Augustine, probably the most illustrious representative of this early North African tradition. Born in Thagaste (today Souk Ahras) and later made bishop of Hippo (today Annaba), Augustine marked the consciousness of not only the scholars with whom he was in contact both in Africa and throughout the Roman Empire but also those of the following centuries, first with the specific positions he took on a whole range of theological problems in his voluminous writings and maybe even more lastingly with his literary-philosophical magnum opus, the *Confessions*. When Augustine died in 430, the Vandals were at the doors of Hippo, and North Africa was about to begin another of its many transformations.

(2) Even though the earliest literary material traces found in North Africa are inscriptions, texts, and poems written in Greek, Punic, and Latin, we contend that the Berbers, the earliest inhabitants of the area, had rich oral traditions that predated these by millennia. Their tradition of tales, songs, and other genres—explored in more detail in the three Oral Tradition sections—not only has lasted until today but is now experiencing what can only be described as a renaissance, with present-day Morocco and Algeria finally inscribing Amazigh as an official language in their constitutions, thus taking the first step toward doing away with the neglect, opprobrium, and repression that were the lot of the native North African languages during the centuries of colonial domination—be it Latin-, Arabic-, or French-speaking.

We therefore open the first chapter—called "A Book of Multiple Beginnings"—to make clear the multiplicity of the area's cultural origins ab initio (with a Berber tale that gives an Amazigh version of how the world and all that's in it came to be created). That such tales were gathered in the opening decades of the twentieth century by Leo Frobenius, whose work—take, for example, his concept of *Paideuma,* culture as a gestalt and a living organism—would be so important to the rich experimental poetic tradition of that century all the way from Ezra Pound to Jerome Rothenberg's later ethnopoetics movement, seems to us a meaningful link between the most distant past and our own and may be described by the phrase—in the poet and cultural *passeur* Michel Deguy's words—"extreme contemporaneity."

The First Human Beings, Their Sons and Amazon Daughters

In the beginning there were only one man and one woman, and they lived not on the earth but beneath it. They were the first people in the world, and neither knew that the other was of another sex. One day they both came to the well to drink. The man said: "Let me drink." The woman said: "No, I'll drink first. I was here first." The man tried to push the woman aside. She struck him. They fought. The man smote the woman so that she dropped to the ground. Her clothing fell to one side. Her thighs were naked.

The man saw the woman lying strange and naked before him. He saw that she had a taschunt. He felt that he had a thabuscht. He looked at the taschunt and asked: "What is that for?" The woman said: "That is good." The man lay upon the woman. He lay with the woman for eight days.

After nine months the woman bore four daughters. Again, after nine months, she bore four sons. And again four daughters and again four sons. So at last the man and the woman had fifty daughters and fifty sons. The father and the mother did not know what to do with so many children. So they sent them away.

The fifty maidens went off together toward the north. The fifty young men went off together toward the east. After the maidens had been on their way northward under the earth for a year, they saw a light above them. There was a hole in the earth. The maidens saw the sky above them and cried: "Why stay under the earth when we can climb to the surface, where we can see the sky?" The maidens climbed up through the hole and onto the earth.

The fifty youths likewise continued in their own direction under the earth for a year until they too came to a place where there was a hole in the crust and they could see the sky above them. The youths looked at the sky and cried: "Why remain under the earth when there is a place from which one can see the sky?" So they climbed through their hole to the surface.

Thereafter the fifty maidens went their way over the earth's surface and the youths went their way, and none knew aught of the others.

At that time all trees and plants and stones could speak. The fifty maidens saw the plants and asked them: "Who made you?" And the plants replied: "The earth." The maidens asked the earth: "Who made you?" And the earth replied: "I was already here." During the night the maidens saw the moon and the stars, and they cried: "Who made you that you stand so high over us and over the trees? Is it you who give us light? Who are you, great and little stars? Who created you? Or are you, perhaps, the ones who have made everything else?" All the maidens called and shouted. But the moon and the stars were so high that they could not answer. The youths had wandered into the same region and could hear the fifty maidens shouting. They said to one another: "Surely here are other people like ourselves. Let us go and see who they are." And they set off in the direction from which the shouts had come.

But just before they reached the place, they came to the bank of a great stream. The stream lay between the fifty maidens and the fifty youths. The youths had, however, never seen a river before, so they shouted. The maidens heard the shouting in the distance and came toward it.

The maidens reached the other bank of the river, saw the fifty youths, and cried: "Who are you? What are you shouting? Are you human beings too?" The fifty youths shouted back: "We too are human beings. We have come out of the earth. But what are you yelling about?"

The maidens replied: "We too are human beings, and we too have come out of the earth. We shouted and asked the moon and the stars who had made them or if they had made everything else." The fifty boys spoke to the river: "You are not like us," they said. "We cannot grasp you and cannot pass over you as one can pass over the earth. What are you? How can one cross over you to the other side?" The river said: "I am the water. I am for bathing and washing. I am there to drink. If you want to reach my other shore, go upstream to the shallows. There you can cross over me."

The fifty youths went upstream, found the shallows, and crossed over to the other shore. The fifty youths now wished to join the fifty maidens, but the latter cried: "Do not come too close to us. We won't stand for it. You go over there and we'll stay here, leaving that strip of steppe between us." So the fifty youths and the fifty maidens continued on their way, some distance apart but traveling in the same direction.

One day the fifty boys came to a spring. The fifty maidens also came to a spring. The youths said: "Did not the river tell us that water was to bathe in? Come, let us bathe." The fifty youths laid aside their clothing and stepped down into the water and bathed. The fifty maidens sat around their spring and saw the youths in the distance. A bold maiden said: "Come with me and we shall see what the other human beings are doing." Two maidens replied: "We'll come with you." All the others refused.

The three maidens crept through the bushes toward the fifty youths. Two of them stopped on the way. Only the bold maiden came, hidden by the bushes, to the very place where the youths were bathing. Through the bushes the maiden looked at the youths, who had laid aside their clothing. The youths were naked. The maiden looked at all of them. She saw that they were not like the maidens. She looked at everything carefully. As the youths dressed again the maiden crept away without their having seen her.

The maiden returned to the other maidens, who gathered around her and asked: "What have you seen?" The bold maiden replied: "Come, we'll bathe too, and then I can tell you and show you." The fifty maidens undressed and stepped down into their spring. The bold maiden told them: "The people over there are not as we are. Where our breasts are, they have nothing. Where our taschunt is, they have something else. The hair on their heads is not long like ours, but short. And when one sees them naked, one's heart pounds and one wishes to embrace them. When one has seen them naked, one can never forget it." The other maidens replied: "You lie." But the bold maiden said: "Go and see for yourselves and you'll come back feeling as I do." The other maidens replied: "We'll continue on our way." The fifty maidens continued on their way, and so did the fifty youths. But the youths went ahead slowly.

The maidens, on the other hand, described a half circle so that they crossed the path of the youths. They camped quite close to one another.

On this day the youths said: "Let us not sleep under the sky any more. Let us build houses." A few of the youths began to make holes in the earth for themselves. They slept in the holes. Others made themselves passages and rooms under the earth and slept in them. But a few of the youths said: "What are you doing digging into the earth to make houses? Are there not stones here that we can pile one upon the other?"

The youths gathered stones and piled them one on the other in layers. When they had built the walls, one of them went off and began to fell a tree. But the tree cried and said: "What, you will cut me down? What are you doing? Do you think you are older than I? What do you think to gain by it?" The youth answered: "I am not older than you, nor do I wish to be presumptuous. I simply wish to cut down fifty of you trees and lay the trunks across my house for a roof. Your branches and twigs I will lay within the house to protect them from the wet."

The tree answered: "That is well."

The youth then cut down fifty trees, laid their trunks across his house, and covered them with earth. The branches he cut up and stored away inside the house. A few of the larger trunks he set upright in the house to carry the weight of the roof. When the others saw how fine the house was, they did even as he had done. Among the youths there was a wild one, just as among the maidens one was wild and untamed. This wild youth would not live in a house. Rather he preferred to creep in and out among the houses of the others, seeking someone whom he could rend and devour, for he was so wild that he thought only of killing and eating others.

The fifty maidens were encamped at a distance. Looking, they saw how the fifty youths first dug themselves holes and tunnels in the earth and how they finally built their houses. They asked one another: "What are these other humans doing? What are they doing with the stones and the trees?" The bold maiden said: "I'll go there again. I will sneak over and see what these other humans are doing. I have seen them naked once and I want to see them again."

The bold maiden crawled through the bushes to the houses. She came quite close. Finally she slid into a house. There was no one there. The maiden looked around and saw how fine the house was. The wild one came by outside. He scented the maiden. He roared. The maiden screamed and, dashing out of the house, made for the place where the other maidens were encamped. All the youths heard the maiden scream, and all jumped up and ran after her. The maiden ran through the bushes and screamed. The other maidens heard her. They sprang to their feet and ran in her direction to help her. In the bushes the fifty maidens and the fifty youths came together, each maiden with a youth. They fought in the bushes, the maidens with the youths. Even the wild maiden encountered the wild youth in the bushes.

It was dark in the bushes, and they fought in pairs. No pair could see the next one. The fifty maidens were strong. They hurled the fifty youths to the ground and threw themselves on top of them. And they said to themselves: "Now I will see at last if the bold maiden lied." The maidens seized the youths between the thighs. They found the thabuscht. As they touched it, it swelled, and the youths lay quite still. As the maidens felt the thabuscht of the youths, their hearts began to swell. The fifty maidens threw aside their clothes and inserted the thabuscht into their taschunt. The youths lay quite still. The fifty maidens began to ravish the fifty youths. Thereupon the fifty youths became more active than the fifty maidens.

Every youth took a maiden and brought her into his house. They married. In the house the youths said: "It is not right that the woman lies on the man. In the future we shall see to it that the man lies on the woman. In this way we will become your masters." And in the future they slept in the fashion customary among the Kabyles today.

The youths were now much more active than the maidens, and all lived happily together in great satisfaction. Only the wild youth and the wild maiden, who had no house, roamed here and there, seeking others to devour. The others chased them, and when they met them, they beat them. The wild ones said to each other: "We must be different from these humans that they treat us so badly. We will do better to keep out of their way. Let us leave this place and go to the forest." The wild ones left and went to the forest, from which, in future, they emerged only to steal children, whom they devoured. The wild maiden became the first teriel (witch) and the wild youth the first lion. And they both lived on human flesh. The other young men and women were happy to be rid of the cannibals. They lived happily with one another. Their food consisted only of plants, which they uprooted.

Translation from Leo Frobenius's French version by Douglas C. Fox

Hanno the Navigator

(Carthage, c. sixth century B.C.E.)

from **THE PERIPLOS OF HANNO**

Record of the voyage of King Hanno of Carthage round the lands of Libya which lie beyond the Pillars of Hercules. It has been engraved on tablets hung up in the Temple of Chronos.

The Carthaginians decided that Hanno should go past the Pillars and found Carthaginian cities. He set sail with sixty penteconters carrying thirty thousand men and women with provisions and other necessities. After passing the Pillars of Hercules and sailing for two days beyond them we founded the first city, which was named Thymiaterion. Around it was a large plain. Next we went on in a westerly direction and arrived at the Libyan promontory of Soloeis, which is covered with trees; having set up a shrine to Poseidon, we set sail again toward the rising sun for half a day, after which we arrived at a lagoon close to the sea covered with many tall reeds. Elephants and large numbers of other animals were feeding on them. Leaving this lagoon and sailing for another day, we founded the coastal cities named Carian Wall, Gytte, Acra, Melitta, and Arambys.

Leaving this place we arrived at the great river Lixos, which comes from Libya. On the banks nomads, the Lixites, were feeding their flocks. We stayed for some time with these people and made friends with them. Upstream from them lived the unfriendly Ethiopians, whose land is full of wild beasts and is broken up by high mountains where they say the Lixos rises. They also say that about these mountains dwell the strange-looking Troglodytes. The Lixites claim that they can run faster than horses. Taking Lixite interpreters with us we sailed alongside the desert in a southerly direction for two days, then toward the rising sun for one more day. We then found at the far end of an inlet a little island five stades in circumference. We named it Cerne and left settlers there. Judging by our journey we reckoned that it must be opposite Carthage, since we had to sail the same distance from Carthage to the Pillars of Hercules as from the Pillars of Hercules to Cerne. From there, sailing up a big river named the Chretes, we arrived at a lake in which there were three islands, all larger than Cerne. Leaving these islands, we sailed for one day and came to the end of the lake, which was overshadowed by high mountains full of savages dressed in animal skins who threw stones at us and thus prevented us from landing. From there we entered another river, which was big and wide, full of crocodiles and hippopotamuses. Then we retraced our journey back to Cerne.

From there we sailed south along a coast entirely inhabited by Ethiopians, who fled at our approach. Their language was incomprehensible even to the Lixites whom we had with us. On the last day we disembarked by some high mountains covered with trees with sweet-smelling, multicolored wood. We sailed round these mountains for two days and arrived in a huge bay on the other side of which was a plain; there we saw fires breaking out at intervals on all sides at night, both great and small. Having renewed our water supplies, we continued our voyage along the coast for five days, after which we arrived at a huge inlet, which the interpreters called the Horn of the West. There was a big island in this gulf, and in the island was a lagoon with another island. Having disembarked there, we could see nothing but forest by day, but at night many fires were seen, and we heard the sound of flutes and the beating of drums and tambourines, which made a great noise. We were struck with terror, and our soothsayers bade us leave the island.

We left in haste and sailed along by a burning land full of perfumes. Streams of fire rose from it and plunged into the sea. The land was unapproachable because of the heat. Terror-stricken, we hastened away. During four days' sailing we saw at night that the land was covered with fire. In the middle was a high flame, higher than the others, which seemed to reach the stars. By day we realized that it was a very high mountain, named the Chariot of the Gods. Leaving this place, we sailed along the burning coast for three days and came to the gulf named the Horn of the South. At the end of it was an island like the first one, with a lake in which was another island full of savages. The greater part of these were women. They had hairy bodies, and the interpreters called them Gorillas. We pursued some of the males, but we could not catch a single one because they were good climbers and they defended themselves fiercely. However, we managed to take three women. They bit and scratched their captors, whom they did not want to follow. We killed them and removed the skins to take back to Carthage. We sailed no further, being short of supplies.

Anonymous translation from Greek

Callimachus (Cyrene, 310–c. 240 B.C.E.)

THIRTEEN EPIGRAMMATIC POEMS

1

I loathe the serial poem, rejoice not
in a road that many people travel,
and hate a beloved who's made the rounds.
No fountain drinks, things public disgust me.
But you, Lysanias, I thought fair, I thought fine.
No sooner said than Echo replies, "But not mine."

2

Kleon of Thessaly, you poor, poor thing!
By the dazzling sun, I didn't know you.
Where've you been, pathetic bag of hair and bones?
Have you caught my luck, been hit hard by heaven?
Now I get it. Euxitheos took off with you.
When you came here, you just ate him up with both eyes.

3

But half my soul still breathes, the other half
off with Love or Death, don't know, but it's gone.
With one of the boys again? I often said,
"Don't take him in, young men, that runaway."
Look for it at . . . for someplace around there
that lovelorn condemned thing is hanging out.

4

Your hunter in the hills, Epikydes, tracks every hare
and the slot of every hind through frost and snow.
Show him a wounded beast, and he won't take it.
That's my way of loving: to pursue my quarry
as it runs away, and to fly right by
whatever lies in my path for the taking.

5

If I came to you in fun on purpose, Archinos, then a thousand apologies, but if I'm here strictly because I couldn't help myself, consider the urgency of it. Strong wine and Love compelled me. One pulled me while the other took away my sobriety. But when I came, I didn't howl about who I was or whose, but kissed the doorpost. If that's a sin, then I'm a sinner.

6

I swear it by the gods, there is
fire hidden under these embers.
I can't trust myself. Don't hold me.
Still waters can gnaw away at a wall.
I fear, my friend, lest the silent
creeper chase me back into love.

7

Menippos, I know that I'm not wealthy,
but, for god's sake, please stop telling me so.
To hear incessant bitter words pains me.
Yes, dear, this is your most unlovely side.

8

On the twentieth of last month, I said,
"I'll get you, Menekrates, no escape."
Today, the tenth, the ox accepts the yoke
in just twenty days. Good for Hermes! Good for me!

9

What an excellent charm for the lovelorn Polyphernos found! You can bet he wasn't completely unschooled, that Cyclops. The Muses make Love very thin, Philip, and learning is a kind of panacea for every ill. And I think hunger has one good to set against its evils, the radical excision of the boy-love disease. I certainly have my reasons for telling Love, "Your wings are being clipped, little guy, I'm not in the least afraid of you." For I have at home both of the charms that will treat this grave wound.

10

If handsome, dark Theokritos hate me, hate him
back times four, but if he love me, love him.
For surely, divine Zeus, by fair-haired Ganymede,
you were in love once, too. That's enough said.

11

We hadn't noticed our guest is wounded.
You saw, though, how stressed out his breathing was
when he took his third drink. And how the roses
shed their petals and fell from his wreath to the ground.
He's on fire. By god, I'm not just guessing,
but being a thief myself, I read the clues.

12

Kallignotos swore to Ionis that no man
or other woman would be dearer to him.
He swore, but it's true what they say about lovers'
oaths, that they never get past the gods' ears.
Now he's on fire for some boy, and the poor girl,
like a ghost town, gets no account or word.

13

May such a sleep be yours, Konopion,
as that you make me take by your cold doors.
May such a sleep as that your lover sleeps
be yours, bitch. You've not a dream of pity.
Neighbors show pity, but you, not a dream.
May white hair remind you of this—and soon!

Translation from Greek by George Economou

Mago (Carthage, pre-second century B.C.E.)

from *DE AGRICULTURA*

These things, Mago of Carthage so reported, so I will record them here . . .

In buying new bulls make sure they are squarely built, with great limbs, long black and robust horns, a wide and curling brow, hairy ears, eyes and lips black, nostrils turned up and open, a long and muscular neck, ample dewlap (falling almost to the knees), breast great, forequarters vast, a spacious belly (as if always full), flanks extended, loins wide, back straight and flat (or even sunken), buttocks round, legs compact and straight (more short than long), knees not weak, tail long and bristly, hair of the body thick and short—of reddish or dark color—and a body quite soft to the touch.

On preserving pomegranates:

Seawater should be brought to a violent boil and pomegranates lowered briefly in it (tied with flax or twine) until they are discolored, and taken for three days to dry in the sun. Afterward, they should be hung in a cool place, so when they are finished and ready to be used, they should be softened in cool, fresh water for one night and the following day. . . . Too, the fresh fruit may be thickly kneaded in potter's clay, and when it has dried white, the fruit hung in a dark, cool place. . . . These methods will preserve all fruit as well as if they were just picked.

Mago of Carthage emphasizes this significance, when at the auspicious beginning of his writings he states . . .

A man who has bought land must sell his town house. That way he'll not be praying to the gods of the city more than to the deities of the country. For any man who keeps his town house nearer his heart has no need of a country estate.

Translation from a Latin version of the lost Punic by Emmett P. Tracy

Lucius Apuleius (Madaurus, now M'Daourouch, c. 123–c. 180 C.E.)

from *THE GOLDEN ASS, OR METAMORPHOSES,* BOOK II

[7] Immediately afterward, I awoke from sleep into a state of panic and joy. I rose quickly, disordered, and drenched in sweat. I was amazed at the clear vision of the powerful goddess in my dream. So I sprinkled myself with seawater, and eager to understand her great command, I recalled over and over the order of her instructions. Then immediately a golden sun arose, dispersing the clouds of dark night, and there a crowd filled all the streets with a triumphal, religious procession. . . .

[8] Lo! this prelude of the great parade gradually marched along beautifully adorned in their emotions and votive displays. One masqueraded as a soldier wearing a sheath! One was girdled in a Greek cloak, made out like a hunter with sandals and a spear! Another was in gilded slippers, a silken robe, and expensive jewelry, with woven hair plaits, imitating the walk of a woman. Far off, there was another in leggings, a shield, a helmet and sword, and an emblem from the games so that you might think a gladiator had appeared. Neither was a magistrate missing—with his functionary rods and royal purple toga—nor one who reinvented himself in a cloak and scepter, woven sandals, and the bearded goatee of a philosopher. Along came a pair carrying different cane rods: one of birdlime for a bird catcher, another with hooks for a fisherman. I even saw a trained bear dressed like a woman being carried in a chair, and a monkey in a woven hat and a saffron-colored Phrygian dress like the shepherd boy, Ganymede, carrying a golden cup. There was even an ass with glued wings walking beside a crippled old man, so that one was Bellerophon and the other Pegasus (though you'd laugh at both!).

[9] Among these playful spectacles of common folk parading everywhere, there arrived the private procession of my savior goddess. And at first came the women, radiant in white garments, rejoicing in their various vestments, blooming in spring garlands, and strewing the ground with flowerlets from their bosoms along the streets where the sacred throng followed . . .

[10] . . . when another appeared carrying in his happy bosom the venerable effigy of my savior goddess: not in the image of a goat, or a bird, or a wild beast, or even a human itself, but by some clever invention a thing which inspired in its strangeness such fear, so far that it was an ineffable token of a more profound sanctity having to be hidden in secret. It was a little urn, shaped in splendid gold and most skillfully hollowed, with a rounded

base and strange Egyptian images on its surface. Its mouth, not particularly elevated, jutted out like a beak into a long spout, and on its other side, a large handle was attached, arching into a broad curve. On top, coiled in a knot and rearing the striped swelling of a scaly neck, was a viper.

[11] Then and there approached the promised beneficence of the omnipresent goddess. The priest (carrying my fate and my very fortune!) came forward, extending in his right hand a sistrum, decorated to the order of the goddess' divine right—it was like a crown to me—oh Hercules, more than a crown! Having endured so many labors, traversed such danger, by the foresight of the great goddess I'd overcome a Fortune which most cruelly wrestled me down. And yet, impassioned in sudden ecstasy, I did not rush forth with unmerciful haste. For of course, I was scared that the solemn procession of the ceremony might be frightened by the sudden appearance of a four-footed animal, so I calmly and gradually hesitated forward, as if with human steps and a bent body, and I gently crept (truly by providence!) through the parting crowd.

[13] Then the priest, whom I was fully able to recognize, was mindful of the oracle of my dream and marveled at the accordance of the foretold offering. He stopped at once, and with his right hand he held out a garland wantonly before my mouth. I was shaking, with my beating heart endlessly throbbing, and the crown, which was interwoven with pleasant roses, was glistening, and I, hungry for what I'd been promised, in my yearning mouth eagerly devoured that gift. Nor did the divine promise deceive me: suddenly the ugly, beastly form was stripped from me. At first the naughty hair shed down, then the thick skin began to contract, the gross belly retracted, the soles of the feet shot through the hooves into toes, my hands were no longer feet but stretched out in their upright function, my extended neck shrunk, the mouth and head became round, the enormous ears went back to their pristine littleness, the bulky teeth returned to small human shape, and that which had tortured me most of all—my tail—disappeared.

The crowds were amazed. The pious ones worshiped the clear power of the supreme goddess and the splendor mirrored by the vision of my dream and the ease of my transformation with a voice both clear and consonant, and putting their hands in the sky, they bore witness to the clear beneficence of the goddess.

Translation from Latin by Emmett P. Tracy

Quintus Septimius Florens Tertullianus

(Carthage, c. 160–c. 220 C.E.)

from **DE PALLIO (THE CLOAK)**

1.1. You who have been always leaders of Africa, men of Carthage, men of rank, men of happiness, I am glad you live in such prosperous times that you can find both the time and the pleasure of censuring clothing! This is the sort of pursuit of peace and plenty. All is well on the part of the empire and on the part of the sky.

However, in the past you too wore your clothing, tunics, differently: they were even famous for their skillful weave, harmonious coloring, and proper size. For they did not fall extravagantly over the legs or shamelessly above the knees, they did not fit shortly at the arms nor tightly at the hands. No, in a fourfold suitable form it fitted men (it was not considered easy to divide its folds with a belt). The outer garment, the pallium, itself also quadrangular, was thrown back from both sides and knit around the neck in the bit of a buckle, and so rested on the shoulders.

Its equivalent today is what is worn by the priests of Aesculapius and has also become yours. This is the way the twin town close by used to dress, and wherever else in Africa there is a Tyrus. But as soon as the urn of worldly loss swung around and the deity favored the Romans, your twin town hastened to change on its own account. Thus it wished to salute Scipio at his landing beforehand through its prematurely Roman attire.

3.1. Animals also change, not in dress but in form. And yet for the peacock its feathers form a dress, a festive dress at that: one that has a deeper hue than all purple at its flowery neck, more golden than all edgings at its gleaming back, fanning out more than any strange robe where its tail lies down; many-colored, parti-colored, changing in color; never itself, always different, although it is always itself when it is different, bound to change color as often as it is moved.

The snake too must be mentioned, though after the peacock, for this animal also exchanges what it has been allotted, namely its skin and its age, for as soon as it senses the coming of old age, it wrings itself into a narrow spot, enters a hole, and at once leaves its skin, being scraped smooth at the very threshold. Abandoning its slough right there, revived, it then snakes its way out. Along with its scales it shakes off the years.

The hyena, if you look closely, is of an annual sex: it alternates between male and female. I keep silent about the stag, that it also controls its own age: having fed on a snake and falling sick it is rejuvenated.

Then we have the four-footed, slowly stepping, lowly, stubborn creature . . . do you think I mean the Pacuvian tortoise? No, I don't. The line applies to another little animal as well, really one of medium size, but with a great name. If you hear about a "chameleon" without any knowledge of it, you will fear something bigger than a lion. But once you come across one, generally in a vineyard, lying in its entirety under a vine foliage, you will laugh right away at the boldness of its name, which is Greek at that. For its body contains no moisture, unlike much smaller creatures.

•

Much needed to be said to arrive well-prepared at man. Whatever you regard as his beginnings, by all means he was naked and undressed when he was fashioned by his maker. It was only later that he grasped wisdom, prematurely, before he was entitled to it. Then and there he hastened to cover the part of his new body not yet meant for shame: for the time being he veiled it with fig leaves. Later, when he was exiled from his birthplace because he had sinned, he was shown into the world, as if into a mine, clad in a skin.

But these are mysteries not for all to know. Come, show us something of yours, a story told by the Egyptians, listed by Alexander, read by his mother, a story about the time of Osiris, when Ammon, rich in sheep, made his way from here to Africa.

Translation from Latin by Vincent Hunink

from SCORPIACE (THE SCORPION)

From a little scorpion the land emits great evil. As many poisons, as many types, as much ruin, as many species, as much pain, as many colors. Nicander writes about it and depicts it well.

Yet of all things, the movement of its tail (the so-called coda, which extends from behind the body and strikes) inflicts the most pain. So this is the scorpion: its chain of knots, from a thin, poisonous vein, rising up in an arc of rage, and drawing at its height a barbed spear like the war-plan of a catapult.

For this reason the war machine with retracted spears is also called a scorpion. Its sting is also an open vein, and it volleys venom into the wound as it pierces. It's well-known the dangerous season is summer. In the south and southwest winds, this ferocity is at work. In terms of remedies, natural things appear most effective; so too magic works; there's a cure by knife and potion. Some, who hope to swiftly avoid pain, drink an immunization, but sex keeps it from working, and then immediately you're at risk again.

Translation from Latin by Emmett P. Tracy

Thascius Caecilius Cyprianus

(Carthage, early third century–258 C.E.)

from *EPISTLE TO DONATUS, 1.1*

You rightly chastise me, dearest Donatus, though I remember myself what I've promised. And now seems precisely the right time to answer your letter, as the mild grape-harvest season and the appointed peace of the ending year allow an unclenched mind to withdraw in earnest reflection. The place fits the season. The pleasant beauty of the gardens becomes the gentle breezes of sweet autumn, soothing and nourishing the senses. For here, one can lead the delightful day in conversation and teach, by learned tales, some sacred sayings to the heart's conscience.

And just so any indecent onlooker might not interrupt our conversation or wild clamor of the household deafen our talk, let us seek this place—the neighboring seclusion grants us solitude—just as the wild drooping of the vines in hanging knots crawls through thick canes, and a leafy shelter has made us a vined colonnade. Rightly, we give our ears this reflection, and while looking into the groves and vineyards, pleasing the eyes with delightful scenes, at once the act of listening instructs our mind, and our eyes nourish it: and yet now your only grace, your only care, is our discourse. Rejecting the allure of pleasant scenes, you have fixed your eyes upon me: with your mouth, with your mind, you are every part the listener, with the love with which you love.

Translation from Latin by Emmett P. Tracy

Lucius Lactantius (Cirta? c. 240–Trier? c. 320 C.E.)

from *DE AVE PHOENICE*

When the Phoenix has finished a thousand years of life
(and long lengths of time become painful to her),
she flees her sweet, familiar nest of the grove
and renews her faded existence in time's turning spaces;
as when the sanctity of the place—in her passion for rebirth—
has been relinquished, then she seeks *this* world
where Death holds reign; and into Syria
(to which she proffered, like an ancient author,
the name *Phoenicia*) she directs her swift flight.
Toward its deserts, untouched, and the tranquil sacred grove
in sequestered woods, lurking beneath the forest
and high on the summit, she makes her way to the lofty palm
(which also bears the Greek name *Phoenix*)
into which no hurtful living creature, or slithering serpent
or any preying bird, can follow. Then Aeolus
confines the winds in vaulted grottoes (so they may
not violate the radiant air, nor the dense clouds
of a South Wind drive off the Sun through the emptiness
of the sky and harm the bird), as there she builds
for herself some nest or sepulcher: for she dies
to live, creating herself from herself, and gathers
juices and scents from the divine wood
which the Assyrians harvest, and wealthy Arabs
(like those picked by the races of Pygmaeans
or Indians or produced in their soft bosom of Sabaean
farmlands). So the Phoenix gathers cinnamon
and the odor of amomum and balsam's mixed leaf,
nor is a stem of sweet cassia absent or fragrant acanthus.
To all this, she adds tender ears of ripe nard and
mixes in the power of myrrh from you, Panacaea.
Then immediately in her nest she contracts her changing
body and on her pyre of life anoints her shriveled limbs:
so at last, upon her own funeral pyre, the spirit
in her and around her and above her inspires her to die.

Translation from Latin by Emmett P. Tracy

Aurelius Augustinus Hipponensis
(Saint Augustine) (Thagaste, 354–Hippo, 430 C.E.)

from **CONFESSIONS**

Book 3

I came to Carthage. Everywhere a medley of shameful loves was clamoring around me. I wasn't yet capable of loving, and yet I loved to love, and with more hidden desire I hated that I was less desirous. I was looking for what I could love, loving love, and I despised surety and a path free of danger. It was all because I was hungry from within, for more internal foods, for you—my God—though I hungered not with that hunger. No, I was without the desire for incorruptible nourishments. Yet I was not satisfied with them, rather more empty, more sick. Because of this, I was not rightly well in my soul, and it exposed itself as ulcerous to the world, piteously desirous to be tickled by the touch of the senses. For if the senses had no soul, they would not be so loved. To love and be loved was sweet to me, better yet if I might have taken pleasure in the body of a lover.

And so I was polluting the vein of friendship with the filth of my desires. I was darkening its purity with the hell of my lust. And yet I wanted to be disgraceful and dishonorable, handsome and cosmopolitan, all with such copious vanity. Indeed I fell in love, and I was yearning to be trapped by it. My God, my Compassion, with how much poison you inflicted that charm on me with all your goodness. Because I was loved, I arrived secretly at the bond of pleasuring. I was happy being bound to those wretched bonds, though I might be scourged with the passionate, cruel switch of jealousy and suspicions and fears and angers and arguments.

Book 8

I collapsed beneath a fig tree, I can't recall how, and unleashed my tears. My eyes, as rivers, burst forth, worthy of your sacrifice, Lord, and though not with these words, but with these feelings, I said to you, "Even you, Lord, forever? Forever, Lord, will you be angry forever? Will you be mindful of my prior sins?" (Indeed I was feeling still attached to them.) I cast out such miserable words: "How long, how long? Tomorrow, even tomorrow? Why not now? Why not this very hour end my disgrace?" So I spoke, weeping in the most bitter contrition of my heart.

Yet then I heard a voice from a nearby house singing songs in constant repetition, whether a boy or girl, I can't recall: "Pick up, read; pick up, read."

At once my expression changed; I began to think: were children likely to sing such things while playing? I had never heard it anywhere. So I rose, suppressing the passion of my tears, and interpreting it as nothing other than a divine commandment to take a book and read the first chapter I might find. Indeed, I had heard of Antony, as he chanced upon a reading from the Gospels, and was chastised, as though what he was reading was speaking directly to him: "Go, sell everything, sell all you have, give it to the poor, and you will have a trove in heaven; come, follow me"; and through such miracles immediately Antony was converted to you, Lord.

So I went back to that place where Alypius sat, for there I had placed the book of the apostles when I had gotten up. I took it. I opened it and read it in silence, that chapter which my eyes had first cast upon: *Not in rioting and drunkenness, not in laziness and immodesty, not in contention and jealousy, but as one must bear you, Lord Jesus Christ, and make no provision for the flesh in desire*. I read no more. There was no need. At once, at the end of the sentence, as if by a light of freedom infused into my heart, all shades of doubt disappeared.

from **DE DOCTRINA CHRISTIANA, BOOK 4**

3.40. So, as children do not grow to speak other than by learning the speech of speakers, then why are orators not able to develop the art of oratory by reading and listening to the orations of orators and, as much as possible, by imitating them? Why not? Do we not experience it? For we know many more who are eloquent without the rules of rhetoricians than those who have learned them, and yet there is none excellent in orations and declamations without having read and listened. . . .

27.1. The life of a writer holds greater weight than the grandeur of his diction. For he who speaks wisely and eloquently yet lives miserably teaches the multitudes eager for learning while his own soul is useless.

from **DE FIDE RERUM INVISIBILIUM**

"But," they say, "those things are in the mind which we can only discern in the mind and which we have no power to understand through the eyes of the body. But you say that we should believe in them, though you don't show them to us so we might see them, nor are they within our own minds, so that we can think and see them." This they say as though one were ordered to believe, as if a thing which he can see placed before him is to be believed. Yet surely we ought to believe in certain temporal things which we cannot see so that we may be worthy of seeing eternal things which we believe.

from **PSALMUS CONTRA PARTEM DONATI**

All you who celebrate peace, now proclaim the truth.

An abundance of sins disturbs our brothers.
For this, Our Lord wanted to forewarn us
and likened the kingdom of heaven to a sea-cast net
gathering numerous fish, everywhere, all species,
and dragging them toward the shore, separating them:
the good ones in buckets, the bad ones released.
Whoever knows the gospels, fearfully knows
that the net is the church, the age is the sea,
and a righteous race of fish has been mixed with sinners.
The end of the age is the shore, and it is time for separation.
Those who broke the nets were content with the sea.
The buckets, which hold the holy, can no longer be reached.

All you who celebrate peace, now proclaim the truth.

Translations from Latin by Emmett P. Tracy

COMMENTARY

Few of his Maghrebian "compatriots" showed much interest in that eminent figure of Christian theology, Saint Augustine. Then, in April 2001, a first international conference was held in Algiers & Annaba, under the title "Africanity and Universality." It was presided over by André Mandouze (1916–2006), professor in Algiers & great scholar of Augustine, & by Abdelaziz Bouteflika, the president of Algeria. Since then, Augustine has officially become part of the national cultural heritage.

Blossius Aemilius Dracontius

(Carthage, c. 455–c. 505 C.E.)

THE CHARIOT OF VENUS

Suddenly Cypris and her dove-drawn chariot
descended from the quarter where the fiery night
wheels its constellations over southern shores.
Her purple doves wore bridles woven out of flowers,
a red rose linked the gently undulating traces,
the birds' beautiful yoke was lilies mixed with roses.
She flicked a purple whip to keep the team on course.
She steered the wing beats; she controlled the feathered oars.

Translation from Latin by Aaron Poochigian

DE MENSIBUS (MONTHS)

January.   The official ensigns of the court proffer sacred honors, exchanging new names in the books of the festival calendar.   February.   The Sun, already in blows, releases the ices of winter, as buds break in swollen shells on the vine.   March.   The rights of Mars stir. In ranks, they threaten cruel wars to rouse the troops and shear the young vines with the scythe.   April. After chaos recedes, the world's young fruits rejoice. The times of night are weighed out with the light of day.   May.   The bejeweled fields show signs of spring through infinite colors; the sweet-smelling turf is constellated in divine flowers.   June.   With the armed harvests swaying like flaxen grain, the farmer reclaims his debt, and the sailor's seas swell.   July.   The damp dwelling of the Moon gives dry harvests and draws off the springwaters, so that the Nile floods.   August.   August holds the warm halls of the Sun, but the name of Caesar applies: it offers ripe fruit, as open ground wears away the dry grain.   September.   Autumn burns partly in multicolored vines, the wine promising the farmers a reward for their labor.   October.   The drunken flow is brought forth by the farmers, dancing, and the joyful country life is properly humbled in wine.   November.   Lazy winter, returning, grows numb, as the olive tree ripens and crops seize the ground which has replenished with interest.   December.   The cold midwinter's snowing loads the lofty mountains in frost, and glacial chill suckles its lambs, nursing under their mothers.

THE ORIGIN OF ROSES

Venus, nurturing goddess, was stricken while avoiding Mars—
and treading barefoot upon fields of flowers
where through placid grasses the profane thorn crept,
for at once, that thorn tore her sole a delicate blow
and poured out blood. The thorn was clothed in red
and though committing the crime, it kept the honor
of her fragrance. So all thickets through the golden fields
are red with blood, and the thornbush makes holy
the heavens. What benefit then, Venus, was it to have fled
bloody Mars when your foot was drenched bloodred?
And rosy-cheeked Cytherea, do you punish these crimes
so that the fiery beauty may hide the long-lasting thorn?
So it was fitting too for the goddess to have been in pain,
as it is with the power of love: as it may avenge the wounds
of love with the honor of affection.

Translations from Latin by Emmett P. Tracy

Luxorius (Carthage, sixth century C.E.)

"THEY SAY, THAT WHEN THE FIERCE BEAR GIVES BIRTH"

They say, that when the fierce bear gives birth, she gently
forms her baby with her mouth,
shines and polishes its pliant, shapeless body
with her lips and, with pious devotion,
once more, tenderly, creates another generation.

The way a master craftsman sculpts
a soft clay limb into life, she molds the flesh
of her exhausted, battered whelp
into something promising.

Nature has surrendered its good duty
to a loving creature—who licks things into shape
first with her uterus, and then
with her wise tongue.

PREMATURE CHARIOT

You always shoot out first and never last, Vico,
because you need to get hold of that part
you've softened with your pitiful, constant stroking.
The only time you're able to, somehow, hold
your horses is when you let the sly guy,
who's paid you off, come from behind.

Translations from Latin by Art Beck

FIRST DIWAN

A Book of In-Betweens: Al-Andalus, Sicily, the Maghreb

The conquest of North Africa was difficult for the Arab Muslim invaders, who up until then had experienced fast and overwhelming victories. Tradition has it that Caliph Omar always warned his commanders against invading this part of the world because "*Ifrikiya,* that means breakup" (a pun on the Arab root *frq,* which means "to separate, to divide"). But religious zeal and desire for gain won out.

Arab historiography has gathered much detail on "the liberation of Africa and Spain" (*fath ifriqiya wa al-andalus*), including these main facts:

· In 647, Abdallah Ibn Sa'd, Caliph Othman's foster brother and the governor of Egypt, vanquished the Byzantine army of the exarch Gregory the Patrician in Sufetula (modern Sbeitla in Tunisia).

· In 670, 'Oqba Ibn Nafa' founded Kairouan, the first permanent Arab and Muslim settlement in Ifriqiya. This military camp was the base for the conquest of Ifriqiya and Spain. It also served as a fallback position for aborted sallies. 'Oqba is said to have led his warriors all the way to the Pillars of Hercules, and there only the sea kept him from advancing. On the way back, he was killed in the Aurès Mountains, during an encounter with Kusaila's Berber troops. His body supposedly rests in the oasis named after him, near Biskra. Oral Maghrebi tradition (at least the Arabophone one) makes 'Oqba Ibn Nafa', aka Sidi 'Oqba, the great conqueror who liberated the Maghreb through Islam.

· The conquest came to a close in 705, after the campaigns of Hassan Ibn No'man el Ghassani and then Musa Ibn Nusayr, marked by the conquest of Carthage in 698 and the defeat of the famous "Queen of the Aurès," the Kahina—an emblematic figure of the "Algerian resistance" in Kateb Yacine's theater. (*Kahina* means "prophetess, magician"; the Arabs gave her this surname. She and her tribe are supposedly of Jewish origin—her name is thus sometimes assimilated to *Cohen*. The sedentary tribes—supposedly opposed to her scorched-earth strategy—accelerated her defeat by helping the Arab invaders.) The few decades at the end of the seventh century and the political upheavals they witnessed were pivotal for the future of the Maghreb. The countries of North Africa would now be definitely cut off from the Latin and Christian cultural sphere of influence and integrated into the Arabo-Muslim world. However, the modalities of this rupture remain insufficiently known and are the object of passionate discussions in which politico-religious arguments, openly admitted or not, fight with historical scientific investigations. The Berber tribes' submission to Islam was quickly completed, despite numerous recurring apostasies, and it is the Berbers who began the conquest of Spain, under the leadership of Tariq ibn Ziyad (who gave his name to Gibraltar) in 711.

This Islamization, though superficial to begin with, would deepen over the centuries. Henceforth, Islam would be the core of all political, social, and religious representations of the Maghreb. It is inside an Islamic structure that the Berbers affirm their originality and their autochthonous genius: messianic movements, Sufism, brotherhoods, maraboutism, and so on. This Islamization was conducted in the Amazigh language, with the core moments happening under the Almohad Dynasty (1147–1269). Arabization, still in progress today, was much slower. Arabic replaced Latin as the civilizational language in the cities. The Hilali invasions of the eleventh century were decisive for this process of Arabization. Some ten or twenty thousand Arab beduins from the Banu Hilal, Banu Sulaym, and Maqil tribes swooped down on the Maghreb like "swarms of locusts," as Ibn Khaldun phrased it. The climate of insecurity their invasion created slowed down the adoption of a sedentary lifestyle throughout these lands. However, they Arabized the Zenata Berbers, who also acquired their lifestyle. Arabic would slowly penetrate the Berber nomad tribes, sparing, more or less, only the Sahara and the mountain chains of the Djebel Neffoussa in Libya; Kabylia, the Aurès, and the Ouarsenis in Algeria; and the Middle and Anti-Atlas in Morocco.

Many states followed and confronted one another: the dynastic quarrels, struggles to control the commercial routes, and skirmishes between nomads and settlers echoed the religious struggles of the caliphate—the Central Maghreb was a privileged area for the Kharijite schism—and often reflected social antagonisms. The uprisings against the central power of the Umayyad caliphs of Damascus and later of Córdoba and the Abbasids of Baghdad contributed to the political commminution of the Maghreb. During these centuries marked by the preponderance of centrifugal forces and the harshness of the divisions, a tendency toward the unity of the Muslim West won out—temporarily—on at least two occasions:

- In the eleventh century, under the Almoravids (al-Murabitun; 1061–1147). Yusuf Ibn Tashfin led these Lamtuna Berbers—veiled nomads originally from Mauritania—into Spain to fight Don Alfonso and the Cid. The dynasty took its name from the famous Saharan *ribat* (fortress-monastery) where Ibn Yassin (d. 1059) preached the Maliki doctrine and organized the first troops destined to fight the Kharijite heresy. The Almoravids were the first to achieve the religious unity of the Maghreb and to create a link with the civilization of al-Andalus.

- In the twelfth century, under the Almohads (al-Muwahhidun; 1147–1269). This dynasty was born through the encounter of Ibn Tumert (d. 1128), the future Almohad mahdi from the mountains of southern Morocco, with Abd al Mumen (d. 1163), a potter's son from the region of Nedroma in eastern Algeria and the first caliph of the empire. The Almohads extended their authority over the whole of the Maghreb and Andalusia. Their name was linked to the teachings of Ibn Tumert, which were based on the affirmation of *tawhid*, the doctrine of the oneness of God. Under the Almohads, the Maghreb experienced a short period of stability and peace, intense economic activity, and a brilliant cultural life, illustrated in particular by the philosophers Ibn Tufayl, the author of the philosophical novel *Hayy Ibn Yaqzan* (see p. 155) and Ibn-Rushd (Averroes). Numerous architectural remains bear witness to the era's artistic quality.

Written literature developed in Arabic, which explains the small number of Berber authors in the Maghreb. A few names do surface, such as those of Ibn Hani (see p. 49) in the tenth century and Abu Madyan Shu'ayb (see p. 96) in the twelfth. Ibn Khaldun's judgment is severe: "Their poetry isn't any better, even today. Besides Ibn Rashiq [see p. 71] and Ibn Sharaf [see p. 137], there is no famous poet in Ifriqiya. Most were freshly arrived immigrants. And their eloquence remains inferior."

It is in al-Andalus that Arabo-Muslim culture shines with exceptional brightness, especially under the dominion of the Umayyads from 756 to 1031. Córdoba rivaled Baghdad in welcoming the great artists and scholars of the age. The cultural cohabitation between Muslims, Christians, and Jews allowed for a deeply original artistic *métissage*. For many poets the collapse of the Córdoba Caliphate marked the end of a golden age. Al-Andalus was the true homeland of poets. The taste for poetry was certainly quickened by training in the Arab language, for which the Qur'an is not the only linguistic model.

The originality of the poetry of al-Andalus lies in its invention of new metrical forms, such as the muwashshaha and the zajal, easily adaptable to music. Breaking with the classical monorhyme Arab qasida, these new forms have stanzas with different rhyme schemes. The muwashshaha classically consists of five stanzas *(bait)* of four to six lines, alternating with five or six refrains *(qufl)*; each refrain has the same rhyme and meter, whereas each stanza has only the same meter. The *kharja* ("final" in Arabic) is the final refrain of a muwashshaha and often appears to have been composed independently of the muwashshaha. What is most fascinating about the kharjas is their language: about a third of those extant are written in Classical Arabic, while most of the remainder are in Andalusian Arabic, but there are about seventy examples either in Ibero-Romance or with significant Romance elements. None is recorded in Hebrew, even when the muwashshaha is in Hebrew (see p. 46).

While the muwashshaha is written in the classical tongue, the zajal uses vernacular Arabic and Spanish. The rise of the zajal, in the twelfth century, coincides with that of the Almoravids, whose mastery of Arabic was deficient. Ibn Quzman (see p. 93) used the zajal to sing of love and compose panegyrics, the latter a genre usually reserved to the classical language. Many Sufis also used the zajal to reach a wider public.

Al-Andalus's Jewish minority found its fate closely tied to that of the Arabo-Muslim community, first sharing its prestige and then its debasement. Despite their status as "protected (i.e., tolerated) ones" *(dhimmi)*, Jews played a major role in the economic, political, philosophical, and literary spheres, in the last of which they used not only Hebrew but also Arabic and Judeo-Arabic in their poetry. A highly elaborate secular poetic production that renews both formal elements and content characterizes the vitality of the cultural symbiosis of al-Andalus. The poets in this anthology showcase the diversity and high quality of this literary production.

Even today, the muwashshaha and the zajal perdure in the music and "Andalus" singing of the Maghreb.

Anonymous Muwashshaha

Skeletal traces of the encampment revive
      my sorrow. Is it possible
    To find solace for my longing heart?
      Die, oh, consolation!

Oh, vestige which predestined my death,
You were thirsty. Here are the tears of my eye
Which pour forth, so quench your thirst at the fountain.
      But, oh, you who have departed, you are to blame for
        my sin. Perhaps the time has come
      For me to die. Then woe! Alas!

Oh, territory of love, are you about to kill me?
This passion is increasing.
Separation came to you right after he turned away.
      Oh, one tested by all grave affairs, how long are
        you going to be sad? How long will you mourn
      And be troubled about a love whose passion wanes and
        is forgetful?

My censurers, I don't want to forget him.
I am suffering because of a white antelope on a hill.
The mention of his name is sweet to my heart.
      But mentioning the name of every beautiful thing is my
        occupation, which consoles and does me good,
      Whereas the core of my heart neglects everyone but him.

How often does the ghost of fantasy make me desire
While preventing a true reunion!
If only he could hear me complain about my condition.
      But he will never pity the one in love, whether he
        conceals or reveals it.
      How many lovers would go astray if he called them?

How often was he my drinking companion!
His mouth with well-arranged pearls is my candied fruit,
And whenever he says, "Yes," my paradise comes closer.
      It is all just a game with me, yet I am satisfied with
        dark red lips which, when he smiles,
      Reveal sweet food that is delicious. I sip from his
        radiant mouth.

I said while death was heading straight for me,
When he said, "Tomorrow I must go,"
And stretched out his hand to me in farewell,

> "I commend to the Lord's protection the one to whom
> I say farewell, and I ask God
> To make my heart patient while he is away. Alas!"

Translation from Arabic by Linda Fish Compton

Some Kharjas

1

I love you so much, so much,
so much, my love,
that my eyes are red with weeping
and always burn.

2

My man is violently jealous; he hurts me.
If I go out, he will harm me—
I can't make a move or he threatens me.
Mamma, tell me what to do!

3

Tell me, girlfriends,
when will my love give me—
O God! when will he give me—
the only medicine that will cure me?

4

My lord Ibrahim
—how sweet you are!—
come to me tonight.
If not, if you don't want to,
I will go to you:
just tell me where to meet you!

5

I love a dear boy
who belongs to another,
and he loves me!!!
But his wicked guardian
wants to keep us apart!

6

Mamma, my lover's
slave boy
is also mine—
for better or worse!

Translations by James DenBoer

COMMENTARY

(1) This *kharja* concludes a *muwashshaha* by the Hebrew poet Yosef al-Katib, & is perhaps the oldest known, from the first half of the eleventh century—the brother, Ishaq, mentioned in the poem, died in 1042, & the poem was written before that. The muwashshaha is a panegyric to Abu Ibrahim Semuel & his brother Ishaq, important Jews at the courts of Granada. After extolling the virtues of the brothers, the poet asks them to listen to his song, that is, the kharja, in which he declares his love "using his best words." The poem is in Hebrew, & the Arabic & Romance words are Hebraicized; in transcription from Hebrew letters to unvocalized Arabic & Romance words the first line reads "tnt 'm'ry tnt 'm'ry   hbyb tnt 'm'ry," with hbyb = habib (lover), the only Arabic term. The triple register, from Hebrew to Arabic & Romance, reflects the Arab,

Hebrew & Christian religious & social divisions in al-Andalus, while highlighting the code-switching between each group. . . . As is usual with Hebrew muwashshahat, this one is replete with biblical allusions, & the lover could be taken as Israel itself.

(2) The muwashshaha is a love poem by Abu Bakr Muhammad ibn Arfa' Ra'suh; because of love, he cannot sleep; his beloved doesn't know the poet's suffering; the poet will die if the lover leaves him. Every time he turns over in bed, the love in his heart grows, he says. "You, you are my best lover"—*amado* is in the masculine gender; experts point out that the use of the masculine in Arabic often includes reference to females as well as males, so there is no necessity to see this muwashshaha as addressed to a young man, though this is possible. The woman who sings the kharja calls upon her mother for help: "Mamma, tell me what to do!" (mam(m)a a gar ke farey)—the topos of the daughter/mother is frequently used in the kharjas, as in other traditional songs. Unusually, the poet introduces the kharja with a question: "How many young women have spoken allusively to their mothers of their fear of a lover?"

(3) The muwashshaha is by Abu Isa Ibn Labbun, an Arab poet who was a lord of Murviedro (now Sagunto) & then a magistrate in the court of King Mahmun of Toledo. It is a love poem, in which the poet accepts the suffering love brings; he asks for a kiss that will save him from death; love has taken possession of his reason & intelligence, & has humiliated him. . . . The kharja is sung (sadly) by some women, sick from love, who share the poet's "condition." The images of love as a sickness—as also in the medieval western European tradition—& the ministrations of the lover as a cure, or a healing, are common in these poems.

(4) The muwashshaha is a love poem by Muhammad ibn 'Ubada al-Qazzaz al-Malaq (of Malaga); it is dedicated to the poet's friend Abu 'Amr, a bachelor, the poet's "amigo íntimo," whose first name is perhaps Ibrahim. . . . The poet & the young woman singing the kharja are perhaps in love with this same Ibrahim. The singer of the kharja is introduced as someone who never stops complaining that her lover is unjust; she sings without hope that he will return. That she stutters over two "ifs" in the fourth line is perhaps an indication of her uncertainty, her anxiousness, her impatience.

(5) This kharja is used by three poets in three different muwashshahat, all of them love poems. The first & oldest is by the Arab poet Abu Bakr Yahya al-Saraqusti al-Jazzar (the Butcher), who wrote until almost the end of the eleventh century. The second is by Abu Bakr Yahya ibn Baqi, who died in 1145. The last is a Hebrew muwashshaha, by Moshe ibn Ezra, who died in 1139. Al-Jazzar's muwashshaha plays with the themes of fire in the heart & tears in the eyes of a lover; he asks for pity from his lover, & speaks the kharja himself, to a friend. Ibn Baqi's muwashshaha says love is good, there is no error in love, nothing bad in his lover—but why is he censured by others? He then praises his

lover's beauty in standard terms, & puts the kharja in his own mouth, attacking the jealous guardian. The Hebrew muwashshaha by Moshe ibn Ezra speaks of his betrayal by his lover, who has let loose the secret of their love; his lover's eyes are the cause of the poet's love, but sometimes they seem ominous (*nefastos*). He puts his kharja in the mouth of a gazelle, whose song reminds him of the spy's presence. . . .

(6) This kharja is used in two different muwashshahat. The first is by al-Saraqusti, the Butcher. . . . It is mostly in colloquial Andalusian Arabic, & contains but two Romance words. In al-Saraqusti's muwashshaha the beloved is described as usual: a sultan, a garden, one beauteous & graceful, a gentle fawn, who so loved the poet she became possessed & called to her mother for help. The identical kharja is also used by Abu Isa Ibn Labbun, a vizier to Abd al-Aziz of Valencia. His muwashshaha has some of the same language as that of al-Saraqusti: the poet has been captured by a fawn who is haughty & oppressive, who shuns him, who doesn't notice that the poet is wasting away—that is, it is darker in tone, & clearly homoerotic. In both poems, however, the kharja is sung by a young woman, expressing the feelings of any lover, male or female.

EDITORS' NOTE. Commentary by James DenBoer, edited by P.J.

Ibn Hani al-Andalusi (Seville, c. 934–
Barqa, Libya, 973)

AL-JILNAR

In tender age amid green branches
the pomegranate tree's daughter looked
like the heart of a falcon or of a hawk
left over by an eagle in its nest,
or like blood gushing from her slit throat
or as if she'd grown up in a land of embers
or been watered by a stream of wine
or as if the times had spared her time's hardships.
She blossomed like a flowering young breast
and showed her red gums through a smile
that tasted like the encounter of two lovers
who have lived a long time apart.

EXTINCTION IS THE TRUTH . . .

Extinction is the Truth, while Life is a lie
among great sermons and frightful omens.
We nourish endless hopes in our hearts
though our lives shall soon come to an end.
We witness our death with our own eyes:
if only our minds could comprehend that!
Our tragedy stems from our eyes that
can see though our minds remain blind.
If we really thought about our bodies,
their weakest part would be eye and eyesight,
and if all those parts were tested,
eye and ear would certainly be left out.
How could I be content with such a life
after I've realized that I'm human?
We remain tongue-tied
when, above us, Destiny speaks.
What is the use, then, of royal wealth,
honor, fortune, and white-footed horses?
What is the use, then, of my wandering poetry
and of my sharp, cutting tongue?
This is a cup I am tired of drinking from,
but I cannot keep away from it.
Shall we let life get the best of us
and surrender without fighting back?
Shall we not take our spears into our hands
and hurl them in piercing clusters?
Alas! Put down both sword and spear
for neither can really save us.
Life gathers us
though we are all separate.
If its fangs did not sow a seed of doubt
in our minds, we could see its true nature.
Times are only what we are cautious about:
great falls and great miseries.
The lion is only a mane and a paw;
his strength is his fang and his claw.
Every day, below his chest, traces
of innocent blood unjustly shed.

He is most feared for his strength;
if only he were merciful when he could be!
I swear the morrow won't see
a brighter morning, but a darker one!
The rising stars will soon be extinct, and so
will the twin lights of sun and moon.
Even if their rising observes a regular cycle,
someday, soon, they will become extinct.
And even if the planets keep spinning all around,
someday they too will disperse and vanish.

Translations from Arabic by Abdelfetah Chenni

COMMENTARY

(1) Born around 934 in Seville to a Maghrebian family, Muhammad ibn Hani, aka Ibn Hani al-Andalusi, was an Ismaili Arab poet who studied in the literary milieus of Córdoba. It is said that his licentious lifestyle & his Shiite religious convictions drew the ire of the populace, &, as Hoa Hoï Vong & Patrick Mégarbané write, "accused of being one of the numerous missionaries whom the Fatimid Imam keeps in Muslim Spain, he has no other choice than exile." After first finding refuge among the Banu Hamdun of M'Sila (in the eastern part of Algeria), toward 958 he offers his services to the Fatimid caliph al-Mu'izz, whose panegyrist he becomes. In the caliph's service he will, like poets often did, accompany the sovereign on his war expeditions (& will thus be present when al-Mu'izz conquers Egypt in 969). He also becomes a great defender of the Fatimid cause against the Abbasids & the Umayyads. While traveling with al-Mu'izz he will be assassinated somewhere between Tunisia & Egypt in 973—it is not known if this is because of an amorous passion or for political reasons.

(2) Reputed for highly imaginative descriptions & panegyrics, he was in his lifetime considered the equal of the great Mashreqi poet al-Mutanabbi (justly famous for his descriptions of armies & battles), especially in his poems on al-Mu'izz's fleet (then the dominant force in the Mediterranean) & on the caliph's well-bred horses—to which he dedicated many verses. The Syrian blind mystic poet Abu al-'ala al-Ma'arri, however, took umbrage, saying that he'd compare al-Hani "only to a grindstone that grinds horns, so much does his poetry crackle & sputter."

Ibn Darradj al-Qastalli (958–1030)

from *ODE IN PRAISE OF KHAIRAN AL-'AMIRI,
EMIR OF ALMERÍA*

In the folds of the stranger's rags
                many strange things are hidden
things that have long before settled
                in the depths of his hurt heart
kindling an old fire darkens
                night despite its blaze—
if the sea should dry up in the heat
                he'll fill it again with disconsolate tears
and when the sea winds die down
                low moans remind us of those we love
and will say—as the sea waves rise and fall
                amid the immensity of dark misery:
Will we survive or will we have
                but the sea as a grave and water as a shroud?
 Suppose we spotted land from far away
                shall we find refuge there and solace from old friends?
Death took advantage of us being far from home
                to beguile and seduce us.
That homeland now out of reach has turned into rubble
                under time's weight or injustice's swords
as old friends separated by distance
                became death's friends, land and sea—
their women mounted on wandering camels
                and roaming desert lands.
O Lord! What happened to their caravan?
                Are they now forced into exile on both land and sea?
Like orbiting planets they have become
                though driven by reins and bridles, anchors and sails.
When the Maghrebian land exiled me
                and dear friends rejected me
the land of Iraq warmly welcomed me
                and the good news reached Khorasan.

The land that banished me is a backward land
        and the life that broke its word to me is a traitor!
Peace on brothers from a hopeless brother
        I wish those times—when I had brothers—would return!
No road would now take me to my wife's
        as separation and oblivion had erased all tracks!

from ODE IN PRAISE OF AL-MANSUR AL-'AMIRI, EMIR OF CÓRDOBA

O wife! Set the will of the unjustly treated free
        so that it may rise into the desert's immensity and take flight!
Perhaps what pained you after separation
        will make the lowly stronger or free a prisoner.
Don't you know that to settle down means to die
        and that the homes of those who have no will become graves?
Didn't you try to read the early birds' omen?
        Didn't they fly to the right to tell you the journey would be safe?
This long journey does scare me
        though the hope of kissing al-Mansur's hand sustains me.
Let me drink the desert's stagnant waters
        until the pure waters of his nobility will quench my thirst
and give revenge for hard times
        as I meet the one who will protect me
for the risks that await the one who dares
        are also part of his human fate.
When she came closer to say good-bye
        her moans and sighs were more than I could bear;
she reminded me of our love and affection
        while from the cradle rose a baby's babble
that sounded like a dumb person's talk
        though it went straight to the heart
where it settled forever helped
        by wide open arms and a soft throat
that make of all noble and beautiful women
        breast-feeders for other children and their own.
I turned away from my child against my will
        to be led on a journey that would last many nights and days

and give wings to my ambitions and push me forward
>   while she yielded to the pain of separation and stepped back.
If she thinks she's said good bye to a jealous husband
>   I too am jealous of the power of her grief over my resolution.
If only she could see me amid the furnace
>   of the desert sun and the hallucinations of the mirage
unaware of the midday heat burning
>   my face till late in the blaze of afternoon
breathing searing desert wind
>   and treading on baking hot stones!
In a coward's life, death takes on many forms
>   while for the ear of the brave, fear is but a faint whistle!
She'd then understand that I fear only injustice
>   and that I have great patience when it comes to grief and pain:
like an emir who braves the dangers of the desert
>   and, if scared, resorts to his noble sword.
If only she could see me on the road at night
>   while my voice keeps the jinns company
braving the desert's scary darkness
>   like a lion roaring in a thick forest
as the stars start shimmering in the sky
>   like a virgin's black pupil in the white of her eye
and the polar stars shine high overhead
>   like crystal cups in a young servant's hands
and the Milky Way in the dark heavens
>   looks like a young man's hair turning white—
I was resolute in my decision despite the scary night
>   as the sleepy stars closed their lids;
then she'll realize that my wishes obey my will
>   and that I deserve al-Mansur's affection and generosity

Translation from Arabic by Abdelfetah Chenni & P.J.

COMMENTARY

(1) Writes Abdelfetah Chenni: "Ibn Darradj is known as the poet of 'exile, separation, geographical nomadicity,' yet he's never been farther than Ceuta in Morocco, & each time he traveled, his family was with him: the man lived more in a nostalgic nomadic world of his own, though he did write excellent poems thanks to this virtual nomadic state of mind. He was a Berber from the Sanhaja tribes, Shia followers of 'Ali, a minority in al-Andalus, unlike the Zenata, who were powerful allies of the then-ruling Umayyad Dynasty, though Ibn Darradj

never mentions his Berber origins in his poetry. He even stood against those Berber emirs who tried to take over power."

(2) The second ode we present an extract of, dedicated to al-Mansur, the emir of Córdoba, besides being a superb poem in itself, is also a major example of the genre of the emulation (*mu'arada*), in this case a "writing-through" (as some of us would say today) of a poem by Abu Nuwas. Beatrice Gruendler, who has analyzed these emulation poems, writes in her essay "Originality in Imitation: Two Mu'aradas by Ibn Darradj Al-Qastalli" (*Al-Qantara* 29 [2008]: 437–65): "Ibn Darradj, known as a poetic genius in his own right and credited for his expertise in *badi'* and virtuosity in motifs, can be expected to realize whatever potential an emulation offered. . . . Abu Nuwas was popular in the East; his poetry became the subject of emulations by Ibn Shuhayd, Ibn Sara al-Shantarini, Abu Tammam b. Rabah al-Hajam and others. . . . Like Abu Nuwas, Ibn Darradj uses the debate with the female character as a transition to the journey towards the praised one. But even within this framework, the poet makes large semantic and structural shifts. The female character is his wife, not an inaccessible beloved, and he introduces the character of an infant son. The wife receives a larger structural role in that the journey is described to her, soliciting her (imagined) approval, whereas Abu Nuwas inserts the journey in the middle of the praise section to show his zeal and exertion in reaching the mamduh ['a man easy to praise, benevolent to his supplicants, indulgent towards the faults of his poets, appreciative of and erudite in poetry' (Gruendler, *Medieval Arabic Praise Poetry: Ibn al-Rumi and the Patron's Redemption* [London: Routledge, 2003], 55)]."

Abu Amir Ibn Shuhayd (Córdoba, 992–1035)

from *QASIDA* (1)

Get up for the rooster's just sung
and water your thirsty heart with wine!
Meditate on Allah's miraculous suras
I've never read the like in any book:
the wine jug's bowing in awe
weeping over the brimming glasses;
the oud sweeps my sadness away
and makes me feel so merry again!
A young one stood to serve us:
a gazelle still suckling her mother
though her haircut made her look
more like a graceful young fawn.

Roses blossomed on her cheeks
and curls like the scorpion's
sting protected her temples.
An innocent sparrow
trusting the cunning fox
she walked toward me
—to become mine!

CÓRDOBA

An old woman who's—on my youth!—a mortal one!
Though—in truth—she's still a young beautiful one!
She seduced many lovers despite her age—
what a seducer she is indeed!
Despite her weakness she shows you
how minds can be turned like waterwheels!
Minds that have been taken in by her love
and found themselves her prisoners!
She's far larger than Cuenca
and more coquettish than Denia!
I agonized over my sad life there—
a lover's agony over his sad fate!

from *QASIDA* (II)

Death has no pity for eloquent speeches
    or for a poet's excellent words!
It spares neither the strong man's heart
    nor the weak man's soul!
It undoes the most powerful knots
    & sobers up the toughest drunk!
It's not strange that my death is near
    for the weak child's become an aging man
though it's strange that inside my chest
    still burns a fire throws off sparks
that keep me alive while death stifles my heart
    & even makes me happy in agony!

"AS HE GOT HIS FILL OF DELIRIOUS WINE"

As he got his fill of delirious wine
and went to sleep—as did his guards,
I closed in on him
like a burglar who knew his way through!
I fell on him like sheepish sleep
and entered his soul like breath,
kissing the white of his throat
licking the dark of his inner lips!
I spent that night enjoying his pleasures
until early dawn smiled at last!

GRAVESTONE QASIDA

O companion, get up, for we're late—
Will we spend all our time asleep?!
He told me: we can't get up
for there is sand & stones above;
remember all those nights we enjoyed
as though life were an eternal feast!
How many merry days we spent
like rainy clouds gathered above!
All this now gone as though it never existed
leaving behind only a readily sad present.

Translations from Arabic by Abdelfetah Chenni & P.J.

COMMENTARY

(1) Abu Amir Ibn Shuhayd came from an aristocratic Andalusian lineage, the Banu Shuhayd—a tribe famous for the purity of its language & for its poetic gifts. The historian Ibn Bassam al-Shantarini provides detailed information: hearing-impaired at an early age, Ibn Shuhayd also suffered in childhood from the misfortune of having a drunken father, who in old age turned pious, imposing his austere religious views on his son. At eighteen, the young poet witnessed the fall of Córdoba, then lived through the depressing Andalusian *fitna* period that would lead to the abolition of the Córdoba Caliphate in 1031. At age forty-three Ibn Shuhayd was laid up by hemiplegia for six months & then died.

(2) Ibn Shuhayd was a close friend of Ibn Hazm (see p. 67), to whom he addressed one of his major late poems. But he may be best known for a prose work he wrote in his youth, *Risalat al-tawabi' wa-l-zawabi* (Epistle of Inspiring

Jinns and Demons; c. 1013–17), an anthology of earlier great Arab poetry with his own mixed in. Robert Irwin has called it "a curious piece of fantasy, composed . . . in order to demonstrate his superiority to such great poets of the past as Imru' al-Qays, Abu Nuwas & Mutanabbi; it is a manifesto of emulation." The poem above beginning "As he got his fill" is a superb *mu'arada* of Imru al-Qais, the famous Mashreqi poet, whom Ibn Shuhayd outdoes in all sorts of ways in spite of keeping nearly all the same words in the first hemistich of the first line—probably so as to point out the challenge he intends to take up.

(3) The matter of emulation (see commentary on Ibn Darradj, p. 57) was much in the air & was central to the poets of al-Andalus while they formed a cultural & poetic identity separate from the place of Arabic origins, the Mashreq. Ibn Shuhayd meets the old great poets in an imagined land of jinns & competes with them. Irwin adds, making an interesting connection between al-Andalus & the European tradition to come: "Ibn Shuhayd's fantasy of the afterlife preceded by a few years that of Ma'arri & may have inspired the latter. . . . One or both of these Arab fantasies may have indirectly inspired Dante's famous *Divine Comedy* & its vision of an afterlife (in which, of course, dead poets make a prominent showing)."

Yusuf Ibn Harun al-Ramadi (d. c. 1022)

HUGGING LETTERS AND BEAUTY SPOTS

when you look at letters tracing a line
some are linked, others stand far apart
see how the former seem to be hugging
and the latter look like gap teeth in a mouth
—yet both are pearls extracted
by thought diving into a pulsing mind

black ink spots on the whiteness of the page:
beauty spots on the lover's lustrous face

SILVER BREAST

Many nights I spent with a glass of wine in my right hand
while my left kept squeezing a young budding breast
like an apple made from silver that was melted down
and then cooled in a perfectly round mold.

GOLD NAILS

She put her palm on her cheek
and kept brooding though not upset
as if her fingers were hiding
a red rose with a lily
or as if her silver fingers
were encrusted with gold nails.

THE SWALLOW

A swallow praised the Lord
in a gibberish that was well understood
with piercing shrieks that quickly resumed
just when you thought they'd come to an end
like a Qur'an reader who will lengthen a pause
to clearly mark it before he goes on.

O ROSE . . .

O rose veiled with a natural blush of shyness
like the cheeks of a black-eyed beauty
we're both strangers here—
you from Pechina, and me from Córdoba
we've met in the home of friends
known for their generous gifts
kissing you in front of them
is not a strange thing
as a stranger would kiss another stranger
when they meet far from home

Translations from Arabic by Abdelfetah Chenni & P.J.

COMMENTARY

(1) One of the early great al-Andalus poets, al-Ramadi was from Córdoba, where he spent most of his life, except for a short period of exile in Saragossa. Different sources set his death date at either 1013 or 1022. There is no complete *Diwan*, or collected poems, & of his other major work, *The Book on Birds*, written in prison, only a section on falcon hunting survives. Though trained in

the Mashreqi writing tradition, he worked in the contemporaneous Andalusian muwashshaha mode, to which he introduced several innovations.

(2) Writes Abdelfetah Chenni: "Zooming in on calligraphic/poetic processes— see the first poem above—or on subtly erotic physical features, or simply on the natural Andalusian landscape around him, with its flowers, trees, & birds, al-Ramadi, using all the artistic & linguistic resources of the al-Andalus tradition, captures those superb instantaneous moments of pure beauty. Maybe most famous for the poems concerning the young girl Khalwa, whom he saw only once & loved for the rest of his life (love at first sight, as immortalized by Ibn Hazm in *The Neck-Ring of the Dove*), he would later also immortalize his passion for a young Mozarab boy he calls Yahia—which makes his passionate/platonic love for Khalwa quite different from the Christianized platonic love of Dante for Beatrice. The last poem in our selection remembers an occasion when al-Ramadi was the guest of his friend Bani al-Arqam in Wadi-Aci, the Guadix of today. It was wintertime, yet he was offered roses brought from Bejana, the Pechina of today. But beyond these lyrical matters, al-Ramadi was also the poet exiled & jailed for his political stance against the Umayyad caliph, & who died in utter poverty."

In all of this, then, al-Ramadi is unquestionably the Andalusian poet par excellence!

Yosef Ibn Abitur (mid-tenth century–c. 1012)

THE "WHO?" OF IBN ABITUR OF CÓRDOBA

who
    ANCHORED the high skies
        set off the wheels for those who shine
who'd
    BE a god as great as El
        could tell El's greatness
who
    COMES to praise El Elohim
        with silence
who
    DID speak & speech became
        the day he pitched his skies
who
    EMITTED utterance & utterance remained
        the day he set his earths

who
    FIXED the ocean's depth
        the day he placed his lines
who
    GLUED earth's clods together
        the day he laid his valleys' floors
who
    HELD its measurements in place
        whose plumb line touched the earth
who's
    IN a king's robe
        fancy garments
who
    JUDGES righteousness
        on country roads
who's
    KNOWN as strong Yah many-powered
        all who stand up bow to him
who
    LETS out secrets drop by drop
        then names them speaking
who
    MAKES speech bring to life without his word
        but him
who
    NARROWED the sea breakers
        into sea deeps
who
    OPENED 300 horses' hooves
        between each wave
who
    PRONOUNCED words
        that broke a channel for the current
who
    QUESTIONED the rain coming
        two drops at a time to wash it out
who
    ROUNDED up the winds in his cupped palm
        trapped the waters in his robe

who
     SIGNALS ninety-nine
          birthshrieks for the mountain goat
who
     TOLD the eagle she could grasp her children
          in between her wings ascending
who
     URGED the dragon
          to bite the goat's womb
who
     VISIONS to every thunderclap
          a roadway of its own
who
     BROKE a channel for the current
          a road for his bolts of lightning
who
     YIELDED to every man
          the number of hairs for his head
who
     YET made each hair unique
          to keep from jamming together
who
     ORNAMENTED what man constructs
          like the beauty of firstborn Adam
who
     SAID that this should be like that
          same form same speech same voice
who
     EXPRESSES commands to his face
          & pays him when he obeys
whose
     FIVE fears were instilled
          in the five great beasts of this world
who
     ORDAINED a fear of mosquitoes
          beneath the elephant's thick hide
who
     FORCED the fear of the squirmer
          on ancient Leviathan

who
>CALLED out loud to show them
>>that he rules over them all

who
>OPPOSES his ways
>>& can soften his heart to peace

who
>REVERSES oppressed & oppressor
>>so oppressor can't break loose

who
>DREW the sudden fear of the locust
>>over the lion's mind

who
>OVERCOMES the scorpion
>>with fear of the squirming spider

who
>BROUGHT the fear of the swallow
>>to the eagle up in the sky

who
>ANCHORED the ends of the earth

Translation from Hebrew by Jerome Rothenberg & Harris Lenowitz

COMMENTARY

The first of the "new poets" of medieval Spain, Ibn Abitur was part of a prestigious Spanish family from the city of Mérida. Besides being a great scholar, he was deeply into *piyut* practice—as in the acrostic (alphabet & poet's name) translated here as such. *Who,* like other pronouns, was itself thought of as a name of God. Ibn Abitur also wrote a commentary on the Bible in Hebrew & enjoyed a relationship with the caliph of the time, for whom he fashioned an Arabic translation of the Talmud. When Moses ben Hanoch's son Hanoch was chosen to succeed his father as a rabbi, Ibn Abitur felt compelled to leave Spain & traveled to the Mashreq, stopping in Egypt before arriving in Baghdad. He eventually went to Damascus, where he died.

Hafsa bint Hamdun (Wadi al-Hijara, now Guadalajara, tenth century)

FOUR POEMS

Ibn Jamil's view is to see the world in toto, for everyone is taken by his gifts.

His manners are like wine with a dash of water, and his looks have grown
more handsome since his birth.

His sunshine face invites the eye, but his aura keeps people at bay.

Translation from Arabic by Abdullah al-Udhari

Good God, I have had it
up to here with my servants!
There's not even one
good egg among them;
they are but ignorant
flaky fools or so artful
& astute that they refuse
to come when I call.

•

He who is generous
reckons the world is kind
& the tides of his favors
lap against every shore;
he has an air of mildness
like a young varietal wine
& his beauty, sweeter
than all of creation.
His face like the sun
in all its grace attracts
the eyes and blinds them
with the intense respect
that it awakes.

•

I have a lover who can't be budged
by reproach & if I leave him he
asks out of spite: have you ever
known a man like me before?
To which I retort, & have you ever
seen a woman quite like me?

Translations from Spanish versions by Joseph Mulligan

Samuel Ha-Levi Ibn Nagrella, called ha-Nagid, "the Prince" (Merida, 993–Granada, 1055)

THREE LOVE POEMS

1

I'd sell my soul for that fawn
of a boy night walker
to sound of the oud & flute playing
who saw the glass in my hand, said
"drink the wine from between my lips"
& the moon was a yod drawn on
the cover of dawn—in gold ink

2

take the blood of the grape from
her red jeweled glass like fire
in middle of hail
this lady with lips of scarlet
thread   roof of her mouth
like good wine
mouth like her body well perfumed:
from blood of corpses the tips
of her fingers are red   thus
half of her hand is like ruby
half quartz

3

that's it—I love that fawn
plucking roses from
your garden—
you can put the blame on me
but if you once looked at my lover
with your eyes
your lovers would be hunting you
& you'd be gone
that boy who told me: pass
some honey from your hive
I answered: give me some back
on your tongue
& he got angry, yelled:
shall we two sin against the living God?
I answered: let your sin,
sweet master, be with me

Translations from Hebrew by Jerome Rothenberg & Harris Lenowitz

WAR POEM

[when we conquered their land destroyed the fortresses & towers subjugated villages & towns & overwhelmed the capital with violence]

I

field where the strong men lie
  puffed up like bellows
    like pregnant women
all together
  slave & noble
    prince & servant
with their king the new Agag they lie
  dung for the earth
    unburied
of a thousand only one was saved
  single grapes
    in a forsaken vineyard
Amalek's memory wiped out in Spain
  his army scattered
    kingdom destroyed

2

we left them to the jackals
  leopards & wild boars
    the flesh a gift to wolves
& birds of heaven
  tore at it
    so full so full
they dragged limbs across
  thorns & thistles
    lions would still their young with
& they tore at it
  so full
    so drunk with blood
hyenas made their rounds
  & night was deafened by
    the cries of ostriches

Translation from Hebrew by Jerome Rothenberg

Ibn Hazm (Córdoba, 994–Niebla, 1064)

MY HEART

I would split open my heart
with a knife, place you
within and seal my wound,
that you might dwell there

and never inhabit another
until the resurrection and
judgment day—thus you
would stay in my heart

while I lived, and at my death
you too would die in the
entrails of my core, in
the shadow of my tomb.

Translation from Arabic by Ammiel Alcalay

from "Author's Preface"

In the aforesaid letter you expressed ideas exceeding what I was accustomed to find in your other communications. Then on your arrival you revealed your intention plainly to me, and informed me of your views with that frankness which has always characterized our relations, that habit of sharing with me your every sweetness and bitterness, your every private thought and public profession. In this you were led by true affection, the which I doubly reciprocate, desiring no other recompense but to receive a like return. It was upon this theme that I composed the following verses in a long poem addressed to 'Ubaid Allah ibn 'Abd al-Rahman ibn al-Mughira, great-grandson of the Caliph al-Nasir (God have mercy upon him!), who was a dear friend of mine.

The passions most men boast them of
Are like a desert's noontide haze:
I love thee with a constant love
Unwithering through all my days.

This fondness I profess for thee
Is pure, and in my heart I bear
True love's inscription plain to see,
And all its tale is written there.

Had any passion, thine beside,
At any time my soul possessed,
I would have torn my worthless hide
And plucked that alien from my breast.

There is no other prize I seek:
Thy love is my desire sincere.
Only upon this theme I speak
To capture thy complacent ear.

This if I win, the earth's expanse
And all mankind are but as dust,
Yea, the wide world's inhabitants
Are flies, that crawl upon its crust.

Of Falling in Love while Asleep

EVERY love affair must necessarily have some original cause. I shall now begin with the most unlikely of all causes of love so that the discourse may proceed in due order, starting as ever with the simplest and easiest example. Love indeed is sometimes caused by things so strange that but for having myself observed them I would not have mentioned them at all. Now here is an instance from my own experience. One day I visited our friend Abu 'al-Sari 'Ammar ibn Ziyad, the freedman of al-Mu'aiyad, and found him deep in thought and much preoccupied. I asked him what was amiss; for a while he refused to explain, but then he said, "An extraordinary thing has happened to me, the like of which I have never heard." "What is that?" I inquired. "Last night," he answered, "I saw in a dream a young maiden, and on awaking I found that I had completely lost my heart to her, and that I was madly in love with her. Now I am in the most difficult straits possible, with this passion I have conceived for her." He continued cast down and afflicted for more than a month; nothing would cheer him up, so profound was his emotion. At last I scolded him, saying, "It is a vast mistake to occupy your soul with something unreal, and to attach your fantasy to a nonexistent being. Do you know who she is?" "No, by Allah!" he replied. "Really," I went on, "you have very little judgment, and your discretion must be affected, if you are actually in love with a person whom you have never seen, someone moreover who was never created and does not exist in the world at all. If you had fallen for one of those pictures they paint on the walls of the public baths, I would have found it easier to excuse you." So I continued, until at last by making a great effort he forgot his trouble. Now my opinion is that his case is to be explained as a pure fantasy of the mind, a nightmare illusion, and falls into the category of wishful thinking and mental hallucination. I have expressed this situation actually in verse.

Ah, would I knew who she might be,
  And how she walked by night!
Was she the moon that shone on me,
  The sun's uprising light?

A mere conjecture of the mind
  By cogitation wrought?
An image that the soul designed,
  Revealed to me by thought?

A picture that my spirit drew,
  My hopes to realize,
And that my sight imagined to
  Perceive in fleshly guise?

Or was she nothing of all these,
  But just an accident
Contrived for me by Fate's decrees
  With murderous intent?

Translation from Arabic by A. J. Arberry

Wallada bint al-Mustakfi (Córdoba, 994–1091)

SIX POEMS

By Allah, I'm made for higher goals and I walk with grace and style.
I blow kisses to anyone but reserve my cheeks for my man.

•

Come and see me at nightfall, the night will keep our secret.
When I'm with you I wish the sun and moon never turn up and the stars
  stay put.

•

If you were faithful to our love you wouldn't have lost your head over my
  maid.
You dropped a branch in full bloom for a lifeless twig.
You know I am the moon yet you fell for a tiddly star.

•

Ibn Zaidun, in spite of his qualities, is unkind to me for no reason.
He looks at me menacingly as if I'd come to unman his boyfriend Ali.

•

Ibn Zaidun, though a man of quality, loves the unbent rods in men's trousers.
If he saw a joystick dangling from a palm tree he'd fly after it like a craving
  bird.

.

Is there a way we can meet and share our love once more?
In the winter I used to wait on hot coals for your visits.
Now I feel worse since you've gone and confirmed my fears.
The night rolls on, but absence stays and patience won't free me from
  longing's grip.
I hope Allah waters the new land that's become our home.

Translations from Arabic by Abdullah al-Udhari

COMMENTARY

Wallada bint al-Mustakfi was the daughter of Muhammad III of Córdoba, one
of the last Umayyad Córdoban caliphs, who came to power in 1024 after assas-
sinating the previous caliph & who was assassinated himself two years later.
Her early childhood passed during the high period of the Córdoban Caliphate,
while her adolescence came during the tumultuous period following the even-
tual succession of Sanchuelo, who in his attempts to seize power from Hisham II
plunged the caliphate into civil war. As Muhammad III had no male heir, al-
Mustakfi inherited his properties, which she used to open a palace & literary hall
in Córdoba. She was an ideal beauty of the time: blond, fair-skinned, & blue-
eyed, as well as intelligent, cultured, & proud. She was also somewhat controver-
sial, walking out in public without a hijab. The first verse of the first poem above
was written on the right-hand side of the front of her robe, & the second verse
on the left-hand side. The love of her life was the poet Ibn Zaydun (see p. 74).

Ibn Rashiq al-Qayrawani (also al-Masili)

(Masila, Algeria, c. 1000–Mazara, Sicily, c. 1064)

from *LAMENT OVER THE FALL OF THE CITY OF KAIROUAN*

Many great men dwelt in that city
their faces shone with pure faith
they worked together to promote religion
and belief in Allah in overt and covert ways.
Many were renowned for their virtue and generosity,
and jealously preserved their respectability.

. . .

And when darkness fell, you would see them
deep in prayer like chaste monks
in the garden of Eden, that honorable place
among the beautiful houris and boys.

. . .

Thanks to its tribunes, Kairouan
was ranked among the world's greatest.
She outranked Egypt—that was fair enough—
and left Baghdad well behind.
When the city greatly prospered
and attracted ambitious pioneers,
as she became a place for all virtues,
as well as safety and faith,
time looked at her with envious eyes
and kept many sorrows in store
—till destiny had decided
to unleash the unavoidable:
troubles caused by various clans
that belonged to the Banu Hilal.
They massacred the Prophet's nation
and defied Allah's punishment during Ramadan.
They violated former treaties and those
under Allah's protection without keeping their word.
They preferred to deceive their neighbors
and take their women as prisoners of war.
They tortured them in the cruelest manner
and let rancor show through their hearts.
The Muslims were divided and humiliated
at the hands of these unfaithful:
some were tortured or could do nothing,
others were killed or put in prison.
They called for help but no help came,
and when they couldn't yell or cry anymore,
they gathered all their belongings
and valuables, whether gold, silver,
pearls, rare ornaments, or crockery.
They went out on bare feet, begging Allah
to protect them and overcome their fear.
They fled with their infants, their children,
their widows, and their spouses.
They kept their virgins safe like gazelles

lest their beauty drive the enemy mad—
chaste beauties covered with shawls
like moons shining on willow trees.

. . .

Sorrow will never disappear after such calamity
just as the eternal cycle of night and day will never end.
If Mount Thahlan had suffered the tenth of it,
its highest peaks would have crumbled!
All the cities of Iraq mourned her,
as did the villages of Syria, Egypt, and Khorasan.
Affliction and sorrow even reached
the farthest countries of the Sind and Hind,
and the land turned into a desert
from al-Andalus to Halwan.
I saw the stars rise but they did not shine,
nor did sun or moon.
I saw mountains deeply afflicted,
as were all humans and jinns.
Even Earth, because of this heavy burden,
has now a definite lean.
Will the nights, after they had separated us,
bring us together again?
Will they restore the land of Kairouan
and bring the city back to life again
after time had stolen its beauty
and caused bloodshed among rival clans?
It stands now as if it had never known riches
nor ever been a sacred land.
Time has duped its people
and cut off the ties that used to bind them.
Now they are scattered, like Saba's peoples,
and err about the lands.

Translation from Arabic by Abdelfetah Chenni & P.J.

COMMENTARY

(1) Abu Ali Hasan Ibn Rashiq al-Qayrawani (also called al-Azdi & al-Masili)
is a product of the flourishing eleventh-century culture of the North African
city of Kairouan on the eve of its demise. Born at Masila in the region of
Constantine circa 1000, fathered most probably by a freed slave of Byzantine
origin who was a client of the Arab tribe of Azd, he traveled as a young man to
Kairouan, where he studied, & at the age of twenty became a poet at the court

of the Zirid al-Mu'izz. When Kairouan fell to the invading nomadic tribes of the Banu Hilal in 1057, Ibn Rashiq composed an elegy to the city, for which he gained fame. He spent his last years in Sicily, where he died in either 1063–64 or 1070–71.

(2) Notes: The poem excerpted here was written after the Banu Hilal invasion of 1051; Mount Thahlan is a mountain range in Hejaz; "like Saba's peoples" refers to a traditional Arab proverb about the biblical Sheba.

(3) See also Ibn Rashiq's critical prose on p. 139.

Ibn Zaydun (Córdoba, 1003–71)

FRAGMENTS FROM THE *QASIDA IN THE RHYME OF NUN*

Now we are far apart
one from the other
my heart has dried up
but my tears keep falling.

In losing you my days
have turned black.
When I was with you
even my nights were white.

It's as though we never spent
that night together
with no third presence
save our two selves made one,

a night our lucky star
caused even gossips
who would spy on us
to turn away their eyes.

We were two secrets
held by the heart of darkness
until the tongue of dawn
threatened to denounce us.

WRITTEN FROM AL-ZAHRA'

From al-Zahra'
I remember you with passion.
The horizon is clear,
the earth's face serene.

The breeze grows faint
with the coming of dawn.
It seems to pity me
and lingers, full of tenderness.

The meandering waterway
with its silvery waters
sows a sparkling smile.
It resembles a necklace
unclasped and thrown aside.

A day like those delicious ones
now gone by
when seizing the dream of destiny
we were thieves of pleasure.

Today, alone,
I distract myself with flowers
that attract my eyes like magnets.
The wind roughhouses,
bending them over.

The blossoms are eyes.
They see my sleeplessness
and weep for me;
their iridescent tears overflow,
staining the calyx.

In the bright sun
red buds light up the rosebushes,
making morning
brighter still.

Fragrant breaths come from
the waterlilies' pome,
sleepyheads with eyes
half opened by dawn.

Everything stirs up the memory
of my passion for you,
still intact in my chest,
although my chest might seem
too narrow to contain it.

If, as I so desire,
we two could again be made one,
that day would be the noblest
of all days.

Would God grant calm to my heart
if it could cease to remember you
and refrain from flying
to your side
on wings trembling with desire?

If this passing breeze
would consent to carry me along,
it would put down at your feet
a man worn out by grief.

Oh, my most precious jewel,
the most sublime,
the one preferred by my soul.
As if lovers dealt in jewels!

In times gone by
we demanded of each other
payments of pure love
and were happy as colts
running free in pasture.

But now I am the only one
who can boast of being loyal.
You left me
and I stay here,
still sad, still loving you.

Note: Al-Zahra' refers to Madinat al-Zahra', the palace complex outside Córdoba. (The ruins are still extant.) The gardens are said to have been more splendid and extensive than those of the Generalife in Granada.

Translation from Arabic by Abdelfetah Chenni

Salomon Ibn Gabirol (Malaga, c. 1020–Valencia, c. 1058)

THE 16-YEAR-OLD POET

I am the prince the song
's my slave   I am the
string all singers songmen
tune   my song's a crown for
kings for ministers a
little crown   am only
sixteen years old but my
heart holds wisdom like some
poet 80 year old man

Translation from Hebrew by Jerome Rothenberg & Harris Lenowitz

from THE CROWN OF KINGDOM

May man profit by my prayer
may he learn the right and straight through it
I have told the wonders of living El in it
in brief not at full length
I set it above all my other praises
I call it the Crown of Kingdom

I

How wondrous your doings my soul knows well
Greatness is yours Adonai   and might and beauty
                              infinity and splendor
Rule is yours Adonai   and overall and richness and honor
The created things are yours   witness above and below
for as they disappear you wear on
Might is yours
our very thought wears out getting at its secret
You are so stronger than we
The mystery of might is yours   the hidden and the hide

Yours is the name hidden from sages
       the power which carries the world over nothing
       the ability to bring the hidden to light
Yours is the mercy
which rules your creatures
      and the good   hidden for those who fear you
Secrets are yours
which thought and reason cannot hold
and life which is unending
  the throne rising over all over
  the pleasance hidden in the height of mystery
Reality is yours
in its lit shade being is

we have said it: "We will live in His shade."

You have drawn a border between two worlds and both are yours:
one for doing and the other for reward
The reward of you you have kept for the righteous
                     kept hidden
for you saw its good and stored it up

    II

You are one   the beginning of all count
      the base of every structure
You are one   the sage of heart gape at your oneness
      and its secret   for they cannot know it
You are one   your unity cannot be diminished or added to
      it cannot want or gain
You are one   not as counted and dealt are one
      for extent and change cannot reach you
      nor description nor reference
You are one   My logic tires setting a limit for you and a law
      so I must guard my way from my own tongue's error
You are one   higher and over low and fallen
      no one   alone   to fall

III

You are real   but earhear and eyesight cannot reach you
                      how and why and where have nothing to do with you

You are real   but to yourself
                  and no one takes part
You are real   before all time you were
                  and dwelt without place
You are real   your secret hidden and who can catch it?
                  Deep   deep   who can find it?

. . .

VIII

You are he   Elohei Elohim   Adonei Adonim   ruling high and low
You are Eloha   all creatures your witness
                  all creation made to serve you honoring this name
You are Eloha   all the made things are your servants and serve you
                  no glory lost where others worship without you
                  the desire of all is to reach you
                  though they are like the blind who seek the highway
                  and stray from the way
                                 This one drowns in ruin pit
                                 this falls in holes
                     yet all think they have struck their wish
                     yet reach waste
Your servants are openeyed   walking the right way
                          never turning off right or left
                          till they come to the palace yard
You are Eloha   keeping made things by your Godness
                  feasting creatures on your Oneness
You are Eloha   no different in your Oneness and your Godness
                  or your Firstness or your Being
It is all one secret
                  and even if all the names are changed
it all comes back to one place

You are wise   wisdom is the source of life and flows from you
      all men are too stupid to know your wisdom
You are wise   the first of every first
      wisdom grew up with you
You are wise   not learn from without you
      not have it from some other
You are wise   shone fixed will from your wisdom
      a worker and an artist   pulling something
                                  from nothing

      as the light is drawn out from the eye
      drawn from lightsource without a tool
      working without any tool
      split and chop
      cleanse and true
      call to nothing and split it
           to being and fix it
           to timeworld and divide it
      measure skies by hand
      a hand joining tents of orbit
      joining the films of creature
      with rings of might
      power beaming on to the edge of creation
                    the lowest
                    the farthest away
                    the curtain's hem

Translation from Hebrew by Harris Lenowitz

Al Mu'tamid Ibn Abbad (Seville, 1040–Aghmat, 1095)

TO ABU BAKR IBN 'AMMAR GOING TO SILVES

When you come to Silves, Abu Bakr, my friend,
Greet with my burning love the spirits who dwell
In that place, and ask if any remember me.
Say this young man still sighs for the white palace,
The Alcazar of Lattices, where men like lions,
Warriors live, as in a wild beast's den,

And in soft boudoirs women who are beautiful.
Sheltered under the wing of darkness,
How many nights I spent with girls there.
Slender at the waist, hips round and abundant,
Tawny hair or golden, deeper than a sword blade
Or black lance their charms would run me through.
How many nights, too, in the river's loop I spent
With a graceful slave girl for my companion;
The curve of her bracelet imitated the river.
She poured out for me the wine of her eyes;
Or again the wine of her nook she poured for me;
Another time it was the wine of her lips she poured.
When her white fingers played among lute strings,
I felt a thrill as when a sword hits and clips
Clean through the sinews of a foe in combat.
When with a languid look she'd shake off her robe,
Like a ray of light surrendering her body was.
The very air around her shivered with desire.
It was a rose opening out of a rosebud.

TO RUMAYKIYYA

The heart beats on   and will not stop;
passion is large   and does not hide:
tears come down   like drops of rain;
the body is scorched   and turns yellow:
if this is it   when she is with me,
how would it be   if we're apart?

By her indifference   I am broken:
dark-eyed gazelle   among her leafage,
stars that burn   on her horizon,
depth of night   shining moon,
rock, then jonquil   in her garden,
bushes too   that spread perfume,
all know me downcast,   wasted as a man,
and are concerned   by my appearance,
how it mirrors   my state of mind;
they ask if I   may not be well,
flaming desire   might burn me out.

Woman, you do   your lover wrong
that he should look   as you've been told.
You say: "What hurts?   What's going on?
What do you want   but cannot wait for?
You're less than just   to doubt my love,
everyone knows it,   here or distant."

God! I am sick,   sick with the love
that makes, beside you,   others puny.
My body frets.   Give thought to this:
I want to see you   and I cannot.
Injustice calls   to God for pardon:
ask him to pardon   your injustice.

*Translations from Spanish versions of the original Arabic by Christopher Middleton &
Leticia Garza-Falcón*

Ibn Hamdis (Noto, Sicily, 1056–Majorca, 1133)

HE SAID, REMEMBERING SICILY AND HIS HOME, SYRACUSE

Because of long-lasting grief, we drive our camels,
and their legs bear us through the wide-open spaces

They frighten the wild cows straying in the desert
whose glances remind us of young ladies' eyes

Virgins, you see their marvelous beauty, as if
they were the type and original of their species

My critic! allow me to set loose my tears:
in moments of the most exquisite patience, I still find nothing to obstruct
    them

I am a man harboring a sorrow that
pricks me at the core of my heart

I believed that my land would return to her people—
but my beliefs have become a torment to me; I have grown hopeless

I console my soul, since I see my land
fighting a losing battle against a venomous enemy

What else, when she has been shamed, when the hands
of the Christians have turned her mosques into churches?

Whenever they wish, the monks strike, and the land fills—
morning and evening—with the sound of church bells

No medicine was able to cure her—
but also how much rust on the sword, how it tires the polisher!

Oh, Sicily! Destiny has deceived her
and she had protected the people of her time

How many are the eyes made sleepless by fear
that had been lulled to sleep by safety?

I see my nation—the Christians have imposed disgrace upon it
when once its glory was firmly established by my people

And the nation of infidels was once clothed in fear of her,
but now she is clad in the armor of fear of them

I no longer see the Arab lions among them
and in their hands you would see the unbelievers become prey

Oh my eye, you have not seen their like—squadrons
of war heroes in battle trampling their enemy

How many a shining sword! You imagine them
radiant shooting stars in the thick of the night

Standing out among the sword edges of the armored warriors
he cuts the helmets from the horsemen

I never imagined that the heat of fire might cool
when it falls upon the palm leaves in the arid heat of summer

Was Calabria not filled with Arab raiders?
Did they not annihilate the audacious Christian generals there?

It was they who opened its gates with their swords
and left its lights like darkest night

Their hands drive on the prisoners of war, white and uncovered:
you imagine them wearing cloaks of hair

They plunge into the sea, every season, toward them—
a sea whose waves are horsemen

Their battleships shoot Greek fire
and the smell of death descends upon the enemies' noses

You see the machines of war with red and yellow caps
like black girls married off as brides

When ovens smoke in the land
you imagine them rivals of volcanoes

Is there in Qasrini any patch of land they still inhabit?
Or has every trace of Islam been obliterated?

Among the wonders that the devils have wrought,
they have burned the houses of the zodiac to the ground

Syracuse became a stronghold for the Christians;
in its monasteries they visit their tombs

They march through a land whose people are below the earth
and have not encountered among them a proud and war-experienced
    person

And if those tombs were to split open, scowling
lions would arise from the graves

But I have seen the lion's covert; when the lion is absent
jackals prance and strut in the pride lands

Translation from Arabic by Karla Mallette

COMMENTARY

Writes his translator, Karla Mallette: "Ibn Hamdis, the premier Arab poet of
Sicily and one of the greatest Arab poets of the Middle Ages, was sixteen years
old when the Normans took Palermo. He left Sicily in 1078/79 and spent the
rest of his life in al-Andalus and Tunisia, leaving the former for the latter after
the Almoravids defeated and deposed his Andalusian sponsor, al-Mutamid.
The best known and best loved of his poems are his qasidas (or odes) remem-
bering Sicily: the *Siqilliyat*. [In the extract] above the poet draws on the images
and rhythms of traditional battle poetry to evoke and lament Sicily's fall to the
Normans."

Ibn Labbana (Benissa, mid-eleventh century–Majorca, 1113)

AL-MU'TAMID AND HIS FAMILY GO INTO EXILE

I will forget everything
except that morning
beside the Guadalquivir
when they were taken onto the ships
like the dead to their graves.

Jostling crowds line both banks
to see them, precious pearls,
adrift on the foam of the river.

Young girls dropped their veils,
clawed their faces,
and ripped their clothes.

The moment they left,
an endless commotion let loose
a clamorous outcry
of farewells and laments.

Translation from Arabic by Cola Franzen

TWO MUWASHSHAHAT

I

How long will the one whose eyes are languid
  yet healthy, not smitten by sleeplessness,
  keep me awake?

My tears have revealed what I would conceal, and my heart yearns for
  the one who treats it unjustly,
A gazelle whose mouth is used to saying no. How often do I desire
  to kiss it!
  It reveals well-ordered pearls. How nice it would be
    if daisies had such fragrant breath.

Is there any way to drink the kisses? How far I am from attaining
that hope!
Before accomplishing that, one must face eyes like swords, which
unsheath glances both brazen and bashful.
He showed us something red amid the white: the cheek
of morning with a glow of twilight in it.

Who will enable me to do justice in praising the Banu 'Abbad and
thanking them adequately?
Those gifts which they gave me were very unexpected. I forgive the one
who envies me because of them.
Doves resemble me among the leaves. The Banu 'Abbad
provided my wings with feathers. Then they put
a ring around my neck.

How magnificent is a king of Ya'rub who has relied on God! He is the
most noble of them in liberality.
And they pour forth like seas and roar like a lion if an embassy
appears.
If they are assailed or summoned, equally they hasten
forth with wine and a vessel of milk out of
generosity.

Time has been good to us and moderate as long as we have had this
dynasty, which has made us heirs of joy.
It brought back words of youth and love, so I said when my beloved
left,
"Send the greeting with the wind for an anxious lover
who does not trust mankind."

2

Thus the light of the shining stars leads the way
To the seated ones when water is mixed with wine in
the glasses.

Accept my excuse, for it is time to devote oneself to
Wine, which is passed around by one who has luxuriant eyebrows.
As you know, he is slender and lean.
Whenever he moves in the meadow of garments,
You see myrtle with its leaves swaying to and fro.

He is human even though he is more radiant
Than the sun and the full moon on a dark night.
My soul belongs to him and is not forsaken.
　　He is a gazelle who hunted the strongest lions
　　With harsh glances which penetrate people's homes.

Let me leave alone the subject of rejection and flight.
Take from me the two reports concerning glory
And say that I am going to talk about the sea.
　　Rashid of the Banu 'Abbad was victorious and generous,
　　And he has made men forget Rashid of the Banu 'Abbas.

His image dispelled darkness by the light of true religion
And so the stars strive to reach his height.
Thus kings are servants of 'Ubaid Allah.
　　So whoever wished to compare you to another in matters of glory
　　Compared in ignorance the light of the sun to a lantern.

Nobility is yours and you are from a noble family.
All see the attainment of favors they hope for through you,
So the one who sings does not leave in his former condition.
　　"Banu 'Abbad, because of you we are enjoying festivals
　　And weddings. May you live forever for the people's sake!"

Translations from Arabic by Linda Fish Compton

Moses Ibn Ezra (Granada, c. 1058–c. 1135)

DRINKING SONG

Bring me that sickly-looking wineglass.
See, when I fill it
it becomes as ardent as a lover's face
and chases off my beelzebubs.

Drink, my friend, and pass the beaker
So I may unburden myself
and if you see me going under
revive me with your minstrelsy.

SONG

Circumstance has estranged my friend.
He has bolted the door
but I will enter the portal
and knock
        despite my enemies.
I will shatter locks with words.
I will break bolts with my songs
and will persuade myself
that nettles are sprigs of balsam.
I will dance and shout to their bitter juice
as if I were drunk on wine
and humble myself
and pretend that hell stream is icy
if it will get me through darkness
                        into his light.
Go now, my song,
take this message to my beloved,
for song is a faithful messenger.

Adaptations from Hebrew by Carl Rakosi

Al-A'ma al-Tutili (b. Tudela, c. late eleventh century–
d. 1126)

WATER-FIRE MUWASHSHAHA

Tears flow, chest burns, water & fire!
                Moments of togetherness, rare moments indeed!
On my life, the censor's harsh:
                life's short, but love's toils long.
Oh hear, here sighs betray the lover
                here tears flow & flow.
Sleep's far away, seeing you—way farther;
                no peace, no quiet—yet no place to flee to.
Oh Kaaba, refuge for all hearts torn
                between a passion that calls & love that answers.

You called this sinner, who returns to you
                here I am, & don't listen to the spy's words.
Let me travel & worship there, no excuses!
                My heart's the gift, my tears the stones.
He's welcome, though he be my death—
                with his supple waist & languid eyes!
O hard heart love sees as soft,
                you taught me thought can think ill.
Since he ran from those brief nights, my tears flow
                as if between my lids stood sharp swords.
I've chosen a lord who unjustly condemns,
                I mean him—but won't give his name;
my justice is weird given his wrong's nature,
                you may ask him for a tryst & refusal.
I have to accept—no matter what
                as my lord who's forgotten & rejected me
He left me imprisoned, a hostage to pain & sorrow
                then sang between love & boldness:
"Mev'l habib enfermo de meu amar que no d'estar?
                Non ves a mib que se ha de no llegar."

Translation & adaptation from various Arabic versions & an English version by P. J. & Abdelfetah Chenni

COMMENTARY

Al-A'ma al-Tutili (the name means "the blind one from Tudela") was raised in Seville, where he familiarized himself with the poetry tradition of al-Andalus—he became one of the best-known muwashshaha & zajal poets of the Almoravid period in al-Andalus (1091–1145)—& he lived in Murcia, where he died young. He is known to have competed with Ibn Bajjah in witty compositions at the court of Ibn Tifilwit, the governor of Saragossa, & was recognized as a major elegiac poet. Karla Mallette, in her essay "Misunderstood" (*New Literary History* 34, n. 4 [Autumn 2003]), calls the muwashshaha above "a particularly tender and elegantly constructed love song. The opening line delicately balances two opposed elements: water (the tears that the lover sheds) and fire (the fire that burns in his heart). . . . The poet mourns the absence of his beloved. He calls out to the Ka'ba to witness his pain (and his contrition); and the Ka'ba, the ultimate goal of the Meccan pilgrimage and thus a sign of spiritual presence, symbolizes in the context of the erotic poem the sort of presence that is denied to the poet, who suffers the absence of his beloved." The realm of "the in-between" (as one of us has called it) is key: as Mallette writes, "The heart on its journey toward the Ka'ba is caught between (*bayna*) 'passion that calls and love that responds' (v. 5); the lover's tears are like swords balanced between (*bayna*) his eyelids (v. 10); the beloved sings the closing kharja 'between (*bayna*) boldness and love' (v. 14). The lover's heart, in short, is fragmented by the absence of his beloved (as the muwashshaha's lines are fragmented into brief, rhyming hemistiches) and craves the unifying presence of the beloved."

The kharja (see pp. 44, 46) is in Ibero-Romance; we decided to leave it as such to give the multilingual & slightly defamiliarizing sense of the original. Translated, it means: "My lover is lovesick—how could it be otherwise! / Don't you see he'll never come back to me again?" Often the kharja is presented as a quotation from a speaker introduced in the preceding stanza. Such Ibero-Romance kharjas are now seen as the first instances of Spanish lyric poetry.

The Spinozas, a band that specializes in Middle Eastern & Andalusian dance music with poetry from medieval Spain & al-Andalus, recorded a contemporary truncated version of this muwashshaha translated by its singer Na'Ti.

Ibn Khafadja (Alcita, province of Valencia, 1058–1138)

THE RIVER

God how beautiful it was
Gliding in its bed, the river

To drink from, more delicious
Than a lovely woman's lips

The loops, bracelets
Everywhere flowers ringed it

Milky Way

Margins of boughs curled like
Eyelashes, clear river iris

A breeze, late afternoon
Teased the boughs
Gold of dusk skimming
Silver water

Translation from Spanish versions of the original Arabic by Christopher Middleton & Leticia Garza-Falcón

Ibn Khafadja is most famous for his nature poems. He lived between the ages of the Taifas & the Almoravids, & his freedom-loving & proud temperament made him shy away from soliciting the favors & protection of any sovereign. In his critical treatise on al-Andalus literature & culture, al-Maqqari, the great Tlemcen-born critic, considers him the al-Andalus poet par excellence. Ibn Khafadja excelled in both his prose & his poetry, with fine descriptions of landscapes, rivers, gardens, & *riad*s (traditional Moroccan houses with interior courtyards) in his native region of Alzira, which he considered the flower of al-Andalus. For him, nature was a being with whom he stood in dialogue & exchanged feelings.

Yehuda Halevi, the Cantor of Zion

(Toledo, 1075–Cairo, 1141)

from *YEHUDA HALEVI'S SONGS TO ZION*

My heart in the east
and I at the farthest west:
how can I taste what I eat or find it sweet
while Zion
is in the cords of Edom and I
bound by the Arab?
Beside the dust of Zion
all the good of Spain is light;
and a light thing to leave it.

And if it is now only a land of howling beasts and owls
was it not so
when given to our fathers—
all of it only a heritage of thorns and thistles?
But they walked in it—
His name in their hearts, sustenance!—
as in a park among flowers.

In the midst of the sea
when the hills of it slide and sink
and the wind
lifts the water like sheaves—
now a heap of sheaves and then a floor for the threshing

and sail and planks shake
and the hands of the sailors are rags,
and no place for flight but the sea,
and the ship is hidden in waves
like a theft in the thief's hand,
suddenly the sea is smooth
and the stars shine on the water.

Wisdom and knowledge—except to swim—
have neither fame nor favor here;
a prisoner of hope, he gave his spirit to the winds,
and is owned by the sea;
between him and death—a board.

Zion, do you ask if the captives are at peace—
the few that are left?
I cry out like the jackals when I think of their grief,
but dreaming of the end of their captivity,
I am like a harp for your songs.

Adaptation from Hebrew by Charles Reznikoff

THE GARDEN

I

You
in Eden's trees:
a myrtle tree
and flowers
or among the stars:
Orion shining
God sent you myrrh
a cluster
purely
his own work:
no perfume maker's
skill
The dove
day that she nested in the tree
the myrtle stole her scent

breathed out as perfume
While with her
do not ask the sun to rise
she does not ask
while with you
for risings of the moon

Translation from Hebrew by Jerome Rothenberg

2

On the wind
in the cool of the evening
I send greetings to my friend.

I ask him to remember the day
of our parting when we made a covenant
of love by an apple tree.

Translation from Hebrew by Carl Rakosi

Ibn Quzman (Córdoba, 1078–1160)

[A MUWASHSHAHA]

Disparagers of love, now hear my song;
Though you be of a mind to do love wrong,
Believe me, moonlight is the stuff whereof
My lady's limbs are made. I offer proof.

Something I saw, full moon in her, alive,
Cool in her balanced body, took me captive;
Her beauty, young, her anklets, with a thrill
They pierced my heart, to cause my every ill.

A lover is a man amazed. Desire
Can drive him mad the moment he's on fire;
Heartsick, when he has had the thing he wants;
Worse, if he's deceived by what enchants.

A lover knows he's not the only one.
His lady's garden gate, she keeps it open:
A challenge—passion hurts him even more.
Whom will she choose? Whom will she ignore?

I'm of a kind a woman's body charms
So to the quick, it's Eden in her arms:
Absolute beauty being all we seek,
We can be melted by a touch of magic.

As for the moon, so for the sun: from both
She draws her power; moon pearls grace her mouth,
Solar fire crimsons her lips, and yet
She's not ambiguous when her heart is set:

Burning in my reflections, day by day,
In every act of mine she has her say;
Even when, if ever, she's at peace,
You'll never find her supine in the least.

Such is my proven moon, my lady love.
Yet of myself she did once disapprove:
Pointing to the marks my teeth had made
Across her breast, then eyeing me, she said:

"Easy does it, not too quick,
I like it slow, and nothing new.
Custom knows a thing or two,
It's to custom we should stick:
Festina lente, that's the trick—
Come at me slow, I'll come with you."

THE CROW

That house, not a stone left standing now,
Yet love does bring me back to where it was.

Some whose hour struck are gone for keeps:
Arcade and all, everywhere the wilderness.
The little dove mourns, with its cooing voice.
You lose a friend—what's to be hoped for next?
Simply seek, and mourn, the trace he left.

The soul went out of me. Sooner touch
Starlight than ever it return.
The turtledove, no matter what

. . .

Ibn Zaid's dive—what was all that noise about?
The busy throng that glittered round the mosque!
Delight in life! But an evil, greater, beat it down:
Look now, barren field, no plough, no seed.
Desert bigger than a man could grow.

Who'd ever tell it was my haunt, with friends,
Loyal, breezy, after a festival,
Me flashy in fine threads from a cabin trunk,
Hearing the plectrum pick at a guitar,
And shrilling in the open air, a flute.

Quzman repents! Let him get on with it.
Among the other lives, his was a feast.
Now drum is mute, and tambourine, the dance is done.
Still the muezzin inches up his minaret,
And prostrate in a mosque the imam prays.

Sinister twin of his, the crow croaks.
Not a dash of salt about him, poor glum thing!
In mourning garb forever, never glad:
All in sight or earshot ugliness for him:
Ah, deadly bird, pitch-black, the bogeyman!

Translation from Spanish versions of the Arabic by Christopher Middleton & Leticia Garza-Falcón

COMMENTARY

Ibn Quzman wrote "The Crow" after the devastation of Córdoba by Berbers egged on by fundamentalist faqihs. He had lived in various cities—Seville, Granada, Málaga, Jaén, possibly Fez—besides his native Córdoba. This is the penultimate poem in the earliest (Palestinian) poetry collection, thus presumably one of his last. The ellipsis marks lines lost in the original.

Abraham Ibn Ezra (1089–1164)

"I HAVE A GARMENT"

I have a garment which is like a sieve
Through which girls sift barley and wheat.
In the dead of night I spread it out like a tent
And a thousand stars pierce it with their gleams.
Sitting inside, I see the moon and the Pleiades
And on a good night, the great Orion himself.
I get awfully tired of counting all the holes,
Which seem to me like the teeth of many saws.
A piece of thread to sew up all the other threads
Would be, to say the least, superfluous.
If a fly landed on it with all his weight,
The little idiot would hang by his foot, cursing.
Dear God, do what you can to mend it.
Make me a mantle of praise from these poor rags.

Translation from Hebrew by Robert Mezey

Abu Madyan Shu'ayb (Sidi Boumedienne)

(Cantillana, 1126–Tlemcen, 1198)

YOU WILL BE SERVED IN YOUR GLASS

Hard times,
Sea that hides its secrets,
Harbinger of the visionary.
Cast your pretensions aside
And take your measures.

You, who believed
That in wounding others, you would be saved,
And that misfortune would only come to others,
This time, evil has spared you.
Above all, don't fool yourself where you shouldn't.

Reason before unleashing your words;
All questions engender a response.

Never does a claimed right die
When there are men behind it,
Even if it appears farther than sun and moon.

You who evoke only in mocking
The weaknesses of others,
The day will come when yours will be displayed.
You who make evil the reason of life,
Don't forget that you bathe in absolute shame.

You,
Sedentary without a home,
The riches that surround you will one day go up in smoke.
Very slowly the coming days will diminish your life,
Like wine dismantles reason.

It's time to leave,
The caravan's moving, and the horsemen as well,
And you are doing nothing for this voyage,
Too sure, you don't really know what awaits you,
The days to come will scarcely give you reason.

Translation from a French version of the original Arabic by Sylvia Mae Gorelick & Miles Joris-Peyrafitte

Hafsa bint al-Hajj Arrakuniyya (Granada, 1135–
Marrakech, 1190)

EIGHT POEMS

Ask the lightning when it roarrips the nightcalm if it's seen my man as it
    makes me think of him.

By Allah, it shakes my heart and turns my eyes into a raining sky.

.

I'm jealous of my chaperone's eyes and of the time and place that claim you.

If I keep you in my eyes until the world blows up I'd still want more.

.

I know too well those marvelous lips.

By Allah, I'm not lying if I say I love sipping their finerthanwine delicious
dew.

•

*Hafsa called at Abu Ja'far's house and handed the porter the following poem, to
be given to Abu Ja'far. As soon as Abu Ja'far saw the poem, he said: "This can
only be Hafsa." So Abu Ja'far went to receive Hafsa, but she had already gone.*

The girl with the gazelle neck is here and longs to meet you.

I wonder if she'll be graced with a welcome or told you're indisposed?

•

If you were not a star I would be in the dark.

Salaam to your beauty from one who misses the thrills of your company.

•

I send my earthrilling poems to visit you like a garden that can't go visiting
but reached out with its floating scent.

•

*After Hafsa had spent the night with Abu Ja'far in his garden, he sent her a poem
telling her how pleased were the garden, the birds, the river, and the breeze with
the way they had spent their night. Hafsa wrote back:*

When we walked along the garden path, there was no smile on the garden's
face but green envy and yellow bile.

And when we stood on the riverbank, the river was not a bubble of rippling
joy, and the dove cooed with spite.

You shouldn't take the world as it looks just because you're good.

Even the sky blazed on its stars to scan our love.

•

*As soon as Hafsa heard of the murder of Abu Ja'far she wore her mourning
clothes and grieved openly for him. She was threatened for mourning him, and
she cried out:*

They killed my love, then threatened me for wearing my mourning clothes.

Let Allah bless those who grieve or untap their tears for the man killed by
   his haters.

Let the morning clouds, like his generous hand, shower the earth that
   blankets him.

Translations from Arabic & comments by Abdullah al-Udhari

Ibn Arabi, al-Sheikh al-Akhbar

(Murcia, 1165–Damascus, 1240)

I BELIEVE IN THE RELIGION OF LOVE
Whatever direction its caravans may take,
For love is my religion and my faith.

Translation from Arabic by Maurice Gloton

"O MY TWO FRIENDS"

O my two friends—
   turn aside at al-Kathib,
pull off the track at La'la',
and seek the waters of Yalamlami.

   There you'll find
those you came to know.
   To them belong my fastings,
my pilgrimages, my festivals.

May I never forget what happened
   at the stoning grounds of Mina,
that day, at the fields of sacrifice,
   at the Zamzam's blessed spring.

   Their stoning ground, my heart—
let them cast their pebbles there!—
   their field of sacrifice, my soul,
their sacred spring, my blood.

Translation from Arabic by Michael Sells

The ransom of a prophet is a beast slaughtered as a sacrificial offering.
But how can the bleating of a ram compare with the speech of Man?
God the Mighty made mighty the ram for our sake or its sake, I know not
    by what measure.
No doubt other sacrificial beasts fetch a higher price,
But they are all less than a ram slaughtered as an offering.
Would that I knew how a mere ram came to be a substitute for the
    Vice-Regent of the Merciful.
Do you not perceive a certain logic in the matter,
The realization of gains and the diminution of loss?
No creation is higher than the stone, and after it the plant,
In a certain sense and according to certain measures.
After the plant comes sentient being, all know their Creator
    by a direct knowledge and clear evidence.
As for the one called Adam, he is bound by intelligence,
    thought, and the garland of faith.
Concerning this said Sahl, a Gnostic like ourselves,
Because we and they are the degree of spiritual vision,
Whoso has contemplated what I have contemplated
Will say the same as I, whether in secret or openly.
Do not consider words contrary to ours, nor sow seed in blind soil.
For they are the deaf, the dumb of whom the sinless one spoke in the text
    of the Qur'an.

Translation from Arabic by R. W. J. Austin

Abi Sharif al-Rundi (Seville, 1204–Ceuta, 1285)

NUNIYYA

Spain has been stricken by a calamity for which there is no consolation;
    because of it, Uhud is fallen and Thahlan lies in ruins.
The evil eye has smitten her Islam, and so deeply has she been afflicted that
    in many provinces and towns not a Muslim is left.

Ask Valencia what is the plight of Murcia! And where now is Xàtiva or where is Jaén?

And where is Córdoba, the home of learning, in which many a great scholar rose to renown?

And where is Seville with all her delights and her sweet river whose waters are full and overflowing?—

Noble cities that were the pillars of the land; and how can the land subsist when the pillars are no more?

As a fond lover weeps at parting from his beloved, bitterly weeps the glorious religion of Abraham

For desolate countries forsaken by Islam and peopled only by infidelity.

Their mosques have become churches: there is nothing in them but bells and crosses,

So that the mihrabs weep, though lifeless, and the minbars mourn, though wooden.

O you who does not heed the warning of Fortune—if you are asleep, yet is Fortune awake!

O you who walk jubilantly, charmed by your dwelling place—is any man beguiled by a fair abode after the loss of Seville?

That disaster made us forget those preceding it, and for all the length of time it will never be forgotten.

O you who ride noble horses, slender and swift as eagles on the field of honor,

And bear keen-edged Indian swords gleaming like fires amid dark clouds of dust,

And chew the cud of ease, powerful and glorious in your homes beyond the sea,

Have you no word of the people of Spain?—yet all night have riders carried their news to you.

How long will the sons of the despised, who are slain and captive, cry for succor and not a man of you be roused?

Why this estrangement between Muslims? O servants of Allah, you all are brothers!

Are there no proud souls, generous and of high courage? Is there none to aid and champion the good cause?

Oh, who will come to the help of a people once mighty but now abased, once flourishing but now oppressed by unbelievers?

Yesterday they were kings in their dwelling places, and today they are slaves in the land of the infidel.

And what if you could see them stricken with consternation, with none to guide them, wearing the garments of ignominy!

Could you but see them weeping when they are sold, the sight would dismay you and throw you into a frenzy of grief.

Ah, such a sundering comes between many a mother and child—as when souls are parted from bodies!

And many a young girl beautiful as the new-risen sun, blushing like rubies and coral,

The barbarian drags to shame by force, her eyes weeping, her mind distraught.

A sight like this melts the heart with anguish, if in the heart there be a Muslim's feeling and faith.

Translation from Arabic by Reynold A. Nicholson

Ibn Said al-Maghribi (Alcalá la Real, 1213–Tunis, 1274)

THE BATTLE

Oh God! The knights' banners
flutter like birds
encircling your enemies.

Lances punctuate the writing
of the swords;
dust like dry sand dries the ink;
blood perfumes it.

BLACK HORSE WITH WHITE CHEST

Black hindquarters, white chest:
he flies on the wings of the wind.

When you look at him you see dark night
opening, giving way to dawn.

Sons of Shem and Ham live harmoniously
in him, and take no care for the words
of would-be troublemakers.

Men's eyes light up when they see
reflected in his beauty

the clear strong black and white
of the eyes of beautiful women.

THE WIND

There is no better procuress
than the wind
because it lifts garments
and uncovers hidden
parts of the body

weakens the resistance
of branches
and makes them lean over
and kiss the faces of pools.

No wonder the wind is used
as a go-between
to carry messages back and forth
between friends and lovers.

Translations from Arabic by Cola Franzen

Abu al-Hassan al-Shushtari (Guadix, 1213–
Damietta, 1269)

MY ART

Tell the *faqih* on my behalf:
loving the beautiful one is my art.

My drink, with him from the glass,
and the *hadra,* with those gathered round,
Close by, good companions.
They lifted the weight from me.

Tell the *faqih* on my behalf:
loving the beautiful one is my art.

What kind of believer do you take me for?
The law revivifies me
and the truth annihilates me.
Know that I am a Sunni.

Tell the *faqih* on my behalf:
loving the beautiful one is my art.

And know that there is no one home
except you, so let's get to the point.
Enter into the arena with me.
Have faith. Don't push me away.

Tell the *faqih* on my behalf:
loving the beautiful one is my art.

If you could see me at home
when I raise the curtains
and my love is naked with me . . .
In union with him, I am made glad.

Tell the *faqih* on my behalf:
loving the beautiful one is my art.

So leave me be and spare me your delusions,
for you lust for yourself
and this world is your boudoir.
Wake up, you will see my beauty.

Tell the *faqih* on my behalf:
loving the beautiful one is my art.

BUT YOU *ARE* IN THE NAJD

How confused you are by two paths and the mountain
when the matter is clearer than fire on the mountain.

You traverse from Sal' and Kazima,
from Zafid and the neighbors of the people of Mecca.

You keep asking about the Najd. But you already are in the Najd.
And about Tihama—this behavior is suspect.

There is no life but for Layla. Go on, ask
about her—your questions are a delusion, they bring a void.

Say what you will about her, for she is pleased
either way, whether it be silent or spoken.

DESIRE DRIVES THE CAMELS

Desire drives the camels on the night journey
    when sleep calls out to their eyelids.

Slacken the reins and let them lead, for they
    know the abode of the Najd as well as anyone.

Prod the mounts, for Sal' is just ahead,
    and dismount just right of the path to Wadi al-Qari.

When you get there, smell that soil;
    it will smell of musk, pungent.

When you reach al-'Aqiq, say to them:
    the heart of the enthralled is back at camp, worn out.

If no one is there, embrace their habitations
   and be satisfied, for earth stands in for water.

Oh, people of Rama, how I long to join you;
   for that I would sell my life, if anyone would buy.

With a lover's hand, I hold fast to the bond of your closeness
even as fate sunders the bond to which I cling.

I bid you welcome, for everything that pleases you
   pleases me, and what you want for me, I want.

Translations from Arabic by Lourdes María Alvarez

Abraham Abulafia

(Saragossa, 1240–Comino, c. 1291)

HOW HE WENT AS MESSIAH IN THE NAME OF
ANGEL RAZIEL TO CONFRONT THE POPE

*Nahmanides: And so when the eskaton arrives   the messiah
will come to the Pope   by command of the Name
and will say   "Send out my people that they may serve
me"   and then he will have come*

   FROM AN ARGUMENT BETWEEN NAHMANIDES
   AND PAOLO CHRISTIANI IN BARCELONA, 1264

This *Book of Witness* is the fourth book of Raziel's explanations . . . until this
year he had not composed a book which might be called "prophecy" . . . and
in that good year the Name awoke him to go to great Rome   He commanded
him in Barcelona in the year "These" and five thousand [1280] . . . in going he
passed through Trani and was taken captive by goyim   because of slanders
the Jews had laid against him   but a miracle was done him   YHVH aided
him   and he was delivered . . . went through Capua . . . and in the month of
AV came to Rome . . . and determined to go before the Pope the day before
Rosh Hashanah   And the Pope commanded his guards   while he was in
Soriano   a certain city a day's walk from Rome   that if Raziel would come
there to speak with him in the name of all Jewry   that they would take him
immediately   and that he would not see him at all   but that they would take
him out of the city and burn him by fire   and there was the firewood behind

the city's inner walls   but this thing was announced to Raziel   He paid no
attention to the words of the speakers   but went away by himself   and saw
sights   and wrote them   and made this new book   and called it the Book
of Witness   it being a witness between him and the Name who delivered
him from the hands of his enemies   For on the day of his going before the
Pope two mouths spoke to him   and as he entered the outer gate of the city
a messenger came out toward him and told him the news   that the one who
sought his life had died sudden death   instant   in that very night he was
slain   and died   and he was delivered   and then caught in Rome by the
Little Brothers   and stayed in their college "Strength" days [= 28] and went
out on the first day of Marheshvan   and I have written this here to say the
praise of the   Holy One Blessed Is He and His miracles and wonders with
Raziel and His faithful servants

Translation from Hebrew by Harris Lenowitz

from **THE BOOK OF THE LETTER**

        And Adonai said to
    Zechariahu the Messenger,
        Raise your voice
            with the tongue
                of your pen,
            write
the word of god, this book with
your three
fingers; and God was
with him as guide, and he wrote
all that was commanded
and he came reciting the words
of God to the Jews circumcised
in the flesh as well as the
dullheaded and poor, but
they paid no heed to the form
of his coming, spoke of him
and his god in unimaginable
terms

Translation from Hebrew by Jack Hirschman

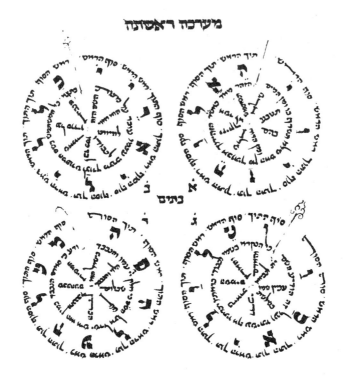

READING INSTRUCTIONS: Beginning at the marker: the outer rims read right to left; the inner rim leads to the inner spokes, & from circle into circle, right to left. The words at top = "first order."

Translation/Text/Gloss

Upper right

outer rim: middle of the first . middle of the last . first of the last . last of the last . first of the middle . middle of the middle . last of the middle . first of the first . last of the first

middle rim (large letters): permutations of the name "72"

inner rim: **be very wary as your fathers warned you of the fire don't be burnt by it & water**

inner spokes: **not to / drown / in it / & wind / that it not / harm you / you not / use**

Upper left

outer rim: first of the last . middle of the middle . middle of the first . first of the first . middle of the last . last of the last . first of the middle . last of the middle . first of the first . last of the first

middle rim (large letters): permutations of the name "72"

inner rim: it on condition anyone who takes the name for his own needs transgresses the command

inner spokes: about said name / was formed / to be / for his own glory / only thus / the prophet / said about / its secret

Lower right

outer rim: last of the middle . last of the first . first of the last . middle of the last . first of the middle . middle of the first . middle of the middle . first of the first . last of the last

middle rim (large letters): permutations of the name "72"

inner rim: whatever has my name I made it for my honor formed it worked it truly & concerning this the name informed

inner spokes: his prophets (be he blest) / about his name / by 3 / ways / of creation / of the skies / & earth / & man

Lower left

outer rim: last of the first . last of the middle . last of the last . middle of the middle . first of the first . middle of the first . first of the middle . first of the last . middle of the last

middle rim (large letters): permutations of the name "72"

inner rim: & know according to the name the one most honored is the one of Israel because the name's own portion is his people & the most honored one

inner spokes: of Israel is / the Levite & the most honored / of the Levites / is the / priest / & the most honored / of the priests / is the Messiah

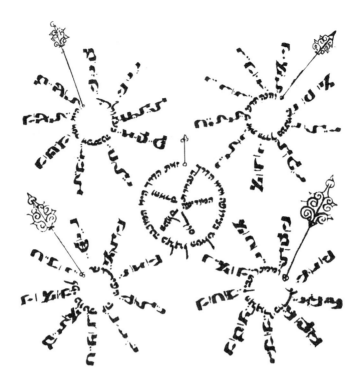

READING INSTRUCTIONS: Right to left & circle into circle toward the center. Larger letters are permutations of the name "72."

Translation/Text/Gloss

Upper right

the rim: o look here now this is the way itself

Upper left

the rim: by which you'll understand the gilgul metempsychosis complete

Lower right

the rim: the one I now write in the circle

Lower left

the rim: the intention of the explanation

Center

the rim: way that may be understood as three-fold gilgul metempsychosis
the spokes: the chosen way / disclosing / secrets / of the world / & man

Translations from Hebrew by Jerome Rothenberg & Harris Lenowitz

Abulafia's poetry of permutations (a kind of medieval "lettrism," etc.) here takes the form of nearly 200 circles, consisting of a discourse on meditation, a set of instructions for specific permutations, & the permutations of the letters themselves. In the present instance the permutations work off the so-called Name-of-72: i.e., 72 three-letter syllables "based on the three verses of Exodus 14.19–21, each of which contains 72 letters . . . . [It] was made up by joining the first letter of verse 19, the last letter of 20, and the first of 21, to form its first triad; the second letter of 19, the penultimate of 20, and the second of 21, to make the second triad, and so on until we have 72 three-letter terms comprising all the letters of these verses" (J. Trachtenberg, *Jewish Magic & Superstition*, p. 94). Abulafia in turn arranges the syllables in rows & columns, then sets them into circles according to instructions ("middle of the first, middle of the last," etc.), which form part of the circles as well. In this way the disciple is led into the circles, must follow their message as an act of concentration.

Abulafia himself writes of the abstracting/spiritualizing process which he then employs & by which the world is apprehended as language/sound: "Know that the method of *tseruf* [the combination of letters] can be compared to music; for the ear hears sounds from various combinations, in accordance with the character of the melody & the instrument. Also, two different instruments can form a combination, & if the sounds combine, the listener's ear registers a pleasant sensation in acknowledging their difference. . . . The same is true of the combination of letters. It touches the first string, which is comparable to the first letters, & proceeds to the second, third, fourth, & fifth, & the various sounds combine. And the secrets, which express themselves in these combinations, delight the heart, which acknowledges its God & is filled with ever fresh joy." Thus the letters—by a process called *dilug* (skipping)—become a basis for meditation "on the essence of one's thought, abstracting from it every word, be it connected with a notion or not . . . [by putting] the consonants which one is combining into swift motion" (from *Sha'are Tsedek*, for which see G. Scholem, *Major Trends in Jewish Mysticism*, pp. 154–55). For Abulafia & others, such processes remain essentially "oral," in the sense of open-ended: an improvisatory meditation on a fixed base (Torah, names of God, etc.) whose true meanings are not "literal" but the occasion for an ongoing process of reconstruction (revelation) & sounding. In touch with Yogic currents from the East, Abulafia's intention here seems clearly mantric; but his practice of a systemic & concrete poetry also closely resembles the twentieth-century lettrism of Isidore Isou, the asymmetries & nuclei of Jackson Mac Low, & the blues kabbala improvisations of Jack Hirschman, all of whom he may have influenced.

Commentary by Jerome Rothenberg, first published in A Big Jewish Book.

Ibn Zamrak (Granada, 1333–1393)

THE ALHAMBRA INSCRIPTION

I am a garden graced by every beauty:
See my splendor, then you will know my being.
For Muhammad, my king, and in his name
The noblest things, past or to come, I equal:
Of me, a work sublime. Fortune desires
That I outshine all other monuments.
What pleasure I provide for eyes to see!
In me, any noble man will take fresh heart:
Like an amulet the Pleiades protect him,
The magic of the breeze is his defender.
A shining dome, peerless, here displays
Evident splendors and more secret ones.
Gemini extends to it a touching hand,
Moon comes to parley, stars clustering there
Turn no longer in the sky's blue wheel:
In the two courts, submissively, they linger
To be of service to their lord, like slaves.
It is no marvel that the stars should err,
Moving across their marks and boundaries,
And are disposed to serve my sovereign lord,
Since all who serve him glory in his glory.
The palace portico, so beautiful
It bids to rival heaven's very vault;
Clothed in a woven raiment fine as this
You can forget the busy looms of Yemen.
See what arches mount upon its roof
And spring from columns burnished by the light
Like the celestial spheres that turn and turn
Above the luminous column of the dawn.
Altogether the columns are so beautiful
That every tongue is telling their renown;
Black the shadow-darkened cornice cuts
Across the fair light thrown by snowy marble;
Such opalescent shimmers swarm about,
You'd say, for all their size, they are of pearl.
Never have we seen a palace rise so high,

With such a clarity, such expanse of outline;
Never did a garden brim like this with flowers,
Fruits more sweet to taste or more perfumed.
It pays the fee required of beauty's critic
Twice and in two varieties of coin:
For if, at dawn, an early breeze will toss
Into his hands drachmas of light galore,
Later, in the thick of tree and shrub,
With coins of gold the sun will lavish him.
What sired these kindred things? A victory:
Still none can match the lineage of the king.

Translation from Spanish versions of the original Arabic by Christopher Middleton & Leticia Garza-Falcón

THE ORAL TRADITION I

PROLOGUE

What do we mean by *oral tradition?* Many researchers and scholars tend to cast the question of orality in some absolute or, perhaps, dialectical opposition to writing. Thereby, however, they situate themselves and the area under investigation in a classically Eurocentric dichotomy of Tradition versus Modernity, and its multiple variations based on specific concrete cases: Barbarity versus Civilization, country versus city, the urban versus the rural, and so on. Through this reductive procedure they keep themselves from apprehending the question's multidimensional subtleties.

To begin with, one has to lift the ambiguity of the term *tradition,* which, though indeed pointing back to an ancient heritage, mainly and simply signifies the retransmission of a given knowledge, the passing along of a range of know-hows: in this sense there exist an oral tradition and a written tradition—that is, a tradition that perpetuates itself by the spoken word and one that uses the written word. Thus the dichotomy Tradition/Modernity loses some of its value, because the oral tradition is not by nature wholly given over to archaisms and conformism, is not necessarily stuck in its formulation or fixed once and for all. In fact it can be the carrier of the new and the revealer of social upheavals (vide the use of oral communications such as cell phone conversations and minimal written adjuncts such as Twitter messages at the heart of the Arab Spring events in Tunisia and Egypt). The written, on the other hand, can easily be the harbinger of a conformist ideology and the carrier of so-called traditional but often reactionary values.

There remains another, even more dangerous confusion: the one that relegates the oral tradition to the universe of spontaneity, of collective creation by (illiterate) masses, and of a presumed popular "simplicity" in contradistinction to the domain of (complex) writing personalized by individual authors-creators, a domain usually reserved to an elite and certain "initiated" social groups. Such a view relies on an ideology or ideologies demanding an ahistoric world where form and content are permanent, where there are seemingly no contradictions inside a given society—in contradistinction to what we witness, namely an actual social reality showing societies to be historically delimited and determined, founded on dynamic conflicts inside and between their constituent groups.

The relationship between the oral and the written becomes more complex in societies where a strong and vital oral tradition survives parallel to one that foregrounds writing, such as those with an Arabo-Islamic culture. One can even suggest that in the Islamic world, writing has a privileged status in the organization of society: it is in a hegemonic situation, for it represents one of the "locations" of power where the dominant culture manifests itself. These societies' written productions in theology, philosophy, law, history, geography, science, and literature are manifold and ancient, covering a vast area of the social field. One can also note that the coexistence of the oral and the written inside such a society was perceived long ago and that it has been the object of many, often rigorous studies. (See, for example, the formidable gathering of oral poetry and anecdotes that al-Isfahani collected for his *Kitab al-Aghani.* See also the work of Muslim traditionalists concerning the gathering of the hadiths—the sayings of the Prophet—or Ibn Khaldun's rather mixed appreciation of oral tales in his *Muqaddimah.*)

In his work *Rappel à l'intelligent, avis à l'indifférent,* the Emir 'Abd al-Qadir attributes superiority to the written over the oral, thus stating a commonplace of Islamic societies (*Le livre d'Abdelkader,* translated by Gustave Dugat [reissue, Tunis: Bouslama, 1980], 117–21). For example: "There are two types of eloquence: the one belongs to the tongue and the other to writing; the latter is superior, for what the pen fixes perdures, [while] what the tongue says disappears after a few years." But the written is only privileged as a way of fixing the word, as a making permanent and a generalization of the oral, which is why reading aloud in front of an audience is one of the manifestations of sociability and of divine blessing.

Writing's mastery inside society remains a weak argument to explain the coexistence of an oral and a written tradition. The complex relationship these two traditions maintain points back to the question of how cultural diversity is created inside a given society. Indeed, the oral tradition is not simply a vulgarization of the written tradition or a late reprise of it but rather often an older, original, and independent conception.

All those collective representations of a group's lived or sublimated realities, of its aspirations, desires, beliefs, of its vision of the world that can be expressed in language, anonymously more often than not, can be considered part of the oral tradition. The expression of these representations is generally codified in the forms they take (such as tales, legends, epic narratives, poetry, proverbs, and sayings) and in the times and places they manifest (for example, fireside gatherings, propitious or ominous occasions, set feasts, and seasonal or other reunions).

In the Maghrebian oral tradition there are two clearly distinct genres:

- One that can be termed magical, which involves a tale that starts and ends with a specific ritual formula and can only be spoken at nightfall. The breaking of such a centuries-old rule risks bringing down punishment, such as turning bald, on one's children or oneself.
- The other could be called prosaic, in that it lacks any magical element in its formal structure. This does not prevent it, however, from addressing matters of the sacred. This genre includes animal fables, hagiographic narratives of the life and doings of the Prophet and his companions, stories of the group itself (its heroes and saints, etc.), songs, proverbs, and nursery rhymes.

As we'll see, animal stories are in the main either comic or tragicomic. The animals most dangerous to humans, such as the viper, the jackal, and sometimes the lion, are always ridiculed. The hedgehog, the donkey, and the turtle turn out to be the "good guys." In this animal universe, humans are clumsy, versatile, improvident, greedy, and inattentive. Such defects call misfortune down upon them. These "childish" stories present an obvious pedagogical, rather than merely ethical, aspect. That they are often told about a specific incident accentuates this aspect. Listening to them forces the understanding that these are in fact examples or parables. They also serve to share messages or underlying ideas. One often uses such indirect means so as not to cause offense to an oversensitive interlocutor by too frontal or obvious a message. Such stories play the role of arousing awareness and still have considerable importance in popular Maghrebian culture.

The oral tradition uses the Amazigh languages or vernacular Arabic, except for the Hilali epic, *Sirat Banu Hilal,* which holds a special place in the cultural heritage of the Maghreb. Indeed, Ibn Khaldun commented on this epic, which starts in Yemen and ends at the edge of the most western part of the Maghreb, in his *Muqaddimah.* Depending on the region, it is recited in either verse or prose form, always in a "less altered" vernacular Arabic. Much work has been and is being done on these *Sirat Banu Hilal* (see pp. 121, 353).

Kabyle Origin Tale: "The World Tree and the Image of the Universe"

The Kabyles' conception of the world is the following: The entire universe rests on the horns of a giant bull. And if he ever moved, the universe would immediately collapse. The earth itself is not a sole entity; it is composed of seven strata of earth superimposed one on the other. And beyond that, the Seven Heavens stretch out above. Humans live on the fifth stratum, counting from the bottom. Between heaven and earth, there are two more worlds. Beyond lies the nothingness from which everything was created.

On the lowest strata live the tiny *tidjal*. These are minuscule creatures that come out of ant eggs. They are meaner, and apparently smarter yet, than ants. On the land of these creatures grows a very powerful tree that towers high above. If this tree were ever uprooted and were to fall, these creatures would immediately have free access to our land and ruin everything, destroy all. Because this is the desire of these tidjal.

That is why all day long these creatures try desperately to fell this powerful tree. They even succeed each day in cutting deeply into the trunk. They dig until no more remains than the width of four fingers, almost to the point, therefore, of bringing down the tree. But in the evening, at the moment where they are so close to their goal, they stop working and say, "Now we will rest; the remainder we will do tomorrow." And the next day, when they want to return to their work and finish digging the rest to fell the tree, they find it intact, as if they had not touched it the day before. In fact, this tree grows back during the night by a height equal to the one that the tidjal had removed by digging during the course of the previous day. Thus, the access that would allow them to reach us remains sealed up—otherwise we would have been ruined and destroyed a long time ago.

Translation from the French Frobenius version by Steven Weber

from *Sirat Banu Hilal* (I)

SULTAN HASSAN EL HILALI BOU ALI, THE TACITURN

Sultan Bou Ali's wife dies, leaving him with three children: Zazia, Hassan, and Fakrun. He now marries Chiha, the daughter of the emir Rizg and sister of Bouzid, who gives him three children: Yahia, Yunes, and Maraï.

At the death of Sultan Bou Ali, the Hilali consult one another to determine his successor, for Hassan, the oldest of the male children, was so taciturn that he was believed to be mute.

The old sage man of the tribe told them:

"Noble assembly, before giving up all hope for him, make him walk with bare feet outside the beaten path among sharp stones and thorns. When he'll be tired, give him shoes and listen to what he'll say then. Right after that, make him walk some more, and when he is exhausted, put him on the back of a mount and remember what he will say; only then start on the way back. A man will reveal himself through his words."

Hassan el Hilali staggered along, his feet bloodied. Shoes are held out to him.

"He who has shoes will climb," he says.

They walk on. When he was exhausted, he is made to ride a mount.

"He who is mounted, is king."

The assembly of notables says: "It is he who will manage our affairs, for his words bear the stamp of common sense." They immediately named him sultan and gave him two councilors: Chiha and Zazia.

OVER WHOM TO WEEP

When a death among the people of the tribe was announced, Zazia bint Bou Ali would adopt different attitudes, depending on who it was.

The deaths of some saddened her deeply. She would weep hot tears and henceforth would assemble the Hilalis each month to tell them, "Let's go weep for and glorify our deceased."

But the death of others left her indifferent. She would bathe, change clothes, make up her eyes, and go, all smiles, to the parents of the deceased to give them her condolences. She'd leave them quickly and would forget the deceased forever.

Many were displeased by this disconcerting behavior of Zazia bint Bou Ali. Resentment grew, and the tribe risked being sundered by discord and thus becoming easy prey for its enemies.

So the Banu Hilalis' elders said: "This woman's beyond the pale. She merits death. Her partiality makes her unworthy of the high rank she occupies among us."

They go to confer with her brother, Sultan Hassan el Hilali Bou Ali, who tells them: "Summon her, ask her for the reasons for her behavior, and if she merits death, kill her."

Zazia comes before the assembly and is asked to explain her actions. She rises to face her judges, draws back her veil, and says:

"O Hilal Bou Ali! Three kinds of men deserve to have hot tears shed over them and to be mourned loudly.

"The first is the one who confronts danger and extinguishes the flames of war.

"The second is the one who receives guests during years of drought and famine, when to offer a sip of water to someone thirsty demands a struggle with oneself.

"The third is the man who is spiritual and eloquent and capable of asserting his rights and defending those of others.

"The rest, O Hilal Bou Ali, are worth no more than the faint glimmers a near-blind man perceives; their life amounts to little more than making women pregnant, to bringing brats into the world that will swell the masses of imbeciles, and to gorging themselves on heaps of asida on feast days in great ceremonial dishes. They deserve neither mourning nor tears."

A deep silence follows these words. Everyone withdraws, regretting whatever they had said against Zazia bint Bou Ali.

WHO IS THE BEST HILALI HORSEMAN?

The young girls of the Banu Hilal want to know who is the best horseman of the tribe. They organize a bet and send Dhaïa, the daughter of Bouzid, and his own daughter Zrara to Sultan El Hilali Bou Ali to ask him this question.

Dhaïa and Zrara address him as follows: "Hassan el Hilali, you owe us an account—don't leave us in uncertainty: who is the best horseman of the tribe when danger strikes?"

Hassan el Hilali answers:

"Zaïdan! Yes indeed, it is Zaïdan—he is the knight who defends and holds the narrow gorges on the days when lance thrusts rain down on the warriors.

"And it is also Dhiab! He is the knight of the skirmish: when the assault begins, it is he who keeps the advancing lines straight.

"And it is also Bouzid! Yes, Bouzid! I feel incapable to enumerate all his qualities. He is the Ethiopian hawk gliding above the bustards. This organizer of great razzias, this explorer of desolate vastnesses, how many tribes have seen him suddenly swoop down and decimate them, leaving owls to screech on fields of ruins.

"All the brave warriors the Hilali women have given birth to taken together do not equal Bouzid."

Dhaïa jumps up full of joy and runs toward her companions, but Zrara, dazed, eyes brimming with tears, remains, facing her father.

"I feel that you have humiliated me before the young Hilali women," she tells him, "and I won't dare show myself in their company henceforth. I counted on you, and you have disappointed me."

"I am the pivot of the millstone, O Zrara," he answers her. "It is I who disperses them and it is I who assembles them. If someone disobeys me, I squeeze him like the bark squeezes the stick."

CHIHA'S ADVICE

Bouzid says:

"They have sent camels against us, cherished camels raised for two years on their mothers' teats, camels whose flanks felt no load for two years.

"When they hear the mule driver's scream or the swords' clash, they start on their run, faster than the head partridge which crazed by thirst makes a dash for the water point."

All three now say:

"Bouzid's spouse has given us an embroidered breastplate so precious it could sate the poor during the years of dearth and said to us: 'Tell us, I beg you, protectors of our family, to whom do you, who are so good, abandon us?'"

Bouzid, turning toward her, replies:

"Hassan el Hilali is your protector. He is the strongest of the tribe. He's also the most magnanimous."

And they answered:

"No Bouzid, don't tell us this. In the name of Allah! If we lose you, we will lose men as precious as the camels entrusted to us by an absent being."

•

Then Chiha advances to make her recommendations to her brother and her children.

"Oh Bouzid! You have seven aunts on your father's side, and seven on your mother's side, and they all have recommendations for you.

"The first, oh Bouzid, is: if someone hails you, answer with 'please' but never with 'ya!'

"The second, oh Bouzid: never go down into a fort in ruins before having discovered the causes of its abandonment, for the one who destroyed it the first time around could destroy it again, even if it was rebuilt by an adept of Sidi ben Aïssa, the great magician!

"Bouzid! Do not camp in the bed of a wadi, because you risk being carried away by the floodwaters of a faraway storm.

"Bouzid! Avoid making noise and yelling loudly at high noon, because the noise echoes and could attract the enemy.

"Bouzid! If you light a fire in the middle of the plain, don't let the flames rise too high.

"Bouzid! If you go toward a water hole, carefully reconnoiter the area, like the jackal at nightfall.

"Bouzid! Don't let the meat grill too long on the fire. . . . Your manly stomach can do the job, once the meat is half-cooked.

"Bouzid! Ask Meraï to take care of your camels, for Meraï is the one who knows best how to do this.

"Bouzid! Put Yahia in charge of your provisions, for Yahia is neither greedy nor a glutton.

"Bouzid! If you happen to get hungry, send Younes to ask for food. Younes's beauty pays off even in the moments of greatest distress.

"And you, my darlings, if you feel that you are in difficulty, put your uncle at the front, for in battle your uncle is a formidable lion."

BOUZID ON RECONNAISSANCE IN THE MAGHREB

Bouzid leaves with his nephews. When they come to the Ksar Nbaoua in Tripolitania they see a mule making its way all by itself and carrying a load of fruit. The travelers take a few of the fruit and the mule stops dead. They leave it there and go on their way, in great haste.

The owner of the animal, not seeing it arrive, goes out to meet it. He finds it standing still on the road, its load dented. He is perplexed, but leaning toward the ground he discovers traces. He thinks for a moment and then says:

"Now the region is trampled by the animal with the rounded hoof. Life's no longer possible here!"

Then he sells everything he owns and leaves the country, saying:

"He who takes off at first warning will find where to live on this vast world. But he who stays motionless will lose life and limb."

.

Bouzid and his nephews camp in the shade of the Ksar Nbaoua.

You can still see the traces of their camels' hooves and the hole in which they baked their bread.

But that day they forget to tie up Meraï, something they usually do at each night's camp, so as to prevent him from using his divinatory skills to fill their hearts with dark presentiments. They did not want to know what fate had in store for them and preferred to trust themselves to God's will.

They said: "In Nbaoua we traced a figure on the ground so as to scrutinize the future."

Meraï raises himself up to inspect it as a connoisseur and says: "Why, O why, my companions, are you so eager to bring about your downfall and ruin?"

Bouzid turns toward him and says: "What did you say, Meraï?"

He answers: "Uncle, all I said was: O eagle, you take to the sky only with a twitching prey in your claws.

"Even he who'll pull our bread up from the pit will die.

"Yunes will be cloistered by Aziza Sfira in a palace with high crenellated walls.

"Yahia will die in the well at Nagoua, where a viper starved for seven years lies in wait for him.

"Meraï will be killed by slaves with thick lips.

"Bouzid, however, will no doubt return home to report what will have happened to our powerful tribes."

They leave right away, abandoning their bread. Bouzid goes back to pick it up. A jackal had ripped it from the walls of the pit. He kills it, roasts it over a fire, takes the bread, and turns back. He rejoins his companions toward noon in Mornag.

The next morning they let the mehari camels graze under the guard of Meraï and Bouzid while Yahia and Yunes walk to Tunis.

Here is how they recall their trek:

"We passed through Tourgha, a place lacking milk. Harmful to male animals, favorable to females, Tourgha makes its inhabitants despair.

"We came through Mesrata, Mesrata the blessed. And there we met a hundred nobles, all from high lineage.

"We came through Majer. There we found apples swaying on branches and bunches of grapes hanging from trellises.

"We passed through Tripoli, the scented city of merchants. One would say—I assure you, an ostrich standing up guarding her eggs.

"We passed through Al Aradh. May God keep them confined in their discomfort. A flight of bustards crosses over this region, even at night, only grabbed by fright.

"We arrived in Ifrikiya—may God not scatter its inhabitants—this country that feeds all the Arabs who live there and all those who immigrate there as well."

Translations & adaptations from Abderrahmane Guiga's Arabic versions by P.J.

Four Tamachek' Fables

Tamachek' is a dialect of the Iskkamaren, part of the Imouchar, or Tuareg of the Ahaggar, also spoken by the Haggar and the Azguer.

THE GREYHOUND AND THE BONE

A greyhound found a bone and started to gnaw it.

The bone said to him: I'm pretty tough.

To which the hound responded: Don't worry, I got all the time and nothing else to do.

THE LION, THE PANTHER, THE TAZOURIT, AND THE JACKAL

A lion, a panther, a tazourit,* and a jackal were friends. One day when they were hunting together they found a ewe, which they killed. The lion took the floor and asked: "Which one among us has to share out this meat?" It was suggested that it should be the job of the jackal, the smallest one among them.

So the jackal did as suggested, cut up the meat into four parts, and said: "All of you, come and get your part."

Tazourit is the name of a carnivorous animal, probably a species of large hyena.

The lion came and said to the jackal: "Which one is my share among these?" To which the jackal answered: "They are all the same; take the one you like."

"Jackal, you don't know how to share." Then he hit the jackal, killing him.

With the jackal dead, they wondered who would do the sharing of the meat. The tazourit told them that she would do it. She mixed up the ewe's meat with that of the jackal and divided the whole into six shares.

Seeing this, the lion asked: "There's three of us; why six parts?"

The tazourit answered: "The first part belongs to the lion, the second is for you as our boss, and the third is for red-eyes."*

"Who taught you this way of sharing?" asked the lion.

"The blow with which you killed the jackal," said the tazourit.

THE BILLY GOAT AND THE WILD BOAR

In the days when the animals were speaking, a billy goat in rut at springtime was calling out, filling the countryside with the noise of his voice. A wild boar heard him and accosted him:

"Hey! My friend, why are you raising such a ruckus?"

"I'm on the track of nanny goats, and usually they give birth when they hear this noise."

"How many kids does she usually give birth to?"

"Two, if she is fecund."

"No more than that!" says the boar. "Come, I'll show you my litter."

Billy goat and wild boar went off together and soon arrived at the place where the sows spent their days. They found five or six of them, each one followed by twice ten young ones.

"Do you see those piglets?" said the boar. "They are all my children. I'm not in the habit of making as much noise as you, and yet I have way more little ones than you."

He who habitually makes noise has nothing inside except noise.

*A nickname for the lion.

THE WOMAN AND THE LION

Kidnapped and abducted by her enemies, a woman however manages to escape en route. She meets up with a lion, who lets her ride on his back all the way to her village. The woman's kin were very happy to see her return and asked her who had brought her back. A lion, she said: "He treated me well, though he had very bad breath."

The lion, who was huddling close to her, heard this and got up and left.

A few nights later the woman, out searching for firewood, met up with a lion again, who said to her:

"Take a piece of wood and hit me."

"I'm not going to hit you; you see, a lion helped me out the other day and I can't know if it was you or another one."

"It was me."

"In that case I certainly won't hit you."

"Hit me with that piece of wood, or I'll eat you."

So she took the piece of wood and hit him and wounded him. The lion told her she could go now.

A few months later the lion and the woman met up again, and the lion said:

"Look at the spot where you wounded me—has it healed or not?"

"It has healed," the woman answered.

"Has the pelt grown back?"

"It has indeed."

"A wound usually heals," said the lion, "but not so the harm caused by harsh words. I prefer a blow from a sword to the words from a woman's tongue." And he carried her off and ate her.

Translations from Adolphe Hanoteau's French versions by P.J.

Kabylian Song on the Expedition of 1856

the marshal going to battle   has unfurled his standard
the soldiers following him   are well-armed and used to war.

unfortunate Kabyles who listen to no counsel
they will be reduced to slavery!

especially the Ayt Iraten   who had been warned long ago.
the Kabyles obeyed   neither Arab nor Turk

and yet the powerful Christian warrior   has come to settle in their land,
he has erected the Sultan's fort   and that's where he'll dwell.

Ayt Lhassan has been forcefully abducted   all the better for him
for the children of Paris always   keep their promises

the generals' standards   blind with their brightness
all march for one single cause   toward one single goal

each one of them   his rank's insignia on the shoulder
vanquished   the Zouaoua have submitted

the columns are camped   beneath Tizibert
the cannon was thundering   the women fled terrified

the Christians wearing their decorations   had girded on their swords
when the signal was given   they marched into battle

Mzian has been razed to the ground   let those who understand think on it!

Translation from French version of M. Féraud by P.J.

COMMENTARY

This song was composed by a *taleb* (student) of the zawiya of Chellata. It has been newly Englished by P.J., following a literal French version by M. Féraud collected in the *Revue Africaine* 2 (1858, p. 331). Tizibert is the rock towering above the mountain pass of Chellata (or *Icelladen* in Kabylian), which is a commune in Kabylia, in the *daïra* of Akbou in the *wilaya* of Bejaïa. Mzian or Mzeguén, depending on how the Zouaoua pronounce it, is the village of the Illoula Omalou burned to the ground on June 29, 1856, by the advancing French army.

Tuareg Proverbs from the Ahaggar

When Orion appears on the Ahaggar's threshold,
the guest will eat his fill.

    •

When Atakor* turns mouflon red, there's but one thing to do:
take your distance.

    •

Necessity makes the snake
walk on its belly.

    •

The viper takes on the color
of the place where it lives.

    •

In his mother's eye the dung beetle is a gazelle.

    •

Let me tell you the proverb of the female mouflon:
"If you leave a mountain, get onto another one immediately."

    •

Aldebaran pursues the Pleiades.
When he catches them
it will be the end of the world.

    •

*The massive Atakor volcanic field is the largest in the Hoggar (or Ahaggar) volcanic province of southern Algeria and covers an area of 2,150 square kilometers. Basaltic (mostly basanitic) scoria cones and lava flows from the Pleistocene or Holocene lie near spectacular older trachytic and phonolitic lava domes and volcanic necks that form some of the most dramatic scenery of northern Africa.

If you want herds, risk the razzia:
you'll drink milk or smell powder.

•

A man who drinks from a jar will never be a good guide.

•

A hundred mice led by a lion are better
than a hundred lions led by a mouse.

•

Hell itself abhors dishonor.

•

One hand, if sisterless,
no matter what, cannot untie a double knot.

•

Better to spend the night in irritation for an offense than in repentance for
vengeance.

•

If a man with a heart hurts you, do him good, and he will blush with the
pain he has caused you.

•

Throw goodness over your shoulder; it will be before you.

•

When doing good, one does it to oneself; when doing evil, one does it to
   oneself.

   •

Magic drinks are made with sweet things.

   •

The violent man
feeds his mother snakes.

   •

Kiss the hand you can't cut off.

Adaptation of H. Basset's French versions by P.J.

SECOND DIWAN

Al Adab: The Invention of Prose

PROLOGUE

The concept of *al adab* sends us back not directly to literature but rather to savoir vivre—good manners, rules of etiquette. The *muaddab* is "l'honnête homme," the gentleman, the honest, well-educated burgher who knows how to behave in society with his polite and polished manners, his dress, knowledge, and so forth. The term's closeness to matters of culture and education explains how *adab* came to refer to a large literary production whose aim was to forge a cultivated being. It is under the Abbasid Dynasty in Baghdad that the adab will develop as both a rule of conduct and a series of writings destined to edify a cultivated public. One of the founding texts is said to be *Al Adab al-kabir* (The Great Adab) of Ibn al-Muqaffa (d. 756). The Umayyad Caliphate in Córdoba promoted this literature, as it wanted to rival Baghdad. The Almohads did the same. Adab deals with a range of modalities, such as licit behaviors, table manners, interactions with women and with friends, sexual and erotic practices, the hagiographies of illustrious people. It is above all when dealing with the rules of conversation that adab touches upon literature, offering the reader various models of discourse, of poetries and didactic récits judged to conform to Muslim ethics. The greatest adab writer was incontestably al Djahiz (Basra, 776–868), whose works were widely imitated throughout the Muslim world.

The adab texts, be their orientation religious or secular, are written in prose, but they often include extracts from poems or whole poems to make the reading more agreeable. They are addressed to a well-off urban citizenry eager to learn and cultivate themselves without disdaining aesthetic pleasure. Ibn Hazm's *The Neck-Ring of the Dove* is a perfect example of the genre (see p. 68), as are Ibn Tufayl's *Hayy Ibn Yaqzan, a Philosophical Tale* (see p. 155) and Sheikh Nefzaoui's *The Perfumed Garden* (see p. 176). These erotic treatises are not considered libertine or licentious works to be read secretly but are part of Islamic exegesis. Most of their authors are imams of irreproachable moral standards.

One can also include Sufi texts, such as those of Ibn Arabi. In fact, Arab authors tend to classify as adab all literary texts, excluding the works of philosophers or historians. We, however, think of adab more in terms of a wider genre of "prose," as against poetry—and thus also present extracts from Maimonides's *Guide for the Perplexed* (see p. 160), Ibn Khaldun's *Muqaddimah* (see p. 171), and writings by Ibn Baja, known as Avempace (see p. 149).

A particular genre of adab called *rihla* develops in al-Andalus and the Maghreb. The word derives, as Stefania Pandolfo tells us in *Impasse of the Angels*, "from the verbal root *rahla*, to set out, to depart, to move away, to emigrate, to be constantly on the go, to wander, to lead a nomadic life." The noun, meaning "travel," thus became the Arabic name of the travelogue, "a classical literary genre of travel writing which blossomed in Dar al-Islam, the 'land of Islam,' from the eleventh to the fifteenth century and lasted in different forms all the way to the nineteenth century." Its origins are in the diaristic writings describing an individual's hajj, or journey to Mecca, though it expanded rapidly to take in other kinds of travels and was in fact a place of literary innovation. Pandolfo further explicates its importance: "The rihla as physical journey and existential displacement was the style and possibility of learning. Across the Islamic world, from one center of learning to another, a constant flow of scholars moved on endless peregrinations: from teacher to teacher, and from text to text. . . . The imperative of traveling for seeking knowledge determined the cosmopolitan character of the centers of learning, where everyone was a foreigner and everyone belonged."

One further aspect of this genre that Pandolfo points out is useful to note: the rihla is also a philosophical genre, of narratives of displacement. It is a genre that might be called cynical. Like the *maqamat* discussed by Abdelfattah Kilito, it is a narrative genre of reflections about the journey-like character of life, the mutability of fate and of the world, the irony of human existence, and what Kilito names *l'identité fugitive* (fugitive identity) in the context of a celebration of instability.

If the ur-rihlas were the travel journals of pious pilgrims undertaking the hajj, the genre developed quickly into geographical and commercial descriptions, *compte-rendus* of diplomatic journeys, and a range of related travel narratives. The most important rihla of Arabic literature remains Ibn Battuta's, a narrative that centuries later is still a fascinating read. The success of the genre in the days of the major political and economic expansion of the Arab world is easy to understand, knowing that it was addressed to a merchant elite that maintained links with a vast part of the world. Often the descriptions of the visited countries focus on curiosities and extraordinary or edifying events or objects. Although they could be seen as belonging to some preethnologic or preanthropologic literature, the rihlas do not aim at reporting or making their readers aware of any otherness or alterity, but, to the contrary, they want to magnify the unity of the Islamic ideal in accordance with the Qur'anic prescription that says, "We made you into nations and tribes, that you may know one another" (49:13). The genre will continue in the Maghreb until the nineteenth century, though with less brilliance than in its heyday.

Ibn Sharaf al-Qayrawani (Kairouan, c. 1000–
Seville, 1067)

ON SOME ANDALUSIAN POETS

As regards abd-Rabbu al-Qortobi [i.e., from Córdoba], though he lives far away, his poetry has reached us in its purest and most modern form, telling us about his sincere repentance, his Marwanid panegyrics, and his Abbasid satire. He is, in all this, a brave knight and a fine blade, as he also shows in his poetry a wide range of knowledge and great capacity for comprehension—writing genuine poetry and leaving a real jewel for his contemporaries and successors to wonder at and appreciate!

As for Ibn Hani Muhammad—al-Andalusi by birth but al-Qayrawani [related to al Qayrawan/Kairouan, Tunisia; see p. 49] by his presence and useful contributions while in that city—his language is like thunder and his writing smoothly narrative in structure and solidly constructed. His lines sometimes lack clarity and meaningfulness, though when meaning becomes clear through his eloquent poetic constructs, it goes straight to the heart like a hard stone thrown from a catapult and hits even those who are hard to please! He writes licentious, uninhibited ghazals—not chaste and pure platonic love poetry—in which the sword is always present! The sultan of the Zab [area of oases around Biskra, Algeria] has shown him his gratitude and contributed to his fame. His sovereign, Sayf al-Dawla ["the Sword of the State"], however, considered him a man who sought to better his life on earth at the expense of life after death because of the weakness of both his mind and his religious faith, for, if he were sensible enough, he wouldn't find it hard to write clear and meaningful poetry without seeking the help of his atheism!

As for [Ibn Darradj] al Qastalli [see p. 52], he is a brilliant poet who knows what he says. Everybody admits that he is an avant-garde poet, very smart in placing words exactly where they should be—particularly when he mentions what he went through in the days of the fitna [Andalusian civil war]. In short, he is the most poetic of all poets in the Maghreb—at all times!

ON POETIC CRITICISM

Literary criticism is a gifted competence that may be improved and updated. I have seen many poets and critics of poetry who were incapable of criticizing a text or distinguishing a good poem from a bad one! There are many, however, who aren't learned in criticism but are fully aware of the deficiencies that may be inherent in poetry—such as ambiguity, vagueness, and contradiction! To become a good critic, the first thing to rely on is patience: never hurry to praise or reject a piece of writing until you have used both eyes and mind to scrutinize it, have studied it in detail and examined it thoroughly. Know that impatience leads to risks, as it is also an unreliable ground, for there exists a kind of poetry that sounds pompous, but don't let it impress your ears! Look at the bait [line or verse] that is like a home: if there is meaning in there, then it is undoubtedly good poetry! But if the bait or the home is empty, with nobody in, then you may consider it just as a corpse!

Likewise, when you hear overused language and stereotyped words that have been used so many times that they have become clichés, don't hasten to underestimate them but instead spot their deficiencies and weaknesses: how many strange *meanings* can and may be expressed in strange ways! Meaning is the soul of poetry, and the word is its bodily appearance! When they match, this is the kind of luck each and every living poet dreams of! But when they don't, the poem is utterly soulless!

Watch out for two things:

· The first is to be so enamored of the poetry of the past that you hasten to appreciate and praise anything you listen to.

· The second is to be so disappointed with contemporary poetry that you don't listen carefully to what is said around you!

Both are unfair positions! Take your time, don't be overhasty, study carefully what is said: it's only then that you can make an unbiased judgment. In the Qur'an Allah has described man's obstinate clinging to the past:

We found our fathers following a certain religion, and we do guide ourselves by their footsteps.

And I've also said—along those lines:

Tell anybody who doesn't see any use in the present
*   but sees everything in the past*
that the past was once present
*   and that the present will someday become past!*

Translations from Arabic by Abdelfetah Chenni

(1) In his *Literary Criticism in Medieval Arabic-Islamic Culture: The Making of a Tradition,* Wen-chin Ouyang writes: "Ibn Sharaf, the sources tell us, is a lesser-known contemporary of Ibn Rashiq al-Qayrawani. . . . We also learn that he held extensive discussions of poetry with Ibn Rashiq, especially in connection with the issues contained in *Al-'umda* ["The Foundation," Ibn Rashiq's major work of adab, below]. . . . Ibn Sharaf al-Qayrawani . . . argued for the notion that *naqd* [literary criticism] was a talent because many [commentators on poetry] had no insight into *naqd* or the understanding of what is good (poetry) and what is otherwise."

(2) In the above extracts, we see the depth of Ibn Sharaf's insight & the soundness of his judgment when hearing a poem for the first time—be it an older or a modern piece of writing. We also wonder at his conception of a bait or tent/home that when uninhabited becomes "soulless" in the same way that a bait/verse/line from a qasida/poem becomes "meaningless" when deserted by the genie or jinn of poetic inspiration. Note how professionally didactic Ibn Sharaf becomes when teaching us how to be patient & not to hasten in evaluating poetry but to fairly & sufficiently study, examine, & scrutinize the text—very basic, simple, & sensible critical advice.

Ibn Rashiq al-Qayrawani (also al-Masili)

(Masila, Algeria, c. 1000–Mazara, Sicily, 1064)

from *AL-'UMDA:* "ON MAKING POETRY AND STIMULATING INSPIRATION"

Any poet—even if he is a laureate, well-versed, brilliant, and in the vanguard—must have found himself in a situation like this one: either a small difficulty, or the absence of inspiration, or the emergence of an unusual mood at that very moment. Al-Farazdaq, a gifted poet in his time, used to say: "I'd rather have a tooth extracted than write one verse of poetry." If that state perdures, the poet is said to be like the hen that cannot lay eggs anymore, or like the well digger who finds a rocky floor and cannot dig any farther, or like an infant who cries so much that his voice is gone. When the poet's words become defective, he is said to have become a dotard. It had been said of the poet al-Dhubyani that his poetry was free of imperfection because he said it when he was old. This is why he was called "the genius"; he grew old but did not turn into a dotard.

The poet is said to have missed the target when he misses meaning. Thus al-Buhturi once said: "I had a discussion with Ibn al-Jahm about poetry, and he mentioned Ajsha' al-Silmi and said that he used to miss the target. I did not understand him then and preferred not to ask. After I had left him, I thought about it and read Ajsha's poetry: I realized that there was not one single interesting verse." ...

When the poet Jarir wanted to write a qasida, he used to do that at night. He would light his oil lamp and go up on the roof. Once there, he would even cover his head to be in complete seclusion. The poet al-Farazdaq used to mount his camel and wander on his own in the mountains, the valleys, and the desert places that had fallen into ruins until language submitted itself to him. He mentioned this in his qasida called "Al-Fa'iya." One day, a young man from al-Ansar boasted in his presence of the poet Hassan Ibn Thabit's poetry. Al-Farazdaq spent the whole night struggling with inspiration, but nothing came. Before daybreak, he rode to a mountain near Medina called Dhubab and started to shout: "Your brother, oh Bani Labni! Your friend! Your friend! Your friend!" He then leaned his head on his camel, and the rhyming verses rushed in all of a sudden: thus was born his famous qasida.

The poet Abu Nuwas was once asked how he made poetry. He replied: "I start drinking until I feel in a state halfway between being still awake and almost drunk. At that very moment, I start feeling overexcited, and that makes it much easier for me to produce poetry."

Ibn Qutayba said: "There are times when making poetry becomes easier for the poet to achieve: at nightfall before slumber, at midday before lunch, and while secluded in prison or during a long journey on his own."

What makes it easier for the poet to get inspired is to lie down on his back. In any case, there is nothing more effective than to start work at early dawn after having just woken up, for at that moment the mind is clear and not distracted yet by either the pleasures or the worries of life, as if newly born. Early dawn is a fine moment, with much purer air and more balance between night and day, whereas in the evening, even though it is also a balanced moment between night and day, the mind is exhausted after a whole day's work and needs to rest in sleep. Early dawn is therefore the most appropriate moment for a poet to make poetry, while the night is best for those who want to learn and study.

The poet Abu Tammam used to overwork himself when making poetry, and that clearly shows in his poems. One of his friends told the following story: "I once called on him and knocked on his door. He asked me to come in, which I did. I found him lying in a very hot room, sweating as if he had just taken a bath, and tossing and turning all the time. I said to him: 'You must feel very hot. Are you ill?' He replied: 'No, it's something else.' He remained in that state for an hour or so and then stood up as if he had a cramp. 'Now I've got it!' he told me and lay back again to write something. 'Do you know what I was doing?' he then asked me. I said I didn't. So he explained: 'I was working on a line by Abu Nuwas, *Like times with their ferocity and leniency*, and I wanted to replace *times* with *the sun* and move along from there. Allah helped me, and I could make it:

I became ferocious, no: rather lenient, no: I actually made this from that.
You, without any doubt, encompass both the plain and the mountain.' "

I swear that if that visitor had remained silent, this verse would have ended with what was inside the room, because painstaking work is too obvious in it. Stories like Abu Tammam's—and even graver than his—did happen to others, such as the poet Jarir. Al-Farazdaq had made a poem in which he said:

I am the death that is going to take you, so see how you can fight it!

He swore he would divorce if Jarir could make a better verse than his. So Jarir went out for the day in the scorching sun and eventually came up with the following:

I am the eternal time that may put an end to death,
so give me something which, like time, is eternal!

Abu Tammam used to impose the rhyme on the verse to make the first hemistich more eloquent. This was rarely practiced, except by those who wrote in a forced, unnatural manner. The right manner for a poet is that he should not write a verse whose rhyme he initially ignores. I myself do not work in this manner; I am incapable of doing so. I usually make the first hemistich the way I want it to be, and then I search among the rhymes for the most adequate one to build the second hemistich. I do that in the same way as the poet who builds the whole verse on the rhyme. I do not see this manner as inconvenient to me in any way, nor does it make me stray from my objective or change anything in the first hemistich, except in very rare instances in which I seek excessive refinement. . . .

When a verse comes spontaneously to mind, many poets hasten to fix it and get rid of any imperfection. This is a quick and easy way for the poet who seeks to put his mind at ease. Others, however, won't fix the verse immediately but prefer to wait until they have brought it to perfection through hard mental work and highly meticulous refinement. This is a much more honorable way for the poet to proceed and shows how skillful he can be. It also preserves him from plagiarism.

I once asked an old master poet about what can help a poet to make poetry. He replied: "Flowers in a garden and relaxation after a bath." Others say it is good food, good wine, and good music than can ease the poet's mind, put him in a good mood, and help him make poetry.

When the people of Quraysh wanted to counter the Qur'an, their most eloquent men started to eat wild nuts and lamb and drink choice wine before going into seclusion. However, when they heard the sura that goes

> And it was said, "O earth, swallow your water, O sky, withhold your rain." And the water subsided, and the matter was accomplished, and the ship came to rest on the mountain Judiyy. And it was said, "Away with the wrongdoing people"

they gave up what they were after and admitted that such language could not have been invented by humans.

It has been suggested that to keep poetry on the leash, one has to sing it. The poet Abu al-Tayyib is said to sing his verse in the process of making it. When he faces difficulty finding the next verse, he stops and resumes singing what he has made so far from the first verse to the last until he gets hooked again. . . .

One should not overlook a relevant piece of writing on the subject by Bishr Ibn al-Mu'tamir, in which he said: "Take from your time only what you can spare, when your mind is really at peace, for it is then, and only then, that the mind becomes as pure as a gem and much readier for extreme focus and attention. It is only then that it will bring to you the finest of all words and meanings, which will seduce both the ear and the heart and prevent the occurrence of error. You should also know that this offers you more satisfaction than a whole day's work full of hardship and resistance. And even if your mind happens to mislead you, you should know that the error can be easily handled at that moment, as it has just originated from a fresh source, much like primal water from a newly born spring. Don't be a perfectionist, for this will lead to complexity, and it is complexity that obscures meaning and makes language unattractive. He who aims at clear meaning should express it through clear words, for clear meaning rightly deserves clear words. They both deserve to be protected from that which may damage them or cause them to be incorrect and from returning to that state in which they were before you managed to reveal their purity. Try to always work toward the following three objectives: The first one is to make your language soft, eloquent, rich, and simple and your meaning obvious, unveiled, and close. Meaning should not address either the public or an elite on an exclusive basis, but it should rather be relevant and appropriate in both cases. If you manage—thanks to the eloquence of your tongue and the fineness of your pen—to make the public grasp the meaning reserved for the elite and to express it through simple language that won't sound dull to the artist or remain obscure to the common people, you are then the most eloquent of all poets. If this first objective does not suit you, and if you see that the words you use do not fit where you intend to place them, and if you feel that the rhyme does not sound as harmonious as it should be with the form of the poem and seems rather "nervous" or "fidgets" there where you have fixed it, you should refrain from forcing both the word and the rhyme to camp in lands from which they both feel estranged. If you fail to make good metrical poetry or eloquent prose, no one will blame you for that. However, if you do not acknowledge your incapacity and persist in making poetry in such a forceful way, you may then be blamed by people less eloquent than you. If you really want to become a good poet and you feel that luck has not been on your side yet, you should be patient and work on it night and day whenever you feel your mind is ready and well-disposed till you achieve improvement. But if you feel that there is nothing to hope for, you will have to shift to the third objective and choose an easier and more motivating trade than that of making poetry. You will have tried your hardest. And never forget that desire alone cannot make the soul yield its best, as both love and yearning can.

Translation from Arabic by Abdelfetah Chenni

COMMENTARY

Ibn Rashiq's famous literary-critical work, *Al-'Umda fi Mahasin al-Shir wa-Adabihi wa-Naqdihi* (The Foundation of the Merits of Poetic Art and Criticism), is in fact a synthesis of three centuries of inquiry by Arab scholars of both East & West into the questions of literary criticism. Amjad Trabulsi has characterized Ibn Rashiq's originality in this work as his manner of presentation: an initial discussion of opposing views followed by an attempt to conciliate between them in an original way. We find this conciliatory spirit in the text above, in which the author concedes the merit of Tradition & the Ancients while simultaneously arguing for the superiority of the Moderns. See also Ibn Rashiq as poet (& the bio in that commentary; p. 71).

Al-Bakri (Huelva, 1014–Córdoba, 1094)

from *KITAB AL-MASALIK WA-'AL-MAMALIK* (BOOK OF ROUTES AND REALMS)

Zawila is like the town of Ajdabiya. It is a town without walls and is situated in the midst of the desert. It is the first point of the land of the Sudan. It has a cathedral mosque, a bath, and markets. Caravans meet there from all directions, and from there the ways of those setting out radiate. There are palm groves and cultivated areas which are irrigated by means of camels.

When 'Amr conquered Barqa he sent 'Uqba b. Nafi', who marched until he arrived at Zawila, and thus all the country between Barqa and Zawila came under the sway of the Muslims. In Zawila is the tomb of Di'bil b. 'Ali al-Khuza'i, the poet. Bakr b. Hammad says about him:

Death betrayed Di'bil in Zawila
And Ahmad b. Khasib in the land of Barqa.

Between Zawila and the town of Ajdabiya there are fourteen stages. The inhabitants of Zawila use a very ingenious method of guarding their town. He whose turn it is to stand watch takes a beast of burden (*dabba*), ties to it a large faggot of palm fronds so that their ends trail on the ground, and then goes round the town. The next morning the watchman, accompanied by his subordinates, goes on a saddle camel around the town. If they see footprints coming out of the town, they follow them until they overtake whoever has made them, in whatever direction he or she has gone, whether thief, runaway slave or slave woman, or camel.

Zawila lies between the Maghreb and the qibla from Atrabulus. From there slaves are exported to Ifriqiya and other neighboring regions. They are bought for short pieces of red cloth. Between Zawila and the region of the Kanim is forty stages. The Kanimis live beyond the desert of Zawila, and scarcely anyone reaches them. They are pagan Sudan. Some assert that there is a people there descended from the Banu Umayya, who found their way there during their persecution by the Abbasids. They still preserve the dress and customs of the Arabs.

It is said that there are great sands there, known as al-Jaza'ir, "the Islands," which have many palm trees and springs but no habitations or human beings, and that the whistling of the jinn is heard there all the time. Sometimes Sudan raiders and robbers stay there to waylay Muslims. The dates pile up there for years without anybody coming far enough to find them until people come foraging for them in years of famine or when they have an urgent need.

From Badis to Qaytun Bayada, which is the beginning of the land of Sumata and from which the route diverges to the land of the Sudan, to Atrabulus and to Qayrawan

The town of Sijilmasa was built in the year A.H. 140/757–58 C.E. Its growth caused the depopulation of the town of Targha, which is two days distant. It also caused the depopulation of the town of Ziz.

The town of Sijilmasa is situated on a plain whose soil is salty. Around the town are numerous suburbs with lofty mansions and other splendid buildings. There are also many gardens. The lower section of the wall surrounding the town is made of stone, but the upper one is of brick. This wall was built by al-Yasa' Abu Mansur b. Abi 'l-Qasim at his own expense, without anyone else sharing the cost. He expended on it [the value of] 1,000 *mudy* of wheat. There are twelve gates, eight of which are of iron. Al-Yasa' built the wall in the year 199/814–15, and in 200 he moved into the town, which he divided among the tribes, as it still continues till this day. The inhabitants wear the face veil (*niqab*), and if one of them uncovers his face, none of his relatives can recognize him.

Sijilmasa stands on two rivers, whose source, in the place called Ijlaf, is fed by many springs. On approaching Sijilmasa this stream divides into two branches, which flow to the east and west of the town. The cathedral mosque of the town is strongly built. It was constructed by al-Yasa', who did it excellently. The baths, however, are of poor construction and bad workmanship. The water in the town is brackish, as it is in all the wells of Sijilmasa. The cultivated land is irrigated with water from the river collected in basins like those used for watering gardens. There are many date palms, grapes, and all sorts of fruit. The grapes that are grown on trellises which the sun does not reach turn into raisins in the shade, and for this reason they are known as *zilli*, "shady," but those which the sun does reach become raisins in the sun.

The town of Sijilmasa is situated at the beginning of the desert, and no inhabited places are known to the west or south of it. There are no flies in Sijilmasa, and none of the inhabitants falls ill with leprosy (*judham*). When anyone suffering from this complaint enters the town, his illness does not develop further. The inhabitants of Sijilmasa fatten dogs and eat them, as do the people of the towns of Qafsa and Qastiliya. They eat grain (*zar'*) when it puts forth its shoots, and this they regard as a delicacy. The lepers (*mujadhdham*, "suffering from *judham*") there are occupied as scavengers (*kannaf*), and their masons are Jews, whom they restrict to this trade alone.

From the town of Sijilmasa you may travel to the land of the Sudan, namely to the town of Ghana. From Sijilmasa to Ghana is a distance of two months' traveling through deserts inhabited only by nomads, who do not stay anywhere permanently. They are the Banu Masufa of the Sanhaja, who have no town to which they may resort, save Wadi Dar'a. Between Sijilmasa and Wadi Dar'a is five days' journey.

The B. Midrar governed Sijilmasa for 160 years. The first of them was Abu 'l-Qasim Samgu b. Wasul al-Miknasi, the father of the above-mentioned al-Yasa' and a grandfather of Midrar. He had met, in Ifriqiya, 'Ikrima the freedman (*mawla*) of Ibn 'Abbas and heard hadiths from him. He owned flocks and often used to seek pasture on the site of Sijilmasa. A group of Sufriyya joined him, and when they had reached forty men, they made 'Isa b. Mazid the Black their leader and put him in charge of their affairs and began to build Sijilmasa. This was in 140/757–58. Others, however, say that Midrar was a smith, one of the Andalusian Rabadis who emigrated after the Rabad events and settled near Sijilmasa. The site of Sijilmasa at that time was a bare plain (*barah*) where the Berbers used to gather at a particular time each year to buy and sell. Midrar used to attend this market with the iron implements he had made. Then he set up a tent there and dwelt in it, and the Berbers dwelt round him, and that was the beginning of its becoming populated, and then it became a town. The first account of its becoming populated is the sounder one. There is no doubt that Midrar was a smith, for his sons who ruled Sijilmasa were satirized on that account. The first ruler of Sijilmasa was 'Isa b. Mazid, but then his Sufrite associates took exception to various things he did so that Abu 'l- Khattab said one day to his companions in 'Isa's council: "All the Sudan are thieves, even that one!" and pointed to 'Isa. So they took him and bound him tightly to a tree on a hilltop and left him there until the mosquitoes killed him. That hill is called Jabal 'Isa to this day.

They sow in the land of Sijilmasa in one year and harvest from that sowing for three years. The reason for this is that it is an extremely hot country with extreme summer heat, so when the grain is dry it gets scattered during harvesting, and as the ground is cracked, the scattered grain falls into those cracks. In the second year they plough without sowing, and do so in the third year too. Their wheat has a small grain and is *sini*, "Chinese"; a Prophet's *mudd* contains seventy-five thousand grains. Their *mudy* contains twelve *qanqal*s, the *qanqal* contains eight *zalafa*s, and the *zalafa* eight Prophet's *mudd*s.

Adaptation by P.J. of an English translation from Arabic by J. F. P. Hopkins

COMMENTARY

Al-Bakri (full name: Abu Ubayd 'Abd Allah Ibn 'Abdal-Azid al-Bakri) is one of the most important sources for the history of the western Sudan. Born to a princely family in Spain that lost its diminutive principality & moved to Córdoba, he lived most of his life in that city & Almería & became known as a geographer, theologian, philologist, & botanist. He died at an advanced age in 1094. Only two of his geographical works survive. Even his major work, *Kitab al-Masalik wa-'al-Mamalik* (Book of Routes and Realms), from which the present selection is taken, is incomplete & its greater part still unpublished. But it is clear that the sections on the Maghreb & the Sudan are the most original & valuable parts of his work. In these sections, his interest in ethnography & in what may be described as social & political history add depth & scope to the dry administrative & geographical material. His descriptions of towns are remarkably precise, & the value of his toponymic material is vindicated by the fact that it identifies, at least tentatively, many places in the modern Maghreb, Sahara, & Sudan.

His knowledge of this region is all the more surprising because it appears that he never left Spain, not even for Morocco, just across the Strait of Gibraltar. But in Spain al-Bakri had access to a wide range of geographical sources.

Abu Hamid al-Gharnati (Granada, 1080–Damascus, 1169)

from *TUHFAT AL-ALBAB* (GIFT OF THE SPIRIT)

Description of the Lighthouse of Alexandria

It was erected by Du'l-Karnayn—blessings be upon him!—and rose to more than three hundred cubits in height. It was constructed using cut stone and had a square base. On top of the square minaret, there was an octagonal minaret made out of bricks, and on top of the latter, a round minaret built with cut stone, each stone weighing more than two hundred *mann*. This minaret was topped by a mirror made of Chinese iron, which was seven cubits in size. One could see everything in it that traveled over the sea coming from all the lands of Rum. If they were enemies, they were allowed to come close to Alexandria. Then, when the sun leaned toward the Occident, the Alexandrians turned the mirror directly to the sun and aimed it at the ships so that the rays struck down on the ships and burned these while they were still at sea, and all aboard perished. The Byzantines paid a tax to insure their ships against fires caused by this mirror. When Alexandria was conquered by 'Amr ibn al-As, the Rum made use of a cunning stratagem: they sent in a troop of Arabized priests who posed as Muslims and turned up a book which claimed that the treasure of Du'l-Karnayn was inside the minaret. The Arabs believed them, as they knew little of the trickery of the Rum and did not know the usefulness of this mirror and the minaret, and they imagined that once they had got hold of the treasure and riches, they would restore the minaret and the mirror to their previous state. They demolished nearly two-thirds of the minaret without finding anything. The priests fled, and so the Arabs realized that it had been a stratagem. They rebuilt the brick minaret but were not able to put the cut stones back in their places. When they completed the minaret, they put the mirror at the summit, as it had been previously. But the mirror had rusted, and one could no longer see things as they had been seen before, and its power to set fire to ships had disappeared. The Arabs regretted having acted thus, as they lost an immense advantage in the process.

In the lower part of the minaret, constructed by Du'l-Karnayn, people entered through the gate, which is raised twenty cubits above ground level. One reaches it through archways made of cut stone. . . .

Passing the gate to the minaret, one finds, at one's right-hand side, a door through which one enters a large chamber of twenty square cubits, reachable from the two sides of the minaret. . . . One finds a door there that leads to a passage; right and left of this passage there are numerous rooms penetrated by light from the exterior of the minaret. Then one comes across a large chamber similar to the first and a passage similar to the first in which there are numerous rooms that lead to another large chamber similar to the preceding one. Then a passage identical to the preceding one leads to a fourth chamber, again resembling the preceding one but having a single door. One has to retrace one's steps, in order to exit through the first door. Many unwarned people get lost and find their deaths because they do not know the configuration of these spaces. I have entered them numerous times in the year 511 [= 1117 C.E.]. Upon leaving, one comes back to the passage that leads up to the minaret, and one climbs a stair to the minaret. Upon turning twice around the sphere, one also finds a chamber similar to the first and small rooms, and in each angle a large chamber like I mentioned earlier. This minaret is one of the wonders of the world. . . .

Chamber Made for Solomon by the Jinns

The jinns had made a room in Alexandria for Solomon—blessings be upon him!—with red marble pillars colored with all kinds of colors, pure as Yemenite onyx, polished as a mirror. The marble reflects so purely that, when looking at them, one can see those who walk behind you. The pillars are three hundred in number, or thereabouts. Each pillar rests upon a marble base and has, in its upper part, a perfectly crafted marble capital. In the middle of this room, there is a marble pillar, one hundred eleven cubits high, made of colored marble like all the other pillars. The jinns had cut the ceiling of this chamber, which is the courtroom of Solomon, from a single green stone, cut to the square. Upon learning of the death of Solomon—blessings be upon him!—they went to lay down the stone on the banks of the Nile, at the far end of the Egyptian territory. Among all those pillars that were in Solomon's courtroom, there was one that moved from east to west, along with the rising and setting of the sun. People observed its moving without knowing what was the cause. Similarly, in Constantinople there was a stone lighthouse on four pillars as well, which also moved from east to west, as witnessed by people. The base lifted from one side to the other side; people inserted pieces of brick, pottery, and stones under the base, and when the base tilted back, it crushed these. Each day, people inserted these objects, and no one knew the cause of it except for Allah the Highest. And it is an extraordinary marvel.

Translation from Arabic by Peter Cockelbergh

COMMENTARY

Born in Granada in 1080, al-Gharnati left his country in 1087, embarking for Alexandria via Sardinia & Sicily. He went on to Baghdad, Abhar, Jibal, & Sakhsin (or Saqsin) on the upper Volga, where he spent a number of years. He also traveled in Balghar (near Kazan on the Volga) & Hungary. In 1160 he was in Baghdad, & later he lived at various places in Khorasan & Syria. He wrote many geographical works, but it seems that his descriptions of most foreign countries are largely anecdotal. In 1162 al-Gharnati was in Mosul, where, on the suggestion of a pious scholar, he composed his *Tuhfat al-Albab* (Gift of the Spirit), from which the above texts are taken.

Ibn Baja (Avempace) (Saragossa, 1085–Fez, 1138)

from *THE GOVERNANCE OF THE SOLITARY,* CHAPTER 13

Some men, as we stated previously, are merely concerned with their corporeal form; they are the base. Others occupy themselves only with their particular spiritual form; they are the high-minded and the noble. Just as the basest among the men concerned with their corporeal form would be the one who disregards his spiritual form for the sake of the corporeal and does not pay any attention to the former, so the one who possesses nobility in the highest degree would be the one who disregards his corporeal form and does not pay any attention to it. However, the one who disregards his corporeal form completely, reduces his longevity; like the basest of men he deviates from nature; and like him he does not exist. But there are men who destroy their corporeal form in obedience to the demands of their spiritual form. Thus Ta'abbata Sharran says:

Our lot is either captivity to be followed by the favor of manumission
Or to shed our blood; death is preferable for the free.

Thus he considers death better than having to bear the favor of manumission. Others choose to kill themselves. This they do either by seeking certain death in the battlefield, as did, for example, the Marwanite in the war with 'Abd Allah Ibn 'Ali Ibn al-'Abbas; he is the author of the following lines:

Life with dishonor and the dislike of death,
Both I consider evil and hard.
If there is no escape from one or the other,
Then I choose to march nobly to death.

Or else they choose to take their life with their own hands. Zenobia did this when 'Amr was about to kill her: "I would rather do it with my own hands than let 'Amr kill me." So did the queen of Egypt whose story with Augustus is given in the histories. So also did certain peoples whom Aristotle mentions when treating of the magnanimous man: they burned themselves and their city when they became certain that their enemy was about to defeat them. All this borders on excess, except in certain situations in which the destruction of the corporeal form (but not the spiritual form) results from magnanimity and high-mindedness. This, for instance, applies to what Fatimah the mother of al-Rabi' (and the rest of the Banu Ziyad) did when Qays Ibn Zuhayr caught up with her. She threw herself off the camel she was riding, and died. But this is one of the special cases in which it is better to die than to live, and in which the choice of death over life is the right thing for man to do. We shall give an account of this later on.

There is another and lower type of the noble and the magnanimous man, which forms the majority. This is the man who disregards his corporeal form for the sake of the spiritual, but does not destroy the former, either because his spiritual form does not compel him to do so, or—despite its compelling him to destroy his corporeal form—because he decides in favor of keeping it. We believe this to be what Hatim al-Ta'i did when he slaughtered his horse and sat hungry, not eating any of it himself or feeding any of it to his family, while his young children were convulsing with hunger. Another example is what thieves do [when they endure hardships and face danger]. However, in the former case, the purpose is to control the body and improve it, while these thieves expend their bodies for the sake of their bodies and have a predilection for one corporeal state rather than another. In the former case—the case of Hatim al-Ta'i and his like—no argument can be adduced for not acknowledging that the action is noble and high-minded, and the nature responsible for it is honorable, sublime, and free of corporeality; it occupies the most sublime position, next only to that occupied by wisdom; and it must necessarily be one of the qualities of the philosophic nature, for without it the philosophic nature would be corporeal and mixed.

In order to achieve its highest perfection, the philosophic nature must, then, act nobly and high-mindedly. Therefore, whoever prefers his corporeal existence to anything pertaining to his spiritual existence will not be able to achieve the final end. Hence no corporeal man is happy and every happy man is completely spiritual. But just as the spiritual man must perform certain corporeal acts—but not for their own sake—and perform particular spiritual acts for their own sake, similarly, the philosopher must perform numerous particular spiritual acts—but not for their own sake—and perform all the intellectual acts for their own sake: the corporeal acts enable him to exist as a human, the particular spiritual acts render him more noble, and the intellectual acts render him divine and virtuous. The man of wisdom is therefore necessarily a man who is virtuous and divine. Of every kind of activity, he takes up the best only. He shares with every class of men the best states that characterize them. But he stands alone as the one who performs the most excellent and the noblest of actions. When he achieves the final end—that is, when he intellects simple essential intellects, which are mentioned in the *Metaphysics, On the Soul,* and *On Sense and the Sensible*—he then becomes one of these intellects. It would be right to call him simply divine. He will be free from the mortal sensible qualities, as well as from the high particular spiritual qualities: it will be fitting to describe him as a pure divinity.

All these qualities can be obtained by the solitary individual in the absence of the perfect city. By virtue of his two lower ranks—that is, the corporeal and the particular spiritual—he will not be a part, the end, the agent, or the preserver of this perfect city. By virtue of this third rank he may not be a part of this perfect city, but he nevertheless will be the end aimed at in this city. Of course, he cannot be the preserver or the agent of the perfect city while a solitary man.

Translation from Arabic by Lawrence Berman

COMMENTARY

Ibn Baja (known in the West as Avempace) represents the ideal of the Andalusian man of knowledge: astronomer, logician, musician, philosopher, physician, botanist, physicist, & poet. He was born in Saragossa & died in Fez in 1138. He worked as vizier & wrote poems (panegyrics & muwashshahat) for Abu Bakr Ibn Ibrahim Ibn Tifilwit, the Almoravid governor of Saragossa, & they both enjoyed music & wine. Ibn Baja also joined in poetic competitions with the poet al-Tutili. He was later the vizier of Yahya Ibn Yusuf Ibn Tashufin, the brother of the Almoravid sultan Yusuf Ibn Tashufin in Morocco. Ibn Baja was the famous author of the *Kitab al-Nabat* (The Book of Plants), a popular work on botany which defined the sex of plants. His philosophic ideas had a clear effect on Ibn-Rushd & Albertus Magnus. In his explanation of the zajal (see p. 44), E. G. Gomes writes: "There is some evidence for the belief that it was invented by the famous philosopher and musician known as Avempace. Its chief characteristic being that it is written entirely in the vernacular."

Al-Idrisi (Ceuta, 1099–Sicily, c. 1166)

from *AL-KITAB AL-RUJARI* (ROGER'S BOOK)

As Roger [II of Sicily]'s domains expanded he wished to learn more about them and other countries by seeking the knowledge contained in the books composed about this science, such as al-Mas'udi's *Book of Marvels* and the books of Abu Nasr Sa'id al-Jayhani, Abu 'l-Qasim 'Ubayd Allah b. Khurradadhbih, Ahmad b. 'Umar al-'Udhri, Abu 'l-Qasim Muhammad al-Hawqali al-Baghdadi, Khanakh b. Khaqan al-Kaymaki, Musa b. Qasim al-Qardi, Ahmad b. Ya'qub known as al-Ya'qubi, Ishaq b. al-Hasan al-Munajjim, Qudama al-Basri, Claudius Ptolemy (Balalmayus al-Aqlawdi), and Orosius of Antioch (Urusiyus al-Antaki). But he did not find what he wanted expounded in detail in them; nay, he found that it was ignored . . . ; so he set in train the operation of which this work is the result.

The First Clime

On the western side this clime begins at al-Bahr al-Gharbi (the Western Sea), called Bahr al-Zulumat (the Sea of Darkness). No one knows what is beyond this sea. There are two islands in it, called al-Khalidat (the Immortal Isles). From these islands Ptolemy started to reckon longitude and latitude. It is said that on each of these islands is an idol (*sanam*) built of stone. Each of these idols is one hundred cubits high and has on top an effigy of copper, pointing with its hands to whatever lies beyond. According to what is reported, there are six such idols. One of them is at Qadis in the west of al-Andalus, and no one knows of any inhabited land beyond it.

In this section the towns which we have marked are: Awlil, Sila, Takrur, Daw, Barisa, and Mura. These towns are in the land of Maqzara of the Sudan.

The Island of Awlil is in the sea near the coast. The famous salt deposit is there. No other salt deposit is known in the land of the Sudan. The salt is carried from there to all the towns of the Sudan. Boats come to this island, and the salt is loaded on them. The boats then go to the mouth of the Nile, which is one day's run from the island. They then proceed up the Nile to Sila, Takrur, Barisa, Ghana, and the other towns of Wanqara and Kugha, as well as to all the towns of the Sudan. The majority of them have no fixed abode, except on the Nile itself or on one of its tributaries. All the other lands in the neighborhood of the Nile are empty waste, where there is no settlement. In these wastes there are arid deserts where water can only be found after two, four, five, six, or twelve days' [marching], as in the arid desert of Nisar, which is on the route from Sijilmasa to Ghana. It extends a fourteen days' journey, during which no water is found. The caravans, to cross these arid deserts, take supplies of water in waterskins carried on camels' backs. In the land of the Sudan there are many arid deserts like this. Most of its terrain is sand that is swept by the winds and carried from place to place, and no water is found there. This land is very hot and scorching. Because of the intensity of the heat and the burning sun, the inhabitants of this First Clime as well as those of the Second and part of the Third Climes are black in color, with crinkled hair, in contrast with the complexion of the people of the Sixth and Seventh Climes.

From the island of Awlil to the town of Sila is sixteen stages. Sila, on the northern bank of the River Nile, is a metropolis, a meeting place for the Sudan and a good market. Its inhabitants are brave. Sila belongs to the domains of the Takruri, who is a powerful ruler. He has slaves and soldiers, strength and firmness, as well as widely known justice. His country is safe and calm. His place of residence and his capital is the town of Takrur, on the south bank of the Nile. Between that town and Sila is a distance of about two days' traveling by the river or by land. The town of Takrur is larger than Sila and has more trade. The people of al-Maghrib al-Aqsa go there with wool, copper, and beads, and they export from there gold and slaves.

The food of the people of Sila and of Takrur consists of sorghum, fish, and dairy produce. Their livestock are mainly camels and goats. The common people wear chemises (qadawir) of wool and woolen bands (kurziyya) wound round their heads. The notables dress themselves in garments of cotton and mantles (mi'sar).

From the towns of Sila and Takrur to Sijilmasa is a forty-day journey at caravan pace. The town nearest to them in the desert lands of the Lamtuna is Azuqqi. It is twenty-five stages away. There one makes provision of water from two to four, five, or six days. Also from the island of Awlil to the town of Sijilmasa is about forty stages at caravan pace. From the town of Takrur to that of Barisa, which is on the Nile going to the east, is twelve stages. The town of Barisa is a small town which has no wall but is like a populous village. Its inhabitants are itinerant (mutajawwilun) merchants, who pay allegiance to the Takruri.

South of Barisa, at a distance of about ten days, is the land of Lamlam. The people of Barisa, Sila, and Ghana make forays into the land of Lamlam and capture its inhabitants. They bring them to their own countries and sell them to the visiting merchants. The latter export them to all the countries. In the whole land of Lamlam there are only two small village-like towns, one called Malal and the other Daw. Between these two towns is a distance of about four days. Their inhabitants, according to the reports of the people of that part of the world, are Jews, [but] infidelity and ignorance have overcome them. When, among all the people of Lamlam, one reaches puberty, he is branded on his face and temples with fire, and this is their mark. Their country and all their settlements are in a river valley, which meets the Nile. Beyond the land of Lamlam to the south there is no known habitation. The country of Lamlam adjoins, in the west, that of al-Maqzara, in the east the land of Wanqara, in the north the land of Ghana, and in the south the uninhabited lands. The speech of the people of Lamlam does not resemble that of the people of Maqzara, nor that of the people of Ghana. From the aforementioned Barisa to Ghana takes twelve days in an easterly direction. Barisa is halfway [from Ghana] to the towns of Sila and Takrur. Likewise from the town of Barisa to Awdaghusht is twelve stages. Awdaghusht is north of Barisa.

There are no fresh fruits (al-fawakih al-ratba) in the land of the Sudan but only dried dates (tamr) that are imported from the land of Sijilmasa or the Zab. These are imported by the people of Warqalan of the desert.

The Nile flows in that land from east to west, and on both its banks grow a reed called sharki, the ebony tree, the boxtree, the khilaf, the mimosa (tarfa), and the tamarisk (athl) in continuous thickets. The herds go there for the midday rest, and the people themselves resort there to seek shade during the scorching heat of the summer. In these thickets are lions, giraffes, gazelles, hyenas, elephants, hares, and hedgehogs. In the Nile are species of fish, big and small, which serve as food for most of the Sudan. They catch, salt, and preserve them. These fish are very thick and oily.

The weapons of the people of this country are bows and arrows, on which they mostly rely, but they also use maces, which they make of ebony with much cunning and craft. Their bows are made of the sharki reed. The arrows and bowstrings too are of reed. The people of this land build their houses of mud because wide and long pieces of wood are scarce there.

Their adornments are of copper (nuhas), little beads (kharaz), strings of glass beads, and the stones called badhuq and lu'ab al-shaykh, "old man's slobber," as well as various kinds of false onyx (mujazza'at) manufactured from glass. All these facts and circumstances that we have mentioned concerning their foodstuffs, drinks, clothing, and ornaments are common to the majority of the Sudan throughout their land, for it is a fiercely hot country.

The townsmen in that country cultivate onions, gourds, and watermelons, which grow very large there, but they have no wheat or any grain other than sorghum, from which they make an intoxicating drink (*nabidh*). The bulk of their meat comes from fish and camel meat cut into strips and dried in the sun, as we have already described. Thus ends the description of all that is in the First Section of the First Clime, praise be to God.

Adaptation by P.J. of an English translation from Arabic by J. F. P. Hopkins

COMMENTARY

In Europe, Abu 'Abd Allah Muhammad al-Sharif al-Idrisi is perhaps the best known of all Arab geographers, no doubt because an abridgment of his work was printed in Rome as early as 1592, thus being one of the first Arabic books ever printed. Al-Idrisi was a descendant of the Banu Hammid Dynasty, which had ruled Malaga till A.H. 447/1055 C.E. As an offshoot of the Idrisids of Morocco he claimed descent from the Prophet. He wrote the book *Nuzhat al-mushtiiqfi ikhtiriiq al-iifiiq* (The Pleasure of He Who Longs to Cross the Horizons), completed by his own account in January 1154 (though there are a few later additions), for the Christian king of Sicily, the Norman Roger II. It is therefore often referred to as the *Book of Roger*. The book was designed to accompany a large silver planisphere, which has not survived. Some of its manuscripts are accompanied by maps, which are on the whole the most accurate & complete of those in the Islamic tradition.

Ibn Tufayl (Cadiz, c. 1105–Marrakech, 1185)

from *HAYY IBN YAQZAN, A PHILOSOPHICAL TALE*

Our forefathers, of blessed memory, tell of a certain equatorial island, lying off the coast of India, where human beings come into being without father or mother. This is possible, they say, because, of all places on earth, that island has the most tempered climate. And because a supernal light streams down on it, it is the most perfectly adapted to accept the human form. This runs counter to the views of most ordinary philosophers and even the greatest natural scientists. They believe the most temperate region of the inhabited world to be the fourth zone, and if they say this because they reason that some inadequacy due to the earth prevents settlement on the equatorial belt, then there is some color of truth to their claim that the fourth is the most moderate of the remaining regions. But if, as most of them admit, they refer only to the intense heat of the equator, the notion is an error the contrary of which is easily proved.

For it is a demonstrated principle of physical science that heat is generated only by motion, contact with hot bodies, or radiation of light. The same sciences teach us that the sun itself is not hot and is not to be characterized by any such mixed qualities. Likewise they teach that it is the highly reflective bodies, not the transparent ones, that take up light best; next are opaque, nonreflecting bodies; but transparent bodies with no trace of opacity do not take on light at all. The foregoing point was proved by Avicenna, using an argument which was his original work; his predecessors do not have it. If these premises are sound, they imply that the sun does not warm earth the way bodies warm each other, by conduction, because in itself the sun is not hot. Nor is the earth warmed by motion since it is stationary and in the same position at sunrise as at sunset, although warming and cooling are apparent at these times. Nor does the sun first warm the air and then the earth by convection. How could it, since we find that when it's hot the air close to the earth is much hotter than that higher up? The only alternative is that the sun warms the earth by radiation of light.

Heat invariably follows light. If focused in a burning mirror light will even set things on fire. It has been proved with scientific certainty that the sun is spherical, as is the earth, and that the sun is much bigger than the earth. Thus somewhat more than half the earth's surface is perpetually lit by the sun, and of the sector of the earth illuminated at any given moment, the most brilliantly lit portion is the center, since it is furthest from the darkness and faces most directly into the sun. Toward the edges the illumination is progressively less, shading into darkness at the periphery. A place is at the center of the circle of light only when those who live there can see the sun, at its zenith, directly overhead. At this time the heat is as intense as it will get. A place where the sun stays far from the zenith will be very cold; places where it tends to linger at the zenith will be very hot. But astronomy proves that in equatorial regions the sun stands directly overhead only twice a year, when it enters the Ram at the vernal equinox and when it enters the Balances at the autumnal equinox. The rest of the year it declines six months to the north and six to the south. These regions, then, enjoy a uniform climate, neither excessively hot nor excessively cold.

I recognize that this statement demands a fuller explanation than I have provided, but this would not further our purpose. I bring it to your attention solely by way of corroborating the alleged possibility of a man's being engendered in this place without father or mother, since many insist with assurance and conviction that Hayy Ibn Yaqzan was one such person who came into being on that island by spontaneous generation.

Others, however, deny it and relate a different version of his origin, which I shall tell you. They say that opposite this island there is a large island, rich

and spacious, and inhabited by people over whom one, a proud and posses-
sive man, was king. Now this king had a sister whom he forbade to marry
until he himself should find a fitting match. But she had a kinsman named
Aware, and he married her secretly, but lawfully, according to their rite.
She soon conceived and bore him a son, but fearing exposure of her secret
she took the infant after nursing him, put him in a tightly sealed ark, and,
attended by a few trustworthy friends and servants, brought him at nightfall
down to the sea, her heart aching with love and fear for her child. She then
wished the child farewell and cried, "Almighty God, you formed my baby
'when it was nothing, a thing without a name.' You fed him in the darkness
of my womb and saw that he was smooth and even and perfectly formed.
In fear of that wicked tyrant I entrust him to your care. I beg you shed your
bounty upon him. Be with him. Never leave him, most merciful God!" She
cast him into the sea.

A powerful current caught the box and brought it that very night to the
coast of the other island of which I spoke. At that very moment the tide
reached a height to which it would not return for another year. It lodged the
little ark in a pleasant thicket, thick with shady cover, floored by rich loam,
sheltered from wind and rain and veiled from the sun, which "gently slanted
off it when it rose and set." The tide then began to ebb, leaving the ark high
and dry. Sand drifted up with gusts of the breeze, damming the watercourse
into the thicket so the water could not reach it. The nails of the box had been
loosened and the boards knocked akilter by the pounding of the surf against
them in the thicket. When the baby had gotten very hungry, he began to
cry and struggle. The sound of his voice reached a doe; and taking it for
the call of her lost fawn, she followed the sound until she came to the ark.
She prodded with her hoof and the baby fought from inside until one of the
top boards came loose. The doe felt sorry for the infant and nuzzled him
tenderly. She gave him her udder and let him drink her own delicious milk.
She became his constant nurse, caring for him, raising him and protecting
him from harm.

This, according to those who deny spontaneous generation, is the story
of his origin. In a moment I shall tell you how he grew up and progressed
from one phase to the next until he reached his remarkable goal. But first I
should say that those who claim Hayy came into being spontaneously say
that in a pocket of earth on that island, over the years, a mass of clay worked
until hot and cold, damp and dry were blended in just the proper way, their
strengths perfectly balanced. This fermented mass of clay was quite large,
and parts of it were in better equilibrium than others, more suited than the
rest for becoming human gametes. The midmost part was the best propor-
tioned and bore the most perfect equivalence to the makeup of a man. The

clay labored and churned, and in the viscous mass there formed what looked like bubbles in boiling water.

In the very middle formed a tiny bubble divided in half by a delicate membrane and filled by a fine gaseous body, optimally proportioned for what it was to be. With it at that moment joined "the spirit which is God's," in a bond virtually indissoluble, not only in the purview of the senses, but also in that of the mind. For it should be clear that this spirit emanates continuously from God—glory be to Him. It is analogous to the sunlight that constantly floods the earth. Some objects, like transparent air, are not lit by it at all. Others, opaque but not shiny, are lit partially, differing in color according to their different receptivities. Still others, polished bodies such as mirrors, take up light maximally; and if these mirrors have a certain concave form, fires start in them from the concentrated rays of light. The same holds for the spirit which flows eternally from God's word to all that is. Some beings, lacking any aptitude to receive it, show no trace of it. These, corresponding to the air of the analogy, are the lifeless, inanimate objects. Others, that is plant species, show its influence to varying degrees in proportion to their capacities; they are analogous to opaque objects. Still others show its impact greatly; these are animal species, and they correspond to the shiny objects of the analogy. The most reflective body, far outshining all others, is the one that mirrors in itself the image and pattern of the sun. In the same way with animals, the one that best takes on the spirit in himself and is formed and modeled in its pattern is man. There is reference to this in the words of the Prophet—God bless him and grant him peace—"God created Adam in His own image."

If this image grows so strong in a man that its reality eclipses all other forms, the splendor of its light setting afire all it apprehends so that it alone remains, then it is like the mirror reflecting on itself, burning everything else. This happens only to prophets, the blessings of God upon them. But all this will be made clear in due course. Let us return to the story they tell of [Hayy's] creation.

They say, "When this spirit was linked with that chamber all the powers of the latter submitted totally to it, bowing to its sway according to God's command. Then opposite this chamber a second bubble formed, divided into three chambers, separated by thin membranes and joined by tiny ducts. This also was filled by gaseous material, like that which filled the first, only not as fine. In these three sacs, partitioned within one, lodged some of the powers that had subordinated themselves to the spirit, entrusted with its preservation and care and with relaying to this first spirit, linked with the first chamber, all their experiences, from the subtlest to the most magnificent. Next to the first, opposite the second, a third bubble formed, filled with its own gaseous matter, denser than either of the others, and with its own set of subordinate faculties, devoted to the protection and sustenance of the spirit.

"These chambers, first, second, and third, in the order I have given, were the first to be created in that working mass of clay. Although they all depend on each other, the dependence of the first on the other two is its need for service, but their dependence on the first is the reliance of the led on their leader or the controlled on what controls them. Still the second and third in their own right are masters, not servants, of all the organs formed after them; and the second has a fuller share of rule than the third. The first has the conical shape of a flame, since it is linked to the spirit and burns with the spirit's heat. The dense matter by which it was enclosed took on the same shape; it developed into solid flesh and was in turn covered by a tough protective envelope of skin. The whole organ is what we call the heart.

"To survive, the heart needed to be fed and maintained to replenish the juices which constantly broke down in the terrific heat. It needed also a sense of what was good and bad for it so it would be drawn to the one and reject the other. The first need was delegated to one organ with powers designed to serve that need, and its second to another. Sensation was in charge of the brain and nutrition of the liver. Each depends on the heart not only because its heat keeps them alive, but also because their specialized powers originate there. Meanwhile ducts and passages were woven between them and the heart, some wider than others, depending on the need. These were the veins and arteries." So, neglecting nothing, they go on to describe the whole anatomy and all the organs, as physiologists describe the formation of a fetus in the womb, up to the termination of the development process, when all the parts were fully formed and the embryo was ready to be. In accounting for the success of this metamorphosis they rely heavily on their mass of fermenting clay and on its suitability to be formed into all the protective membranes and the like which would be needed in the forming of a man.

When the embryo was ready these coverings were sloughed off as if in labor; and the clay, which had already begun to dry, cracked open. His food supply thus vanishing, the newborn infant got hungrier and hungrier and began to cry, whereupon the doe with the lost fawn responded. From this point on both factions give interchangeable versions of his upbringing.

They agree that the doe that cared for him was richly pastured, so she was fat and had plenty of milk, to give the baby the best possible nourishment. She stayed with him, leaving only when necessary to graze. The baby grew so fond of her he would cry if she was late, and then she would come rushing back. There were no beasts of prey on the island.

Translation from Arabic by Lenn Evan Goodman

Musa Ibn Maimon, called Maimonides

(Córdoba, 1138–Fostat, 1204)

from **THE GUIDE FOR THE PERPLEXED**

Chapter 39

Heart [*leb*] is an equivocal term. It is a term denoting the heart; I mean the part of the body in which resides the principle of life of every being endowed with a heart. Thus: *And thrust them in the heart of Absalom.* And inasmuch as this part is in the middle of the body, the term is used figuratively to designate the middle of every thing. Thus: *Unto the heart of heaven; The heart of fire.* It is also a term denoting thought. Thus: *Went not my heart,* which means that thou wast present in my thought when this and that happened. In this sense it is said: *And that ye go not about after your own heart,* which refers to your following your thoughts; and: *Whose heart turneth away this day,* which means that his thought is discontinued. It is also a term signifying opinion. Thus: *All the rest of Israel were of one heart to make David king*—that is, they were of one opinion. A similar meaning is to be found in the dictum *But fools die for want of heart,* which is intended to signify: through the deficiency of their opinion. And in the same way this meaning is to be found in the dictum *My heart shall not turn away so long as I live*—the meaning of which is: my opinion shall not turn away from, and shall not let go of, this matter. For the beginning of this passage reads: *My righteousness I hold fast and will not let it go; My heart shall not turn away so long as I live.* In my opinion it is with reference to this meaning of *yeheraph* that the expression *shiphhah neherephet le-'ish* (a handmaid betrothed to a man) is to be explained—the term *neherephet* being akin to an Arabic word, namely, *munharifa* (turned away), that is, one who turns from being possessed as a slave to being possessed as a wife. *Heart* is also a term denoting will. Thus: *And I will give you shepherds according to My heart; Is thy heart right as my heart is?*—that is, is thy will like my will in rectitude? Sometimes the word is figuratively applied with this meaning: *That shall do according to that which is in My heart and in My soul,* the meaning of which is: he shall do according to My will; *And Mine eyes and heart shall be there perpetually*—that is, My providence and My will. It is also a term denoting the intellect. Thus: *But an empty man will act his heart,* meaning that he will cognize with his intellect. And similarly: *A wise man's heart is at his right hand*—that is, his intellect is directed toward the perfect things. This use is frequent. It is in this sense—I mean that indicative of the intellect—that the term is applied figuratively to God in all the passages in question, save certain exceptional ones where it is sometimes used to indicate the will. Every passage should therefore be understood according to its context. In this way *heart* is applied to the intellect in the verses *And lay it to thy heart, And none considereth heart*, and all the others that are similar. In the same way Scripture says: *But the Lord hath not given you a heart to know,* in a way analogous to its saying: *Unto thee it was shown that thou mightest know.* As for the dictum of Scripture *And thou shall love the Lord thy God with all thy heart*—in my opinion its interpretation is: with all the forces of your heart; I mean to say, with all the forces of the body, for the principle of all of them derives from the heart. Accordingly the intended meaning is, as we have explained in the commentary on the Mishnah and in the *Mishneh Torah*, that you should make His apprehension the end of all your actions.

Chapter 40

Air [*ruah*] is an equivocal term. It is a term denoting air; I mean the element that is one of the four elements. Thus: *And the air of God hovered.* It is also a term denoting the blowing wind. Thus: *And the east air brought the locusts; West air.* This use of the term is frequent. It is also a term denoting the animal spirit. Thus: *An air that passeth away and cometh not again; Wherein is the air of life.* It is also a term denoting the thing that remains of man after his death and that does not undergo passing away. Thus: *And the air shall return unto God who gave it.* It is also a term denoting the divine intellectual overflow that overflows to the prophets and in virtue of which they prophesy, as we shall explain to you when speaking of prophecy, in the way in which it is proper to mention it in this treatise. Thus: *And I will take of the air which is upon thee, and I will put it upon them; And it came to pass that when the air rested upon them; The air of the Lord spoke by me.* This use of the word is frequent. It is also a term denoting purpose and will. Thus: *A fool uttereth all his air,* his purpose and will. Similarly in the verse *And the air of Egypt shall be made empty within it, and I will make void the counsel thereof;* it says that Egypt's purposes will be divided and its governance will be hidden. Similarly also in the verse *Who hath comprehended the air of the Lord, or who is familiar with His counsel that he may tell us?* Scripture says that he who knows the ordering of His will or apprehends His governance of that which exists as it really is should teach us about it—as we shall explain in the chapters that will deal with His governance. In all cases in which the term *air* is applied to God, it is used in the fifth sense; in some of them also in the last sense, which is that of will, as we have explained. Thus the term should be interpreted in every passage as indicated by the context.

Chapter 41

Soul [*nephesh*] is an equivocal term. It is a term denoting the animal soul common to every sentient being. Thus: *Wherein there is a living soul.* And it is also a term denoting blood. Thus: *Thou shalt not eat the soul with the flesh.* It is also a term denoting the rational soul; I mean the form. Thus: *As the Lord liveth that made us this soul.* And it is a term for the thing that remains of man after death. Thus: *Yet the soul of my lord shall be bound in the bundle of life.* It is also a term denoting the will. Thus: *To bind his princes according to his soul,* which means: through his will. Similarly: *And deliver not Thou him unto the soul of his enemies,* which means: Thou will not deliver him to their will. In my opinion this is similar to: *If it be according to your soul to bury my dead,* which means: if it be according to your purpose and will. And similarly: *Though Moses and Samuel stood before Me, yet My soul could not be toward this people,* the meaning of which is that I have no will toward them—that is, I do not wish that they endure. In all cases in which the term *soul* is applied to Him, may He be exalted, it has the meaning of "will," as has already been set forth by us with regard to the dictum of Scripture: *That shall do according to that which is in My heart and in My soul*—the meaning of which is: in my will and purpose. One should interpret according to this sense the verse *And his soul was grieved in the misery of Israel,* which means that His will refrained from rendering Israel miserable. This verse was not translated at all by Jonathan ben Uziel, for he took it as using the term *soul* in its first sense, thought that he had met with a case of affection being ascribed to God, and accordingly refrained from translating it. However, if the term is taken in its last sense, the interpretation of the verse is very clear. For it is preceded by the statement that the providence of God, may He be exalted, had abandoned them so that they were perishing, and they implored God for help, but He did not help them. However, when they had gone far in repentance and their wretchedness had increased and the enemy had dominated them, He took pity on them, and His will refrained from letting their misery and wretchedness continue. Know this accordingly, for it is strange. In the words of Scripture: *in the misery of Israel, in* is used instead of *from.* It is therefore as if he had said: *from the misery of Israel.* Many instances of this use of *in* have been enumerated by the linguists. Thus: *And that which remaineth in the flesh and in the bread; Remains in the years; In the stranger and in the native of the land.* This use is frequent.

Translation from Hebrew and Arabic by Shlomo Pines

Ibn Jubayr (Valencia, 1145–Egypt, 1217)

THE TRAVELS OF IBN JUBAYR: SICILY

The Month of Ramadan the Venerated, A.H. 580
[December 6, 1184–January 4, 1185]

*May God in His grace and favor let us share His blessings and during
it accept our prayers. There is no Lord but He.*

On the morning of the first day of this month we observed before us the
Mountain of Fire, the famous volcano of Sicily, and rejoiced thereat. May
God Most High reward us for what we have endured and end our days with
the best and most magnificent of His favors. May He animate us in all cir-
cumstances to gratitude for what He has bestowed on us. A favorable wind
then moved us from that place, but on the evening of Saturday the second
of the month its force increased and drove the ship with such speed that in
but an instant it had brought us to the mouth of the strait. Night had fallen.
In this strait the sea is confined to a width of six miles and in the narrow-
est place to three. The sea in this strait, which runs between the mainland
and the island of Sicily, pours through like the "bursting of the dam" and,
from the intensity of the contraction and the pressure, boils like a cauldron.
Difficult indeed is its passage for ships. Our ship continued on its course,
driven by a strong wind from the south, the mainland on our right and the
coast of Sicily on our left.

When it came to midnight on Sunday the third of the blessed month of
Ramadan, and we were overlooking the city of Messina, the sudden cries
of the sailors gave us the grievous knowledge that the ship had been driven
by the force of the wind toward one of the shorelines and had struck it. At
once the captain ordered that the sails be lowered, but the sail on the mast
called the *ardimun* would not come down. All their efforts they exerted on
it, but they could do naught with it, because of the strain of the wind. When
they had labored in vain, the captain cut it with a knife piece by piece, hoping
to arrest the ship. During this attempt the ship stuck by its keel to the ground,
touching it with its two rudders, the two shafts by which it steers. Dreadful
cries were raised on the ship, and the Last Judgment had come, the break
that has no mending and the great calamity which allows us no fortitude.
The Christians gave themselves over to grief, and the Muslims submitted
themselves to the decree of their Lord, finding only and clinging and hold-
ing fast to the rope of hopefulness in the life to come. In turn the wind and
the waves buffeted the ship until one of its rudders broke. The captain then
threw out one of the anchors, hoping to take hold with it, but to no purpose.

He cut its rope and left it in the sea. When we were sure that our time had come, we braced ourselves to meet death and, summoning our resolution to show goodly patience, awaited the moment or the time of destiny. Cries and shrieks arose from the women and the infants of the Rum. All with humbleness submitted themselves to the will of God, and "men were despoiled of their manhood."

We, meanwhile, were gazing at the nearby shore in hesitance between throwing ourselves in to swim and awaiting, it might be, relief with the dawn from God. We formed the resolve to remain. The sailors lowered the longboat into the sea to remove the most important of their men, women, and effects. They took it one journey to the shore but were unable to return, and the waves threw it in pieces on the beach. Despair then seized our spirits, but while we were suffering these vicissitudes, dawn shone and aid and succor came from God. We made certain of our eyes, and there before us was the city of Messina less than half a mile away.

We marveled at the power of Great and Glorious God in the management of His designs and said: "Many are taken off in death upon the threshold of their house." The sun then rose and small boats came out to us. Our cries had fallen on the city, and the king of Sicily, William himself, came out with some of his retinue to survey the affair. We made speed to go down to the boats, but the violence of the waves would not allow them to reach the ship. We at last descended into them at the end of the terrible storm. Our deliverance to the shore was like that of Abu Nasr from destiny. Some of the chattels belonging to men had been destroyed, but "they took comfort that although without plunder, they had returned in safety." The strangest thing that we were told was that this Rumi king, when he perceived some needy Muslims staring from the ship who had not the means to pay for their landing because the owners of the boats were asking so high a price for their rescue, inquired concerning them and, learning their story, ordered that they be given one hundred *ruba'i* of his coinage in order that they might alight. All the Muslims thus were saved and cried, "Praise be to God, Lord of the Universe." . . .

Recollections of the City of Messina in the Island of Sicily
May God Restore It (to the Muslims)

This city is the mart of the merchant infidels, the focus of ships from the world over, and thronging always with companies of travelers by reason of the lowness of prices. But it is cheerless because of the unbelief, no Muslim being settled there. Teeming with worshipers of the Cross, it chokes its inhabitants and constricts them almost to strangling. It is full of smells and filth and churlish too, for the stranger will find there no courtesy. Its markets are animated and teeming, and it has ample commodities to ensure a luxurious life. Your days and nights in this town you will pass in full security, even though your countenance, your manners, and your tongue are strange. . . .

The finest town in Sicily and the seat of its sovereign is known to the Muslims as al-Madinah and to the Christians as Palermo. It has Muslim citizens who possess mosques and their own markets in the many suburbs. The rest of the Muslims live in the farms of the island and in all its villages and towns, such as Syracuse and others. Al-Madinah al-Kabirah ("the great Palermo"), the residence of their king, William, is, however, the biggest and most populous, and Messina is next. In al-Madinah, God willing, we shall make our stay, and thence we hope to go to whichever of the western countries that Great and Glorious God shall at His will determine.

Their king, William, is admirable for his just conduct, and the use he makes of the industry of the Muslims, and for choosing eunuch pages who all, or nearly all, concealing their faith, yet hold firm to the Muslim divine law. He has much confidence in Muslims, relying on them for his affairs and the most important matters, even the supervisor of his kitchen being a Muslim, and he keeps a band of black Muslim slaves commanded by a leader chosen from among them. His ministers and chamberlains he appoints from his pages, of whom he has a great number and who are his public officials and are described as his courtiers. In them shines the splendor of his realm through the magnificent clothing and fiery horses they display, and there is none of them but has his retinue, his servants, and his followers.

This king possesses splendid palaces and elegant gardens, particularly in the capital of his kingdom, al-Madinah. In Messina he has a palace, white like a dove, which overlooks the shore. He has about him a great number of youths and handmaidens, and no Christian king is more given up to the delights of the realm or more comfort and luxury-loving. William is engrossed in the pleasures of his land, the arrangement of its laws, the laying down of procedure, the allocation of the functions of his chief officials, the enlargement of the splendor of the realm, and the display of his pomp, in a manner that resembles the Muslim kings'. His kingdom is very large. He pays much attention to his Muslim physicians and astrologers and also takes great care of them. He will even, when told that a physician or astrologer is passing through his land, order his detainment and then provide him with means of living so that he will forget his native land. May God in His favor preserve the Muslims from this seduction. The king's age is about thirty years. May God protect the Muslims from his hostility and the extension of his power.

One of the remarkable things told of him is that he reads and writes

Arabic. We also learned from one of his personal servants that his 'alamah is: "Praise be to God. It is proper to praise Him." His father's 'alamah was: "Praise be to God in thanks for His beneficence." The handmaidens and concubines in his palace are all Muslims. One of the strangest things told us by this servant, Yahya ibn Fityan, the Embroiderer, who embroidered in gold the king's clothes, was that the Frankish Christian women who came to his palace became Muslims, converted by these handmaidens. All this they kept secret from their king. Of the good works of these handmaidens there are astonishing stories. It was told to us that when a terrifying earthquake shook the island, this polytheist [a Muslim would deem William to be so, since he accepted the dogma of the Trinity] in alarm ranged round his palace and heard nothing but cries to God and His Prophet from his women and pages. At sight of him, they were overcome with confusion, but he said to them: "Let each invoke the God he worships, and those that have faith shall be comforted." . . .

In Messina we lodged at an inn and stayed there nine days. Then, on the night of Tuesday the twelfth of the holy month of Ramadan and the eighteenth of December, we embarked on a small ship sailing to al-Madinah. We steered close to the shore, so that we might keep it within sight. God sent us a light breeze from the east that most pleasantly urged us on our way. So we sailed along, bending our gaze on the continuous cultivations and villages and on the fortresses and strongholds at the tops of the lofty mountains. To our right we saw nine islands [Aeolian or Lipari], rising up like lofty mountains in the sea, close to the shores of Sicily. From two of them— Vulcano and Stromboli—fire issues unendingly, and we could see the smoke ascending from them. At the close of night a red flame appeared, throwing up tongues into the air. It was the celebrated volcano. We were told that a fiery blast of great violence bursts out from air holes in the two mountains and makes the fire. Often a great stone is cast up and thrown into the air by the force of the blast and prevented thereby from falling and settling at the bottom. This is one of the most remarkable of stories, and it is true.

As for the great mountain in the island, known as the Jabal al-Nar ["Mountain of Fire," Etna], it also presents a singular feature in that some years a fire pours from it in the manner of the "bursting of the dam." It passes nothing it does not burn, until, coming to the sea, it rides out on its surface and then subsides beneath it. Let us praise the Author of all things for His marvelous creations. There is no God but He. On the evening of Wednesday following the Tuesday we have chronicled, we came to the port of Shafludi [Cefalu], between which and Messina lies a day and a half's sailing.

Translation from Arabic by R. J. C. Broadhurst

Ibn Battuta (Tangier, 1304–Marrakech, 1369)

from *RIHLA:* CONCERNING TRAVELS IN THE MAGHREB

I left Tangier, my birthplace, on Thursday, 2 Rajab 725 [June 14, 1325], being at that time twenty-two years of age, with the intention of making the pilgrimage to the Holy House at Mecca and the tomb of the Prophet at Medina.

I set out alone, finding no companion to cheer the way with friendly intercourse and no party of travelers with whom to associate myself. Swayed by an overmastering impulse within me and a long-cherished desire to visit those glorious sanctuaries, I resolved to quit all my friends and tear myself away from my home. As my parents were still alive, it weighed grievously upon me to part from them, and both they and I were afflicted with sorrow.

On reaching the city of Tlemcen, whose sultan at that time was Abu Tashifin, I found there two ambassadors of the sultan of Tunis, who left the city on the same day that I arrived. One of the brethren having advised me to accompany them, I consulted the will of God in this matter, and after a stay of three days in the city to procure all that I needed, I rode after them with all speed. I overtook them at the town of Miliana, where we stayed ten days, as both ambassadors fell sick on account of the summer heats. When we set out again, one of them grew worse, and he died after we had stopped for three nights by a stream four miles from Miliana. I left their party there and pursued my journey, with a company of merchants from Tunis. . . .

On reaching Algiers we halted outside the town for a few days, until the former party rejoined us, when we went on together through the Mitija, the fertile plain behind Algiers, to the Djurdjura, the mountain of oaks, and so reached Bejaïa. The commander of Bejaïa at this time was the chamberlain Ibn Sayyid an-Nas. Now, one of the Tunisian merchants of our party had died, leaving three thousand dinars of gold, which he had entrusted to a certain man of Algiers to deliver to his heirs at Tunis. Ibn Sayyid an-Nas came to hear of this and forcibly seized the money. This was the first instance I witnessed of the tyranny of the agents of the Tunisian government.

At Bejaïa I fell ill of a fever, and one of my friends advised me to stay there till I had recovered. But I refused, saying, "If God decrees my death, it shall be on the road with my face set toward Mecca." "If that is your resolve," he replied, "sell your ass and your heavy baggage, and I shall lend you what you require. In this way you will travel light, for we must make haste on our journey, for fear of meeting roving Arabs on the way." I followed his advice and he did as he had promised—may God reward him!

On reaching Constantine we camped outside the town, but a heavy rain forced us to leave our tents during the night and take refuge in some houses there. Next day the governor of the city came to meet us. Seeing my clothes all soiled by the rain, he gave orders that they should be washed at his house, and in place of my old worn headcloth sent me a headcloth of fine Syrian cloth, in one of the ends of which he had tied two gold dinars. This was the first alms I received on my journey.

From Constantine we reached Bône, where, after staying in the town for several days, we left the merchants of our party on account of the dangers of the road, while we pursued our journey with the utmost speed. I was again attacked by fever, so I tied myself in the saddle with a turban cloth in case I should fall by reason of my weakness. So great was my fear that I could not dismount until we arrived at Tunis. The population of the city came out to meet the members of our party, and on all sides greetings and questions were exchanged, but not a soul greeted me, as no one there was known to me. I was so affected by my loneliness that I could not restrain my tears and wept bitterly, until one of the pilgrims realized the cause of my distress and, coming up to me, greeted me kindly and continued to entertain me with friendly talk until I entered the city.

The sultan of Tunis at that time was Abu Yahya, the son of Abu' Zakariya II, and there were a number of notable scholars in the town. During my stay the festival of the Breaking of the Fast fell due, and I joined the company at the praying ground. The inhabitants assembled in large numbers to celebrate the festival, making a brave show and wearing their richest apparel. Sultan Abu Yahya arrived on horseback, accompanied by all his relatives, courtiers, and officers of state walking on foot in a stately procession. After the recital of the prayer and the conclusion of the allocution the people returned to their homes. . . .

Some time later the pilgrim caravan for the Hejaz was formed, and they nominated me as their qadi [judge]. We left Tunis early in November, following the coast road through Susa [Sousse], Sfax, and Qabis [Gabès], where we stayed for ten days on account of incessant rains. Thence we set out for Tripoli, accompanied for several stages by a hundred or more horsemen as well as a detachment of archers, out of respect for whom the Arab brigands kept their distance.

I had made a contract of marriage at Sfax with the daughter of one of the syndics at Tunis, and at Tripoli she was conducted to me, but after leaving Tripoli I became involved in a dispute with her father, which necessitated my separation from her. I then married the daughter of a student from Fez, and when she was conducted to me I detained the caravan for a day by entertaining them all at a wedding party.

Ibn Battuta returns to the Maghreb and the city of Fez in Morocco in November of 1349 [C. E.], twenty-four years after he set out on a journey which had meanwhile gotten him as far as Quanzhou in China.

I arrived at the royal city of Fez on Friday, at the end of the month of Shaban of the year 750 [A. H.], and presented myself before our most noble master, the most generous imam, the commander of the faithful, al-Mutawakkil Abu' Inan—may God enlarge his greatness and humble his enemies. His dignity made me forget the dignity of the sultan of Iraq; his beauty, the beauty of the king of India; his fine qualities, the noble character of the king of Yemen; his courage, the courage of the king of the Turks; his clemency, the clemency of the king of the Greeks; his devotion, the devotion of the king of Turkistan; and his knowledge, the knowledge of the king of Java. I laid down the staff of travel in his glorious land, having assured myself after unbiased consideration that it is the best of countries, for in it fruits are plentiful, and running water and nourishing food are never exhausted. Few indeed are the lands which unite all these advantages, and well spoken are the poet's words:

Of all the lands the West by this token's the best:
  Here the full moon is spied and the sun speeds to rest.

. . . The dirhams of the West are small, but their utility is great. When you compare its prices with the prices of Egypt and Syria, you will see the truth of my contention and realize the superiority of the Maghreb. For I assure you that mutton in Egypt is sold at eighteen ounces for a dirham nuqra, which equals in value six dirhams of the Maghreb, whereas in the Maghreb meat is sold, when prices are high, at eighteen ounces for two dirhams, that is a third of a nuqra. As for melted butter, it is usually not to be found in Egypt at all.

The kinds of things that the Egyptians eat along with their bread would not even be looked at in the Maghreb. They consist for the most part of lentils and chickpeas, which they cook in enormous cauldrons and on which they put oil of sesame; *basilla,* a kind of pea which they cook and eat with olive oil; gherkins, which they cook and mix with curdled milk; purslane, which they prepare in the same way; the buds of almond trees, which they cook and serve in curdled milk; and taro, which they cook. All these things are easily come by in the Maghreb, but God has enabled its inhabitants to dispense with them, by reason of the abundance of meat, melted butter, fresh butter, honey, and other products. As for green vegetables, they are the rarest of things in Egypt, and most of their fruit has to be brought from Syria. Grapes, when they are cheap, are sold among them at a dirham nuqra for three of their pounds, their pound being twelve ounces.

As for Syria, fruits are indeed plentiful there, but in the Maghreb they are cheaper. Grapes are sold there at the rate of one of their pounds for a dirham nuqra (their pound is three Maghrebian pounds), and when their price is low, two pounds for a dirham nuqra. Pomegranates and quinces are sold at eight *fals* [copper coins] apiece, which equals a dirham of our money. As for vegetables, the quantity sold for a dirham nuqra is less than that sold for a small dirham in our country. Meat is sold there at the rate of one Syrian pound for two and a half dirhams nuqra. If you consider all this, it will be clear to you that the lands of the Maghreb are the cheapest in cost of living, the most abundant in good things, and blessed with the greatest share of material comforts and advantages.

Moreover, God has augmented the honor and excellence of the Maghreb by the imamate of our master, the commander of the faithful, who has spread the shelter of security throughout its territories and made the sun of equity rise within its borders, who has caused the clouds of beneficence to shed their rain upon its dwellers in country and town, and who has purified it from evildoers and established it in the ways alike of worldly prosperity and of religious observance. After I had been privileged to observe this noble majesty and to share in the all-embracing bounty of his beneficence, I set out to visit the tomb of my mother. I arrived at my hometown of Tangier and visited her, and went on to the town of Ceuta, where I stayed for some months. While I was there I suffered from an illness for three months, but afterward God restored me to health.

Translation from Arabic & edits by H. A. R. Gibb, revisions & subedits by P.J.

COMMENTARY

Ross E. Dunn opens his book *The Adventures of Ibn Battuta* by citing Henri Cordier as quoted in Joseph Needham's *Science and Civilization in China:* "Westerners have singularly narrowed the history of the world in grouping the little that they know about the expansion of the human race around the peoples of Israel, Greece and Rome. Thus have they ignored all those travelers and explorers who in their ships ploughed the China Sea and the Indian Ocean, or rode across the immensities of Central Asia to the Persian Gulf. In truth the larger part of the globe, containing cultures different from those of the ancient Greeks and Romans, but no less civilized, has remained unknown to those who wrote the history of their little world under the impression that they were writing world history." And indeed one of those great non-European explorers is the Tangerine Hajji Abu Abdullah Muhammad Ibn Battuta, also known as Shams ad-Din, a Moroccan Berber Islamic scholar known for the record of his travels & excursions published in his *Rihla*.

Ibn Battuta traveled for close to thirty years, covering almost the entire known Islamic world and beyond, extending from the Maghreb, West Africa, southern Spain, and Eastern Europe in the west to the Middle East, the east coast of Africa as far south as Tanzania, the Arabian Peninsula, the Indian subcontinent, Sri Lanka, the Maldives, Central Asia, Southeast Asia, and China in the east. The distance he traveled far surpassed that of his predecessors and his near-contemporary Marco Polo. As Dunn puts it: "His narrative offers details, sometimes in incidental bits, sometimes in long disquisitions, on almost every conceivable aspect of human life in that age, from the royal ceremonial of the Sultan of Delhi to the sexual customs of women in the Maldive Islands to the harvesting of coconuts in South Arabia. Moreover his story is far more personal and humanely engaging than Marco's."

Sultan Abu 'Inan, the Marinid ruler of Morocco, commissioned the *Rihla* in 1356, after Ibn Battuta's final return to Morocco, and asked Ibn Juzayy, a young Andalusian scholar, to record Ibn Battuta's reminiscences and experiences as a travel diary. The form is rather classical and even conventional, and it is the content that prevails and has kept interest in Battuta's work alive over the centuries in the Muslim world—and since the nineteenth century in the West as well. Given the nature of the present book, we have chosen to concentrate our excerpts on Battuta's travels through his own region, the Maghreb.

Ibn Khaldun (Tunis, 1332–Cairo, 1406)

from THE MUQADDIMAH, AN INTRODUCTION TO HISTORY, BOOK 6

Section 54: "The craft of poetry and the way of learning it"

Poetry in the Arabic language is remarkable in its manner and powerful in its way. It is speech that is divided into cola having the same meter and held together by the last letter of each colon. Each of those cola is called a verse. The last letter, which all the verses of a poem have in common, is called the rhyme letter. The whole complex is called a poem. Each verse, with its combinations of words, is by itself a meaningful unit. In a way, it is a statement by itself and independent of what precedes and what follows. By itself it makes perfect sense, either as a laudatory or an erotic statement, or as an elegy. It is the intention of the poet to give each verse an independent meaning. Then, in the next verse, he starts anew, in the same way, with some other matter. He changes over from one poetical type to another, and from one topic to another, by preparing the first topic and the ideas expressing it in such a way that it becomes related to the next topic. Sharp contrasts are kept out of the poem. The poet thus continuously changes over from the erotic to the laudatory verses. From a description of the desert and the traces of abandoned camps, he changes over to a description of camels on the march, or horses, or apparitions of the beloved in a dream. From a description of the person to be praised, he changes over to a description of his people and his army. From an expression of grief and condolence in elegies, he changes over to praise of the deceased, and so on. Attention is paid to retaining the same meter throughout the whole poem, to avoid one's natural inclination to pass from one meter to another, similar one. Since the meters are similar to one another, many people do not notice the need to retain the same meter.

The meters are governed by certain conditions and rules. They are the subject of the science of prosody. Prosodists restricted their number to fifteen, indicating that they did not find the Arabs using other natural meters in poetry.

The Arabs thought highly of poetry as a form of speech. Therefore, they made it the archive of their sciences and their history, the evidence for what they considered right and wrong, and the principal basis of reference for most of their sciences and wisdom. The poetical habit was firmly established in them, like all their other habits. The Arabic linguistic habits can be acquired only through technical skill and constant practice of speech. Eventually, some sign of the poetical habit may be obtained.

Of the forms of speech, poetry is a difficult thing for modern people to learn, if they want to acquire the habit of it through study as a technique. Each verse is an independent statement of meaning suitable for quotation by itself. It requires a kind of refinement of the poetical habit, for the poet to be able to pour poetical speech into moulds suitable to this tendency of Arabic poetry. A poet must produce a verse that stands alone, and then make another verse in the same way, and again another, and thus go through all the different topics suitable to the thing he wants to express. Then he establishes harmony among the verses as they follow upon one another in accordance with the different topics occurring in the poem.

Poetry is difficult in its tendency and strange in its subject matter. Therefore it constitutes a severe test of a person's natural talent, if he wants to have a good knowledge of poetical methods. To press speech into the moulds of poetry sharpens the mind. Having Arabic in general does not suffice. In particular, a certain refinement is needed, as well as the exercise of a certain skill in observing the special poetic methods which the Arabs used.

Let us mention the significance of the word *method* as used by poets and what they mean by it.

It should be known that they use it to express the loom on which word combinations are woven, or the mould into which they are packed. It is not used to express the basis upon which meaning rests. That is the task of the vowel endings. It also is *not* used for perfect expression of the idea resulting from the particular word combination used. That is the task of eloquence and style. It also is not used in the sense of meter, as employed by the Arabs. That is the task of prosody. These three sciences fall outside the craft of poetry.

Poetical method refers to a mental form for metrical word combinations which is universal, in the sense of conforming with any particular word combination. This form is abstracted by the mind from the most prominent individual word combinations and given a place in the imagination comparable to a mould or loom. Word combinations that the Arabs consider sound, in the sense of having the correct vowel endings and the proper style, are then selected and packed by the mind into that form, just as the builder does with the mould or the weaver with the loom. Eventually the mould is sufficiently widened to admit the word combinations that fully express what one wants to express. It takes on the form that is sound in the sense that it corresponds to the Arabic linguistic habit.

Each branch of poetical speech has methods peculiar to it and existing in it in different ways. . . .

Word combinations in poetry may or may not be sentences. They may be commands or statements, nominal sentences or verbal sentences, followed by appositions or not followed by appositions, separate or connected, as is the case with the word combinations of Arabic speech and the position of individual words in respect to one another. This teaches a person the universal mould which he can learn through constant practice in Arabic poetry. This universal mould is an abstraction in the mind derived from specific word combinations, to all of which the universal mould conforms. The author of a spoken utterance is like a builder or a weaver. The proper mental form is like the mould used in building or the loom used in weaving. The builder who abandons his mould or the weaver who abandons his loom is unsuccessful.

It should not be said that knowledge of the rules of eloquence suffices in this respect. We say: they are merely basic scientific rules which are the result of analogical reasoning and which indicate by means of analogical reasoning that the word combinations may be used in their particular forms. We have here scientific analogical reasoning that is sound and coherent, as is the analogical reasoning that establishes the rules concerning the vowel endings. But the poetics that we try to establish here have nothing to do with analogical reasoning. They are a form firmly rooted in the soul. It is the result of the continuity of word combinations in Arabic poetry when the tongue uses them. Eventually, the form of those word combinations becomes firmly established. It teaches the poet the use of similar word combinations and how to imitate them for each word combination that he may use in his poetry.

The scientific rules that govern the word endings or syntax and style do not teach poetry. Not everything that is correct according to analogical reasoning, as used in connection with Arabic speech and the scientific grammatical rules, is used by poets. They use certain ways of expression which are known and studied by those who have expert knowledge of poetical speech and the forms of which fall automatically under those analogical rules.

Therefore, we have stated that the moulds in the mind are the result of expert knowledge of Arabic poetry and speech. Such moulds exist not only for poetry but also for prose. The Arabs used their speech for both poetry and prose, and they used certain types of divisions for both kinds of speech. In poetry, these are metrical cola, fixed rhymes, and the fact that each colon constitutes a statement by itself. In prose, as a rule, the Arabs observed symmetry and parallelism between the cola. Sometimes they used prose rhymes and sometimes straight prose. The moulds for each kind of expression are well known in Arabic.

The author of a spoken utterance builds his utterance in the moulds used by the Arabs. They are known only to those who have expert knowledge of Arabic speech, such that in their minds they have an absolute universal mould, which is the result of abstraction from specific individual moulds. They use that universal mould as their model in composing utterances, just as builders use the mould as their model and weavers the loom. The discipline of speech composition, therefore, differs from the studies of the grammarian, the stylist, and the prosodist. It is true, though, that observance of the rules of those sciences is obligatory for and indispensable to the poet.

When all these qualities together are found to apply to a spoken utterance, it is distinguished by a subtle kind of insight into those moulds which are called methods. Only expert knowledge of both Arabic poetry and Arabic prose gives that insight.

Now that the meaning of *method* is clear, let us give a definition or description of poetry that will make its real meaning clear to us. This is a difficult task, for, as far as we can see, there is no such definition by any older scholar. The definition of the prosodists, according to whom poetry is metrical rhymed speech, is no definition or description of the kind of poetry we have in mind. Prosody considers poetry only under the aspect of the agreement of the verses of a poem with respect to the number of successive syllables with and without vowels, as well as with respect to the similarity of the last foot of the first hemistich of the verses of a poem to the last foot of the second hemistich. This concerns meter alone and has nothing to do with the words and their meaning. We must have a definition that will give us the real meaning of poetry in our sense.

We say: poetry is eloquent speech built upon metaphoric usage, and descriptions; divided into cola agreeing in meter and rhyme letter, each colon being independent in purpose and meaning from what comes before and after it; and using the methods of the Arabs peculiar to it. . . .

Section 55: "Poetry and prose work with words, and not with ideas"

Both poetry and prose work with words, and not with ideas. The ideas are secondary to the words. The words are basic. The craftsman who tries to acquire the habit of poetry and prose uses words for that purpose. He memorizes appropriate words from Arabic speech, so as to be able to employ them frequently and have them on his tongue. Eventually, the habit of classical Arabic becomes firmly established in him. As we have mentioned before, this comes about as follows. Language is a habit concerned with speech. One tries to acquire it by repeated practice with the tongue, until one has acquired it, as is the case with all other habits.

Now, tongue and speech deal only with words. Ideas are in the mind. Furthermore, everyone may have ideas. Everyone has the capacity to grasp with his mind whatever ideas his mind wants and likes. No technique is required for their composition. But the composition of speech, for the purpose of expressing ideas, requires a technique. Speech is like a mould for ideas. The vessels in which water is drawn from the sea may be of gold, silver, mother-of-pearl, glass, or clay. But the water is one and the same. The quality of the vessels filled with water differs according to the material from which they are made and not according to the water in them. In the same way, the quality of language and eloquence in its use differ according to different levels of attainment in the composition of speech, depending on the manner in which an utterance conforms to the situation that it wants to express. But the ideas are one and the same.

A person who is ignorant of the composition of speech and its methods, as required by the Arabic linguistic habit, and who unsuccessfully attempts to express what he wants to express is like an invalid who attempts to get up but cannot, because he lacks the power to do so.

Adaptation by P.J. of an English translation by Franz Rosenthal of the original Arabic

Sheikh Nefzaoui (Nefzaoua, southern Tunisia–c. 1434)

from **THE PERFUMED GARDEN**

The Names Given to Man's Sexual Organs

Know, O Vizier (to whom God be good!), that man's member bears different names, as:

Ed de keur, the manly member.
Ed kamera, the penis.
El aïr, the member for generation.
El hamama, the pigeon.
Et teunnana, the tinkler.
El heurmak, the indomitable.
El ahlil, the liberator.
Ez zeub, the verge.
El hammache, the exciter.
El fadelak, the deceiver.
Al naasse, the sleeper.
Ez zodamne, the crowbar.
El khiade, the tailor.
Mochefi el relil, the extinguisher of passion.
Ei khorrate, the turnabout.
El deukkak, the striker.
El aoauame, the swimmer.
Ed dekhal, the housebreaker.
El khorradj, the sorter.
El aouar, the one-eyed.
El fortass, the bald.
Abu aine, the father of the eye.
El atsar, the pusher.
Ed dommar, the strong-headed.
Abu rokba, the father of the neck.
Abu qetaïa, father of hairs.
El besiss, the impudent one.
El mostahi, the shame-faced one.
El bekkaï, the weeping one.
El hezzaz, the rummager.
El lezzaz, the unionist.
Abu laaba, the spitter.
Ech chebbac, the chopper.

El hattack, the digger.
El fattache, the searcher.
El hakkak, the rubber.
El ourekhi, the flabby one.
El motela, the ransacker.
El mokcheuf, the discoverer.

Concerning the names *kamera* and *dekeur,* the meaning is plain. *Dekeur* is a word which signifies the male of all creatures and is also used in the sense of "mention" and "memory." When a man has met with an accident to his member, when it has been amputated or has become weak, and he can in consequence no longer fulfill his marital duties, they say of him: "The member of so and so is dead," meaning that all remembrance of him will be lost and his generation cut off at the root. When he dies they will say, "His member has been cut off," meaning "his memory has disappeared from the world."

The *dekeur* also plays an important part in dreams. The man who dreams that his member has been cut off is certain not to live long after that dream, for, as said above, it presages his loss of memory and the extinction of his race.

I shall treat this subject more particularly in the section on dreams.

The Names Given to Woman's Sexual Organs

El feurdj, the slit.
El keuss, the vulva.
El kelmoune, the voluptuous.
El ass, the primitive.
Ez zercour, the starling.
Ech cheukk, the chink.
Abu tertur, the one with a crest.
Abu khochime, the one with a little nose.
El guenfond, the hedgehog.
El sakouti, the silent one.
El deukkak, the crusher.
Et tseguil, the importunate.
El fechefache, the watering can.
El becha, the horror.
El taleb, the yearning one.
El hacene, the beautiful.
En neuffakh, the one that swells.
Abu djebaha, the one with a projection.

Elouasa, the vast one.

El dride, the large one.

Abu beldun, the glutton.

El makaur, the bottomless.

Abu cheuffrine, the two-lipped.

Abu aungra, the humpbacked.

El rorbal, the sieve.

El hezzaz, the restless.

El lezzaz, the unionist.

El moudd, the accommodating.

El moudïne, the assistant.

El mokeubbeub, the vaulted one.

El meusboul, the long one.

El moli, the duellist.

El mokabul, the ever ready for the fray.

El harrab, the fugitive.

El sabeur, the resigned.

El maoui, the juicy.

El moseuffah, the barred one.

El mezour, the deep one.

El addad, the biter.

El zeunbur, the wasp.

El harr, the hot one.

El ladid, the delicious one.

As regards the vulva, called *el feurdj*, the slit, it has got that name because it opens and shuts again when hotly yearning for the coitus, like the one of a mare in heat at the approach of the stallion. This word, however, is applied indiscriminately to the natural parts of men and women, for God the Supreme has used this expression in the Qur'an, chap. XXXiii, v. 35, "*El hafdine feuroudjahoum ou el hafdate.*" The proper meaning of *feurdj* is "slit, opening, passage"; people say "I have found a *feurdj* in the mountains," viz., a passage; there is then a *soukoune* upon the *ra* and a *fatcha* upon the *djine*, and in this sense it means also the natural parts of woman. But if the *ra* is marked with a *fatcha* it signifies the deliverance from misfortunes.

The person who dreams of having seen the vulva, *feurdj*, of a woman will know that "if he is in trouble God will free him of it; if he is in perplexity he will soon get out of it; and lastly if he is in poverty he will soon become wealthy, because *feurdj*, by transposing the vowels, will mean the deliverance from evil. By analogy, if he wants a thing he will get it; if he has debts, they will be paid."

It is considered more lucky to dream of a vulva as open. But if the one seen belongs to a young virgin, it indicates that the door of consolation will remain closed and the thing which is desired is not obtainable. It is a proven fact that the man who sees in his dream the vulva of a virgin that has never been touched will certainly be involved in difficulties and will not be lucky in his affairs. But if the vulva is open so that he can look well into it, or even if it is hidden but he is free to enter it, he will bring the most difficult task to a successful end after having first failed in it, and this after a short delay, by the help of a person whom he never thought of.

Adaptation by P.J. of the 1886 English translation from Arabic by Richard Burton

Al-Hasan Ibn Muhammad al-Wazzan al-Fasi (Leo Africanus) (Granada, c. 1488–1554)

from **TRAVEL DIARIES**

Why This Part of the World Was Named Africa

In the Arabian tongue, Africa is called *Ifrikiya,* from the word *Faraka,* which in the language of that country means "to divide." There are two explanations of why it is called thus: The first suggests that it refers to the fact that this part of the world is divided from Europe by the Mediterranean Sea and from Asia by the Nile. The second explanation claims that the name *Africa* is derived from one Ifricus, the king of Arabia Felix, said to have been the first who had ever inhabited these parts. This Ifricus waged war against the king of Assyria, and being at length driven from his original kingdom by the latter, he crossed the Nile with his whole army and moving westward hurried on until he got to the region around Carthage. This is also why the Arabs imagine the area surrounding Carthage and those lands west of it as constituting all of Africa. . . .

The Manner and Customs of the Arabs Inhabiting Africa

The Arabs, having very different mansions and places of dwelling, live in a diverse and various manner. Those who inhabit the lands between Numidia and Libya lead a most miserable and distressed life, differing much in this regard from those who dwell in Libya. However, they are said to be far more valiant than those other Africans and commonly exchange camels in the land of the Blacks; they also have vast numbers of horses which in Europe are called Barbary horses. They take great pleasure in hunting and pursuing deer, wild asses, ostriches, and other game. Nor should it be omitted to state here that a great number of those Arabs living in Numidia are quick-witted and proud of their skills in writing poems. To these poems each man will consign his loves, his successes at hunting and in battle, and any other worthy act—done for the most part in rhyme, following the Italian manner. . . .

On Fez

Hostelries

Fez has some two hundred very well constructed hostelries. Some are extremely spacious, especially those close by the great temple, and all are three stories high. Some have 120 rooms, some more. All are fitted out with fountains and latrines with sewage systems for the evacuation of waste matter. I never saw any comparable buildings in Italy, except for the College of the Spaniards in Bologna and the palace of Cardinal de Saint-Georges in Rome. The doors of all the rooms give on a corridor.

Despite the beauty and size of these hostelries, they constitute detestable lodgings, because they have neither beds nor bed linens. The innkeeper provides the guest with a blanket and a mat on which to sleep. If the renter wants to eat, he has to buy the food and give it to the kitchen to be prepared. Not only foreigners lodge at these inns, but also all the city's widowers who have neither house nor family. They live one or two per room and have their own bedding and cook their own meals.

The worst, however, is to be lodged with certain individuals who are part of a brood called the El-hiwa. These are men who dress as women and wear women's ornaments. They shave their beards and go as far as imitating women's voices and manners of speaking. What am I saying—they even spin and weave! Each one of these abject beings has a concubine and behaves toward him exactly as a wife would toward a husband. In these inns these people also have women whose mores are those of the prostitutes one finds in public houses in Europe. It is allowed there to buy and sell wine without getting into trouble with the functionaries of the court, and thus these inns are continuously frequented by all those who live most deplorable lives. Some go there to get drunk, others to assuage their lust in the company of venal women, others finally to hide from the court because of illicit and shameful actions, of which the less said the better. The innkeepers have an *amin,* or consul, and pay an annual fee to the governor of the city. They are further obligated to provide on certain occasions the armies of the king or the princes with a large part of their personnel to cook for the soldiers, as there are very few others qualified to do this job.

If the law that binds the historian had not forced me to tell the truth, I would certainly have been happy to pass over this part of my description in silence. I would have preferred not to have to put any blame on the city in which I grew up and was educated. But truth be told, apart from this vice, the kingdom of Fez is inhabited by the most honest people one can find in Africa, and with these people the innkeepers have, as they say, no traffic at all. The latter frequent only despicable lowlifes of the basest provenance. No lettered person, no merchant, no artisan speaks to them. They are also prohibited from entering the inns close to the temple, as well as any markets, steam rooms, or private homes. They certainly cannot become innkeepers anywhere near the temple, where the merchants of a higher class tend to stay. The whole population wishes them dead. But given that the lords and princes use them for the needs of the army, as I reported above, they are permitted to live out their dishonest and despicable lives.

Mills

Inside Fez there are some four hundred mills, that is to say buildings that contain millstones, though there may well be a thousand millstones in all, as a mill is a large colonnaded room housing at times four, five, or even six millstones. A part of the surrounding population has their grain ground in the city, and there are certain merchants, called flour men, who rent mills, buy grain, mill it, and then sell the flour in shops they also rent. This profession is quite lucrative, as all the artisans who do not have the means to buy grain buy ready-milled flour in these shops and bake their bread at home. But more important and well-off people buy the wheat and have it ground in certain mills reserved for the city dwellers, for about two *baiocchi* per *roggio*. Most of these mills belong to the temple and the colleges; few belong to individual owners. The rental is high and comes to about two ducats per millstone.

Poets Writing in the Vulgar Tongue

In Fez there are also many poets who compose poems in the vulgar tongue on various subjects, and especially on matters of love. Some describe the love they feel for women, others the love they have felt for boys, and mention without any consideration and without the least shame the name of the child they love. Each year, on the occasion of the Mouloud, the celebration of the Prophet's birthday, these poets compose a poem in honor of the latter. The poets are brought together early on the morning of the feast day on the square of the chief of the consuls. They climb on the bench that serves as the chief's seat and each one recites his poem in the presence of a large audience. The poet who is judged to have recited his verses in the best and most agreeable manner is proclaimed that year's Prince of Poets and considered as such. Back in the days of the great Merinid sovereigns, the reigning king was in the habit of inviting the town's scholars and savants to his palace, where he would throw a party to honor the poets and ask that each one, standing on an elevated platform, recite his poem to the glory of Prophet Muhammad in the presence of the king and before all those who attended. Then, following the judgment of competent people, the king gave the most highly appreciated poet the sum of one hundred ducats, as well as a horse, a female slave, and the clothes he wore that day. All the other poets would receive fifty ducats, so that all of them would have some recompense when they took their leave. But due to the decline of the dynasty, this custom disappeared some 130 years ago [i.e., in A.H. 800/1398 C.E., when Sultan Abu Said Uthman ibn Ahmad came to the throne].

Translation by P.J. from A. Epaulard's 1956 French version

Al-Hasan Ibn Muhammad al-Wazzan al-Fasi, better known in the West as Leo Africanus, was born in Granada around 1488 & died in 1554, possibly in Tunis or in Italy. His family left Granada sometime after the Christian conquest of that Muslim kingdom in 1492, settling like numerous other exiled Andalusians in Fez, Morocco, where he studied at the al-Karaouine university. As a young man he accompanied his uncle on a diplomatic mission in the Maghreb, reaching as far as the city of Timbuktu (c. 1510), then part of the Songhai Empire. He was later captured by European pirates somewhere in the Mediterranean & sold into slavery. Presented to Pope Leo X, he was baptized in 1520 & freed. The pope, recognizing his abilities, asked him to put together a survey of his knowledge of the continent of Africa. For many years his book, dictated in Arabic, translated into Italian, & published by Giovanni Battista Ramusio as *Cosmographia dell'Africa* (Description of Africa), was the only known source of information on Sudan. A twentieth-century rediscovery of the originally dictated manuscript revealed that Ramusio, in smoothing the grammar of al-Wazzan's text, had colored many neutral details to make it more palatable to Christian European audiences; French & English translators added further embellishments. Modern translations which incorporate this manuscript are thus more true to the original—though we are in dire need of a good & reliable contemporary English version.

A BOOK OF MYSTICS

PROLOGUE |

From early on—and parallel to a legal communal practice—an individual mystical stance, Sufism, arose to unsettle and deepen matters of faith and the vision of the sacred in Islam. Sufism (*Tasawwuf* in Arabic) was not born of the meetings with Christianity or Buddhism after the Arab conquest. It is a mysticism whose essential source remains the Qur'anic revelation and the imitation in all circumstances of the "perfect man," that is the Prophet Muhammad, who is considered the first link in the chain (*silsila*) of Sufi initiates.

The fundamental concept of Sufism is *walaya*, closeness to (or approaching, friendship with, or nearness to) God. The ritual practice of Islam, as defined by the Qur'an and the Sunna, is the "legal" means of bringing the faithful close to their Lord. However, this codification of piety dissatisfied certain believers, who desired to liberate their souls from all secular contingencies.

The first Sufis distinguished themselves from other believers by renouncing earthly belongings and practicing retreat and meditation. Reading the Qur'an was their essential spiritual nourishment—which is why orthodoxy did not oppose them with brute force, at least at the beginning. Parallel to the ulama (Muslim religious scholars), the Sufis elaborated an original and much richer reading of the Qur'anic revelation, more closely concerned with the hidden meaning of the divine message. This esoteric reading is the basis of Sufism's concepts, specifically *fana* (from the Arabic verb meaning "to pass away" or "to cease to exist")—the complete denial of self and the realization of God through self-annihilation (via prayer and ecstatic states of meditation)—and *mahabba*, divine love. Sufism's personal quest is open to all believers, without gender distinctions.

Sufism started to develop in the Orient and quickly acquired vast authority. In the eighth century, Rabi'a al-'Adawiya (d. 801), a Sufi woman from Basra (in present-day Iraq), was renowned for her renunciation of the world and love of God and wrote mystical poems highly appreciated even today. But it is above all in the ninth and tenth centuries that Sufism develops as a formal mystical system and forges an original conceptual apparatus with its own terminology. This was achieved thanks to the contributions of such famous mystics as Abu Yazid Bistami (d. 874), Junayd of Baghdad (d. 910), and above all Mansur al-Hallaj (d. 922), who was tortured and executed in Baghdad for having said "*Ana al-haqq*" (I am the truth), a formula considered sacrilegious as it identified the creature with the Creator (*al-haqq* being one of the names of God). Most Sufis did not in any way publicly defy the Law; they simply thought that the exterior ritual was not sufficient to create unity with God. Their erotic and bacchic poetry was not to be read literally, but it contained a hidden meaning that only initiation allowed access to. Because of its indifference to Islamic ritual, however, Sufism did draw the ire of certain Muslim jurists.

In 1046 al-Qushayri wrote his famous *Epistle on Sufism* (*Al-Risala al-qushayriyya fi 'ilm al-tasawwuf*) describing the spiritual itinerary (*tariqa*) and its different stages (*maqamat*), distinguishing between the station (*mawqif*) and the state (*hal*) of the believer desiring mystical unification with God. Al-Qushayri also tried to reconcile religious orthodoxy (Sunnism) with mystical aspiration (Sufism). But it is above all the great thinker al-Ghazali (1058–1111) who imposed Sufism as one of the sciences of the law of religion, through his magnum opus, *Revival of Religious Sciences* (*Ihya 'ulum ed-din*). Through the depth and clarity of his analyses; the compass of his knowledge in the domains of philosophy, religion, and mysticism; and his exemplary attitude, al-Ghazali removed all suspicion from Sufism. He himself opted for this "intuitive" way of approaching God and ended his life renouncing the public world in which he had been such a shining light.

Spreading throughout the Muslim world, Sufism gave rise to a considerable literary production in Arabic, Persian, Turkish, Urdu, and other languages. The Muslim West would give birth to the Great Master (*as-Shaykh al-Akbar*) of Sufism, the Andalusian Ibn Arabi of Murcia (1165–1240; see pp. 98, 195), whose large oeuvre would be *the* monumental synthesis of Sufism. Across the centuries, his ideas will profoundly mark those of many other Sufis and thinkers, including Emir Abd El Kader (see p. 271).

Sufism would also obviously shape the religious perception of the Maghrebians—who contributed to it with their own specific genius. There were many Sufis from al-Andalus and the Maghreb whose fame went far beyond local notoriety, such as Abu Madyan Shu'ayb (see pp. 96, 189), Abdeslam Ibn Mashish Alami (see p. 192), and Abu al-Hassan al-Shushtari (see p. 199). Their poems continue to be sung in the spiritual concerts (sama') of the Maghrebian brotherhoods.

Sufism did not remain for long as an individual(istic) contemplative stance in the margins of society. The great Sufi masters and their disciples were also directors of conscience, with the aim of educating, organizing, and reforming people's mentality. From the end of the twelfth century on, the orders, or brotherhoods (*turuq*, the plural of *tariqa*), they founded would develop and spread across the lands of Islam. But one would have to wait for the end of the fourteenth century for Sufism to be no longer a solitary individual's path but totally taken into hand by the turuq and their spiritual masters. The first tariqa is the Qadiriya, founded after the death in 1166 of the great Baghdadi mystic Abdelkader al-Jilani by his sons. It would shine throughout the Muslim world—and especially brightly in the Maghreb, as the oral tradition shows—and is the mother tariqa from which all the ensuing ones have come. Sidi Abdelkader al-Jilani is the most revered saint of North Africa. One finds *maqam* (stations with small *koubbas*, i.e., domes, cupolas) celebrating his memory in a number of towns and other places, particularly in western Algeria. Many legends and tales claim that these maqam are in places that the saint—who had a gift for ubiquity—passed through. He is the champion of the widow and the orphan, the patron saint of the poor and the destitute.

The rise of the Sufi brotherhoods profoundly marked the Berber world. North Africa gave birth to tariqa-founding masters such as Abu al-Hassan as-Shadhili, who was born in Ceuta in 1196 and died in Egypt in 1258 while on a pilgrimage to Mecca; Sheikh Mohammed ben Aissa (1465–1526), the founder of the Isawa, at whose mausoleum in Meknes, Morocco, multitudes of faithful go into trances to the sound of bewitching music; Sidi Ahmed at-Tijani, who was born in Ain Madhi, Algeria, in 1737 and died at Fez in 1815 and whose Tijani brotherhood is very powerful in sub-Saharan Africa; Moulay al-Arabi ad-Darqawi of the Banu Zeroual in Morocco (1737–1823), whose disciples fought the Turks and the French in Algeria; and Sheikh as-Sanusi (1787–1859), whose tariqa marked the history of Libya.

It is thanks to the turuq that the teachings of the Sufi masters perpetuated themselves in the Maghreb and continue against all odds to nourish the Maghrebian imagination. Poetry, as a means of communicating at a range of levels beyond the most trivial linguistic one, has always been a favorite mode of the Sufi masters in forming, inscribing, and transmitting their experiences and thinking. It is therefore not surprising that in a Maghrebian context, Sufism and poetry have remained closely related over many centuries. As one of us writes in an essay called "Manifesto of Maghrebian Surrealism," Sufi poetry has always included what one could call surrealist dimensions, even though its twentieth-century French (and international) literary avatars (which rarely, if ever, acknowledge such roots) are but pale late versions of the Maghrebian originals:

Ibn al-Arabi manuscript page.

For a long time the Maghrebian has been a surrealist without knowing it. Take for example the following statement by Ibn Arabi:

"In what I have written I have never had a deliberate purpose, like other writers. Glimmers of divine inspiration illuminated me and nearly overcame me, so that I couldn't free my mind of them except by writing down what they revealed to me. If my works show any kind of formal composition, this form is not intentional. I have written some of my works on the behest of Allah, sent to me during my sleep or through a revelation."

To conclude, "it is finally into Maghrebian Sufism that surrealist subversion inserts itself: *'Psychic automatism in its pure state,' 'amour fou,'* revolt, chance meetings, etcetera."

Abu Madyan Shu'ayb (Sidi Boumedienne)

(Cantillana, 1126–Tlemcen, 1198)

THE QASIDA IN RA

By command of the Almighty His splendor has been magnified,
And with majesty and glory establishes His divine decree.

He—whose judgment inexorably governs creation,
According to what was set down as a record in the Primordial Book.

All praise is Yours! There is no granting what You forbid,
And no forbidding what You abundantly bestow.

Your will is preordained and Your judgment is piercing—
Your knowledge encompasses the seven heavens and the earth.

Your command subsists between the kaf and the nun,
[Executed] more swiftly and easily than the blink of an eye.

When You say, "Be!" what You say has already been,
And Your pronouncement of it is never repeated.

You were, and nothing was before You; You were, and nothing was
Other than You, yet You remain when mortal beings die.

You determined the fate of creatures before creating them,
And that which You determined was a predetermined command.

You loom above the seven heavens as a conqueror,
And You see what You have created, yet You [Yourself] are not seen.

Lords affirm that You are [their] Lord—
If they denied [You] they would taste the torment of one who disbelieves.

You have put on the cloak of grandeur, and there is not
Anything other than You, Enthroned One, to be exalted.

You it was who named Yourself the Conqueror,
And You are the God of Truth—certainly and beyond doubt.

You raised the firmament to its utmost height,
And then restrained it so it would not engulf the earth.

You fixed the sun and full moon as ornaments
For it, and stars, rising and setting.

You set down the earth, then spread it out,
And made rivers and seas flow upon it.

You created towering mountains and peaks on it,
And caused its waters to pour forth, overflowing.

You it is Who has overwhelming power over [the universe];
You created a fully formed creature out of moist clay,

[Then] endowed him with intellect, hearing, and sight,
And established him as a hearing, seeing individual.

You paired him with a mate from one of his own kind,
And brought forth progeny from them, who multiplied.

Yours is the greatest bounty, by which You guided us,
And made us believers in a pure, primordial religion.

After [our] ignorance You allotted us a [great] responsibility,
And a "manifest light," as an illumination for hearts.

So glory be to You, oh God, the Grand and Exalted,
Blessed be my Lord, most Majestic and Great!

How much grace have You clothed us with as an honor!
You have covered the naked one with it and continue to shield him.

How many misfortunes and calamities have You eased for us,
Have you warded off from the slave who errs and slackens!

We have erred and sinned often, yet You still
Remain merciful with us, near to us, and watchful.

Were evildoers and sinners not among us,
You would surely create a sinful people in order to pardon them.

Oh Lord, prepare repentance for all of us,
And set aside our errors with preordained forgiveness.

Then bless the Unlettered One and preserve him,
Who came to us as a messenger, an apostle and bearer of good tidings.

And to [his] family and companions [give] the purest greetings,
Exuding musk and ambergris for all time.

THE QASIDA IN MIM

Return to us the nights that have been lost to us,
And erase, by Your favor, that which has issued from us.

How much we have sinned, yet out of generosity You forgive [us];
How much we have erred, yet we still hope for Your good pardon!

Nothing but You have I—You are the recourse of my sorrow;
I have been ignorant, and possess nothing but Your indulgence.

Not for a single day have I turned toward anyone but You,
For in all the world I own nothing but Your favor.

How much respect I display in [my] love [for You]!
No friendship do I hope for, other than Your affection.

Were I to have a thousand tongues with which to express
Thanks to You, I would not stop thanking You for a single day.

Translations from Arabic by Vincent J. Cornell

COMMENTARY

Abu Madyan Shu'ayb ben Al-Ansari d'Al-Hussayn, also known as Sidi
Boumedienne, was a master of Sufi mysticism & a poet. The founder & prin-
cipal source of Maghrebian & Andalusian Sufism, he was born into a family
of Arabic origin in Cantillana, near Seville, in 1126 & died in 1198 in Tlemcen,
Algeria—the city whose patron saint he is. He studied in Seville & Fez, where
he received his religious education & came under the influence of the teachings
of the Berber ascetic Abu Yaza, Abdelkader al-Jilani, & al-Ghazali (through
Ibn Hrizim & Abu Bakr Ibn al-Arabi, Abu Yaza's master). He went into the
Atlas Mountains to ask to be initiated by Abu Yaza himself.

After his pilgrimage to Mecca & studies in the Middle East, he settled in Bejaïa, the flourishing & highly literate capital of the Hammadids. His reputation for knowledge and holiness—like that of Ibn-Rushd (Averroës) before him—worried the Almohad sultan Abu Yusuf al-Mansur, who called him to Morocco, a country he would not reach. Abu Madyan died in El Eubbad, a suburb of Tlemcen, on November 13, 1198. His mausoleum, a major pilgrimage site for Tlemcenis, was erected there.

Ibn Arabi called Abu Madyan the professor of professors, in which capacity he was the spiritual guide of the Sufi saint Abdeslam Ibn Mashish Alami.

Abdeslam Ibn Mashish Alami

(Beni Aross region, near Tangier, 1163–1228)

AS-SALAT AL-MASHISHIYAH (THE SALUTATION OF IBN MASHISH)

It seemed useful to us to leave at least one of the chanted song-poems in an Arabic transliterated into Roman letters so that the reader may try to read—aloud would be the best way—what such a work sounds like, to get a sense of the musical quality of the language & the ecstatic effect such a prayer-poem might have on the singer-reciter. The original's richness of sounds is of course lost in the English translation, in this case an anonymous one we located on the web & have added as an interlinear aid to approaching this medieval hymn.

Allahumma salli ʻala man minhu-n-shaqqati-l-asrar
O Allah shower Your blessings upon him from whom burst open the secrets,
wa-n-falaqati-l-anwar
from whom stream forth the lights,
wa fihi-rtaqati-l-haqaʼiq
and in whom rise up the realities,
wa tanazalat ʻulum Adama fa-aʼjaza-l-khalaʼiq
and upon whom descended the sciences of Adam, by which all creatures are made powerless,
wa lahu tadaʼalati-l-fuhum
and blessings upon him before whom all understanding is diminished.
fa-lam yudrik-hu minna sabiqun wa la lahiqa
None of us totally comprehend him, whether in the past or the future.
fa-riyadu-l-malakuti bi-zahri jamalihi muniqa
The gardens of the spiritual kingdom blossom ornately with the resplendence of his beauty,
wa hiyadu-l-jabaruti bi-faydi anwarihi mutadafiqah
and the reservoirs of the World of Dominion overflow with the outpouring of his light.

wa la shay'a illa wa huwa bihi manuta

There is nothing that is not connected to him,

idh lawla-l-wasitatu la-dhhaba kama qila mawsut

because if there were no intercessor, everything to be interceded for would vanish, as it is said.

salatan taliqu bika minka ilayhi kama huwa ahluhu

So bless him with a prayer that is worthy of You, from You, as befits his stature.

Allahumma innahu sirruka-l-jami'u-d-dallu bika 'alayk

O Allah indeed he is Your all-encompassing secret that leads through You to You

wa hijabuka-l-a'azamu-l-qa'imu laka bayna yadayk

and he is Your Supreme Veil raised before You, between Your Hands.

Allahumma alhiqni bi-nasabihi wa haqqiqni bi-hasabihi

O Allah include me among his descendants and confirm me through his account

wa 'arifni iyyahu ma'rifatan aslamu biha min mawaridi-l-jahl

and let me know him with a deep knowledge that keeps me safe from the wells of ignorance,

wa akra'u biha min mawaridi-l-fadl

so that I might drink to fullness from the wells of excellence.

wa-hmilni 'ala sabilihi ila Hadratik

Carry me on his path to Your Presence

hamlan mahfufam bi-nusratik

encompassed by Your Victory,

wa aqadhif bi 'ala-l-batil fa-admaghuhu

and strike through me at the false so that I may destroy it.

wa zujja bi fi bihari-l-Ahadiyya

Plunge me into the seas of Oneness,

wa-nshulni min ahwali-tawhid

pull me out of the morass of metaphorical Unity,

wa-ghriqni fi 'ayni bahri-l-Wahda

and drown me in the Essence of the Ocean of Unicity

hatta la ara wa la asma'a wa la ajida wa la uhissa illa biha

until I neither see, nor hear, nor find, nor sense, except through It.

wa-j'ali Allahumma-l-hijaba-l-a'zama hayata ruhi

O Allah make the Supreme Veil the life of my spirit

wa ruhahu sirra haqiqati

and his soul the secret of my reality

wa haqiqatahu jami'a 'awalimi

and his reality the conflux of my worlds

bi-tahqiqi-l-Haqqi-l-Awwal

through the realization of the First Truth.

Ya Awwal Ya Akhir Ya Zahir Ya Batin

O First! O Last! O Manifest! O Most Hidden!

Isma' nida'iy bima sami'ta bihi nida'a abdika Zakariyya
Hear my call as You heard the call of your servant Zachary
wa-nsurni bika laka
and grant me victory through You, for You,
wa ayyidni bika Laka
and support me through You, for You,
wa ajma' bayni wa Baynak
and join me to You
wa hul bayni wa bayna ghayrik
and come between myself and anything other than You—

Allaaah! Allaaah! Allaaah!

According to some, each -aaah should extend for approximately twelve counts. This is the end of "As-Salat Al-Mashishiyah," but these lines customarily follow it:

Inna-l-ladhi farada 'alayka-l-qur'ana la-radduka 'ila ma'ad [Qur'an 28:85]
Indeed He Who ordained the Qur'an for you will return you to the station of
your Ultimate Destiny.
Rabbana 'atina min ladunka Rahmatan wa haiy' lana min 'amrina Rashada
[Qur'an 18:10]
O Lord grant us from Your Presence Mercy and endow us, whatever our outward
condition, with sure Guidance!
Inna-Llaha wa malai'katahu yusalluna 'ala-n-nabi ya ayyuha-lladhina 'amanu
sallu 'alayhi wa sallimu taslima [Qur'an 33:65]
Indeed Allah and His angels shower blessings upon the Prophet. O you who
believe, shower blessings on him and greet him abundantly.
Salawatu-Llahi wa sallamuhu wa tahiyyatuhu wa Rahmatuhu wa barakatuhu
'ala sayyidina
Muhammadin
May the Sublime Blessings of Allah, His Peace, Greetings, Mercy, and Grace, be
upon our Master Muhammad,
'abdika wa nabiyyika wa rasulikan-Nabiyyil-Ummi wa 'ala alihi wa sahbihi
Your Servant, Prophet, and Messenger, the Unlettered Prophet
— and also upon his family and companions.
wa sallim 'adada-sh-shaf'i wa-l-watri wa 'adada kalimati
Rabbina-t-tammati-l-mubarakat
Upon him be Peace multiplied by all even and odd numbers, and multiplied also by
the inconceivable number of the perfect and blessed words of our Lord.

Subhana rabbika rabbil izzati 'ammaa yasifoon wasalamun 'alal mursaleen
waal-hamdu lillahi rabbil 'alameena [Qur'an 37:180–83]
Glorified be your Sustainer, the Lord of Glory and Mercy, beyond all which
they attribute, and Peace be upon the Messengers, and Praised be Allah, Lord of
the Worlds.
Alfu salaam—Alfu salaam— lfu Alfi sallaamin fi qulubina
Thousandfold Peace, Thousandfold Peace, Thousand-Thousandfold Peace in
our Hearts
wala hawla wala quwwata 'illaa billahil 'aliyyil 'adheem
and there is no Power and no Strength except with Allah, the High, the Exalted.

Ibn Arabi, al-Sheikh al-Akhbar (Murcia, 1165–
Damascus, 1240)

OUR LOVED ONES

Where are my loved ones
by God tell me where they are

As I've seen their apparitions
will you let me see them for real

How much I want them O how much
and how I hoped to come close to them

Far from them I'm safe
among them I'm not

Maybe my happiness lies between
leaving them and finding them again

So that my eye may enjoy their sight
and that I no longer sigh: where are they?

Translation from Arabic by Abdelwahab Meddeb & P.J.

I WISH I KNEW IF THEY KNEW

I wish I knew if they knew
  whose heart they've taken
Or that my heart knew
  which high-ridge track they follow
Do you think they're safe
  or do you think they've perished
The lords of love are bewildered
  in it, ensnared.

"GENTLE NOW, DOVES"

Gentle now, doves of the thornberry
and moringa thicket,
don't add to my heartache
your sighs.

Gentle now,
or your sad cooing
will reveal the love I hide,
the sorrow I hide away.

I echo back, in the evening,
in the morning, echo,
the longing of a lovesick lover,
the moaning of the lost.

In a grove of Ghada,
spirits wrestled,
bending the limbs down over me,
passing me away.

They brought yearning,
breaking of the heart,
and other new twists of pain,
putting me through it.

Who is there for me in Jam',
and the Stoning-Place at Mina,
who for me at tamarisk grove,
or at the way station of Na'man?

Hour by hour
they circle my heart
in rapture, in loveache,
and touch my pillars with a kiss.

As the best of creation
circled the Kaaba,
which reason with its proofs
called unworthy.

He kissed the stones there—
and he bore the pronouncement!
What is the house of stone
compared to a man or woman?

They swore—and how often!—
they'd never change, piling up vows.
She who dyes herself red with henna
is faithless.

A white-blazed gazelle
is an amazing sight,
red dye signaling,
eyelids hinting.

Pasture between breastbones
and innards.
Marvel,
a garden among the flames!

My heart can take on
any form:
gazelles in a meadow,
a cloister for monks.

For the idols, sacred ground,
Kaaba for the circling pilgrim,
the tables of the Torah,
the scrolls of the Qur'an.

I profess the religion of love;
wherever its caravan turns
along the way, that is my belief,
the faith I keep.

Like Bishr,
Hind, and her sister,
love-mad Qays and the lost Layla,
Mayya and her lover Ghaylan.

Translations from Arabic by Michael Sells

"WHO IS HERE FOR A BRAVEHEART"

Who is here for a braveheart
   who halts at Sál'in and hopes
Who for a braveheart
   lost in the hollow desert,
    love-burned, love-mad, gone sad
Who for a braveheart
   drowned in his tears
   drunk from the wine
    of her open mouth

Who for a braveheart
   burned by his own sighs
   led astray and abandoned
   in the beauty of the glow between her eyes.

The hands of desire
   played on his heart
What is there to hold against him
   Where is his crime?

Translation from Arabic by Michael Sells

Abu al-Hassan al-Shushtari

(Guadix, 1213–Damietta, 1269)

LAYLA

There is no life but Layla.
When in doubt ask everything about her.

Her mystery emanates in everything
and because of that everything praises her.

Her beauty is widespread; its fullness, concealed.
The witness says:

She is like the sun, its light radiant,
yet when you seek it, it turns to shadow.

She is like the mirror, in which images appear
reflected, yet nothing resides there.

She is like the eye, which has no color,
yet in it appear colors in every hue.

Hers is the right course, even if I suffer;
her evidence is in the removal of the cloak.

Her injustice is just. As for her justice,
it is grace; my brother, ask for more.

In her meadow, there is none but her
so she alone is invoked.

A wonder, she remains distant, nowhere.
Then union draws near, hands full.

And union with her brings us fullness;
distance from her, division; both are mine.

In union, there is no difference between us;
in division, confusion upon me.

In her raiment, her ambiguity is displayed,
for everything is mirrored in her.

She unveiled one day for Qays, and he turned away,
saying: O people, I loved no other.

I am Layla, and she is Qays. What a wonder!
How is that what I seek comes to me from me?

Translation from Arabic by Lourdes María Alvarez

Othman Ibn Yahya el Sherki
(Sidi Bahlul Sherki) (Tétouan region, seventeenth century)

from **AL-FIYACHIYA**

Why am I so worried
about my fortune?
Why should I complain?
My Creator is my Benefactor.

I am His weak creature
and He is the Almighty.
That which is hard for me
for Him becomes so easy.

I am just a slave
and Destiny has all matters settled.
He can see me, while I can't.
Out of semen He shaped me inside a womb.

He says: "Be!" and so it is,
from the Beginning and all new again.
He reigns over all His creatures
and rules His kingdom as He pleases.

Out of semen He shaped me
in the darkness of a womb
and offered me all kinds of riches
and fed me all kinds of food.

I came out completely naked
and He decently clothed me.
He still protects me
and is far above the wisest of all men.

I was born naked—I was born ignorant.
He enveloped my soul in a decent cloth
and made me drink from His holy spring
and made Earth my bed and the Sky my roof.

Praise be to Him our Benefactor!
We must praise Him at all times
for all the good He bestowed upon us
and for both Sky and Earth.

Earth is His kingdom, and I'm one of His subjects.
Men are His creatures, and I'm one them.
He is the One who bestows fortune
so let's not be too demanding, and accept whatever comes. . . .

To you life means to entertain yourself:
seeking only pleasure and careless about the rest.
Take a rest, my heart,
and be happy with just a little!

Discard what your Self wants most if you want to get rich,
for your Poverty lies in your virtues!
He who can't oppose his desires
shall suffer all his life!

Be strong and fight your Self!
Don't let yourself drift away—keep Desire out of your mind
and root out every single seed of it, for your Self wishes you ill!
Look at you: how weary you are!

Some people told me: "Be wise, old fool!
Forget your worries and know what you say!
Build your walls on solid foundations,
for your foundations threaten to fall."

I replied: "Are you being fair to Him?
From Him I see only the good.
How many lie buried under the ground?

Who am I to be in the world what I want to?
The world is worth nothing to me!
Why do you call me a fool
when you can see me carrying hard, heavy stones?
What do you want from me? Just leave me alone!"

They told me: "Be quiet and humble, old fool,
when you enter the mosque!"
To which I replied:
"Who am I to refuse to be humble?!
My hair has turned white
and it's time for me to depart
as if I had never existed!
I am from Earth, and to Earth I shall soon return."

Earth is my Origin and that of all creatures.
Earth is where I am like a plant deeply rooted.
I prefer to see my flesh and bones
turn into weeds and earthworms.

Earth was the Beginning of all Creation:
from Earth we all sprouted, and to it we shall return.
It is said that those who lie there shall someday rise
so I won't mind resting anywhere you wish,
for Earth embraces all men alike:
the ragged and the richly clad,
those wearing large cotton belts,
chechias, turbans, or Yemeni brocades.

. . .

On Him who feeds the birds I rely,
for He certainly is my Protector!
He designs the course of my life
and all things happen as He wishes!

They said my mind was constantly upset.
I said: "He is the One who knows!"
They said I have changed my mind.
I said: "No! No! No! My mind won't feed me."

They said: "Why don't you work?"
I said: "Work is an honor to me!
I will tighten my belt and toil all day long

till I save up enough and savor
the tasty flesh of pigeons!
But I will never, ever beg
any of my brothers
nor any other person in the world!"

They said: "Life is tasteless."
I said: "Because of heartless men!"
They said: "Be a beggar."
I said: "Begging kills his man!"
They said: "Get married."
I said: "Who suits me?"
They said: "But you have no money."
I said: "Thank God!"

When lightning strikes and the wind blows,
I recall those nights
when I was so happy.
But then those were only ghosts!

My heart lies in the East, while in the West
I feel a complete stranger!
Each time lightning strikes
I recall a strange thing:
everyone wonders how I can be there and here!
To them I must look like
a bird whose feathers have been cut.

If you meditate on this poem
you will discover a hidden garden
where meaning flowers in various colors
nurtured by the noble Othman Ibn sidi Yahya.

Translation from Arabic by Abdelfetah Chenni

Translation from Arabic by Abdelfetah Chenni

COMMENTARY

We have omitted a number of redundant quatrains & double lines from this poem that were probably interpolated: such later additions are of course the fate of all poetry that comes from an orally based background. Most of the poem is arranged into quatrains, except where there is dialogue that shouldn't be interrupted, where we merge two quatrains into one—exactly as in the original version.

Notice the similarity of a number of images & metaphors with those of el

Mejdub's quatrains (see p. 215). A few terms, etymological, geographical, & Sufi, need explaining: "Fool," *bahlul,* is the nickname of the poet; *batin* conveys the Sufi notion of the invisible known only to a few Sufi masters. The line "I feel a complete stranger!" translates the Arabic *gharib,* used here to refer to the Sufi notion of estrangement from the physical world. This term derives from the same root as *gharb,* "West." East and West are geographical locations (Mashreq & Maghreb) that also refer to the bipolarized Sufi notion of human existence: the physical & the spiritual. *Sherki* (the Eastern) is the second word in the nickname of the poet: *Bahlul Sherki* means "the Eastern Fool."

Ahmed Ibn 'Ajiba (Tétouan region, 1747–1809)

QASIDA

My Beloved has let me drink the wine of his love
 and I am filled with the wine of this passion.
While He was pouring me to drink, my thirst increased
 and my heart, with nostalgia, was full to the point of bursting.
Were the entire universe, heaven and earth, filled with the cups
 of the wine of love, my thirst would not be quenched.
And even if, drawing from the springs of the two worlds, I drank in
 love with each of my breaths, I would not weary of drinking.

Awakened by love's intoxication, some find discernment; I,
 remaining in the tavern, enjoy the wine of general knowledge.
How smitten I am by wine, in which is my repose,
 my relaxation, my perfume, a beneficent plenitude!
Drunken, we have drowned in the splendor of its Beauty;
 And before its radiant light our senses have vanished.
The daily sun has appeared, glorious,
 and in its presence no star can further shine.
The protective curtain has risen before the universe of our Lord
 and we have hastened toward the light of the Beloved.

He said to us: Welcome you are! Here is my Beauty
 in real nature; rejoice in it!
O cohort of lovers, take full enjoyment in Our presence,
 for here resides the object of all desire!
Beware, beware of separating from My lovers
 through some lack of propriety, a source of separation.

Act well toward friends in all respects,
  and contemplate My beauty, for it is I who unite the whole!
In distance as in proximity, in ease
  as in trials, look at Me with a submissive heart.

Do likewise, whether you feel upon you My satisfaction or My
  anger, for it is I who make manifest all things, and decree them.
To expansion belongs an etiquette that must be respected,
  at the risk of seeing your feet slip, then your heart:
Modesty, reverential fear, glorification of My beneficence,
  holding in the tongue, always too prompt to escape.
And if the night of contraction falls upon you, in darkness,
  welcome it with constancy, for the light will shine anew.
Be calm and resigned before what happens,
  the ineluctable destiny that comes from the Lord.

To poverty corresponds an etiquette through which
  the aspirant realizes his relationship to the illustrious master of Sufi
  science.
May he renounce the world, raising his aspiration,
  may he be altruistic and with a heart ready to give,
Humble and retiring before the Almighty;
  may he be the companion of a sheikh who holds the essential lore.

Submission, respect, sincere love:
  conforming to them perfectly, therein is the whole way.
Raise not your voice in his presence,
  and do not laugh, for laughter is an occasion for mourning.
In no way go against him,
  for he sees with the light of clairvoyance.
And do not cast your glance toward any source other than his,
  for you would be thrown, broken, lost in arid solitude.
Do not leave the nest wherein you receive an education which,
  in the long run, will give you incessant lights,

Until you see the time of your majority arrive
  and, manifestly, you are made firm in the truth.
Thus, lights will come to your assistance from all sides,
  and you will quench the thirst of your peers who come to follow you.
Remain steadfastly on the path of the revealed law,
  for it protects against those misfortunes which break one's back.
Grasp it with two hands, like the miser his treasure, for the highest

perfection you can attain is the respect of prescriptions.
He who is closest to God is he who, in secret, contemplates
and, outside, draws from the sources of the law.

It is he who receives heritage completely
who is showered with the greatest riches, for he follows the footsteps of
the Friend.
May God's prayer and His salvation be upon him,
for both are addressed with respect to the Intercessor.
May God be satisfied with all the companions,
with the family of the Prophet, and with those who have followed him.

MAXIMS

If one did not stop in the shadows of things,
the heart would be illuminated by the sun of gnosis.

If it were not for shackles and obstacles,
the suns of realities would be seen to shine.

If there were neither individual will nor free will,
the shadow of otherness would withdraw from the heart.

If they were not passions and desires,
aspirations would become real in less than the wink of an eye.

If they were not bad tendencies and defects,
invisible secrets would make themselves manifest.

Without the struggle with oneself,
the secret of the elect would not appear.

Without the company of true men,
no one knows how to distinguish imperfection from perfection.

Without the company of the great,
the hearts and their depths cannot be purified.

Without the service of true men,
no one can reach the degrees of perfection.

Translation by David Streight after a French translation by Jean-Louis Michon from the original Arabic

Mystical Poetry from Djurdjura

"TELL ME, YOU SAINTS FROM EVERYWHERE"

Tell me, you saints from everywhere,
who lives in the forests?
Lions and wild boars.
Who lives in the branches?
Owls and falcons.
Who frequents the assemblies?
Bureaucrats and brigands.
I beg you, lion, don't abandon me to the wild boar.
I beg you, owl, don't abandon me to the falcon.

"THOSE WHO REMEMBER KNOW IT"

Those who remember know it,
O scholars and savants!
We love and cultivate the rose.
When I open the irrigation channel,
all its petals bloom,
and that rejoices us, men and women.
But now she's taken up by others.
I see animals grazing her.
Her master's death saddens her.

"WHAT DWELLING DID I RAISE IN AYT-IDJER"

What dwelling did I raise in Ayt-Idjer
Fashioned with fastidious labor!
I was so happy to see it stand.
Alas, deceitful construction—
I wept before inhabiting it,
For it collapsed in the noon sun.
But I praise God,
For I have paid my debts,
So much so I haven't a patch of land left.

"BIRD, SOAR UP INTO THE SKY"

Bird, soar up into the sky
and then with plaintive cries
land in the midst of the Ayt-Bougherdane.
Take my greetings to Sidi Mohand ou-Saïd,
the man with the powerful ancestry.
Carry on toward the Ayt-Houari,
who, big or small, all learned the sacred text,
and to the Ayt-Sidi-Ali-ou-Athmane,
Who transform a cane into a tree.
Carry on to the Ayt-Ouelhadj,
Whose blows transform the mountain.
O saints! I implore you
When at noon I disembark in Jidda.
Happy the pilgrim who, his tasks absolved,
in plenitude crosses the oceans.

Translations by P.J. of Youssef Nacib's French translations from Arabic

Two Shawia Amulets

AMULET AGAINST POISON AND POISONOUS ANIMALS

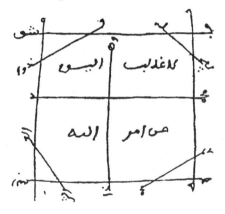

AMULET TO "UNKNOT" HEADACHES AND NEURALGIAS

*These amulets, meant to protect against occult forces such
as jinns and the evil eye or natural dangers such as illnesses
and poisonous animals, traditionally consist of writing in
Arabic characters done with saffron-colored water or ink
from burned wool on paper or animal skin. They are worn
enclosed in a little leather bag or a silver locket.*

THIRD DIWAN

The Long Sleep and the Slow Awakening

The long period of North African cultural slumber from the fourteenth to the nineteenth century is marked by a stagnation of the literary genres that had shone brightly in previous centuries. With the fall of Granada in 1492 and the ensuing Spanish and Portuguese threats, the Maghreb starts to fold back upon itself. Algiers, Tunis, and Tripoli will call upon the Turks to help contain and repel the Christian aggressors. From the sixteenth to the nineteenth century, except for Morocco, the whole northern part of the Maghreb becomes theoretically a part of the Ottoman Empire, though most of Algeria and Tunisia, despite their being vassals of the Sublime Porte, are in fact quasi-independent states. It is also during these centuries that the borders of the three core Maghrebian countries begin to firm up and their capital cities set up definitively along the shores of the Mediterranean and the Atlantic (this also being, of course, the age of the famed Barbary pirates).

The written production of this period is essentially concerned with matters of law, theology, and mysticism. However, as a consequence of the Arabization of the Maghreb, a popular poetry will start to develop in a sort of Arabic Maghrebian koine, forged by the *meddahs,* the local poets. This poetry, called *melhun,* is deeply appreciated even today by Maghrebis. Among others, Leo Africanus signals this taste for poetry, in his *Description of Africa:* "They love poetry and recite, in their vulgar Arabic, very elegant verses, even though that language be corrupted today. A poet with local renown is much appreciated by the lords who will pay him lavishly. I can't tell you the purity and grace they put into their verses."

Despite the melhun's capital importance for Maghrebian culture, many of the advocates of classical Arabic continue to consider it an inferior, minor genre. In fact, the word *melhun* refers to the act of making mistakes and committing barbarisms (Berberisms?) in Arabic. At the same time it indicates that this poetry was composed to be sung. The poetic form of the melhun is the qasida, which doesn't differ in structure from the classical Arabic poem of some fifty (or even up to a hundred) monorhyme verses. What does make the specificity and liveliness of this literary production, separating it from a servile and sterile imitation of the old, established, and by now academic Mashreqi genres, is the use of what Dante in his culture called the "vulgar tongue."

This poetry kept Maghrebian culture awake and alert during what some have called the dark centuries. It exalts the chivalric values and love in a rich, image-laden, and luxuriant language that is, however, all too often mired in stereotypes. Praise (*madh*) of the Prophet and his ten companions, mystic love, religious virtues, patience before the vicissitudes of life, death, and the Last Judgment are recurrent themes.

Starting in the sixteenth century in Algeria, popular poetry exalts the virtues of the warrior and the struggle against the infidels, for the Spanish threat is real. Sidi Lakhdar Ben Khlouf, for example, composed a celebrated poem in ninety-nine verses (*Qissat Mazagran ma'luma*) concerning the Battle of Mazagran, in which he himself took part. In the nineteenth century, resistance to the French conquest gave rise to singer-poets of renown such as Mohammed Belkheir (1835–1905).

Earthly love, erotic games, and the pleasure of the senses are also major themes of *chi'r melhun* (the poetry of melhun). Verses that celebrate loved ladies—named Meriem, or el-'aliya, or Fatma of the long painted eyelashes, or Sa'diya, and so on—still make today's many lovers of *chaabi* (a musical genre born in Algeria at the beginning of the twentieth century) dream. These texts, altered and modernized, also enrich *raï* music, a folk style originating in Oran in the 1930s (see Cheikha Rimitti, p. 518).

Though their works are sung and celebrated throughout the Maghreb, the poets of melhun are for the most part from Morocco and the west and south of Algeria. The chi'r melhun was particularly developed in the regions around Fez and Meknes in Morocco and in the Dahra region and the area of Biskra (the Hodna) in Algeria. It is easy to discern a shared inspiration: chi'r melhun is an extremely elaborate genre of a nearly classical facture, especially when compared to the popular poetry that is routinely recited throughout the Maghreb.

Although preserved in writing, melhun poetry is not much disseminated, except orally, because the owners jealously guard and keep secret their manuscripts. Small publishing houses have compiled, edited, and published partial collections of some poets, such as Sidi Lakhdar Ben Khlouf, Ben Msaieb, and al-Maghraoui, and today researchers and scholars in ever-greater numbers are gathering and analyzing this essential corpus of Maghrebian literary artifacts.

If the poets of what one could call the high melhun constitute the core section of the Third Diwan, we have added some texts—including popular oral versions of melhun, such as "The Poem of the Candle" (*Qasida as-shma'*), gathered in Morocco by Stefania Pandolfo in the 1980s (p. 251), and Amazigh texts gathered and translated into French by Taos Amrouche—to remind that even given the expansion of Arabic language in the Maghreb during those centuries, Berber culture was alive and active.

Finally, we have inserted a few of the prose writers of that time, such as Al-Maqqari (writing on those Andalusians who had fled to the Maghreb) and al-Yusi (on local geography and wider cultural concerns).

Sidi Abderrahman el Mejdub

(Tit Mlil, early sixteenth century–Merdacha, Jebel Aouf, 1568)

SOME QUATRAINS

dirty and ugly they saw me   there goes an empty head they said
in fact I am more like an open book   there's much useful stuff inside this head

.

o my heart I burn you   and if you want I will do more
o my heart you shame me   because you like who doesn't like you.

.

neither think nor search too much   don't always be despondent
the planets are not fixed   and life's not eternal

.

don't play with your best friend's feelings   and if people insult him, ease his mind
who loves you, love him more   but if he betrays you, don't ever be his friend again

.

all I've had in life is one goat   but I've written beautiful quatrains
many are fulfilled through God's favor   yet claim those favors as their own
    labors

    •

travel and you'll get to know people   and owe obedience to the noble
the fathead with the potbelly   sell him for a dime

    •

my heart's between a hammer and an anvil   and that damned blacksmith
    has no pity
he keeps hammering and when it cools   he kindles the fire with his bellows

    •

my weak heart can't bear any pain   and by God you are barbarians
you supported me when I was strong   and let me down when I grew weak

    •

o you who sows the good grain by grain   o you who sows the bad lot by lot
the good multiplies and rises   the bad withers and wastes away

    •

don't think of this time's tightness   see how wide time is in God
difficulties wipe out the weak   but men wipe out difficulties

    •

I suggest to you devourer of sheep heads   throw those bones in a well
laugh and play with the people   but before all shut your mouth

    •

silence is abundant gold   and words destroy good ambiance
say nothing if you see something   and if they ask say no, no

    •

o friend, be patient   hide your burden
sleep naked on thorns   wait for a brighter day

.

the good old days are gone   hard ones are here
who dares speak the truth   will have his head cut off

.

don't get in the saddle before you bridle   and tie strong knots
think twice before you speak   or you'll live to regret it

.

I made snow into a bed   and covered myself with the wind
I made the moon into a lamp   and went to sleep in the starry night

.

misery should be hidden away   and covered under a veil
cover the wound with the skin   and the wound will soon heal

Translations from Arabic by Abdelfetah Chenni & P.J.

Sidi Abderrahman el Mejdub (also transcribed as Majdoub) was a Moroccan
Sufi poet whose poems, or at least stanzas thereof, have become part of popu-
lar culture throughout the Maghreb & given rise to a range of proverbs (e.g.,
"doubt is the beginning of wisdom"). Born (exact date unknown) in Tit Mlil,
on the coast of the Atlantic Ocean between El Jadida & Azemmour, he lived
during the rise of the Saadi Dynasty under the reign of Mohammed ash-
Sheikh & Abdallah al-Ghalib & died in 1568 in Merdacha, Jebel Aouf. His
tomb, which attracts many visitors even today, is in Meknes. His surname—el
Mejdub—refers to someone who is illuminated, mad, enraptured; the *jdub* was
the dancer who led the other dancers of ecstatic Sufi brotherhoods into the
jedba, the dance that resulted in trance. If someone stays in this trance state his
whole life, he is called a *mejdub*. The French scholar Alfred-Louis De Prémare
wrote in his 1988 book *La tradition orale du Mejdub:* "Epileptic kid, or young
man surprised by the irruption of mystic ecstasy? Exalted Malamati secretly
affiliated to an active politico-religious grouping, or respectable sheikh of a

rural zawiya? Miserable troublemaker from El Qsar or missionary preacher of a Sufi current in full expansion? Holy man or con man? Popular bard or composer inspired by a dhikr? Sidi Abderrahman was doubtless all of the above at different points of his life ... or was these according to how he was judged, or recuperated. At any rate, this kind of personage is deeply rooted in the Moroccan landscape, in its social ramification, in its mental environs."

Sidi Lakhdar Ben Khlouf (Mostaganem region, sixteenth–seventeenth century)

from *THE HONEYCOMB*

The best of my poetry begins   with God's name and with yours.
Your love resides at the root of my heart   and is as precious as a single eye.
As often as the bee makes honeycomb   after honeycomb.
O Mohammed! Oh my Lord!   May God bless you in eternity!

O my god! Bless and greet our Prophet   century after century.
As many times as there are stars in night's darkness   and drops in the
     falling rain.
As there are tortoises and fish swimming in silence   in the depths of the
     sea.
My threads are stretched between my loom's beams and my work   a shirt
     and a coat
Purple silk threads   the like no silkworm can make.

God has blessed you praised you   then sent you a thousand salutations.
Without you there would be no resplendent light of paradise   no burning
     fire of hell.
We need you in this world and in the next   o you on whom rest our
     foundations.
Save my father and my grandfather from the fire   my mother and
     grandmother too!
Be kind to my soul and my body   nurse me so that I may heal from what's
     ailing me!

Apply your medicine to me   that I be delivered from the invisible demon's
     obsession.
Is the devil redoubtable?   I have a living God inside me, though my eyes
     can't see Him.

I just need to say "I take refuge in my God"   and the words of the Qur'an will seal its mouth.

The graces of God's book suffice me   as nourishment and as weapons.

Thanks to it I prevail all alone   over these assailants, my weaknesses and Satan.

Through a ruse perfidious Satan   has sown discord among us, O people!

By surprise he attacked us on our left   and we're afraid that our religion will be split.

Protect us and keep us safe, Lord,   and damn him a thousand times!

Awake and asleep I denounced him   I gave him a terrible blow!

I hit him with a steel rod   and administered two hundred blows of the whip.

O Mohammed!   Do not abandon the poet and his tribe!

I want to make a pact with you   the pact of someone who keeps his word.

On the tumultuous Day of Judgment   no one but you will gratify us with kind deeds

That day of great thirst when water will not flow in the rivers   when the unbelievers will live in infamy

When they will be thrown into a flaming fire   so horrible, so dark, so intense.

. . .

I prove negligent though death is at my heels   and I am weighed down by sins.

When I fall asleep I am like an oxen   when I awake I'm as alert and evil as a viper.

That's how I spent my life   but I hope intensely that God will forgive me

Before I come to die   if he does consider me one of his submissive creatures.

Yet I am scared: how to get rid of the terror of this world   and the terror of the next.

The she-camels raised their lament toward you publicly   witness to your vast prestige.

The birds' warbling ceaselessly evokes your name, O chosen one!   So does the soldiers' drumbeat as they raise their shelters and tents.

And the schools resound with the voices of the scholars and their students   in the study circles that guide toward goodness.

And the frogs at the edge of the pond   spend night upon night repeating your name.

I pray earnestly for God to make my joy last   you are my happiness and he
  fills me with elation.
Kindnesses accrue to me   and my benefits grow larger day by day.
It's in the waves of a sweet and limpid ocean   that I'll wash off my stains.
Your bright light shines on my cheeks   a pomegranate flower opening
  amid roses.
I've dunked my bread in a delicious cream   and achieved ascendency that
  way.

Sincerity of intentions is enough for me   how can Lakhal have erred?
I have had ninety-nine visions   and the Giver keeps granting them to me.
The prophet of the right way has rewarded me   and, O Lord, has accepted
  my demand.
God created city dwellers and country fellows   all will be plunged into
  felicities as if in honey.
Only the Jew will not partake   if he dies without pronouncing the
  shahada.

I end my song invoking the prayers   of Prophet Ahmed to the cloud
The guide whose beauty is indescribable   and in whom we rest all our
  hopes on the day of Resurrection
In consideration for the one who nursed him   Halima of the tribe of the
  Banu Saad.
May he keep us from the burning fires of hell   that devouring furnace!
May he guide us forthwith to the eternal gardens   the blessed community
  of Muslims and me, Lakhal!

Translation by P.J. of Ahmed Amine Dellai's French translation from Arabic

COMMENTARY

Sidi Lakhdar Ben Khlouf, considered one of the great singers of the prophet
Muhammad, belonged to the Ouled Khlouf tribe, whose patron saint he now
is. He lived in the sixteenth & seventeenth centuries & took part in the Battle
of Mazagran (1558) against the Spanish led by the Count of Alcaudate, who
died in the fighting. Sidi Lakhdar recounts this battle in the qasida that starts,
"O rider, from over there, I arrive just now . . . " In a testamentary poem he
bids his tribe & his family members good-bye, sharing his last will with them,
& tells us that he has lived more than 125 years & that since the age of forty,
following a pilgrimage to the mausoleum of Sidi Boumedienne in Tlemcen, he
has dedicated himself exclusively to praise of the Prophet, who had asked him
in a dream to change his name from Lekhal ("the Black One") to Lakhdar ("the
Green One"). Today's lovers of chaabi greatly esteem his melhun.

Abdelaziz al-Maghraoui (Tafilalet, 1533–1593/1605)

from **A MASBAH AZ-ZIN (O BEAUTIFUL LAMP!)**

o beautiful lamp heal the lovesick with your renowned beauty o lalla of all
*   flowers*
have mercy shine & call on the lonely lover o full moon

o you whom the lord's made so beautiful you outdo all jealous beauties
with grace & softness & majesty o cradle rocking in the breeze

a flower on which the soul feeds & soul of all flowers shine on all flowers
    by daylight
your deep sea has flooded the rivers whose swelling brought along many
    riches

you outdid the famous abla with your grace & beauty that make the soul
    ecstatic
you're the sharp scimitar shines when unsheathed on dust-blown
    battlefields

I love you o gazelle wanders in the desert & settles by the camp you make
    me cry
you possess my soul I'm your humble servant for the rest of my life

o beautiful lamp heal the lovesick with your renowned beauty o lalla of all
*   flowers*
have mercy & call on the lonely lover o full moon

he who's been let down by such beauty how should he feel but miserable &
    wretched
mourned like a poor fool who's lost his mind

have mercy & soothe the pain of the lovesick for beauty bears no grudges
a night with you to me is the happiest of all aid-feasts

black & soft eyes & bright cheeks & dresses when will those breasts be
    merciful
are they twins or small apples placed right where they belong?

from **PEACE BE UPON YOU O SHINING PEARL!**

in the name of Allah I start my poem with these lines
       the lord's name should be known overtly & covertly
an honorable credit for the poet who mentions your name
       the secret of all that's said is Allah's the greatest
in praise of the one the lord has honored & chosen
       he showed him evidence & gave him victory
let your blessing be thorough & everlasting
       respect & reverence & dignity
Peace be upon you O shining pearl—Muhammad the most generous of men!
. . .

where will the tyrant hide as you'll always be there to judge
       your effort can't be ignored
your kingdom is great & you know all its secrets
       you who created male & female
the devil lulled me into a sinful life
       I spent all of it like a drunk
my mind kept seeking pleasures until my hair turned white
       though today the burden's become too heavy
Peace be upon you O shining pearl—Muhammad the most generous of men!
. . .

now my poem is over having said what I wanted
       in an elaborate way to the last *bait* & line
you who understand the secret signs in poetry
       take its necklace set with gems & shining red rubies
shielded by the rich merchants' protective chests
       smell that breeze as it blows the scent of those stones
the poet Abdelaziz says in this perfect poem:
       he wrote it in praise & honor of the sayyid of all men

Translations from Arabic by Abdelfetah Chenni

COMMENTARY

(1) Sheikh Abdelaziz al-Maghraoui, of the Tafilalet region in southern Morocco, was the supreme qadi (religious judge) of Fez & one of the few poets appointed to the court of Sultan Ahmed al-Mansur Saadi, the sixth sultan of the Saadi Dynasty. Acknowledged by many Maghrebis as one of the earliest melhun poets, he & Sidi Lakhdar Ben Khlouf (see p. 218) belong to the same Berber tribe, the Maghrawa, based in the Chelif Valley & the mountains of the Dahra in Algeria. Both ensured a smooth transition from Ibn Quzman's Andalusian zajal to the Maghrebian melhun.

(2) Al-Maghraoui innovated melhun metrics by creating a meter of his own, blending the first & second hemistiches into a longer line & forcing the syntax to adapt to this length—though the zajal's linguistic heritage & Andalusian ghazal imagery remain evident in his poems. In the first extract, from the ghazal *A Masbah az-Zin*, the line's expanded length is easily detectable.

(3) In the second extract, from the poem "Peace Be upon You O Shining Pearl!," al-Maghraoui opts for a different variation in meter—an innovative one for his time: he omits the caesura between the first two hemistiches by blending them into one verse (as he did in the previous poem), then adds a third & final orphan hemistich (though always on the same line), with a caesura this time. The last stanza not only points out the mystical Sufi way of writing poetry brimming with meanings hidden to the uninitiated listener or reader but also refers to the poetics that al-Maghraoui adopted to "[say] what [he] wanted in an elaborate way to the last bait & line."

(4) Nearly every melhun poet's repertoire evolves along two extremes: when young, the poet leads a turbulent, fun-seeking life, pursuing pleasure in wine, kif, women, & music (almost the sole topics of his ghazals); as he grows older & (possibly) wiser, he tends to be more religious & writes mystical Sufi poems, mainly medihs in which he repents & asks for forgiveness.

Mawlay Zidan Abu Maali (d. Marrakech, 1627)

"I PASSED . . . "

I passed by a beautiful tomb in the middle of a cemetery
on which flowers had formed a carpet
so I asked whose grave this was.
And I was told, "Pray for him respectfully—it is the grave of a lover."

Anonymous translation from Arabic

COMMENTARY

Mawlay Zidan Abu Maali of the Saadi Dynasty was the sultan of Morocco from 1603 to 1627, residing in Marrakech. He progressively lost authority, & the country fell into anarchy: Morocco was in a state of civil war, warlords took territory from Zidan, Salé became a sort of independent republic, & the Spanish captured Larache in 1610 & then al-Ma'mura (now Mehdya). Due to strange circumstances during the civil war, Zidan had his complete library transferred to a ship, whose commander stole it & brought it to Spain, where the collection was transmitted to the Escorial.

Al-Maqqari (Tlemcen, c. 1591–Cairo, 1632)

ON THOSE ANDALUSIANS WHO TRAVELED TO THE EAST

"Among them was Abu Ishaq al-Sahili, known as al-Tuwayjin or al-Tuwayjan, the celebrated scholar, the upright man for whom thanks are given, the renowned poet, a native of Granada from a family of rectitude, wealth, and trust. His father was the *amin*, the head, of the perfumers' guild in Granada. As well as being the amin he was a scholar and lawyer, proficient and versatile. He was well versed in the law of inheritance (*fara'id*).

"This Abu Ishaq was in his youth a notary in the lawyers' street of Granada. He departed from al-Andalus for the East and made the pilgrimage and then traveled to the land of the Sudan. He made his home there and found high favor with its sultan. He died there, may God have mercy on him." Here ends a summary of the words of the emir Ibn al-Ahmar in his book *Nathir al-juman fi man nazamani wa-iyyahu al-zaman* (The Spread of Pearls in the Poetry of My Contemporaries).

Abu 'l-Makarim Mindil b. Ajurrum said: "It was related to me by one whose words may be trusted that the death of Abu Ishaq al-Tuwayjin took place on Monday, 27 Jumada the Second 747 / October 15, 1346, at Tunbuktu [Tombouctou], a place in the desert which is one of the provinces of Mali, may God have mercy on him." Then he vocalized *al-Tuwayjin* with *i* after the *j* and said: "This is how he vocalized it with his own tongue, may God have mercy on him. Those who call him al-Sahili name him after his maternal grandfather."

Among them was the excellent imam, the litterateur Abu Ishhaq Ibrahim b. Muhammad al-Sahili al-Gharnati. Al-'Izz b. Jama'a says: "He came to us from the Maghreb in the year 724/1324, then returned to the Maghreb in that year. We have heard that he died at Marrakech in the 740s/1340s."

Al-Sarakhsi says: "I heard that some people brought Ya'qub al-Mansur an elephant from the land of the Sudan as a present. He ordered that they be rewarded but did not accept it, saying: 'We do not wish to be one of the "owners of the Elephant."'"

He says in his rihla when mentioning the sayyid Abu 'l-Rabi' Sulayman b. 'Abd Allah b. Amir al-Mu'minin 'Abd al-Mu'min b. 'Ali, who was at that time governor of Sijilmasa and its districts: "I met him when he came to Marrakech after the death of al-Mansur Ya'qub to take the oath of allegiance to his son Muhammad. I found him to be an old man of striking appearance and excellent character, eloquent in Arabic and Berber. These are some of his words in a letter of reply to the king of the Sudan in Ghana, complaining to him of the detention of some traders: 'We are neighbors in benevolence even if we differ in religion; we agree on right conduct and are one in leniency toward our subjects. It goes without saying that justice is an essential quality of kings in conducting sound policy; tyranny is the preoccupation of ignorant and evil minds. We have heard about the imprisonment of poor traders and their being prevented from going freely about their business. The coming to and fro of merchants (*jallaba*) to a country is of benefit to its inhabitants and a help to keeping it populous. If we wished, we would imprison the people of that region who happen to be in our territory, but we do not think it right to do that. We ought not to "forbid immorality while practicing it ourselves." Peace be upon you.' "

"The faqih Abu 'Abd Allah Muhammad al-Qastallani said to me: 'I went into the presence of Abu 'l-Rabi' in the palace of Sijilmasa. He had before him leather mats upon which were the heads of the rebels, the Kharjites who had robbed travelers on the highway between Sijilmasa and Ghana, and he was scratching the ground with an ebony stick, saying: 'No wonder that his enemies' heads are a reply when swords are his letters.' "

Abu 'l-Rabi' died after the year 600/1203–4.

Adaptation by P.J. of the partial English translation from Arabic by Pascual de Gayangos

COMMENTARY

Abu-l-'Abbas Ahmad Ibn Muhammad al-Maqqari was a member of an illustrious family of scholars originally from Maqqara, a town southeast of Msila in Algeria, that had lived for many centuries at Tlemcen. He was born in Tlemcen c. 1591 & died in Cairo in 1632. His anthology *Nafh al-ttb min ghusn al-Andalus al-rattb* (The Fragrant Scent from the Tender Branch of al-Andalus) is a compilation of sometimes little-known historical & biographical material related to al-Andalus from earlier sources, much of which he located in the library of the Saadids at Marrakech. Al-Maqqari preserved the only known extract from the rihla (travel book) of al-Sarakhsi, who had come from the East to the Maghreb & was at the Marrakech court of the Almohads from 1197 to 1203. Al-Sarakhsi's accounts are an important source for the relations between the Almohads & the Sudan at the end of the twelfth century.

Al-Yusi (Middle Atlas, 1631–1691)

from **AL-MUHARAT**

[Two seasons]

In spring, given that it is a moderate season, the forces don't accumulate, nor can foods hurt, constrained as they are by the season. There is thus no risk in being very active, physically and sexually. Bloodletting can be performed on a serene, quiet, gratifying day. On that day one will avoid worry, annoyance, any painful experience, too much thought, bookish study, or sexual activity. Long nights, fasting, and diverse exhaustions should be kept for a full day, when there is neither hunger nor satiety. . . .

During summer, given its burning and dry nature, one should abstain from any heat stemming from food and drink. Thus avoid honey, garlic, birds, pigeons. One should eat fresh and humid things: fatty veal in a vinegary sauce or prepared with squash. Also cucumber and watermelon. Wear light clothing; reduce physical exercise as well as sexual activity. Avoid staying up late, and sleep longer at siesta time.

[The city and the country]

Man resorts to the urban mode of living to enjoy commerce and industry, and all the other techniques his system of living can accommodate, and also to gain mutual aid, and in view of religious or secular advantages. In general, all of this can only be achieved by the gathering of many people likely to furnish the markets, each trade, art, technique, or activity lending one or more specialists. Now, these conditions are not present inside a single family, or even inside a single tribe. They result from the variety of the mix and the size of the mass. This is so for two reasons. First, because such is the opinion of the collectivity that takes on those needs. And then, because natural law does not want a small group to keep the exclusivity of knowledge, or have sole use and possession of religious or secular advantages, or free itself from other creaturely characteristics so as to constitute an order proper and useful to itself, by excluding any consideration of the others. To the contrary, in His solicitude and wisdom, God has widely distributed qualifications and advantages among the humans. Thus it is that one finds a savant among such and such a group, a poet among another, in yet another an artisan or a merchant, in such manner that mutual aid can be complete and that everyone can participate in God's beneficence by taking on a specific task.

Translations by P.J. of Jacques Berque's French versions of the original Arabic

Abu Ali al-Hassan Ibn Masud al-Yusi, considered by many to be the greatest Moroccan scholar of the seventeenth century, was a close associate of the first Alaouite sultan, Rashid. Born in a Berber tribe, the Ait Yusi, in the Middle Atlas Mountains, he left his native village at a young age for a lifelong pilgrimage. He received his baraka (a flow of blessings & grace) from Sheikh Mohammed ben Nasir al-Dari of the Nasiriya tariqa of Tamegroute. His best-known text, *Al-Muharat,* contains many autobiographical passages & is remarkable for frank discussions of his childhood misdeeds, the pleasures of his conjugal sex life, & other intimate details.

Ahmed Ben Triki (Ben Zengli)

(Tlemcen, c. 1650–c. 1750)

from *TAL NAHBI* (MY PAIN ENDURES . . .)

My pain endures and my eyes shed tears every day;
    separation causes unbearable pain that has no reason to be!
Her name's engraved in my burning heart;
    I found no cure or counsel for my pain!
My hair's turning white, O lord, after separation
    from those I love and wish to be with again!
Such separation's made my heart bleed
    and tears run down my cheeks all day long!
I miss them so much I'm wasting away in despair;
    my tears rage like ocean waves against these sad days!
All this is so unfair I wasted my life
    wandering in lands of exile and feeling low!

from *SHA'LAT NIRAN FI KBADI* (BURNED TO THE DEPTHS OF MY SOUL!)

Burned to the depths of my soul!
    It's no use to shed tears, though I cried so much!
My eyes are sore from weeping;
    I wish I could visit the sacred *bait* where I can rest!
    Peace be upon the prophet al-Hadi!
If I could visit the *bait* of the full moon

clouds would disperse & my troubles dispel!
It's years I haven't slept with peace of mind
       as I've been in love since a child with this beautiful maiden!
Her braids as dark as darkness fall well below her belt
       and reach her legs—happy is he who caught a glimpse!
Darker than an African *zinj* or blackberries—
       her soft, killing eyes cast a spell on her admirers!
Her forehead makes me sigh as it shines
       with beauty on all her virtues!
       Peace be upon the prophet al-Hadi!
From that stunning beauty show
       arched eyebrows over the eyes
and eyelashes sharp as scimitars
       make you fall under their spell
and cheeks as pearls
       toppled with amber—
roses and poppies
       blossom in between!
       Peace be upon the prophet al-Hadi!

. . .

My *hal* longs for peace;
       my heart needs a rest!
I long to see the shining light
       with eyes wide open!
Like apples or bitter oranges,
       orange flower water mixed with wine!
Fruit of fertile trees
       ripen at dawn and dusk
and show insistently offered
       at sun set and rise
sublime work of art by the lord
       in the bosom—O delight!

Translations from Arabic by Abdelfetah Chenni

COMMENTARY

(1) Born in Tlemcen, Algeria, Ben Triki started writing poetry at an early age &
learned much from his sheikh & master, the poet al-Mendassi, as he acknowl-
edges in one of his poems. Ben Msaieb, his contemporary (see p. 232), is reported
to have said of him: "Ben Triki is possessed by a great jinn, but this jinn was
mistaken when he chose such a home!" The nickname Ben Zengli, which refers to
Ben Triki's father, may be understood as "tough, coarse" but also "rich, wealthy."

(2) The first extract is from "My Pain Endures . . . ," written in Jebel beni Zenaten, near Oujda, Morocco, in 1652, after the Ottoman authorities had banished Ben Triki from Tlemcen. He composed many of his major poems during that period of exile & painful separation.

(3) The second extract is from "Burned to the Depths of My Soul!," a religious poem with an innovation which Ben Triki was probably the only melhun poet to dare. Rumor has it that he wanted to prove to his sheikh, al-Mendassi, how creative & brilliant he could be at writing poetry. The sheikh is said to have liked the poem & raised no criticism whatsoever. The whole qasida is a descriptive praise of the holy Kaaba. Ben Triki transposes mystical Sufi ghazal devices originally applied to the love of God/the beloved to the description of a place, hence the insistence on its physical features.

Sid al Hadj Aissa (Tlemcen, 1668–Laghouat, 1737)

A *BORNI* FALCON SONG

Take off my boots and spurs, Abu Kaltum.
It has been a long, exhausting day.
My shoulders ache from the weight of these
starry-breasted *borni* falcons with piercing eyes.
I rested for a day or two, then got bored of
doing nothing and felt so sad.
Let us rejoice now and head to our Sahara
riding on crests scattered with wild jujube bushes.
I dashed through a fertile *guerara*, then to a denuded one
to hear my companions' excited *haihaia* yell.
She was instantly flushed out of her nesting bed
looking like a sleepy maiden slave who had drunk
too much wine the night before.
Terrified she was by the strength of her new master,
whose presence she was unaware of until he came
swooping down on her faster than an arrowhead,
scattering whole flocks of flying birds with his shrill cries.
He tore open her robe and kept scratching her pretty face
until it turned a sooty, baking *tajin*.
She then thought of her poor mate and feared for him
for the houbara bustard homeland was no secret anymore.

A *TURKLI* FALCON SONG

Oh Abu Souar! Rub your bird with oil to excite him
and mount a steed that can catch up with mine.
Under me is a thoroughbred that brings tears to my eyes
as he dashes forward into the wind.
No sooner had I let my bird go
than he caught a houbara and a red hare!
I chased them away with tough riders, though,
great hunters that deserve not the slightest blame.
I search the desert, then return home loaded with game.
My *turkli* and I enjoy wintering in the Sahara.

Translations from Arabic by Abdelfetah Chenni

Sid al Hadj Aissa belonged to a noble family: his father was Aissa ben Brahim
& his mother, Mahbuba, was the daughter of Si al hadj Bou Hafs, an important
sheikh from the famous western tribe of Ouled Sidi Cheikh. Sid al Hadj Aissa
was a very pious man, a Sufi saint who left Tlemcen in 1694 for Oran, then joined
the tribe of the Harrar for a short while before going to Ben Bouta in Laghouat,
where he founded a zawiya. He is said to have made predictions about the French
invasion of Laghouat. He was a fine poet too, especially when extolling his hunt-
ing birds. *Borni* are falcons with a red hue, while *turkli* have a dark brown hue.

Al-Hani Ben Guenoun (Mascara, 1761–1864)

from *YA DHALMA (O UNFAIR LADY!)*

To the qadi of love I went crying
    & made a plea to end my pain.
When I told him my story he said:
    "Of course we all feel sorry for the lovesick!"

Praised be the lord for what he created—
    in you he melted beauty, glory, & generosity!
The moon feels ashamed to show itself at night;
    the lion dreads the killing looks in your eyes.
I love no one but you, O sultana of the gazelles—
    your like can't be found anywhere today!
Because of you your folks are now jealous of me!

My pain endures as your love persists;
        you torture my heart, though everybody's sound & safe!
You didn't allow me to come to your place;
        he who's been banned won't let his heart settle down!
You didn't have mercy & made no generous gift;
        before the lord I'll settle a score with you!
Your folks are men of great tents, O noble lady—
        fearless warriors who're brave & generous!
I know your father's brother was a hero
        who died like a strong & fierce lion!
Al-Hani Ben Guenoun misses your shadow—
        O girl, I can't face hell alone!
For you I'll make orphans of the sons of my tribe, O unfair lady!

You torment my heart—I'm worn out!
        When night falls all my wounds reopen!
I lost repentance & feel like waning away,
        O girl with painted nails & eyes & eyebrows!
Kind & tough like al-Halaili the horse rider
        you leave me at a loss—I swear!
The cheeks' roses hang from high branches!
        The beauty spot makes the zealot a true sinner!
That cute nose drives me crazy—
        I'll banish anyone who won't forgive & forget!
My heart won't wake up; a thick cloud veils it!
For you I'll make orphans of the sons of my tribe, O unfair lady!

The days of love I spent in sweat & tears—
        no, I'm not fit for that battle!
A humble servant obeys your orders;
        your slave, who sold his soul to love!
I'll hate all of them who hate you—
        when you're sick I'm devastated!
I fear people's eyes & their gossip,
        each night awake, though my body's asleep!
For your love I've sinned—that fear's made me a mystic!
        If I repent—sure I'll win you in the afterlife!
For you I'll make orphans of the sons of my tribe, O unfair lady!

Translation from Arabic by Abdelfetah Chenni

(1) From the eighteenth-century western High Plateaus of Algeria (Mascara region), Ben Guenoun's qasida *Ya Dhalma* traveled far to reach the eastern Arab-Andalusian city of Constantine in the nineteenth century, where two great figures of the *malouf* (a local version of the ancestral Andalusian music) adopted & sang it: the Arab Sheikh Mohamed Tahar al-Fergani & the Jewish Sheikh Raymond Leyris (whose daughter married the famous Jewish-French singer Enrico Macias, then a young musician in Sheikh Raymond's orchestra).

(2) Melhun poetry has truly encouraged Maghrebian musicians to innovate in melody & rhythm, though always in harmony with the lyrics & vocals. In the early twentieth century, Sheikh Abdelkrim Bastandji made Ben Guenoun's poem into a major Andalusian musical work, adapting it & introducing six other modes/melodies to the original melhun mode called *dheil* (as used by Sheikh Hamada in his western Bedouin version), which are *rhaoui, zeidane, sika, h'sein, Iraq,* & *mezmoum.* Each of these fits a specific stanza according to the poet's mood, state of mind, emotions, & so forth. In the same stanza one melody may be combined with another if need be, for instance when the poet switches to a different emotional state. No wonder, then, that Ben Guenoun's *Ya Dhalma* is rightly called *seb'iyit as-snai'i,* or "the masterpiece with the seven melodies." This poem shows the continuity in creativity made possible by inventive & innovative research into potential common grounds between the structural metrical patterns inherent in melhun poetry & Andalusian muwash-shaha musical melodies.

Sidi Mohammed Ben Msaieb (d. Tlemcen, 1768)

from **O PIGEON MESSENGER!**

I am tired of being blamed—o pigeon—and of tears rolling down my face
    like raindrops
you didn't bring any news nor felt pity   though you know I'm in great
    pain
I beg you to ask the one who left me   how can she forget me
how can I be happy when she is far away   every day I burn a little more
        go and greet my beloved with kohl-lined eyes
        tell the slender one   to stop rejecting me
        she has broken her promise   though she has sworn
        she is of noble lineage   but she's too hard
        tell her I'm so scared   she won't be kind to me again

I spent last night with her—o pigeon—and I was so happy I wish you were
   there
tambourine and r'bab and oud sang their melodies   flute and gasba woke
   whoever was drunk
candles burned in candlesticks and wine   flowed in glasses like water in
   streams
       go and greet my beloved with kohl-lined eyes
       how beautiful that night was   in the company of my beloved
       venus twinkling above the palace   in which we both slept
       far from any watching witness   or envious eyes
       we kept drinking from our glasses   all night long
her cheeks were in blossom—o pigeon—and a bright forehead showed
   through her hair
like a full moon piercing thick clouds   the twelfth and thirteenth nights
   of the month her eyes and lids like spears and arrows   made me fall
   under her spell
       go and greet my beloved with kohl-lined eyes
       how soothing it was to meet her again   after all the trouble and
          pain
       separation lasted too long   and kindled the fire of love
       I couldn't stand it anymore   nor could I find the cure
       so from her lips I drank   an old healing wine
a light breeze started blowing—o pigeon—when the morning star showed
   at dawn
and the birds that awoke to the notes of the strings started warbling in
   their nests
what else can I do when the wine is so sweet   but embrace my beloved
   tightly
       go and greet my beloved with kohl-lined eyes
       be careful young man   don't be a fool
       lest you fall in love with some girl   and be under a spell
       fill the glass to the brim   and make the beauty drink
       always welcome your guest   with a glass of wine first
       beside the sublime Aishah   with kohl-lined eyes
       I lay last night—o how I wish   it had lasted forever—
       go and greet my beloved with kohl-lined eyes
this song was written after eleven hundred—o pigeon—and widely known
   in the forties

since his childhood Ben Msaieb has loved girls   how can he be patient?
how can he rest?

I won't rest and I won't sleep without the one   with black hair and black
eyes and lids

I am tired of being blamed and of tears   rolling down my face like
raindrops

Translation from Arabic by Abdelfetah Chenni

COMMENTARY

Writes his translator, Abdelfetah Chenni: "Born in Tlemcen, Algeria, Sheikh Mohammed Ben Msaieb first learned how to use a loom and make a living from it before he started weaving lines into poetry by the end of the seventeenth century. He is said to have had a narrow escape just when the Turks were about to behead him for his political position against Ottoman rule, and he fled to Morocco, where he lived for a few years. It was there that his poetry came to a turning point: from ghazal to medih and other religious genres. His Moroccan experience led him to Sufism and to Mecca, a long journey that he described in one of his poems. Today, Ben Msaieb's language remains accessible despite all the changes that the vernacular has witnessed over the centuries, and many of his poems have been sung in the local traditional *hawzi* music. His poetry belongs to the old tradition of the melhun, though it is urban rather than nomadic."

Mohammed ben Sliman (d. Fez, 1792)

THE STORM

Friends, yesterday my beloved visited; it was the middle of Ramadan,
and it was as if I had gathered honey and roses,
but I was accused of breaking the fast—
why shouldn't I have done so, after so much solitude!
Isn't the sick person advised not to fast?

After the long drought, the storm makes its drum rumble;
saber at the ready, lightning routs the defeated cavalry;
while the wind, that intrepid rider,
after a short rest is ready to rumble.

The downpour attacks, standard flying,
victorious showers that have the torrents on the run,

and wherever the eye turns
my overflowing heart sees only green.

From the fields in bloom rises perfume—
spring, a king with no rival,
and restful shade
have invented marvelous new clothes.

Joyous inventor, Spring dispenses his riches:
roses, wild flowers, concerts of birdsong—
in a festive garden
where the bee gathers nectar among the roses.

Friends, yesterday my beloved visited me, in the middle of Ramadan,
and it is as if I had gathered honey and roses,
but I was accused of breaking the fast;
why shouldn't I have done so, after so much solitude!
Isn't the sick person advised not to fast?

Translation from Arabic by Abdelfetah Chenni & P.J.

COMMENTARY

Mohammed ben Sliman was born in Fez in the middle of the eighteenth century & died there, thirty-five at most. He is seen as the precocious genius of Moroccan melhun, & various singers still perform the poem above. While translating it, we have been listening to a version recorded by the Ensemble Melhun Amenzou of Marrakech.

Boumediene Ben Sahla (Tlemcen, late eighteenth–early nineteenth century)

from WAHD AL-GHAZAL RIT AL-YOUM (I SAW A GAZELLE TODAY . . .)

I saw a gazelle today   wandering alone on the way,
running scared in the desert—   the Arabs called her a jinn!
If she could be bought   I'd spare a hundred sultanis!
I saw a gazelle today that tormented me, O listeners!
Even though I could spare a hundred   that won't be enough!

As I look into her eyes   I feel I have to sing about her
for all beauty is hers—   she's torturing me, O listeners!
I saw a gazelle today that tormented me, O listeners!
All beauty's gone to her—   she with the languid eyes!
The perfect body—   which sets my heart ablaze!
Her forehead—a shiny full moon   makes me shiver with love!
I saw a gazelle today that tormented me, O listeners!
Eyebrows & eyelashes like swords;   jewels hanging down a shiny forehead.
I stared at her all the time   feeling crazy about her!
I've lost my mind, I'm sure—   should you try, you'll forgive me!
I saw a gazelle today that tormented me, O listeners!
When I keep silent, my friends,   I can hear demons inside me!
I hear a string plucked in my head   but no one starts singing!
In spite of the oud & wine in the glass   I find no one to entertain me!
I saw a gazelle today that tormented me, O listeners!
Fall in love & you'll see what I had   to go through because of this gazelle
I once met on my way & since then   she's driven me crazy!
When I cry no one feels any pity!   When I stifle my pain it hurts so much!
I saw a gazelle today that tormented me, O listeners!
What can I do? I need help!   No description fits her beauty!
This gazelle is so gorgeous   my words can't describe her!
Her hair's soft as silk   & black as a Sudanese!
I saw a gazelle today that tormented me, O listeners!
Black, yellow, & of all colors!   Her eyes do cast a spell!
Her neck's a fine bough from   a ben tree or the stem of a lily!
Her mouth an agate   or pure gold set with coral!
I saw a gazelle today that tormented me, O listeners!
When will this fire be quenched   O you who understand my poem?
I didn't know I'd roam the high seas   when my pirate took me on that
    schooner!
I beg the merciful Lord   forgive my sins!
I saw a gazelle today that tormented me, O listeners!
Be kind to me, O friends!   Look for the bough of the ben tree
the one who lives beyond my reach   in the district of Laqran!
She left me with a tormented mind—   O Lord, give me patience!
I saw a gazelle today that tormented me, O listeners!

Translation from Arabic by Abdelfetah Chenni

A weaver by trade—from Tlemcen, Algeria, like many poets of the urban mel-
hun (see the commentary on Ben Msaieb, p. 234)—Ben Sahla, acknowledged
by his peers as "the Tlemceni sheikh," lived in the eighteenth century, an era
marked by oppressive Ottoman rule. He denounced political & social injus-
tice in many of his poems & was even forced to flee Tlemcen for the plains of
Anqad on the Moroccan-Algerian border. In this, his life was not very differ-
ent from that of the other exiled poets of western Algeria (see, e.g., Ben Triki,
p. 227; Ben Brahim, p. 237). The poem above is a muwashshaha that has lost
many structural features of the original Andalusian form through an innova-
tive melhun touch by the Tlemceni sheikh. Even today it is a masterpiece of
the Tlemceni hawzi musical repertoire & confirms the intimate historical link
between melhun poetry & Andalusian music (for more on this connection, see
the commentary on Ben Guenoun, p. 232).

Mostefa Ben Brahim (Safa) (Boudjebha, Sidi Bel Abbès province, 1800–1867)

SADDLE UP, O WARRIOR!

hedda (1)

Saddle up your mount—O warrior!   Ride off to al-Bahja—O companion!
Ride nonstop to az-Zohra.   Go hand her my message,
the one with the slender waist!   My gazelle lives in Oran.
Let your horse gnaw at his reins &   run as if after a prey in the Sahara,
like a pirates' schooner fending   the sea when pushed by a gale!
Let him thunder ahead with just   a spur as a true thoroughbred!
Before darkness surprises you   depart & spent the night riding.
You'll drink a few glasses of wine   before you meet my men the next day.
Greet my brothers Belkacem &   Lahbib & Ali
when they all have greeted you   don't forget al-Bachir & al-Mhalli.
Greet Ben al-Yemmem   Dahmane & she who drives me crazy.
Tell this noble assembly   I'm suffering, O my men!
In her absence I can't sleep!   You're the only ones who can help me!

frech (1)

My *hal* is indescribable: I can't compare it to any other!
Each night I feel tormented—   pains come & pains go!
I miss her—the moon crescent!   I miss her shadow—the lovely one!

Love drives me crazy—desire   is a throbbing pain!
My spoiled lover's beauty seduced   me with the red rose of her lips!
Black eyes look darker in their white   & poppies blossom on her cheeks!
Light shining from the crescent   on the tenth of the month!
High mountains separate us—   her country is far away!
I lost my mind because of her   there's no reason left to me!

hedda (2)

After I'd sent word to her   I saw my messenger come back.
As I saw the boy from far away   my mind flew off to him—
I lost patience & asked him   to tell his story right away!
He answered saying: "Yes   I am the one who roams the desert
though yesterday I was heading   to the town when I saw
a crowd of young girls in a garden   who strutted along before me!
They looked like a swarm of doves   nesting on the roof of a palace!
One of them pulled down her veil   to show a loving shiny cheek
as though she ripped the clouds with   the piercing sparkle of her
     bracelets!"

frech (2)

She said: "By the name of Allah, O boy!   I beg you to keep my secret!
I feel so miserable as if in jail   because of the one I miss so much!
I'm willing to bear any pain   as long as I may see my lover again!
*The black-eyed one defeated me—   my miserable face is clear to
     everyone!"*
I told her: "I'm a falcon   tomorrow at dawn I'll fly off
should heavy rain or clouds fall   or should I dig my own grave!"
She begged me: "Bring me word   from Safa or let him come to me!"

hedda (3)

Before the new day broke   I saddled up the best of my horses—
the one that looks like a pigeon   his mother from the Sahara his father
     from the Tell!
A dark night it was with striking   lightning and roaring thunder!
I flew off for fear of her blame   at ten sharp I was with her!
I stood before her arms   smelling musk & rich perfumes
turned on by the thirst of love   & speaking words of gold in my poem
     to her!

Translation from Arabic by Abdelfetah Chenni

Mostefa Ben Brahim, also called Safa, is a widely known melhun poet thanks to the singers of the Oran region, who have never stopped adapting his poetry to hawzi, *bedui,* modern, & raï music—a poetry that is profoundly lyrical, eloquent, & concise at the same time, singing the praise of tribal values & individual achievement. Born in 1800 in Boudjebha, in the Oran region, he was educated at the Derqawa Mhajia zawiya, where he studied the Qur'an, law, & the mystical texts of the tariqa & soaked up the melhuns of Orani poets such as Sidi Lakhdar Ben Khlouf (see p. 218), Ben Msaieb (see p. 232), & Ben Guenoun (see p. 230). Ben Brahim's relationship to Emir Abd El Kader's resistance to French invasion remains uncertain. He was said to have been the qadi, or judge, of his native village, & the French administration named him the *caïd* in charge of gathering taxes from the Ouled Sliman populations, whose territory spreads over the Sidi Bel-Abbès province. His poetry from that period tells of his love adventures, & half his diwan comprises erotic songs about the beauties Fatimah, Aishah, Mamiya, Yamina, Zohra, & many others whom the "hunter of gazelles," as he liked to call himself, had seduced.

Starting in 1841, his administrative harshness & licentious life caused him problems. In 1845 he was forced into exile in Fez, Morocco; there he composed poems brimming with nostalgia for his native land & regrets for the separation from loved ones but also biting satires against the inhabitants of Fez. Thanks to the intervention of his friends & his son Hachemi, who was a brilliant student in Algiers, Ben Brahim was allowed to return to Boudjebha, where he died in 1867.

Mohammed Belkheir (El Bayadh, south of Oran, 1835–1905)

MELHA!

Your leg's as fine as a cutting blade
in the hands of a famed sheikh;
your jingling *r'dif* around your ankle
teases me until late at night
like an early marching army
with its musical brass band
or a lost nomad caravan
fleeing the sultan's wrath in the dark.
O Lord! Make her suffer
the same pain I now suffer!
Make *Melha* feel tormented
and let my tormenting jinn possess her!

MOROCCAN EXILE

Counsel me, O sultan of all horse riders—
you who set the prisoner free from the Rumi's jail!
I beg you, O knight & saint of the saints,
in the name of the almighty lord!
Neither my state nor my troubles seem to upset you
as I wander among wandering people—
Berbers from the Tell & the Guir
who'll laugh at me & blame you for that!
My people are gone & I remain alone,
feeling sad when I think of the ones I love!
Sometimes the moon shines at night
sometimes the night is so infinitely dark!
I went into exile but regret nothing.
I live now in the kingdom of Moulay Ali,
protected by the saint & sultan,
patron of the western gate,
market of old Fez.

EXILED AT CALVI, CORSICA

Stop asking!
My fate depends on the almighty lord.
I'm waiting for the saint of saints,
Sid Sheikh, to come on his white mount.
I miss him & miss my kids too,
& that troubles my soul.
With Sheikh Bendouina my lifelong friend
I am prisoner in Calvi,
where we're both held hostage.
I need to breathe & want to flee
the infidel's country for my Muslim lands.

Translations from Arabic by Abdelfetah Chenni

In his foreword to Mohamed Belkheir's *War & Love Poems*, Jacques Berque writes: "Bard of nomadic bravery and eternal desire, Belkheir makes use of pure poetic forms to propose a timeless message for tomorrow and always." Belkheir was a self-taught poet from the tribe of the Rzeigat (in the southwestern High Plateaus). He took part in the second insurrection of the Ouled Sidi Cheikh (1881–84) against the French occupation of western Algeria. He was a fierce Bedouin warrior & coordinated between the various tribes of the region. He was finally captured & sent to a jail in Calvi, on the Mediterranean island of Corsica, for nearly nine years.

Si Mohand

(Icheraiouen, At Yirraten, c. 1840–Lhammam-Michelet, 1906)

THREE POEMS

> *This is my poem:*
> *If it's God's pleasure, it will be beautiful*
> *And spread far and wide.*

> *He who hears it will write it down,*
> *He will not let it go,*
> *And the wise man will agree with me:*

> *May God inspire them with pity.*
> *He alone can preserve us:*
> *When women forget us, we have nothing left!*

•

I have sworn that from Tizi Ouzou
All the way to Akfadou
No one will impose his law on me.

We will break, but without bending:
It's better to be cursed
When the chiefs are pimps.

Exile is inscribed on the forehead:
I prefer to leave my country
Than to be humiliated among these pigs.

If I hadn't lost my mind
I would have condemned the kif
Unworthy people take advantage of.

It is a source of inequality:
It has enriched the slave;
The wise man has stayed behind.

Oh my God, what an injustice!
How can you tolerate it?
Isn't it soon the turn of the poor?

from **SI MOHAND'S JOURNEY FROM
MAISON-CARRÉE TO MICHELET**

1. His departure with his pipe as only viaticum

What a subject for meditation
Is the case of Mohand or Mehand
Who had lost his mind!

He had studied and chanted the Qur'an,
Once he had been strong
Now he is plain pitiful.

The end no doubt is quite near
But his only viaticum is
His pipe, his only companion.

2. From Maison-Carrée to the Alma

From Maison-Carrée to the Alma
My disposition soured,
I traveled very fast.

Oh wise one, understand:
My misery's great,
Greater than anybody else's.

It unveiled itself in the dry kif
Which has changed my face:
It refuses to see my white hair.

3. From the Alma to Thenaya

From the Alma to Thenaya
Boredom grabbed me
By the pleats of my djellaba.

I left at dawn
I walked without stopping!
The sun came down on the peaks.

Without shame I collapsed in a café
Dying of fatigue
And begging the pardon of the saints.

4. From Thenaya to Bordj Menaël

From Thenaya to Menaël
My misery deepened
And I broke my pipe.

In anger I let myself blaspheme
My mood changed
And I decided to walk barefoot.

It took ripe old age
For me to start to revolt
And be handed the worst ordeals.

Translations by P.J. from Mouloud Feraoun's French versions

COMMENTARY

Si Mohand (or Mhand) was the major poet of Kabylia in the late nineteenth century. He was born to a wealthy family & educated in traditional Islamic sciences (hence his title *Si,* "doctor"). His life was marked by the strong repression that followed the 1871 Kabyle revolt against French colonial rule, which saw his father sentenced to death, his paternal uncle exiled to New Caledonia, & all his family's possessions confiscated. Unlike his mother & brothers, who emigrated to Tunis, Si Mohand preferred to stay in Algeria, where he worked as a day laborer & had other menial jobs. He never settled anywhere but spent his life wandering around Algiers & other towns & villages in & around Kabylia. Traditional accounts of his life mention a visit he paid to the pious Sheikh Mohand ou-Lhocine, with whom he sustained an epic poetic duel, & his journey on foot to Tunis, where he met his brothers but was badly welcomed. He died of tuberculosis at fifty-seven in the Sainte-Eugénie hospital in Michelet. His poetry—oral compositions in Amazigh—was written down early in the twentieth century by Amar Said Boulifa & commented on most recently by Younes Adli in his book *Si Mohand ou Mhand: Errance et révolte* (EDIF, 2000). Our selection is based on *Les Poèmes de Si Mohand* (Editions de Minuit, 1960) by Mouloud Feraoun (see p. 284).

Mohamed Ibn Seghir Benguitoun

(Sidi Khaled, c. 1843–1907)

from **HIZIYA**

I'm grieving dear friends   over the loss of the most beautiful one
her body lies beneath the ground   my heart forever buried with it.
How I wish yesterday had lasted forever   how happy we both were then
like flowers in the meadows   in the first days of spring.
The young woman I'd cherished   like a shadow had vanished
the young gazelle I'd tamed   had been taken away.

. . .

Her long hair falling down her back   a waterfall of scents and rich
    perfumes.
Her eyes like bullets in warriors' rifles   aiming at you ready to fire.
Her cheeks shining like bleeding roses   or blossoming carnations at dawn.
Her mouth, pure ivory glistening with a smile   her saliva, ewe's milk or
    fresh honey.
Look at the neck as white   as the heart of a date palm
or a crystal lamp   set in gold necklaces.
Her bosom smooth as marble   hides two twins my hands have caressed.
Her body, the softness of cotton   or light snowflakes in a dark night.
Her belly so cherished   held captive by a large belt
falling in loose folds   down to her feet.
Can you hear the tinkle   of her silver *khalkhal*
between her leather slippers   and her fleshy calves?
In Bazer we camped   I was happy then.
Every morning as I pulled open   the curtain of my tent
I saw my beloved swiftly tread   the green dewy grass.
After having spent all the summer in the Tell   we went down south to the
    Sahara,
our homeland we now miss   my beloved riding
in a closed *bassour* carried   by the strongest of our camels.

. . .

Feasts broke out at each halt before the night   the *baroud* roar excited
   my stud.
In the middle of the riders   my winged breed,
like a jinn, swiftly disappeared   beyond the dusty camping site.
Her height, that of our tribe's banner;   her smile, a row of genuine pearls.
H'mida's shining daughter told me   all her love in veiled words.
She looked like a tall date palm   struggling against the raging wind.
Alone in the middle of the palm grove   eventually she got pulled away
when thought to be well-protected   thus had decided my almighty Lord.
In Oued Itell we were camping   when the most beautiful of them all
said farewell to this world one night   she hugged me for the last time
and I held her tight against my chest   before Destiny took her away
like a young date palm just planted   then swept away by the wind.
Like a fool I wandered in the desert   up and down hills and ravines.
She's gone my gazelle with kohl-lined eyes   leaving me to my grief and
   folly.
Daughter of a great man   she was clad in a silky shroud
her sleeping body rocked by the heavy step   of the camel carrying her.
She was laid on a stretcher, my sweetheart   with long black eyelashes.
Her litter twinkling—a lonely star at dusk   in a cloudy sky stabbed by a
   rainbow.
She had torn my heart away since I was a child   all the pain I had endured!
They took her to the country of Sidi Khaled   where by night she was
   buried.
My tattooed sweetheart will never again   look at me with her gazelle eyes.
They let the earth fold its arms around her   like a date palm between the
   souagui.
I beg you gravedigger not to let a single stone   hurt the body of the one I
   once loved
nor even the smallest grain of sand   hide her stunning beauty!
. . .

The sun that rose   shone, then faded away
in the middle of an eclipse   the morning of a bright day.
The moon that grew   full in Ramadan withdrew
when darkness came and forced her   to say farewell to the starry universe.
This poem is dedicated   to the most beautiful one
Ahmad's daughter   famous Dhouadia.
Twenty-three she was   the one who stole my heart
and for whom my love   will never die.

. . .

With these hands   shaking today
I once tattooed her   right where her breasts spring.
I gently traced the perfect contours of a line   that went softly all the way
   down
between her cherished breasts   blue as a dove's neck
the line, so pure, adjusted   to the softness of their curve
the letters of my name were then encrusted   in the delicate flesh of her
   fragile wrist.

. . .

Between her death and this writing   three days have passed.
She said good-bye to me   and will never come back.
Written in the year twelve hundred, add ninety   plus the remaining five
the writing of Ibn Seghir   forever will be remembered.
In the month of al-Eid al-Kebir   this poem was born
to tell you about   the one you once saw alive.

Translation from Arabic by Abdelfetah Chenni & P.J.

COMMENTARY

(1) Mohamed Ibn Seghir Benguitoun (or Ibn Guitoun), from the tribe of the Ouled Sidi Bouzid, was born, probably, in 1843 in Sidi Khaled, an oasis known for its poets & respected for its learned sheikhs, about 110 kilometers southwest of Biskra, Algeria. He studied at the Rahmania zawiya, a traditional Sufi school, in Sidi Khaled. Some sources claim that he was a *khetatri,* a day laborer paid for pulling water from wells to irrigate palm plantations & orchards. It is said that Sayyed, Hiziya's cousin, solicited Benguitoun three days after her death to write a poem that would immortalize her beauty & his love for her in exchange for his horse. *Hiziya* is one of the few love poems Benguitoun wrote & probably the only one that has made him famous beyond the limits of the Sahara.

(2) Adds the translator Abdelfetah Chenni: "The beduins' poetic resources are rooted in an environmental time & space totally foreign to English language & culture. Nomadic semes risk looking like distant galaxies. To the Western reader, a camel gurgling at dawn suggests no meaningful mental image, & the dozen different names a nomad gives to his date palm remain untranslatable culturally as well as linguistically. Both signifier & signified, even when translated 'successfully,' cannot be the same, for they will have been forced out of & away from their meaningful landscape. Hence the necessity, for the translator, to make the host language as tolerant as it can be, inviting as many semantic &

lexical items to be adopted, accepted, & hopefully integrated so as to achieve a better 'perception' of the others' outer & inner worlds."

(3) The web site of the Algerian Embassy to the United States says: "Currently, the Biskra Cultural Agency is in the process of finalizing collection of data on the life of Hizia to create a database, leading to its inclusion in the national cultural heritage."

Sheikh Smati (Ouled Djellal, near Biskra, 1862–1917)

MOUNT KERDADA

Move over—oh Mount Kerdada—and go away!
You are hiding the caravan of my beloved from my view.
Without my gazelle I have no way to see,
for your clouds cover my eyes and make me blind.
Oh you, the highest of all mountains, I fear going mad
in your country and so appeasing my enemy's envy.
I may lose my mind after separation or be at a loss
and so be missed by many beduin poets.
I fear my absence will make her forget about me,
or listen to those who like me not.
If I am a praiseworthy man and close to the saints,
may Allah answer my only prayer
and grant me the best of all obedient steeds,
a genuine thoroughbred with fine features
and a mirrorlike sparkling coat,
less than one year old with his fill of summer fodder;
he will slide like a sailboat into the desert,
asking me to lean on his windswept mast.
I won't close my eyes till I start off
long before the morning star is wide awake.
From Boussada I shall depart to see early farmers
watering their orchards at Aouinat-al-Ma.
Loussif's grave will soon be visible beyond
al Magtaa, at the foot of those bare hills.
From there to al Hamal, home to the perfect *Qutb,*
Sheikh Ben Belgassem, healer of my wounded soul.
I shall leave him in peace and ride on eastward

to Foum al Ounk, then Messad now being very close.
I shall leave Mount al Sammara behind, still heading east
through the Ben Zrigui gorge to al Dhaiya.
On the way I shall greet Sheikh Sidi Lakhal Boudhina,
then force the pace all the way to al M'higan.
At Ain al Malh I shall soon take a rest,
and have coffee with a few friends of mine
before I leave Lashan a long way behind.
I shall then be most lenient with him carrying me home
through the remaining hills and valleys.
Beyond Mount Lakraa that faces us now
we shall soon come out into the open,
across the vast plains of the Sahara,
where he will lose his temper and go wild,
faster than a gazelle fleeing from her hunters.
Like a falcon he will fly way beyond al Batma
till his breath comes out in short pants.
I shall then slow him down all the way through the lowland,
now that I am getting close to the one I miss most:
we have reached Ouled Djellal at last!
If you want to ask me for my name,
I will now spell it for you: *sin, mim, ta,* with a final *ya,*
and if you cannot read, it is *SMATI,* you old fool!
Allah created me a poet
to poke the fire that burns every lover's heart.
Mine cannot stand her absence any more,
she whose name is: *ain, ya, shin,* and the *ha* to heal my wound—
Aisha, oh my friends, is far away!

Translation from Arabic by Abdelfetah Chenni

COMMENTARY

Writes the transcriber & translator Abdelfetah Chenni: "His full name was Djaflafi Ahmad ibn al Buhali, from the tribe of Ouled Sassi. Born 1862 in Ouled Djellal (about one hundred kilometers east of Biskra), he died in 1917. He was educated at the Rahmania zawiya of Sheikh al Mokhtar & the Tijania zawiya of al Ghrib, both in Ouled Djellal. An adventurous horseman always on the move, he spent most of his life between Djelfa, Boussada, & Laghouat, where his friend Ben Kerriou lived. Kef Kerdada is a mountain in Boussada. The poem is an imaginary journey from Boussada to Ouled Djellal. The poet already missed Aisha, whose caravan had just left for Ouled Djellal."

Mohamed Ben Sghir (Tlemcen, late nineteenth century)

LAFJAR (DAWN)

look at the sky overhead—source of light!
though earth's inhabitants cannot reach it
look at mars—you who're indifferent!
its beauty clearly enlightens the world
look at mercury that comes to you—o traveler!
above the globe & amazing ignorance
look how neptune shines on deserts
he's put his *ruh* in creation—he who's everything!
look how saturn visibly walks toward you
above the seventh of the perfect secrets!
men's war—o you who's asleep!
look at the dance of the heavenly bodies—
they've lit man's ignorance with their dazzling light!
know the truth if you want to be pure—
lafjar comes upon you from an illuminating science!
o you who listen to me—Yabriz & Nakir!
he who commands the wiliest of foxes & wolves—
he who swiftly responds to the challenge
must protect all beasts
can the hedgehog wage a war against the ogre?!
the eagle may easily be recognized among falcons—
he fears the slightest sound & the beasts of the mountains
if you walk by the caves
—Tlemcani *bendir* & its ceremonial procession—
tell the one who's neither weak nor bragging
that Mohamed Ben Sghir is an unsheathed sword!

YA'L-WARCHAN (O DOVE)

o dove go to essaouira's sons
who live in tlemcen
greet them with peace from allah
pray for their glory & light
that they come back the way they've left
from the lion gate you'll take your flight o dove
you'll ask for protection from sidi mogdul patron of the harbor

his news has reached istanbul
take care & be cautious
fly way beyond those rocky heaps and hilly lands
touch with your wings moulay durayn saint of regraga
glory of our holy land
tomorrow at dawn
you'll purify yourself when you hear
the first call for prayer

Translations from Arabic by Abdelfetah Chenni

COMMENTARY

A native of Tlemcen, Algeria, Mohamed Ben Sghir was (re)discovered by Georges Lapassade when the latter participated in the Conference on Musicology at the Melhun Poetry Festival in Essaouira, Morocco. Lapassade spent a long time asking Essaouira's *khazzanes* (conservators) for the ancient poetry manuscripts they were known to preserve in wooden chests—in vain! (One of them actually had a copy of *al-Fajr* in a chest in the suq when the French researcher met him; unfortunately such unhelpfulness is a problem in the Maghreb when trying to collect this precious melhun heritage.) Lapassade had to travel to Marrakech to locate a copy, which he later translated into French. Ben Sghir was a follower of the Aissawa Sufi brotherhood, & *Lafjar* clearly shows the Sufi touch. His reference in *Ya'l-Warchan* to the Regraga (an Essaouira tribe & a place of pilgrimage) points to the ancient religious & spiritual symbiosis between the monotheistic religions in the Maghreb: seven saints representing all the Regraga tribes of the Chiadma territory in southern Morocco between Safi & Essaouira, who were Christians back then, reportedly made the pilgrimage to Mecca to meet the prophet Muhammad well before Islam was introduced into North Ifrikiya. These tribes converted to Islam & have held their yearly saints' festivals ever since.

Abdallah Ben Keriou (Laghouat, 1869–1921)

"OH YOU WHO WORRY ABOUT THE STATE OF MY HEART"

Oh you who worry about the state of my heart,
who will soothe you?
My heart has left with the fleeing gazelle.
Here is the camp where that treacherous one lived
with her painted eyelashes—she left it deserted.

O my messenger, leave—take this letter,
put it into the hands of the most gracious one, and return.
Bring back good news, be her messenger,
And show me our shibboleth.
Despite me my tears run down faced with this encampment;
the sight of its ruins tortures me.
The encampment of my beloved is deserted: why come back to it?
It reminds me of my past, and my passion takes fire again.

Translation by Abdelfetah Chenni & P.J.

COMMENTARY

Abdallah Ben Keriou was unquestionably the poet of true love. Born in the Saharan town of Laghouat, he followed in the steps of his father as an assistant judge. He was a learned man not only in poetry but also in other sciences, particularly astronomy. Knowledge of the heavenly bodies proved useful for his poetry. Perhaps the most famous of his poems is *Gamr al-lil* (Moon of the Night). One night, walking with a friend in the dark streets of Laghouat, he raised his eyes to watch the sky but saw instead the face of a beautiful woman he'd love for the rest of his life & dedicate all his poetry to. Though he tried to keep her name secret, their love story came to be known & the woman's family sent word to the French military governor, who exiled Ben Keriou to el-Golea, a town far south, in the Sahara. In the old Arab tradition of passionate love, like Majnun's for Layla, Ben Keriou wrote poems to that beauty he saw only once until he died, blind & utterly frustrated.

Hadda (Dra Valley, southern Morocco, late twentieth century)

THE POEM OF THE CANDLE

The following is from Stefania Pandolfo's Impasse of the Angels *(pp. 152–54). She sets the scene:*

Hadda does not move. From the roof, someone yells to go home while he still can. Between us, on the floor, the candle.

He concentrates on the flame, as bright as the fire of a house, his house, in the darkness of the room. Then, he starts reciting a poem, as if to the candle itself—herself, in Arabic candle is feminine.

With pressing insistence a Poet questions a Candle about the source of her pain: Why do you cry when others rejoice? With blind obstinacy he tries *to cheer her up, to make her forget her sadness and enjoy the pleasures of this world. If it is a love who turned away from you . . .*

The Candle listens, then speaks. She is Light, and speaks with clairvoyance. Her vision springs from her incurable wound, her awareness of estrangement and death. To be alive is to have one's body fissured by a wick.

Hadda the Poet, Hadda the Candle

Tell me
I implore you Candle
Why cry when others rejoice
    tears streaming down on your stick
Consumed by longing
you liquefy
Set ablaze by passion
you give light
Everything is forgiven to the one in love
Yet I find no way around your tears
If it is a love who turned away from you
you must forget him
Remember: those who betray never win
Despise him because of his wrongs

Candle of ours, candle of pleasure
You too lose yourself in the presence of beauty
Surrounded by girls dancing the hadra
Daughters of the best from every tribe
Rejoice, rejoice o Candle! Rejoice in the spectacle of that show of licit
    beauty
You saw reddened cheeks
Big eyes, blackened with kohl
You saw young men displaying their pride
each ready to fight a lion
Thus spoke the Poet.

Then, She spoke:
I'll show you, clever one
What has befallen me
And you'll say, "Beware of the wound!"
You did not divine my uncanny story
    in its disguise
I, who sit in the place of honor in celebrations

The craftsman who molded me
to challenge the gas lamp
He hollowed my body with skill
lured me with many a trick
And then planted at the core of my body a wick

"To set her ablaze," says Hadda, interrupting his recitation and looking at me for the first time. The roar of the rain covers his words. As if realizing for the first time, he pauses, dismayed for a moment. "God save us!" But the spell of the candle is stronger. Her light is an ecstasy born of pain, it is a movement of dying. Her vision comes from her wick: the inscription of death on her body, the mortal trick, poisonous gift of the craftsman.

They squeezed me and took the honey
    then put me aside and said
"It will serve to put down in front of the guests"
By her, the room is lit
She burns throughout the night

"The Poet keeps pushing the candle," comments Hadda, interrupting his recitation again; "he can't understand. He tells her about the advantages of life. The Candle, then, comes down to his level, and ironically proposes to get back to the happy mood."

She said to him:
I have seen it all
and today, it's enough my dear Poet, let's not spoil the party
Let's stick to our rhythms and lutes
    and with our drums dance away this night
This is a word of wisdom
    if you wish to hear
Wise people say, forbearance is rewarded
We thank the present company
And those who challenge us, we ignore

COMMENTARY

Stefania Pandolfo writes (in *Impasse of the Angels,* p. 348n103): "*Qasida as-shmaʿ,* 'the poem of the candle,' belongs to a genre of popular oral poetry in colloquial Arabic called *l-malhun* (from the verbal root *lahna,* to compose, to set to music). It has also been adapted to other styles, and was performed by the Moroccan pop band Jil Jilala. The poetic genre of l-malhun is related to other genres of oral poetry in colloquial language, such as that of *rasma,* specific to the poetic tradition of the Dra' valley. . . . Like rasma, a poem of malhun is composed to be sung, within a metrical mold that is first given as a tune for the voice. The wording of malhun poems, however, tends to be less hermetic than in rasma compositions, and hence more accessible to a large audience. Poems often make use of everyday language and celebrate or mourn events from daily life. This is why, with the spread of the media and the commercialization of audiotapes, l-malhun has become something close to Morocco's national poetry in colloquial Arabic. The scholarly and mediatic attention dedicated to it during the nationalist period and after independence contributed to its reputation. (The other poetic and musical genre associated with the national image and mediatically spread nationwide is al-Andalusia, also known as *al-ala*, a genre of *taqsim* instrumental music and sung poetry in classical Arabic, and originally from Muslim Andalusia. Both l-malhun and al-ala remain, however, mainly urban genres.)

"According to Hadda, and in general in the view of people from the Dra' valley, the style of l-malhun—which blossomed in the traditional urban environment of cities such as Marrakesh and Meknes—is an urban refinement and instrumental adaptation of compositions that originated elsewhere, namely in the south. A genre known in the Dra' valley as *aqallal* (from *qala*, 'to speak or recite') is viewed as the ancestor of l-malhun. The poem of *sh-shma'*, 'the candle,' used to be sung by Hadda in this style."

A BOOK OF WRITING

An abstract quest for meaning, Arab calligraphy is a meditation on the sign, on Arabic writing, the vehicle of the divine message. It is also an aesthetic form that enters the domain of abstraction. Islam is said to reject all forms of the figural, with representational imagery supposedly proscribed. Indeed, that is what one has to conclude after examining Islamic art, but in fact this is not a doctrinal point. The relationship with representation remains controversial. Islam developed in a beduin culture that had very few image-based representations. On the other hand, this culture highly admired rhetoric, song, and poetic metaphor. Both the voice and the sign thus play important roles in the study of the sacred book: the voice in that the Qur'an is chanted, and the sign in codifying these readings. Indeed, writing becomes one of the most important Islamic arts, maybe as a response to the divine injunction: *Iqra* (read, or recite). This injunction to gain knowledge through reading will pass through dedicated work on the letters of the alphabet.

Muslims were intent on distinguishing their religion from Christianity and its use of representation in sacred art. To achieve this, they developed abstraction, to communicate with the sacred and the divine through channels that are not image-based. The sign marshals the gesture of the one who traces the calligraph and the gaze of the one who contemplates. Calligraphy also becomes the basis for decorative motifs in frescoes and architectural structures. It is a complex art in which aesthetic sensibility and mathematical research come together. Scale and proportion are extremely precise. The work of writing is done with a reed pen whose nib is cut according to a variety of models (pointed, flat, wide, fine, etc.), differing from Chinese calligraphy, which uses a brush. Despite the variety of the Islamic calligraphic corpus, it has a conceptual unity that transcends regional distinctions. Art based on Arabic writing, extending to the work of contemporary painters and designers, remains a core characteristic of Muslim identity.

There exist a great number of calligraphic styles; they fall, however, into two main categories:

1. Those in the Kufic script, which is said to have originated in the (now Iraqi) city of Kufa at the beginning of Islam. Kufic calligraphy is geometric and angular; it insists on verticals and horizontals, and on the angles. The first Qur'ans were written in this script. Kufic varies by country and era. Austere to start with, its letters will become more sophisticated, even braided or animated, with some ending in animals or faces. This kind of calligraphy developed strongly in al-Andalus and the Maghreb.

2. Those in the cursive script that starts to develop in the tenth century and is characterized by very delicate tracing of the letters. This style of calligraphy is invested in the curve, roundedness, the circle. It is less austere and more decorative. Floral motifs abound. There are six distinguishable cursive styles, and the most often encountered is Neskhi, a simple and highly readable style much used in Iran and Turkey. One of the most celebrated calligraphic styles, the *tughra* (see for example, the seal of Süleyman the Magnificent), shows an ample and majestic sweep, reflecting imperial grandeur.

The Qur'anic text is the core inspiration of calligraphy, which becomes a means of exploring the mystery of the letter and the hidden sense of the verses. One's gaze loses itself in the labyrinth of letters to open slowly toward an illumination. This art must not incite distraction or sheer pleasure but has to guide the spirit toward a meditation enhanced by the abstraction of the works. Sufism deeply influences most calligraphers, who work on the concept of the errant gaze that can only find and center itself after long concentration and meditation on the names of God. The appearance of things leads one astray; only concentration on the essence permits one to find the way. The author and the end user of this calligraphy are united in a single quest for meaning, the basis of which is the sacred letter.

The Ottomans developed a "figurative" calligraphy based on verses of the Qur'an: for example, the one that represents a flame starts from the *Ayat* (verse) of the Light; the one that uses fruit is based on the verses that evoke paradise; and others involve a kneeling believer, animals, and a boat with sails. There also exist Persian calligraphies in military manuals of the eighteenth century that represent warriors, war machinery, and so forth.

Today the poetry, maxims, and other such text in get-well cards, birth and marriage announcements, and similar items appear in a secular calligraphy with the whole array of angular and cursive styles. The Iraqi calligrapher

Hassan Massoudi and others have popularized this decorative calligraphy by adding color to it. Billboards, posters, business and institutional logos, political ads, and magazines often use calligraphs to stimulate the imagination of their customers—see, for example, the logo of Al Jazeera, the Qatari television channel.

Starting in the 1950s, the Arab world saw the rise of a school of painting based on the written sign, initiated by the Moroccan artist Ahmed Cherkaoui (1934–67). The painters of this school, inspired by the work of calligraphers, inscribed abstract Western painting into the universe of Arabo-Berber culture.

Archaic Kufic Script

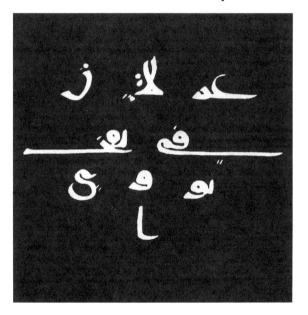

Variants of letters from a Qur'an incorrectly attributed to Caliph Uthman.

Polychrome Maghrebian Script

From al-Qandusi's remarkable twelve-volume Qur'an (completed 1849).

Maghrebian Script

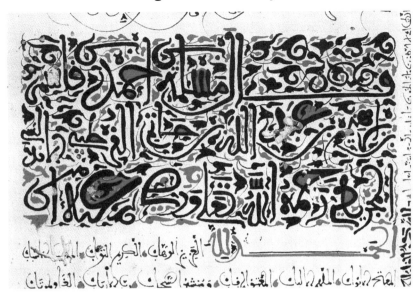

Within this one word (from 1850) is a contrast between the rectilinear and curvilinear styles.

Maghrebian Cursive Script

Andalusian Cursive Script

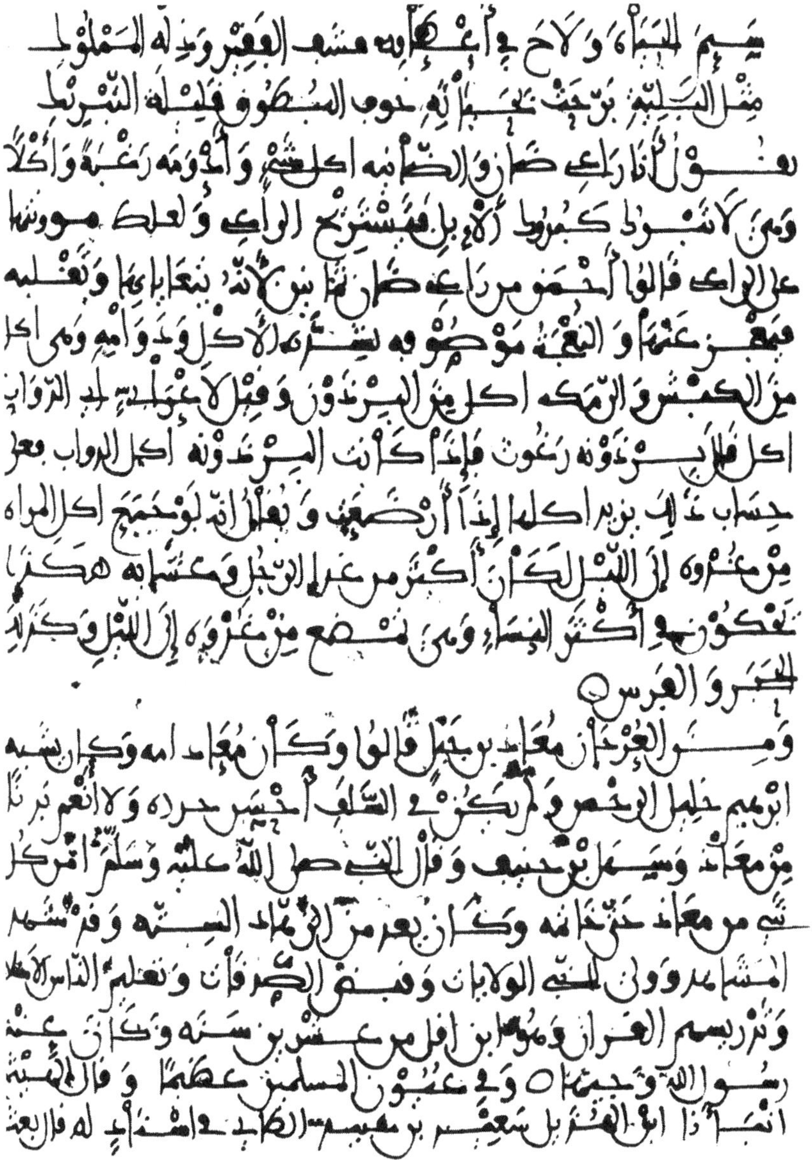

Al-Qandusi

A BISMILLAH

COMMENTARY

Our choice of calligraphic visuals is of course mostly interested in Maghrebian examples. Al-Qandusi was maybe the major nineteenth-century calligrapher. Born in 1790 in southwest Algeria, he is known to have been living in Fez by 1828, where, besides doing his calligraphy, he was also an herbalist. He died there in 1861. Although Fez has his shrine, most of his works are now in the National Library in Rabat, Morocco.

Maghrebian Script:
The Two Letters *Lam-Alif*

*Standing alone with vocalization, these letters
(pronounced la) signify "no" or "not."*

Maghrebian Mujawhar Script

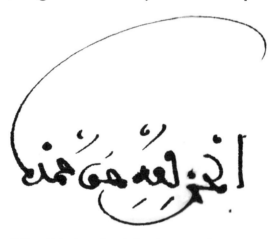

Calligraphic laudatory formula from the nineteenth century.

FOURTH DIWAN

Resistance and Road to Independence

At the end of the eighteenth and the beginning of the nineteenth century, the Maghreb seems apart from the "new world" arising in Europe. The region is configured into several autonomous states even though Morocco does not pledge allegiance to the Ottoman sultans. These countries are united by a common language and their Arab-Andalusian heritage. The Islamic brotherhoods played an important role in structuring the social body and as ramparts against colonial intrusion. Centers such as the al-Karaouine Mosque, the university in Fez and the Zitouna Mosque in Tunis continued to train ulamas, Muslim scholars of religion and law.

In Morocco the Alaouite Dynasty maintained the country's independence until 1906 when the Algeciras Conference placed it under international control; in 1912, a Spanish protectorate was set up in the north and a French protectorate in the south. The Regency of Algiers, created in 1525 when Hayreddin Barbarossa captured the city, reached its apogee in the seventeenth century when a majority of European states signed treaties with it and paid regular tribute to protect their fleets in the Mediterranean against pirates. In the next century, revolts against the imposition of ever-heavier tax burdens crippled the regency. After the French landing at Sidi Ferruch in 1830, it collapsed in a few weeks, and the Arabo-Berber inland and desert tribes resisted the invaders. The rise of Emir Abd El Kader is due in great part to the unprecedented circumstances of the colonial conquest.

Tunisia seems more dynamic—indeed, the Husainid Dynasty, in power since 1705, had acquired real autonomy in relation to the Sublime Porte. Bey Ahmed I (who reigned from 1837 to 1855) started a process of modernization culminating in 1861 in the promulgation of the first constitution of the Arab world. However, Tunisia was unable to realize its entry into the modern world as French troops, after invading in 1881, imposed the status of protectorate on the country with the Treaty of Bardo.

The firm hand of the Qaramanli Dynasty governed Libya from 1711 until

1835, when the Sublime Porte imposed its authority on the country by forming two *wilayat*, or districts—Tripolitania and Cyrenaica—which the 1912 Treaty of Lausanne gave to Italy.

Mauritania stayed basically apart from the various movements occurring in the north until the French entered it in 1902. Back in the tenth and eleventh centuries, Mauritania had had an important religious effervescence, which gave rise to the (Berber) Almoravids. It was only in the fifteenth century, with the arrival of the Arab tribes of the Banu Hassan from Egypt, that the Sanhadja Berbers were Arabized through widespread intermarriage. From the eleventh through the fifteenth century, cities like Tinigui and Chinguetti became important Islamic cultural centers whose influence radiated throughout sub-Saharan Africa.

French colonization caused major upheavals in the North African countries, whose economic development and social (dis)integration primarily disadvantaged their Muslim majorities. Algeria, a settler colony, experienced the greatest shocks. It was only in the third decade of the twentieth century that a Frenchified urban elite arose in Algeria and started to express identitarian demands through a literature freed from clichés and folkloric stereotypes. This Francophone literature broke with colonial Algerianism to bear witness to the country's deep reality. In Morocco and Tunisia, where the traditional elites were not wiped out, Arabic remained a living language, and it is Tunisia that gives rise to the most original modern Arab poet of his day: Abu al-Qasim al-Shabi (see p. 282). Libya stayed apart from the French-dominated Maghrebian countries, and the Senussi brotherhood strongly influenced its cultural and political choices.

The colonial era's educational system explains why its Algerian authors were essentially Francophone. We include a few of European extraction, such as Jean Pélégri and Emmanuel Roblès, and of Caribbean origin, such as Frantz Fanon, because they contributed to the long march toward independence. The Arabophone Algerian writers don't compare well with their counterparts from the Middle East, Egypt, or Tunisia. Prisoners of a sacralized language and archaic forms, they stand outside the reworking and rethinking of the language of writing and the deconstruction of forms that occurred in the Arab literature of their time. There are, however, two exceptions: Mohammed Laïd al-Khalifa (1903–77) and Mufdi Zakaria (1913–77), the "national poet" and author of the national hymn "Qassaman" and many patriotic songs. Despite the classicism of their style, these two occupy honorable places in Arabic poetry.

The colonial period was a great moment of confrontation between the colonized and modernity—which they had to face in a major and unequal struggle. But artists and intellectuals did exchange ideas across borders, and at some moments Paris was the true Arab capital.

Emir Abd El Kader (Mascara, 1808–Damascus, 1883)

MY SPOUSE WORRIES

My spouse worries, though it is she who knows me best.
"Don't you know, O princess of my hearth, that my many rides
through the country ensure the safety of the tribe?
Fearlessly I face the narrows of death
and defend the women in the days of terror.
The women are confident as long as I am there,
while my *khalkhal* spouse doesn't even trust her husband.
It is I who take care of the young riders—
lion cubs without experience.
When my wounded horses grow weak, I urge them on:
"May your endurance equal mine, and your worth too!"
In times of war I generously risk my life,
and yet, in times of peace, my soul's salvation is what means most to me.
Go ask the French; they'll tell you of the massacres
wrought by my saber and throbbing lance.
Go ask night; it will tell you how I tore
its black hide in nighttime raids.
Go ask the desert, hills, and wide-open spaces—they'll tell you
how I stormed over plains and mountains in breathless cavalcades.
My only desire is to confront the enemy
with my warriors and beat his formidable soldiers.
So don't you worry about me!
Know that, even as a corpse attacked by worms, I'll still confound my
    enemies!

Translation by P.J. from a French version

I AM LOVE

I am Love, Lover, Beloved all in one,
    the one in love: secret or blatant target of his own desire.

I say "Me," but is there another here than Myself?
    I don't cease being dazzled and demented by the subject of "Me."

In me is all the waiting and hope of men:
    for whoever wants "Qur'an," for whoever wants the "Book of
    Discriminations,"

For whoever wants "Torah," for who wants "Gospel,"
   flute of the Prophet-King, Psalm or Revelation,

For who wants "mosque" in which to pray to his Lord,
   for who wants "synagogue," for who wants "bell" and "crucifix,"

For whoever wants the Kaaba to piously kiss the Rock,
   for whoever wants images, for whoever wants idols,

For who wants retreat into solitary life,
   For who wants dance halls and to fondle the girls . . .

In "Me" that which was, in "Me" that which exists:
   for Us, in truth, the "Me" is sign and proof!

Translation by Sylvia Gorelick & Miles Joris-Peyrafitte from a French version

THE SECRETS OF THE LAM-ALIF

These symbols we make for men but they will only be
understood by those who know.

(KOR. 29:43)

Know that God proposes symbols by His acts as well as by His works, for the purpose of a symbol is to lead to understanding, in such a way that the intelligible object becomes as evident as the sensible object which symbolizes it. Among the symbols which He proposes by His acts is the creation of the letters of the alphabet. Their lines contain, in fact, secrets which only one endowed with knowledge and wisdom can grasp. Among all these letters is found the *Lam-Alif,* which conceals subtle allusions, secrets and innumerable enigmas, and a teaching.

Among these secrets is the fact that the combination of the two letters *Lam* and *Alif* in the *Lam-Alif* is analogous to the combination of the divine Reality with the forms of the creatures. From a certain point of view these are two distinct letters and, from another point of view, one single letter. In the same way, the divine Reality and the forms of the creatures are two distinct things from a certain point of view and one and the same thing from another point of view.

There is also the fact that we do not know which of the two branches of the *Lam-Alif* is the *Alif* and which is the *Lam.* If you say, "It is the *Lam* which is the first branch," you are right. If you say, "It is the *Alif*" you are also right. If you say that you are incapable of deciding between one or the other, then you are right again.

In the same way, if you say that only the divine Reality manifests itself and that the creatures are non-manifest, you speak the truth. If you say the opposite you also speak the truth. And if you confess your perplexity on this subject, you speak the truth again.

Among the secrets of the *Lam-Alif*, there is also this: God and the creature are two names which in fact designate one and the same Named, which is the divine Essence which manifests Itself through both. In the same way the *Lam* and the *Alif* are two designations which apply to one and the same "named" for they constitute the double name of the single letter.

Another secret: just as the form of the letter which is called the *Lam-Alif* cannot be manifested by one of the letters which constitute it independently of the other, so also it is impossible that the divine Reality or the creation manifest independently of each other. God without the creation is non-manifested and the creation without God is deprived of being.

Another secret: the two branches of the *Lam-Alif* unite and separate. In the same way God and the creatures are indiscernible with respect to the essential reality and are distinct with respect to their ontological degree, for the ontological degree of the creator God is not the same as that of the created servant.

Another secret resides in the fact that the writer, when he writes the "*Lam-Alif*," sometimes begins by writing the branch which appears first in the completed form of the *Lam-Alif*, and sometimes in that which appears second. So it goes with the knowledge of God and the creation: sometimes the knowledge of the creation precedes knowledge of God—this is the way referred to by the formula, "He who knows his soul knows his Lord." This is the way of the "itinerants" (*al-salikun*); on the contrary, sometimes the knowledge of Allah precedes the knowledge of the creation. This is the way of election and divine attraction (*jadhb*), that is to say, the way of the "desired" (*al-muradun*).

Another secret is that [when the *Lam-Alif* is pronounced] the ordinary perception grasps only the sound *La*, which is the named, although there are two letters, the *Lam* and the *Alif*. In the same way ordinary perception does not distinguish the two "names"—"God" and "creation"—[which inseparably constitute the total reality] although they are in fact two distinct things.

Another secret is that when the *Lam* and the *Alif* combine to form the *Lam-Alif* each hides the other. Similarly, the divine Reality, when it "combines" with the creatures in a strictly conceptual mode (*tarkiban ma'nawiyyan*), is hidden to the eyes of the spiritually veiled, who see only the creatures. Conversely, it is the creatures that disappear in the eyes of the masters of the Unicity of contemplation (*wahdat al-shuhud*), for they see only God alone. Thus, both God and the creatures hide the other [as the *Lam* and the *Alif*] but from two different points of view.

Among the secrets of the *Lam-Alif* there is also this: when the two branches, the *Lam* and the *Alif*, merge together, with the result that the form

La disappears to the eye of the observer, the significance attached to this form disappears also. In the same way, when there is the state of extinction (*fana'*)—which the men of the way also call "union" (*ittihad*)—the worshipper and the Worshipped, the Lord and the servant, disappear together. If there is no worshipper, there is no Worshipped; and if there is no servant, there is no Lord. For, when two terms are correlative, the disappearance of one necessarily brings about the disappearance of the other, and therefore they disappear together.

It is for you to pursue these analogies, and to discover what they teach!

Mawqif 215.

Translation from Arabic by a team under the direction of James Chrestensen & Tom Manning

COMMENTARY

Praised by an adolescent Rimbaud & celebrated by a young Kateb Yacine (see pp. 321 & 554), the Emir Abd El-Kader occupies a paradoxical place in Algeria: founder of the modern Algerian state, hero of the resistance to the French conquest from 1832 to 1847, refined man of letters, this prominent ancestor remains cumbersome, because too complex to fit in any clichéd vision in the national(istic) pantheon of images. A lucid humanist, open to progress in human affairs, he was a precursor of the renaissance (*Nahda*) in Arab letters. His early poetry, fed by the *mu'allaqat*, resounds with an exalted epic lyricism. But his genius comes to full flower in exile in Damascus, as he rereads Ibn Arabi, whom his father taught him. In his *Kitât al-mawâqif* (Book of Stations) he retraces his spiritual progress, in the process renewing the traditional Arab genre of mystical writing with exceptional virtuosity.

Mohammed Ben Brahim Assarraj (Marrakech, 1897–1955)

POEM I

Tell me, I beg you: Have you ever seen someone of feebler mind than me?
Is there a single man on this earth as lunatic as I?
Yet how I pride myself on my knowledge and refined culture!
When in fact there is no ignoramus who should pretend less than me to
ignorance.

I am, of course, an upright man,
Yet my behavior stifles my virtue,
And thus I'm not virtuous, while being it.

Let a beautiful face pass by,
And at its sight my impatient reason takes leave.
My gaze follows the face: good-bye occupation, if, in fact occupation there
    was.
Have I recognized the gorgeous passerby? If so, I'm at peace;
If not, I can't stop questioning and twisting in the wind any which way.

Often I could have been found with nothing to cover my back or my feet.
But while the crisis kept getting worse—
(Everyone knows that misery and friends tend not to get on well!)—

Suddenly hope's smile peeps through,
The dawn of happiness breaks from among fearsome darknesses.
Forgetting adversity I immediately set about to give with pride
And I sure am generous when I give.
I can easily squander everything that way,
Forgetting even to restore clothes and babouches.
I throw myself body and soul among the mass of ignoble people.
I am not made for them, and they are not made for me.
My whole life I have let pass in such total contradiction:
Serious I am when I joke, and I make fun when seriousness is in order.
God has decided that I remain childless,
With no affectionate mother, with neither companion nor parents.
I am a stranger, though I live in the city that witnessed my birth;
I am alone, though I have innumerable friends.
Anger, when it carries me away, turns me fiendish,
Yet so indulgent am I that I offer glory to those who humiliate me.
When it's a matter of sinning, I come running,
But on the road to heaven, with feet tied, I can't take a single step forward.

Thus I lead an infernal existence and do nothing to please the Lord,
And therefore I implore you, O Merciful One! Don't create man in my image!

POEM II

to al-Baghdadi, the pasha of Fez

To extinguish the coals smoldering in his heart
He makes a river spring through his eyelids, flooding his torso.
In fact, there are tears that in their very abundance ease the heart.
Let ours thus flow:
Better than anyone we do appreciate the scope of our misery.

To face such misfortune I turned toward patience,
But patience, itself impatient, abandoned me.
What is there more unbelievable than to see
Shepherds set themselves up as overlords and legislate?

Here's a "weird one" who's never had anything but rope as a belt,
An idiot who has ever only led sheep into the mountains,
And now he's become the master of Fez!
He mistreats and tortures the city's youthful elite:
In such extremities it is to God alone that one addresses one's complaint,
From Him alone can deliverance come.
The echo of these calamities has crossed the borders:
Young people who are being sequestered, tortured, humiliated
Though they have committed no crime.
Let this coarse man be told that his whip
Makes ten million Moroccans groan:
There are those among them who keep silent, not knowing how to express
   their pain;
Others, to the contrary, who've had enough and who cry out—
They all suffer the pain that eats them up.
Can you imagine a sick person ignoring his pain?
They have not been subjected . . . while being subject.
Let's suppose they're at fault: their due then is a just
Judgment, one that doesn't err because of blunders or excess.

Translations from Arabic by P.J.

COMMENTARY

Also known as the poet of "the red city of Marrakech," Mohammed Ben
Brahim Assarraj, a teacher & journalist, was a man known to have written
poems for both King Mohammed V & his opponent el Glaoui. His biographer
Omar Mounir claims that "he was considered a nationalist by the French, a
traitor by the nationalists, an alim by the man in the street, and a rascal by
the ulamas." Many of his poems have been set to music & are still popular in
present-day Morocco, for example in Karima Skalli interpretations.

Tahar Haddad (Tunis, 1899–1935)

from *MUSLIM WOMEN IN LAW AND SOCIETY*

Introduction

Woman is the mother of all mankind; she carries the child inside her and in her arms. It is from her that he gets the character that will manifest itself later on in life. She suckles the child at her breast, nourishing him with her blood and soul. She is a faithful companion and a wife who fills a gap, and takes away her husband's loneliness. She sacrifices her health and comfort to satisfy her husband's needs, helps him overcome obstacles, and showers him with love to ease all hardships and sorrows. She infuses him with life and rejuvenates him. She makes up half the human race and half the nation, fully contributing to all aspects of human activity. If we despise woman and ignore her humiliation and degradation, we are in fact showing contempt for ourselves and are satisfied with our own humiliation and degradation. However, if we love and respect her, and endeavor to help her achieve her full potential, this is a demonstration of love and respect for ourselves in our quest to fulfill our own potential.

We are accustomed to viewing women as being separate from men, as though they do not play a role in shaping man's character and life, or, more specifically, man's social development and failures. In doing so, the bitterness of disappointment is seeping into all aspects of our lives. Unless we identify the underlying causes of this growing failure, we will be unable to eliminate them.

Woman is viewed in two different ways in society today: there are those who support her and those who oppose her. However, in the West they look at things differently than in the East. Indeed, the differences are as great as those between their women and ours. In Europe, they attach a great deal of importance to the upbringing and education of women, and the sexes work together so that women can perform their tasks in the home as well as raising the children. As women enjoy civic freedom they are able to fully develop their talents, both materially and morally, for the good of the family and society as a whole so that they can fully participate in life's pleasures. Both women, themselves, and European society as a whole have benefited from their activities. European women are different in that they have progressed equally alongside men. They have an equal share in the nation's economic output and governance. They share all burdens with men and are their equal in everything. This has become an increasingly powerful trend among Western women. Opponents argue that this means women are neglecting their traditional role as housewives, child bearers, and educators. They believe that a woman's involvement in public affairs will undermine her efforts at home since she will have no time left for anything. Furthermore, opponents argue that women competing with men in the job market has contributed to an increase in unemployment in various countries across Europe, even though in their view a woman is not capable of doing men's work, or at least not as well as they do. Supporters of women, on the other hand, regard their activities during and after the Great War as clear evidence of future achievements. Success on the part of women should be regarded as a success for the nation and as adding strength to its thriving productivity both economically and morally. This constitutes a clear benefit as long as it does not affect the children. Indeed, if the fact that a woman works outside the home affects the upbringing of children, which is a specifically female task, we should establish more nurseries in order to alleviate women's domestic responsibilities until they are eventually removed. European countries have heeded this and have enabled women to become Members of Parliament and take up leading public office.

Conversely, in the East our women continue to live behind a veil. Those among us who support women's emancipation realize that education and instruction in the sciences of life are the only factors that can improve their lives. It will help them accomplish their duty in the home and towards the family, and enable them to give birth to children who will grow up to have jobs that make their country proud and allow them to achieve success in life. The proponents also consider that it is a woman's natural and lawful right to use her civil freedom in a way that directly benefits her and, like men, to seize the opportunities that life has to offer. The opponents of women, on the other hand, regard this amount of freedom as exceeding the bounds of isolation that is necessary to prevent temptation and inhibit intimacy with men. They also hold that in order to live and do their duty, women only need a small amount of knowledge, restricted to the family domain, which does not require the establishment of various scientific institutes. The advancement of the nation does not depend on men being forced to grant women social freedom. In support of this, they cite as evidence the rise of Arab civilization which depended merely on men's efforts.

This is our attitude toward woman in the East, and our view on her advancement. In Tunisia, we have failed, more than any other Eastern country, to raise the status of women in any way. While some of us at least talk about this, the majority of the people are completely indifferent to it. Some influential people among them believe, however, that we can advance ourselves as a society without advancing women, as in Arab civilization in the past. If we look at the position of women beside Arab-Muslim men when they were conquering kingdoms, we can see that it was women who filled men with the spirit of greatness that was the driving force behind the success of that civilization. Some people believe that this was the secret of success, rather than the knowledge of religious sciences and literary genres, such as poetry and prose. However, women would have had a greater impact on this civilization if they had been more educated, cultured and had enjoyed more freedom. Perhaps this spirit of the past still exists among us men. While women advance in their honorable tasks, in order to save their country and defend it, they instill both life and courage in us men. Yet, we persist in foolishly looking backwards while we see other nations advancing and being granted victory in life.

If we examined the origin of our tendency to deny progress to women, we would see that this is primarily due to the fact that we regard them as an object to satisfying our desires. While we may choose to exaggerate in denying women's rights we ignore the overall good that we will all gain through their progress, the trend of progress is marching on forcefully, and neither we, nor women can stop it. Women are proceeding along this path, without guidance, which increases the deep-rooted and complicated sense of chaos. We ought to abandon this futile stubbornness and instead work together to salvage our lives by establishing comprehensive grounds for the advancement of women which, in turn, ensures the advancement of society as a whole. In so doing, we will purify the water of life before it becomes putrid, and destroys life.

The French authorities here in Tunisia have, for some time now, been investigating Tunisian women's progress, in accordance with a policy based on setting up educational programs for Muslim girls in primary schools specifically for them. The government also seizes every opportunity to pave the way towards enhancing the development of Muslim women. How can we then remain silent, bewildered, and resentful in this sweeping current? Are we waiting to be swept down the drain?

It is essential to introduce social reform in all aspects of life, and it is particularly indispensable when it is related to our own existence. I, without a doubt, do not consider Islam as an obstacle in the way of progress. In fact, Islam is completely innocent of the accusations leveled against it as being a factor in delaying reform. Nothing could be further from the truth inasmuch as Islam is the endless source and strength of this reform. It is the fantasies of our own beliefs that are the cause of our destruction, in addition to dangerous and abominable customs that have stiffened our necks against change. This is what has made me write this book on women in the *shari'a* and society, to show who is right, and who has gone astray. In doing so, I hope I have discharged a duty which I owe first to all men and second to my nation.

Tunis, 10 December 1929

Translation from Arabic by Ronak Husni & Daniel L. Newman

Tahar Haddad was an author, scholar, & reformer born in the medina of Tunis in 1899 to a family of poor shopkeepers; from early on he worked in the suq to help the family make ends meet, which would indelibly mark him & shape his future political stance & involvements. He attended the Great Mosque of Zitouna from 1911 until his graduation in 1920, then became a notary public but left this career to join the political party al-Destour, which he quit when unsatisfied with the leadership. The need for modern education would remain a leitmotiv in Haddad's thought, together with interests in workers' & women's rights. In the 1930 book *Muslim Women in Law and Society*—arguably the first Muslim feminist treatise in history—he advocated expanding women's rights & criticized contemporary interpretations of Islam that inhibited women. He died of tuberculosis in 1935, & his work fell into oblivion after his radical ideas were condemned as heretical & anti-Islamic—until, after independence, Tunisia's first president, Habib Bourguiba, who was an admirer of Haddad's, implemented some of his recommendations.

Jean El Mouhoub Amrouche (Ighil Ali, 1906–Paris, 1962)

ADORATION OF THE PALM TREES

At night the palm trees shed heavy tears.
Their shadows bend over the sea
Nearly soundless
Like the scattered souls that weep
In the serene immobility of the stars.

Palm trees,
For whom the tremor of your lowered hands
And your mute sob in night's vertigo?

Palm trees,
For whom the call of the distant seas,
The warm perfumes,
The anguish,
That rest in the gold of your half-open hearts?
For the cold kiss of the moon?

Will he come, the naked Child, with the enormous eye,
To spread his desire over all your silences,

And in the nameless sky
Will unhoped-for love be born,
And then shoot up into the fullness of the stars?

Oh palm trees,
The shivering coat of your blue'd hair
And the shadow of your swaying bodies
Each day have sung the delirious suns of these dazzled shores.

The hour when the big sleep
Will bend our heavy nakednesses toward earth
Has rung, far away, on the dream's high plain.

On our forehead we carry the somber diadem
And our hearts made heavy with the impossible love
Adore throughout the night and the music of the stars
The wound that your friends the leaves put to sleep,
And the endless sob of your fallen branches.

25 February 1932

Translation from French by P.J.

COMMENTARY

I have said nothing that belongs to me
oh tell me the origin
of the words that sing in me!

J.E.M.A.

Somewhat forgotten in independent Algeria, Jean El Mouhoub Amrouche has begun to arouse the interest of scholars again—witness the numerous recent essays on his work. Born in 1906 in Ighil Ali (Kabylia) to a family converted to Catholicism, he spent his childhood & adolescence in Tunis. After attending the Saint-Cloud Ecole Normale, he taught at different high schools in Tunisia & Algeria. In Tunis during the 1930s he befriended Armand Guibert (poet, translator, & publisher; Tunis, 1906–90), with whom he coedited the magazine *Cahiers de Barbarie,* in which he published his first poems. During World War II he met André Gide in Tunis & joined the Gaullists in Algiers, where he became the director of the magazine *l'Arche.* He also produced radio programs in Algiers & later in Paris for Radio France. His interviews with Gide, Giuseppe Ungaretti, François Mauriac, & many others remain exemplary. Although dismissed from his radio job by Michel Debré, the French prime minister, Jean Amrouche never ceased to plead the cause of an independent Algeria. He died on April 16, 1962, from cancer, just after the Évian Accords—which led to the independence of Algeria—were signed.

A torn & flayed being, highly cultured & principled, as his *Journal* (published in 2009) shows, he was the first to shape the French language to the lyricism of "the eternal Jugurtha" (the title of one of his major essays, published in 1946). In the three collections of poems he published, *Cendres* (1934), *Étoile secrète* (1937), & *Chants berbères de Kabylie* (1939), there is no place for a reductionist folklore or sterile provincialism; the poems develop with a purity of style rarely achieved by Francophone Algerian poetry. Despite being anchored in the tradition of Stéphane Mallarmé, Amrouche, his modesty hiding his pain, spoke loudly to the questions of the place & the audience for literary expression.

Abu al-Qasim al-Shabi (Tozeur, 1909–Tunis, 1934)

LIFE'S WILL

When people choose
To live by life's will,
Fate can do nothing but give in;
The night discards its veil,
All shackles are undone.

Whoever never felt
Life celebrating him
Must vanish like the mist;
Whoever never felt
Sweeping through him
The glow of life
Succumbs to nothingness.

This I was told by the secret
Voice of All-Being:
Wind roared in the mountains,
Roared through valleys, under trees:
"My goal, once I have set it,

And put aside all caution,
I must pursue to the end.
Whoever shrinks from scaling the mountain
Lives out his life in potholes."

Then it was earth I questioned:
"Mother, do you detest mankind?"

And earth responded:
"I bless people with high ambition,
Who do not flinch at danger.

I curse people out of step with time,
People content to live like stone.
No horizon nurtures a dead bird.
A bee will choose to kiss a living flower.

If my mothering heart
Were not so tender,
The dead would have no hiding place
In those graves yonder."

Translation from Arabic by Christopher Middleton & Sargon Boulus

COMMENTARY

(1) Write the editors of *Modern Arabic Poetry* (Columbia University Press, 1991), from which this translation is taken, about Abu al-Qasim al-Shabi: "Tunisian poet whose rise to poetic prominence in the twenties immediately ushered Tunisian poetry into the current of avant-garde Arabic poetry of the time. He was influenced by north Mahjar poetry and by translations from the French Romantics, and was himself a true Romantic. He combined the two opposing trends—the one positive, strongly rejecting traditional social and political shackles and seeking to awaken people to progress and revolution, and the other negative, seeking seclusion in Nature, away from people's ignorance and submissiveness. His only volume, *Songs of Life,* appeared in 1955, many years after his death."

(2) Al-Shabi's best-known poem remains "To the Tyrants of the World," which was used as an anthem & rallying cry in both Tunisia & Egypt during the events that came to be known as the Arab Spring. We have not found a good English translation of the poem qua poem, but here is a decent prose rendering by Adel Iskandar, which NPR used while covering events on Tahrir Square: "Oppressive tyrant, lover of darkness, enemy of life, you have ridiculed the size of the weak people. Your palm is soaked with their blood. / You deformed the magic of existence, and planted the seeds of sorrow in the fields. / Wait, don't be fooled by the spring, the clearness of the sky or the light of dawn, for on the horizon lies the horror of darkness, rumble of thunder, and blowing of winds. / Beware, for below the ash there is fire, and he who grows thorns reaps wounds. Look there, for I have harvested the heads of mankind and the flowers of hope, and I watered the heart of the earth with blood. I soaked it with tears until it was drunk. The river of blood will sweep you, and the fiery storm will devour you."

Mouloud Feraoun (Tizi Hibel, 1913–Algiers, 1962)

from JOURNAL, 1955–1962

1st April 1958

It is a month now that I haven't opened this notebook, in which, for the past three years, I have been in the habit of consigning, of writing down, my fears and feelings of helplessness and confusion, or my pain and anger. What's the point of restating these same things in a different form one more time? During any given month of war, what else can have happened than that which will have happened during any other month? I live here as if outside the world, overwhelmed: far from our small villages, the echoes of which no longer reach me; far from the Muslim town to which, though I can see it, I remain a total stranger; from the European city where weariness is great, as is the edginess, due to a calmness that everyone knows to be deceptive and loaded with bad surprises—tears and mournings; far, finally, from the political agitation where one-upmanship, lies, and madness seem in the process of becoming the normal manifestation of human intelligence and prominence.

Since Ak's arrest—he is now in a camp but out of danger—I have not one connection with my own. Friends have stopped thinking of friends, maybe accusing one another mutually and in secret of being cowards or traitors, who knows?

E[mmanuel] Roblès gets away every time he can and comes over to have a chat with me. He, on the other hand, barely sees anyone anymore. Despite his rather optimistic temperament, he is as discouraged as I am.

Tonight we went on a visit to Algiers. By chance we met Camus, who was happy to see me and whom I may see again. I would like to talk with him. I think that's what he, for his part, wishes too.

3rd April

I have news from home, via Titi. If you can call it news. I know all of those things. The village is empty of young people. The men who have stayed and the women live in a continuous state of terror. Which has become a state that is bearable. The men have a haggard look, which they will retain to the end of their days. They have lost, so my sister tells me, any arrogance and sense of superiority in relation to women. They flaunt their weakness and cowardliness with a recklessness that seems to indicate that they find much pleasure and relief in being thus. Everyone has taken the habit of speaking in a low voice, the finger ready to lay itself on the lips. As a rule, it is agreed, admitted, recommended to go into rapture before the exploits of "our brothers," to never doubt their invincible courage or the cowardliness of the French soldiers, who at each encounter fall like acorns do here when the north wind blows. Given this, one mustn't trust anyone, for words understood wrongly can be interpreted wrongly; the troubles that could arise from this are never foreseeable. One has to convince oneself once and for all that "the brothers" are powerful, infallible, and rigid, like the eye-for-an-eye law that has become dark flesh. Who can tell you that the soldier who questions you, or the SAS [Sections administratives spécialisées, created in September 1955 by Jacques Soustelle, the governor-general of Algeria, and in charge of "pacification"] captain are not in cahoots with them? My poor sister, whose heart was heavy, lowers her voice, asks if she can be heard from outside, feels relieved, makes so bold as to start being critical, and then, once launched, just try to stop the verbal flood that suddenly pours out like a confused and interminable scream of revolt, like an abscess being lanced, like a somber sky that in a sudden rage comes clean.

Everybody understands that "the brothers" are not infallible, are not courageous, are not heroes. But we also know that they are cruel and hypocritical. The only thing they can give is death, but to them one has to give everything. They keep on ransoming, commandeering, destroying. They keep talking religion, prohibiting everything they have the habit of prohibiting, plus whatever else it pleases them to prohibit. One is forced to call them *brothers* and venerate them like gods. But when one of them commits treason and starts to denounce his hosts, one has to quickly forget this two-faced brother—though without holding it against the others or haggling over your contribution. Everybody's participation is requested. At present, the women watch over the wounded, carry them on their backs in case of an alert, bury the dead, collect the money, stand watch. The members of the resistance mobilize the women, and so the soldiers start to arrest and torture women.

A new world may be slowly emerging from the ruins, a world in which women will wear pants, literally and figuratively, in which the remainder of the old traditions concerning the inviolability of woman, literally and figuratively, will be swept away as something of a nuisance.

Thus all the peaceful attempts at emancipation that had run up against the general stubbornness and had not managed to gain an inch on the road toward freedom for that poor creature have found radiant revenge today, given that tomorrow the women of Algeria will have nothing left to envy other women. Except, perhaps, this: education.

But meanwhile they first have to take part in unjust fights, in torture, in the sufferings and mournings those scoundrels have heaped upon the country. The scoundrels are those who have accepted such a price for an illusory and problematic happiness; also those who hold the reins and refuse any wise solutions: the privileged ones who do not want to give up any part of their privileges, the ambitious ones willing to climb over mountains of corpses, ready to pay for their extravagant paradise with an incommensurable hell for the others.

It happens at times that some poor guy, whose nerves suddenly fray, will suffer from a sort of lucid insanity and will start to talk, talk, talk. At the *djema,* in the café, everywhere, he says what he thinks of his "brothers." And the people watch him aghast and feel sorry, because they know that there is nothing that can be done to make him shut up. And in a way, they take pleasure in listening to him, given that what he is saying he is reading in their hearts. He speaks, they listen, and then they go home in sadness, while he goes somewhere else and keeps talking. Oh, this doesn't last! On some morning he will disappear. God have mercy on his soul. One week, two weeks, or a month later they find him, in the bushes somewhere, disfigured, half eaten by the jackals or hanging from a tree, eyes put out, an ironic grin on the face. At the djema there's also ironic grinning, they say he had earned that noose, and the terrorist in chief complacently recounts the details of the summary execution. Then major sins are discovered in his past and he gets classified among the traitors whose death is enough to wipe clean the village's disgrace.

Who will say one day that Mohand Ouamer, seventy-five years old, and "Dangerous," thirty years old, are heroes of a sort? And others, no doubt, nearly everywhere else, who were aware of the risks they ran, and accepted them coolly?

At any rate, that multitude of individual tragedies, those obscure and gratuitous deaths simply condemn violence and can only bear witness to human dignity. Those who are accused of treason and who die as traitors are not worth any less than the heroes—or any more. They don't love the soldier, the Frenchman, France any more, for the cup of humiliations that runneth over has been filled indiscriminately by the different masters that come and go, and the nameless terror that has taken hold of all hearts is inspired by the same unfettered beast whose undifferentiated cruelty can take this or that shape in turn.

To the same tally of stupid death one could add the deaths of those guileless ones driven to the guerrilla as one is driven to suicide. They start as lookouts and then become terrorists of their own free will or by force; they get involved and committed, begin to run away from the soldiers, to live in the field near the village; and finally they become draft dodgers, true outlaws into whose hands the ALN [Armée de libération nationale] charitably puts an old hunting rifle at some point, with the rather obvious design of having it recuperated some day by the French soldiers, who, on that day, will add one more fellagha to their tally of kills, shot down because "dangerous and armed." Kids just good enough to have themselves killed after having lived through the unspeakable fear of hunted game animals.

Translations from French by P.J.

COMMENTARY

(1) Mouloud Feraoun was an Algerian Francophone writer of Amazigh extraction whose real name was Aït-Chabane, Feraoun being the name the colonial administration imposed on his family. Born in Tizi Hibel, Kabylia, in 1913, he studied at the Bouzareah Normal School, where he met Emmanuel Roblès (see below) & worked for some years as a schoolteacher & principal. In 1934 he wrote his first book, the autobiographical novel *Le fils du pauvre*—which he self-published in 1950 & of which Le Seuil published a heavily censored version in 1954. In 1951 he was in correspondence with Albert Camus. In 1960 he was named the inspector of social centers (created as an initiative of the French anthropologist & resistance fighter Germaine Tillion) in Château-Royal, near Ben-Aknoun. The French OAS (Organisation de l'armée secrète) assassinated him & five of his colleagues on March 15, 1962—four days before the cease-fire that marked the end of Algeria's war of independence. His *Journals 1955–1962* (Le Seuil, 1962), from which the extracts above are taken, came out posthumously in France; James D. Le Sueur, Mary Ellen Wolf, & Claude Fouillade published their English translation as *Journal, 1955–1962: Reflections on the French-Algerian War* (Bison Books, 2000).

(2) In 2005, Caraf Books, a University of Virginia Press series, published Lucy R. McNair's English translation of *Le fils du pauvre* as *The Poor Man's Son: Menrad, Kabyle Schoolteacher.* Writes Assia Djebar (see p. 563): "Feraoun's novel is more than just a testimony in which he recounts the daily life of his Berber mountain village, the emigration of his father to Paris, and especially his adolescent efforts to succeed in becoming a teacher rather than a simple shepherd. Through its austere authenticity and the modesty of its form, it became a classic for young Algerians, and marked, moreover, the birth of the post-colonial Francophone literature of the Maghreb."

Emmanuel Roblès (Oran, 1914–Boulogne-Billancourt, 1995)

from **MIRROR SUITE**

I

In a smile's mirror
My sky opens beating
With so many storms

It is then that dawn's born
And rushes toward you

In the mirror of your eyes
The windows explode
On a country of milk
Of honey and of reeds
And are born the sighs
Of the lovers embracing

Other mirrors are born
Those of unreason
And those of fate
Reflections strange reflections
Of our love that trembles
In the starry river

II

The arrows of the sun
In the mirror of time
Hit collapsed castles
On a beach of crystal and wind
Riddled with wrecks with shredded flanks

Shadow towers in skirts of ivy
Ruined bastions and crumbling ramparts
I walk in these reflections without touching earth
Caught as in an abandoned child's anguish

III

All the emotions of slow awakenings
Tremble in the mirror
Mornings when soul comes back to life
On the shore of slumbering marshes

And this pale attentive mask watches me
With the cold eye of reason
From deep down in this shimmering abyss
Where an inexpressible anguish ripples

Translation from French by P.J.

Emmanuel Roblès was an Algerian-French writer, born in Oran in 1914. His father died before his birth, so he was raised by women. The father's absence would prove central to his oeuvre, he himself suggests. At the Ecole Normale in Algiers (a city he loved & would live in later) he met Mouloud Feraoun (see p. 284). In Algiers he also spent time with young writers grouped around the bookshop owner & publisher Edmond Charlot, who had just brought out Albert Camus's *L'envers et l'endroit*. Roblès worked on a BA in Spanish while writing for *l'Alger républicain*, which was edited by Camus—& published Roblès's novel *La vallée du paradis* in installments. World War II interrupted his studies, so he worked as a war correspondent, visiting much of the Mediterranean theater & surviving several plane crashes. After the war he tried living as a freelance writer in Paris but returned to Algiers in 1947 to found the literary review *Forge*, probably the first serious attempt at a Franco-Maghrebian synthesis. Among the contributors were Mohammed Dib (see pp. 297, 547), Kateb Yacine (see pp. 321, 554), Jean Sénac (see pp. 315, 540), Ahmed Sefrioui, & Malek Ouary. The same year, he wrote *Les hauteurs de la ville*, a novel sparked by the events of May 1945 & awarded the Prix Fémina in 1948. He also started a career as playwright, became one of the first French translators of Federico García Lorca, & traveled the world (the USSR, Indochina, China, Mexico, Japan, etc.), trips that resulted in a number of books. Later, in Paris, he edited a book series for Le Seuil called Méditerranée, publishing Feraoun & Dib, among others. He was also involved in cinema, collaborating with Luis Buñuel & Luchino Visconti. He died in 1995 in Boulogne-Billancourt, near Paris. Our extracts are taken from *Cristal des jours* (Paris: Le Seuil, 1990).

Edmond Amram El-Maleh (Safi, 1917–Rabat, 2010)

from *TAKSIAT*

Isso Imzoghen! He returned home, as every year, to resume the interrupted reading of a great book, so clearly did things speak to him, humming with infinite voices, resonant pathway of his life. The mere sound of his own name, which he enjoyed repeating aloud in deepest solitude, sent up a gusher of luminous landscapes from his native city, knotted into his own memory-engorged flesh. This time again, as with each return, something was ripening in him. Within himself he heard the rustling of a slow meditation, like a silkworm—so he imagined—spinning in its cocoon. He could already see himself putting the final touch on a piece of work, though he had no idea what it would look like or where it was headed, if not down the slope of a strong desire, irresistible and dark.

But already, before all else, came a name, a title, the bud of sonorous sensuality from which the work would unfold, as if he were palpating a fertile belly: "Taksiat," like the distant echo of the famous Maqamats, songline of an epic in embryo. From certain angles, as he knew and feared, there was a kind of resonance, a similarity that tended to recall the category of the mechanical, the vehicular, which, in the Buddhist way, contained both lesser and greater vehicles. He tried to shake off his doubt, assuring himself that it wasn't time to decide yet, and besides, after all, why shouldn't an epic spring from the asphalt, like Aphrodite surging from the sea!

Brothers of purity, of the humble day-to-day, taxi drivers united, the *Tareqa Ikhouann Taksia*—are they not the ardent and zealous servants of Modernity-as-city? Isso Imzoghen, whose combustible imagination caught fire from the slightest spark—God knows how often he had been reproached for this—liked to think of them as walking or wandering philosophers in the manner of Aristotle's Peripatetics or Houday's Mostazilites, retracing the utopic body of the mega-metropolis, inventing its life, its path, second by second, like a sponge soaking up its air, its sky, its breath, the labor of its innards, the violence of its groin, the stale bread, the hunger in its gut, the huge surge of its laughter, the provocation of its sunlight, more like a mirror than a sponge, set ablaze by the incandescent lava of its volcanoes, the pharaonic explosion of its monstrous appetites, of its dislocated members in the orgasm of its countless joys, its deliriums, vaginas, abysses of insatiable truth, anus, solar anus as it's so well put, ruins that glorify, the triumphant fecality of matter, idolatry, in quiet obscurity the Phallus made God, for there lay the grain of a truth that burned everything in its path, rejecting all the halts, the traps that Isso strove to set for it. Still, as Isso knew quite well, no brain already consumed, no eye however mobile and quick to scan would succeed in discerning this grain of truth, for, as Isso, tired out and a bit confused—oh! just barely!—admitted to himself, nothing of the sort existed, his desire was drifting elsewhere along indecisive paths. Incorrigible Isso Imzoghen! What did he care! What he pursued assiduously was the sensuality of words, their unhoped-for capacity to provoke explosions, sensations of orgasmic delight. If he had wanted to he could have stopped there, accused himself in some manner, and confessed that adhering to the underbelly of these duplicity-laden words was the living flesh of a dual sensuality, mobility itself, the witness floating in the ragged hole of a cloud, shedding light on the game of seduction, but he did not want to entrust the subtlety of eroticism to the insipid inertia of paper. Fateha's graceful body had to slip away, had to glide into the tenderness of his gaze, the rise of desire knotting in his throat, crudely anticipating her mouth open to passion, those young buttocks, warm sand pouring through a hand's circling caresses, the triumphant abduction of this gentle, superb body, whose looming presence he felt like some imperial summons. Who would ever suspect for a minute such amorous transports in a man whom age should have pacified? Not even the taksist, of course, in whose presence Isso, following a well-thought-out strategy, had settled himself on the front seat. These men, however, Imzoghen told himself in his candid, deluded naiveté, are undoubtedly gifted with the powers of those sovereign beings of the kingdoms of the night, capable of reading signs traced in sand, song, and bird flight, the entrails of the sacrificed beast, the trail of stars shooting across a mute sky, the writing inscribed on the forehead, or in the abyssal waters, of a mere glance.

Isso had invented an opening gambit, as if he were coming to seek their advice, perhaps because he had a certain penchant for jinns, almost an affinity, convinced as he was that they circulate everywhere, beings in the full sense of the word.

Salam aalik, aalekoum salam, sabah el hkeir! An incantation, the words of the tribe: by opening the door to seat himself next to the taksist, Isso obtained access to mutual recognition and exchange. Yes, Isso was an archaic being, but it is very difficult to take full measure of this, to say exactly how, by escaping time or being annihilated by it, his memory held no birth certificate, no record at all, a fact unsurprising in this country.

The taksist, a young man of wholly citified appearance, returns the greetings warmly, waits to hear in what direction he is to go, and glances somewhat perplexedly at the rather extraordinary character he has just picked up. Out of courtesy for him, he doesn't ask any direct question. Driving down the Anfa Boulevard towards the famous Place de Verdun, their attention, Isso's and his, is simultaneously drawn to the imposing silhouette of a man crossing the wide street in the middle of an indescribable free-for-all. The man himself is a symbol, a revelatory sign begging to be deciphered: A black hat perched on his head, black suit coat, almost like a frock-coat, impossible to button up, held in check by an impressive gut, the identity of the person poses no doubt, the long black beard invading the entire face completes the picture, like a signature. Sherif! Isso is delighted to hear himself addressed this way, not only because he is reassured by this mark of attention, but also because it proved to him that respect and a sense of dignity have not been completely lost—"Sherif! You see that man, he's a 'Hakham,' you know what a 'Hakham' is?" Semantic subtlety, identificatory fuse, everything depends on Isso's answer. Will he recognize the word "Hakham" as the Judeo-Arabic designation for rabbi and thus display to the perplexed taksist the marks of an adherence? "Mentabaa el hal," of course, a response in the affirmative. Perhaps Isso has mistaken the intentions of his taksist, the latter not searching to probe further, the conversation moves on, yet Isso still appreciates the subtlety of the thought, the man, another hypothesis, knew what was what without missing a beat. You understand, ya Sidi, ou Allah! You're from around here, ould el bled, Isso felt pure delight! Soon, alas, no one will speak in this fashion, so many fruits have perished from this earth, it was an inventory of them he was making, that lovely language, made of flesh and life, of face to face encounters, convivial talk, commanding the upright stance, opening up the most beautiful vistas of imagination, ould el bled, enta dial na, you are one of us! You know, you remember how it used to be, yes, you must know, you come from that time, tbark allah aalek, may God give you his blessing! It's hell, now, you see, we loop around like in a medina, shoulder to shoulder, elbowing our way through. It's a totally different world now, I'll tell you a story: They say a blind man living in the neighborhood made a habit of crossing the avenue where we're driving now by counting to twelve from one curb to the other, but one day, counting to twelve, he found himself in the middle of the roadway and was almost run over by a car, the boulevard had just been widened to twice its size. The parable of the blind man, Imzoghen was charmed, transported by metaphor, yes, the whole country is one big parable! Starting with those parabolic antennas, parasols open to the sky that have blossomed on the balconies of luxury apartment buildings, the era of miserable couscous-tins, of makeshift substitutes, is over. Now modernity, arriving from far off climes, descends from the sky, sweeping along a chaotic flood of violent images, war, massacre, famine, a whole world of barbarity unveiling itself tragically in the very heart of that arrogant Western civilization, reminding those who continue to refuse to believe that it is there, towards and against centuries of lies, total alienation, that's where barbarity was born, as paradoxical as it may seem. Parable, parable! Beware! said Isso Imzoghen, while taking another cab to the port station this time, beware of getting entangled in the foils of all this complex and seductive symbolism! Make sure you curb this old discourse that you know so well because you've carried it in you all this time, this torrent of outraged violence that grabs you by the throat! Discontented with himself! Why did this vehemence, this sort of crude condemnation, crop up inconveniently at the slightest provocation?

Translation from French by Lucy R. McNair

COMMENTARY

Born in Safi to a Jewish family, Edmond Amram el-Maleh moved to Paris in 1965, where he worked as a journalist & philosophy teacher. He started to write in 1980, at the age of sixty-three, traveling back & forth between France & Morocco. He stated that in spite of his long stay in France, he had devoted his entire literary life to Morocco. From 1999 until his death he lived in Rabat.

Of the novel *Parcours immobile* (Maspéro, 1983), his first book, emblematic of the rest of his work, he said: "This book reflects a desire to deepen more and more the sense that I'm rooted in the Moroccan culture, where I've tried not to copy but to relive my experience of a young Moroccan Jew who fought against colonialism and as a militant within the communist movement." Annie Devergnas-Dieumegard suggests that "in this novel can be found the basic features of his works, which belong to both the autobiographical and the historical genres, as it depicts the Jewish Moroccan society throughout the first half of the twentieth century. The theme of personal death—the memories of an unhealthy childhood—is linked to the account of the progressive disappearing of this community in the middle of the century. But it is essentially el-Maleh's writing style which is remarkable. Nonchronological, metaphorical, close to orality, almost without punctuation, it gives true historical facts a puzzling subjectivity. . . . This singular writer, whose works cannot be parted from his life, uses writing as the only way to keep alive his own past, along with the remembrance of the now-vanished Jewish community of Morocco."

Mouloud Mammeri (Taourirt Mimoune, Kabylia, 1917–Aïn Defla, 1989)

from *L'AHELLIL DU GOURARA: TIMIMOUN*

There is but one God, our master
Blessed be you, sent by God
Father of my Lady Rekia?
And for one, one is my Lord
And for two, my mother told me:
"My son, watch out for love!"
And for four, in full gallop spread toward me
And for five, as many fingers on my hand.

Girls are like standards:
Poor is he who has none.

There is but one God since Masinissa
There is but one God all the way to the *zawiya*
Of Sidi Hadj Belkacem
Your standard, O Tigorarin
I'll make a pilgrimage to Aougrout
To Sidi Omar
Sidi Omar-Ou-Mhemmed
Of the descendants of the last Sidi Abbad.

Fatma, daughter of my uncle
Give me a sip of water.
But where is the water, my God,
So that I may give to Ahmed my cousin?

My jug is near the *seguia*
And I have no *tazouda* with me
The *zenzmiya* is too precious:
Only the dove drinks from it.
—Which dove, my God?
—The pillar of the house
As soon as I hear that one of them is ill
I fall ill and sick is my heart
All my members are sick.

I'll love who'll love Aishah
I'll hate who'll hate her
All Aishahs are doves
Mares from Bousemghoun
I'm ashamed
Shame is in me
It is in me, it is in my heart
Since the time I was a child
I haunted the love of the girls
My Lord God, mercy,
Forgive your creature rebellious
Since the time of my childhood.

Translation from Mouloud Mammeri's French version by P.J.

COMMENTARY

(1) Born on December 28, 1917, in Taourirt Mimoune, Kabylia, Mouloud Mammeri is the only Algerian writer of his generation to have finished high school (at the lycée Louis-le-Grand in Paris) & university (Faculté des Lettres d'Alger). Drafted into the army during WWII, he took part in the fighting in Italy, France, & Germany, experiences echoed in his novel *Le Sommeil du juste* (1955). In 1947 he started a teaching career in Algeria, & he published his first novel, *La Colline oubliée*, in 1952. It is a staggering work in which the implacability of tragic fate closes in on the hero, who tries to separate from his clan. The book, oracularly, lays out Mammeri's own later death. In 1957, forced to leave Algeria, he settled in Morocco, staying until Algeria became independent. From 1968 onward he worked, via cultural anthropology, to give a new life to

the Amazigh language & its popular poetry. He taught Berber studies at the university of Algiers, but the political powers often censored him. From 1969 to 1980 he directed CRAPE (the Center for Anthropological, Prehistoric, and Ethnographic Research) at the Bardo Museum in Algiers. He also conducted detailed research on Si Mohand's *isefra*s (see p. 241) & on the Tuareg ahellil & headed the first national union of Algerian writers for a time but left over disagreements on the role of writers in society. In 1980, the ban on his conference on Kabyle poetry in Tizi Ouzou (the capital of Kabylia) triggered a popular antigovernment movement demanding that Amazigh be recognized as an official language of the country. In 1982, in Paris, he founded CERAM (the Center for Amazigh Studies and Research) & the magazine *Awal* as part of the EHESS (Ecole des Hautes Etudes en Sciences Sociales). The same year, Editions Plon published his novel *La Traversée,* which tells of the rise of fundamentalist Islam in Algeria & was banned in that country. Returning home from a symposium in Oujda on Amazigh culture & identity, Mammeri died in a car crash. For his funeral—at which no Algerian official was present—more than two hundred thousand people gathered around the cemetery of his native village.

(2) Mouloud Mammeri's 1980 response to his detractors: "You make me the cantor of Berber culture, and it is true. This culture is mine; it is also yours. It is one of the components of Algerian culture, it contributes to enrich it, to diversify it, and for this reason I want (as you should too) not only to maintain but to develop it."

(3) In *L'Ahellil du Gouara,* Mammeri gathered & translated ahellil texts, a poetic & musically polyphonic genre in Zeneta Berber specific to the Saharan Gourara region, whose capital is Timimoun.

Mostefa Lacheraf (Sidi Aïssa, 1917–Algiers, 2007)

from COUNTRY OF LONG PAIN

Country of long misery that comes from the same invisible assault charging space all the way to the summit. Here it is now like a serpent of fauve sand and stones: it walks with an unheard screeching, in a song of eternity wherein the rumors of men and beast mix with the muted latencies of plants and water.

Lizards and caterpillars, artemisia flowers, vivacious asphodels and the hoofs of the herd on the mat silex, and the distraught wind that weaves and reweaves. Life moves stealthily in a soft reptation of down, of animal silks, of mica, of tender avalanche along the flanks of the dune where the fennecs slide. And the sun gazes at us, terrible and fraternal in the black of the eyes, in the prodigious agate where the measure of the world establishes itself, where from a great distance the reptilian movement organizes itself and where the interminable day reflects in us.

Witnesses, O witnesses! What is it that you see? where was the strange? All millennia curl up inside a childhood, memory has lived through the ages of the earth. What is to come is on the same roads and less than astonished the old man and fills the candid youth with wonder. And the staggering feet that carry him along the trace and the hands full of crude rattles have already reinforced grip and stride.

Like the bitter and flowery rosebays, first wisdom is to begin with some shade along the absent waters under the heat wave.

And when the flood returns to the shore tattooed with subtle footsteps, the birds have already flown off again toward the rare watering places carrying along in their beaks the rose's bitterness and the loam's thirst.

True! The children too were weak, chirping their arid innocence, but autumn came. Derisory shade along the riverbanks, meridian that flattens itself flat on the ground, ocher and warm like infamy's redness, tomorrow we'll be far away from this chiaroscuro game!

Never again will the fever find pleasure in its shivers at the edge of the swamps; never again will love be made in the oppressive siesta under the perfumes of ambergris and sweat. Summer and its stupor ebb; henceforth the seasons obey the vigils. Noon, wide-eyed, night upright, and the hours of the day are an awake dawn. The child that had been stumbling rejoins the man on harder paths. In terms of age, there will only be left the age of memory, and your days are equal when Death has struck.

For death no longer awaits the breath that trembles
The doleful or bedridden end
The sleep of death pangs in the humidity of the hospice
A monotonous youth hurries toward its high places
All dressed up, with no shroud, without balm or benzoin
A smell of saltpeter impregnates the young bodies,
An immaterial musk brightens their too new blood.
The prayer surrounding them is fragrance from the fountain of youth,
Breath that quivers from mouth to mouth
A vast respiration where the dead confound themselves to stay among us.
Down to the stone, down to the thorn,
To the thistle of the fallow fields
A swirl of anger still stirs the ground around the carnage
And where blood flowed, grass bristles.

Fresnes prison, December 6, 1960

Translation from French by P.J.

Born in 1917 south of Algiers, Mostefa Lacheraf studied at the Sorbonne & later taught at the lycée Louis-le-Grand in Paris; by 1939 he had joined the PPA—the Algerian People's Party, from which the FLN (National Liberation Front) eventually emerged. Lacheraf is better known for his work as a historian & for his political career than for his poetry—though the latter isn't any less important. A major intellectual, truly bilingual, he contributed articles & poems to magazines such as *Fontaine, Simoun, Les Cahiers du Sud, Cahiers internationaux, Présence africaine, Esprit,* & *Les Temps modernes* starting in the late 1940s. In 1954 he published *Chansons des jeunes filles arabes,* a book that is both a translation & a true creation. He also wrote prefaces for *Matinale de mon peuple* (1961) & *Algérie, capitale Alger* (1963) by Anna Gréki (see p. 329). As an essayist—his core vocation—he wrote his best-known work, "Pays de longue peine" (Country of Long Pain), which dates from the 1950s & is extracted above. Often reprinted & anthologized, it shows great rhetorical mastery & a sustained lyricism.

Mohammed Dib (Tlemcen, 1920–La Celle-Saint-Cloud, 2003)

from **OMBRE GARDIENNE**

Guardian Shadow I

Fasten your doors
Women, bitter sleep
Will flow through your nerves,
Water, sand have erased
The trace of your steps,
Nothing belongs to you.

Distant and sparse
The glimmer of stars,
Opaque the land around,
Dark the ancestral homes
That shelter your repose.

Fasten your doors,
I am the guardian:
Nothing belongs to you.

Guardian Shadow 2

Yet I will sing so softly
That sorrow will barely
Seem to trouble your sleep;
Peace be upon you, mothers, brides,
The blood-sucking tyrant
Will be dust in your winnows.

I walk across the mountain
Where the coming spring
Is clothed in scented herbs;

Hear me women, hear me,
When daybreak softens
I will scour your doorsteps.

And I will cover with song
The wailing cries of time.

Guardian Shadow 3

Do not ask whether
The wind that trails
The mountain peaks
Kindles a hearth:

Whether it be joyful,
Whether a pauper's fire
Or a signal for the watch.

Still soaked in dew, fabulous
Women, may you dream
The night behind sealed doors.

I walk, I walk:
The words that I bear
Forth on my tongue
Are a strange herald.

Dawn Breaks

Dawn breaks and the landscape
Is drawn in blood, in wind,
Pale thunder and silence.

Borne on a beautiful voice
An endless song weaves unfettered
Over the hills—Oh, how to live?

I dwell in a house of frost, riven
By a deadly wind—yet you murmur:
"Let the exile come to an end;

The new mint has flowered,
The fig tree has given its fruit,
Let the grieving come to an end."

In tormented times you alone,
Lavender maid of the solemn heart,
You alone may bear this song.

The Crazed Hour

The crazed hour roams. Dark
You will recognize her
By her pall of dark hate,
Her pall of wind and cries.

Born of ancient calcites
And ocean fires,
Her doves offer death
A strange resplendence.

You will recognize her:
It is the hour of grief, the hour
Of russet blood on the vines,
Harried by the light.

Nursery Rhyme

One.
With flame
And with blade, this game
Unravels the landscape.

Two.
Among the living
Eyes turn words
Into desolate spearworts.

Three.
A shadow a hostage,
A hostage a shadow
And so?

Four.
It snows.
Silence
A hostage a shadow.

Five.
It is but a touch of snow
And all is lost,
All is lost.

Six.
Reaper's
Half somewhere else
Half-a-watching.

One, two,
Three, four, five,
Six deaths.

Etc.

A Voice

This morning half-opens its eyes
To the mist, the solitude
And the scarce flowers of the steppe.

Over there, dry grasses in flame
And far beyond, the flutter of a sail
—Where is this woman who walks?

I survey this reddened land
And wonder: this alone perhaps
Is what keeps my heart steadfast.

All at once a voice arises
To answer me in the haze
Of an infinite trembling light:

"Let the years spin the thread
Of the seasons, for youth is my home,
Young I am reborn, as young

As this day soaked in morning dew
And yet so cold. Love me!"
And the wind echoes: Love me . . .

Translations from French by Madeleine Campbell

COMMENTARY

. . . one step into the design and all space is surpassed there is no more space there is only the path you engrave in this paraphrase of calligraphy you must go search the writing that searches and writes you but.
M.D.

Born in Tlemcen, Algeria, in 1920 to a family of artisans who loved Arabo-Andalusian & *hawzi* music, Mohammed Dib is one of the fathers of modern Maghrebian literature, his vast oeuvre stretching from colonial days to the first decade of the twenty-first century. He is one of the rare Algerian writers completely & exclusively possessed by the need to write. He explored all forms: novel, short story, poetry, children's books, essays, tales, plays. Upon the completion of his great fiction trilogy (*L'incendie*), Dib moved to Paris in 1959, where he lived—except for a year in Los Angeles & repeated visits to Finland—until his death in 2003. Though primarily known as the author of more than thirty novels, Dib was also a poet of sizable output—because before all he very consciously & self-reflexively worked on writing as writing. (Interestingly enough, it was not a French writer who brought him, at fifteen, to literature but the English novelist Virginia Woolf, especially her *To the Lighthouse* & *The Waves,* although later on, when he started to write, he said he had to unlearn the seductive lusciousness of her style by training himself in short, clear sentences.) Paul Vangelisti, one of Dib's American translators, comments in his postface to Dib's novel in verse *L.A. Trip* (Green Integer, 2003) on "the stillness of the book in which the reader not only reads but, perhaps more importantly, is read by the book. For me Dib revealed poetry as an ultimate inability to communicate, whose motive force springs from this very lack or failure: 'you are no longer the one who asks questions begs for self-expression but they but they / cradle where destiny grows a little tamer a little calmer.'" As Dib suggested in his last interview, "To become Westernized is the exact meaning of the Arab verb translated more generally as 'to exile oneself.'" For him then, the West is "the country of exile, of the soul's exile," but the term itself has "a mystical connotation more than a geographical one. In Islam the notion of purgatory does not exist, and yet this 'occidental exile' comes close to it, and at any rate it is not a pleasant place. I haven't really known it as such. For me it was more a question of breaking away from a landscape rather than of going into exile. This rupture wasn't really difficult, because I never really loved the sun. I feel better here, under a changing, animated sky. Truly I wouldn't wish on my worst enemy to always have to live under a sky that's always pure, certain of itself, hard. Anyway, for a writer, the passage from culture to culture becomes a strength, an advantage, because it sharpens the senses. It forces one to look more deeply into the hell hidden inside man, and that's a gain for literature." For more Mohammed Dib, see also pp. 547–549.

Bachir Hadj Ali (Algiers, 1920–1991)

DREAMS IN DISARRAY

I dream of laughing islets and shady streams
I dream of green cities silent at night
I dream of white-blue villages with no trachoma
I dream of deep rivers, wisely lazy
I dream of protection for the convalescent forests
I dream of harbinger sources of cherry orchards
I dream of blond waves crashing pylons
I dream of derricks the color of May First
I dream of languorous lace on burned trails
I dream of slender factories and deft hands
I dream of cosmic libraries in moonlight
I dream of cantinas Mediterranean frescoes
I dream of red tiles at the summit of Mount Chelia
I dream of curtains gathered at the windows of my tribes
I dream of an ivory light switch for every room
I dream of a bright room for every child
I dream of a transparent table for every family
I dream of a flowered cloth for every table
I dream of elegant purchasing power
I dream of lovers delivered from secret transactions
I dream of couples agreeing harmoniously
I dream of men well-balanced in the presence of the woman
I dream of women at ease in the presence of the man
I dream of rhythmic dances in stadiums
And of peasant women shod in spectacular leather
I dream of geometric tournaments between high schools
I dream of oratorical duels between peaks and valleys
I dream of summer concerts in suspended gardens
I dream of modernized Persian markets

To each according to his needs
I dream of my valiant people cultivated good
I dream of my country without torture without prisons
I scrutinize with myopic eyes my dreams in my prison

Translation from French by Sylvia Gorelick & Miles Joris-Peyrafitte

OATH

I swear on the reason of my bound-up daughter
Howling at the passing airplanes
I swear on the patience of my mother
Waiting for her child lost in exodus
I swear on the intelligence and kindness of Ali Boumendjel
And the broad forehead of Maurice Audin
My brothers my hopes broken in full swing

I swear on the generous dreams of Ben M'Hidi and Inal
I swear on the silence of my villages taken by surprise
Buried at dawn without a tear without a prayer
I swear on the horizons of my shores broadening
As the wound deepens ruffled with blades
I swear on the wisdom of the Mujahideen masters of the night
I swear on the certainty of the day seized by the night transfigured
I swear on the raging waves of my torments
I swear on the wrath that beautifies our women
I swear on tested and true friendship on deferred loves
I swear on the hatred and the faith that keep the flame alive
That we bear no hatred for the French people.

Translation from French by Kit Schluter

COMMENTARY

Bachir Hadj Ali is a child of the casbah of Algiers, where he was born in 1920 to a modest Kabyle family. He went to Qur'anic school & to French grade school but could not continue to study at teachers' college level, as he had to work to help his family make ends meet. In 1945 he joined the Algerian Communist Party (PCA), becoming its secretary-general in 1951. Starting in 1948, he edited *Liberté*, the party's newspaper.

Hadj Ali knew the prisons of the colonial regime, clandestinity during the war of independence, and then the prisons of the Boumediène regime, and he bore witness to the tortures suffered there—their sequels remained with him for the rest of his life—in a work called *L'arbitraire,* published by Editions de Minuit in 1966. A long-lasting friendship linked him with the painter Mohammed Khadda, from the end of the 1960s until their death a few days apart in May 1991. Tahar Djaout (see p. 615) wrote later that month in the weekly *Algérie-Actualité:* "Bachir Hadj Ali has not asked us to remember the names of his torturers; he has forbidden us to respond to hatred with hatred. That is why, without forgetting the trials he went through, we will remember much more his songs that plead for joy, that say the 'red carnations' and the 'dreams in disorder.'"

As a musicologist, Hadj Ali frequented the masters of *chaabi,* among them El Anka. His poetry was nourished by zajal, the poetic form in vernacular Arabic closely related to the muwashshaha (Ibn Quzman—see p. 93—was the Andalusian master of that form). His 1961 book, *Les Chants pour le onze décembre,* proved a great success. If his poetry was militant and politically *engagée,* it could also be intimist and love-directed. The letters he wrote to his wife while in prison in Lambèze—published in Algiers in 2002 as *Letters to Lucette, 1965–1966*—are an ode to beauty, love, and hope, firmly linked to the body. The poems gathered in *Actuelles-partitions pour demain* (1980) are as tight and spare as Japanese haikus.

Jean Pélégri (Rovigo, 1920–Paris, 2003)

OPEN THE PEBBLE

It was then, in the days that followed—or perhaps it was that very evening (he no longer remembered very clearly)—that Slimane had found that which he had been missing, the beginning of History, or rather, above all, the way to tell it to other people. The means. *The idea.* That which at once tells history and explains it—because until then, it could be said, it had simply been walking around within him. Okay, for a long time, even—but without speaking to him exactly (like someone who would occasionally see, on the farm, and from afar, another Arab—for example, the other Slimane in his great burnoose—walking a ways away in the vines or olive trees of the wadi, but without encountering him, without seeing his face, because the other man, every time he is approached, hides himself in the trees, escapes—seeming to say that he has the secret, and that it is not time yet. Until the day when both men, in the cabin in the north part of the wadi, meet, coalesce— and the other starts to speak for Slimane, *in his stead*).

Before him, on the raffia carpet, he has the two-colored flag with, in the middle just where it needs to be, the rock—and he thinks he is going to make them come, so that they hear History, all of the Arabs from the farm. It's even possible that he thinks they are already there, sitting all around, with, behind their backs, the wadi pebble. HE TELLS THEM.

First, everyone must look carefully at the rock, for a good moment, both the rock and he who is speaking, so that already, without paying attention, they make the mixture. "This rock," he begins, "that one there upon the flag, between the star and the sliver of moon, this rock is more than thousands and thousands of years old, perhaps much older even—*it is before time. It is older than all the soil there is on the plain, older than the wadi.* IT IS *the piece of the Great Rock that we see out there* [he shows them], *in the cloud atop the mountain—the true piece.* . . . And yet, FIRST, we may think that it is a rock like any other, the Arabic pebble. Nobody can know *at first* that within it lies a secret, *es-sserle-kbir,* the great secret that explains every-thing. Nobody can—AND PERHAPS AT FIRST ONE MUST NOT . . . " (And then, all of a sudden, while all the brothers are watching the rock:) "This rock, O brothers, that rock—perhaps it is named Slimane, *or Sidi Slimane.* . . . *Perhaps still it is named Oumranne, Lakhdar, or Saïd.* . . . No matter, it is not important. . . . The name that it bears, by God alone on the Day of Judgment can be given—for He, when He gives the name, He gives the Commandment. The rock, whether it has this name or any other, needs not but obey."

(Then he who is speaking takes a break—just as the child breaks when he has already rewritten, in the necessary way, nearly the whole Great Book: *the khetma-break*—such that all those listening think, each one, that it is of him that one speaks—and that, at his side, his guardian observes. And then, all of a sudden:)

"THIS ROCK HAS KILLED A MAN"

(He says the thing like that, gesturing to the rock upon the flag—so that each thinks that it is perhaps him, and that *at the same time,* seeing as it is a rock, he does not ask himself the questions immediately. So that he may understand, already, that it has only *served* in killing. Nothing more.)

One day it killed him by separating itself from the Great Rock. (And then, he who is speaking tells all of History, *speaking for the rock*—until tonight in the mountain, where, in falling, it had chosen: because of the heat, because of the cold, because of the water, the time that passes, the erosion. Because of the secret.)

"PERHAPS" (he now says again) "PERHAPS THIS ROCK IS NAMED SLIMANE?" (For God, sometimes, in he who seems like the others, in the pebble, sometimes He hides what no longer is believed possible.)

"IT IS UP TO GOD TO RESPOND."

(It is at this moment that, with his two hands, he takes the rock from upon the flag, the pebble, and holds it up to show to the others. And at first, with his finger, he makes them see the small line that runs around it, the crack, hardly visible:)

"Sometimes in the pebble that seems good for nothing, the pebble of the wadi or the one crushed by a farm wagon, sometimes within, as in the depths of a well, there is the secret, the reason, the reason that made it break off and that explains everything. The reason that must be sought at length . . . for, in order to find it, O brothers, you must not search without—you must search WITHIN! . . . YOU MUST THINK OF OPENING THE PEBBLE." (And he opens it—the two pieces—one in each hand:)

"Sometimes in the old, worn-down pebble there is *the Snail* [and he gestures to it], *the hidden Snail, the Snail before time* . . . " (And then, to finish, he places the pieces before himself, gently upon the two-colored flag—in the correct place between the star with five points and the moon—and he begins, Hélal:)

"THE ARABIC SNAIL!" (The others, at this moment—with, behind their backs, the wadi pebble—begin to understand, to see in a new way Slimane, Sidi Slimane. Without asking themselves questions, they look upon the stone, the stone-snail, then . . .)

Translation from French by Kit Schluter

COMMENTARY

Although less known than many of his contemporaries, Jean Pélégri—a close friend of the likes of Mohammed Dib & Kateb Yacine, & associated with painters such as Baya & Abdallah Benanteur—was a prolific poet, novelist, film scenarist, actor, & playwright, as well as a professor of literature. As Dib wrote in 2003: "Jean Pélégri, an Algerian by birth, is one of the greatest of today's writers, greater than Albert Camus at any rate, though he remains unknown and ignored in France. Why? Because, to mark his belonging to the Algerian territory, he has piss-marked its borders so strongly that he has created another French language for his usage. This the French public has begrudged him and has made it turn away from him." And Jean Daniel wrote in *Le Nouvel Observateur* in the year of Pélégri's death: "No French writer from Algeria— the *pied-noirs,* as we ignorantly call them—with the possible exception of the poet Jean Sénac, accepted Algeria completely for what she is and for what she has always been the way that he did. No one so naturally felt like a son of Algeria in all her forms: Arab, Berber, Spanish, French . . . as Jean Pélégri did: not Gabriel Audisio, not Emmanuel Roblès, not Jules Roy nor Albert Camus. From his novel *Oliviers de la justice* to *Maboul,* Pélégri sings a veritable *cante jondo* of rural Algeria in all of its baroque complexity. With Kateb Yacine's *Nedjma, Le Maboul* is the only Faulknerian novel of our literature."

Nourredine Aba (Aïn Oulmene, 1921–Paris, 1996)

from *LOST SONG OF A REDISCOVERED COUNTRY*

. . . And all of a sudden one morning,
comes
a sky riddled with many-sided ornaments,
air loaded with incense,
a morning of roads stretching out to the horizon
to infinity
and interlaced like couples.
And one morning
with trees and the entangling
of their branches
like stylized inscriptions . . .
   . . . Tomorrow I will depart
   before the sun
   is high in the sky . . .
   . . . Beyond, there is MEMORY
still shivering
with a mixing of wings
and as if invaded
by a legion of centipedes.
I see it fully
like a strange rose window at the mast of this darkness,
I count the fragments
of its stunning stained glass
crucified in their leading,
I see them here and there
flower and disappear
in a row of florescence
the eyes cannot bear.
I count the paths
branches of leafy boughs
which trail through the crossroads of my life
like boundary markings,
but the branches are dried
and as if fallen from a tree
one had sucked dry of its sap! . . .
   . . . Tomorrow I will depart
   before the sun
   is high in the sky . . .

. . . Yes, but here is the challenge of the
riddle:
the greater the light
the more darkness becomes dense within me . . .
    . . . One must go naked
be quartered to the marrow,
scrape the bone, polish it
to ashes
carry these memories to the red of the sun
until the first flowering of its sterile sands! . . .
      . . . HERE PERHAPS? . . .
      . . . I walk. The sky is burning.
   The sand broils.
. . . HERE PERHAPS? . . .
. . . The sky and sand as far as the eye can see, everywhere,
sky and sand so close to one another
so exactly identical
that it would seem possible to invert them . . .
     . . . HERE PERHAPS LIES? . . .
     . . . The idea is disturbing to me: to have
for roof
of the world
this immense stomach without end of the desert
bellowing with these organs
forcing a path through this deluge of meteors . . .
     . . . HERE LIES PERHAPS
     FOSSILIZED? . . .
      . . . I walk, the sky is burning, the sand
broils.
In this incandescence the wind picks up
on the dunes in cones, in spheres, in pyramids,
its repertory of graphic signs
ever erased but always begun again . . .
     . . . HERE LIES PERHAPS
     A WORLD FOSSILIZED? . . .
      . . . I walk, the sun is high, on the heels
of these arenas without end, I pull forth a sea of gems
and the irresistible delirium carries me off
from bank to bank of these waves of powder
where an agonizingly abrupt fall

and all the rumbling pulverizes
ribbons of salt . . .
. . . HERE PERHAPS LIES FOSSILIZED A WORLD WHICH
WAS CLOSE TO ME? . . .
   . . . I walk, my steps plant the shadow of their
trace
and follow me like enormous ants.

Translation from French by Cynthia T. Hahn

COMMENTARY

Born in 1921 in Aïn Oulmene, near Sétif, where he graduated from high school, Nourredine Aba was drafted into the army in 1943 & served until 1945. He reported on the Nuremberg Trials as a journalist. He soon began to militate for independence & was thrown in jail for engaging in subversive activities. After 1962, he lived in France, & he died in Paris in 1996. In 1990, he created the Aba Foundation to encourage young Algerian writers. Aba worked in all genres, but he was above all a poet & a humanist playwright marked by World War II, the Algerian war of liberation (see *La Toussaint des énigmes*, 1963, & *Le Chant perdu au pays retrouvé*, 1978), & the Palestinian conflict (see *Montjoie Palestine*, 1970; *L'Aube à Jérusalem*, 1978; & *C'était hier Sabra et Chatila*, 1983). His is a politically engaged writing that tries before all to touch its readership & bring home its message of love & fraternity, a writing that is the witness of an whole era.

Mohammed Al-Habib El-Forkani

(Tahannaout, 1922–Rabat, 2008)

"IN A MISERABLE WORLD"

In a miserable world
Here I am, toward you refuge of free men.
Despite the rest, I've accepted
The call launched in midstruggle.
I walked toward you, unhesitating, fearless,
Happy to be your companion: you are too.
Your enclosure fences the spring
Where souls are reborn. Refuge of the just.

On your flanks of pride
The meaning of life resides and the secret unveils itself.
If I have defended tyrants,
If they throw that at you, weapon of their vengeance, with masked face,
I have defended truth when a generous society
Yelled its contempt, despite the violence of the vile.

"MY YESTERDAY PURSUES ME"

My yesterday pursues me
Judges me through time
Laughs, plays tricks on me
Mocks my life, insults it
& through my prison of boredom
It drags shards of mirages.

I make an inventory of space
Searching for a dreaming tomorrow
I crush insects
They swirl about my dark road
In search of a shore of light.
Will I cradle a lost ship there?

I finally pull up the veil
Perceive the direction of the path
Gather stars into my heart.
Night becomes my privilege.
I am going toward my source.
Toward the valley of shadows. Master. Free.

Translations by P.J. from French versions of the original Arabic

COMMENTARY

Born in 1922 in Tahannaout in the region of Marrakech, Mohammed Al-Habib
El-Forkani died in Rabat in 2008. This Arabophone writer was an emblematic
figure of the nationalist movement—exiled & jailed several times by the colo-
nial institution—& was active in politics, poetry, & historical research. The
poems presented here were gathered & translated from Arabic into French by
Mohammed Benjelloun Touimi, Abdelkebir Khatibi, & Mohammed Kably in
Ecrivains marocains du Protectorat à 1965 (Paris: Sinbad, c. 1974).

Frantz Fanon (Fort-de-France, 1925–Bethesda, Maryland, 1961)

from **ON NATIONAL CULTURE**

It is clear therefore that the way the cultural problem is posed in certain colonized countries can lead to serious ambiguities. Colonialism's insistence that "niggers" have no culture, and Arabs are by nature barbaric, inevitably leads to a glorification of cultural phenomena that become continental instead of national, and singularly racialized. In Africa, the reasoning of the intellectual is Black-African or Arab-Islamic. It is not specifically national. Culture is increasingly cut off from reality. It finds safe haven in a refuge of smoldering emotions and has difficulty cutting a straightforward path that would, nevertheless, be the only one likely to endow it with productiveness, homogeneity, and substance.

Though historically limited the fact remains that the actions of the colonized intellectual do much to support and justify the action of the politicians. And it is true the attitude of the colonized intellectual sometimes takes on the aspect of a cult or religion. But under closer analysis it clearly reflects he is only too aware that he is running the risk of severing the last remaining ties with his people. This stated belief in the existence of a national culture is in fact a burning, desperate return to anything. In order to secure his salvation, in order to escape the supremacy of white culture the colonized intellectual feels the need to return to his unknown roots and lose himself, come what may, among his barbaric people. Because he feels he is becoming alienated, in other words the living focus of contradictions which risk becoming insurmountable, the colonized intellectual wrenches himself from the quagmire which threatens to suck him down, and determined to believe what he finds, he accepts and ratifies it with body and soul. He finds himself bound to answer for everything and for everyone. He not only becomes an advocate, he accepts being included with the others, and henceforth he can afford to laugh at his past cowardice.

This painful and harrowing wrench is, however, a necessity. Otherwise we will be faced with extremely serious psycho-affective mutilations: individuals without an anchorage, without borders, colorless, stateless, rootless, a body of angels. And it will come as no surprise to hear some colonized intellectuals state: "Speaking as a Senegalese and a Frenchman. . . . Speaking as an Algerian and a Frenchman." Stumbling over the need to assume two nationalities, two determinations, the intellectual who is Arab and French, or Nigerian and English, if he wants to be sincere with himself, chooses the negation of one of these two determinations. Usually, unwilling or unable to choose, these intellectuals collect all the historical determinations which have conditioned them and place themselves in a thoroughly "universal perspective."

The reason being that the colonized intellectual has thrown himself headlong into Western culture. Like adopted children who only stop investigating their new family environment once their psyche has formed a minimum core of reassurance, the colonized intellectual will endeavor to make European culture his own. Not content with knowing Rabelais or Diderot, Shakespeare or Edgar Allan Poe, he will stretch his mind until he identifies with them completely.

> The lady was not alone
> She had a husband
> A fine, upstanding husband
> Who recited Racine and Corneille
> And Voltaire and Rousseau
> And old Hugo and the young Musset
> And Gide and Valéry
> And so many others as well.
>
> René Depestre, *"Face à la nuit"*

In some cases, however, at the very moment when the nationalist parties mobilize the people in the name of national independence, the colonized intellectual rejects his accomplishments, suddenly feeling them to be alienating. But this is easier said than done. The intellectual who has slipped into Western civilization through a cultural back door, who has managed to embody, or rather change bodies with, European civilization, will realize that the cultural model he would like to integrate for authenticity's sake offers little in the way of figureheads capable of standing up to comparison with the many illustrious names in the civilization of the occupier. History, of course, written by and for Westerners, may periodically enhance the image of certain episodes of the African past. But faced with his country's present-day status, lucidly and objectively observing the reality of the continent he would like to claim as his own, the intellectual is terrified by the void, the mindlessness, and the savagery. Yet he feels he must escape this white culture. He must look elsewhere, anywhere; for lack of a cultural stimulus comparable to the glorious panorama flaunted by the colonizer, the colonized intellectual frequently lapses into heated arguments and develops a psychology dominated by an exaggerated sensibility, sensitivity, and susceptibility. This movement of withdrawal, which first of all comes from a petitio principi in his psychological mechanism and physiognomy, above all calls to mind a muscular reflex, a muscular contraction.

The foregoing is sufficient to explain the style of the colonized intellectuals who make up their mind to assert this phase of liberating consciousness. A jagged style, full of imagery, for the image is the drawbridge that lets out the unconscious forces into the surrounding meadows. An energetic style, alive with rhythms bursting with life. A colorful style too, bronzed, bathed in sunlight and harsh. This style, which Westerners once found jarring, is not, as some would have it, a racial feature, but above all reflects a single-handed combat and reveals how necessary it is for the intellectual to inflict injury on himself, to actually bleed red blood and free himself from that part of his being already contaminated by the germs of decay. A swift, painful combat where inevitably the muscle had to replace the concept.

Although this approach may take him to unusual heights in the sphere of poetry, at an existential level it has often proved a dead end. When he decides to return to the routine of daily life, after having been roused to fever pitch by rubbing shoulders with his people, whoever they were and whoever they may be, all he brings back from his adventuring are terribly sterile clichés. He places emphasis on customs, traditions, and costumes, and his painful, forced search seems but a quest for the exotic. This is the period when the intellectuals extol every last particular of the indigenous landscape. The flowing dress of the *boubou* is regarded as sacred and shoes from Paris or Italy are shunned for Muslim slippers, *babouches*. The language of the colonizer suddenly scorches his lips. Rediscovering one's people sometimes means in this phase wanting to be a "nigger," not an exceptional "nigger," but a real "nigger," a "dirty nigger," the sort defined by the white. Rediscovering one's people means becoming a "filthy Arab," of going as native as possible, becoming unrecognizable; it means clipping those wings which had been left to grow.

The colonized intellectual decides to draw up a list of the bad old ways characteristic of the colonial world, and hastens to recall the goodness of the people, this people who have been made guardians of truth. The scandal this approach triggers among the colonists strengthens the determination of the colonized. Once the colonists, who had relished their victory over these assimilated intellectuals, realize that these men they thought saved have begun to merge with the "nigger scum," the entire system loses its bearings. Every colonized intellectual won over, every colonized intellectual who confesses, once he decides to revert to his old ways, not only represents a setback for the colonial enterprise, but also symbolizes the pointlessness and superficiality of the work accomplished. Every colonized intellectual who crosses back over the line is a radical condemnation of the method and the regime, and the uproar it causes justifies his abdication and encourages him to persevere.

If we decide to trace these various phases of development in the works of colonized writers, three stages emerge. First, the colonized intellectual proves he has assimilated the colonizer's culture. His works correspond point by point with those of his metropolitan counterparts. The inspiration is European and his works can be easily linked to a well-defined trend in metropolitan literature. This is the phase of full assimilation where we find Parnassians, Symbolists, and Surrealists among the colonized writers.

In the second stage, the colonized writer has his convictions shaken and decides to cast his mind back. This period corresponds approximately to the immersion we have just described. But since the colonized writer is not integrated with his people, since he maintains an outsider's relationship to them, he is content to remember. Old childhood memories will surface, old legends be reinterpreted on the basis of a borrowed aesthetic, and a concept of the world discovered under other skies. Sometimes this precombat literature is steeped in humor and allegory, at other times in anguish, malaise, death, and even nausea. Yet underneath the self-loathing, the sound of laughter can be heard.

Finally, a third stage, a combat stage where the colonized writer, after having tried to lose himself among the people, with the people, will rouse the people. Instead of letting the people's lethargy prevail, he turns into a galvanizer of the people. Combat literature, revolutionary literature, national literature emerges. During this phase a great many men and women who previously would never have thought of writing, now that they find themselves in exceptional circumstances, in prison, in the resistance, or on the eve of their execution, feel the need to proclaim their nation, to portray their people and become the spokesperson of a new reality in action. . . .

Much the same could be said about poetry. After the assimilation period of rhyming verse, the beat of the poetic drum bursts onto the scene. Poetry of revolt, but which is also analytical and descriptive. The poet must, however, understand that nothing can replace the rational and irreversible commitment on the side of the people in arms. Let us quote Depestre once again:

> The lady was not alone
> She had a husband
> A husband who knew everything
> But to tell the truth knew nothing
> Because culture does not come without making concessions
> Without conceding your flesh and blood
> Without conceding yourself to others
> A concession worth just as much as
> Classicism or Romanticism
> And all that nurtures our soul.

> René Depestre, *"Face à la nuit"*

The colonized poet who is concerned with creating a work of national significance, who insists on describing his people, misses his mark, because before setting pen to paper he is in no fit state to make that fundamental concession which Depestre mentions. The French poet René Char fully understood this when he reminds us [in *Partage Formel*] that "the poem emerges from a subjective imposition and an objective choice. The poem is a moving assembly of decisive original values, in topical relation with someone whom such an undertaking brings to the foreground."

Yes, the first duty of the colonized poet is to clearly define the people, the subject of his creation. We cannot go resolutely forward unless we first realize our alienation. We have taken everything from the other side. Yet the other side has given us nothing except to sway us in its direction through a thousand twists, except lure us, seduce us, and imprison us by ten thousand devices, by a hundred thousand tricks. To take also means on several levels being taken. It is not enough to try and disengage ourselves by accumulating proclamations and denials. It is not enough to reunite with the people in a past where they no longer exist. We must rather unite with them in their recent counter move which will suddenly call everything into question; we must focus on that zone of hidden fluctuation where the people can be found, for let there be no mistake, it is here that their souls are crystallized and their perception and respiration transfigured.

Translation from French by Richard Philcox

Jean Sénac (Béni Saf, 1926–Algiers, 1973)

DAWN SONG OF MY PEOPLE

for Baya

You said simple things
woman, worker of the morning
the forest grew in your voice
trees so deep that the heart is torn by them
and knows the weight of song
the mildness of a clearing
for the upright man who demands
a word of peace
a word of the size we are

You drew out of his solitude
the prowler who follows you filled with his shadow
the one who would like to write the way you see
the way you weave the way you sing
bring to the others the wheat
the goat's milk the couscous
and so dense in the heart and so strong in the blood
everyone's goodness
the impetuous charm of men in their solidarity

Speak O quiet flower weaver of promises
prelude to the certain awakening of the barley
say that soon the steel will refuse the throat
soon the *douar* will broach night
You teach me to think
to live as you are
of the Morning torn from the dark dwelling.

Algiers, 1949

NEWS IN BRIEF

for Mustapha Kateb

Bidonvilles bidonvilles
in the thistles anger
builds its nest
bidonville

One night a scream in the city
freedom
a thousand tigers lying in wait
awake the stubborn foreheads

Freedom
life's so close
death's on lookout

Whose fault
a man's
accused of screaming
accused of killing

It's but an abscess draining
bidonvilles
freedom

It's but a ear of wheat rising
in the blood
toward the good.

THE JULY MASSACRES

For the national holiday of free men
they massacred my friends
brown skin on gray cobblestones
O Paris how sad you are
sad and severe with my race

Here's the rootless tree
here's the beaten bark
the closed flower the burned fruit
and your big humid sun
freedom

Should one have escaped the injustice
the wound opened in the douar
the sun and the hunger of Algiers and Tunis
for the freedom of Rochechouart

O my double-crossed people
frustrated thrown into the shadows
my people savaged in its quiet hope
violent naïf my people of humans
who lose heart the sea and find blackness

One has to stand up while being torn
stand straight under the neon lights as they debase you
this taste of oleander and this smiling blood
that's the cold freedom of Paris

You'll bring it back like a pure bee
it will make the day in the houses' whitewash
it will write for all peace on the seasons
O fresh O joyous companion

This summer death is our salary
our break our dignity
comrades death and under your eyelids
the just morning of July

They massacred my friends
they raised the Bastille
they executed the flames and the scream

O Paris how sad you are
cactus blood covers the Seine
Paris of Beauty of Justice of Misery
how sad and severe you are for the exiles!

Algiers, 14 July 1953

Translations from French by P.J.

COMMENTARY

(1) Jean Sénac is without a doubt the poet with the most important oeuvre in Algeria, in terms of both quantity & quality. A very generous man & a major discoverer of new talent, Sénac lived through all the dramas, the joys, & the disasters of Algerianity. A vast part of his writings, deposited at the National Library of Algiers & in the archives of the city of Marseilles, remains unpublished. The published volumes—such as *Poèmes* (1954), *Soleil sous les armes* (1957), *Matinale de mon peuple* (1961), *Citoyens de Beauté* (1967), & *Avant-corps* (1968)—give us entry into a warmhearted, baroque universe, illuminated by a fraternal sun. Sénac sings love, freedom, & beauty with a certain naïveté & at times grandiloquence, though always with a treasure trove of scintillating images. His poetry resonates with the hope that Algeria, in his eyes, possesses. The revolution was not some abstract, bureaucratic concept for him but a body vibrating & part of a vivid inner life, with the elements of nature called to join the celebration. The assassination of the poet left his work unfinished & created major sorrow among all the poets he had welcomed with such ease:

The fires of my poor hood light up the future
This year I have received the lanterns of
Djamal Imaziten Hamid Nacer-Khodja
Boualem Abdoun Hamid Tibouchi
Abdelwahab Abdelghani Habib Tengour
Aïcha Bernier Abdelhamid Laghouati
Sebti's fort & Bey's hold up well
Happy new year then
Uphill road with aloes
From silex to jasmine the sign fortifies itself

(Akmoun manifests it)
Vertebral chorus—the Andalusian arc!—
Saw edge of fresh teeth, oh youth!

Alger-Reclus, 1971–1972

(2) We have divided Sénac's contribution, featuring him first here in the Fourth
Diwan, to foreground his involvement with Algeria's road to independence,
& then again in the Fifth Diwan (see p. 549) with poems that postdate the war
years of the 1950s.

Malek Haddad (Constantine, 1927–Algiers, 1978)

THE LONG MARCH

I am the final point of a novel that begins
Let us not forget everything above level zero
I sustain my romance intact between my eyes
Then, denying nothing, I set out once again
I am the final point of a novel that begins
No need to distinguish the horizon from the sky
You cannot dissever the music from the dance
And within my burnous my house survives
I am the final point of a novel that begins
Of my two Saharas I compose my song
I sustain my romance intact between my eyes
I am in truth the *pupil and the lesson*

Often I recall having been a shepherd . . .
Then in my eyes there's that long-suffering look
Of a fellah who watches in his unbreakable hands
The history of a country where the orange tree will be born
Often I recall having been a shepherd
I have sliced the galette
I have parted the figs
My daughters
   I have married well
It has no equal
To the gun
   To the task
      Than my eldest son
My wife was the finest in the valley.

Among us the word *fatherland* has a taste of anger
My hand has caressed the heart of palm trees
The handle of my ax opens an epic
And I have seen my grandfather Mokrani
Finger his beads watching eagles pass
Among us the word *fatherland* possesses a taste of legend

Daddy!
Why have you deprived me
Of fleshly music
See:
    your son
        learning to speak in another tongue
Words that I have known
Since I was a shepherd lad

Ah my God the night so much night in my eyes
Mummy calls herself Ya Ma while I say *Mother*
I have mislaid my burnous my gun my pen
And I bear a first name falser than my deeds
Ah the night my God but what's the good of whistling
Fear you're afraid fear you're afraid fear you're afraid
Since a man stalks you like some frightful mirror
Your school friends and the streets the jokes
But since I tell you I'm a Frenchman
just look at my clothes my accent my house
I who turn a race into a profession
Saying *Tunisian* when I mean "tradesman"
I who think of a Jew as some wretched homegrown
Soldier? Come on then, my sister wears no veil
And in the lycée didn't I take all the prizes for French
For French for French for French . . . in French?

Ah my God the night so much night in my eyes

Translation from French by Robert Fraser

Born 1927 in Constantine, Malek Haddad, a grade school teacher's son, always felt exiled inside the French language. After finishing high school in his hometown, he went to study law in Aix-en-Provence ("I could stay fifty years in this Provence I love & understand, this Provence that has inspired a number of my books, though without being a Provençal poet," he writes in *Les zéros tournent en rond*). He gave up his studies after 1954 & worked as a farm laborer with Kateb Yacine, contributing to various magazines & radio programs & writing poems & novels.

His much-contested essay *Les zéros tournent en rond,* published by Maspéro in 1969, condemned him to silence because it discredited all those who perpetuated colonial alienation by writing in French. After Algerian independence in 1962, Haddad moved back to Constantine & wrote for the national media. He was director of cultural affairs at the Ministry of Information from 1968 to 1972. The literary magazine *Promesse,* which he launched to promote young writers, did not last long. In 1974 he was named secretary-general of the Union of Algerian Writers. Struck down by cancer, he died on June 2, 1978, in Algiers.

Like the work of all the Algerian writers of his generation, his is marked by the struggle for independence, especially his prose texts. His poetry, of simple construction, remains lyrical, the image aimed at producing emotion in the reader. The poet often resorts to humor to create an effect:

And with peace returned
The dove will say
Give me a break
Now I'll be a bird again

Because of his extreme position concerning writing in French, Haddad triggered many concealed & malicious feelings of guilt in relation to that "foreign language," which muzzled many authors, to the benefit of the bureaucracy in power.

Kateb Yacine (Guelma, 1929–Grenoble, 1989)

NEDJMA, OR THE POEM OR THE KNIFE

We had readied two glasses of blood
Nedjma opened her eyes among the trees

A lute made the plains foam and transformed them into gardens
As black as blood that would have drunk the sun
I had Nedjma under the fresh heart inhaled banks of precious flesh
Nedjma ever since we started to dream many stars have collapsed behind
    us . . .
I had foreseen you as immortal as the air and the unknown

And now you die and I lose myself and you can't ask me to weep . . .
Where Nedjma are the dry nights we carried on our backs to shelter other
    slumbers!
The fountain where the saints galvanized the *bendirs*
The mosque to think the white smooth as a silk rag
The sea whistled over the faces thanks to the moons suspended in the water
    like balls of frost skin . . .
It was that poem of Arabia, Nedjma, that should have been preserved!

Nedjma I have taught you an all-powerful diwan but my voice caves in I am
    in a deserted music no matter how hard I try to throw away your heart it
    comes back to me decomposed
Yet we were named in the epic we have scoured the land of complaint we
    have followed the weepers when they laughed behind the Nile . . .
Now Algiers separates us a siren has made us deaf a sly windlass uproots
    your beauty
Maybe the charm has passed Nedjma but your water fuses under my
    deferent eyes!

And the mosques crumbled under the sun's lances
As if Constantine had arisen from the fire by more subtle arson
Nedjma was eating unhealthy fruit in the shade of the brushwood

A poet forsook the city followed by a sly dog
I followed the walls to forget the mosques
Nedjma smiled and dipped the fruit into her chest
The poet threw pebbles at us in front of the dog and the noble city . . .

And the emirs gave gifts to the people it was the end of Ramadan
The mornings rose up from the hills' steepest heat a perfumed rain opened
    the cacti's bellies
Nedjma held the reins of my horse grafted crystals on the sand
I say Nedjma the sand is filled with our footsteps gorged with gold!
The nomads are watching us their screams puncture our words like bubbles
We will no longer see the palm trees grown toward the tender hail of the
    stars
Nedjma the camel drivers are far and the last stage lies to the north!
Nedjma pulled on the reins I was saddling a dromedary muscular like an
    ancestor.

When I lost the Andalusian I couldn't say anything I agonized under her
    breath I needed time to name her
The palm trees wept on my head I could have forgotten the child for the
    leafage

But Nedjma slept remained immortal and I thought I touched her
   disconcerting breasts
That was in Bône in the easy days of the jujubes Nedjma had covered me
   with enormous palm groves
Nedjma slept like a ship love bled under her immobile heart
Nedjma open your great eyes time passes I'll die in seven and seven years
   don't be inhuman!
Search the deepest basins that's where she flows when her eyes close the
   nights like trapdoors
Cut up my dreams like serpents or else carry me into Nedjma's sleep I
   cannot bear this solitude!

Translation from French by P.J.

from **NEDJMA**

IX

. . . There could be no doubt that Rachid was very disturbed; he smoked,
slept hardly one night out of two, lying awake or roaming the city alone
or with me, for I attached myself to him as much as to Mustapha, though
unable to link them in the same friendship. As for Rachid, if he talked to
me at all (feverish words, outbursts followed by sullen silences), it always
seemed to be against his will. I felt our relations had become strained at the
same time that they were growing stronger; he was pretending to be calm
now; but he grew thinner from day to day, grew completely taciturn; then an
attack of malaria kept him in my room over a week; after violent fits of fever
that made his teeth rattle, sitting on the bed with a handkerchief tied around
his head, he collapsed into a strange light sleep, interrupted by seizures of
violent delirium, sudden awakenings that kept me up all night, impatient
and feverish in my turn, anxious as I was not to disturb Mustapha, who lay
against the wall, imperturbably unconscious, leaving early every morning as
though fearful of contagion, or foreseeing that Rachid would confide some-
thing to me when he awakened. . . .

   "Do you understand? Men like your father and mine. . . . Men whose
blood overflows and threatens to wash us back into their old lives like dis-
abled boats floating over the place where they capsized, unable to sink with
their occupants: we have ancestors' spirits in us, they substitute their eternal
dramas for our childish expectations, our orphan patience bound to their
paling shadow, that shadow impossible to dissolve or uproot—the shadow
of the fathers, the judges, the guides whose tracks we follow, forgetting our

own way, never knowing where they are, whether they're suddenly going to shift the light, ambush us, resuscitate without even coming out of the ground or assuming their forgotten outlines, resuscitate just by blowing on the warm ashes, the desert winds that impose the journey and the thirst upon us, until the hecatomb where their old, glory-laden failure lies, the one we'll have to bear after them, even though we were made for unconsciousness, for frivolity in other words, for life. . . . Yes, those are our fathers; every wadi ransacked, even the smallest brook sacrificed to the confluence, the sea where no springs recognize their own sound: agony, aggression, the void—the ocean—haven't we all seen our origins blurred like a stream in the sand, closed our ears to the underground gallop of our ancestors, played on our fathers' graves? . . . That old pirate Si Mokhtar, the fake father who brought me to this city, lost and abandoned . . . Do you know how many sons, how many widows he's left behind, without even forswearing himself? . . . He was my father's rival. Who knows which of them is Nedjma's father? . . . The old bandit! He told me about it a long time ago, before the last time we were in town, he followed me here without seeming to, knowing I was looking for his presumed daughter, Nedjma, he had introduced me to her himself; but he had talked to me before, in snatches, always in snatches, no one else could talk like that: ' . . . I wonder what came of all the old nights,' he used to say, 'nights of drinking and fornication; nights of rape and burglary, fights in every city we went to; fights in hallways and on terraces; fights in procuresses' houses . . . ' The chorus of women, women seduced and abandoned, he didn't think he'd forgotten a single one, the only ones he kept quiet about were the ones in our own family, for Si Mokhtar was descended like me from Keblout; he told me that later, when we were sailing on the Red Sea, after dropping off some pilgrims for Mecca. . . . That was before our last stay in Bône, long before. . . . And the old pirate told me a little more every day, but I still didn't understand his clown's confession, although he had already hinted at most of it: a congenital liar's story—caught in his own tricks, reduced to spitting out the truth by the sudden materialization of his own lies: ' . . . What escapes me,' he said, 'is the spawn, the vengeful spawn of all the mistresses seduced, the married women whose second husband I became just long enough to confuse the chronology of blood, to abandon one more piece of property to the suspect rivalry of two progenitures—one, tradition, honor, certainty, and the other, the offspring of a dry root that may never sprout, yet everywhere green and growing despite its obscure origin. . . . ' And the bandit, the second husband, neither polygamist nor Don Juan but only the victim of his monumental polyandry, cared no more about eliminating his legitimate rivals than he wanted their prolific wives. But he almost wanted to seduce their children, like a tree too high to attract the moss that would save it from the icy embrace of the deadly altitude; it was late to recognize his children, to see the childhood velvet climbing toward him—a childhood that was really his own, one he created by himself, and finally it was Si Mokhtar who capitulated, bending his trunk, ripping out his dead roots, seeking a hitherto alien lichen. . . . He was on the brink of the grave, stripped of the ancient luxuries of blood, a despot rejecting everything, not foreseeing that he was emptying his heart and only bringing the banal moment of his fall that much closer; it was no use appealing to paternity courts, to orphanages, not to mention to the mistresses who wouldn't look at his shadow any more. Not even a man in the street to proclaim at the hour of his death: 'I am the child of this corpse, I am a bud of this rotten branch'; but Si Mokhtar would end his days in ridicule; the clandestine wives had left him in doubt, as if, after accepting the sowing, they had annihilated or concealed the harvest; all the old pirate had left was the horrible conviction that the products of his crimes would always be secret, until they flowered around him, a grove where the plunderer finds only insomnia, the illusion of waking renewed while the sudden and studied matriarchal vengeance that all women must satisfy sooner or later takes its course, sacrificing to the primitive polyandry from which men have reaped only survival—women enjoying the fruits, men picking up the pits, each taking root despite the other—and now it was Si Mokhtar's turn to endure the matriarchal flight: the abandoned women who were poisoning his death drop by drop, weighing down his depraved body with the burden of the long, sticky tears he had blindly made them shed, from which rose now the ghost of a son like Kamel, husband of another problematic daughter . . . I will not speak her name again. And Si Mokhtar even had a semblance of certitude about Kamel, who had quite innocently invited him to his wedding, and he had brought me with him, probably so my presence would keep him—at the time I knew nothing, or almost nothing— from perpetrating some scandal or other. . . . Kamel's mother had been one of Si Mokhtar's few Constantine mistresses whom he had kept for several years, partly because he was sure of being her only lover and partly because he hated the class of puritanical nobility to which her husband belonged; finally, a curious rivalry had just developed among the deceived husband, who had his mistress too, Si Mokhtar, who wanted to get this mistress away from him after having already supplanted him in his wife's favors, and my father, who was then Si Mokhtar's closest friend: my father and Si Mokhtar had heard that the puritan, Kamel's legitimate father, had a foreign mistress, contrary to the sacred principles, the wife of a Marseillais notary who had run off with a Bône landowner. . . . "

Translation from French by Richard Howard

Born on August 2, 1929, in Guelma, Kateb Yacine came from a Berber family literate in Arabic; back in the past, their ancestor Keblout had revolted against the French occupation. On May 8, 1945, when the demonstrations of Sétif & Guelma broke out—historians today put the number of Algerians killed by French army & police units at fifteen thousand at least—the young Yacine was a boarder at the Sétif high school. He was arrested on May 11 & held for two months, after which he was not allowed back into school. During his detention his mother became insane. In 1946 he published a volume of poems, *Soliloques,* in Bône (today Annaba). Taken with the nationalist ideas of the PPA (Algerian People's Party), he toured Algeria & France, giving talks. From 1947 until his death, on October 28, 1989, Yacine's life was one long errancy through the world, through love & every kind of writing: journalism, poetry, plays, novels . . . His personality arouses passionate responses. Despite the numerous articles & studies devoted to him & his work, the author still perplexes, impenetrable & limpid at the same time, like the people that vibrated inside him & tore him apart. He is the only Maghrebian writer who became a mythic figure in his own lifetime.

In 1956 he published *Nedjma,* hailed as a major event by the greatest of the Parisian critics. *Nedjma* is a novel but also a poem of *amour fou,* mad love, & an ancient tragedy. Nedjma is a woman whose name translates as "star," "unreachable," "rebellious," & "indecipherable." It is essential to read this book—& to let oneself be carried away by its astounding, spellbinding style, to believe in its mysteries, to love it & grow irritated with it so that that unknown, Algeria, may unveil herself. Or the loved woman! Like all great precursor texts, it becomes clearer over the years, without, however, losing any of its power. *Nedjma* has marked all Francophone Maghrebian literature—deeply. Maghrebian authors never wrote again as they had before.

In 1959 Kateb created an Algerian theater with *Le Cercle des représailles,* in which the Algerian drama becomes a classical Aeschylean tragedy. In 1970, his *L'Homme au sandales de caoutchouc* expressed tangible solidarity with Vietnam in its struggles against American imperialism. These plays, because written in French, were not performed in Algeria, & after *L'Homme au sandales de caoutchouc* Kateb stopped writing in French. Wanting to be closer to his people, he dedicated himself entirely to a theater in the Algerian vernacular Arabic. His exemplary play, often reworked for a given occasion & through time, called *Mohammed, Grab Your Suitcase,* played throughout the country & in the working-class suburbs of the great European cities with strong concentrations of immigrant workers.

Through his popular theater, Kateb had hoped to get out of *la gueule du loup,* the wolf's clutches or the lion's maw, & to find again "at the same time his mother & his language, the only inalienable treasures," which he regretted having lost, as he writes in his last great text, *Le Polygone étoilé* (1966). In 1984 he started to write again, encouraged by Jacqueline Arnaud, but death came too quickly, leaving the work incomplete. The funeral was turbulent. Goodbye, revolution. Algeria was tilting into a long, dark night. For more by Kateb Yacine, see p. 554.

Ismaël Aït Djaafar (Algiers, 1929–1995)

from **WAIL OF THE ARAB BEGGARS OF THE CASBAH**

I would like to break out in rage
in howling arm-raving rage
in a fury like people who know
how to rage

by smashing their
fists down on tables, breaking them
to get what they want
I want to cut loose
on account
of sweet little Yasmina
who didn't want to die
but who's dead
a few days ago
on the Rue Franklin Roosevelt.

Khouni Ahmed is a 42-year-old
beggar . . .
But with stomachs full, the children of Charlemagne
sing a song
they learn at school:

> *Frère Jacques! Frère Jacques!*
> Dormez-vous
> > Ding! Dung! Dong!

The cold is mute
The cold says nothing
It simply kills
kills people
by natural causes;
it especially kills poor people who have only mattresses
of cardboard to sleep on
and wrapping
wrapping
wrapping
paper with which to cover themselves.

When it has a good day,
that goddamn current of icy air
which freezes every stone and wrapping paper, and who's wrapped in
it,
twirling and romping on through
the arcades of the Rue de la Lyre,
Charlemagne,
hopscotches
from male sleeper
to female sleeper
and from the sleeping child
to the sleeping old man
and from the tubercular sleeper
to the BCG* one,
and so on
for 500 yards of cardboard
and wrapping paper
and 127 mummified cadavers
in the arcades.

Before dying, little
Yasmina
        slept there
        with her little papa
        who murdered her
        simply
        abruptly
        with the fatherly pat
                        (and not at all nasty)
of a hardworking conscientious
peasant, who sows the tiny nine-year-old
seed
in the furrow
on the treads of a big truck passing
and grinding by.

Translation from French by Jack Hirschman

*BCG is bacillus Calmette-Guérin, a tuberculosis vaccine.

Ismaël Aït Djaafar is a child of the casbah of Algiers & the author of one single book: *La complainte des mendiants arabes de la Casbah et de la petite Yasmina tuée par son père*, published in Algiers in 1951, reprinted in January 1954 in Jean-Paul Sartre's *Les Temps Modernes*, & then reissued & staged several times. Here is what Kateb Yacine (see p. 321) wrote in his preface to the 1987 Bouchène edition: "Aït Djaafar and I are born in the same year, 1929, a year of world crisis, and we met when we were twenty, in the days of the great hopes. . . . I loved the caricatures he would show me from time to time, in the small cigarette shop where he helped his father, on Rue Patrice Lumumba. . . . To begin with a miscellaneous news item: the nearly daily drama, turned banal, of a young girl assassinated by her father. You had to be Aït Djaafar to make a poem out of it. And what a poem! A long wail of pain, so violent that afterward you discover in it the imminence of the storm, the announcement of the November events. This complaint, by itself alone, is enough to make a poet of Aït Djaafar."

Anna Gréki (Batna, 1931–Algiers, 1966)

THE FUTURE IS FOR TOMORROW

For all my sisters.

The future is for tomorrow
The future is for soon enough

The sun of our hands takes on a wild light
in the naked anger that rises to our mouths,
multiple memory makes the future ripen,
this memory sweet to the tooth. In prison
being free takes on the single sense of our loves,
love the precise voice of these endless struggles
that have thrown us in there, standing
on the graves of olives and men.
The cruelty of our life will be understood and justified.

The future is for tomorrow
The future is for soon enough

The future expresses itself very badly like
a hesitant tongue. And the doubters,
blue with fear, declare they've lost their minds,
the past remains future in this still-born flash
of those who devoured the earth, lived with backs turned

and invent the idea of being free, this eighth sin,
a capital one like capital punishment.
But the stubborn dawn inseminates our nights,
the guillotined future lifts its head again.

    The future is for tomorrow
    The future is for soon enough

The guillotined past lifts its head
and these women, proud of their bellies
crimson from giving birth, every dawn
these women blue with patience
who have too much voice to learn how to keep quiet
with their hands—the leaves—on our feverish bodies
with the leaves—their hands—planted in the sky
wisely move the frontiers of life
like taming a star, like killing it.

    The future is for tomorrow
    The future is for soon enough

Beyond, the closed walls like clenched fists,
through the bars that circle the sun
our thoughts are vertical and our hopes.
The future coiled in the heart rises towards the sky
like arms raised in a gesture of farewell,
lifted and rooted in the light
as a call, a sign of love, of return, oh life!
I draw you to my breast, my sisters,
builders of freedom and tenderness,
and I tell you till tomorrow because we know

    The future is for tomorrow
    The future is for soon enough

EVEN IN WINTER

Even in winter the day was nothing but a sweet orchard
When the Guerza Pass would swell under the snow
The grenadines were scarcely more than fruit—only
Their leather skin bloodied by gluttony
We'd hide in the bristling scrub to laugh

And the guns were only seeking game.
And if the granite mountain was blown up
By dynamite, it was my father the teacher
plowing along the road in his Citroën.
None of the houses needed doors.
Because the faces opened up in faces.
And the scattered neighbors were simply being neighbors.
The night didn't exist because one slept through it.

It was in the Aurès
At Menaa
The mixed municipality of Arris
As they say in the newspapers
My childhood and the delights were born there

At Menaa—a mixed community of Arris
And after twenty years my passions
Are the fruits of their choices
From the time when the birds who'd fallen from their nests
Would also fall from Nedjaï's hands
To the depths of my Shawia eyes

Chilly as an iris
My friend Nedjaï
Naked under his blue robe
Would run in the shadowy evening
Slipping on the grey scorpions
Of Oued El Abdi.
Beyond the brilliant jackals
That laugh with their throats wide open.
And standing in a sharp angle, smooth
From the height of his stilts
to see clearly he'd launch
The moon with a slingshot.

Now there is the war too in my village;
It has folded up its kilometers of joy
Like the grey under-wings of a butterfly
Polymorphous and brooding under tin roofs.
On all the germinating happiness that has disappeared

Outside . . . no more orchards with their sweet silks
That made the wind sweeter than a bee.

No longer the sound of Nedjaï's bare feet
On the roots of my childhood, buried
under the sediment of fear, of hate, of blood
because it is the blood that beats in Oued El Abdi
and rolls the scorpions fat like the wounds
that will be the sole survivors of the martyred bodies.

It is the war
The sky foaming with helicopters
Blown up by dynamite
Hot earth gushes and slides
In a sauce of honey
Along the bursts of blue faience
Of white sky
The sounds of propellers
Have replaced the sounds of the bee

Aurès is shivering
Under the caress
Of secret transmitters
The breath of liberty
Being divulged by electric waves
vibrates like the stormy fur of a wildcat
Drunk with a sudden oxygen
And finds the way of all breasts

The sounds disappear
In the balmy atmosphere in time
It is the mute war
Behind the doors of Batna
On the screen of my youth I follow
a silent combat
in slow motion

In the light of my age I admit.
That everything in this world that touches me to the soul
comes from a mountain range painted pink and white on the maps
in the fifth-grade geography book
and resembles it through I don't know what liquid joy
in which my childhood had faded.
Everything I love and do now

Has its roots back there
Beyond the Pass of Guerza at Menaa
Where I know that my first friend will wait for me
Because he has grown in the flesh of my heart. If
The world that surrounds me has aged by twenty years
He keeps in his skin my Shawia loves.

Translations from French by Kora Bättig von Wittelsbach & Gail Holst-Warhajt

COMMENTARY

Colette Anna Grégoire, who adopted the pseudonym Anna Gréki, was born in Batna in 1931, the daughter of a grade school teacher, & interrupted her university studies in Paris to join the struggle for Algeria's independence. Arrested in 1957 & jailed at Barberousse (the infamous civil prison in Algiers), she was expelled from Algeria & could only return after independence in 1962. She completed her BA in French literature in 1965 & became a high school teacher in Algiers. She died in childbirth in 1966, leaving her work unfinished. Gréki only published one volume of poems in her lifetime, *Algérie capitale Alger* (P. J. Oswald). The work was published in Tunisia in 1963, with a facing-page translation into Arabic by Tahar Cheriaa & a preface by Mostefa Lacheraf (see p. 295). Gréki's poetry is marked by her political choices—& charged with the promise of a better future, despite the horrors of the colonial war; she praises the courage of the women who have joined the struggle & tells of her closeness to her native land, the Aurès.

Henri Kréa (Algiers, 1933–Paris, 2000)

from *LE SÉISME AU BORD DE LA RIVIÈRE*

Scene I

. . . Young maid.—I wanted to tell her the story
of a princess who played hopscotch at
her palace doors with a fish
whom she followed, a slave to his entreaties
for seven years during which
she was in turn
beggar and orphan
lover and lovelorn

she was even suspected of theft
though she was but a mute accomplice
as the fish made her cover his game
in the shops where she worked
cleaning the floors of the wealthy
She dealt with grief as with a cheating spouse
married to the king's son
she bore him seven children
whom the fish stole in succession
taking care to cut off one little finger
from each of these innocents
to place them in the sleeping maid's mouth
who found herself seven times
accused of the most heinous crime
/though she knew the culprit she never absolved herself/
her distraught lover had her imprisoned
in a henhouse where one fine day
he found the mother surrounded by her children
the fish had no doubt completed his task
since he was never seen again.
/This raucous dream where the captive smiles at her betrayer/
is but a whimsical subversion of the tale
for the normal course of things
often alters its sublimation
which is starkly refuted by reality
in a doomed flourish of hope
that soars as the phoenix
from its burning nest.

Scene 2

Voice

I am reminded of a love slain
by the rules of the game
a love that rose above illusion even
as it sought the fount of knowledge.
The crime had been premeditated

according to experts
from those climes where the cold
renders men as dimwitted
as a spinning top.

The crime was perpetrated
with a fitting sangfroid
to place the poet first among equals
in a crowd. How very futile, he reflected,
to have once thought himself a hermit.

CLANDESTINE TRAVELERS

For Hubert Juin

I

We lived in abject poverty
In a garret
Its skies so close
Yet forbidden
We barely had enough bread
To avoid death
Our clothes wearing thinner
By the day
We had driven apart
Both child and mother
We said nothing
Hoping always
For tomorrow's mystery
To wring from us
A little more misery
Yet forever
Passionate and unbowed
In spite of it all
Truly, madly, deeply
We loved life.

2

The twilight is golden as a market day
And the earth is laden with rocky clouds
And the water in venomous spasms
Is returned to the rim of the sky

3

Water embodies itself

4

At the thought of frost
Its course is encrusted
On the pale bed of its restless night
And the grass is painted blue by the force
Of its light
Dissolved by the sun
Before it too disappears

5

O how love pretends indifference . . .

Translations from French by Madeleine Campbell

COMMENTARY

An Algerian-born poet, dramatist, & novelist whose work deals with alienation & identity, nature, heroism, & moral & social change in his home country, Henri Kréa, like the hero of his first & only novel, *Djamal* (1961), had a French father & an Algerian mother. He attended secondary school in Blida & later in Paris, at the Lycée Henri IV. Starting in 1955, he published his poetry with P. J. Oswald (in Paris) & collaborated on a number of artists' books with illustrations by Matta & Abdallah Benanteur, among others. Living in Paris from the early 1960s on, he kept himself increasingly apart from the publishing & literary scene, though he continued to write quietly. He died there in December 2000.

Kréa's oeuvre includes novels, plays (*Le Séisme au bord de la rivière*, 1958), and above all poetry—unhappily but unsurprisingly too little known, given the small editions in which it was published. The title of his 1960 collection, *La Révolution et la Poésie sont une seule et même chose* (Revolution and Poetry Are One and the Same Thing), lays out what he saw as his process, which evolved toward a more intimate relation with the world.

THE ORAL TRADITION II

More Kabylian Origin Stories

THE ORIGIN OF SHOOTING STARS

When God drove Satan out of Heaven, the latter returned to earth.

One day he stole a haystack from some humans. The criminal angel took his plunder at night and flew into the air. In his mad rush, he dropped armfuls of hay, which caught fire in the sky.

This is what we now call shooting stars.

THE FIRST ECLIPSE

An old sorceress who wanted to cast spells made the lunar star fall into a big dish of couscous, causing the first eclipse in human history. This phenomenon created a great panic among men.

As she wanted to push the limits of her achievement, she also wanted to capture the sun. Like she did for the moon, she prepared her large dish, invoked some magic formulas, and the miracle was produced. She took a sickle and frantically beat the water in its large dish. The bubbles from the emulsion rose into the sky in myriads. The amount produced was so extensive that in a few moments the sun darkened, decreased in volume, and . . . fell with all its weight on the plate.

The day turned into a horribly black night, thus creating widespread panic.

Upon discovering the distress that she had caused, the sorceress was seized with remorse and considered the gravity of her act. Those who knew her begged her to restore the luminous disk to its usual place.

The darkness had lasted too long. The sorceress had to act quickly before the world sank into eternal darkness. This was the first known solar eclipse in human history.

The old sorceress tried to restore the light by any means, but in vain. The men gathered around her began to panic. They approached her, torches in hand, threatening to burn her alive. Filled with remorse, she began to invoke God in these terms:

Oh, my God!
What a grave error I have committed:
I brought down the sun,
Which illuminated men,
I have taken their light
And now they threaten me with death.

God, angry, responded to her:

The sun will retake its place
On only one condition:
Give in exchange
The life of one who is dear to you.

Cornered, having no choice, the old sorceress was forced to accept the deal. The sun retook its place for the price of one human being. This was the first human sacrifice in the world. Since then, the solar star shines in the firmament.

THE ORIGIN OF MENSTRUATION

At the time of the appearance of the first humans on earth, men had periods under their right armpit.

One day a couple went to the village festival. It was that time of the month for one man. He put a towel under his arm and accompanied his wife. Upon arriving in front of the *tajmaat* (the agora of Kabyle men), he raised his right arm to greet them. But he dropped his towel. To hide his "shame," his wife rushed to pick it up. Panicking, she did not know where to hide it. She had only one idea: to put it between her legs. Since periods were contagious, the woman got them, and the man found himself to be cured ever since.

Today, during her menstrual period, the woman need not prepare meals, work in the garden, plant, pray, or fast.

Translations from Djamal Arezki's French versions by Steven Weber

The Magic Grain: A Tale

May my tale be beautiful and unfold like a long thread!

Long ago, in a village, there were seven brothers. They got together and said:

"This time, if our mother gives birth to a boy, we will go into exile. We'll run away."

The day their mother was to deliver, they left the village behind and waited, seated in a circle.

Settoute, the old witch, came up to them and said:

"Welcome to your brother!"

They answered her:

"Damn you!"

And they set forth immediately.

Settoute had lied. She wanted the seven brothers to go into exile. The family was increased not by a son but by a daughter.

The mother watched over her. When she was grown, the girl would go fill her goatskin at the spring. But one day she met Settoute there, who was drawing water with an acorn cup. The girl said to her:

"When will you be done filling your pitcher with that cup? If you're not in a hurry, let me get by!"

Settoute replied:

"How dare you speak like that, you whose seven brothers went into exile the day you were born?"

The girl returned to the house with her goatskin empty. Fever took hold of her. Her mother in tears drew close to ask:

"What's wrong, my child? Just a little while ago you went out healthy and happy. What evil things did they say to you?"

The girl then told her, but she asked her mother to explain Settoute's words.

"My child," swore her mother, "your seven brothers said to one another: 'If an eighth son is born, we will run away without seeing him, without knowing him.' It's been fifteen years since they left, and we haven't heard a word."

The girl declared:

"I will go search after them and bring them back."

Her mother tried to restrain her:

"What's the use? We looked all over for them. I only have you now."

But the girl replied firmly:

"Since they don't know me, they won't run away from me."

So her mother gave her a horse, some provisions, and a black girl to accompany her. She gave her in addition the Magic Grain, which the daughter slipped into her bodice, and told her some very important advice:

"On your way, you will come across two springs. One is for black women, and the other is for white women. Take care not to bathe in the spring for blacks or to drink its water! You will be changed into a black girl!"

The daughter promised to heed all the wise counsel, and got on her horse.

So she started off, followed by the black girl. From hill to hill, stopping point to stopping point, the mother called her daughter. The girl, who heard her thanks to the Magic Grain, would thus respond to reassure her. And the Grain transmitted her weak and distant voice.

When the springs came into view, the black girl rushed toward the water for white women and bathed in it. The daughter approached the spring for blacks, drank from it, and plunged in. Then, when she was getting on the horse, she lost the Magic Grain.

As she drew farther away from the place where it had fallen, the girl heard her mother's voice less and less. There even came a moment when she could no longer hear it at all. And her skin was darkening, while the black girl's skin was getting lighter.

When the black girl had become completely white, she turned to her companion and said arrogantly:

"Get down off your horse!"

But the girl refused. As soon as she had reached a big boulder, she started to sing in a plaintive voice:

"Rise up, rise up, boulder,
boulder, rise up,
so that the land of my parents
can appear to me!
A nasty black girl tells me:
'Get down so that I can climb up!'"

A melancholy echo responded:

"Go ... Go ... Go ...!"

The frightened black girl did not insist. But a moment later, impatient, worn out, she said again:

"Get off the horse, I say!"

The girl called her mother in vain. Since the Grain no longer replied, the black girl forced the daughter to get down. She stripped off the girl's clothes in order to put them on herself. Then she got on the horse and struck a dignified pose. The poor girl had to follow on foot.

At last the travelers reached the village where the seven brothers lived: the house was pointed out to them. They had left to go hunting. . . . The girls waited for their return. In the evening, when they came back, the black girl drew toward them, kissed them, and said:

"My dear brothers, I have lived long enough now that I see you! Settoute insulted me. She told me that coming into this world I had chased you from our home. Settoute—may she burn!—deceived you. And now here I am! Must I stay among you or will you accompany me back to the home of our father and mother?"

They replied:

"Rest a few days. We'll think about it."

The black girl settled in to look after the house of the seven brothers. The daughter had to serve her and lead the camels to pasture. Each morning the black girl would give her a coarse biscuit made of barley flour. No sooner did she arrive on the heights than the daughter would start to sing with a plaintive voice, surrounded by the seven camels entrusted to her:

"Rise up, rise up, boulder,
Boulder, rise up,
So that the land of my parents
Can appear to me!
The black girl stays at home
While I look after the camels,
Weep, camels, as I weep!"

She set the barley biscuit on a stone and let herself starve. Six camels did as she did and wept with her. Only the seventh, which was deaf, took the opportunity and ate. The six camels also became as thin as nails.

One day the youngest brother wondered:

"What's going on? Since that servant came here, she's only been wasting away. And the camels are wasting away like her. There must be a reason."

He resolved one morning to go out before the girl, to get to the spot where the camels grazed and hide himself nearby. He saw the girl hike up to the top of the hill. He saw her set the biscuit on top of all the others she hadn't eaten, piled up on a stone. And he heard her sing with a plaintive voice:

"Rise up, rise up, boulder,
Boulder, rise up,
So that the land of my parents
Can appear to me!
The black girl stays at home
While I look after the camels,
Weep, camels, as I weep!"

The youngest brother came out of his hiding place and questioned the girl. He said:

"Who are you, creature?"

She answered him:

"Me? I am your sister. When I was in my father's house, I went one day to the spring, and there I found Settoute, who was drawing water with an acorn cup. I told her: 'Give me your turn!' (I was in a hurry.) She replied: 'How dare you speak like that, whose seven brothers went into exile the day you were born?' I told my mother: 'Explain to me what Settoute meant by those words.' She explained, and I went off in search of you. My mother gave me a horse, a Magic Grain, and a black girl. On the way I came across two springs: I used the wrong one. I bathed in the water for blacks, and I lost the Grain that connected me to my mother. The black girl, who bathed in the water for white women, turned white, and I turned black. But I am the one who is your sister."

The youngest of the seven boys returned among his brothers and repeated to them what he had just learned. But they didn't believe a word of his story and told him:

"How shall we recognize that this servant is really our sister?"

So they consulted the Old Wise Man. They told him how the camels were wasting away and how they wept; how they shared in the sorrow of the servant girl who looked after them. The Old Wise Man listened to them and said:

"One thing could not be changed for the real black girl: her hair. Her skin may well have become white as milk, but her hair will remain frizzy. The girl whose hair is smooth, she is your sister. But the black girl will not want to remove her head scarf in front of you. So announce to them both that you've bought them some henna and say: 'Today is a holiday. We would like you to dye your hair with henna in front of us.'"

The seven brothers brought the henna. The servant crushed it into a powder and mixed it into a paste, which she offered to them. So the oldest one ordered the two girls to take off their scarves. The servant obeyed, and her hair spread out in skeins of silk down to her waist. But the black girl cried out:

"My dear brothers, how could I uncover my head in front of you? I would be ashamed! When you've gone out, I will coat my hair in henna."

The youngest brother tore off her scarf. And a mass of spiky hair appeared, sticking up toward the sky.

The seven boys surrounded the black girl and said in a menacing tone:

"So you are the black girl? You have stolen our sister's place!"

They turned toward their sister to ask her:

"What would soothe your heart?"

She answered:

"I would like her head for an andiron, her foot to poke the fire, her hand to shovel the ashes."

So they slit the black girl's throat. They burned her up and spread her ashes outside. Then they brought their sister some water drawn from the spring for white women. She bathed with it. Her face and her body became as light as before. The seven brothers were able to go back to their favorite pastime: hunting. Their sister prepared the meals and kept house.

In the spring of the following year, where the black girl's ashes had been scattered grew a mallow stalk. The girl cut it and made a dish with it that she offered to her seven brothers when they came back from hunting. They all ate with a great appetite. The seven boys were then changed into wood pigeons and the girl into a dove.

And they all took off into the sky.

My tale is like a stream—I have told it to Lords!

Translations from Taos Amrouche's French versions by Jason Weiss

Kabyle Proverbs

—The cat says:
    May God damn the people
    here in this house
    & may he make them go blind
    so I can steal
    all I want

—But the dog says:
  May God make these people
  be fruitful & multiply
  & then have them each
  give me treats
  A mouthful from everyone
  so I can feel full

—Toss me one of your babes, says the Ogre
  Or I'll blow your house down

—Walk following your feet
  Not following your eyes

—You sold me rotten onions
  I slipped you a counterfeit coin

—Who dares tell the lion: *your mouth smells like shit?*

—Whoever has beauty has status
  Even the god of the dead stands in awe

—The rock said: "This head hurt me bad."
  The clump of earth replied: "There's nothing left for me to say."

—Those near to you are still your best bet:
  Marry them, don't sell them off.
  For good or bad, this is the hand you've been dealt.
  You can never get rid of them.

—One hand to caress you
  the other to burn a hole
  through your skin.

—The rats on the outside
  drive off those in the house.

Translations by Jerome Rothenberg from Taos Amrouche's French versions

Songs

CHILDREN'S RAIN SONG

Judeo-Arabic, Morocco

o the rain drop drop drop drop
o the farmers' little sons
o the landlord Bu-Sukri
o the trip down by the river
o his tumble down the well
o his mother's red tarboosh
o the one-eyed man one-eyed
down the silo in the dark
the wind the wind o the bellows
o my uncle o the bellows
it's the blacksmith's bellows
blacksmith gropes his way around
then calls out children
o my children in the forest
they call Papa
buy a shirt or Papa
buy a black shirt
shirt with carrot-colored sleeves
we eat it all up
whatever there is to eat

"O NIGHT LIGHTS OF JEW TOWN"

A Song of the Hara

Judeo-Arabic, Tunisia

o night lights of Jew Town
lift me up carry me
to my grandfather's house
my grandfather o my sultan
took out his cashbox & gave me
four coins that he gave me
to fix up my shoes
—my shoes are at the judge's

but the judge is unhappy
his wife screams all morning
at the roast meat sausages—
black maid o unwashed maid
lift your eyes to heaven
sky's dripping water
the married couples sitting
with apples in their hands
smells of acid & perfume
—o jews o jews
have you seen my uncle Moseud
playing the *gayta* & the lute
while the little dog bites at him
& I say "that's all right!"

Translations by Jerome Rothenberg

from *The Adventures of the Jew*

Judeo-Arabic, Tunisia

I. THE BRIDE WHO WAS TOO LARGE

One day a cry rose from the wedding house. Everything was ready, the guests were seated, the hors d'oeuvres were piled up in the kitchen, and the orchestra was waiting. Everybody's waiting for the bride. And where's the bride? Why, there she is! She's climbing up the stairs, she's starting to come through the door. My God, what agony! The door's a little low, while she, the bride, the lovely woman, is too large, she's taller than the door. How will she get inside? What can we do for her? We waste ourselves in huddles and discussions. This is a disaster without end. Should we renounce the bride? Should we smash the door? While everyone is at it, someone says: "Call the Jew. Only the Jew can rescue us from this disaster."

Someone goes looking for the Jew. He arrives, looks at the bride, looks at the door, raises his clenched hands, and brings them crashing down on the bride's head. The bride says "ouch" while drawing in her head. He tells her: "Go and enter now."

People throw themselves upon his neck and hug him. Someone showers him with gold.

2. THE TAIL OF THE COMET

Once the Jew traveled into a country of yokels. He passed by an orchard, where he spotted a stream of running water. The day was warm. He took his handkerchief, dipped it in the water, and stretched himself out in the shade of the tree. He stretched himself out for a siesta. He fell asleep. Evening came, but the Jew was so tired that he went on sleeping.

The people came out into the city for the evening, and the muezzin climbed the minaret of the mosque to call them to prayer. He turned from side to side, and as he faced that tree (in the shadow of which the Jew was sleeping), he said: "My God, the tail of the comet!" And he began to cry: "The tail of the comet! The tail of the comet!"

When they heard him, the people began to run in all directions, weeping, shouting: "It's the end of the world, the tail of the comet has appeared." The noise startled the Jew, who woke up astonished and said: "What's going on? They're saying that the world's in ruins!" He walked down to the city. Seeing the people in tears, he asked them: "What's wrong? Has some catastrophe befallen you?" They answered: "Don't you see? It's the end of the world, the tail of the comet has appeared." The Jew raised his head and saw that they were looking at his handkerchief (which he had hung up in the tree) and trembling. He told them: "That's it, huh? Tail of the comet, huh? What will you give me to get rid of it for you?"

"What will we give you? Why, what will we give you! We'll dress you up in gold: just lift this affliction from us, that's all we ask of you."

He told them: "Stay right here, don't budge."

The Jew went out of the city, came to the orchard, examined his handkerchief to make sure it was dry, folded it in four, put it in his pocket, and came back down.

He told them: "See, I've lifted this affliction from you." The women looked at one another and uttered cries of joy, the men embraced one another. And the Jew, loaded down with all his heart desired, made his way to Tunis.

They're out there, and we're back here.

Translations by Jerome Rothenberg

More Riddles and Proverbs

from the Ayt Souab, Anti-Atlas, Morocco

RIDDLES

—What is whitewashed without an opening? The egg.

—What leaves as an old man and returns as a young man? The waterskin.

—There's always three of them, all the way to the country of the Ihahen: the hearthstones.

—What is long and throws no shadow? The road.

—Two blacks, always girded: kettle and couscous pot.

—What is long, though thyme be taller? The road.

—What carries a little sickle wherever it goes? The scorpion.

—One enters, two knock on the door: cock and balls.

—A mineral known to the whole world but not yet exhausted: salt.

—What creature satisfies all men by taking all need from them and yet men do not like it? Death.

—Name a well into which only its own cord descends: the cleaning rod and the gun.

—Among the creatures that don't talk, which one did God tell what to do? The bee.

—Among the creatures that don't talk, to which did the Prophet talk? The ants.

PROVERBS

—Who calls on the wind can't weep in the straw.

—Who wants flour better use his legs to turn the millstone.

—Only your hand can scratch your itch.

—Who asks scholars to read him the whole Qur'an shouldn't complain when they empty half his butter jar.

—The hearth provides only for its own needs.

—Lack of patience will give you the runs.

—Who shuts up will be saved.

—Be content with little and you'll eat your fill.

—Stand apart and you won't be splattered.

—Fire is different for the one it warms than for the one it burns.
—Ask for directions and you won't get lost.
—Who wants to eat a lizard calls it by another name.
—The thatch doesn't fuel the oven.
—Only two hundredweights can hold up one hundredweight.

Adaptations & translations by P.J. from Jean Podeur's French versions & dialectical Arab transcription

Satirical Nomad Poem

Constantine region, Algeria

his saber's a stalk of devil's dung,* its guard's made of clay;
    wading through a field of purple salsify, he mows them down.
his rifle's hammer's made of sparrow-wort, the trigger's flour dough,
    the flint a sliver of friable sandstone.
he hunts gerbils, & mice too—& brings home
    two thousand canned frogs

Translation by P.J. from a French version by Marc Arnaud

Saharan Gharbi/Western-Style
Anonymous Nomad Songs

I

I love you so much, don't you know that?
I love you so much; will you blame me for that?

How sorry I felt for the camel,
and how sorry I felt for his screams,
when his throat was slit and his blood gushed out.
The girls kept him tied and refused to set him free.

  *Asafoetida.

2

Oh horse breeders!
Go south and spread the news.
Will someone do me a favor
and reach the southern star?

My beloved hasn't her like among women
when she gracefully walks about
like an arched cloud in the west
struck by blazing lightning.

She wore a tinkling *khalkhal* around her ankles
and a finely chiseled silver necklace
when she snuck down the path to the river
and met her hiding man.

3

My land lies amid distant green valleys
and the indigo of faraway hills.
Facing al Maiymuna in the west
and Sidi Khaled to the east,
Djebel al-Hodna stands erect
like a mirror for the slender Derrajiyate.
He who has long left his loved ones
can only cry over his fate.

4

The summer has come!
There is no green grass left.
Every leaf in my land has dried.
How sad is my heart!

O Sahara, what's wrong now
that the rainy clouds have come?
Your ruling masters are hiding
but I keep praying to these hills.

Translation from Arabic by Abdelfetah Chenni

Writes the compiler & translator Abdelfetah Chenni: "Those Saharan Gharbi/ Western-style anonymous nomadic songs are wonders, particularly when, as I do, you recall your grandmother's sad, soothing voice singing the magical words in their Gharbi melody. Saharan melhun poetry is easily distinguishable from urban melhun [see Ben Msaieb, p. 232], not only because of the obvious linguistic & thematic differences but mainly because of the spirit that inhabits the beduin qasida [see Benguitoun, p. 244, & Sheikh Smati, p. 247]. This spirit also entails a qualitative difference in musical terms when these texts are sung: both vocals (usually solo) & instruments (such as the *gasba*, a reed flute) are particularly expressive in Saharan Bedouin melhun."

The Derrajiyate are women from the Ouled Derraj tribe.

from *Sirat Banu Hilal* (II)

SADA BETRAYS HER FATHER FOR LOVE OF MERI

We are still with you in this popular tale that in the vulgar tongue describes the stages of the Banu Hilal's wanderings.

My brothers, after Bou Zid's lament about himself, his health, and his past and present situation, our tale now returns to Sada, the daughter of Znati Khlifa.

Time went by and became long for Sada as she obtained nothing from Meri, and she told herself: "How much longer will he be jailed close to me like a bird, while I suffer bitterly! I have to tell the Banu Hilal how to war with my father; if Znati Khlifa doesn't die, I will never be able to marry Meri."

So what will she do now? She decides to go out at night and walk to the Banu Hilal's camp to incite them to fight her father. But when she reaches the walls of the city, she finds the gate closed and the night porter refusing to let her cross the threshold. A long discussion ensues as Sada tells him:

Oh Mansur, you the porter,
open the gate in the wall
let the virgin go visit
the encampment of the beduins.

He said to her:
      Sada I'm afraid
of something unexpected
they'll call me a prankster
and I'll fall prey to sadness

—Come on, man
I won't betray you
just a moment and I'll be back
with you instantly
—Oh, virgin, no, no
I'm scared to be punished
I'll be in trouble
and they'll tear me to pieces
—Oh shut up
shush those worries
it's dark night now
nobody will see us
—Oh best of mistresses
wait for morning
when the land will be lit
and dawn will have come
—Oh porter, why
all these worthless words?
I'm not going to wait,
in an hour or less . . .
—Virgin, go away
your father has instructed me
if he was to find out he'd throw me
into one of his bottomless jails
—By god, oh porter
why this reservation?
Offer your pity to this youth
and you'll reap honors and well-being
—No, turn back, it's better,
enough! Don't insist
I'm scared of the Emir
Khlifa, son of Mohrane
—Listen to me, porter
open the door and raise me up
you can't stop me
and this sally is necessary.

The porter tried as best he could to dissuade Sada from going out, but he found in her not the slightest desire to renounce. She left under the veils of the night and came to the tent of Sultan Hassan. She stayed outside; the black man came toward her. Sada was the most beautiful of the Zenati girls, and she loved Meri with a very great love. The singer went on:

The black man went on order of his Hilali master
to see who was coming toward them
he returned with a lively step to the sultan
hurrying, pushed by a violent wind.
"Tell me, Massud, what's so important?
Speak quickly and give me the news."
Massud answered: "I saw a magnificent thing,
the work of the Creator, the One, the Victorious,
resembling the polar star, gem among the stars
on her face the flowers of rosebushes bloom
like the gazelle in freedom running wild
her cheeks are a burning sun
onto her shoulders her hair cascades
like a dark night,
they fall in thick braids down her back
her teeth are like shining gold
when she smiles they resemble the light of dawn
God has given her total beauty
hers is a priceless splendor."
The king went out and saw her with his own eyes
and found the slave's words to be true.
The king said: "By god, this is a happy moment
that thing there dizzies the mind.
Ask, O young girl, whatever you want
your wishes shall instantly be fulfilled."
"Let me make the following suggestions right away
I'm in a hurry and have to return to the palace
my father and family are tough in battle
and they don't submit to saber or fire
by God, I've lingered too long
using a ruse I came to you
send for Diab immediately, do not wait
it is he who will save the encampment from danger
this is the straight road and the voice of salvation
it is the only true way out."

She went to Sultan Hassan's tent, and Chiha came out to meet her and
asked about Meri, Yahya, and Younes; then Sada stepped toward Sultan
Hassan and said to him: "It is necessary that my father be killed by no
one else than Diab; if you want to seize the city, the answer is Diab Banu
Ghanam." He answered her: "How to go about it?" "Go bring Diab back
from the western parts."

Lord Hassan had quarreled with Diab, hadn't he? He can't send for him, and tells himself: "No matter that the encampment will be destroyed, wiped out! Send for Diab and tell him to fight Znati Khlifa? No, a thousand times no, may the Banu Hilal's camp be exterminated, I don't care." He incited the Banu Ghanam to fight Znati Khlifa. Every day the latter killed a hero from among them, and this until he had exterminated eighty men from among the Banu Zaghba of Diab's family. All valiant knights, and Sultan Hassan watched each fight as a spectator. Diab's father, called Ghanam, was an old man of seventy-five, an old man carrying a heavy load of painful years that had brought the death of his son Judge Bu Dir, of his grandson Nasr, of Khfaji Amer, of Hamza and Brahim and other war heroes. Finally, unable to bear it any longer, he went up to the palace of Znati Khlifa and met him face to face. An old man of seventy-five! What did Znati Khlifa say?

Oh old man, you have come   led by your fate
you throw yourself into the fire   the incandescence of quick war
this will be your last day   your life will come to an end
of this earth you will take leave   killed, engulfed
turn back   consider your person
your head is white on the outside   empty on the inside
today your fate has given you   into my hands
you will leave   shredded to dust by my horses' hoofs
a whirlwind from the sky   has thrown you down here
Znati moves toward you   a torrent raging with flood waters
your hour has come   you'll cross from life into death
as far as war is concerned   you lack all cunning
as far as I'm concerned   it will be my feast
your blood will remain   splattered over the ground
then I'll wipe out   any traces you've left
your mind is small   your intelligence limited
go back to your tent   and fulfill your pious rituals
worship God the One and Only   the Venerable One
you will have fulfilled   what your duties ask of you
for what pushes you   into this war like scorching fire?

•

Ghanam has prepared himself   for his battle with Khlifa
and answers   with clear and sensible words.

•

Znati rushed forward   lets out a great scream
pouncing   and advancing
thrown upon a live fire   flaming
he is an evil devil   his thrust's poisonous.

And now Mister Ghanam addresses Znati Khlifa in response to the lat-
ter's speech:

You think I have no   strength left
I'm still the horseman warrior   pouncing on his enemy
you are about to suffer an ordeal by my hands
this date will remain   forever engraved in the annals
war, you should know   is the beduins' business
and for as long as there have been men   the prerogative of the hilali

.

And the two met up like a pair of infidels
and whirlwinds of dust envelop their horses
Ghanam is riding his best charger
in battle it zigzagged like a pigeon
from dawn until darkness
covers the light of the day
and lowers the veils of night and all is darkness
the saber sounds loudly like violent thunder
and you can't tell the white from the black combatants
and blood runs like the water of the sea
and war, like all-devouring fire, roars
since dawn has shown its first light
and even before the sun's appearance
Ghanam has thrown himself into the warring furnace
like a lion he thrashes about and his thrusts are fierce
but he stumbles and falls upon the ground
Znati turns toward him advancing for the kill
Ghanam's family and brothers all together surround him
and drag him away so that he not be lost and shredded
and between them hard battles were fought
and their war dragged on and lasted three days.

Translation & adaptation by P.J. of Lucienne Saada's French version

FIFTH DIWAN

"Make It New": The Invention of Independence I

The countries of North Africa came into their independence in different contexts and after vastly different experiences and struggles—something that had lasting repercussions, including differently shaped futures for each of them. The often violent upheavals of indigenous societies caused by colonialism, although indisputable, varied depending on local circumstances. The Algerian case could be seen as exemplary in this regard. Indeed, the country was colonized in the middle of the nineteenth century after a long and arduous conquest opposed by a very spirited and persistent resistance. Several different politics of integration were applied to appropriate this territory and include it in the French nation, but with no success as far as assimilation was concerned—and these measures uprooted the peasantry and disintegrated the traditional social frameworks, leading to the extinction of the local elites and undereducation in the Arabic language, which was pushed back exclusively into the religious sphere. "French Algeria" was a settler colony and not simply a protectorate like Tunisia or Morocco, so the relations between the communities there always remained antagonistic. Finally, the Europeans had to leave each of these countries—either en masse, as in Algeria, right after an independence won after a total war that lasted eight years, or else progressively, as in Tunisia and Morocco, where the confrontations were shorter and less passionate and lethal. Note also that the Algerian Jewish minority of Berber origin was naturalized as early as 1870 through the Crémieux Decree, thus cutting it off from other indigenous groups, while in Tunisia and Morocco the Jewish minority had the same status as the native Muslim populations (see Jacques Derrida's reflection on the Crémieux Decree in his essay *The Monolingualism of the Other, or The Prosthesis of Origin*, p. 478). This explains the much greater implication of the intellectuals from a Jewish background in Tunisia and Morocco in the struggle for independence, as shown by the examples of Albert Memmi and Edmond Amram El-Maleh (see p. 289).

If there was a good side to the evils of colonialism, it was that it woke the Maghrebians up, forcing them to think of themselves as having one autonomous identity (or several) and to find the adequate forms to articulate these identities. As in the other African states, independence forced the Maghrebians to get down to the task of constructing a nation-state, which demands a mobilization of civil society around a vision of a shared future. That the world age in which this happened was the cold war obviously had specific impacts on the task at hand. Of course writers and intellectuals—in a Gramscian vision of the "organic intellectual"—were asked to put their shoulders to the wheel. However, the coming to power of undemocratic regimes that had no inclination to let artists and critical thinkers roam freely did not favor the cultural and artistic renaissance one might rightly have expected.

After gaining its independence in 1956 following a relatively short period as a French protectorate, Morocco reinstalled its monarchy and its King Mohammed V, whose prestige was great among not only Moroccans but all Maghrebians. His son Hassan II succeeded him in 1961 and was noticeably less popular. Hassan started a conflict with Algeria in 1963—known as La Guerre des sables (The War of the Sands)—that would have sequels in the memory of the Algerian army. He had to face the Casablanca riots of 1965 and, as could be expected, repressed them violently, declaring a state of emergency that would last until 1970. Several aborted coups marked his reign. In November 1975, the king triggered the Green March in an attempt to annex Western Sahara. His regime was especially merciless to the political opposition and left-leaning intellectuals, many of whom were assassinated (the Ben Barka Affair being a salient example of this) or spent unconscionable amounts of time in jail—to mention but a few: Abraham Serfaty, Abdellatif Laâbi (see p. 668), and Saïda Menebhi, who died in prison after a hunger strike. Today Hassan's son Mohammed VI, who succeeded him in 1999, conducts a somewhat more open policy bent on reconciliation and conducive to a cultural and artistic renewal, though the monarchy's *mainmise* on the wealth of the nation continues unabated, via a few international and a series of national companies beholden to the king that enrich his family and the chosen few.

After Tunisia acceded to independence on March 20, 1956, Habib Bourguiba, the leader of the Neo-Destour nationalist party, abolished the monarchy of the Beys and became the first president of the Tunisian Republic, in November 1959. He gradually established a single-party secular regime with hints of socialism, though he abandoned his more progressive policies following the riots against the collectivization of land in the Sahel in 1969. In 1975 Bourguiba was proclaimed president for life. Paradoxically, police repression did not diminish the fighting spirit of the Tunisian General

Trade Union (UGTT), and the Tunisian League for Human Rights was created in 1977. Despite a climate of corruption, clientelism, and floating uncertainty about the future linked to the president's illness, civil society kept developing, just as Islamic fundamentalism did, despite fierce repression by the iron fist of Zine el-Abidine Ben Ali, then the minister of the interior—who, on November 7, 1987, removed Bourguiba from power on the pretext of senility. Elected president with more than 99 percent of the vote, Ben Ali set up a police state using the excuse of the struggle against religious terrorism. The corruption orchestrated by his wife's clan, the Trabelskis, the level of unemployment among an often highly educated youth, and the wear and tear of the exercise of power caused the eventual collapse of the regime. The Tunisian revolution, the beginning of the Arab Spring, sparked by the self-immolation of young Mohamed Bouazizi on December 17, 2010, is still a work in progress. Rather than resolving the cultural strife between modernist-secular and traditional-religious factions, the rise of Islamist parties and their coming to power through parliamentary elections has brought the conflict to a head—leaving the future uncertain at the time of this writing.

The independence of Algeria, on July 5, 1962, after an eight-year-long armed struggle in which close to a million people lost their lives, was painful to say the least. The summer of that year saw the mass exodus of the *pieds-noirs* ("black feet," the name given the French born in Algeria) and violent conflicts between the leaders of the FLN (the National Liberation Front) and those of the ALN (National Liberation Army). On September 4, the army entered Algiers and effectively took power. Ahmed Ben Bella (1918–2012) was nominated president of the Algerian state and elected first president of the People's Democratic Republic of Algeria in September 1963—with the FLN as the sole party. The coup of June 19, 1965, called a "revolutionary leap," did not question the regime itself but only the bad management and the demagogy that were tarnishing the image of the state. Colonel Houari Boumediene became president of the Revolutionary Council, whose aim, in his words, was to create a "serious democratic state, governed by laws and founded on morals." Starting in 1971, Boumediene and the council set in motion a triple revolution—agrarian, industrial, and cultural—by triggering, after long debates, radical reforms that reorganized agriculture, the socialist management of the national companies, and the democratization of education.

At Boumediene's death, the Revolutionary Council appointed Chadli Bendjedid, the highest-ranking military officer, as a candidate for the presidential election. The Chadli era was characterized by a surface liberalization and a cultural opening, though the regime pursued a policy of Arabization while repressing the Berber movement. The progressive abandonment of the country's socialist direction and achievements and the rise of unemployment among the more and more highly educated youth ended in the popular uprisings of October 1988. In an attempt to redress the situation, the regime moved toward democratization by opening the political game and allowing the creation of political parties. This move benefited the Islamist currents, which under the label of FIS (Islamic Salvation Front) gained a majority of votes in the first round of legislative elections in December 1991. The army put a stop to the elections, claiming that the (forced) resignation of President Chadli had created a "constitutional vacuum."

This disguised coup led to a hidden civil war that lasted for a decade (and indeed is still smoldering today). The transition was assured by Mohamed Boudiaf, one of the "historic leaders" of the November revolution, but he was assassinated after six months. Without getting into the details of this story "full of sound and fury," suffice it to say that one had to wait for the election of Abdelaziz Bouteflika to the presidency in 1999 to see the country regaining its confidence. In 2004 he sought and gained a second mandate. Today Algeria seems tired, and its youth, desperate to find viable jobs, dream only of leaving. A disillusioned climate of wheeling and dealing amid a profound weariness, not to say exhaustion, paralyzes most creative activity. A constitutional amendment permitted Bouteflika to seek and gain a third term in 2009, following a traditional practice of Arab heads of state.

Libya was the first North African state to accede to independence, in 1951, under a monarchy headed by Idris I, the grandson of Sheikh Senussi, the founder of the brotherhood that carries his name. In December 1955, Libya became a member of the United Nations. One year later the Libyan American Oil company discovered oil, and it became the major African oil producer by the 1960s. The country then began to develop and to come out of its isolation. In 1969, Colonel Muammar Qaddafi overthrew the monarchy to install a Jamahiriya, a direct democracy of the masses, as outlined (in a not uninteresting way) in his *Green Book* (in imitation of Mao's *Little Red Book*), though in fact this dream of a "third way" (different from the capitalist-parliamentarian and authoritarian-socialist ways) quickly turned into a dictatorship headed by Qaddafi's clan. His regime, toppled in the latest installment of the Arab Spring in 2011, though extremely long-lasting— for over forty years—was also extremely fantastical and unpredictable, on both the national and the international scene. This is not the place to go into details about the disconcerting politics of the Guide of the Libyan Revolution, but what is certain is that his regime's demagogic authoritarianism, combined with the embargo imposed on the country, did not favor cultural or artistic activity in an area still strongly marked by tribal structures and the predominance of the group over the individual.

The aspirations toward and hope for a unified Maghreb, which had cemented the struggles for independence by the various national Maghrebian movements, were strongly put into question once individual states obtained their independence. The different regimes used ambiguous nationalist rhetoric and played at political one-upmanship while keeping a tight control on their borders. The complex evolution of the cultural, and especially literary, developments since independence has reflected all these vagaries. The Francophone poets and writers went on publishing in France and the Arabophone poets and writers in the Middle East or their own countries, depending on the political climate. Specifics of literary developments can be found in each country's subsection.

LIBYA

Contemporary Libyan literature is rich and shows signs of great fecundity. Back in the nineteenth and early twentieth centuries, what came to be known as the Arab Renaissance—*al-Nadha*—emanating from the Mashreq, only reached Libya late and without exerting a major influence. But autochthonous oral traditions, always present, came to a new and powerful flowering, spurred on by the sufferings and injustice visited upon the Libyan people by Italian colonialism. Core figures in this resistance and renewal movement were Sulaiman al-Barouni, the publisher of the *Muslim Lion* newspaper, and the prominent poet Rafiq Al-Mihadawi, whom the Libyans considered highly, calling him the national poet.

Contemporary Libyan writing, however, remains for much of the world limited to one name, that of the most famous Libyan novelist, Ibrahim al-Koni, rightfully considered one of the great prose stylists in modern Arabic. Minimally distributed and sparingly translated, Libyan literature has a width and a depth that are relatively little known even to the Arab-speaking public—never mind in the West. For a long time it was confined to small intellectual and artistic circles, due to the lead weight of repression that Muammar Qaddafi's authoritarian regime extended over cultural and political matters. During its forty-year reign, for example, the regime allowed only one publishing house to function in the country, which published only authors who at least acted as if they supported the government. Starting in the early 1990s, censorship laws were somewhat loosened, creating a breath of fresh air that allowed for a measure of literary renewal, so that in 2007 some 120 new literature and poetry titles were published through the official publishing house. As Ashur Etwebi (see p. 373) says: "An active world of literature and poetry has developed in Libya over the past thirty years. Little is known about this in Europe, because to the West, Libya did not exist on the world map until recently." Indeed, the Tunis-based Tunisian-Libyan publishing house Maison arabe du livre has published some major works of Libyan narrative literature.

It is in the domain of the short story that Libyan literature has excelled in terms of both quantity and quality, with Ali Mustapha Mosrati and Khalifa Husien Mustafa being among the genre's major voices. The past decade has also seen the emergence of Arab-language poetry of a modernist facture. It is thanks to translations into English by the Libyan-American poet Khaled Mattawa (see p. 384) that much of this poetry began to gather a wider audience beyond the borders of Libya. It will be fascinating to observe developments in the post-Qaddafi era.

Muhammad al-Faituri (b. al-Janira, Sudan, 1930)

THE STORY

And Bidpai said:
the thieves have stormed
across the harbor mole,
they've broken the ship's mast
and plundered its precious cargo,
the captain is still
searching through the alleys
for his old telescope.
It is this story, Dabshalim,
I see unfolding, chapter by chapter.

INCIDENT

And Bidpai said:
while the clowns laugh
the corpse is dangling
like a windless flag
from the gallows,
the sun is white-haired in the sky.
It could well be, Dabshalim,
that what we see with open eyes
comes sated with the blindness of the core.

THE QUESTION AND THE ANSWER

—With what sword shall I
strike down tyranny?
—With the sword of the weak of the earth,
Bidpai answered.
—What fire will burn
the winding sheets of death?
—The fire of humiliation,
Bidpai said.
—And how might I make man anew?
And Bidpai answered:
—You will make him if you fall
while standing up for him.

Translations from Arabic by Sargon Boulus & Peter Porter

COMMENTARY

Muhammad al-Faituri was born in 1930 in al-Janira, Sudan, to an Egyptian mother & a Sudanese father with Libyan family ties. He spent his childhood in Alexandria, Egypt, before moving to Cairo, where he studied Islamic sciences, philosophy, & history at al-Azhar University until 1953. That year, he published his first book of poems, *Songs of Africa*. His other poetry collections include *Sunrise and Moonset, Music of an Errant Derwish,* & *Lover from Africa*. He has been in the employ of the Libyan government ever since becoming a Libyan citizen. His poetry has taken on wider horizons as he has come to address the large Arab audience & to write about political freedom & other Arab problems.

Ibrahim al-Koni (b. Fezzan region, 1948)

from **ANUBIS**

Dusk

WITH THIS BLOODY ESCAPADE commenced my break with the herds. Thereafter my animal kin shunned me and braved the heights to cross over into unknown realms.

The gazelles migrated to the north, crossing lofty, sand-strewn peaks to cast themselves into the mighty sea of sand. The Barbary sheep clans migrated to the south, scaling the circle of southern mountains and crossing into the trackless deserts that lead to mountain chains with surging peaks, about which the tribes recount fantastic legends as part of epics handed down from their forefathers. I first followed the gazelles' trail in their journey northward but then retraced my steps rather than tackle the sandy slope that cast me down to the oasis one day, for I remembered that gazelles are a species extraordinarily hard to capture when traversing sandy ground. I conjectured, on the other hand, that I could catch up with the herds of Barbary sheep, which are slow creatures on the difficult plains that dot the southern desert before it reaches the mountain chains of whose impregnable heights fantastic legends are narrated. The hope for escape for Barbary sheep is always weaker when they enter a sandy area. The hope for escape for gazelles, conversely, is weaker when they enter mountainous terrain, as time-honored proverbs assert.

I scaled the mountain but had trouble ascending the highest boulders leading to the summit. So I fell back on my wits and sought easier passageways through the chain's westward extension. That took me the whole day, and dusk fell before I discovered a gap. As darkness overtook me, I cast about for a sheltered place where I could spend the night. Stretching out in a hollow at the base of a column-like boulder, which was suggestive in its majesty of an idol, I surveyed from my lofty perch the low-lying areas where my oasis looked a modest plot no different from the groves of acacia or retem in some of the valleys of the northern desert. When I cast my eyes upwards, the bare, dispassionate sky spoke to me in a stern tongue. As it addressed me, I pondered the cause for the temporary insanity that drove me to pursue creatures that shunned me. Had gluttony motivated me to chase after them? Was gluttony an illness, a need, or an appetite? Was I pursuing them and risking my life in their pursuit out of a longing to capture beauty, which for some unknown reason I felt I could not live without? Was my pursuit motivated by fear of solitude? Was my pursuit occasioned by some other unknown cause? Was I pursuing because man must always pursue, so that even when he finds nothing to pursue, he invents a prey, albeit fictitious, deceptive, or imaginary? Was I pursuing them merely out of stubbornness, because these creatures that had so recently constituted my kin had banished me from their ranks in the course of one day, leaving me a fugitive, alone, and shunned, so that I resembled no one so much as a bastard, desert Anubi? Or did my motivation actually lurk deep within a whispering appeal that told me this rejection was not a rejection but a portent embracing an awe-inspiring truth related to my truth, which no stratagem had allowed me to discern in myself?

I wondered and wondered until my head hurt so much it was ready to burst open. Sleep carried me off before I could reach any answer to any question. I awoke to a dawn that was still cloaked in darkness. I sped away at that early hour, acting on the counsel of the Barbary sheep community, which recommends: "Travel in the morning, rising at dawn, in order to reach your destination."

I struggled past the stone monoliths until dawn receded and a firebrand was born on the horizon. I climbed a forbidding cliff face and found I was ascending the mountain's summit from its western side. Because of the gloom, I was not able to discern the full extension of its foothills. I groped my way through a relatively easy opening but was unable to make out the lay of the land until the darkness was routed and light prevailed. The region was filled with mountainous knobs of gloomy hue and modest elevation. These were spaced out and scattered at some points and in other locations smack dab together. They rose at times and fell in other places till the plains terminated them. All the same, their average height remained constant, even though they were paralleled at the rear by true mountain peaks. Thus the oasis at the bottom appeared to be in a pit rather than on a plain.

I discovered dung from Barbary sheep on the sandy blazon encircling the haunch of one of these knobs. When I rubbed it between my fingers, I found it was still fresh, but the ewe's trail disappeared where the sandy band terminated. So I made for the heights, knowing that Barbary sheep would typically be satisfied with no other type of refuge. I persevered till midday without finding a single ewe. My throat was parched, my tongue and lips were dry, and my body had shed its sweat reserve. I saw that I had forsaken sound counsel when I failed to respond to the inner voice that had advised me all along to desist and turn back before it was too late. I searched for a shrub or boulder that would afford me some shade until the noonday heat passed, but the soil was of that grievous type the tribes say was cursed at some time; a fiery heat emerging from the center of the desert had scorched it, wiping out all vegetation until even plant seeds had disappeared. The only crop its dirt produced was stones.

I resolved to turn back but thought I would never survive unless I found a place where I could shelter from the siesta-time heat. I committed another error for once again I ignored the little voice and went forward, hoping to run across some shade behind the hill, which was bathed by waves of mirages.

I pressed forward, but the hill retreated ever farther away the more I advanced toward it, as if fleeing from me. I remembered the tricks mirages play in the northern desert and felt certain that I had fallen out of the pan into the fire and that confusion had once again led me into harm's way. My vision was blurred, and I started to see double. My body shook from a weakness that struck without warning. I felt dizzy, dropped to my knees in a grim, eternal solitude, with a scorching earth beneath me and a furnace overhead. Only then did I understand that my crime lay not in venturing farther into the desert than I should have, but in entering the desert in search of anything other than water. I realized at last that although the fates had provided me with everything I needed, I had rebelled and set forth in search of something I had never needed. I deserved the fury and punishment of the sun-baked earth.

I perceived clearly that a sip of water was all I needed. Why had I disdained the bold stream, the springs, and life in general to set out like a madman in search of a figment of the imagination and a lie, substituting for life a shadow of life? Now I had landed myself in life-threatening isolation, where I was searching for a drop of moisture in a rocky desert. I did not even dare to think about the copious supply of water I had left behind, since all I dreamt of was some shade to shelter me from the blazing sky and to preserve in my body all of the lost treasure I could salvage.

I crawled for a distance, but the scorching earth burned my hands. I licked them and fell on my stomach and elbows. I began to wriggle forward on my belly like a snake but was not able to wriggle far. I lay on my back. My face was burned by the punishing sun and my back by the punishing earth. I burned until I no longer felt the inferno. I sensed I was about to pass out. I do not know how long I was unconscious, but the sip of water that saved my life certainly preceded the prophecy I heard from the mouth of the emissary who stood above my head: "It is not wise to neglect what we have in order to search for what we lack."

He placed the mouth of his water-skin in my mouth, and the water poured down my throat. I could feel it flow through my body and spread into my blood, restoring my faculties to me. I regained the ability to use my hands and grasped the water-skin with thirst's insanity, attempting to empty it into my belly in one gulp, but the emissary seized it, pulling it away from my mouth. "This is the answer," he said. "This is the secret. It is all about greed."

I was thirsty. I had returned in an instant from a trip to the unknown. My dream was to provision myself with more of the antidote that had rescued me from the ghoul's grip. I made a sign with my eyes. I begged with my eyes, because—like others who have fallen into the ghoul's grip and then miraculously returned to the desert of the living—I had lost the ability to speak. Even so, the apparition kept the water-skin out of my reach while he proclaimed sagely: "You had a comfortable living bestowed on you, but you betrayed your covenant."

My tongue, however, stammered with the wisdom of the thirsty: "Water!"

"You received water and betrayed it by setting out on a journey. Where are you heading? Where?"

"Give me a sip, and I'll tell you a secret."

"No one who has disavowed his secret has a secret."

"Did I disavow my secret by setting forth in search of food?"

"We provided you with the fruit of the palm for nourishment. So don't lie."

"Dates are a lifeless form of nourishment."

"Lifeless?"

"Any nourishment devoid of that riddle named beauty is lifeless food."

"Beauty is a treasure that gives life, not a deadly ordeal."

"How can one seize beauty, master?"

"Beauty always evades us if we set out to search for it."

"Master, I have never dreamt of obtaining anything so much as I've dreamt of obtaining beauty. When, however, I departed one day to search for my father, I lost my way and was not destined to return, for I found myself stuffed into the jug of metamorphoses."

"Do you see? This was your punishment. You should not search for anything you do not find in your heart. You are beauty. You are your father. You are prophecy. You are the treasure!"

He chanted his words as if reciting verse. He swayed right and left, as if in a trance. He uttered groans of pain reminiscent of those of people overcome by longing. My faculties were restored and life began to pulse through my body. I said, "I gave up searching for my father one day and decided to look for Targa, but the spirit world cast me into an oasis whose name I don't even know."

"What the spirit world wishes for us is always nobler than what we wish for ourselves."

"I don't understand."

"The oasis whose name you don't know is real, but Targa is a false illusion."

"I don't understand."

"Targa too is a lost oasis."

"I've heard members of my tribe speak of caravans that left for Targa."

"Caravans that leave for Targa don't return. It is the lost caravans that head for Targa."

"Targa is lost, the law is a lost set of prophetic admonitions, and the people of the desert are a lost tribe. Are we, then, bastard children of heaven like Anubi?"

"Each one of us is Anubi; each a fleeting shadow."

"But . . . who are you?"

"I am a fleeting shadow."

Because of my fatigue, dizziness, and ordeal-induced daze, I was not able to make out his features clearly, but sparks in my heart tried to tell me something. "Has the spirit world not brought us together before?" I asked.

He stuck to his enigmatic response: "I'm naught but a fleeting shadow."

The sparks in my heart illuminated a corner veiled by darkness, and I pulled myself together and struggled onto my elbows. I clung to his blue veil, which gleamed indigo in the twilight. Unaware of what I was doing, I shouted, "Not so fast! You are my father! Are you my father?"

He stared at my face for a time. His eyes narrowed to slits, but when he opened them again I detected an attractive smile in them, the smile of a child who has received what he wants. I struggled against vertigo once more but heard his prophetic admonition clearly: "What need for a father has one whose father is the heavens?"

"I heard a maxim saying that a father is the antidote for misery and that a creature who has never discovered his father will never be happy. So, who are you?"

He continued to gaze silently at me. The childish smile in his eyes twinkled brighter and became more affectionate and tender. I smiled too, for I sensed intuitively that he was preparing to give me some good news. I wished he would be quick to quench my thirst for the truth before my heart grew confused and I passed out again. He, however, took his time, deliberately I supposed. Just when I felt the whispered onset of unconsciousness I heard him say: "I'm you!"

Translation from Arabic by William M. Hutchins

COMMENTARY

Ibrahim al-Koni was born in 1948 in Libya of Tuareg descent. He spent his childhood in the desert & learned to read & write Arabic when he was twelve. He studied comparative literature at the Maxim Gorky Literature Institute in Moscow & then worked as a journalist in Moscow & Warsaw. One of the essential Arabophone writers of this age, he has published some fifty books—of short stories, novels, poems, aphorisms, & so forth—translated into a range of languages. Available in English (besides *Anubis,* extracted here) are the novels *Gold Dust, The Animists, The Bleeding of the Stone, The Puppet,* & *The Seven Veils of Seth*—but no volume of poetry or essays. In 2008 he received the Sheikh Zayed Prize for Literature for his novel *Nida'ma kan ba'idan* (Calling the Distant). His oeuvre as a whole is profoundly inspired by the desert & the nomadic culture of the Tuareg. As he put it in a recent interview: "As is inevitable with one's birthplace, the desert buries enigmatic signs in the souls of its natives that slumber deep within and one day must awake. The signs that my Great Desert planted within me have made me a poet and a seeker after the truth of this world."

Ashur Etwebi (b. Tripoli, 1952)

from **OF SOLITUDE AND A FEW OTHER MATTERS**

Solitude: pursuing his fleeing dreams, a young girl turning her head toward us at the crossroads, a scarf revealing a lily neck as it slips off, a green bird beating its wings looking at life for the first time, water gurgling above thirsty rocks, nipples hardening on blossoming breasts, winter investing Abidine Square, deserts that no longer count the years, an old man nodding, smiling, at the top of the mountain.

Thus solitude arrives, thus stupor remains hanging from the side of a book.

•

It's as if you were staring at emptiness
as if your soul had become a dwelling for scarlet spiders
a pillow for the skull's viper
and the sly dragon's fire.
The head of the tribe did not speak
with two pale fingers he stirred the sand
his gaze running over your deeply hidden valley.
The sun clambers up the carpet of hours
you leave with a river about to disappear.
We dance together and laugh for a long time.

•

A bird before a lit bread oven, from its wings fall the dreams of ripe figs.
I see a mouflon with golden horns roll its dreams before him,
the sighs of scared people folded on his back
I see a field where the waves of an amorous sea feast on food and drink
I see the palm trees' calm and perfidious seduction's agitation
I see a world standing on two legs waiting for its sacred incense
I see what you don't see.
Is it the Last Quake predicted by Alif and Mim
Or is it Alif an outstretched column striding ahead on the straight road.

•

A woman without desire
her stone roses, sumptuous

her breasts, two salted rivers
her face, ambiguous cruelty
her belly, planes, horses, and bulls
in her arms the days sleep white
white like the sun
   the white
   sun.

   •

Two kites
Two saffron roses
Two transparent threads of glass
Tell of the sufferings of earth and sky
So said to me the man died from cold

   •

A bird in the neck
around the neck a jasmine necklace exhaling a desire of humid loam
"Done, the awakening of the fire," I said aloud
"don't raise the feet above the frivolous marble," said the taciturn chamberlain
"the passersby crossing the bridge asleep dream of a faraway childhood,"
said a raised iris.
"afraid of slanderers he hid his dark words under his hat," insinuated the
gestures of the royal orchestra conductor or at least that's what the royal
analysts explained.

"move your hands, make us hear the ardent iron's clatter and smiling
bravely step up to the edge of the abyss," said the young bride while
lighting sticks of sandalwood.

   •

may your crown have three pyramids
so that you'll be granted fairness wisdom and a long life
the witches of the south advised you
the short hammer, grab it with your right hand
so as to ground your power
and may men submit to you like slaves
the old blind man from the land of truffles advised you

fasten bunches of ripe black grapes to your chest and drape a garland made
of last year's corn around your neck
the devoted guardian of the western gate advised you

make my throne from the four pillars forest's cypress wood you'll soak the
wood for a long time in olive oil
do not hammer any nails into the wood, let it stand for forty days facing the
sea, forty guards shall watch over it without their breath ever touching its
surface, anoint it with the menstrual blood of forty virgins and none of you
may say a word of this in either of the two worlds
you advised your men in the first year of your reign

·

from the heart of the oak forest he patiently watches over the sea
algae float over his body, feed off the salt of his dreams
hunter of naked words, he lays the balls of light down on two mountains
                and carefully sieves the waves of the sea, one by one.
the oil flask gently absorbs the perplexity of the shore
and the shiver of the wait.

·

the dark blue exchanges his old new dream with the debauched apricots.
On the western section of the great arc stars that don't lift a hand in the
immense space and don't murmur anything sit down.

·

in the universe's belly button, the throne of eternal poems struts about like a
royal vessel—neither noise nor silence
the earth brings its wine out from under its mantle and offers a drink to the
shepherds come from beyond the desert.

·

who is hiding their body in the clay?
maybe the seller of truffles? Or is it the thief of laughter?

·

in the high room, a bed and red apples
the poem worms through the window, on the threshold the butterflies weave
the sheets of faraway winter
in the high room temptation burgeons on the blue walls, the cup runneth
over with forbidden desires
two flasks swimming through the air pour the live beings' seminal liquor
into a river of "compression and expansion"
the male and female swimmers, into their game, follow their bodies boiling
with life, offer their bare busts to the caresses of the supreme stallion and
rend without sinning the stream of lasciviousness.

    •

a body dies when it looses the shiver
a tongue gets drunk on the tea of words
vagabond clouds have picked your apple and the song has lost its virginity
the guardian of the lantern has fallen asleep before the gypsy dancers
appeared
the pomegranate of the soul leans over my body repeating the words of the
decrepit lands
that is why I stand fully upright in front of the door of heaven, I the pepper
red

    •

Translation from Arabic by Samira Hassan ben Ammou & P.J.

COMMENTARY

Ashur Etwebi, born in 1952, is a Libyan poet, novelist, & translator. He is a
member of the League of Libyan Writers. His books include the poem collec-
tions *Balcony Poems* (1993) & *Your Friends Have Passed through Here* (2002),
& the novel *Dardanin* (2001). In an essay he speaks to the importance of early
listening: "As I come from a place where an oral tradition of literature plays a
major role in our culture, I find it amazing to see how simple words can turn
into magnificent images and tales. I still recall the part where, when Siaf Ibn
Di Yazan helps the giants in defeating their enemy, the Guol, he was rewarded
with betrothal to the princess, and on the wedding night he realized that he
could not have normal sex with his bride, because the size of her vagina was so
big as to be his grave; the idea of a vagina as a grave captured my imagination,
revealing the relationship between sex and death, pleasure and pain. Of course,
he managed to escape."

Faraj Bou al-Isha (b. 1956)

WHERE DOES THIS PAIN COME FROM?

where is it leading to?
I pick at my wounds,
like a nomad spurring his donkey
impatient to reach
the end of the century.

HERE I AM

tossing at your feet
the knowledge I have gained
from my mistakes.
I waited for your arrival
and picked at my soles
for meaning.
What good is this step
or that step?
This is how
I became stranded
in the mud of modesty.

WAIT

do not leave yet.
Let me rearrange the world
for you.

SLEEP

the doves have subsided
the tiger slouched
and the ox now ploughs.
The camel tossed its rider
dying of thirst
and went on its own.

Sleep
the snake dreams of another poison
the ghoul has devoured
the children of fantasy
and my grandmother
has made a pillow
of the tales we loved.
Sleep
the earth is your palace
and your terrace
is the seventh sky.

Translations from Arabic by Khaled Mattawa

COMMENTARY

An Arabophone poet born in Libya in 1956, Faraj Bou al-Isha has worked as a
primary school teacher & later as a journalist & writer. He published his first
poetry collection in 1987, then two in Cyprus (1992 & 1993). He left Libya for
Cyprus in 1988 as a political refugee from the Qaddafi regime &, with the poet
Fatima Mahmoud (see below), established *Modern Scheherazade*, a magazine
concerned with Arab women's issues. He now lives in Germany & writes for
the Arabic newspaper *Al-Sharq al-Awsat*.

Fatima Mahmoud (b. Tripoli, mid-twentieth century)

WHAT WAS NOT CONCEIVABLE

In harmony
we entered the climate of water
in harmony with the law
of the tree.
In harmony
we pronounced grass, recited hedges.
In harmony—a horizon
                    of carnations.
A bundle of lavender.
                    We tapped on the silence
                    of abandoned gardens,
walked—

the road massaging its back
with the sun's ointment
and staring at the choked
 sidewalks.
 The patrolman
 inhabits
 the first line,
 sucks out the blood of language,
 strips the alphabet
 of its dots
 and tears out
   the plumes of speech.
He confiscates the states of narcissus.
He muffles
the coronets of the flowers,
buries alive the jasmine leaning out
 of the gardens
 of the gaze.
The fence is the noose of geography
around the waist of drowsy grass.
And time . . . wilts.
 In the first clarity
 of an approaching poem
 the boy
 washes
 from his chaotic face—
 the dust of starved herds
  led by hollowed men
  to the official stable.

 •

With staring pebbles
the beautiful children stone them,
and the math lesson embalmed
in the teacher's throat
emaciates the leap year.
The patrolman prepares
shackles
for the window
a lock

for the wind
and for the rest of eternity "invents"
     an accusation
     a torturer
     and a scaffold.

  •

I climb the thickets of laughter.
I return
to the branch its features
to the wind its shape
to the hedge
  its pebbles.
We glare
at the frontiers of NO,
and our loud singing
flashes.
We adjust our watches
to the patrolman's
        pulse rate.
Our country   two embers away
was
an oven.

  •

Carnations
  lean closer—
     the glass expands
     the forest widens.
Carnations write their crimson
autobiographies.
I read—
     what was tenable
     of the water's
     verse
     and what was inconceivable
        of your face and my country

  •

I leave for your seed
my fields
and the whiteness of the page.
I search for your hand,
a sentence
in active voice
in the season of fires—
      I smear the whiteness
      with the ashes
      of the era . . .
and search
for your hands . . .
  an iris of ecstasy
  in
  the season of desires

   •

Carnations
  flee
Carnations
  spill their crimson autobiographies
I said:
  the ember is the master of fire
  the ember
  is its dust . . .
  Then I became confounded . . .
  what
  to offer . . .
  the master's repulsive . . .
        and delicious mouth
I am singed with happiness
endowed
with the stamps of hollowness
lips
dipped in counterfeit songs
a scented
morning and our faces . . .
  are spat out
  in handsome
  editions . . .

What
    to offer
        the master's repulsive
        delicious mouth

   •

I tossed
my heart to him
my hands to him

   •

The land
is only two wheat spikes away
—and now—
an iris.
Carnations . . . draw us
in blood
spilled on
the patrolman's uniform.
  He rolls us
into clusters
in the imagination's vineyard.
Blood is
our secret ink,
blood
our aged fire.

Translation from Arabic by Khaled Mattawa

COMMENTARY

Fatima Mahmoud is an Arabophone Libyan writer. She worked as a journalist in her home country from 1976 to 1987, then moved to Cyprus, where she started a magazine (*Modern Sheherazade*) focusing on Arab women's issues, for which she served as the chief editor. She later returned to Libya but had a confrontation with, she says, the "dictatorial political regime" concerning the absence of freedom of speech. In 1995, Mahmoud was forced to seek political asylum in Germany, where she currently resides. She has one book of poems—*Ma Lam Yatauasar*, or *If It's Not?* (1984)—& a new collection forthcoming.

Laila Neihoum (b. Benghazi, 1961)

MELTING SUN

"Things fall apart,"
Tide not turning.
Melting away profoundly
In darkness
The sun.

And I,
Like every other day
A global world-sized wreck
Glaring white,
A hollowed art
Flattened pastures,
Facing an abandoned cave
Where a tear is
The only water
Spilled into
Emptiness.

And I
Said to be a big star
Whom night made sunset
Believe in
So what?
A mere light gleam
Where fate
Grins its last laugh?

And I
What if I had not been,
My parents' sculpture
And was expecting my shadow
To change its direction
Running over my euphony
Eclipsing me
Partially
Wholly
And what if I jump over obstacles
In the eclipsed noon

Into darkened sea waves
To see terror in your
Blindfolded eyes
And what if,
Oh trembling ones,
I,
Coming out
In mid-eclipse,
Purified my soul of you?

Translation from Arabic by Laila Neihoum & Mohamed Hassan

COMMENTARY

Laila Neihoum is a journalist, poet, editor, & translator. She was the first Libyan author to join the International Writers Program at the prestigious University of Iowa Writing Program. She edits & contributes to a number of Libyan journals & newspapers, including *Albait* (which she also directs), & the magazines *Almouatamer, Almajal,* & *Four Seasons.* She oversees the *Kol El Fenoun* newspaper & writes a weekly column on English-language authors for the daily *Al Jamahiriya.* She has published a collection of her own short stories & edited an anthology of poems by young Libyans, *Teseneon* (Poets from the 1990s), & a collection of global short stories, *Ofoq min lazaward* (Azure Horizons).

Khaled Mattawa (b. Benghazi, 1964)

from EAST OF CARTHAGE: AN IDYLL

I

Look here, Marcus Aurelius, we've come to see
your temple, deluded the guards, crawled through a hole
in the fence. Why your descendant, my guide and friend,

has opted for secrecy, I don't know. But I do know
what to call the Africans, passportless, yellow-eyed,
who will ride the boat before me for Naples, they hope.

Here the sea curls its granite lip at them and flings a winter
storm like a cough, or the seadog drops them at Hannibal's
shores, where they'll stand stupefied like his elephants.

What dimension of time will they cross at the Hours, loop
tight plastic ropes round their ankles and wrists?
What siren song will the trucks shipping them back

to Ouagadougou drone into their ears? I look at them
loitering, waiting for the second act of their darkness
to fall. I look at the sky shake her dicey fists.

One can be thankful, I suppose, for not being one of them,
and wrap the fabric of that thought around oneself
to keep the cold wind at bay. But what world is this

that makes our lives sufficient even as the horizon's rope
is about to snap, while the sea and sky ache to become
an open-ended road? That's what we're all waiting for,

a moment to peel itself like skin off fruit, and let us in
on its sweetness as we wait, smoking, or fondling provisions,
listening to the engine's invocational purr. In an hour

that will dawn and dusk at once, one that will stretch
into days strung like beads on the horizon's throat,
they will ride their tormented ship as the Dog Star

begins to float on the water, so bright and still,
you'd want to scoop it out in the palm of your hand.

2

A pair of Roman fists robbed of spear and shield;
the tiles of the tapestries mixed in with popcorn

that slipped from the buttery hands, aluminum
wrappers smudged with processed cheese;

countless cigarette butts surround the fallen
columns and beams with a fringe of tarnished foam;

pairs of panties still hot with forbidden passion . . .

The ruins are not ruined.
          Without all this garbage
packed, stratified, how else to name our age?

3

Earlier, I had walked the market of Sabratha, changed
to its people, but like my old city brought me back to me.
The petty merchants, all selling the same goods, shouted out
jokes to each other. A Sudanese waiter carried a tray
with a giant pot of green tea with mint. Among the older men,

their heads capped with crimson shennas, I kept seeking
my father's face. An old lust wafted past me when the abaya-clad
women, scented with knock-off Chanel, sashayed by.
The sawdust floors of the shawarma and falafel eateries,
the sandwich maker dabbing insides of loaves

with spoons of searing harissa, my mouth watering
to a childhood burn. Pyramids of local oranges,
late season pomegranates, radish and turnip bulbs
stacked like billiard balls, and the half carcasses of lambs
as if made of wax and about to melt off their hooks,

the trays of hearts, kidneys, brains, and testicles arrayed
in slick arabesques. The hand-woven rugs where
the extinct mouflon thrives, mincers, hairdryers, and toasters,
their cords tentacles drooping from rusty shelves.

It was as if my eyes were painting, not seeing, what I saw,
my memory slowly building the scene until it assembled whole.
What face did my face put on in the midst of transfiguration?
I know what the eyes of the men my age said, settled now
in comfortable middle age, about the life I left behind.

True, I did envy them the asceticism of their grace,
where a given horizon becomes a birthright—to drive or walk
past the same hills all your life, to eat from the same tree
and drink from the well that gave you your name.

4

Though for centuries the locals broke the statues'
limbs and ground them to make primitive pottery,
enough remains to echo all that has disappeared:

you and the woman leave the towpath, and you brace her
against the trunk of an oak. It's not the moonlight, but refractions
from suburban homes trapped under cloud-cover
that make her bronze skin glow among glistening trees.

First, God made love:
    the canopy like the inside of an emerald,
her lips a rush of cochineal. Then a route of evanescence
brought her from Carthage into these living arms, here.

5

"A nice time," he tells us, how he and four
cousins crossed the desert heading home
on top of three years' worth of meager pay
(the tarp ballooning, a giant dough) roped to a truck.

Wearing the goggles of the welder he'd hoped
to become, he looked at the sky and wondered "what
those flying, smoke on their tails, thought of us."

Later, deported in a cargo plane, he handed
the Tuareg soldiers one of his fake passports,
and they, like "space aliens" (in shabby uniforms,
sunglasses, tribal veils), poured into his face.

As the propellers' hammering calmed to
a shuddering hum, he saw the stars, "hundreds
of them like gnats," swarm Mt. Akakous's peak.

"My next road is the water," he says, serving
us tonight, and we promise, if the coffee is good,
to put him on the next boat to the moon
                    shining over Syracuse.

12

At last they set to sail. They slaughter a rooster,
douse blood on the Dido figurehead adorning the prow.
The seadog opens a canvas bag and pulls out a hookah.
His Egyptian assistant fills the smoke chamber with seawater,

twists the brass head into it, caking the slit with sand.
He fills the clay bowl with apple-flavored tobacco,
wraps it with foil, pokes it tenderly with a knife.
He picks embers from the going fire, places a few

on the aluminum crown, and inhales and blows
until the bottom vessel fills with a pearly fog,
the color of semen, I think, then hands the pipe hose
to the seadog who inhales his fill and hands it over

to the travelers in turn. The air smells sweet around us,
the breeze blows it away and brings it back tinged with iodine.
Their communion done, they embark, except the one who
stands, the dead rooster in his hand, as if wanting

to entrust it to us, then digs a hurried hole to bury it in.
The boat, barely visible, leaves a leaden lacy ribbon
aiming directly for the burnt orange sun. As it reddens,
for a moment, their standing silhouettes eclipse it.

Then the sea restores its dominion, dark as the coffee cooling
in our cups. Dangling from the vine arbor, the lights reflect
a constellation on the table's dark top. I trace my fingers among them,
hoping conjecture would shine on the mind's calculus.

Between my unquiet eddies, Marcus Aurelius,
and the coursing water, the travelers' moment sails,
its tentacles sewing a rupture I had nursed for too long.

COMMENTARY

Khaled Mattawa was born in 1964 in Benghazi, Libya, & emigrated to the
United States in his teens. He is one of the major Arab-American writers at
work today, as a poet, essayist, & translator from Arabic into English. He is
the author of four books of poetry, *Tocqueville* (New Issues, 2010), *Amorisco*
(Ausable, 2008), *Zodiac of Echoes* (Ausable, 2003), & *Ismailia Eclipse* (Sheep
Meadow, 1996). He has translated a number of books of contemporary Arabic
poetry, by Adonis, Saadi Youssef, Fadhil Al-Azzawi, Hatif Janabi, Maram
Al-Massri, Joumana Haddad, Amjad Nasser, & Iman Mersal. Mattawa has
coedited two anthologies of Arab-American literature & has been awarded the
Academy of American Poets' Fellowship Prize & a range of other prizes.

TUNISIA

The years that preceded Tunisia's independence were essentially given over
to mobilization for nationalist causes, and thus its literary production of the
1950s was neither very innovative nor critically oriented. The order of the
day was political engagement with the people toward independence.

However, the massive push for schooling in both Arabic and French, set in
motion by the regime of President Habib Bourguiba, led to the flowering of
a bilingual generation. Writers started experimenting with innovative tech-
niques such as using dialectical Arabic—at least for dialogues within prose

compositions or for modern poems in the vernacular that insist on marking their distance from the traditional structure of the melhun—and exploring the marvelous and the fantastic without, however, completely breaking with realism.

In an interview, the poet Midani Ben Saleh spoke to the warm, communal, and optimistic atmosphere of those days: "In our free time we would meet once a week at the Hotel Aux Jeunes with the great novelist Béchir Kheraïef to read our poems and short stories to him in a warm and intimate atmosphere, far from any dogmatic or fanatic mind-set. During the sixties we met predominantly at the café L'Univers. . . . And despite our sharp divergences and differences, the holy bond of fraternity was enough to unite us. Even on those days when I didn't have any money whatsoever, my meal and my bottle were guaranteed."

Lorand Gaspar and Salah Garmadi (see p. 399) founded the magazine *Alif,* which was active and central from 1971 to 1982 and with a primarily literary and poetical focus, in contradistinction to, say, the near contemporary Moroccan magazine *Souffles,* which was much more politically and ideologically outspoken. In its twelve issues, *Alif* published, besides dossiers on Georges Perros, Saint-John Perse, and George Seferis, French poets such as Yves Bonnefoy, Jacques Réda, Michel Butor, and Pierre Oster, plus Arab, English, Hungarian, and central Asian poets, and of course Maghrebian poets such as the Algerians Jean Sénac (see pp. 315, 549), Tahar Djaout (see p. 615), and Hamid Tibouchi (see p. 604), the Tunisians Moncef Ghachem (see p. 405) and Garmadi, and the Moroccans Tahar Ben Jelloun (see p. 682) and Mohammed Khaïr-Eddine (see p. 659).

This new generation tried to break sexual and religious taboos while according a privileged place to writing. Tahar Hammami (1947–2009), for example, experimented with the use of the local vernacular in his poetry, and with Habib Zannad founded the literary movement *Fi ghayr al-amoudi wal-hurr* (Nonmetrical and Free Poetry) in the 1970s.

It is interesting to note that Francophone literary productions come later and issue primarily from authors belonging to the Jewish community, such as Claude Benady (see p. 390) and Albert Memmi. This is because the teaching of Arabic was more highly developed in Tunisia, where the elites were in closer contact with Egypt and the Near Eastern countries. Contrary to what happens in Algeria and Morocco, where the Francophone literary production is quantitatively and qualitatively important from the 1940s on, one has to wait for the 1970s to see major Francophone writing in Tunisia, with the publication of, for example, *Nos ancêtres les Bédouins* by Garmadi in 1975, *Talismano* by Abdelwahab Meddeb in 1979 (see p. 409), or the work of Ghachem or Mohamed Aziza (see p. 401), or the poetry of maybe the best-known of contemporary women poets from Tunisia, Amina Said, the Paris-based author of over ten volumes of poetry (see p. 425).

In the introduction to their 1981 anthology of Tunisian literature, Taoufic Bakar and Garmadi write:

> If we had to sum up Tunisian literature since independence, we would say that it is an unceasing reworking of forms and languages with the aim of showing reality more clearly, a reality felt as a double hunger for bread and freedom in the face of the coming to power of a neo-bourgeoisie jealously guarding its interests and its prerogatives. Confronted by this state of affairs, so profoundly opposed to the great ideals of the independence movement, the new generation of writers, who came for a great part from the modest and often poor rural social classes, judge that everything in the order of the words and in the order of things needs to be changed if it does not help advancement on the road toward social justice and democracy.

Their hopes were soon shattered, as the censorship imposed during the past three decades by the regime of Zine El Abidine Ben Ali has had repercussions on the aesthetic and thematic choices of those Tunisian poets who lived in their home country, no matter which language they wrote in. Paradoxically, poetic research, at a distance from political problematics, has led to innovative formal experiments in Arabic. The events in February 2011 which brought down the Ben Ali regime and heralded a vaster Arab Spring across the Maghreb and beyond are still too close for us to allow any prognostication as to their influence on the development of a new Tunisian literature—except to state our optimism and hope for renewal.

Claude Benady (Tunis, 1922–Boulogne, Hauts-de-Seine, 2000)

THIRST FOR A COUNTRY . . .

Sometimes
at the season of transhumance
I get such a thirst
for a country with no maps
no barbed wire
a desire for earth to shape
like loam,
to rebreathe life into dead
things

make the stone alive inside
myself
so that a cloister of nothing but sun
may erect itself
where hedges of wild grasses would be a prayer
and the broken branch a summer song.

STRUGGLE

SAY IT ALL
Gather the present
dear dilapidated one.

Speak of angels
ripe carriers of stars.
Speak of plains
velvety swaddling clothes
and the wailing of the wind.
Speak of those breasts
each night kisses below the sky.

Say it all:
then to undo oneself.
Say it all about the dry tree
with the hidden groundwater.

Man resembles man.
Man resembles loam
triumphing over the earth.
He has a recluse thirst
of the light flows aimed at
the small of his back.
With flows of resin
also between the hard trunks
that come and go
as morning gives the nod.

Man resembles this:
resembles the immensity of the high night
in its found again lands,
resembles what makes itself loved.

Man resembles salt
that eats into his love,
resembles the child at play
with his anger
and tracks the sun's
spoor.

Skirt the soft seasons
and open one's arms
to the mounting fever
of daily hungers.

Say it all
while following the dotted line
of the road.

And start over again.
Say it all.
Gather the present
dear dilapidated one.
And then, in each hand
the gaze wide
open on our Future.

Translations from French by P.J.

COMMENTARY

Born in Tunis in 1922, Claude Benady set up as a bookseller in France. He published a number of novels, including *Les remparts du bestiaire*, & a number of poetry collections: *Les cahiers de l'oiseleur, L'or du sablier, La couleur de la terre, Recommencer l'amour, Le dégel des sources, Un été qui vient de la mer, Marguerite à la source, Les étangs du soleil,* & *Hors jeu de mots*. He was the editor in chief of the magazine *La Kahéna* & founded the magazine *Périples*, which introduced French avant-garde poetry to Tunisia. He died, totally forgotten, in France in 2000. Here is how Benady, the Tunisian Jewish exile, expressed the sense of uprootedness & nomadicity: "We went exploring virgin spaces, not as conquerors but as humble pilgrims in love with roots and with stones, with plants to pamper, with birds to protect. We went, the ones toward the Levant, the others toward the Sunset, without passports but with the same identity and respect in the heart for fresh bread, wine, and the olive. We went with different languages, but we made the same solemn vow of allegiance to the Master, companion of the tops, in order to learn humility, the meaning of the word *given*, the measure of equitable sharing. We went as innocent children, between the light and the dark, between the ignorance and the hope of an unlimited welcome."

Al-Munsif al-Wahaybi (b. Kairouan, 1929)

THE DESERT

In the beginning the desert
was the ashes of a woman
inhabited by a storm.
Hidden secrets echoed,
and the silent poet
lay down on its grasses alone
or sat between its light
and shade, looking for something
that had disappeared
in its endless, rust-colored mirrors.

At the beginning, the language of the desert
was grass blooming against the wall of wind,
tall palms swaying in the season of seeding
and cinders carried by air
to the blue welcome of warm sand.
She was our first fountain, our mother,
who held us, then gave us away
to the age of waiting cities.

IN THE ARAB HOUSE

The deep blue of the earth
tempted me, and I came.
It was an Arab house
dedicated by wind to eloquent silence.
   I wished good night to the grasses of the garden,
then went away.

A woman awaits me.
She has fixed a spear at the threshold of the tent,
completed her beauty rituals, lain down
on the sands, and slept.
   As I move toward her in the dream,
the star of the guest will see me
and follow my steps.

"Sir, oh sir,
you who stealthily came to me in the dream,
spread out in my body—
the morning star has entered our tent
and alighted in the mirror of frothing days."

CEREMONY

Embarrassed, you reach God's door.
Your face is pale, your spirit aflame.
This difficult love, Lord, has set me astray in the land,
won't you stretch a compassionate hand to save me?
He says, are you only a wayward desire
clamoring like wind when its routes are blocked?
If you should crave the fire of the Beloved,
do not alight,
they've lost their way who have come down before you.
And silence your hands when you approach my Kingdom,
only your foolhardy heart shall give the knock.

But I left my camel at His banks,
until sheets of rain enveloped it.
Solitary at last, God revealed Himself in my words,
a river following His waters.
The bathed spirit kindled for passion of Him
but His old love tempted it away.

Translations from Arabic by Salma Khadra Jayyusi & Naomi Shihab Nye

COMMENTARY

Writes Salma Khadra Jayyusi on Al-Munsif al-Wahaybi: "Born in the city of
Qairwan, which has been a center for Islamic learning for many centuries, he
completed his early education in his home town before going to study Islamic
philosophy and literature at the University of Tunis. After graduation, he
became a teacher in Qairwan and went to teach for three years in Libya. He
published his first collection, *Tablets,* in 1982. . . . His poetry reflects his Islamic
and mystical interests as well as his deep rootedness in Arabic culture, which
he frequently celebrates. He uses vibrant imagery and a diction rich in mystical
allusions, free of contemporary poetic gloom and anger."

Midani Ben Salah (Nefta, 1929–2006)

IN THE TRAIN WITH THEM

The train, in the gust, hugged the horizon,
hungrily devoured the vastness of the plains.
Its cry echoed back from the face of the mountain.
The mountain, scared, writhed like a dwarf,
humbly faded away, vanquished by this dragon.

Time, as if broken, seems no longer to recognize
either its points of departure or its points of arrival.
And so here I am sitting with my companions
while in quick successive flashes
the windows unrolled their dazzling drawings.
The vineyard itself and the ever so proud palm tree
started to gallop in a headlong race,
forever wiping themselves out under veils of dust.
Thousands of herds of cows and sheep
snatched up by the desert, drowned in the mirages,
suddenly grabbed by panic, vanished into nothingness.
Here we are, my soul and I, living a thousand torments,
my present gashed and slashed by pain and suffering,
my past fading behind the clouds,
my wandering future exile and anguishing fog.
Suddenly an unexpected voice cried in the air:
"Metlaoui! Metlaoui! Five-minute stop!
Those who get off here, do so now!"
I immediately forgot the strange shapes and visions
and started to curiously ogle
all those who got off and those who got on:
all were carrying their eternal misery on their bodies,
while enthralling women got on,
having long ago abjured their veils.
As gay as a spring day, they show off their charms:
dressed most sexily and wearing ornate jewelry
they sow their ardent temptations into the air.
Astonished and pleased I asked my friend:
who are these women as beautiful as stars?
These women are whores, my friend answered.
Then I cried out: My God, the danger!

Our jubilant train was turning into a party,
joyous nuptials, a happy festival,
while totally pleased my friends and I
watched as between the lips and fingers of the ladies
of the night the happy cigarettes glowed.
Looking at me then one of the beauties said:
"Hey, you over there, the young one, don't you smoke?"
Night suddenly fell on the earth all around,
but it couldn't fall on the hearts of our gathered company.
Lights appeared, large beautiful smiles
that from afar addressed friendly greetings:
it was Gafsa-the-wildcat who slept there, dreamy
while we were rolling along in this magic tube.
The demented one stopped, breathless, gasping as if in a trance.
"Get up, young one, get up quickly, darling,
Go, run from here to the nearest tavern,
and bring us back some divine bottles."
Not knowing what to answer, I took off running,
devoured by worries and shyness.
Quickly I put my hand into my one and only pocket,
fingered my coins to count them.
Yesterday I had sold my mother's jewels.
O earrings, great chance of my life!
Having given all my coins to the taverner,
I ran back at full tilt, as if I'd lost my mind,
but amply provisioned with bottles of wine,
for all my companions, for all those whores.

The train started up again and went on its way,
while drunkenness dripped from our glasses,
and fire radiated from our vermillion cups.
The group we were was charmed by it all,
exploded with joy, redoubled its licentiousness.
But with night advancing, we ran out of wine:
the songs started to congeal in our swooning throats.
Later on a voice screaming loudly woke me up:
"This is Tunis-the-Green! This is the capital city!"
And now I've arrived in the capital city
and our silly little game is over.

Translation by P.J. from Taoufik Baccar & Salah Garmadi's French version of the original Arabic

Midani Ben Salah was born in Nefta in 1929. After studying at the Zitouna in Tunis, he received a degree in history from the University of Baghdad. He taught history in Tunis & took part in the creation of several cultural & humanitarian associations. A well-known & influential figure, Ben Salah was the president of the Tunisian Writers Union from 1991 until 2005, the year before his death. He authored a dozen volumes of poetry, with much of the writing, as the critic Imen Abderrahmani suggests, "under the influence of [his] Sufi experience . . . [and] a mosaic of symbols and myths such as those of Sisyphus, Ur, Tammuz, Ishtar, etc." In an interview with the Tunisian press, Ben Salah stated: "What characterized my generation at the end of the '40s and in the '50s was an intense thirst for literature, art, and knowledge. . . . We held steadfast to our faith in the avant-garde role of the intellectual and in the necessity for the writer to come down from his ivory tower and to mix with the crowd."

Noureddine Sammoud (b. Kelibia, 1932)

THE EYES OF MY LOVE

Your eyes, my love,
are two beautiful butterflies
in a perpetual verdure.
Two pearls
on a ground of pure mother-of-pearl
ceaselessly thirsting
for the blue of the sea.
Two doves
in quest of a nest of tenderness
warm and peaceful.

Your eyes
are two jewel
boxes of gold and silver.
Two boats
loaded with flowers
and drifting on a vast green space
dreaming of diamantine purity
close to shores

with marble cliffs
with amber sand.
And deep down two islands
where no boat has berthed
not even in dream
only Sinbad in his long
errancy passed close by
and in a time long
gone only Ulysses, captive of Calypso,
tasted the delights
of their fine liqueur,
and nearly forgot his country.

Your eyes, my love,
are two cities
whose mystery was never violated by a gaze.
I gaze into them and see the peacefulness:
evenings it's Beijing, a forest of pearls,
mornings it's Isfahan and its enchanting streets.

Your eyes
are lakes of tenderness
I look into them and see
shadows and lights.
I see the impossible.
How often have I traveled through them
into a world that makes one lose one's head
as if erring through the museum of marvels!
I gaze into them and see
the gateway to the world of perfumes.
Imagination then is ready to
penetrate the divine secrets.

Your eyes, my love,
are two rivers of wine
of an eternal drunkenness
that flow in the depths of my conquered heart,
two nights when it is good to be awake
under the sweet brightness of the moon.

Your eyes are beyond
what my words are capable of
what my lute can express
marvelous universe
where my gaze founders
without being able to touch
their secret depths.

Translation by P.J. from Taoufik Baccar & Salah Garmadi's French version of the original Arabic

COMMENTARY

Born in 1932 in Kelibia, Noureddine Sammoud is an Arabophone poet & prose writer who has published a dozen or so volumes over forty years. He has experimented with all sorts of poetic genres, from classical & neoclassical versification to free verse. In his book *Essais sur la littérature tunisienne*, the Tunisian literary critic Malek ben Amor calls him "the poet with the most experience in different versification techniques."

Salah Garmadi (Tunis, 1933–1982)

OUR ANCESTORS THE BEDUINS

they are there
no one can deny them
no slogan can efface them
they are the inherited majority
depth coiled in maghrebian palm leaves
untamable root

the Moroccans still keep watch over the Tunisian street
the Tunisians still fry doughnuts for the children of Bejaïa
in Constantine a man of the people offered a sheep's
head and declared we are one single people

our fresh air children make themselves siamese
our naked legged women will give princesses
our adolescence will cry out
go straight little guy go straight ahead
our mouths are modest yet want to say it all already
and our Einsteins will be majestic in their jellabas

the African snow is holding back man's foot
the march-exile back of wanderers gives shape to the hubbub-instinct wave
in quest of subsistence
and Ghardaïa eyes' delight by the ochers
and the blues in shadow earth Ghardaïa with nocturnal gaze of
tutelary owl caress and commerce like Jerba adulated Ber-
ber sister
and Roufi has balconies
lost image mirage found again in the hollow of the palmed wadi
Hassi Messaoud
dune from which tumbles the friend at Allah's call
stony ground where man persists and acts

Translation by P.J. of Salah Garmadi's French translation from his original Arabic

COUNSEL FOR MY FAMILY AFTER MY DEATH

Should I one day die among you
but will I ever die
do not recite over my corpse
verses from the Qur'an
but leave that to those whose business it is
do not promise me two acres of Paradise

for I was happy on one acre of land

do not partake of the traditional couscous on the
third day of my death
it was in fact my favorite dish
do not scatter bits of fig on my grave

for little birds of the sky to peck at
human beings are more in need of them
don't stop cats urinating on my grave
it was their habit to piss on my doorstep every
Thursday
and it never made the earth shake
do not come to visit me twice a year at the cemetery
I have absolutely nothing with which to welcome you
do not swear by the peace of my soul that you are
telling the truth even when lying

your truths and your lies are of no interest to me
and the peace of my soul is none of your business
do not pronounce on the day of my funeral the ritual
phrase:
"in death he preceded us but one day we shall meet again"
this type of race is not my favorite sport
should I one day die among you
but will I ever die

put me on the highest point of your land
and envy me for my untouchability

Translation by Peter Constantine of Salah Garmadi's French translation from his original Arabic

COMMENTARY

Born in Tunis in 1933, Salah Garmadi was schooled at Sadiki College & later
studied English & Arabic in Paris, obtaining an *agrégation* in Arabic literature.
A specialist in comparative linguistics, he was a founding member of CERES
(Centre d'études, de recherche et d'éducation socialiste) & a cofounder of the
progressive magazine *Attajdid*. He published one volume of poems in vernacu-
lar Arabic—*Al-lahma al-hayya* (Living Flesh)—in 1970, & another in French,
Nos ancêtres les Bédouins (Our Ancestors the Beduins), in 1975. He also trans-
lated Tahar Ben Jelloun (see p. 682), Rachid Boudjedra (see p. 580), & Malek
Haddad (see p. 319) into Arabic. He died in a car accident in 1982. Faced—as
many Maghrebian writers of his generation were—with a linguistic dilemma,
Garmadi accepted the hybrid nature of his condition: "To a deathly silence I
prefer the rift, and to the mute mouth, even as little as a murmur."

Shams Nadir (Mohamed Aziza) (b. Tunis, 1940)

from **THE ATHANOR**

I

A mask left me stranded at the beginnings of the world
and my delible ashes for a long while swirled
   in the depths of Punic Tophets.
And my powerless breath wore itself out, for a long time
   at the pediments of Roman glory.
O my lifeblood, my Numidian vigor.

There has always been roaming, always the wind,
And the exultation of sands as vain armies of crystal.
And the damp shelter of hillside caves in the steppes
    of exile.
And bare tufts, always there, in the hollow
    of a summer brought forth.
Always, always, the tenacious, fragile
    dream
of a riverbank where to land is to be reborn
naked, reconciled,
and living
at the pace of swaying palm trees.

    II

O my lifeblood, my Numidian vigor—
How can I track you down to the mystery of nascent flesh?
How can I recognise you through the petrified forest
of illicit signs?
How can I find your deep-rooted trace again, twisted as I am
by the mark of Falsehood?
If I wrenched off my mask
my flesh would fall into shreds.

    III

The clamor of exile on the shores of Surt!
The time has come to desert this garden of mirages.
I was lulled by so many lies,
amused by so many charnel houses.
On stone-strewn shores, asbestos-laden strand,
the Caribbean bird dulled its sumptuous plumage
and the clumsy jungle banished the resurgence of water.
    So I unfurled my sails
    before the winds of departure.
    Plough, O prow, the fertile field
    where jellyfish dream.
    Seadrift, subsea tornado,
    and lightning spasms gush forth.
    Douse my eyes with ocean water
    to wash away an overly quick dream

    O torrents of the depths.

XXIX

On the face of the astrolabe, the present keels over.
   It was a beautiful flotilla
        before it was decimated . . .
   Here a frigate named Freedom
      sinks with almighty hiccoughing.
   Over there a caravel called
      Astrology
      or Medicine
      or Algebra
      or Philosophy
      vanishes utterly in aqueous miasma

Here and there

The glaucous cold of the deep
   Embraces me
   Drowns me
When will I ever cease to founder?

XXX

It is time to dream . . .

   I bring the standard of my reason
   to the foresail mast
   and I surge out of the deep
   and I walk on water
   in search of you, Occulted Iman
          masked prophet
    I walk
We will turn the red earth of Canaan green
We will seed you, barren belly of Selma
and we will invent a time that has no memory
   to break bread under the tents of Kedar
   to grow vines on the slopes of Mount Hermon and Atlas
   to inscribe renaissance on the inner walls of our time here
And we will invent a place without enclosure
   to assemble recognized brothers
   to restore freedom of speech and thought to the city
   to banish the time of wolves

We will ENDEAVOUR
to accomplish the reign of joined hands
and hearts in accord
And from the foresail mast
We shall fly our standard of hope

ECHOES FROM ISLA-NEGRA

for Pablo Neruda

Come on, love poem, lift yourself up from
among this broken glass, the time has come to sing

PABLO NERUDA, *MEMOIRS*
(CONFIESO QUE HE VIVIDO: MEMORIAS)

Desiring only the woman with hair of sea foam
   Rippling under my gulfweed hands
Desiring only her lichen eyes
   Revealing the semblance of the sea
Desiring only her lips of coral
   Making seahorses rear
Desiring only her body
   Dune nourished by the wind's innermost sources
Desiring only union
   Undertow of tides enraptured by full moons
Desiring only perdition
   In the burial yards of sand, alluvial sediment of night
Desiring only resurrection
   Under the snow of almond trees, in estuaries of dawn

Translations from French by Patrick Williamson

COMMENTARY

Shams Nadir is the pseudonym of the poet, novelist, & essayist Mohamed
Aziza, born in 1940 in Tunis. After studying literature & sociology, he worked
as a director for Tunisian radio & television. In the 1970s he started a career as
an international civil servant at the United Nations Educational, Scientific and
Cultural Organization. Aziza signs his essays on art in Arabo-Islamic civiliza-
tion with his own name but uses the pseudonym for his creative work in poetry
& prose. His texts exalt travel & the crossing of cultures in a quest for the uni-
versal. Writes Jean Dejeux: "Shams Nadir excels, thus, in rooting his particular
culture in a larger Islamic tradition, and in opening it to the wider resonances
of a multiple universe."

Abderrazak Sahli (Hammamet, 1941–2009)

CLERARE DRAC

Aracrure braclé --------------------------craliténe
Dracnien éractrouk-----fractourte ----------------
Cracline harcain-------------------iracroa-----
-------------------- Mrac - Lirve ------------------
----------------- Nrac - Mire ------------------
Oracpendle prac-croche------------------qura-coche
----------------- Rac - Chile -----------------
Grac-voure------ Tracande------------Wractourme
Vraclitor wracamre-------------------------
Xractorme---------------------Yrac-codre-----
---------------- Zrac - Lide ------------------
---------------- Tra --- Lindre ----------------
---------------- Tra --- Linde ----------------
---------------- Tra --- Lafre ----------------
------------------Tralfe ----------------
----------------Trable ----------------
-------------------Trile ----------------
---------------- Trible ----------------
Trile---Triglette----Tragle---Trigare ----------------
---------------- Tra --- Linde ----------------
---------------- Tra --- Lide ----------------
---------------- Tra --- Lafe ----------------
Tralfe, Trable, Tralbe, Tryge, Trolbe, Tragle
Triglatte, Trigarre, Trawbe, Tribse, Trisme,-
Trasme, Trasle, Transle, Tresne, Treste, Tre-
esbe, Trebse, Trabse, Trize, Traze, Trawbe.--
----------------- TRA - TRA - TRA----------------

--Trabize,
--Trazile,
--Trazite,
--Trazide, Tracile,
----------------------------Tradique, Tracibe, Traline
-------------Tralixe, Trabse, Tramine ----------
--Tralite,
Trate, Trale, Trane, Trabe, Trafe, Trave,----------
---------------Traxe, Trade, Trage,----------
Tra - Tra - Tra----------------------
----------------Tra-e, Tra-i,---------------------Tra-k,
Tra-O, ----------------Tra-p, Tra-Q, Tra-r, Tra-tr,
---------Tra-U, Tra-Ve, -------------Tra-Wa, Traxe,-
----------------------------------Traye, TraZe. ----------

--------- TRA - TRA - TRA,
---- TRA - AAAa,
-- TRA - Ze,

-

COMMENTARY

Abderrazak Sahli was a poet & visual artist who was born in Hammamet, Tunisia, & died there in 2009. An active participant in numerous poetry & art festivals & other events in France & Tunisia, he was one of the rare Arab-language poets to work in sound & visual performance poetry. His work has been published by *Doc(K)s* magazine & in the volume *Illisibles-Modifications* (Shakespeare and Company, 1978).

Moncef Ghachem (b. Mahdia, 1946)

MEWALL

All my life from way before I was born and my life is of all ages
I love my young earth drinking the roots of the day
I love the reddening of the flames on her sands
I love dawns over the mountains
I love her aroma and her fruits
I love her moon meridians

encircling her women
with her burning blood
I love these bodies immeasurably

on the hip of my ancestor
when she comes up from the sea
tattooed in red
on her ardent coals camel
brandishing her saber's lightning
her standard flutters open between wind and rain

in the honey of her lioness's breast
in her nomad flesh
in her name of sun and foam
lives the prophet
from her comes all sweetness and all strength
from her all mystery and all knowledge
she inhabits limpidity as well as the storm
the free sister of the free man
her call I'll answer today and tomorrow
I loved her passionately
and I love her and am ready to fall

I love each tree
   each village
   each drop
      of this country
divided by the tyrant the fake pharaoh the corrupt one
this country of wolves howling
behind the scattered herd
excluded and frustrated mother
they keep drowned
the taste of your shadow turns bitter
the owner and the oppressor beat you
my heart where are you where's your youth
that loved you passionately
and that loves you and cries out

I love they have imprisoned me in Bordj-Erroumi
they have tortured me burned me
have forbidden you my sleep
I truly love and I am the rose in the desert
I pierce the cold breath of night and become drunkenness
I become the mouth for which the fruit ripens

for the feast I am the chant that beats
and my nightingale voice swirls
singing my love and her clear face
I am your lover since childhood
that childhood of mine which remains with the children
and in you I love my wheat and my olive tree
my almond tree and my palm tree
you are so beautiful and alive
and I shall never be subdued

mist and fog and power of unhappiness will pass
forbidden roads nights of tears hemorrhages
and I'll come to meet you before dawn
I'll put my hand on the cheek of my popular street
and I will call my people
the assassins have come by
and they did not get me
I had absented myself and here I am
I come back toward you star of the orient

I was dead I have risen from the dead
I have returned
to see the children
and to raise myself from your hands
to see the children
in their eyes the black stone
the split ball
the rusted lightning bolt
the pain of the starved one
in their eyes the sadness of eagles
the destroyed laughter
the decapitated light

the children on whom everything depends
and their restless words
and their days of bitterness chapped from the cold
and their hands buried in trash and shoe polish
the children whose hands will destroy the castles of lies
and that this year's strike has transformed into black birds
that the traps toppled
that the tombs cradle . . .

Translation by P.J. from the author's French version of his original Arabic

Born in Mahdia in 1946 to a family of fishermen, Moncef Ghachem is a Francophone poet who has published numerous books of poetry often rooted in his childhood—the colors & smells, the fauna & the flora of the sea, & the identity of his native city. He belongs to the generation of disenchanted postindependence Maghrebian writers, saying in a recent interview: "I situate myself among the poetic currents of the '70s, an important current in the various Maghreb countries . . . which has continued a poetry of resistance, breaking with neither its content nor its form. This is a polyglot current, as the [Moroccan] poet Laâbi [see p. 668] has said, and I agree with him. This poetry has been taken up in its principal themes and aesthetic forms by Tunisian, Algerian, and Moroccan poets. My particularity consists in being biologically, geologically linked to the Mediterranean via my origins. I have been a fisherman since earliest childhood and am a poet of the sea and of childhood." Ghachem lives between Mahdia & Sidi Bou Said, where he works as a press attaché. In 2006 he received the International Léopold Senghor Prize for his lifetime achievement in Francophone poetry.

Fadhila Chabbi (b. Tozeur, 1946)

THE BLIND GODDESS

And the blind goddess, when we touched her
like a twinkling of the eye.
On the dry shore her hurried gait . . .
And in her face when sun and moon quarreled,
and in her step when the sea pecked a drop of life
the water receded—having become pregnant—for a time.
How can the letter be Seeing, Omnipotent,
a peer to the belated, jealous god.
And in the blind goddess when she dimmed
and the earth came to be
and it was the insolence of the ages.

I left nothing behind me.
No, I forgot nothing.
The words were thrown in the trash
and the expanse of whiteness.
The wolf is kind to the lamb . . .
That sentence I tore to shreds.
No eyewitness besides a fly rubbing its wings
beneath the autumn sun
and the heavy silver silence of a dying century,
to be born wrapped in waters of ferocity after ten meters deep
the sea snake slithers from one culture to another . . .

Translations from French by Yaseen Noorani

COMMENTARY

The poet & novelist Fadhila Chabbi, a cousin of Abu al-Qasim al-Shabi (see p. 282), was born in Tozeur in 1946. A professor of Arabic, she started her career as a writer in 1988. Her first volume of poems, *Earth Smells,* stands out for its modernity, a writing that refuses traditional Arabic meters. In 2000 she published *The Rise of Things* & in 2002 *Prayers in Where;* she has been awarded a number of literary prizes. "To write," she says, "is to play with language like a god."

Abdelwahab Meddeb (b. Tunis, 1946)

from **TALISMANO**

Alphabet, are you not a seed to flower in the monotheistic desert? Calligraphy, might you then be the orphan of meaning, profanation of the tomb containing the hieroglyphic remains and finery of the gods? The Chinese, who have conserved their ancient system of writing, who have allowed it to evolve, demonstrate the extent to which it is possible to avoid this division. Their words are other deserts; they repudiate the memory of voices to better preserve the alliance with the objects they mean to designate.

To test our conjectures, one need only single out the behavior of an atheist in the following places: here he is in China, where we find he is a calligrapher, Taoist, in harmony with the world, untouched by crisis; in Europe, we discover he is a painter, Christian, feeding on pity and resentment, misfortune and mortification, pornography and nihilism, individualism and pathology of an institutionalized sense of self, disease to be spat out of the social body—rare among this fauna are those who can hope to transform into blacks, Chinamen, dervishes, barbarians; and finally, he can be found in the Islamic, either Christianly contaminated, or regressively pantheistic, brainless, lost, Sufi, vernacular, all complaint and compassion, imitating jubilance, crushingly archaic, revivifying the reliquary of the ancient—always preaching, able to remain ante-Islamic, pagan by body.

But our East surely knows that China remains to be heard. Must we, by necessity, single out the disturbing beauty, bending and dancing, of the sinicized Arabic calligraphy that reiterates the Name above the mihrab of the Canton mosque? Eastern winds, sister Asia, we need only seek inspiration there in our impatient preparation to take part in the procession, even while eliminating the Name and supplanting it with the void, hearts' delight, gift of Hallaj, which controls the corrosive art of calligraphy.

How then can someone write, when at first he practiced calligraphy and only later honed the language that, from the very beginning, fascinates thanks to its mastery of what seems to be a chimerical sort of power?—only to be found irreconcilable with the psychological facility for blasphemy, thrilling fear of the void, boundless experience of textual adventure, in pursuit of bodies and sex; soon revealed as a pseudo-atheist, deceived by the morbidity of religion, cut off from his hierological being.

I write calligraphy that dances; the hand first seductive, then trembling; I divert this too logical language through openings where it can breathe; like this, coming and going, digressing, true to the body, forgetting to do away with the father, sailing, poisoning, flashing of spears, silent night shimmering, silver coats of armor and depersonalizing helmets: irony has it that this writing of mine should import the image of the *Battle of San Romano,* by Uccello, Paul of the Birds, and his *Story of Noah,* badly damaged by the flooding Arno: words, spears that score out the homogenous spectacle from behind the text and destroy more than they reveal: spears that move through the foundries of Shanghai to acquire their springy pliability, shock absorbers for comfortable carriages: the museum image that emerges in this here-and-now where I write turns into something manufactured, so that memory loss and physical frailness have taken me back to the Zituna besieged by a ritual becoming more and more focused as the unexpected but considered density of the text develops, locus where so many wayfaring energies cross paths—where time, more amorphous than space, furls and unfurls: unfamiliar labyrinth where I've lost my memory and bearings: anxiety of one who discovers himself to be writing while escaping from the world, delighted, sailing on the clouds beyond, dancing away.

Translation from French by Jane Kuntz

In the flux of thought, the fragment imposes itself. Between silence :
pause, the verse speaks the discontinuity that cuts me off from the
Writing drifts from language to language. It translates my double gen
The subject bears witness. The hand traces. The written, making
ance for the truth perceived by the senses, accelerates the journey
mind between languages. Though the languages be multiple, there
one table. The part of it that I retrieve through a decision that defi
will brings writing back to an anterior passivity. An active passivity,
forget that, you, a man practiced in the unification of contraries. Wh;
you'll do, you won't break the circle of the gift. I watch the sky unc
ing itself. The sun drags bits of tulle between clouds to mend the f
ment. With one hand I draw the curtain. With the other I open the bc
come across the "liminary," engraved in memory, an incipit that exca
the arabesque of its capital letters from the azure and gold of the illun
tion. Confronted with the beautiful page, I am dazzled by the letters
introduce "The Cow," the longest sura, placed at the head of the Book.
initiatic letters—الم: aleph, lam, mim—open five other suras. Scattered
tials, reticent to make up a word. Will I submit them to the sovereignt
meaning, between effusion and plenitude, between wealth and blame? \
I sound their mystery? On the shores of pain and promise, in the nega\
interrogative mode, the aleph, the laureate, stands up straight. It is the ¢
that subsists and encompasses. It throws its straight shadow upon the si
that transcribe the language. In it, multiple, moving points. It is the pr
ciple from which the letters derive, as the numbers derive from the one.
commands the alphabet to reside in the twenty-eight lunar mansions. T
lam is the letter of proximity and autonomy, of union and of separatio
Decomposed into l.a.m., it contains the aleph, the first, and mim, the int
gral. In its median position, the aleph is a bridge between the beginning an
completion. The book starts with three letters that span the three degree
of the voice. While the aleph is produced far back in the throat, the lam i
articulated by the middle of the palate and the mim by the lips. Orphaned
these three letters suggest from the start the trilateral rule that distributes
most of the radicals in the language. They are enthroned above the words.
When you pronounce them, the flesh shivers and thought lays its first stone.
In each of these letters the verb is incarnated. They are haunted by Hebrew.
From one letter to the other, the same thread weaves different cloths. To the
aleph straight as a one corresponds the figure with three members of the
oblique aleph. The one grows under the shadow of the other, under a sky
crossed by the lightning bolt that whips my blood in the heart of the desert.

Behind those alphabets I look toward the foundational Orient. Between the two rivers, the fertile loam draws the nomad, as soon as he leaves the hostile climate, like it did the Akkadian ancestor. Invoking the god Shamash, patron of travelers, I recognize the Arabic word for sun, the ogre that devours my herds on the arid steppe. In my dialect the Akkadian voice illuminates each morning. As soon as I name the sun I invent writing. The clay baked in the heat of the day rests in an earthen tomb. Despite its vaunted friability, I exhume it barely chipped. The tablet on which the stylus had traced the phonographs of Sumeria fills my hand. I leave Babylonia and the Semitic domains to celebrate the announcement of language by a people gone now for several millennia. Its ascendancy, its flowering remain obscure. Claimed by no one, Sumeria is everyone's heritage.

Translation from French by P.J.

COMMENTARY

Born in Tunis in 1946, Abdelwahab Meddeb was raised in a traditional, scholarly Muslim family & started to learn the Qur'an at the age of four from his father, Sheikh Mustapha Meddeb, a scholar of Islamic law at the Zituna, the great mosque & university of Tunis. At age six he began his bilingual education at the Franco-Arabic Collège Sadiki. In 1967 he moved to Paris, where he studied literature & art history & where he has lived ever since as a poet, scholar, & broadcaster (he has a weekly show on Arab & Muslim culture called *Cultures d'islam* on France Culture, part of French National Radio). Until his recent retirement he was a professor of comparative literature at the University of Paris X–Nanterre. A prolific poet, novelist, essayist, & translator, he was also the editor of the influential international French-language literary journal *Dédale*. He has published twenty books in French, including *Talismano* (Paris: Christian Bourgois, 1979; reprint, Paris: Sindbad, 1987), *Phantasia* (Paris: Sindbad, 1989), *Aya dans les villes* (Saint-Clément: Fata Morgana, 1999), *Matière des oiseaux* (Saint-Clément: Fata Morgana, 2001), & *L'exil occidental* (Paris: Albin Michel, 2005), a series of essays on the work of the Persian Sufi mystic Suhrawardi & the question of exile. His 2002 book-length essay *La Maladie de l'islam* (Paris: Seuil), published in English under the title *The Malady of Islam* (New York: Basic Books, 2003), has attracted considerable international interest. He followed this with a book-length interview with Philippe Petit, *Face à l'islam* (Paris: Textuel, 2004), & three further volumes of essays on the question of Muslim culture & modernity. His most recent book is *Printemps de Tunis,* a meditation on the spring 2011 revolution in Tunisia.

Muhammad al-Ghuzzi (b. Kairouan, 1949)

FEMALE

Do you not see that we pitched our tent on the banks of night
And called out to you to enter in safety
So that we could wash your face at night with seawater,
Your face where ancient terror dwells?
Did you not crave sanctuary of the wind, and we gave you shelter?
Did you not tremble and we called to you
To drink our wine from earthen vessels,
That wine whose praises you have sung?
Did we not call upon you to seal in the blue of night
A covenant with the land you seek?
This is your drawn countenance
The water birds enter it in flocks
And this is your house, open,
                               pledged to the flood tide of the sea.
The Female called out your name, saying:
"Do not betray me, Master,
Descend into my body, cleanse
With night rituals its estrangement;
Of antique cedar wood is our bed,
And full of gladness is the night; be with me."
Why did you lose her, Master? They say she cast
Her girdle and earrings to the waters of the sea,
They say we saw her before people crying out:
"Who of you can restore to me my Master, whom I love,
A young man like the cypress tree, all the birds of evening
Are reflected in the depth of his eyes;
I invited him into my mother's house,
I said, do not saddle your horses for the valley of God
That path has no guide and winter is on the roads,
What should you seek?—God is here in my body."

Why did you lose her, Master?
They say we saw her, face to the sea, arms open, calling:
"Come to me now, my body celebrates you."
Why did you lose her, Master? Here you return
Dust on your shoulders, heavily burdened,
In your open face the osprey finds a home.

Descend in safety, let's wash
Your face at night with seawater,
Your face where ancient terror dwells.
Did you not crave sanctuary of the wind, and we gave you shelter?
Did you not tremble and we called to you
To drink our wine from earthen vessels,
That wine whose praises you have sung?
Did we not call upon you to seal in the blue of night
A covenant with the land you seek?
This is your drawn countenance
The water birds enter it in flocks
And this is your house, open,
                              pledged to the flood tide of the sea.

QUATRAINS FOR JOY

When joy surprises me, I ripen
Before the gathering of figs and grapes,
And call to my master, who is one with my soul:
"Pour out your wine for all, my body is the cup."

When joy surprises me, the sea
Floods in upon the thresholds of the night
Carrying in a basket all the fruits of the season
And I make myself a necklace of the sea's treasures.

When joy surprises me, I cry out:
"Master, alight at my side,
I will hide you tonight in the cloak of my love,
Here's my body flowering for your wayward stallions."

When joy surprises me, I come forth
With my loosened hair, following my lovers,
I open my breast to the bird flocks, "Who," I say,
"Will repair to the regions of the Female if lovers go?"

When joy surprises me, I come forth
From my hidden cities and kindle my incense burners,
And bless the tree of my body; then all I've hidden
shows on my face and my secret is out.

When joy surprises me, I inhabit
The incandescent kingdom of lightning,
Sleep with the sap in the heart of the leaf,
Return when the palm branch is heavy with dates.

When joy surprises me, I cry out,
"Priest of the Nile Valley, here are my fish
Dead, and my horse is slain before me.
With what chant then shall I open this requiem?"

When joy surprises me, I go
To the soothsayer bearing my broken pitcher
And he lays his hands on my chilled body and declares,
"For seven nights shall this glad face be grieved."

When joy surprises me, I behold
A hawk perched on the castles of the winds.
I loosen my locks over my face and cry,
"From what frontiers does this portent come?"

When joy surprises me, and its white gulls
Alight on my body, I see my shroud
Through my ecstasy, and so I strew
All I possess on the waves and I depart.

Translations from Arabic by May Jayyusi & John Heath-Stubbs

COMMENTARY

The poet, playwright, & literary critic Muhammad al-Ghuzzi was born in
Kairouan in 1949, where he finished his grade & high school education before
completing a PhD in Arabic literature at the University of Tunis (where he
now teaches) in 1989 with a dissertation titled "The Masks in Modern Arabic
Poetry." Sufi mysticism, classical Arabic poetry, & the universe of the fairy tale
mark his work. Abdul Kader El-Janabi & Bernard Noël, in their anthology
Le poème arabe moderne (Paris: Maisonneuve et Larose, 1999), characterize
al-Ghuzzi's importance thus: "His mastery of rhythm and image, his ability
to invoke childhood in a few words, and his passionate desire to unravel and
keep unraveling all the mystical lights, without becoming fixed in any single
Sufi order, imbue each poem with a cosmic illumination able to imparadise the
reader's soul."

Moncef Ouahibi (b. Kairouan, 1949)

from *UNDER SARGON BOULUS'S UMBRELLA*

I got up this morning
Fog was swallowed whole over the Euphrates
Over its rocks, a frog was becoming green
as if nothing had happened
not a corpse floating
not a ship in sight

Iraqis were going
from one exile to another
At every station they stop
We see one man standing under the rain

As the train crawled in the afternoon noise
I was thinking: life is truly slow
Like the first step in a dance
It is a bolero dance and we are between two dates:
We are born by coincidence
and we die by coincidence too
Maybe we will sprout some day in the stem of wild chicory
Maybe we will shoot some day in the violet of its blossoms
It usually rains in Kirkuk at this time
Mount Zarakos is ginning its cotton.
I have mentioned that I "forgot my umbrella"
I will get off at the last station

The trees have only spread a drooping blue sheet
at their feet (are they warding off the sun with this shade?
What, then, have they prepared for winter, their talons?)
Trees are black here like Iraqi women at Kadhimiya
swallowing their own shadows (the secret of this feminine
   presence is the wound
gazing at us through its triangular opening
in gaping, silk underwear)
about to . . .
In a light that comes
and does not come.

Iraqis were going
from one exile to another
At every station they stop
We see one man standing under the rain

Would the earth have sprouted all these flowers
were it not for the wound?
Give thanks to this light!
It was arranging objects from Baghdad to Khanaqin
with a furry brush:
a land to be ploughed between the hills' thighs
It tames the sky's horizon
Pine trees shake off their frost (I mean tiny shards)
as silver dewdrops fall on my window
to flash in their boats
which are tied to an anchor at port

Color has the smell of trash
when the sun becomes blue
behind restaurants at bus and train stops
People still have dog food to eat
and dogs have their excrement
All we need in al-Sayyab's Basra is spiky wine,
arak the color of sugar,
and beer like piss at Ibn Harma's tavern
that's what I called him
It's Noah's Ark except that its prophet seaman
did not peel the water's face with it before the flood
He did not carry animals on it
It was a urinal for drunken sailors
(a sculpture thrown to the waters by Marcel Duchamp)
They come in the night of wolves
One by one they sit at their tables
gazing with mute eyes
caught in their shadows
as if afraid they would talk in their sleep
Their food, or bait, is smoked fish, and a bag of candy
When Ibn Harma dozes off in the fog
and the river's water shimmers like zinc
white, then blue, then white

they depart
as if walking in the verses of his wine songs
drunk in the light towering over Sindbad's land ·
as if an island is floating there
as if Atlantis can be observed
on the margins of water . . .

Iraqis were going
from one exile to another
At every station they stop
We see one man standing under the rain

Snow has the taste and smell of fires
Its beads are swollen with silent water
The earth is water
so let us flow through it to this Iraq
(Its mapmakers in the dark are bent
over a book of sand where winged fish fly
like one turning the globe from one side to the other
to stop at cities of the Babylonian diaspora)
We are running, but water is ahead of us
It even becomes distant whenever our steps sink
We don't come and it doesn't come

Thanks for this light
Its arrow pierces the mud
When I am about to die in the Euphrates
I am alive and still, like palm trees
When I die, I withdraw like a fish to its still water
whispering to the dead:
You who walk the earth!
Sleep well so you can dream!

They dreamed of all these flowers for him
and he woke up to eat two of them
They dreamed of two hands, a farmer's hands, like my father's
They dreamed of more
than two hands and two lips for him

Iraqis were going
from one exile to another
At every station they stop
There was a broken umbrella
and you have to find the one who had raised it, and if . . .
then you have to find the hand
to be like an echo

Translation from Arabic by Sinan Antoon

COMMENTARY

Moncef Ouahibi was born in December 1949 in Hajeb El Ayoun, Kairouan, where he teaches Arab language & literature at the university. He has published seven collections of poetry, among them *Tablets* (1982), which gathers the poems of the 1970s; *Tablets II: The Mountains Come from the Sea* (1991), a retelling of cities visited; *The Timbuktu Manuscript* (1998), which interrogates the history & legends of Tunisian cities; & the volume *Mitavizika wardat al Raml*, which won the Abu al-Qasim al-Shabi Award in 1999. His work has been translated into several languages. He has also written the scenarios for several films, such as *A Country That Resembles Me* & *Paul Klee in Hammamet and Kairouan*. In the essay "Poetry and Knowledge," Ouahibi suggests that "poetry is not an object of knowledge but could well be its origin."

NOTE: Sargon Boulus (1944–2007) was a pioneering Iraqi poet. Ibn Harma was an eighth-century poet known for his wine songs & an encomium to Baghdad's founder and ruler, Abu Ja'far al-Mansur.

Khaled Najjar (b. Tunis, 1949)

STONE CASTLE

In the windows of sand
in death
in a chalk-drawn circle
in castle walls

your liquid name, beloved,
was an old journey,

  a song
that comes with the wind to my house in winter.

It was the lantern of the orchards
long dimmed by the tide.
It returned
as a moon above the banks of death
and in its waning reflected
lights from the islands.
They remain at the bottom of the river
to celebrate a feast for my sorrow by the walls
of Mary Magdalene's home.

It was my face
and my stone castle.

BOXES

They stole my childhood from me
and my madness.
They stole my winds
from the wooden crates
where I kept my clothes.
And from the gates of the South
they stole the croaking of my frogs
and my mother's mirrors.

POEM I

And I return to the old house from travel.
Things regain their old taste
and their sad silence.
At night I will walk by my loved one's windows
the way autumn passes by
because the wind still brings back the bitterness
of old days
and takes from the sand
all that we said
the day you first saw me.

POEM 2

Like the sun under water
your face,
like time
a crucifix in my night.
In the memory of days,
lakes from a star
bring the wind back to my house
and give me
our childhood that died
the way butterflies die
in a summer without shores.

POEM 3

When I was young
I walked to the gates of the South
listening to the gushing of springs at night.
When I was young and innocent
like the shells of dreams,
the butterflies on the roof were my stars
and the shadows of horse carts
were my angels.

POEM 4

Across the bridge
an angel passes sobbing.

POEM 5

I hold a candle and flowers
in the silence of my hand.
I hold a mirror, a sock, a cloud
in the silence of my hand,
and your singing is lost

in a distant summer
among paraffin lamps.
I hold a notebook and doors
and the sea,
and butterflies
and the sadness of eternity.

Translations from Arabic by Khaled Mattawa

COMMENTARY

Born in Tunis in 1949, Khaled Najjar studied literature at the university in
his hometown, which led him to teaching & literary journalism. He has con-
tributed to a range of Arabic-language magazines, including *Alif,* founded by
Lorand Gaspar & Salah Garmadi (see p. 339), & edited the bilingual magazine
Le livre des questions. A poet in the lyrical tradition, he is also a translator of
French poets, such as André Velter, into Arabic. His first volume of poems,
Poèmes pour l'ange perdu, came out in London in 1990. The French poet &
critic Jean Fontaine called this work "the vast metaphysical periplus of the nov-
ice toward the core through memory and the inverse of habit." Given his small
output, Najjar tends to keep away from the limelight of literary scenes.

Tahar Bekri (b. Gabès, 1951)

from **WAR TO WAR**

The sea doesn't know where all this water comes from
Off desert shores thirsting for so many rivers

A single wing is not enough for the seagull
To salve its wave-burns and wind-burns

All these leaves that fall to the tyranny
Of winter don't prevent the bird from perching

On the branches free and invincible
His song fed on snow and on sun

What is wrong with the earth that it keeps moaning
Under the rubble the palm tree thunderstruck

After so many nights slashed by lightning bolts
Primroses flattened by hellish boots

I build you up again seasons of veins
Of trees, and the light's blood

Beyond the borders beyond the walls
If you tremble you stir up my dust

How can we let the child eat
Cakes of clay amidst crocodile tears

Shadowy faces numbers beyond counting
Towers of pride hippopotami heavy in mud

From you I have the green orange's rage
All those cracks in the wind's rift

Like a gaping fissure in the caesura
Give me buds instead of all these graveyards

from **I CALL YOU TUNISIA**

I

And you live within me earth
Bow on the violin's cheek
In the untameable sea's neighing
The fleeting notes unwound in skeins of foam
Envying rebellious hair
Its gallop of memories
Down to that waist a mane
That could free a thousand and one riders
Season guided by the Milky Way why
Have you set my boat adrift
In absence without an anchor
Its ropes frayed by so much forgetting

II

They opened at dusk
Those flowers mingled with night's amber
Where a dream tosses restlessly
In the hive of insomnia
Its honey going from eye to eye
Nectar surprising the bees' probes

Like a sudden shower
Sometimes the storm told you my anger
At not having been born
A pomegranate tree or a flowering orange tree
To offer you my fruits
But is it from thunder's grumblings
That orchards are born

For you I have picked
A bouquet of roses
With petals of light
Perfumes diffused without fanfare
I am the stem climbing the stake
Of your arms which console my walls
When the storks fly off will you tell
Of all the distance they crossed
I am not a summer cloud
That wanders lightly
But the heavy sky of its rainstorms
Lover of hardened autumns
The seed that rises
In blackened earth
For the best grain

Paris–Tunis 2010

Translations from French by Marilyn Hacker

COMMENTARY

Born in Gabès in 1951, Tahar Bekri—who writes in French & Arabic—has lived in Paris since 1976. He has published some twenty books (poetry, essays, art books) & been translated into a number of languages (Russian, English, Italian, Spanish, Turkish), with his work being critically analyzed in various university settings. In an article in *Jeune Afrique* from October 1997, the critic Ridha Kéfi describes Bekri's poetry as "all of luminous transparency, in ample murmurs and limpid melodies" evoking "vast crossings of time and space, real or imaginary, where Orient and Occident are continually reinvented." A specialist of Maghrebian literature, Bekri teaches at the University of Paris X–Nanterre.

Amina Said (b. Tunis, 1953)

"CHILD OF THE SUN AND THE EARTH"

child of the sun and the earth
until day pulls evening's shadow toward itself
I roam through the thinned threads of clouds
through the wave which ignores me
following the fevered curve of stars
which burn out in the sea's ink
I go to sleep on the dunes' whiteness
listening to the dead breathing
in their fields of asphodel

child of the sun and the earth
I lean over the last well on the island
to spy on the secret dance
of scorpions under the stone

rocked by my grandmother's story
as she puts incense in the *kanoun*
I bite into the honeyed carob-fruit
when night comes I bend over the echo
that the forbidden cistern sends back to me

child of the sun and the earth
I go with my father to his father's gardens
where hundred-year-old olive trees keep watch
I climb the white mulberry-tree, the pulley creaks
comings and goings of the long-memoried camel

child of the sun and the earth
I recite the sacred verses
the only girl among the boys
sitting on the woven mat of the Koranic school

child of the sun and the earth
I travel in the walls' arabesques
in the nightingale's pure song at the lemon-tree's crown
in books' mysterious sentences
in the glow of my mother's grey eyes

"I AM A CHILD AND FREE"

I am a child and free
to live in perpetual Sunday
sun perched on the horizon
in each thing's clarity
earth contemplates its seasons
I have no place or dwelling
life is everywhere and nowhere

from the cistern on the terrace the grandmother draws
water for the mint and basil
grinds the salt and spices
wages her daily battle with the real world
the breeze swells out stripes on the curtains
the lamp still glows
I play beyond the pictures

in my father's gardens
the trees bear ancient fruit
whisper in the birds' language
well-water sings in the furrows
beneath my steps sand-paths are born
I inhabit the day's innocence
pure beginning with no before or after

from a little house built like a boat
I let myself flow into blue emotion
a sea-horse ballet brushes
against fallen stars
sea-urchins blossom on the rocks
seaweed glitters on my wrist
only the moment lives in what I gaze at

I am a child and free
I have no place or dwelling
how vast the sky is when the whole
world is a poem
it's broad daylight on earth
night has not yet been created
I have a foothold in all of time

Translations from French by Marilyn Hacker

Moncef Mezghanni (b. Sfax, 1954)

A DUCK'S SPEECH

1

The poet's mother said: O son, may God kill poverty!
I have no money
to buy ink
Your father left nothing
but a wild duck's feather

2

With that feather the poet wrote
the most precious poems
The mother wrote them down
in the ink of popular memory
until they rang in the palace's ears
and the ruler decreed:
"We have decided
to execute poverty
We have decided
to give the poet golden pens,
silver inkwells,
pink notebooks,
and finally,
a pile of paper money"

3

The poet became a member of the palace's body
Had a party there to celebrate
the publication of his book of poems
Respected critics were taking notice
They kept hailing his prophetic vision
until a woman at the back of the hall stood up
All ears waited upon her lips
as silence listened
to the breathing of those celebrating
until interrupted by the poet
whispering into the MC's ear:

"Please, take the microphone closer to her lips
I know this woman
I know the woman's face from her eyes."
It had been a long time
but forgetfulness is mute delirium

4

The woman stood there
She was so happy her lips were exposed
She screamed into the microphone:
"I am the poet's mother
He died whitening the teeth of power
What a shame!
May God curse harlotry!
With a duck's feather
he used to write poems of gold,
but with a golden pen
he has only written
a duck's speech"

THE LAND OF NARROW DREAMS

I

When I reached my ninth month
I was bored of swimming
in my mother's pool

2

When I descended
never to return
I smelled the earth's air
and cried for the first time
They cut the umbilical cord
and I dreamed
of crawling free

3

When I crawled
I dreamed of walking

4

When I walked
I dreamed of racing the winds
I wished I had wings
I envied the bird
when I was young
and dreamed of getting old

5

My beard sprouted and my eyes became red
when I saw enormous sorrow
enveloping the world

6

When I saw that enormous sorrow
had enveloped the world
I decided that I must change the world

7

When I got out of prison
(I was accused of destroying the world)
I was carrying glasses
and dreamed
of changing myself

8

When I entered the golden cage
my wife changed me
My children grew
and dreamed of changing the world
Frankly,
I was afraid
for them
I threw my cane at them
I threatened to change
their mother

9

But my children
advised me
to change my glasses
and threatened
to destroy the house

Translations from Arabic by Sinan Antoon

Moncef Mezghanni was born in Sfax in 1954. A consciously experimental
Arabophone poet, he first became known through his public readings, an oral-
ity that characterizes the whole of his poetic production. In 1982 his epic poem
*The Murder of Ayyache the Ksibien and His Excuses for Coming Back from
the Dead in a Future War* made him a celebrity. He has published six volumes of
poetry to date, as well as several books of stories for children. He is the director
of the Maison de la Poésie in Tunis.

Adam Fet'hi (b. 1957)

THE BLIND GLASSBLOWER

first movement

The girl asks her father: How do you write?
He is blind.
I look long into myself, he says, until I see a hole in the paper.
I put a word in the hole. Then, like a glassblower, I blow
into the word so it grows a little. This way,
sometimes, I get a poem.

Then what? The girl asks.

Nothing, darling, worth mentioning,
other than that I
might fall in the hole and then won't come back.

430   *Fifth Diwan I*

another movement

The girl asks her father: How do you find your way?
He is blind.
I get lost for a long while within myself, he says. Until I feel a thread
of light. I put my mouth on the light. Then, like a glassblower, I blow
into the thread so that it grows a little. This way,
sometimes I find my way.

Then what? The girl asks.

Nothing, darling, worth mentioning,
other than that I
may reach the end of the thread without arriving.

CAVAFY'S WHIP

The prickly pear,
thorny, of wily fingers, friend to Tunisians on wedding nights
(when the grains of chance ripen) and Eid mornings, when
halawa calms
the tufts of burnouses.

The prickly pear,
wily, of thorny fingers, polite in this, preserves
your cry "What will we do without barbarians?"
And it doesn't stand up for its kind
when called
a Berber fig, for example

How polite
too, like Dido's bull, when it wags its tail with joy at your enduring
    question
"What will we do without barbarians?"
Wondering how its skin can lose the kind, to become
a Berber city, the first last letter
of its name,
Carthage, for example

Trapped in their bodies (last of the birds of majesty),
they come to the end of the journey, stumbling over one obstacle after
    another,
carrying money sacks of dreams on their shoulders
to a place where there is no window for fresh air
other than Berber poetry. As if the wild man
said, here they are
in their cages of refinement
politely watching their kind
die out,
being replaced with blind names,
the virtuous citizen, for example

Why then say they were a kind of solution, the Berbers?
Or were they the dissolution of the kind?
Or were they the front ranks of ostriches, crossing, disburdened
of their dreams, one sack at a time, in order to
arrive quickly
not knowing
where?

The caravan slept while they walked.
It slept, Cavafy.
The cracking of your whip will not incite them: "What will we do without
    barbarians?"
That was a whip for another sleep.

Now tell me:
What can we make without dreams?

Translations from Arabic by Camilo Gomez-Rivas

COMMENTARY

Adam Fet'hi (real name: Fet'hi al-Qassimi) taught Arabic in a high school in
Tunis until 1995. Since then he has worked on literary programs on Tunisian
radio & television. He has published five poetry collection since 1982 & is also
well-known as a songwriter for many famous singers in the Arab world. He has
translated more than twenty-five books of poetry, fiction, & film scenarios—
among them Baudelaire's *Flowers of Evil*—into Arabic.

Dorra Chammam (b. Tunis, 1965)

from REEFS AND OTHER CONSEQUENCES

I have a nostalgia for my mother's womb.

Everything I've been able to say or make, keep, commit or dismantle, issues from this nostalgia: to return to my mother's womb . . .

. . .

Each time I decide to take my existence in hand, an insidious game gets underway. I veer back and forth . . . And I boil over.

And I disavow my body. And my spirit . . .
Then, I disappear into the denaturement of the world.
And I lose my footing. And I'm no longer anything.
Except perhaps, a few words,
the sensation of profound boredom, of nonsensical fears and
the impression that everything loved ensnares us.

Shouldn't we purify the dross, cease writing our knowing phrases with all those references we pass off and impose in the lecture theatres of the world?

Shouldn't we simply try to approach an apnoea in the nadir of ourselves, to skim the internalised bookstall, come back and tell each other?

One times, three times, x times, no-times . . . And I break myself and curl up, mend myself the better to break myself . . . And I shut myself in and clam-up inside a scarified self and this body I cover in bruises, for want of loving either of them.

Well, even if I often deny it, I do posses one certainty, with all the conviction of a buried truth: *angelic states are the preserve of infernal places.*

My reality regards me: I know, I've always been nostalgic for my mother's womb . . . It occurs to me I have some sort of amnio-acid syndrome.

Abandonment and the void regard me, they observe me, watch me. Everything else is a kind of senselessness, an insanity.

. . .

I've always had a serious problem with emotional management. I'm not some decorative architect.
I have a memory fitted with a dial that doesn't belong to anything but itself.
I compare it to an x-ray facsimile of a pleuritic thorax.

It comes from *a contrario* all the things I'd like to say and never said . . . Worse, it itself always communicates something entirely unrelated to what I'm thinking.

Happiness is unknown to me, still less its *recipe*. If I had to describe the idea of happiness, it'd be analogous to an epilepsy of absence, a state of unreality, a sort of trance in which you believe you see something which straightaway you forget.

A little like an innate lobotomy

As for illusions of happiness, they indeed reign in a world that's become a type of Hollywood Boulevard from which all the cults of appearance and unbridled consumption emerge.

To be consumed so as to be loved, rolling about in a lubricious sweat, hot for it, all forms of impotence forgotten now thanks to Viagra, weightlifting, body lotions, hormone supplements, competitive sports, jet-setting, cosmetic surgery; newborn child of standardisation, delivered like cloned pulp and hemoglobin, for hungry old women who keep their daughters in the shade . . .

. . .

Blissfully, I look on as age ambiguates, chiselled good looks resurrected by the surgeon's knife, the millennium's new superhero . . .

Zombified, I watch this new mutant race which in spite of itself has a geriatric stink under all the layers of plastic and facepaint, gummed-up with false teeth, eyelashes, unguents and every artifice known to man. The stink of their relentless pursuit, refusing ever to be caught offside against Time. And the senile allure, so *young,* so *fun,* so *high,* so *punchy,* even with their osteoporotic hipbones splintered by stiletto heels . . .

Alarmed, I listen to tales of siliconated women, atomised into a fleshy mist when the airplane they're flying in pierces the sound barrier . . .

Horrified, I steer between this hell of deceiving paradisos and its sufferers, and all the johnny-come-latelys, the opportunitists and fake devotees, the bogus gurus, gigolos, false friends and ignominious wind-merchants *happiness* trails in its wake.

Disembodied, I try to flee this abominable Island of Dr. Moreau, but straight away the mad doctor's on my trail, harrying me, hunting me down. Rather death than these bodysnatchers.

. . .

I've always lived inside the mirages of haunted *characters*; characters who're at the same time me and not at all me. Mirages that reflect my *true characteristics* like funfair mirrors.

. . .

From time to time they slip through in enigmatic, worried groups. To stare at me for protracted periods. Writing on my knees with my face buried in a notebook. Then just as they came, they disappear again.

Choppy waves carry me off on some inner-sea whose desert islands exist only to remind that I've always lived inside a mirage, haunted by effigies which both resemble and do not resemble me.

To better escape my truth.

Witness, victim, judge and above all jury of my own existence. I twist myself inside out, change constantly, chameleon-like, turning about the axis of a psychic geography I'm equally the slave of and the arena.

And I speak/write/witter-on that I don't know anyone. Just characters: dead, undead, spectres, knots, winds, reefs and other consequences.

Translation from French by Louis Armand

COMMENTARY

As a poet & a prosist—though her prose, often autofiction, reads very much like poetry without being "poetic" in any simpleminded way—Dorra Chammam is the author of *Récifs et autres conséquences* (Le Nef, 2008), *Les Anges ne répondent* (Autres temps, 1999), *Le Divan* (Le Nef, 1989), *Le Miroir* (L'Or du temps, 1997), *Baisers de sang* (Mirage, 2005), & *La Profonation* (L'Or du temps, 1998). In 1992, the Tunisian president Zine El Abidine Ben Ali awarded her a Medal of Honor in recognition of her poetry. She works as a journalist for the Tunisian newspaper *Le Renouveau* & lives between Paris & Tunis. Evaluating her own & her work's relation to her country, she writes: "Tunisia has a vital artistic life with men and women able to express themselves and write and paint in total liberty without censorship. . . . It is not dangerous to be a poet in Tunisia. My book *Profanation* would have sent me to prison in Algeria. It's very daring and erotic and could be seen as disturbing in puritanical countries. Men like *Profanation* more than women do. Women may feel it reveals too much about them and gives away our small secrets. I exposed them, but I didn't betray them. . . . My aim is to leave something after me. Arabs think living today is important. The future will bring an uncertain tomorrow. Tunisians are not like that. We feel immortal. We do enjoy the present but feel the future will be better. I try to convey that when you enjoy the present with clear-sightedness, it can only make the future better. The younger generation understands what I mean."

Amel Moussa (b. Tripoli, 1971)

A FORMAL POEM

In the old house
where my grandfather composed his formal poems
I live as a concubine in my kingdom,
my dress is wet,
and on my head I place a crown.

In the old house
where the jug is tilted
water seeps out
mixed with prayers.

In the old house
where my first cry echoed,
I spread the soil of lineage
for us to sleep on,
one soul stacked next to another.

In the old house
where my grandmother was throned a bride
I search for her shawl
and place it for my shoulders to kiss.

In the old house
I cross ancient nights
and carry food to dervishes.

In the old house
I hand away my embers as a dowry
to lovers bathing in rain.

In the old house
Love wears us like a cape
and the courtyard becomes
twice its size.

LOVE ME

I carry me on my fingertips.
I carry me on the galloping of my vision.
I wrap myself with a swaddling of my skin.
I embrace me, longing for myself.
I bless my flowing, my gushing.
I cradle me in my chest.
I glove these budding hands with poetry.

I claim revelation,
my engravings are on stone.
My image carries water to thirst,
and bait to fishermen's nets.
I spend the tolling of evening bells
sculpting.
I sleep in my own shade.
I wear my Bedouin nature
to spite cities.

I stroll within me
when I weary myself.
I enter a garden
that does not entice myself against me.
I love my impossible self,
the one whose feet
the earth does not know.

Translations from Arabic by Khaled Mattawa

COMMENTARY

The Arabophone poet Amel Moussa was born in Tripoli, Libya, in 1971. While still very young, she moved to Tunis, where she has lived ever since. After finishing her thesis on religion in Tunisian society for the sociology department of the University of Tunis, she started writing for several Tunisian newspapers. Her first collection of poems, *La femelle de l'eau* (1996), was prefaced by the writer & politician Mahmoud Messadi. Her poetry, in which Sufi influences are visible, steers a course between the sensual & the spiritual while always mindful of the exacting problems the world at large is facing. Her work has been translated into French & Italian.

Samia Ouederni (b. 1980)

FOR TUNISIA

This is just a footnote, though a microcosmic one
  perhaps, to the greater curve
Of the elaboration; it asks no place in it, only insertion
  hors-texte as the invisible notion of how that day grew
From planisphere to heaven, and what part in it all the
  "I" had . . .

JOHN ASHBERY—"SORTES VERGILIANAE"

Do not fill their voices with smoky air
because shut mouths of despair are blocking their spit, their revived
    viruses,
their weaknesses to tell the story
when the noise of a rolling stone is swearing at god.
Shall I, at least, say
that memory is decayed
that history is dismayed;
the past is dead deeds
and mythological dates are the land's seeds
as the sheep have forgotten about the wolf's teeth
clacking?
Shall I say that Eternity
means not a Calvin Klein's perfume
but looms above their hats and doom
denying all celebrity?
Or will you forget someday
that trees have their leaves to be lost
over heartless pebbles and frost?
I have learnt from history that dam-builders
will be forever damned.
When the water will rise with the people's tears,
it will spare none.
Shall I tell about a woman's cry
amid sounds and swear-words?
Or loudly my voice will tell of
female shapes whose bodies have been displaced from time and space
in fashion magazines?
Can I turn on a TV pretending to re-appropriate history

or will its waves bring about voiceless shouts?
Now, when writing is fired by scientific neutrality that cries:
"I AM THE WORLD!"
Can I, at last, see purged tongues laying down their sandals and feet
with no chance even to cheat
or tell what their hearts hide?
Will I be hanged when they will understand?

(1998)

MAURITANIA

In Mauritania, a country often called "the land of a million poets," as throughout the Maghreb, though maybe even more so, literature is indistinguishable from song, chant, music—and poetry is thus the core genre, with prose only coming to the fore recently. Until the twentieth century, Mauritanian literature was mostly confined to the geographical space of the different ethnicities, with nomadic Arabo-Berber influences to the north, and African—essentially Peul (Fula) and Soninke—influences to the south of the Senegal River.

In the north one has to distinguish between classical Arabic-language poetry (*shi'r*) and popular poetry in the Hassaniya language (*ghna*). The latter language's name comes from the beduin Hassan tribe from the Maqil group, who both raided & Arabized the Sanhaga Amazigh nomads of the southern Sahara. As Catherine Belvaude explains: "The *shi'r* obeys rigid rules and is the prerogative of men of letters, and its practice is limited to men only. It consists of imitations of the pre-Islamic (*jahiliya*) and Abbasid-era poems. In *ghna,* the rules are much more flexible, and in it you find an always renewed authenticity; everyone, including women, can compose in this genre. There even exists a form of *ghna* specific to women: the *tabra'.* One can further distinguish another genre inside *ghna,* namely an improvisational duel between two poets who answer each other, the *gta'.* Finally, there exists an intermediate genre between *shi'r* and *ghna* that is called *azrayat.* Traditionally the poetry was conserved and transmitted by the *ruwat* (singular: *rawi*), who learned a poet's oeuvre by heart" (*Ouverture sur la littérature en Mauritanie: Tradition orale, écriture, témoignages* [Paris: L'Harmattan, 1989]).

In traditional oral literature, one of course finds the genres we have already mentioned in our prologue to the Oral Tradition I: tales, proverbs, and so forth. Unfortunately, space does not permit us to reproduce any of the specifically Saharan Mauritanian versions of these here.

We have concentrated in the main on contemporary Francophone Mauritanian poets, as they are the ones who have renewed the literature of their country this past century, linking it to the wider poetics of negritude, and keep doing so today. One of our poets, Djibril Zakaria Sall (see p. 447), has been seeding his French with his Pulaar mother tongue and is slowly moving back to composing in this African language. In fact, one of the great Mauritanian poet-scholars of the past century, Oumar Ba (see below), though he wrote mostly in French, also collected and translated a range of materials from Pulaar. On the *Jeune Afrique* website, Tirthankar Chanda sums up the current situation as follows: "From now on it's bye-bye, negritude, hello, Mauritanian-style hybridity. Be they of Moorish or black-African origin, the Francophone poets of Mauritania today draw their inspiration as much from Peul, Soninke, and Wolof mythology as from the abundant Hassaniya poetic tradition. . . . They claim their country, rich in its hybridity, torn between its Arabicity and its Africanicity."

Oumar Moussa Ba (Senegalese village bordering Mauritania, 1921–1998)

WELL-KNOWN OXEN

You tell me you had the law on your side?
And those oxen I see
In the chief's heard?
If I call them
they'll answer to their nickname.

THE BANU EYO-EYO

A glorious ancestry
does not fill the belly.
How many from Torobé
have served as *cornacs* to the new master?
The white master
is a mount available to
procurer families.
Have patience—
the distant day no doubt exists . . .
The day that will never come,
does not exist.
Even moonless nights
end with dawn.
From North to South
we sleep
helmeted in our certainties.

PLEA

Yes, my father was Ly,
My mother Ly,
My ancestor the Almany Youssouf.
But as soon as the most holy
Long for the diadem
The colonizer knocks on the door.
Food, women, & power,
In living memory, are never rejected.

PEUL POEM

he who gives up tilling the fields
to engage in partisan political battles
his voice will become hoarse
& fights & famine will make for
a calamity will undo his family

SONG OF THE WASHERWOMAN

Sure, I didn't brave the lightning storm
as successfully as Sekou Touré.
Elsewhere my partner Guélel Touré,
incapable of mastering the least problem,
even nausea, has gone under.
Mamadou, the sycophants honor you
with mouths wide open: DIA
happily the ~*dia* moved aside
the vile dog won't take aim at you.
Africans, Houphouet, for the colonized,
false friend likes to swing the whip.
Useless to think of Ibrahim Ndaw—the kid,
the ostrich crawling forever in the dust, unable to win!
But with Father Lamine, son of Ibrahima,
you surround yourself with divine protection.
To lean on Modibo Keita
means to ensure the present!
All unanimously count on Senghor,
always strong,
always a noble man of his word.
Don't be afraid, the issue is the Mali Federation,
for the rest the Moor, abject, would yell: "No way!"

Translations by P.J. from Oumar Ba's French translations of his Peul originals

COMMENTARY

Oumar Moussa Ba was one of the major scholar-poets of Mauritania as the country & Africa generally moved out of colonialism. He was born just across the border in Senegal (in 1921) to a marabout family that had always been Mauritanian (he once humorously explained that his village was in Mauritania but its cemetery, just across the river, was in Senegal). A self-educated man who, however, later in life received a graduate degree from the Sorbonne, he produced an astounding oeuvre, composed on the one hand of translations & transcriptions of poems, sayings & narratives from the Pulaar language (*Poèmes peuls modernes* [Nouakchott: Etudes Mauritaniennes, 1965], published in Pulaar & French) & on the other hand his own writings in French, celebrating Sahelian Africa, its crepuscular nature, its myths, & its great men (*Odes sahéliennes* [Paris: La Pensée universelle, 1978]). He is a true precursor & the first published Mauritanian Francophone poet.

Tene Youssouf Gueye (Kaédi, 1928–1988)

THE MEANING OF THE CIRCUS

Distant carillons of the Great Copper Clock
veiled echoes of bugles and the song of crowds (choir of
great communal feasts, syncopated applause descending
into the depths along green abysses)
we climb back up the dreams to the blue height of stars
all the way to the sonorous circus tiers
resplendent in light.

Now we're back in the front rows of the
grand circle in its heavy red drapes and bathed in
pink sunsets where slight whiffs of dead
roses float. The distinguished and smiling gladiators
are still there, on the lookout for wild animals and shadows, their
great wrestler torsos masked with fine silks.
The call rises in anguish, toward far meridians of
human treason: here we are at the hearings of grand
indictments on those contending on bronze high-warp carpets and muddy
   sands;
we remain voiceless on the shores of other seas,
our gazes fixed on the horizons over there under the Tropics
and the spirit of the abysses.
The Hottentot tethered to his hills of the Transvaal (and my Texan
brother outsmarting his troubles at the threshold of nightclubs),
the Kakongo from Angola in his death-dealing maquis (and
my brother in Arizona soaked in tequila), spatters on the other side of the
   Kalahari,
(and my other brother at the forbidden threshold of his native
   Palestine . . .).
And the prostrate crowd suddenly rises, scrutinizing
the faint light in the east where the silhouettes of mercenaries are moving;
we sharpen our lances humid from easy dews,
lying in wait for shadows come down from the sky toward Bissau.
Our elite lancers charging faraway citadels
behind the Great Gorilla, the Great Circus shuts up and watches
the distinguished gladiators descending into the arenas of this Night
so high and spattered with knowing stars.

We shiver in unison with the hours, toward those other
seashores shaken by thunderstorms heavy with the scents
of jungles and swamps: Smith and N'Komo, Salazar
and Roberto, Verwoerd and Luthuli, great puddles of night
in the clearings of Kivu, screech of conniving rockets
returning from monsoons of violence.

Translation from French by P.J.

COMMENTARY

One of the major voices in modern Mauritanian Francophone literature, Tene
Youssouf Gueye was the author of several novels & volumes of poetry (among
others, *Les exilés du Goumel,* 1968; *A l'orée du Sahel,* 1975; *Sahéliennes,*
1975; & *Rella,* 1985, all from Les Nouvelles Editions Africaines). He was the
president of the Mauritanian Writers Association & an important civil ser-
vant after the independence of his country, serving as a delegate to the United
Nations Educational, Scientific and Cultural Organization. Politically active,
he stood up with other Mauritanian intellectuals for the rights of Mauritanians
of African descent who were being discriminated against. As early as 1986,
a group of Afro-Mauritanians was arrested for having written & distributed
a document called *Manifesto of the Oppressed Negro-Mauritanians,* which
offered proofs of racial discrimination while asking for the opening of a dia-
logue with the powers that be. The government's reaction was a vendetta that
proved to be the darkest & bloodiest page in the country's history. Gueye
was thrown—with many others—into prison by the dictatorship of Colonel
Maawiyya Ould Sid Ahmed Taya & died in the infamous Walata "mouroir" in
1988, though his reputation has been rehabilitated by later governments.

Assane Youssouf Diallo (b. 1938)

from **LEYD'AM**

FORBIDDEN
At my horizon's edge
FORBIDDEN
In the square
FORBIDDEN
Even on the public bench
FORBIDDEN
In the bar

A noise of rough metal
Of amplified clanking
Symphony of spontaneous weeping
Impetuous river of universal indignations
Capital event:
My race is born again
A new dignity

Blues
a link slowly breaks
bright with FREEDOM

.

Tam-tams that roll the essential language
Where the brotherly voices mix
I want to plug up the earth holes on the grains
Harvest the millet ears
Crush my lice during the hour of rest in the fields
Rinse my laughter
With the little *mourtoki* twig
Sing the *lélé* to the virgins
In our nocturnal assemblies

Near the fleeing flames
Of the fire of the circumcised
Sitting down I hugged tight my round
Shadow which
Was hopping about
And rhythmed
The intrusive virgins' threnodies
But the interdict nailed me down
And chewed at my double.

.

I yelled all along the roads
The crossings of heaven opened their doors for me.
In the red dust of time
The finger of the Ancient One
Drew my path.

In night's silence I listened to
the limpid voice
the renewed wisdom.

Grandfather, tell me
What is it your eyes are gazing at?
Do they see ancient things?

Yes, Taniraguelam
Look at the house over there.
Do you see?
There was a big stone
as high as two huts
one on top of the other.
It was the year of the big wind.
I broke,
I carried,
I dragged that stone
It dug deep into the earth
Much of my blood stayed there.

The spirals of time turn
Taniraguelam
Be happy.

Translation from French by P.J.

COMMENTARY

(1) "*Mi amoyi / n'garé n'gamoyen dinguiral managal / dinguiral belngal*" are
the opening lines of Assane Diallo's poem *Leyd'am*—they are in Pulaar, not
French, unlike the rest of the poem, & translate as "I am going to dance / Let's
go dance on the big public square / the pleasant public square." They have the
enthusiasm of the poet & his vernacular, though the poet clearly wants the
switch to French, to have his work read beyond the borders of Mauritania. This
is a familiar quandary for many, if not most, African poets.

(2) Diallo, writes Tirthankar Chanda in *Jeune Afrique*, "sings woman, through
whom the reconciliation with the native country becomes possible. His poem
Leyd'am (1967)—a word that means 'territory' in Pulaar—recalls Aimé
Césaire's mystical fusion with his country, Martinique. Causing, possibly, a
sense of déjà vu, which kept this late current of negritude writing from having
the success it merited."

Djibril Zakaria Sall (b. Rosso, 1939)

TO NELSON MANDELA

All is dark around me
My ideas are gagged
And the world works backward
God! I am alone on the balcony of Life
And the entrance of Hell flowered with screams
of crackling sparks, the smell of flesh
rhythmic dance of SATAN liberated
Satan crowned by mage Satan.
. . . BACCHUS is of the fête
Today the eau-de-vie will flow
from wells of injustice and trampled honor
to the dregs of the barrel of oblivion
then . . . the unconscious will erect its ramparts:
—Come it's the arch in profound misery
The mother strangles her child and bathes herself in his blood
—The child decapitates his father and stones his mother and from
the other side incest unravels in sin
God! I am alone on the balcony of life
and no longer recognize myself . . .

Here furtive looks intersect
crushed like a shadow on the potency of the dream
Mimicry willed in the glaze of extroversion
facing the pedestal of evil incarnate
The hopes shed their leaves the expectations stiffen
the truths are killed the lies cried at the auction
in the plastered and pernicious mourning of the castrated word
All have lost their tongues all have lost their eyes:
We must cross our arms listen and wait
till the curtains of calico fall on the glacial Silence
of choked bitterness and of senile pleasures;
Come! Come! it's the banquet of the fear of the hunger
of the terror:
The gravedigger the hangman the cemetery keeper
are in the front seats—dressed in crimson
"Here only the candidates of black death are admitted,

of death accidentally provoked, hazy, and made-up"
God! I am alone on the balcony of life
and no longer recognize this bloody world, useless and caustic

My hope strung on a rotting thread
inhales a mortal perfume
and from time to time I revolt
Facing Eternity a woman of the night in ruptured flowers
scatters in the night birthing an odor of poison
and of aborted death
My future is not rose
That of others is morose.
It's total confusion and evil is king.
Cruel fate!
I no longer dare to guard—my shadow hunts me
It is there lying in wait, merging with itself
scraping the walls, ears on the lookout.
But I'll no longer speak even to myself.
And it is there that my silence is violated:
"You once thought of suicide"
And it's the trial, the waltz of lawyers.

Five years of prison for having thought of suicide
Inquisition!
Now I must descend into the dark jail
Good-bye, Sun!
Good-bye, moon!
Good-bye, everyone!
Five years of prison! It's death before my time
It's death in slow motion
Ah let me write my will
And why in fact?—As I have nothing to bequeath
But if . . . one truth—the nontruncated truth
It will triumph one day in the blood spurting from everywhere
And from my hole of exile I will laugh
and my laughter will make the earth tremble like thunder
and the gaping crevices will engulf lies
and vendors of mended promises

I've done nothing—I've said it and yelled it high
They could only listen to the absurd voice
of vengeance.

They assassinate innocence on the negative path
of blind force.
No remission of sorrow
no amnesty
no grace
Nor tears
Nor sighs
Nor prayers
Soften their heart of stone
They are made of marble and their consciousness of granite
God! I am alone on the balcony of life.
and no longer recognize this inhuman world.

    When will the bell of all this toll?
I don't know—
But on that day the truth will triumph
and all will know that red is the blood of the negro
and that red is the blood of others.

Nouakchott/Dakar/Lagos, August 1980

Translation from French by Sylvia Gorelick & Miles Joris-Peyrafitte

COMMENTARY

Djibril Zakaria Sall was born on April 23, 1939, in Rosso, in the region of
Trarza, to a Peul family. It was in the late 1960s, as he was working as a police
inspector, that he discovered his calling: "I was twenty-eight when I started to
write; it was in the police station in October 1967, and all of a sudden I started
to produce verse after verse—a flame had lit up inside me. I started to write
in little notebooks handed out as ads by Mazda. In two years I wrote some
twenty-five poems that I sent to Leopold Senghor, who exhorted me in a letter
to give up rhyme and concentrate on black-African poetry, which is rhythm
and image!" He published his first book of poems in 1970 & has published
some eight volumes since. He also started to write in his mother tongue, Pulaar,
exploring its literary possibilities: "I find more freedom there because it is my
language. The vocabulary is right at hand. No need to check the Larousse dic-
tionary. Everything's available. When I come across a grammatical problem, I
immediately check with an uncle or brother. . . . I write in the Latin alphabet
but then bring the work to one Amadou Oumar Dia, who corrects the orthog-
raphy of my Pulaar transcription. So I started [to write in Pulaar], and it is
good, because it is my language . . . the language of my land, and you've got
extraordinary things that do not exist in the French language."

Ousmane-Moussa Diagana (Kaédi, 1951–Nouakchott, 2001)

from *CHERGUIYA*

My country is a pearl—discreet
As traces in sand
My country is a pearl—discreet
As the murmur of waves
Below an evening's rustle
My country is a palimpsest
Where my insomniac eyes wear out
Tracking memory.

Translation from French by P.J.

COMMENTARY

With those lines the poet & linguist Ousmane-Moussa Diagana (who died in 2001, barely fifty) addressed his country in his first volume of poems, *Small Dream Notes for an Amorous Symphony* (1994). These verses, writes Tirthankar Chanda in *Jeune Afrique,* "sum up the principal themes of Francophone Mauritanian poetry: nationalism, the African memory, the violent split between those from the north, the Arabo-Berber nomads ('the sons of the clouds'), and those of the south, the black-Africans ('the people of the river'). Like a pearl, Mauritania is a crossbreed between the water of the Senegal River and the sands of the Sahara."

Mbarka Mint al-Barra' (b. al-Madhardhara, 1957)

POETRY AND I

The sin is that I wasn't a stone
  And the troubles of the world make me sleepless
And I shield myself with poetry
  And it keeps me company when I'm far from home
And poetry is my satchel that I will always carry with me
  It holds the taste and fragrance of the earth
It holds thickets of prickly branches
  It holds palm fronds loaded with dates
It paints all the stories of love in my language

Its colours form the spectrum from grape to dawn
And I said bring the most beautiful of stringed instruments
   So the universe may know how music flows
And play its soothing melody
   That brings justice to those who are in love
Letters burden this world of mine
   Trouble leeches ink from the quill
Trouble leeches ink from the quill
   When I read of the longing of lovers I burn

Literal translation from Arabic by Joel Mitchell; final translation by the Poetry Translation Workshop

The Poetry Translation Centre's website notes: "Mbarka Mint al-Barra' is a Mauritanian poet and teacher writing primarily in Arabic. She is very active in the cultural and literary life of her country, and has achieved some renown elsewhere in the Arab world. She frequently takes part in literary festivals in other Arab countries.

"In the country of the million poets, as Mauritania is often called, al-Barra belongs to the third generation of poets. Like many of this group, she resorted to the use of dialogue in her poems and a narrative style to address the realities of Mauritanian society. . . . She borrows images from religious texts, ancient Arab history and classical Arabic texts to portray conditions in her country. The symbolism of the religious stories is particularly effective in a country deeply rooted in Arab-Islamic traditions. Al-Barra uses both free verse and rhymed poetry, borrowing images from her own environment, which explains the frequent use of palm trees and sand."

Aïcha Mint Chighaly (b. Kaédi, 1962)

PRAISE ON THE SITE OF AFTOUT

O my beloved, remember the past,
Your flowing tears (full of) nostalgia
At the sight of Dagreg and Toueijilatt
From the height of Lahrach
There next to the wells.
And there, the place called Limé
The delightful backwater of Weymé Bameyré
Just a short morning (walk) away.

Before you get there, is the Kedan pass.
And over there a little further on,
The ould Moilid gully.
Before that you see many trees and clearings.
And there is Djeb, silhouetted against the West.
O my beloved, do not let yourself be led
Into a dead-end, for to the east are the cliffs.
That was the domain of the Moors.
In these places, there are no longer music lovers
Nor caravans passing alongside herds of deer.
There is no other divinity but God.

NOSTALGIC SONG ABOUT LIFE

Oh! These are uncertain times.
Even one moment of pleasure
Is sure to be followed by days of pain.
Today I went past the old camp ground
And I saw the baobab branch which used to
stand behind the tents.
This baobab branch was burned all black.
Oh! Such sadness and desolation.
The one who burned that branch is ignorant.
There is no other divinity but God.
O my beloved, speak.
Because I am too shy, I cannot
Come see you at your parents' house.
And you, you did not take the precaution of leaving
and going away
So that I could find you.

Translations by J. Crews of Sheikh Mohammed el-Arbi's French translations from Arabic

COMMENTARY

(1) Born in 1962 in Kaédi, Aïcha Mint Chighaly is the daughter of Yuba al-Mokhtar ould Chighaly, one of the best-known griots of the past century. The Chighaly family comes from the border area with Senegal but moved to Nouakchott in 1982. Aïcha owes her reputation in her country to her abilities as a singer & a player of the *ardin* harp but also to the family heritage in music & poetry. She is always accompanied by her band, made up of her brothers & her sister-in-law, all of whom studied with her father. She launched her international

career in 1996 with her first CD for Maison des Cultures du Monde in Paris & since then has toured Japan & many countries in Europe, Africa, & the Gulf.

(2) The music of the griots of Mauritania is called *azawan* & is a very scholarly art, following strict theory & played by professional musicians with a long & specialized training. The songs are accompanied by three instruments: the ardin harp, a woman's instrument made of half a calabash, with eleven or fourteen strings; the *tidnit*, a four-stringed lute played exclusively by men; & the *tbal* kettledrum, made from a hollowed-out piece of wood, which can reach one meter in diameter.

WESTERN SAHARA

Joseph Mulligan contributed not only all the translations and commentaries in this section but also the material for this prologue. Much of the background information here appears in "Lucha y resistencia en poesía saharaui," an excellent essay on and selection of Sahrawi poetry by Pablo San Martín and Ben Bollig, published in the Patagonian journal Confines *15 (January 2009).*

In 1976, after the final Spanish military forces left their ex-colony in the Western Sahara but before the referendum by which the old colony could have gained international recognition as an autonomous state (something its people, the Sahrawis, and the United Nations had long been demanding) could be held, Morocco and Mauritania, eager to expand their borders, both sent armies into that vast territory populated by one hundred thousand people. While the UN opposed the occupation, it did nothing to stop it, and the Sahrawi-led Polisario Front could not thwart the Moroccans or the Mauritanians. In little time, thousands of Sahrawis died or disappeared, and the majority of the survivors were forced into the refugee camps of Tindouf, in neighboring Algeria. By 1982 the Polisario had managed to push back the Mauritanian troops and to corner the Moroccans. The latter, in response, began constructing gigantic fortifications—walls to divide the desert in two. By 2009 there were around 2,700 kilometers of walls in the Western Sahara, guarded by 130,000 Moroccan soldiers. To this day, about two-thirds of the Western Sahara is under Moroccan control and one-third, Sahrawi.

As the forces were colliding in the 1970s and 1980s, the Sahrawi population was dispersed across the region, away from El Aaiún, from Tiris, from Amiskarif, toponymic towns that, once home to many, had become emblems of a confiscated past. Bahia Mahmud Awah, Mohammed Ebnu, Chejdan Mahmud Yazid, Limam Boicha, and Zahra el Hasnaui Ahmed are part of a generation that has lived most of its life during this political stalemate. They oppose the Moroccan occupation and demand autonomy for the Western

Sahara. In the 1980s, many of these poets crossed the Atlantic to flourish in an abundant and pluralist Caribbean. Cuba, for many Sahrawis, was an essential *mawqif:* not that "resting place" we often hear about (i.e., not another "refuge") but "a (momentary) stance in relation to and with space," as one of us has written; it is "horizonal, . . . active, in motion" ("Notes toward a Nomad Poetics: 1996–2002," in *A Nomad Poetics,* by Pierre Joris [Middletown, CT: Wesleyan UP, 2003], pp. 47–48). The *vuelta* through Cuba repeats the Sahrawi's nomadic and hybrid history: "I keep dodging those who raise no / dust cloud on the road" (Awah). The combination of blurred borders and political violence that dispersed the Sahrawis to Algeria, Spain, and Latin America has stoked deeply nostalgic poetry: "To die and come back to life / in the atlantic underbelly" (el Hasnaui).

These poets are known as the *Generación de la Amistad saharaui,* a group formed in 2005. Their writing is intimately linked to the Latin American poetry of José Martí, Mario Benedetti, and Pablo Neruda, in addition to the Spanish tradition of Garcia Lorca and the Generation of '27. Many Sahrawis, after studying in Cuba, returned to the camps at Tindouf or moved to Spain, continuing their nomadic *andares.* In Tindouf, radio provided a major outlet for the dissemination of resistance media, among which poetry was an essential element. Rather than embracing the formal aesthetics of their Spanish and American brethren, the Sahrawis seem to embrace the notion of autochthony common to indigenist poetics that gravitate toward a sort of social realism—"We exist / by translating the hieroglyphs / of eternal hardship"—unrelenting in its democratic politics—"We exist / with empirical proof and calendars" (Boicha). Some argue that the struggle in the Sahara, with its calls to delegitimize the old regime at the turn of the millennium, contributed significantly to the recent Arab Spring. These poems get their power from the defiance of an oppressive state, with pacifist and humane sincerity, outspoken anger and sorrow, bearing the weight of the dead and disappeared, in verse that is both politically and poetically committed: "A storm rises on the horizon / and I am prepared" (Ebnu).

The contemporary Sahrawi lyric is defined by a poetics in which the embattled Sahara ever looms, giving rise to patriotic and defiant aesthetics. "Every revolution," says Yazid, "has its poetry, its literature, its music . . . corresponding to the times in which it is lived. My poetry is not a pamphlet but rather just that which falls to me to write." Thus, it is a poetics of responsibility, born from the confluence of political defiance and human affection. "Our poetry," he continues, "joins protest with intimacy, because the best way to show the world suffering is to talk about what one feels" (quoted in "Chejdan Mahmud y Luali Lehsen: 'Escribimos para liberar al Sáhara,'" by Juan Luis Tapia, in *Ideal,* May 12, 2011).

Bahia Mahmud Awah (b. Auserd, 1960)

THE BOOKS

The books spoke to me
of disastrous, unjust wars
& also showed me
how to hate them,
how to reproach them.
Into the guts of
my century
the books guided me.
For I have seen
day-laborer poets,
groundskeeper poets,
window washer poets.
Poets
who stoke letters
where the sky englobes
the deserts' immensity.
But I've also seen
that a day-laborer poet's
word is worth
as much as a tulip
in Constantinople.
Waiting on the road
for more than thirty years waving
at the indifferent gait
of many caravans
that would not notice
my face already gaunt
from years of waiting.
Nobody said,
poor guy sentenced to the immensity
of his wait.
Nor did they think to say
I had died

on the road.
While their caravans pass me by
I raise my arms, stiffened
with the conviction
of a statue of liberty
that not even time could topple.

I HAVE FAITH IN TIME

I keep escaping to the infinity
of time.

I keep sidestepping false
starts.

I keep dodging those who raise no
dust-cloud on the road.

I keep evading those who don't believe
in the day
tomorrow will bear.

But I do believe in you,
today, tomorrow and for centuries
to come
and thus
my escape to the infinity of time.

A POEM IS YOU

A woman behind bars
shouts out:
What is a poem?
& a poet in exile
replies:
It's you.
We, the power,
the logos
of verse & poem.

ORPHAN AT A STARBUCKS

Amiskarif, in the jungle
of the West,
perhaps
your name tastes like nothing.
I feel the sum of
your majestic letters bruise,
& turn you
into the pyramid of Tiris
& the fief of its gazelles.
But to me, Amiskarif
sounds
more like a treasure
between Tiris's toasted breasts.

COMMENTARY

Bahia Mahmud Awah—born 1960 in the southern region of the Western
Sahara—graduated from the University of Havana in Cuba & then returned
to the Tindouf refugee camps to direct Spanish-language programs on Sahrawi
National Radio for four years. He went on to study journalism & translation
theory in Spain & has contributed to news & cultural publications. He collabo-
rates with Suerte Mulana, a cultural organization, & is a founding member of
the *Generación de la Amistad saharaui*. He has contributed to several antholo-
gies, including *Aaiún, gritando lo que se siente* (2006), *31. Treinta y uno, Thirty
one* (2007), *Um Draiga* (2007), *Don Quijote, el azri de la badia saharaui* (2009),
& *La fuente de Saguia* (2009). His own publications include *Versos refugiados*
(poems, 2007) & *La maestra que me enseñó en una tabla de madera* (prose,
2011).

Zahra el Hasnaui Ahmed (b. El Aaiún, 1963)

VOICES

To all the Sahrawi voices locked in graves and jails;
those voices that, nevertheless, bring down more than walls.

Perhaps you think your voice does not reach me,
that the evil sirocco carries it off
before it fills my senses.

Perhaps you dream that the echo is mute
the mirror blind and your lines
cowardice.
Your clones pile up,
and in a riot they fight
in black and white
to leave my throat.
Sometimes I spit,
almost always I gobble
down wrath and blood,
and peace and dirt.
I would like to chain
your hands to mine
and swing open the roof
top up to the stars.
I would like to wash
the anger from your eyes.
Thirty voices
thirty times
repeat the history,
because no one or thing
ever could or can tame
the voices that brush
against the soul.

"THEY SAY THAT THE NIGHT"

To that childhood friend, clearly present in the distance, my Rio Saguia

They say that the night
repossesses
your indigo, violet,
and cobalt tones.
That on your lap
the salty kisses
dried up.

They say that
the sonata
of wind
becomes a
symphony of
chaotic notes
conducted
by fear.

Ignore the spears
of the serpent.

I will return,
wrapped in cloaks
of red stars,
to clean up
the contaminated water.

To die and come back to life
in the atlantic underbelly.

GAZES

*Dedicated to Fatimetu. This friend had to inform her mother, one morning, that her
fourth brother had died in battle. The evidently shocking answer of her mother, "Prepare
breakfast and send the kids to school," I understood once she added, "let us not allow
him to have died in vain."*

Gray dawn dyed red forebodes the worst.
You shoot an inquisitive look, understanding, accepting,
Gash in the heart, serene expression.
Your orphan tear contrasts my downpour
Of pain, your calm against my blustery awakening.
My eyes exclaim: Scream! Cry! Pull out this merciless
Spear launched by ignorant ambition.
Your relatives take me in, consoling, comforting.
Like a craftsman fearful of fragile work, you breathe in, fold up, and,
With obstinate parsimony, cherish his scanty belongings in your trunk.
Get up, you whisper, the sun has already risen.

Zahra el Hasnaui Ahmed was born in El Aaiún, the capital of the old Spanish Sahara. After the Moroccan invasion, she first went to study a thousand kilometers away from El Aaiún & then to Madrid, where she received her degree in English philology at the Universidad Complutense. She then returned to the Sahara, where for several years she lived in the refugee camps of Tindouf & collaborated on Spanish-language programs for Sahrawi National Radio. She currently resides in Spain & has contributed to several Sahrawi poetry anthologies, including *Aaiún, gritando lo que se siente* (2006), *Um Draiga* (2007), & *31. Treinta y uno, Thirty one* (2007).

Mohammed Ebnu (b. Amgala, 1968)

EXILE

To Mario Benedetti

My exile is nearly congenital,
like the perennial echo of the mountains of Tiris.
The wind whips my *haymah* of exhausted pleas,
but looking into the distance, as always, I pray for where one returns to.

A storm rises on the horizon
& I am prepared.

Each day my exile is greater & wider
like my dreams, like the hope for a return.

Next to the door I always keep my luggage.
Though my luggage fits in one of my pockets,
like the sand I carry in my lungs.

CHILDREN OF SUN AND WIND

We still live on the corners
of nothingness
between the seasons' north & south.

We still sleep with stone
pillows under our arms
like our parents did.

We chase the same clouds
& rest in the shade of naked thorn trees.

We take our tea in fiery sips
walk barefoot so as not to startle the silence.

& from a distance
we still stare at the mirage's
peripheries, as if at the evening
sunsets into the sea.

& the same woman who stops
at crepuscular *atalayas* to greet us
in the center of the map
greets us & dissolves
in the eyes of a child who smiles
on the lap of eternity.

We still wait for another dawn
to begin anew.

MESSAGE IN A BOTTLE

In silence
I greet you with wandering eyes
over the radio waves.

In silence
I send you ignited verses
& the voice of a poet who sang to you
even after death.

In silence
on these coasts that face you
I've entrusted the waves with
a message of freedom in a bottle.

In silence
after my voice grows hoarse
I shall keep shouting your stormy name,
your pain, your wounds, your solitude.

In silence
I shall keep counting
the paces that separate
your city from the dunes
lodged in my several hearts.

COMMENTARY

Mohammed Ebnu (born in the Western Sahara, 1968) studied literature at the Instituto Superior Pedagógico de Pinar del Río, Cuba. He has contributed to the anthologies *Añoranza* (2003), *Bubisher* (2003), *Aaiún, gritando lo que se siente* (2006), *Um Draiga* (2007), *31. Treinta y uno, Thirty one* (2007), & *Don Quijote, el azri de la badia saharaui* (2009). He has also published two collections of his own: *Voz de fuego* (2003) & *Nómada en el exilio* (2008). A founding member of the *Generación de la Amistad saharaui*, he lives in Spain.

Chejdan Mahmud Yazid (b. Tindouf, 1972)

SIROCCO

Day is always already
made eternal.
Fatimetu grabs her *melhfa*
and wraps her unfazed face
with a run of the mill cloth.
Other sad stares
invoke some mystery.
From the viscera
of a feeble abode
peace is writhing
and, in passing,
pisses off the flies.
There in the shadows
some boy babbles
then
some derisive sermon
is given
and distant realms

corrode our throats.
At the edge
of the *haymah* and *la nada*,
the day grew bitter,
and no one wanted
to damn the gods.

THE EXPECTORATED SCREAM

A drama that's been written
on spurious tablets
of high-profile circles.
They crack down on the streets
today in the city of cold springs:
the tireless soul, going to and fro,
tries, at all cost,
to calm the nerves.

From a shady side street
or insidious avenue,
they arrive, like swarms of flies,
the soldiers of discord
and with their weapons spray down
the angst of the foggy air.

The drama of the Sahara
is still pure of flawed
tongues and distant gazes.

Meanwhile
our blood
will still be shed
over here and there
for the great inalienable reason:
of wandering through the breeze
of the authentic Saharan air.
Aroma of myrrh and beduin stares
shall, therefore, replenish
our rootedly nomadic life.

ENOUGH!

Enough! Furious streets
rise up and state
the grave allegations.
Enough! Houses swarm
with exorbitant anger.
And, enough! Because this
no longer can wait.
At times like these there's no
anger left to quell and pent-up rage
blazes inside the
downtrodden heart.
Spirited cities of the grim
Sahara rise up
once again to scream:
Enough! Enough! Enough!

COMMENTARY

Born in 1972, Chejdan Mahmud Yazid grew up in the refugee camps of Tindouf.
Like many of his contemporaries, he studied at the Universidad de Havana,
Cuba, where he received a degree in Hispanic philology & began to write. He
has contributed to the contemporary Sahrawi poetry anthologies *Bubisher*
(2003), *Aaiún, gritando lo que se siente* (2006), *Um Draiga* (2007), & *31. Treinta
y uno, Thirty one* (2007). His poem "¡Basta!" (Enough!), from the anthology
Aaiún, dedicated to the Sahrawi Resistance for Peace, translated into & read in
Arabic & Spanish alike, won the award for best poem at the IV Festival: Palabra
del Mundo in Mexico City. In 1997 he went to the Canary Islands for a PhD in
literary theory. In January 2002 he began working for the Red Cross of Spain
as a counselor in an immigrant support center, where he also teaches Spanish.

Limam Boicha (b. Atar, 1973)

THE ROADS OF THE SOUTH

Don't forget to say
the names of God
if you go down the roads of the South.

On the planes of Tiris
the dust is having a blast
after the blessings.

A toast breaks the nostalgic song
from the Valley of Sadness
to the Heart of the Scorpions.

When the moon bundles up
old lady night is left alone
in the silhouette of a hearth.

A ship of burning ash
inebriated with anxiety
is drinking dirt in the bay.

Among the travelers
she is there nude,
with her shiny black hair
that reaches her thighs.

Handcuffed by bandages & henna
she walks among the ageless stones
through regions that have no lakes.

Between kisses & rainstorms,
between hugs & promises,
something smells like contraband.

Don't forget to say
the names of God
if you go down the roads of the South.

BOUGHS OF THIRST

In the shade of a thorn tree
two bodies shudder
before their nakedness
while half a desert
separates them & their *ma al-ayún*.
In the Bay of Santiago
someone beat a drum & crooned
an entrancing primitive chant
in Hassaniya or Amharic
in Mandinka or Castilian.
A letter in Catalan arrived

from the Font de Canaletas,
with map & all,
announcing that stray, still
unbranded camel
would make a good water trough.

EXISTENCE

We exist
as the unalterable identity
of this life in itself.

We exist
by translating the hieroglyphs
of eternal hardship.

We exist
among collapsing wells
without the miracle of grass.

We exist
with empirical proof & calendars.

COMMENTARY

Limam Boicha was born in the Western Sahara in 1973. In 1982 he arrived in Cuba, a land he would come to embrace. He went on to study journalism before returning to the refugee camps of Tindouf, where he collaborated on Sahrawi National Radio. He is a member of the *Generación de la Amistad saharaui,* & his poems have appeared in the anthologies *Añoranza* (2003) & *Bubisher* (2003). He has also published a collection of his own, *Versos de la madera* (2004). He lives in Barcelona.

A BOOK OF EXILES

One could argue that the major constant of the Maghreb over a period of millennia has been continuous movements of people(s): the immigration of whole peoples, small tribes, or even individuals and the emigration of groups and individuals at similar rates—all of these moves sometimes forced by wider historical-political circumstances, at other times by the desire to find economic or other opportunities elsewhere. Obviously, our gathering reflects this nomadic reality throughout its various diwans and books, but it seemed useful for us to present late in the anthology a small section devoted to more or less contemporary moves in both directions.

The first concerns the diaspora leaving the Maghreb, and the opening figure is the strange symbolist poet Mario Scalési, born in Tunis in 1892—though of a Maltese mother and an Italian father—who died in Palermo, Sicily, of tuberculosis at thirty. If it may be difficult to see in him the classical Maghrebi, Scalési is, however, one of those characteristic Mediterranean figures who have peopled the southern edge of this sea for millennia. The Tunisian critic and scholar Ali Abassi speaks of Scalési's oeuvre as "elegiac," which links it to an "omnipresent lyricism" throughout the twentieth century. Even though Scalési's poems are formally anchored in nineteenth-century symbolist poetry, he links to a more avant-garde tradition, maybe unknowingly, in one poem (not reproduced here) called "Amour bilingue"—"Bilingual Love"—which is written in a mix of French and Italian.

This specific title is picked up many years later by the Moroccan poet and essayist Abdelkebir Khatibi (see p. 654), who calls one of his book-length essays *Amour bilingue,* a superb meditation on the general Maghrebian situation of a native bilingualism (Arabic and French in his case). Exactly this essay will be picked up by another diasporic Maghrebian philosopher we have inserted into this section, namely Jacques Derrida, who answers Khatibi in another book-length essay, *The Monolingualism of the Other, or*

The Prosthesis of Origin, extracted here, in which Derrida—who until then had been the "metropolitan," or Parisian, French philosopher par excellence—starts to relocate and think through his Jewish Maghrebian origins in his usual brilliant manner.

Even more central to this diasporic section is the Arabist Jacques Berque, born in 1910 to French parents (his father was an Arabist scholar of distinction) in Frenda, Algeria. After studying in Algiers, he worked in Morocco as a civil servant, administering the Seksawa tribe at Imi n'Tanout in the High Atlas. This stay led to his first major book, *Les Structures Sociales du Haut Atlas* (1955), one of the most thorough anthropological studies of Amazigh culture ever undertaken, from which our extract is chosen. Berque went on to become not only the preeminent scholar of the Maghreb and, beyond, of all Arab cultures but, given his gifts as a writer and linguist, also a major translator of classical Arabic texts, most notably the pre-Islamic corpus of the *Mu'allaqat*, the "Odes"—his translation of which may be the best non-Arabic version of these poems we have. Late in life he settled in the Landes region in the southwest of France, from where the Berque family had come. He died there, in Saint-Julien-en-Born, in 1995.

Following Derrida's is a selection by his close friend Hélène Cixous. For her, born in Oran to a German Ashkenazi Jewish mother and a French *pied-noir* Sephardic Jewish father, the diasporic Maghrebian roots have grown more central, as for Derrida, as her work as a writer, feminist, and philosopher has progressed. Hubert Haddad, a Tunisia-born writer with a massive oeuvre of prose and poetry, closes out this section.

But of course the nomadic fluxes also move in the other direction, and we have included three writers who claim the Maghreb as home though they come from outside. Paul Bowles, maybe the best known of these, was an American-born composer and writer who elected Tangiers as his home for more than half a century and is possibly the English-language writer who has done the most to bring the Maghreb and its writers to the attention of the West. (Beyond his text here, see also his translations of Mohamed Choukri, p. 648, and Mohamed Mrabet, p. 523.) The Spanish writer Juan Goytisolo, after years of exile in Paris to escape Francisco Franco's repression, also settled in the Maghreb, finding deep affinities with the land, its people, and a culture that would profoundly influence his writing. Another fascinating example of cultural migration is Cécile Oumhani, a poet born in Namur, Belgium, of French, Scottish, and Tunisian stock who has decided that she wants to be known as a Maghrebian writer.

Mario Scalési (Tunis, 1892–Palermo, 1922)

SYMBOLISM

At my memory's roots great candles were alight;
The flowers of my past whose perfume has expired
Shed leaves from stalks which fell into black water's night,
Bearing away with them dead hopes of things desired.

And the despotic shadows which now haunt my mind
Have pitilessly banished my sunny-coloured dreams;
Sad galley-slave bent down upon the oar, I find
That I crave sobs at night with less ruddy-coloured gleams.

In the pure spring morning's air, and at the edge
Of the divine bocage where the memory dies,
I saw upon your sacred lip the trembling pledge—
That sweet laugh of coralline which floats in future's skies.

NEW YEAR'S GIFT

So that I counter your siren's sharp dart
And bind to my fate your fat with firm hold,
I want to buy you, to mark the year's start
   A flask of bright gold.

Into this flask from old Pisa, enchased
With a goldsmith's ruby flowers on its bole,
My love which singes my lip I'll have placed
   With some vitriol.

But the sun will eclipse its cruel face,
My vesperal heart I feel weeping too.
Oh! Were I but able to burn your face
   Without harming you!

SUNRISE

From lagoon's deep gloom emerges
Rayless and vermilion globe
Which from darkness upwards surges
Drapes o'er hill and sea its robe;
And with rose and moiré glitter
Makes aware the bird which sleeps
Piercing lakes still darkly bitter,
And midst reedy shallows creeps.
—Happy he whose heart, translated
From its anguished grief, O dawn,
With exquisite calmness sated,
Of your fiery lightness born.
Happy he whose dream devises
All your gilded flowers, O sun,
And believes that with you rises
Naked Love, who mocks death's fun!

WORDS OF A DYING SOLDIER

The fire from German guns today has crushed my knees
And pierced my lungs. O flowers in the vale, so dear!
To my soul, ready to fly, memories appear.
Not till it's lost can the day's sweetness truly please.

Tomorrow will my friends dig hollows, and in these
Will lay the dead without a pang, without a tear.
There we shall hallow a reunion serene, sincere
With the warm earth where ruddy corn sprouts at its ease.

So be it. The first love decrees that I expire
For the ecstasy and pride which fashions his empire;
O native soil, you were my first love, premier bliss.

France, fair Amazon, lover of strength supreme,
Clasp me in your fecund bosom, flesh and dream:
In dying I bestow on you the nuptial kiss.

to His Majesty William II,
Emperor of Germany

Kaiser, I love you; and your ermine
is my sun of Messidore.
Ardent apostle of my doctrines,
I am His Majesty Death.

Translations from French by Lieutenant Colonel Roger E. R. Robinson

Jacques Berque (Frenda, 1910–Saint-Julien-en-Born, 1995)

from "TRUTH AND POETRY": ON THE SEKSAWA TRIBE

Durkheim's sociology has been the topic of a nasty quarrel apropos of the "parts" it accords to the group and the individual. I will not get involved in it after the lucid developments recently dedicated to this question by G. Gurvitch and G. Davy. But I will yield, so to speak, to the natural inclination of the exploration, namely to the *taqbilt*s Seksawa of the High Atlas. What can be found, after having looked at the country, its cantons, its villages, its houses, are men who gave shape to all the rest. And among these men a number of great figures emerge: those of characters that were at the front of the scene, some twenty or twenty-five years ago, at the moment of the pacification.[1]

The Heroes

At the moment of the pacification, the High Atlas Mountains are in a full-fledged tyrannical phase. Cyclical or not, a phenomenon of personal power has developed that prevails over the old tendencies of spontaneous democracy in the higher cantons. Press accounts have popularized the great names of Glauoi, Gund'afi, L'ayyadi, and, more importantly for our region, Mtuggi. The terrain of these characters extends over the entire High Atlas, from Mogador to Demnat, as well as from Chemaia to Sous. So far for the material dimension, that of a helping hand, of expeditions, of clever victories, and of defeats soon countered. Another, more subtle dimension of intrigues extends to Fez and expands to the scale of Morocco as a whole, bearing on and amplifying the former dimension.

---

1. The following subsection has as a principal source the direct survey of survivors of that era.

The same does not hold for our mountain potentates. On the one hand, they have less space. It has nothing in common with the space in which their fathers moved about in the fourteenth century, the time of the "kings of the mountain." On the other hand, their stakes are to a large extent a function of the stakes of the main protagonists, or, in the case of the Seksawa, of the great Mtuggi. The latter already is a pious, wily old man and friend of the arts. He reigns with absolutism over a large, haughty tribe: people from calcareous lands, taller and more vigorous than the mountain people, and most dominating because of a solid military staff, a better warfare and feint technique, greater breakaways. Si Abelmalek Mtuggi brings about a restoration after the disaster endured by al-Hiba before Marrakech. Henceforth, he maintains a sort of administration between the mountains and the French that is alternately helpful and reluctant, discreetly offended by our ventures and sourly attached to its mediating role—a policy of flux and reflux affecting the middle Seksawa.

On our mountain, at least three conquerors are held in a stronghold. Violent and sly characters, strong with instincts and machinations, quick on the ambush and the powder, and even more so on the well-formulated intrigue, on the agile volt, and on the poison in the sauce. The high lands of a. H'adduyws have the *amghar* Ah'med Umulid of Tasa, the purest. The Idma have a malicious old man, with an only falsely venerable beard, Lh'ajj H'fid'. The a. Lah'sen have their boss Mokhtar, which makes all the difference. The latter dies in June 1926. We are witness to the first submission of the high Seksawa, a. H'adduyws included. It is a wholly nominal one. The veil *lght'a* covering the tomb of Lalla Aziza, a sort of "zaimph" à la Flaubert, is solemnly brought to the Imintanout bureau, as a token of unity. Let's take to this crucial moment in the Seksawa history to sketch one of its great figures.

The "boss" Mokhtar was a fierce warlord, who more or less dominated the whole east-west diagonal through the Seksawa lands. His methods are expeditious. They are those of all times and all countries: disposing of the adversary at the lowest cost. The following is an example of how our hero gets rid of his adversary, the "boss" Chtittihi of the a. Musa. Between them rages that old competition of alternating assassination attempts and kind words, of gunshots and cups of tea. A first time, Mokhtar barely escaped a bombing: gunpowder had been amassed below the room where he dined, located on a higher floor. The henchman, the host's proper son, lights the fuse, and from below calls for his father, thus warning him to leave right away. This sign, and a stroke of luck, has the boss move quickly toward an opening: the explosion hurls him safe and sound on a dunghill. The bomber's father is killed.

But here is the epilogue. In May 1907, the two chiefs start peace negotiations. Mokhtar's emissary and Chtittihi meet. They even brought along a relic of Lalla Aziza. But they had left it in the reception room. Chtittihi sends his man to fetch it and is left alone with the emissary, who sinks his hand into his *chkara* and pulls from it a fine gun. Chtittihi falls on the floor of his native wadi. The murderer strips him of his valuables and joins Mokhtar. The *amghar* immediately marches his troupes toward the villages of a. Musa, which capitulate. The body of Chtittihi is brought to the victor, who hands it over to the Asstif marabouts. One can feel a Homeric scene of intercession coming up.

These savage adventures characterize the group and the era. They abound in the history of the mountains, but even more so, perhaps, with the Seksawa, whose old chronicles are full of these deadly banquets—a remake of antique legend. Mokhtar is the virtuoso of such feints. He is all sharpness, slyness. I would nearly say cruelty, if it weren't for careful planning, which makes it all tactics, rather than instinct.

Individual Psychologies

Let's dig deeper. The great figures of the *amghar*s today no longer have counterparts of the same type. And, furthermore, on that level the analysis would come close to the political essay, which is not at all our endeavour. I shall want to call for more humble characters, in an intentionally unelaborated and incomplete form. As such there won't be a "portrait" or "collective psychology" of the Seksawa. Not because its method is outdated, but because of the materials at hand. We have not yet arrived to a point, in Maghreb studies, to come up with the laws that connect several character types into one coherent whole, or that, on the contrary, tease out a fundamental incoherence between these types. We are restricted to a method of sampling. Let's therefore limit ourselves to collecting here a fair amount of, as Stendhal said, "small real facts," which the surroundings offer by the hundreds. They are for the better part short accounts, letters, reports of encounters. Materials awaiting a psychology of the Maghrebi groups.[2]

Choral Poetry as a Document

But would the analysis not lack precision and even sincerity if it pretended to forget everything that is usually gathered under the label of "the pictur-

---

2. Berque collected "raw materials" which cover different domains: return from the Orient, rediscovering the country, sacrilege, salvation by the a local saint, other apparitions of the saint, diplomatic correspondence of the good old times, the story of Yamina Amazuz, bewitchment and politics, property claims, the joyous military, suicide, Medea. —Trans.

esque"? Would that be very scientific? As a whole, these kinds of images, of chants, enter perhaps more profoundly into the intimacy of beings and things than a well-concocted study. An artist has certain states of graces that a sociologist does not enjoy. Without remorse, the latter can, moreover, put to work—in order to exploit—the elements of literary expression as a basis for an often arid and barbaric analysis. Especially when that expression is local or indigenous.

The whole reality of the Atlas comes to us, indeed, preceded or perhaps sustained by chants. Whence the importance of restoring the so powerful sonorous core of that life. Colonel Justinard has been working in this field for many years now. But he is the man of Gund'afa and of Tiznit. Should we content ourselves, then, with impressions by analogy? Certainly, we are in the Shleuh music domain, and the language, the workmanship, and the inspiration repeat what, through Justinard, we had already glimpsed of that lyricism that is at once closed off and delivered. In our case, it is rather an acridity and cleverness that is expressed, an unblinking conscience too, malicious and virulent in its epigram, equivocal in its praise, always awakening. The chorus is the journalist of this society. But how can such a dry matter transform itself into sudden alchemies of freshness? These complicated and charming people reject all irresponsibility, even that of the bard; in the face of bitter realities they maintain a wicked fidelity that miraculously knows how to become chant.

This poetry has inspirers that combine the lyric trance with a journalist's precision. It is, to use a familiar proverb, "gut science," *'ilm l-krucha*. Recently, in Hutjan, a known composer started to work only after inhaling breath that got him full to bursting, exhaling again through hoarse groaning and panting: then the poem was born.

The *ined'd'amen*, a hierarchy, rules among poets, based on how much pleasure they take in improvising sentences and balancing rhythms. These privileged share with the *poeta vates* the mysterious aptitude of feeling hidden things, of foreseeing the future. On a lower level is the simple coryphée, or *rraïs*, leader of the dance, animator of the play, inventor of phrases (some of which will become notorious). Lower still is the circumstantial improviser whose voice proposes to the chorus a theme the whole group picks up, which is precisely the genre called *amarg*. Topical affairs take a large part in this poetry, in the form of a satire or a panegyric, *tazzrart*, pl. *tizzrarin*. An invented story may crop up, too, in which case it is romanticized legend or a fairy tale, *lqiççt*.

In the latter case, we are proceeding toward recitation, or rather to individual psalmody. Yet most of the time the figure and voice of this poetry remain collective. It is the *ah'wach*, which is above all a communal dance.

Its goal or occasion is the intensification of the group's life, and, through rhythm, an association of it to an important circumstance, brotherhood, alliance, marriage, etc. Its social, nonreligious, and civil character opposes it, for example, to ecstatic dances of certain brotherhoods. But the gestures are the same, as well as the exaltation they both provoke. So, despite very different starting points, a certain interlacing of these two types of manifestations can be seen.

Essentially, the *ah'wach* consists of a movement of a lined-up group of men, accompanied by rhythmic waddling back and forth, of simple steps and clapping palms. A recitative alternates with the incredibly dry and nervous sound of those hands and feet.

In a more rich form, the *assga,* there is an exchange of call and response between two half choruses of men and women. Because the women evidently participate too. They are never absent from anything at all in this communal life. One can see them rushing about in cheerfully laughing little groups. The disgrace in the lines of their clothing that flaunt their hips (the colors save everything). The *sinus* of fabric that leans on the small of the back serves as a bag and swells with the most miscellaneous things. They give an impression of being walking tables on the mountain slopes. But the legs of these tables are young and supple: one should see them cross ditches and hills along their long trotting and dancing march. And the upsurging chests are sometimes very beautiful. The white of the skirts, the red of the shawls and waistbands, the headpieces made of silver coins clickety-clacking on the faces and chests animate the green penumbra of the *assais,* under the grotesque walnut trees.

Of course, such a rapid evocation cannot meet the precise analyses this institution requires. Sound and film recordings, sketches would be essential. They would reveal, in the Seksawa land alone, an entire geography of dance, and many folkloric varieties. Here, the musicians have a feather in their turban: without doubt to clean their flute. In Fensu, the coryphée gets her inspiration from greedily inhaling some drafts of kif. In Imt'ddan, the female dancers adorn themselves with a tuft of grass on their heads. Finally, in several cantons in a well-defined quadrilateral—a. Chaib and a. Bkher in Demsira, a. H'adduyws in Seksawa, people from the Aghbar and of the high Gedmiwa—the dance itself takes a specific form. It is a Pyrrhic dance, called *tiskiwin,* that is, so to speak, "powder horns," or, more subtly, as some would have it, a dance of the ram with ritual remnants.

Some On-the-Spot Notes—Butaghradin, 17.III.49 [March 17, 1949]

The white court of the *Amghar.* A tight row of spectators squatting against the walls. It is night. An acetylene lamp bearer, immobile, illuminates the dancers up front. A male half chorus livens up, becomes more and more passionate, clapping hands and beating feet. The other half chorus consists of adolescents with partially shaved heads. But near midnight, the matrons, till then only spectators, enter the game and begin the dialogue with the men. Sometimes forming a round that encircles the round of men, and sometimes facing them in a lineup parallel to the men. The 'allàm "coryphée" guides them with a both nervous and cordial cudgel. The lineups get mixed up. The colors, with yellow and red dominating, blend in the outburst of costumes, the hammering of naked heels. In all likelihood, the European visitor, for most official reasons, has only witnessed the beginning of these feasts, where women seem to be the guards of an antique freedom. As for the poetries, what follows are some notes taken here and there, as a contribution to the Berber *diwan* that our scholars have begun to assemble: "For sure I will pay all taxes / but my husband has to talk to you . . . / a new river floats. / Water. No more grazing nor thirst . . . / The farmers, with their mares, have descended / from the plain to work the *bekri* / each of them can choose from the fillies / but the poor only have the *mazuziat* . . . " (ait Lah'sen). "The river is full, the word steady. / Justice strengthens. / Joy from the earth to the heavens. / The wind scatters the birds. / But Sidi Benaïssa gathers them together again" (ait Musa). "There's a reservoir of tea in the village, / of which the *amghar* is the *amazzel* . . . / He brought us a light: / don't forget to bring a second. / It's a feat to walk on one's hands / but if you don't want to fall, / it's better to walk upright . . . " (Wanz'id').

Translation from French by Peter Cockelbergh

Jacques Derrida (Algiers, 1930–Paris, 2004)

from *THE MONOLINGUALISM OF THE OTHER, OR THE PROSTHESIS OF ORIGIN*

Chapter 2

. . . So this meeting—which had just opened, as you recall—was an international colloquium. In Louisiana, which is not, as you know, anywhere in France. Generous hospitality. Invited guests? Francophones *belonging,* as we strangely say, to several nations, cultures, and states. And all these problems of *identity,* as we so foolishly say nowadays. Among all the participants, there were two, Abdelkebir Khatibi and myself, who, besides an old friendship, meaning the blessing of so many other things from memory and the heart, also shared a certain destiny. They live in a certain "state" as far as language and culture are concerned: they have a certain status.

In what is so named and is indeed "my country," this status is given the title of "Franco-Maghrebian" [*Franco-Maghrébin*].

What can that possibly mean to say, I ask you, you who are fond of meaning-to-say [*vouloir-dire*]? What is the nature of that hyphen? What does it want? What is Franco-Maghrebian? Who is a "Franco-Maghrebian"?

In order to know *who* a Franco-Maghrebian is, it is necessary to know *what Franco-Maghrebian is,* what "Franco-Maghrebian" means. To put it the other way round, by inverting the circulation of the circle in order to determine, *vice versa, what it is to be Franco-Maghrebian,* it would be necessary to know who is, and (Oh Aristotle!) above all who is the *most* Franco-Maghrebian. As a model, let us use a logic that would be, say, of the Aristotelian type: we model ourselves upon what *is* "most this or that" or what *is* "the best this or that," for example, upon the entity [*l'étant*] par excellence in order to reach down to thinking the being of what is *in general,* proceeding that way regarding the being of the entity [*l'être de l'étant*], from theology to ontology and not the reverse (even if actually things are, as you will say, more complicated, but that is not the subject).

According to a circular law with which philosophy is familiar, we will affirm then that the one who is *most,* most purely, or most rigorously, most essentially, Franco-Maghrebian would allow us to decipher *what it is to be* Franco-Maghrebian *in general.* We will decipher the essence of the Franco-Maghrebian from the paradigmatic example of the "*most* Franco-Maghrebian," the Franco-Maghrebian par excellence.

Still, assuming there were some historical unity of *a* France and *a* Maghreb, which is far from being certain, the "and" will never have been given, only promised or claimed. At bottom, that is what we must be talking about, what we are talking about without fail, even if we are doing it by omission. The silence of that hyphen does not pacify or appease anything, not a single torment, not a single torture. It will never silence their memory. It could even worsen the terror, the lesions, and the wounds. A hyphen is never enough to conceal protests, cries of anger or suffering, the noise of weapons, airplanes, and bombs.

Chapter 3

So let us form a hypothesis, and leave it to work. Let us suppose that without wishing to hurt Abdelkebir Khatibi's feelings, one day at the colloquium in Louisiana, far from his home and from mine, also far from our home, I make him a declaration through the loyal and admiring affection I feel for him. What would this public declaration declare to him? Approximately the following: "You see, dear Abdelkebir, between the two of us, I consider myself to be the *most* Franco-Maghrebian, and perhaps even the *only* Franco-Maghrebian here. If I am mistaken, in error, or being misleading, then, well, I am certain someone will contradict me. I would then attempt to explain or justify myself in the best way I can. Let us look around us and classify, separate, and take things one group at a time.

"A. Among us, there are Francophone French speakers who are not Maghrebian: French speakers from France, in a word, French citizens who have come here from France.

"B. There are also among us some 'Francophones' who are neither French nor Maghrebian: Swiss, Canadians, Belgians, or Africans from various Central African countries.

"C. Finally, among us there are French-speaking Maghrebians who are not and have never been French, meaning French citizens: yourself, for example, and other Moroccans or Tunisians.

"Now, as you can see, I do not belong to any of these clearly defined groups. My 'identity' does not fall under any of these three categories. Where would I categorize myself then? What taxonomy should I invent?

"My hypothesis is, therefore, that I am perhaps the *only* one here who can call himself at once a Maghrebian (which is not a citizenship) and a French citizen. One and the other at the same time. And better yet, at once one and the other *by birth*. Birth, nationality by birth, native culture—is that not our theme here? (One day it will be necessary to devote another colloquium to language, nationality, and cultural belonging, *by death* this time around, by sepulture, and to begin with the secret of Oedipus at Colonus: all the power that this 'alien' holds over 'aliens' in the innermost secret place of the secret of his last resting place, a secret that he guards, or confides to the guardianship of Theseus in exchange for the salvation of the city and generations to come, a secret that, nevertheless, he refuses to his daughters, while depriving them of even their tears, and a just 'work of mourning.')

"Did we not agree to speak here of the language called maternal, about birth as it relates to soil, birth as it relates to blood, and birth as it relates to language, which means something entirely other? And about the relationships between birth, language, culture, nationality, and citizenship?

"That my 'case' does not fall under any of the three groups that were represented at that time, such was, at least, my hypothesis. Was that not also the only justification, if there was one, for my presence at this colloquium?"

That, roughly, is what I would have begun by declaring to Abdelkebir Khatibi.

What you want to listen to at this moment is the story that I tell myself, the one that I would like to tell myself, or that, perhaps on account of the sign, writing, and anamnesia, and also in response to the title of that meeting, the title *Renvois d'ailleurs* or *Echoes from Elsewhere,* I am limiting, without a doubt, to a little fable.

If I have indeed revealed the sentiment of being the only Franco-Maghrebian here or there, that does not authorize me to speak in the name of anyone, especially not about some Franco-Maghrebian entity whose identity remains in question. We will come back to that, for all of that is, in my case, far from being so clear.

Our question is still identity. What is identity, this concept of which the transparent identity to itself is always dogmatically presupposed by so many debates on monoculturalism or multiculturalism, nationality, citizenship, and, in general, belonging? And before the identity of the subject, what is *ipseity?* The latter is not reducible to an abstract capacity to say "I," which it will always have preceded. Perhaps it signifies, in the first place, the power of an "I can," which is more originary than the "I" in a chain where the "*pse*" of *ipse* no longer allows itself to be dissociated from power, from the mastery and sovereignty of the *hospes* (here, I am referring to the semantic chain that works on the body of hospitality as well as hostility—*hostis, hospes, hosti-pet, posis, despotes, potere, potis sum, possum, pote est, potest, pot sedere, possidere, compos,* etc.—).

To be a Franco-Maghrebian, one "like myself," is not, not particularly, and particularly not, a surfeit or richness of identities, attributes, or names. In the first place, it would rather betray a *disorder of identity* [*trouble d'identité*].

Recognize in that expression "disorder of identity" all its seriousness without excluding its psychopathological or sociopathological connotations. In order to present myself as a Franco-Maghrebian, I made an allusion to *citizenship.* As we know, citizenship does not define a cultural, linguistic, or, in general, historical participation. It does not cover all these modes of belonging. But it is not some superficial or superstructural predicate floating on the surface of experience.

Especially not when this citizenship is, through and through, *precarious, recent, threatened,* and more artificial than ever. That is "my case"; the at once typical and uncommon situation of which I would like to speak. Especially not when one has obtained this citizenship in the course of one's life, which has perhaps happened to several Americans present at this colloquium, but also, and above all, not when one has lost it *in the course of one's life,* which has certainly not happened to almost any American. And if one day some individual or other has seen their citizenship *itself* withdrawn (which is more than a passport, a "green card," an eligibility or right to vote), has that ever happened to a *group* as such? I am of course not referring to some ethnic group seceding, liberating itself one day, from another nation-state, or giving up one citizenship in order to give itself another one in a newly instituted state. There are too many examples of this mutation.

No, I am speaking of a "community" group (a "mass" assembling together tens or hundreds of thousands of persons), a supposedly "ethnic" or "religious" group that finds itself one day deprived, as a group, of its citizenship by a state that, with the brutality of a unilateral decision, withdraws it without asking for their opinion, and *without the said group gaining back any other citizenship. No other.*

Now I have experienced that. Along with others, I lost and then gained back French citizenship. I lost it for years without having another. You see, not a single one. I did not ask for anything. I hardly knew, at the time, that it had been taken away from me, not, at any rate, in the legal and objective form of knowledge in which I am explaining it here (for, alas, I got to know it in another way). And then, one day, one "fine day," without, once again, my asking for anything, and still too young to know it in a properly political way, I found the aforementioned citizenship again. The state, to which I never spoke, had given it back to me. The state, which was no longer Pétain's "French State," was recognizing me anew. That was, I think, in 1943; I had still never gone "to France"; I had never been there.

In essence, a citizenship does not sprout up just like that. It is not natural. But, as in the flash of a privileged revelation, the artifice and precariousness of citizenship appear better when it is inscribed in memory as a recent acquisition: for example, the French citizenship granted to the Jews of Algeria by the Crémieux decree in 1870. Or, better yet, in the traumatic memory of a "degradation," of a loss of citizenship: for example, the loss of French citizenship, less than a century later, for the same Jews of Algeria.

Such was, indeed, the case "under the Occupation," as we say.

Yes, "as we say," for it is actually a legend. Algeria has never been occupied. I mean that if it has ever been occupied, the German Occupant was never responsible for it. The withdrawal of French citizenship from the Jews of Algeria, with everything that followed, was the deed of the French alone. They decided that all by themselves, in their heads; they must have been dreaming about it all along; they implemented it all by themselves.

I was very young at that time, and I certainly did not understand very well—already, I did not understand very well—what citizenship and loss of citizenship *meant to say*. But I do not doubt that exclusion—from the school reserved for young French citizens—could have a relationship to the disorder of identity of which I was speaking to you a moment ago. I do not doubt either that such "exclusions" come to leave their mark upon this belonging or non-belonging *of* language, this affiliation *to* language, this assignation to what is peacefully called a language.

But who exactly possesses it? And whom does it possess? Is language in possession, ever a possessing or possessed possession? Possessed or possessing in exclusive possession, like a piece of personal property? What of this being-at-home [*être-chez-soi*] in language toward which we never cease returning?

I have just emphasized that the ablation of citizenship lasted for two years, but it did not, *strictu sensu,* occur "under the Occupation." It was a Franco-French operation, one even ought to say an act of French Algeria in the absence of any German occupation. One never saw a German uniform in Algeria. No alibi, denial, or illusion is possible: it was impossible to transfer the responsibility of that exclusion upon an occupying alien.

We were hostages of the French, enduringly [*à demeure*]; something of it remains with me, no matter how much I travel.

And I repeat it: I do not know whether there are other examples of this in the history of modern nation-states, examples of such a deprivation of citizenship decreed for tens and tens of thousands of people at a time. In October 1940, by abolishing the Crémieux decree of October 24, 1870, France herself, the French state in Algeria, the "French state" legally constituted (by the Chamber of the Popular Front!) following the well-known act of parliament, this state was refusing French identity to—rather, taking it away again from—those whose collective memory continued to recollect or had barely just forgotten that it had been lent to them as if only the day before and had not failed to give rise, less than half a century earlier (1898), to murderous persecutions and the beginnings of pogroms. Without, however, preventing an unprecedented "assimilation": profound, rapid, zealous, and spectacular. In two generations.

Does this "disorder of identity" favor or inhibit anamnesia? Does it heighten the desire of memory, or does it drive the genealogical fantasy to despair? Does it suppress, repress, or liberate? All of these at the same time, no doubt, and that would be another version, the other side of the contradiction that set us in motion. And has us running to the point of losing our breath, or our minds.

Translation from French by Patrick Mensah

Hélène Cixous (b. Oran, 1937)

LETTER-BEINGS AND TIME

. . .

> *Let her*
> *letter go*

But it is not of these letters that I wished to speak. I wished to speak of the letter that I have been (following) as if in a dream ever since I sent it, a morning in April at least twenty years ago, and maybe fifty, ahead of myself, ahead of time, above the waters of the Deluge, which I sent, in the place of my eyes, to see if by chance the land my mother, I mean Algeria, might not have resuscitated, I wished to speak of the letter to which I had spoken one day, as one goes and talks to a letter in the place of the addressee, by way of transference, by way of hypallage. The letter to Zohra Drif. As the young Balzac will have written to his letter, in the place of Mme de Berny, as he will have written a letter to his letter, like this: "Go my letter! appear with all the morning's graces, the companions of the dew, etc. . . .

How many things I have to say! I will begin by asking forgiveness for. . . . . ."

Me too, a long time ago, I put a letter in the place of Algeria, the one that I love. How many things I had to say!

It is now thirty-five years that I have not wanted to go to Algeria, I say to myself, I never thought of going there, I always thought of not going there, I wanted rather not-to-go-to Algeria, each time that I could go to Algeria it didn't happen finally, there are countries where I end up always not going, I don't do anything for this, on the one hand I have my reasons, on the other hand there are the circumstances, for Algeria it is not that I didn't want ever again to go there again, I wanted rather to go there for sure, better not to go there than to go there the wrong way, I couldn't go there any old way, it is much too dangerous, I have always taken care to retain the hypothesis that admits as probable a trip to Algeria, but I have always simultaneously admitted the contrary hypothesis: it is possible that I will never manage to go to Algeria. In reality. In the (first) case I would retain what I call "my algeri-ance," a vast set of rather disparate reflections sprung up around the notions of country, native country, original country, names of countries and around this word *country,* that is *pays,* which burrows down into the mental wax and spreads in the heart of the one who says it *la paix et la pagaille,* peace and chaos, the one like the other. If a country is recognized for what it sows, then Algeria is a great country I said to myself. I didn't want to go to Algeria and thus I preserved intact the ideal beauty of the Jardin d'Essais, as it was invented by my father in a first moment then reinvented in another part with my friend Jacques Derrida, I hoped not to go to Algeria long enough, and thus to keep the Jardin d'Essais like a reedition of Paradise on earth, and like a personal, unique and destinal paradise as this Jardin of literary Essays attempted by the one and by the other.

Algeria. To go there as in a dream, that would be the ideal I said to myself. To go there as *a dream,* I dreamed. To go there in such a magic, such an intense powerful, light, fleeing, total fashion that I would have been there even while being as if I was not there myself but another, with the force but the impunity, and even the immunity of a letter. If I could have sent myself there, sent it to myself. Letter-being. It's like for the letter to Zohra Drif that I had had the idea and the need to write. I had thought to write a letter to Z.D. in 1960, perhaps it was in 1958. For the first time. Finally I didn't write it. I didn't really think it either. I had as it were felt the light touch of a letter pass over me. It was clear but vague, that's it, it was the beginning of an impulse, one goes and then, no, but it would have been written clearly to Zohra, it's me in the gathering of the circle who lacked precision, I had the desire, the quivering wings, the letter fluttered at my window, not very far not so close, creature of the morning's dawn, then I rose and I thought I'd perhaps dreamed it. I will write a letter, it will be impossible, dear Zohra I am writing to you, from which moral political ethical philosophical viewpoint I have no idea, I have always dreamed of blowing up trains and walls if you do it I have no doubt of being happy because the inadmissible thing is admissible the blood that you speak is the same in my language, next the ideal would be to blow up the separations I wanted to tell you but my voice was separated from me it would have been necessary to begin a sentence by *we* I don't doubt the impossible, what I have most despaired of you are doing, I am on the left side of your dream, you realize almost all the irreparable desires that it made me so sad to have for nothing, if I am not you are

next I will reread this letter, it will be crossed out everywhere, I will have to block out almost all the words, that is, the words were blocking out their meaning to me, I will cleave them, I will zap them with a Z, I will leap a fence, I'll take a breath, I'll not zadvance, what do I have in common with Zohra except the silent weight of fits of zanger in the classroom, I will open the door we can blow up the door, everything impossible will be easy, I will write: I am amazed I see the just person, which I will never be, I see the resemblance to you, I am not against blows from a golden lance and the exultations of bombs

while I was living *in the letter,* sometimes in my place, sometimes in the place of Zohra at least the one whom I imagined to be Zohra, a happiness took hold of me, that I had and have never known elsewhere. It was a happiness of relief. The contents of this happiness was triumphant. I can thus enjoy a happiness that is not mine, I can be in the freedom of someone other, I can be free because of an other liberty that Z takes for me.

The letter is a tangle. No one can untangle what I think from what I think. Violence, justice revolt, courage, right, everything is all tangled up.

What is certain is that it stayed with me. A letter that I did not write. There are dozens of letters that I did not finally write to my beloved, that I was going to write, that I wrote passionately during the night, I signed with fire, I got up, the letter returned to the other world. They did not stay with me. I realize today that the letter to Z.D. is the only one to have reached the ineffaceable.

The idea occurs to me at this very instant, May 8, 2006, that perhaps the decision to go to Algiers was taken already with this letter and by all the innumerable, imperceptible circumstances, gestures, consequences contained in this sheet of paper, under the name of Z.D., perhaps this letter that has stayed with me has mingled itself with me, its totally invisible phantom atoms have spread into those regions about which we know nothing where our future events foment, so that the decision taking shape slowly, being secreted for decades, will naturally have the slow irresistible force of an accumulated seism that has been stewing for a thousand years.

The fact remains that no one today could say if I wrote *the letter* to Z.D. in the end or if I did not write it in the end. I put *time* into it. That makes any evaluation difficult. With time the letter will not have failed to change, and often. In the beginning it was an impulse, but a tenacious, seductive one. I saw myself writing in five minutes an enthusiastic spontaneous letter. Rapid. Because of its improvised character, I would not weigh my words. The idea that it would be a total surprise for Zohra did not embarrass me, between us there was none of those virtual spaces in which letters might appear, moreover the idea that we knew each other only superficially had no weight, my impetus, my soul's passion swept aside these considerations. I could thereupon surmise that Zohra on her side could not have the least idea of what was stirring within me, since 1951 on the one hand and since forever likewise. It was objectively impossible that she had the least intimation of my Algerian turmoil. All these ideas that might have cut off my impetus were dispersed by the breath that animated me in the blink of an eye. What prevented me from writing this letter, which, to summarize, was a burst of laughter, a jubilation rather than an argued missive, was the question of the address. I was nineteen years old perhaps I was no longer in Algeria, but to say I was in Paris would be exaggerated, I was in a state of mist, but in the corridors of Paris. Everything solid, brilliant, bleeding, sparkling, breathing, carnal was in Algiers, in Paris I floated in a gaseous state, I dragged through the dust, I didn't breathe. The sky? Terrible. So even the sky can be sullied by the soot of a country even the clouds suffered from a lack of lightness. To come back to Algiers, to Zohra, to the letter, I didn't have the address of Z. Not-to-have-the-address of the person to whom I wanted at all costs to write was as if I were still in Algeria wanting at all costs to speak to, touch, find I knew exactly what and whom, but I didn't know how, *where,* to reach her, the telephones were always cut off, the iron gates raised in an exaggerated way up to the first floor without handle, without doorbells, the street names unknown, and it began again. If only I had been able to write to Z.D. in care of the Lycée Fromentin where we had been in the same class three years before the letter. But that was not to be done. The letter would not be transmitted. I would not be advised. I would fall into the category of one of those destinerrances whose tragic models I have seen to my sorrow, before finding them gathered malevolent identified as the very fate of humanity, under the appellation invented by my friend J.D., all the letters that are supposed to have arrived, and with which Shakespeare, Balzac, Stendhal make literature weep, those promises of life, which do not fail to get lost and which are transformed into messages of death, they are veritable bombs. The lycée was not my friend, it was Zohra's enemy, it was neither a post office, nor a home, our French extheater antiZohra on the one hand anti-me on the other. The hypothesis that I could write to the Prison. "Z.D. Prison"—which one?— seemed to me a version of the letter addressed in care of the lycée. I saw everywhere hostility, rejection, scorn that would greet on the one hand a request signed by the one who I then was from the point of the enemy, on the other hand the addressee considered otherwise but from the same point of view. Two different combined hostilities, one addressed to the neitherthis northat being, judaic, exdeFrancified reFrenchified, which was my image seen from the French Fromentin point of view, the other turned against the Arab Muslim being, ex-boarding student at the Lycée Fromentin from there passed over from one day to the next into the recesses of the Casbah that she leaves with a basket full of fatality—there was no chance. Logically. I wanted my letter to arrive, or rather, I wanted it not to be stopped on its way. I couldn't address it except to "Zohra Drif, Algeria."

Translation from French by Peggy Kamuf

Hubert Haddad (b. Tunis, 1947)

A QUARTER TO MIDNIGHT

for Abraham Hadad

what is your most beautiful memory I asked her
at a quarter to midnight
while she drowsed in her dirty dress
her two faces superimposed according to the quantum hypothesis
you did not see me
in the grass or in the wave
the sun is so blue
that night starts over
the whole earth is covered by a thousand brilliant springs
can the word empty be empty
like my soul
does the word time last me
such a long time
plain, gentle plain
her memory collapses in the garden garage
at a quarter to midnight
woman I've lived with
winter night forest
exquisite periphery
a living island dreamed in the obscurity
the island of lost words
the island we read like a book
with its flowers, its parrots
its deep-sea divers in the heart of lead
now I'm going closer to the center
I crush the shadow of lovers in a charcoal fire
a blind painter who collects ruins
dreaming of a golden flame
at a quarter to midnight
hunted by wind, the traveler
contemplates her past through her phalanxes
in the crystal pool she plunges
she plunged
in great secret, she is transformed
she seems to rejuvenate
and become another woman

memories come to her that she has not lived
or that she has forgotten
as if another existence had been given to her
as if she had entered the body and thoughts of another
younger each night, younger, freer
different
as if every night she truly became another
from oblivion and darkness
who are murderers
they made flags from shrouds
peace is a treasure we cannot praise too much
sometimes you see a wolf in wolf's clothing
she wanted to die or make herself openwork
the horse struck by loves
passes back and forth behind the window
double song that kills and saves
when the lightning's flint pierces cranial skin
I only listen to time
the poem uncurled at the bottom of a thought
all is a matter of nudity
she runs her luck by miracle
she has nothing left but the garden and her bees,
her biography interrupted at the edge of a miracle
her companion, lover of trap doors
goes through life encircling the invisible
evening breeze, a child's head turns in all directions
but what is life, without you, without her
we must wait for night
my hearing tricks certainty
like a woman imprisoned by her tattoos
she says in madness if I had an apple I'd be cured
even a vomited apple
and those who don't understand will die
on the path of border patrolmen
profusion of the real
blaze of space and time
eyes close to end it
with the worship of deaths
taut like Ulysses' bow
around a deeply thought secret
the vague wings of reality

everything is inside of everything
the fire in the fire
the engine in the engine
a death in a death
the haunted house in the little girl who harbors everything
the manuscripts burn up
the years depart as dust
who will come save us
I have missed sight
I am dying of blindness
on the edge of a Byzantine carpet
the air's trembling irises have no more perfume
my eyes shut on other eyes
which roll at the bottom of a lava pit
it was before time bolted
when memory confused itself with light
and shadows
with these immutable things we think we see
the night, your forgetfulness, the snow on a bridge
past the doorstep
jugglers invent the universe
head and bones travel
face against earth, vast country
the instant sculpts the statue of the flood and of the clouds
I will rediscover the heirs of my glory and my fortune
said Katherine Mansfield to her rotten breasts
mares and sea horse carry me
in the great forge of metamorphoses
these monsters bear witness to our most secret errors
the illusion comes in, what good is it to dream
I was in an unknown city
people questioned me
I didn't know why
at the end they asked me to return an object
something important
which the people of this city valued terribly
they became threatening, a first blow fell
then there was a stampede, jolts and percussions
the old Lynch dance
but I did not have the object
I was on my knees
they continued to tear out my organs

a beautiful woman screamed that's enough, I have it
brandishing a sort of chicken gizzard
stuffed full of pebbles
she opened it with her teeth
I felt a prodigious relief
the pouch was empty and whistled strangely
someone threw a black cloth over me
blinded I thought it was too late
pointless to explain myself further
as someone must keep watch
at a quarter to midnight
she called him a comedian again
without understanding that at the bottom of her nothingness
burned her last impressions of reality
and who will make the inventory of lost time
these eternities past at the bottom of the water
under nourishing clocks
a streetlamp across the way spills its light
an ax beheads the hours by slight anachronism
color, violence of the truth
light is the arch of a god
he was a very large dark man
his eyes were never seen
he always wore the same abyssal mask
we called it the face dispenser
yet his hands were empty
his voice was never heard
but when we saw him once
we searched him for his eyes
we turned at every moment
we even chased after his shadow
the unknown never shows itself twice
one day inevitably the eye froze in a mirror
it was him it was no one
in a dream he returned
to lift our mask
sell it to me at the price of flesh
I do not want to be a shadow
it is this way that once in life
I would have bought my own face from a mute conjurer
whose eyes were never seen
so that she could not forget me

she and her two faces
she and her four eyes
we never saw one another again
look at me eyes night trench
the devious lady wore a black blindfold
her soul aimed at the fierce night in me
I found her door one evening
at a quarter to midnight
the truth gathers the sand of statues
in its chests of salt
wind of the instant—is this death
I will go into the sharp light
she was a young girl like another
she left me I left her
I never looked her so fully in the face
tortured angel beautiful memory

Translation from French by Sylvia Mae Gorelick

COMMENTARY

(1) Born in Tunis in 1947, Hubert Abraham Haddad went into exile with his parents at the age of three when they moved to Belleville & Ménilmontant in Paris & then to the working-class suburbs. He lived the difficulties of the immigrant, between a father who worked as a peddler & a mother of Algerian origins suffering from personality troubles, as depicted in his autobiographical narrative *Camp du bandit mauresque* (2005). Always focused on poetry, Haddad started a poetry magazine with surrealist leanings, *La Mouvance,* while still an adolescent, in which he published the likes of Stanislas Rodanski, Charles Duits, Robert Lebel, & Isabelle Waldberg. Since publishing his first volume of poems, *Le Charnier déductif,* in 1967, he has brought out books at an ever-faster rhythm—be they novels, narratives, collections of short stories (close to thirty), poetry collections (eleven to date), or collections of essays (five), a number of which have gathered prizes in France & beyond. A true Renaissance man, Haddad also works in the theater & is a painter with a number of exhibitions to his credit.

(2) Haddad, in an interview: "All humans, wherever they may be from, are in the same place of presence, of being as a question, as soon as they evolve and incarnate themselves in the space of symbolization, of language. This is as true of the poet as of the illiterate shepherd. We are all *in the same place of the cultural fact, of the civilizational space,* if you want. To write is to read inside oneself, and to read is to meditate the orality that crisscrosses our dreams, that of the bards and singers."

Paul Bowles (New York, 1910–Tangier, 1999)

from **AFRICA MINOR**

This saint-worship, based on vestiges of an earlier religion, has long been frowned upon by the devout urban Moslems; as early as the midthirties restrictions were placed on its practice. For a time, public manifestations of it were effectively suppressed. There were several reasons why the educated Moslems objected to the brotherhoods. During the periods of the protectorates in Tunisia and Morocco, the colonial administrations did not hesitate to use them for their own political ends, to ensure more complete domination. Also, it has always been felt that visitors who happened to witness the members of a cult in action were given an unfortunate impression of cultural backwardness. Most important was the fact that the rituals were unorthodox and thus unacceptable to true Moslems. If you mentioned such cults as the Derqaoua, the Aissaoua, the Haddaoua, the Hamatcha, the Jilala, or the Guennaoua to a city man, he cried, "They're all criminals! They should be put in jail!" without stopping to reflect that it would be difficult to incarcerate more than half the population of any country. I think one reason why the city folk are so violent in their denunciation of the cults is that most of them are only one generation removed from them themselves; knowing the official attitude toward such things, they feel a certain guilt at being even that much involved with them. Having been born into a family of adepts is not a circumstance which anyone can quickly forget. Each brotherhood has its own songs and drum rhythms, immediately recognizable as such by persons both within and outside the group. In early childhood rhythmical patterns and sequences of tones become a part of an adept's subconscious, and in later life it is not difficult to attain the trance state when one hears them again.

A variation on this phenomenon is the story of Farid. Not long ago he called by to see me. I made tea, and since there was a fire in the fireplace, I took some embers out and put them into a brazier. Over them I sprinkled some *mska,* a translucent yellow resin which makes a sweet, clean-smelling smoke. Moroccans appreciate pleasant odors; Farid is no exception. A little later, before the embers had cooled off, I added some *djaoui,* a compound resinous substance of uncertain ingredients.

Farid jumped up. "What have you put into the *mijmah?*" he cried.

As soon as I had pronounced the word *djaoui,* he ran into the next room and slammed the door. "Let air into the room!" he shouted. "I can't smell djaoui! It's very bad for me! "

When all trace of the scent released by the djaoui was gone from the room, I opened the door and Farid came back in, still looking fearful.

"What's the matter with YOU?" I asked him. "What makes you think a little djaoui could hurt you? I've smelled it a hundred times and it's never done me any harm."

He snorted. "You! Of course it couldn't hurt *you*. You're not a Jilali, but I am. I don't want to be, but I still am. Last year I hurt myself and had to go to the clinic, all because of djaoui."

He had been walking in a street of Emsallah and had stopped in front of a café to talk to a friend. Without warning he had collapsed on the sidewalk; when he came to, he was at home and a drum was being beaten over him. Then he recalled the smoke that had been issuing from the café, and knew what had happened.

Farid had passed his childhood in a mountain village where all the members of his family were practicing Jilala. His earliest memories were of being strapped to his mother's back while she, dancing with the others, attained a state of trance. The two indispensable exterior agents they always used to assure the desired alteration of consciousness were drums and djaoui. By the time the boy was four or five years old, he already had a built-in mechanism, an infallible guarantee of being able to reach the trance state very swiftly in the presence of the proper stimulus. When he moved to the city he ceased to be an adept and, in fact, abandoned all religious practice. The conditioned reflex remained, as might be expected, with the result that now as a man in his midtwenties, although he is at liberty to accept or refuse the effect of the specific drum rhythms, he is entirely at the mercy of a pinch of burning djaoui.

His exposition of the therapeutic process by which he is "brought back" each time there is an accident involves a good many other details, such as the necessity for the presence of a member of the paternal side of his family who will agree to eat a piece of the offending djaoui, the pronouncing of certain key phrases, and the playing on the *bendir* the proper rhythms necessary to break the spell. But the indisputable fact remains that when Farid breathes in djaoui smoke, whether or not he is aware of doing so, straightway he loses consciousness.

One of my acquaintances, who has always been vociferous in his condemnation of the brotherhoods, eventually admitted to me that all the older members of his family were adherents to the Jilala cult, citing immediately afterward, as an example of their perniciousness, an experience of his grandmother some three years before. Like the rest of the family, she was brought up as a Jilalia but had grown too old to take part in the observances, which nowadays are held secretly. (Prohibition, as usual, does not mean abolition, but merely being driven underground.) One evening the old lady was alone in the house, her children and grandchildren having all gone to the cinema, and since she had nothing else to do she went to bed. Somewhere nearby, on the outskirts of town, there was a meeting of Jilala going on. In her sleep she rose and, dressed just as she was, began to make her way toward the sounds. She was found next morning unconscious in a vegetable garden near the house where the meeting had taken place, having fallen into an ant colony and been badly bitten. The reason she fell, the family assured me, was that at a certain moment the drumming had stopped; if it had gone on she would have arrived. The drummers always continue until everyone present has been brought out of his trance.

"But they did not know she was coming," they said, "and so the next morning, after we had carried her home, we had to send for the drummers to bring her to her senses." The younger generation of French-educated Moslems is infuriated when this sort of story is told to foreigners. And that the latter are interested in such things upsets them even more. "Are all the people in your country Holy Rollers?" they demand. "Why don't you write about the civilized people here instead of the most backward?"

I suppose it is natural for them to want to see themselves presented to the outside world in the most "advanced" light possible. They find it perverse of a Westerner to be interested only in the dissimilarities between their culture and his. However, that's the way some of us Westerners are.

Not long ago I wrote on the character of the North Africa Moslem. An illiterate Moroccan friend wanted to know what was in it, and so, in a running translation into Moghrebi, I read him certain passages. His comment was terse: "That's shameful."

"Why?" I demanded.

"Because you've written about people just as they are."

"For us that's not shameful."

"For us it is. You've made us like animals. You've said that only a few of us can read or write."

"Isn't that true?"

"Of course not! We can all read and write, just like you. And we would, if only we'd had lessons."

I thought this interesting and told it to a Moslem lawyer, assuming it would amuse him. It did not. "He's quite right," he announced. "Truth is not what you perceive with your senses, but what you feel in your heart."

"But there is such a thing as objective truth!" I cried. "Or don't you attach importance to that?"

He smiled tolerantly. "Not in the way you do, for its own sake. That is statistical truth. We are interested in that, yes, but only as a means of getting to the real truth underneath. For us there is very little visible truth in the world these days." However specious this kind of talk may seem, it is still clear to me that the lawyer was voicing a feeling common to the great mass of city dwellers here, educated or not.

Juan Goytisolo (b. Barcelona, 1931)

DAR DEBBAGH

why me, him, and not the others, them?: imperturbably leaning on the battlemented parapet of the esplanade with their binoculars, polaroids, glasses, kodaks, movie cameras, a tame, motley flock paying close attention to the polyglot commentaries of the impeccable official guide: a stereotypic dragoman in a white djellabah and an inverted red flowerpot, possessed of a number and a badge that properly identify him and invest him with learned, benign authority: a patronizing attitude underlined by the condescending gesture with which he points to the perverse souls in that lucrative hell in which you are rotting away: to that *lasciate ogni speranza, voi ch'entrate* that tacitly, gloomily presides over your foreordained fate: *voici le quartier des tanneurs, Messieurs-dames,* the picturesque old tannery: as the docile members of the flock observe, peer, lie in wait on the top of the wall, fleetingly appear at the cannon embrasures, riddle the condemned men with their weapons, aim threatening telephoto and zoom lenses at the creatures in the tanning pits: heat, an overpowering stench, clavicles sticking out, skinny rib cages, gnarled arms, nothing but skin and bones: for you, for me, the damned, the object of neutral curiosity or indulgent disdain immortalized in the images of a souvenir album, smiling, puffed up with pride, selfassured, *naal d-din* ummhum, I shit on their dead: and once again the why, why, O Lord, always them and never me, shame, humiliation, disgust, and they call this living: questions, questions, in the stinking, stifling circular prison, nothing foredoomed me to this death, I was born light and free as a bird, I've dreamed of eden ever since I was a youngster, you measured the vastness of desert expanses, roamed wherever you pleased amid the dunes: the nomad's way of life, tending flocks, wandering freely, listening to folktales in the heat of the tent, the origin and epitome of your rudimentary sensibility: plans, fantasies, illusions to which one clings desperately, like a shipwreck victim to his life preserver: a necessary compensation in the face of a harsh, cruel reality: working slouched over, bent almost double in the stinking hole, plucking off the bits of fleece stuck to the animal's skin, dressing the hide, laying the skins out flat in the sun, enduring the brutal mistreatment, the stench, the flies, trying to escape: getting out of there, fleeing with your suffering fellows, swearing never to come back, walking like a robot through the great free and alien city, heading toward the graceful silhouette of the Kutubia, stretching your hands out, palms joined, toward the minaret, invoking the justice of Allah, beseeching him to receive you in his kingdom, taking refuge in the higher certainty of eden, remembering the exact description of paradise: sweet repose, a cool place to sleep during the heat of the day, a garden full of trees and vines, shady bowers, exquisite silks, rivers of honey, abundant fruit: effacing the memory of your experience in the great city: digging like a mole, buried in a pit even darker and narrower than the pits of the tannery: re-creating: gently flowing streams, incorruptible water, milk whose delicious taste never changes, maidens in the bloom of youth, nuptial pavilions, wine that does not intoxicate: going back nonetheless: scorching air, a camel parched with thirst, a sere, barren plain: a life sentence, wretched slavery, men swarming like locusts, empty ears of grain with nothing left but bristles: an orphan still, filthy, in tatters, the smell of hides stubbornly clinging to my skin, bearing with you the crushing burden of humiliation, downfall, decrepitude, his miserable portable poverty: enveloped in the scorn and reproof of the elect, unwittingly contaminating their air: go on, yes, go on, don't stop, don't pay any attention, walk along like a blind man, never let your eyes meet theirs: making your way through the native quarter on foot, becoming inured to the fear of those who warily move away as you draw near, retracing his footsteps in a delirious daze without stretching out my black beggar's hand to believers or to infidels: paying, paying, forever paying, for a roof overhead, light, food, paying, paying, that's what we were born into this world for!: the pit again, standing knee-deep in mud, scrubbing skins, dressing the hide, laying it out in the sun like a stiff tortoise pounded flat: deaf to the noisy presence of the onlookers watching from the bastion in the wall up above: the puzzled, perplexed flock awaiting instructions and explanations from the guide: a package tour flown in on a jet, on a direct flight from the industrial smog of Pennsylvania: oh dear, look down there at those men, it's just unbelievable!: straw hats, dark glasses, their proboscises protected from the sun by little sheets of cigarette paper or unnerving plastic noseguards: bearing a vague resemblance to creatures from outer space or victims of an accident just out of the hospital: absorbed in rapt contemplation of the condemned men peopling that vivid illustration of Dante's minutely detailed, geometrical delirium: of his body bent nearly double, his back scorched by the sun, his skull wrapped in a ragged turban, his pants legs hunched up around his thighs: vainly attempting to hide from others' eyes the one and only luxurious gift that God has given you: a dusky, pulsating ace of clubs, the involuntary cause of their derision, envy, stupefaction: seemingly submissive, but in reality intractable, rebellious, pertinacious, ever ready to poke its head out below the lower edge of the cloth at the slightest provocation or moment of inattention on your part: your condemned fellows know this, and refer to it periphrastically each time that you inadvertently display it as you straighten up after bending over: a discreet homage to the dimensions of a weapon that had aroused jealousy and awe in the days, at once so recent and so long ago, of your brief, ephemeral youth: working, continuing to toil away, to struggle with the animal skins, standing up to your knees in the filthy water, resting your eyes by gazing at the insubstantial shadow of the mosque, dimly aware of the guide's explanations and running commentary for the benefit of the tourists standing far overhead on the wall: closing your eyes, escaping, fleeing, blotting out the inferno, the outside world, paying no attention to their cameras, ignoring these spectators as they are ignoring me, all they want is to enjoy the show, to take advantage of the view from that impregnable fortress, a way of killing time: walking through the city, turning your palms toward the Kutubia, searching for an explanation of the disasters that have overtaken you, repeating your questions: penury, orphanhood, a merciless sun, a motionless, arrested, empty present: calling up memories of your childhood sheltered from hunger and storms, when you ran freely about the pasturelands, your gaze capturing life itself, your mother assured you that you would be the best, the strongest, the most beloved: today he is shunned by one and all, I bear the stigmata of misfortune, his friends avoid him in terror: you are the walking leper, the monster, the carrier of the plague: fleeing the horror, joining the other condemned men, seeking refuge in the tannery: a naked, dull gray, lunar expanse riddled with little round pits, like the scars of a stubborn case of smallpox: one for each condemned man: down into the hole, splashing about in the mud, dressing hides, a living death: aware of extraterrestrial eyes staring at your bent back, your bony arms, your skinny legs: the useless weight of your inflexible tail bound to your thighs by your trousers: restlessness, excitement, tumult among the lady spectators from Pennsylvania: the blonde beauty, in an exquisite white dress, whispers to her neighbor, focuses her binoculars on him, appears to lose herself in profound thought: a fluffy hairdo set in waves, like the top of a vanilla ice cream cone: patriotic, presbyterian, antisegregationist, abrahamlincolnesque blue eyes:

meticulously outlined red lips of a pinup girl or a fashion model: a living example of the basic civic virtues of the Pilgrims: abstemiousness, frugality, a firm belief in the merits of fair play, progress, individualism: doubtless the wife of an executive with polarized sunglasses and a plastic nose, directly transported by air from the offices of Koppers or US Steel: all at once finding herself standing on the edge of the pit in which you are struggling with the hides: pretty, polite, spotless, betraying not the slightest sign of repugnance: apparently deeply interested in the traditional method of tanning skins and its breathtaking, fascinating exoticism: or perhaps in the sudden, scandalous proportions that your bare, absolutely functional tool has assumed: as cunning and crafty as a fractious, mischievous child; suavely releasing it from the pressure of the cloth and giving it its freedom, a proud and noble warrior: courteously offering his hand to the woman, helping her down to the sumptuous bed of the tanning pit: plunging her in the mud up to her knees, clasping her tightly in your eager, filthy arms, pressing my violent body to hers, sullying her pure white garments, voraciously kissing her red lips: still paralyzed with shocked surprise when with clumsy hands you pull up her skirts, paw her delicate pubis, her smooth convergent thighs, her silky black triangle: rubbing her vulva, introducing your sticky fingers in her vagina, lubricating, readying, preparing the way for the contained fury of your instrument: taking your pleasure, wallowing with her in the dirty water, kneading her breasts, straddling her hips, coupling within full view of the horrified tourists in the mirador, paying no attention to their exclamations and outcries, effacing your previous differences in pigmentation with slime and unbridled lust: the two of you burning, burning with passion as the ex-blonde creature laughs and hurls insults at the cuckolded executive, leaning his elbows on the edge of the tower, peering through his binoculars: *iwa, el khal ka idrabni, yak? ila bghiti tchuf ahsen ma-itjaf-ch, axi hdana!*: no, that's not how it is, she stays up there with him, with the others, blonde, inaccessible, perfect, at the top of the crenelated wall: heat misery flies for me, everything for them, I fooled myself, they fooled me, I was born free and happy, I watched over the flocks, the shade of the trees was a promise and a symbol of the cool shade that awaited me in eden, young girls and boys followed me, we made love to each other in the dunes: like fire, yes, like fire, faces, garments, smiles, sprinkle the whole thing with gasoline, cigarette lighter, matches, whatever, my eyes flamethrowers, destruction, trails of phosphorus, screams, human torches: the pits again, animal skins, the dead desolation of the tannery, beauty close at hand and unattainable: without a voice, my tongue useless to me, no one willing to listen to what he has to say: they have ears and do not hear, they look at me and do not see me, my presence is an illusion, you are transparent, they are contemplating a specter: dressing hides, scraping off the fleece, putting up with the stench, abandoned to his fate, just a few yards away from the mosque: your long appendage hangs down like a dead weight, love eludes you, as empty as a mirage: useless to say *ya baad-lah ghituni:* they are immunized, and continue on their way, keeping their distance: a powerful spell binds him to the tannery, forces him to return to the pit day after day, to wander through the native quarter like a sleepwalker: the freedom of the public square, its open spaces, seem forbidden and inaccessible to me: dreaming, continually dreaming of them, of losing his inability to speak, of recovering my voice, of addressing the crowds that flock about the entertainers in the halca: pouring out a rush of words for hours on end: vomiting up dreams, tales, stories till you've emptied yourself out: and then waking up again, succumbing to the curse, returning to the pit, getting stuck in the mud: walking along with my flaccid pendulum dangling inertly, a shadow of myself, my youth and vigor suppressed, barren, apathetic, a craven coward

watch the freak, it would be perfect for the sketch, you could show him on the stage!

a pair of bearded men are watching him, run after him, catch up with you, try to strike up a conversation with me

vu parlé fransé?

no, you don't understand them, what do they want from me, they're talking European, a crowd gathers round us, they insist that you go with them

venir avec nu, you understand? *nu aller vu payer: tien,* here's some *flus* for you!

taking off with them like a whirlwind, public gardens, long straight avenues, buses, horse-drawn carriages, clanging bells, squealing brakes, human rivers, the Kutubia, Foucauld Square, the Club Méditerranée, ocher taxis, traffic cops, hustle and bustle exhibitions, speeches, dances, gymnastic feats

bold jaunty young

the evil spell miraculously broken

they take him away, you are, I am in the irregular polygon of the main square

Translation from Spanish by Helen R. Lane

Cécile Oumhani (b. Namur, 1952)

YOUNG WOMAN AT THE TERRACE

There was a time when the poet traveled on his quest across the desert. Figure as light as a shadow, devoted to a poem of sand and ashes, he went his way along the ridges of dunes, his eyes streaming with light . . . A shadow drawn with letters like scars on a wounded body, he is the memory of all poems, of the yearning for words that keeps flooding into that silent part of ourselves. Today still on the horizon, the white city dances, promise of the steppe. It dances and whirls, devoted to the curves of the sign inscribed on the page and to the voices that rise and chant. The wind rises. Far up into the sky, it blows away dried petals of jasmine, sacrificed dreams, and unspoken words. The wind rises. The young woman holds back her hair as it seeks to soar away. She holds her breath at the edge of a forbidden land. Her heart is throbbing with words. A thousand paths that she must not name go through her, spaces that are both mute and heavy with presence. The white city floats in front of her. Freed from the ground, it seems to quiver towards other possible ways of being. The young woman leans over the mirror of life, over there towards the dazzling buildings where she can see a maze of alleys. Her long locks of hair spread on the page, scatter words that come like so many flights of birds. Her long locks of hair perfumed with ambergris and what has been kept so long in the darkness of a hidden room, she writes with her flesh, about the hopes and the pains that dwell inside her. She writes, as light as a shadow, at the front of the terrace. She writes, furtive presence against the sky behind her, out and away from the tiled corridor that contained her whispers, mercilessly buried by the days and the others. She stands in front of the blaze of the sky in the distance. And she wavers, overwhelmed by what she can see inside her and outside, over there, where the alleys disappear. Her fingers are steady as they run across the page. Upright, she lets the torrent rush into her, where images gush forth, the impetuous storm of the word she has conquered. She inhales the evening breeze, the threshold of a new depth and the others' humming, where she can recognize herself, glances given and taken back, words lost halfway between hesitant lips. She listens to them, for the invisible orchestra takes up the phrase which is hers. Leaning over the city, she listens to it, pausing for the moment when she will take up her own song, the song which is theirs, with her voice, made up of words and colors, on the fringes of rites and what should not be uttered. A melody that will be both a lament and a call, as poignant as the hand of a child stretched out to a mother who is walking away.

Further on, she listens to the murmur of the sea and feels the salt drying on her mouth, inscribing her skin with a myriad of white grazes. Crystals shining in the daylight to say what is faraway and yet inhabits her, and inhabits them too, runs through their days and nights, the slow long-lasting burn of something that cannot be, but which we love so much as to bite deep into our lips. Faraway dunes, faraway sea, where other ways of being can be dreamt up, where light, airy architectures can be built, the end of wounds and regrets, dwellings for those we love, and who will be born tomorrow. In comes the night, a vast wave where she can coil up, leaning against the wall, and see the golden glow of lamps light up the faces of the passersby. In comes the night, and she does not know whether the secret murmur comes from inside her or outside. She gives herself up to the words and dark spaces that lead her away toward times that are both ancient and new, following yet another poem of embers.

COMMENTARY

Cécile Oumhani, born in Namur, Belgium, in 1952, grew up in a rich multicultural atmosphere & remains marked by the insights & responsiveness of her mother, the Scottish painter Madeleine Vigné-Philip. Married to a Tunisian, she teaches English literature at a Paris university & has published several collections of writings. Here is how Regina Keil-Sagawe, her German translator, describes Oumhani: "A novelist and poet who started to publish in 1995, she brings a fresh and new gaze on the Mediterranean, a gaze both luminous and tender, full of a melancholic sensuality that brought her immediate attention from critics and the admiration of the reading public."

THE ORAL TRADITION
III

This section does not present what are usually understood as oral tradition materials, as those are nearly always considered anonymous (though note Jerome Rothenberg's strictures against such simplifications in his various anthologies and essays concerning ethnopoetics and oral traditions), while the texts included here are nearly all signed by their authors. However, all—with the exception of Hawad (see p. 529), whose trajectory is more complex—can be assigned to the category of bards and popular tellers of tales. Masters of a revisited orality, they draw their inspiration from the day-to-day lives of working-class people whose spokespersons they are. The record and cassette industry in the 1940s and 1950s, the videocassette industry starting in the late 1970s, and finally CD-ROMs have permitted a wide distribution of their productions—much wider, in fact, than the distribution of books, which is hindered by a lack of bookshops and language/reading barriers (for more on this, see the introduction and prologue to the Algeria section of part 2 of the Fifth Diwan, and elsewhere).

The poets presented in this final section gathering oral traditions compose and sing in Amazigh or vernacular Arabic, and what they sing is often the exile and tribulations of those who emigrated to France to find work, the oppression of women, the arrogance of those in power, the despair of the young—while clinging to the dream of a just world down here.

We have not included in this collection the likes of the Moroccan Jil Jilala and Nass El Ghiwane, groups that have revolutionized Maghrebian music by drawing on the Gnawa tradition, because their songs are structured in a traditional poetic model. Their contribution is above all musical.

Aissa al Jarmuni al Harkati (Sidi R'ghis, now Oum El Bouaghi, 1885–Aïn Beïda, Oum El Bouaghi province, 1946)

POEM ABOUT HIS COUNTRY, THE "WATAN"

Oh tent, why are you so sad?
Those who put you up have left.
My beloved remained a hostage,
a *borni* falcon with broken feathers.

You can't break camp
and lead away your camels
until you beg the *rumi* captain
who won't deign to consent.

Soldiers' feet have trodden my land
long after I have forgotten.
My people have broken camp
and left me all alone.

QUATRAIN ABOUT THE JEWS AT A WEDDING PARTY IN THE "HARAT LIHUD" QUARTER IN CONSTANTINE

You are Jews and your black veils are pretty,
and how beautiful is your women's talk!
My fate is to die with so much pain inside
for I don't know how I can forget your beauty!

QUATRAIN ABOUT THE SUFI SHEIKH SIDI MUHAMMAD BEN SAID'S YOUNG WIFE WHO HAD DIED THE NIGHT BEFORE

She left and her people broke camp,
from the mouth a tooth has fallen.
Oh my eyes, weep for the one who was my age
now that she's gone forever.

TWO QUATRAINS ABOUT HUMAN EXISTENCE

I am tired of always forgiving
those who would burn me alive.
I feel as tired as the musk rose
of the dry hot summer breeze.
Can someone tell me what's wrong with me?
Everyone I try to get close to steps away at once
as if I were carrying embers in my hands,
or deadly scorpions in my burnous's hood!

TWO QUATRAINS ON THE SHAWIA PEOPLE SUNG AT THE OLYMPIA IN PARIS (1936)

We are the Shawia. Don't you ever think
we have become cowards!
We are now returning to our country,
but we'll soon be back!
We'd rather fight in the open
and everyone gets his right.
When I call my people for help,
the last is always first to come!

POEM ABOUT EDUCATION

I went west into exile to become a learned man.
But neither the West nor the East enlightened my mind.
I can write the letter ب and stretch out the ن
but I keep forgetting all the verses of the Qur'an!

He who is not learned,
why should he mess up with pen and inkpot?
And he who has never been an adulterer,
why does he speak ill of respectable women?

TWO LYRICS FROM AL HARKATI'S RECORDED SONGS

Oh Horse Breeder!

Oh horse breeder, will you slow down?
Turn your horse and hit the road,
go to Baya and tell her Muhammad has sent you.
She said: Oh my brother, spread word about me
among the tribes you meet on your way.
I am a true *'amriya*, from a noble clan,
and in every raid my name is mentioned!
I said: Oh noble woman, how could you forget?
Perhaps your heart is unfaithful.
I sent you word two years ago,
and now I am on my way,
feeling tired before nightfall.
Man's best friends are his horse and his gun,
and he who chases women is a fool!
Yet sin is my *mektub* from Allah;
I shall soon be in your arms,
and our lips will then meet in a kiss.

The Slender One

My eyes followed them till they disappeared,
then my mind wandered and pain wrecked my soul.
Oh starling, why did you choose the Tell as your exile?
The well is too deep and the rope treacherous.
You are slender and silk is your dress,
your cheek is the sun and the moon your guard.
You are slender, and this drives me crazy;
your chest and mine are entangled silk threads.
A date palm that bears no fruit has to be felled,
a girl that has no lover is doomed to age alone.

Translations from Arabic by Abdelfetah Chenni

(1) His full name was Merzugui Aissa ben Rabah al Harkati, & he belonged to the Shawia tribe of al H'rakta. Born in 1885 in Sidi R'ghis (a *wilaya* of Oum El Bouaghi, Algeria), he died in December 1946 in Aïn Beïda (another Oum El Bouaghi *wilaya*). He never went to school but started singing at the age of eighteen. He wrote his own songs, which he then performed at weddings. Thanks to his Jewish agent, he recorded most of his songs in Tunis, France, & Germany, & he was the first Maghrebi to sing at the Olympia Hall in Paris, in 1936. On the day he died, his cousin the *guessab* (flutist) Muhand ou Zin broke his *guasba* (reed flute) & swore never to play again, a vow he fulfilled.

(2) Adds his transcriber & translator, Abdelfetah Chenni: "What I like most in his poetry is the powerful imagery and the 'seemingly' superficial ambiguity of his interwoven themes and intricately overlapping thoughts. Most of what he says is expressed in image form, often riddle-like, and the reader is required to make an effort to guess what Aissa actually intends to say: metaphor used as a coded language. All his poetry was spontaneous/instantaneous—orally produced on the spot as a reaction to a situation, either during wedding ceremonies or while chatting with friends. Most of the texts above have never been recorded as songs (except for the last two), and very few people know of their existence. Many of his poems are in the form of quatrains that remind one of those by Si Mohand [see p. 241]."

Qasi Udifella (1898–1950)

FOUR POEMS

I'll start with *Sbih*
the beautiful name
preserves the soul

he sent us the true prophet
for the happiness of all
his name precedes Noah's

what road hasn't he opened for us
giving perfect intelligence of it
even to the infant in the cradle

it is his name we call upon
every instant we proclaim
that we shall leave this world

you the eloquent one
invoke God every moment
and flee this cadaverous life

we shall watch over His road
everything's done by His permission
and all grace comes from God

.

my heart refuses tranquility
my legs totter weakly
oh God spare me further tribulations

the pillars of Islam are collapsing
very few are still standing
the whole structure is lopsided

brothers and allies hate one another
with rage in their hearts
they all go astray

it is the masters
that create the obstacles
they have monopolized everything
they get together to plot evil
never good
they want their recklessness to perdure

they hang on to this world
abandon piety
take pleasure in shoring up riches

alas you the clerics who chant
you who are well considered
can't you see that our religion is up for sale

and yet God has promised
that if we are united
our turn will come

.

the whiter my hair gets the more I rave
lost I am
by God not knowing where I'm going

we are all without hope
we flee action
truth totters along close to its end

most people have lost their spirit
let me tell you straight out
when one gets up the other falls down

who says the truth is trapped by it
all nobleness is adulterated
all that remains is a gaggle of schemers

the older I get the stranger what I hear
absentminded mind take heed
food's been rationed

better dead and buried
than to suffer an injustice
that refuses to die

·

these are the words of a Kabyle
who is not done yet
each day he speaks up more

he appreciates the good
he is no wali
but wants to leave clear omens

long ago we hugged the walls
we were informers
now we'll change our ways

the full moon has risen
illuminating Algeria
be wise get what I'm saying

for a long time we didn't see her anymore
oh all those tribulations
and illegality reigned in commerce

now comes modern science
opening the eyes of those people
who search for their roots

on the history of the Ansar
question the scholars
and on the Hegira too

Translations by P.J. of French translation from Amazigh by Tassadit Yacine

COMMENTARY

Qasi Udifella belonged to the Kabylian Aït Sidi Braham tribe from the Taggourt area. He left a large oral corpus, composed between 1936 & 1950, the year of his death, an important period for Algeria, as it saw major reforms of the ulama, the first nationalist parties gaining ground, the Muslim Congress of 1936, World War II, the Sétif events of May 1945, & more. Early on, Udifella's corpus benefited from transcription by Hadj Boubekar, an imam from the same tribe, into Arab characters (thus preserving what otherwise might easily have been at least partially forgotten or dispersed), which was then translated (into French) & analyzed by Tassadit Yacine (also originally from the same tribe) in her book *Poésie berbère et identité: Qasi Udifella, héraut des At Sidi Braham* (Paris: Maison des Sciences de l'Homme, 1987). In her introduction she tells how Udifella's fellow villagers thought that he was possessed by a *taruhanit*, a female jinn, who fed him his verses. He himself loved to say that his gift came to him by fate, &, like Si Mohand (see p. 241), he could not but be at the rendezvous. One day the village had been turning a Moorish café into a school, a decision that brought into the open the power relationships among the village's political clans: those who backed the administration, the ulama, or the Algerian People's Party (PPA). Udifella, returning home, held his head & composed his first poem: "We are building a new mosque / we are substituting knowledge for play." But he felt that poetry was competing with prayer, for just as he wanted to start to pray, a poem would come to him. He told his problem to a sheikh, who solved it thus: "God knows that you want to pray, but your heart leans toward poetry." Since that day, Udifella never stopped making poems.

Mririda N'aït Attik (Megdaz, c. 1900–c. 1930)

THE BAD LOVER

Leave me, soldier without sense or manner!
I can see that you are full of contempt,
Your hand raised, insults on your lips,
Now that you have had what you want from me.
And you leave, calling me a dog!
Sated with my pleasures,
You'd have me blush for my trade,
But you, were you ashamed
When you pushed gently at my door,
Up like a bull?
Were you coming to play cards?
You turned yourself into something humble,
Agreeing right off to my demands,
To losing all your pay in advance.
And the more your eyes undressed me,
The more your rough desire put you in my power.

When you finally took off my clothes
I could have cursed your soul for the asking!
I could have cursed your mother
And your father, and their ancestors!
Toward what paradise were you flying?

But now that you've calmed down,
You're back on earth,
Arrogant, rough and coarse as your *djellaba*.

Guest of mine for the moment, my slave,
Don't you feel my disgust and hate?

One of these days
The memory of tonight will bring you back to me
Conquered and submissive again.
You'll leave your pride at the door
And I'll laugh at your glances and your wishes.
But you'll have to pay three times the price next time!
This will be the cost of your insults and pride.

I'll no more notice your clutching
Than the river notices a drop of rain.

WHAT DO YOU WANT?

What do you want, girl of the village below?
To marry me, is that what you are thinking?
It is said that you are hardly unfriendly,
and I too dream of holding you.
Here is my only piece of silver.
The peddler will sell you perfumed soap,
a comb, a mirror—what do I know?
But by my neck, I'll bring you a red scarf
from Demnat if you want.

What do I need, son of the high pasture,
with a piece of silver or silk scarf?

Then tell me what you want—
to marry me? What do you think,
pretty girl of the village below?

You make me laugh, son of the high pasture.
I don't care about money or a scarf,
and even less about marriage.
I expect from you
what you expect from me.
And satisfied, we will leave each other.
What I want, strong son of the high pasture,
what I want is the shelter of this bush,
where you will lie on my breasts—which I hold
out to you—and in a moment
happiness sweeter than milk,
while my eyes lose themselves in the sky.

THE BROOCH

Grandmother, grandmother,
Since he left I think only of him
And I see him everywhere.
He gave me a fine silver brooch
And when I adjust my haïk on my shoulders,
When I hook its flap over my breasts,
When I take it off at night to sleep,
It's not the brooch I see, but him!

My granddaughter, throw away the brooch.
You will forget him and your suffering will be over.

Grandmother, it's over a month since I threw it away,
But it cut deeply into my hand.
I can't take my eyes off the red scar:
When I wash, when I spin, when I drink—
And my thoughts are still of him!

My granddaughter, may Allah heal your pain!
The scar is not on your hand, but in your heart.

Translations by Daniel Halpern & Paula Paley of René Euloge's French versions from Tashelhiyt Berber

COMMENTARY

Mririda N'aït Attik was a Moroccan poet who composed in Tashelhiyt Berber. She was born around 1900 in Megdaz in the Tassaout valley. René Euloge, a French civil servant based in Azila from 1927, put her poems to paper, translated them into French in the 1930s, & published them in his book *Les chants de la Tassaout* (Editions de la Tigherm, 1956). Our selection is based on an English version of this work, *Songs of Mririda, Courtesan of the High Atlas* (Unicorn Press, 1974).

The Song of the Azria

I am beautiful Azria
I am unfaithful Azria
I am the tender fruit
of a tree with tight clusters
I smile at everyone
I hate marriage
and for no prize
will I admit slavery
I wear no veil
I hate all cloth
my happiness is
beauty and youth
my black eyes'
mysterious gaze

has the power
to enthrall my lovers
my Queen Kahina face
is more than bait
my mouth is made of honey
perfectly real
he who tastes it once
will return for more
my chest and its high breasts
draw in the holiest looks
while below my belt
lies nature's sacred temple
where the faithful come to sin
in love my heart
often lies for
I am Azria
remorseless Azria
I accept the weak and the strong
I am carefree Azria
and my life is my life
my pride comes from my freedom
my life is crazy gaiety
from the most noble to the ugliest
my lovers are innumerable
I am Azria the dancer
who makes women jealous
I am the singer
I am the crooner
my gorgeous voice
opens all doors

Adaptation by P.J. of Y. Georges Kerhuel's French version

COMMENTARY

This eponymous song, arranged by Y. Georges Kerhuel & included in the *Encyclopédie de l'amour en Islam*, vol. 1 (edited by Malek Chabel), speaks to the specific situation of the Shawia Berber society of the Aurès mountains (northeastern Algeria). Mathéa Gaudry, a lawyer at the Appellate Court in Algiers, wrote about the Shawia courtesans in a treatise on Aurès culture in the 1920s: "The power of the Shawia woman does not pale with time. Knowledge of occult sciences, the prerogative of the elders, only reinforces it. . . . The Azria is a courtesan who receives who she wants and goes where she wants. She sings, dances, plays cards, smokes, and goes to cafés. No triviality in her manners; to the contrary: a tranquil self-assurance and often a natural distinction are her mark. Her courtiers' enthusiasm surrounds her. They all show her a quasi-religious submission. When she intervenes, a fight will stop immediately."

Slimane Azem (Kabylia, 1918–Moissac, France, 1983)

TASKURTH (THE PARTRIDGE)

When I found her crouched under a rock
she was in deep mourning—
"Was it the eagle that struck her,"
I wondered, "or was she scared of the owl?"
But it was the hunters who broke her wings!
When she raised her eyes to look up at me
I saw her swollen eyelids
as she sighed & confided her pain:
"My babies have just flown away into exile!"
Where have they gone?
Injustice leaves a bitter taste in the mouth—
when it strikes it spares no one!
"What's the use of crying now?" said I
in a consoling tone. "You're just rekindling
your old pains! Even far away they won't forget you—
make sure you won't either,
for you should always remember that
these times of blind oppression
are never to be forgotten!
Someday'll come when you'll be happy again—
that day you'll know your little ones
won't stand your absence any more!"
"It broke my heart to see them fly away,"
said she—giving a moan! "It's the fear of the hunters
that made them fly away & disperse into the skies.
I'm scared their exile'll last forever,
for how could they return?
How I wish I could be more patient!

Will they forget their old mother,
who'd toiled for them all her life?"

Times are hard! Thus our lord has decided!
This is how the world goes round!
Today our fists are tied,
but the little ones'll soon fly back home
as sure as any pain will not last & must—
someday—come to an end!

Translation by Abdelfetah Chenni from French version by A.B. of the original Kabyle

COMMENTARY

From the sparse vegetation of the northern Saharan chotts (salt lakes) to the scrubland of the Tell, the partridge has been from time immemorial an emblematic bird in the Algerian collective imagination & folklore, often representing the ideal beauty of the loved woman. In Slimane Azem's song, however, it appears as the protective & loving Algerian mother, mourning her children, who have been forced into exile by the French colonial enemy, the "hunter." Exile, separation, & homesickness are recurrent themes in Azem's lyrics & poetry. Born into a poor peasant Kabyle family, he was self-taught & separated twice from his country: first when he emigrated to France for a living, & then when he was banned for political reasons. After being banned, he never "flew black home" to his native land as he'd always wished, but died in France—in exile. The founding president of the Association Euroberbère announced in a 2011 press release that on July 10 of that year the Algerian government officially agreed to repatriate Azem's body to his "*tashkurth* motherland."

Cheikha Rimitti (Tessala, 1923–Paris, 2006)

HE CRUSHES ME

he crushes me / he makes me broil
he makes my mouth water like *makrouds* in honey
he turns me on / he drowns me
he tempts me / he rocks my cradle
he caresses my back & sleep turns sweet
he tickles me / he rams me
he burns me up & I forgive him
he seduces me / he tempts me
he trills me / ah! ah! ah!

let's swim
if we die / too bad
he shakes me / he bakes me
I'm neither sick nor fine
he hugs me / he squeezes me he tweezes me
& beauty's a winner
barely out / I find her again
he lights me up / he nibbles me down
I have my arms around him so afraid he'll run away
I have to drink / he makes me drunk
two nights & two days / & his demons haven't calmed down
he whips me / he blues me / he nettles me, he pounds me
he & I in bed we're like devils
he shakes me / he makes me sick / he crushes me, ah! ah! ah!
poor me
he bakes me / he shakes me
give me the liquor of your molar
he capsizes me / he tempts me
we're front page news, it's too much
he rubs me, he floods me, he makes me drink
I say "I'm leaving" & I spend the night
oh no! oh no! oh no!
misfortune's upon me / I've gotten bad habits
he crushes me / he irrigates me
he makes me drunk / he thrills me / he blues me

THE GIRLS OF BEL ABBÈS

my love, I've heard your call, how far away it seemed to be

we are the girls of Bel Abbès, we are not lost girls
I'll make a pilgrimage to Sidi el Hadri & he'll give me a child
my reason has left me, carried away by the son of Maïcha

death? we'll all die, only god will remain
the black horse's forelock brings luck
engraved on my love's pistol, a star & a crescent

in the green door's frame Zohra arches her back
her blond hair falls over her white flesh
lala la la la . . .

THE WORST OF ALL SHELTERS

exile, my friend, goes hand in hand with hard patience
ah! the worst of all shelters!
my hair's turned white
the days have gone under & are forgotten
now I want a roof of my own
but the douar is deserted, only ruins remain
this beautiful assembly's dispersed
oh! the return to the old place!
my hair's turned white
my friends, had you suffered like me, you'd understand
many men are missing
only buildings remain
oh! the return to the old place!
white farm, green olive trees
those brave olive trees, oh my men!
the oil of the olive, the fish in the sea
there's bravery, oh my men!
I remember those who're absent
oh! the return to the old place!
may God take into his peace those who've died for the country
oh! the return to the old place! oh! my land!
falling, he yelled: mother's family house is in ruins!
let's intercede for the parents & the heroes
the parents, the parents
my father & my mother cursed me. oh it's hard, it's hard!
do not forget the parents
take care of your parents, & they'll bless you
me, I weep on exile, o you men!
I weep on exile, homesickness squeezes the heart in France
oh my men! oh my friends!
may God give patience to those who are in France
oh my men! oh my friends!
exile's called & dispersed the assemblies
ah! the worst of all shelters!
the worst of all shelters!
oh my friends!

Translations by P.J. from French versions by Marie Virolle from the original Arabic

Cheikha Rimitti was the grand old lady of ur-*raï* music & one of the great voices of the twentieth century. Writes Marie Virolle in *La chanson raï* (Karthala Editions, 1995): "Vernacular Algerian Arabic cries in Rimitti's throat, popular culture weeps in Rimitti's songs, the poetry of western Algeria vibrates in Rimitti's voice. . . . Family feasts, brotherhood events, studios, galas, salons, forests, hangars, cabarets, cafés, tents, terraces, on warm earth under starry skies, no place where one sings with the people was foreign to her." Rimitti—who got her name from the French phrase *remettez-moi ça,* meaning "pour me another round," & started singing in bars & other places of ill repute—learned to sing in the rigorous school of the beduin melhun qasida. Her first major success was also her first (but not last) major thematic breakthrough, a scandalous manifesto song called "Charrak gattaa" (Tear It, Rip It!), which goes, in part, "& Rimitti will sew it up again. / Let's do our things beneath the covers, / move after move. / I'll do whatever my lover wants. / I fell for the wholesaler in fruit, / the one with the dove on the turban." It's easy enough to hear the title as referring to virginity & the song as a rebellious call for free love in a puritan Islamic society. At her last concert, at the Zénith in Paris, two days before she died, in her early eighties, she was carried off stage in triumph—otherwise she might have sung all night long.

Kheira (b. Tunisia, c. 1934)

YOU WHO REBEL AGAINST FATE, RISE AND FACE WHAT GOD HAS ORDAINED

Declare that there is no God but Allah, and He who has sinned should implore his pardon.

Once upon a time there was a perfume merchant who was married to his cousin. She was dearer than life to him and they lived happily. They were filled with joy and merriment. He called her Lilla al-Nsa, "the mistress of women," and she called him Sidi al-Rjal, "the master of all men." They manifested a deep love and mutual devotion which defied description. But their happiness was not complete: in her sleep she would heave a deep sigh of unhappiness. This discomforted the husband and he tried to understand the reason for her uneasiness. He could not remember failing to see to her well being. He had always provided fine clothes and jewellery for her to wear and she was well-fed. He became preoccupied and worried. This didn't go unnoticed by a venerable old man, who enquired about his anxiety. The husband told him: "I have a problem. It's my wife . . . she always heaves a deep sigh in her sleep. I can't imagine why. She lacks for nothing: clothes, jewellery, money. I provide everything she could possibly want." The elderly man replied: "I know the answer. Get a black billy-goat and take it to the house. Keep it out of her sight. When she goes to sleep, after midnight, kill the goat, open it and remove its heart while it is still warm and put it on her chest and listen. You will hear why she sighs." He replied: "God bless you." He did as the old man suggested. *Life was different in those days; wives did not question what their husbands did. There was mutual trust.*

A new day is born and he who prays for the Prophet will be blessed. He brought the billy-goat to the house and hid it in the cellar. On the same night he pretended he was tired and suggested going to bed early. When he was sure she was fast asleep he killed the goat, removed its heart, lit a candle, placed the heart on her chest and asked: "Why do you sigh?" The heart answered: "Because of the indignity I have to suffer, I will be a beggar for a year, a thief for a year and a whore for a year." As soon as the word "whore" was uttered, the candle dripped on her cheek and woke her. Seeing the bloody heart, she asked what was going on. As he had no secrets from her, he told her what was awaiting her. It sorrowed her and she broke out in lament: "Time is fickle, why does it harbor hostility to me? How can I disgrace my cousin after such a life of luxury and pampering? I'd rather die than disgrace my beloved husband." *Indeed no one knows what destiny has in store for us.*

The following day, after her husband went out to work, the indignity of the previous evening was still preying on her mind. So she decided to take her own life. She took out a sharp knife, cut her throat, and fell to the floor, unconscious. Her hour had not come yet. *In those days, there were no doctors and no emergency calls.* When she was discovered she was soon washed and laid out and buried. After the last person left, she received a blow and heard a voice saying: "You who rebel against fate, rise and face what God has ordained for you."

She rose up from her grave. She had nowhere to go and didn't want to go back to her house. She stood at the cemetery gates and started to beg. When night fell, she took refuge in a mausoleum. The next day she bought a dress and got rid of her shroud. For a whole year she begged. The following year she became a thief. She would steal purses, watches, anything. She grew tired of stealing. In the meantime, she got to know some prostitutes and was soon drawn into their way of life. She had a good voice and became famous and was in great demand for weddings, like Shafia Rushdi in those days.

The husband, after the funeral, came back home, sad and heavy-hearted. He swore he would never marry again after he lost his beloved cousin. The first year passed, then the second, and the third, and he was still alone. Well-meaning neighbors and relatives tried to reason with him and talk him into remarrying: "It was God's will, *Qadha wa Qadar*, that your wife died; we shall all take our turn, bear it with patience [patience is an article of faith], otherwise you will be damned." But his heart was broken forever. They eventually persuaded him to marry again. For the wedding they decided to engage the famous singer to entertain the guests. She had taken a stage name. When she arrived at the house, she recognized her house and her husband. She stood singing before the guests. At the end of the evening she sang an improvised verse which went: "How strange for me to be here tonight, singing at my husband's wedding in my own house . . ." The husband understood the message, rose to his feet, wrapped his cloak around her and took her to the bridal chamber. He called the witnesses, canceled the marriage-contract with the new bride and sent the guests away, and they lived safely and procreated until death did them part.

Translation from Arabic by Monia Hejaiej

COMMENTARY

Writes Monia Hejaiej, who recorded, transcribed, & translated this & forty-six other tales by Tunisian women in her book *Behind Closed Doors: Women's Oral Narratives in Tunis* (Rutgers UP, 1996): "Kheira [was] a sixty-two-year-old single woman who live[d] with her brother, his wife and children in Le Bardo, to the west of Tunis. At first, I was interested in Kheira's singing ability because I was told she had a good voice and knew a large repertoire of traditional female songs. But soon I realized that tale-telling was another of her talents. . . . Despite her strict religiosity, she was considered 'a first class entertainer,' and was in great demand at wedding ceremonies and family celebrations. This was due to her authority in and extensive knowledge of *qwa'id* (traditional rules) and her large repertoire of stories and religious songs, many of which added a strong ethical dimension to her repertoire."

Mohammed Mrabet (b. Tangier, 1936)

SI MOKHTAR

A VERY OLD RIFFIAN who lived in Boubana had four sons. Before he died he divided his land equally among them. The three younger men thought only of selling their share, but Si Mokhtar, the eldest, loved the place where he lived, and did not want to see it change. And so he bought his brothers' shares from them, and went on living in his father's house.

The orchard had all the hundreds of pear trees that his father had planted during his long lifetime in Boubana, and there were six deep wells on the land. In the garden Si Mokhtar grew the vegetables he needed for himself and many more. What he did not need he sold. Behind the house there was a clearing that always had been there, because nothing would grow there, and beyond that he had built a fence out of high canes and covered it with vines. The fence hid a patch of kif and a patch of tobacco. Between the two he had left a small place where he could sit.

Si Mokhtar had two big dogs. The white one was chained at one end to guard the kif, and the black one at the other to guard the tobacco. A farmer who lived nearby came every day to help him with his work. During the season when the pears ripened, the man would come with his donkeys each morning before daybreak, and he would find the crates of pears that Si Mokhtar had piled the day before, ready to take away. He would put them on the donkeys and ride off to the city. When he had sold them all, he would buy Si Mokhtar's food and two kilos of horsemeat for the dogs, and set off for Boubana. He would get back to the house as Si Mokhtar was waking up.

Each day it was the same. Si Mokhtar would open the door and step outside. The farmer would go past him into the kitchen with the food, and Si Mokhtar would walk to the well, fill a pail with pure cold water, and begin to wash. When he had finished and dried himself he would lift his face to the trees and say good morning to them. I'm still alive for you, he would tell them. And hamdul'lah, you're still alive for me. Then he would go inside and light the fire and put on the water for tea. For his breakfast he always ate a loaf of fresh brown bread spread with sheep's butter and wild honey. Si Mokhtar was no longer a young man, but he was still healthy. The teakettle stayed on the fire and the farmer sat and ate with him. But he would eat only a small piece of bread and take only a sip or two of tea, and it was difficult for him to swallow even that much. Si Mokhtar would say to him: You get up earlier and work harder than I do. I'm much older than you are, and yet I eat twice as much as you. The farmer would look at him, shake his head, and say: Your body's not like mine. It's strong. Mine isn't.

Si Mokhtar would ask him if he had sold everything and if everyone had paid cash, and the farmer would tell him what he had sold and bought, and how much money he had got and what he had paid out. They would go over each thing as they ate, and count the money that was left. After he had smoked three or four pipes of kif, Si Mokhtar would get up and go outside to pick pears. He put each pear carefully into a crate as he picked. When he grew tired of picking he would water the flowers and weed the vegetables for a while. After that he would wash his hands and feet, and go behind the fence to sit in his own spot between the kif patch and the tobacco patch.

There he would smoke a few pipes and lie back and look up at the sky for a while, before he got up to go in and prepare his midday meal.

One day he went behind the fence to his spot. He sat down and began to smoke and drink tea, thinking about the world, and he looked at the kif growing beside him. It was a fine, light, silvery green. He looked at the tobacco and saw that it was very dark. Soon he leaned over and sniffed of the kif. It smelled sweet and fresh and spicy. And when he sniffed of the tobacco it had a rank odor. He turned to the kif: Yes, you're poison, he told it. If you catch a man you take a little of his blood right away. Then he looked at the tobacco and said to it: But you, your poison is really poison. When you catch a man you may not take his blood then, but a day can come when you'll take it all. He thought a while, and began to laugh. His laughter grew louder, and he looked up at the sky. But he was not crazy. He was thinking of the time that had not yet arrived in the world. The kif he was smoking made his thoughts shoot ahead, and he was able to see what was going to happen. Finally he spoke again. In the time that's coming, there's going to be fighting among men over both of you, he said to the kif and the tobacco. And he got up still laughing, and went out into the orchard to pull dead leaves off the plants. Soon he came to the clearing where nothing grew. He stood for a moment looking down at the ground, and he told it: I'm sorry. I can't give you water and I can't give you food. If I do, I'll lose the thing I love, the thing that makes me happy. I can't give you anything, because I want to stay this way always, with the same life I have now. When the good hour comes each evening I'm happy, and I live with my thoughts. He walked on slowly and watered his trees, and afterwards he went to wash. He ate his supper, made a pot of tea, and went to sit in the clearing. It was the good hour. He spread out his small sheepskin on the ground, set his pipe and his glass of tea on it, and one by one lighted all the carbide lamps that he had put around the clearing.

He sat down and waited. After a while the small slugs began to come out and move around. This was what Si Mokhtar loved more than everything else. The slugs were of many different colors, and they crawled this way and that, and touched each other, and went on. For Si Mokhtar they were always something very beautiful and very rare. Not many people can watch a thing like this every evening, the way I can, he thought. And he stayed very still, looking at them, for many hours, until he grew sleepy. Then he blew out all the lamps and went into his room and slept.

Not far away, above the valley where he lived, a French army officer had bought a piece of land and built a house on it. For a year or more Si Mokhtar saw the workmen come each day, and he was sad when the house was all finished and the Nazarenes came to live in it. Whenever the Frenchman and his wife had guests, they sat on the terrace in front of their house and looked down across Si Mokhtar's land. They could see the word ALLAH written out in Arabic letters by the plants in his garden, and the five-pointed star made by the flower-beds. They would look at the shady orchard and the gardens down below, and then out at their own empty land where there were only cactuses and rock. They thought it was wrong that a Moslem should have all those trees and flowers when they had none. And at night, when Si Mokhtar lighted all the lamps around his clearing, the officer would look down from his window and see the lights flickering among the trees, and he would curse in anger. Sometimes he would see a man in a djellaba stand up and walk around for a moment, and then he would see him disappear as he sat down again. What's he doing down there? the Frenchman kept saying to himself.

One day at noon, when the sun was hot, Si Mokhtar stepped out into the clearing and saw one of the slugs lying alone on the bare ground. This had never happened before, and it astonished him. He bent down and whispered to it. Poor thing, what are you doing here? You'll die if you stay here in the sun, and you mustn't do that. You've got to go on living with your brothers. He shed a tear or two, took a leaf from a tree, and put the slug on the leaf. With the leaf in his hand he walked over to where there was some wet grass beside the well, and set the leaf down in the grass. All afternoon long he kept going to look at it, but it was still on the leaf. At twilight, when the slugs came out and began to move around, he picked up the leaf with the slug on it and carried it over to put it with the others. Then he went to prepare his evening tea. But that night as he sat watching the slugs he began to worry, and soon he bent over and said to them: Something's wrong. It's not the way it was. If I'd only known the Nazarene was going to buy that land, I'd have bought it myself, and he'd never have come to live so near us. It's too bad he got it before I found out. He was quiet for a while, and then he told them: That Nazarene is going to spoil the life we have together. He put his head to the ground and looked closely at his slugs for such a long time that he fell into a trance.

The officer was standing by his bedroom window in the dark, looking down at the lights that burned around Si Mokhtar's clearing. Each minute he felt more angry and nervous. Soon he told his wife that he was not coming to bed. He dressed and went out to the stables. There he got onto his horse and rode into the city to the barracks. He woke up four soldiers and told them they were going to ride with him to Boubana. When they got there he said: You go down there and see what that savage is doing, and come back here and tell me.

The four soldiers went down to Si Mokhtar's land and began to pound on the gate and call out. The dogs made a great noise with their barking. This brought Si Mokhtar out of his trance, and he was very angry. He jumped up and ran to unchain the dogs. Then he opened the gate. The two dogs rushed out like two bullets and attacked the soldiers. Two of the men fell, and the other two ran. When the two on the ground had been badly bitten, they scrambled to their feet and ran after the others towards the highway, firing four shots back at the dogs as they ran. The dogs stopped barking and went back to the orchard. Si Mokhtar chained them up again. He was still very angry.

He went into the house and came out with an axe. Then he ran out into the dark after the soldiers, and went on running until he got to the highway. When he saw them standing in front of the officer's house he shouted: What do you want of me? Where did you ever meet me? Why do you come in the middle of the night and disturb me? I don't want to know you or see you. This is my land, and I live here with my trees and my slugs.

The soldiers kept asking him what he was doing with all those lights burning, but they did not try to go near him. When he heard their questions, he began to swing the axe in the air. You want to know what's in there with the lights? he cried. What difference does it make to you what's there? Everything I have is there! My life is there! But you'll never get to see it!

He ran back to his house and put the axe away. In his bedroom he sat down trembling, smoked four pipes of kif, and fell asleep. When he awoke in the morning he was still trembling. He thought a moment. Then he went out to the clearing and began to spread dirt over the bare patch of ground, and on top of the dirt he poured water. He looked sadly at the clearing, and said to it: I've given you food and I've given you water.

When evening came he went to the place and looked. There was nothing moving. No slugs came out. He waited for a long time, but nothing happened. Then he knew everything was finished, and he began to sob. He blew out the lamps and went to bed.

In the morning he got up very early before the farmer had come, and walked all the way to the city. It was many years since he had been there, and the noise and confusion made him feel that he was about to explode. He rushed this way and that through the streets, sometimes running like a crazy man, until finally he found his way back to the road that led out to Boubana. When he got to his orchard he went in and walked behind the fence to the place between the kif and the tobacco. He let the two dogs loose so they could run around, and sat down to smoke. But his heart was beating very hard and his head was hot.

After his second pipe he began to feel very ill. I'm going to die, he thought.

He could feel the dark growing inside his head, but in spite of that he sat up and began to write with his forefinger in the dirt beside him. *This is our land. If you are my brothers and you love me you will never sell it.*

And Si Mokhtar died then, just as he had expected. And the two dogs put their noses together and began to speak with each other. The black dog lay down beside Si Mokhtar, and the white one went running out of the orchard. He crossed the river and climbed up the side hill to the cemetery, and from there he ran on to Mstakhoche until he got to the house where Si Mokhtar's brother lived. There he barked and scratched at the door. When the man opened the door and saw the dog's eyes, he said to his wife: Mokhtar is dead. And he leapt onto his horse, and with the dog running behind, galloped down to Boubana. Si Mokhtar lay there, with the black dog lying beside him. He read the message written in the dirt, and he bent down and said to Si Mokhtar: I swear to you, *khai*. We'll never sell it.

Transcription & translation by Paul Bowles

COMMENTARY

Mohammed Mrabet (Mohammed ben Chaib el Hajjem) was born in 1936 in Tangier. His forebears were Riffian Berbers from the Banu Ouraaghil tribe who moved to the M'sallah quarter on the outskirts of the city. For a while he made his living as a fisherman, barman, & boxer, & he traveled as far as the United States but returned to Tangier in 1960. That same year he met Paul Bowles (see p. 493), who recognized his gifts as a storyteller & recorded, translated, & started to publish his tales. Meanwhile, Mrabet also began a career as a visual artist, showing in galleries in Europe & America. The core collections of his tales are *Love with a Few Hairs* (Peter Owen, 1967) & *M'Hashish* (City Lights, 1969), & he wrote an autobiography, *Look and Move On* (Black Sparrow, 1976). The story we reproduce comes from *The Boy Who Set the Fire* (Black Sparrow, 1978). Mrabet, on his storytelling: "When I tell a story I don't know where or why it began, how it will continue or when it will end. A story is like the sea, it has no beginning and no end, it is always the same and still it keeps always changing. When the ears want to hear, a voice begins to speak. Today the ears don't want to hear but the eyes want to see. And when the pen forms words the story becomes a rock and rocks never change."

Hawad (b. north of Agadez, 1950)

from **HIJACKED HORIZON**

I

Chaos,
chaos,
chaos and vertigo,
o bottomless well,
well of dreams we hollow out,
each night endlessly,
under the feet of all authority
that wants us to kneel
in history's peat bogs.

Before turning my back on hope
and jumping into vertigo's stirrups,
I heard talk of
fraternity and solidarity,
women and men
ready to offer their teeth
to bite the steamroller
in Paris, London, Berlin.

But in the streets of those precipices
human deserts cities
sight-breaking abysses,
I have not met a single eye
on which to lean a gaze
tottering toward the chasm.

Ha! Only curs' droppings
circled by a posse
of green flies.

You, Gypsy cousin, and you, Basque woman,
and you, the black-tressed Andalusian,
by the bitter and tough
spinal cord of our backbones,
by the gaping wounds of
our strut-covered backbones,
I swear to you, not one
companion remains,

gaze crazed by the conjunctivitis
of determination,
pumice stone, lynx eyes,
hope concentrated
in the fragile stem
of a listing ideal,
liana shadow of pain
sailing against the tempest,
fire of its own illusions.

On the whole of this earth,
its back racked with cowardice,
no free and rebellious head
except for my camel's,
its proud stride and gaze,
lordly and nostalgic,
pouring its incredulity
over the world at dusk.

2

And this arm an echo shot forth
from cemetery and dunes
the desert of deserts
strangles the canons, inheritors
of French colonialism
from the north to the south of the Sahara,
what handcuffs could drag it
back into the tomb of the banana
and *couscoussouïa* States of Africa?

No fetters!
So let's let
the sun's breath and the mirages
rally to the spirit of ubiquity.

You, shadow,
my shadow on the summits,
as you know the answer,
continue to follow me.

Weave, weave, vulture,
vulture, weave, weave!
Go on thrashing the vertigos,

pride and paradoxes
of the camel's sons,
leaving behind the salted pastures
to graze the fetters and locks
that bind the cities
to the beat-up hump
of their eclipse.

Eclipse of day,
imminence of apocalypse and of irony,
here's a dawn without face or surname,
lacking even a neck
on which to hang a name.
Only scree
of thunder and darkness.

An Air France plane,
filled with champagne and *folies bergères*,
crash-lands in the middle of the desert
on a camp of interrupted nomads,
a hearse of radioactive discharges.
Hi, you, our host,
when you return to their country,
over there, where they live,
if their complicit silence permits them
to interrogate you concerning us,
tell them loudly that we are standing straight,
a knee on the furrow of our souls.
And tell them also
that with elbow and toenails
we file down their handcuffs
that fetter our ankles and arms.

And with our teeth
we still hold up
the arches of the sky.
And when we gnaw and melt down
the joints of their chains
in the blood and puss puddles
of our clavicles,
our phalanges knead and mix
a gruel of limestone and rock flint

to feed the volcanoes
and earthquakes
that will scallop tomorrow's
yokes.

Gog and Magog, we are the allies
of the Mongols and Tatars,
ready to gulp down
borders and prisons.
We are the clandestine
raiders of your sleep
and of your shelters' shade.

Paris, here I am
preceding my head,
this eternal pirate head,
figure of pain,
I am coming, here I am
chewing the tobacco of irony.
Don't look for me down here
in your sewers, I say to you,
I am too high and too low
to be seen.
I am the ancient nightmare
of a sleep braced
in the shell of its insomnia,
the inconsolable
and inexhaustible gray cancer
between the cells of your prisons.

Capricious evil that is mine.
Before I blossomed
in my mother's womb,
I was already the messenger
of my death and birth.
I am coming, here I am,
I am coming, I am coming,
preceding my destiny,
and before all, I say to you,
do not look for me
and don't wait for me,
neither in the past nor in the future,

Top: Hawad poem in cursive tifinagh.
Bottom: Hawad poem in "vocalized" tifinagh.

I am not of your clock,
don't belong
to the linear track of your time.

I am the present moment,
the betrothed huddled
in the heat of your veins,
mania swarm allergy
nerve-gnawing termite.
And I decant my escort of larvae
into the electronic mice
of your logic.

I am coming, I am coming, I am coming
following the vulture,
shadow of my ancestor,
vulture, weaver of the black capes
and red shrouds
of the sacrificed.

Translation from French by P.J.

COMMENTARY

For the nomad, thought exists only while walking or singing;
all that is nomadic has therefore either to be sung or walked to be true. H.

Hawad is a Tuareg poet now living in the South of France. He belongs to the
tribe of the Ikazkazen, part of the larger federation of the Kel Aïr, whose origi-
nal space of residence & roaming lies between the Aïr & the Tasmena in the
southwestern Sahara. Raised in the traditional Tuareg world, learning its cos-
mology & poetry, he followed the transhumance of the tribe's cattle & trav-
eled with the merchant caravans from the Sahara to the Mediterranean coast.
Early on he was introduced to Sufi thought & met itinerant Sufi groups; later
he stayed in a range of Sufi monasteries on the Libyan-Egyptian border & at
nomadic camps around Baghdad. From childhood on he was familiar with tifi-
nagh, the written version of his Tamajaq (Tuareg) language, which he now uses
to write down his poems & for painterly calligraphy. (An example of a Hawad
poem in tifinagh—in cursive & "vocalized"—is given below). He then trans-
lates his poems into French with the help of his wife, the ethnologist Hélène
Claudot-Hawad (on whose work these notes are based).

Lounis Aït Menguellet (b. Ighil Bouammas, 1950)

LOVE, LOVE, LOVE

I opened the closet
That I had closed in my youth.
The love book that I had left
Was covered with dust
The dust that covered it,
I shook it off
The book said: Who is waking me up?
Not knowing it was me.
Even the pages did not recognize me

The book that I had written had forgotten me
As if what it contained
Did not evolve from me
As if another hand had written it
and I was not present
Love that we were ashamed of
All are preaching you today
They beautify you and call you Tayri
To me your name brings pleasure
How many times have we used it to recall
O my heart the times of my flame
That fire has now died
It has turned into ashes
Carried by the wind it has left me
My youth with it has gone
The traces which remained
Have been covered by the snows of time

The song that could resuscitate it
Does not recognize the sites anymore
Look Tayri what I have become
How much I have changed
But to me the way I have known you
That way your face has remained
Tell me Tayri
You left me at the crossroads
Do you remember when we met

We made the sun shine on our days
The days that betrayed you
Have ended betraying me too
Each has dealt me a blow
Hitting me and missing you

More, more, more

I still talk about you
As if time stood still
Even when I look at your face
I can hardly believe that it is too late
Let me believe in my dream
If you understand me do not blame me
That is all that I have
Times for me will not change

Nothing, nothing, nothing

Nothing is softer than you
And nothing is more bitter
When I believed in you
You held your arms open
You taught me how
My youth has remained with you
It betrayed both of us
Old age has forbidden your name

Today, today, today

Today, I looked and I saw
Between us a fence of many years
You have not felt the burdens of time
They have fallen only upon me
You know that my friends drink
They have known you before their old days.
They will remain heart-broken

It is over, it is over, it is over

It is over I realize it is too late for me
It is not like the days of my youth
My words are not beautiful anymore
I will burn your book

I will keep your shadow
Only to be reminded of you
It is not under ground
But it is in my heart that I will bury you

Love, love, love

Translation from Tamazight by Rabah Seffal

COMMENTARY

A carpenter by trade, it is no wonder that through all these years of singing &
writing his own lyrics, Lounis Aït Menguellet has carved such beautiful shapes
from the language of his Berber ancestors. He writes with modesty & humil-
ity—exactly as great poets do, far from the spotlights of fame & noisy political
protest. In the ancestral oral tradition of philosopher-poets like Si Mohand
(see p. 241), he writes a poetry that keeps questioning his human existence &
the destiny of his people. Today Aït Menguellet is acknowledged as one of the
greatest Algerian poets & singers.

Mohammed El Agidi (Morocco, twentieth century)

"TELL ME SUNKEN WELL"

Tell me Sunken Well
Where are they who drank from you on summer days
Tell me Sunken Well

Where are those who lived here tell me maddened one
Riding his horse he was beating the drums of war
When the news of war arrived
He covered the desert riding his dark-eyed
They left with their camels and women
No fear in the day of the strike

Trembling rumble of drums

Noise of gunfire, listen to its whistling.
Women shouting ululations, young men arrayed side by side

Tell me Sunken Well
Where are they who drank from you on summer days
Tell me Sunken Well

I questioned you, answer my question
Where is it gone, vanished from here, with its women and tents
I reached its place, the wind blows empty
The broken can't fly without wings
The departed maddened my mind
Longing for them adds sorrow to my heart

How to heal the wound, what to do?

My sleep is light, I wake all night, I can't forget or retreat into oblivion: my
    demon brings me their ghosts in flesh and blood

Tell me Sunken Well
Where are they who drank from you on summer days
Tell me Sunken Well

Where is the untied, combed hair
Where the hair loose in silk threads down to the feet
Where the belts and the veils
Where the scarves flapping loose on the girls' heads
Where the hair braided and rolled up
Where the different qualities of cloth

Where are the different qualities of cloth?
Where is the breeze at the shadows of dawn
Lifting the tents as if they were departing
Like an army approaching, bringing support to the king

Tell me Sunken Well
Where are they who drank from you on summer days
Tell me Sunken Well

The Well was wrapped by its camels,
They sat around it group by group
And the herds ran freely on the hillsides
One neck crying, the other screaming out
It shined the herdsmen's hearts
as the shepherds drove the herd back in the corral

Our Lord makes of our lives what he wants
The story of what happened has forever vanished
we'll never find it or join it back together
We implore God with every joint of our bodies
Our loved ones have disappeared, God have mercy

Tell me Sunken Well
Where are they who drank from you on summer days
Tell me Sunken Well

It was beautiful, its beauty showed,
shining curves on the desert hills
He used to come back tired from herding
Girls played friendly games like unripe young camels
And this happened in the land of rosemary
of oregano, thyme, and chamomile . . .

How many loves are stolen away

Gathering & translation from Arabic by Stefania Pandolfo

COMMENTARY

Writes Stefania Pandolfo in a note to the editors: "This is an oral poem passed on from generations in the Arabic language and intonation of the formerly Arab tribes that lived in the region west of the Wed Draa, moving between the Draa Valley and the Atlantic Ocean. It is an old poem that I recorded from a young poet in Zagora, whose name is Mohammed El Agidi [mentioned in her book *Impasse of the Angels*]. He was young then and had an amazing voice, and because he had been to school all the way through high school, unlike the old oral poets with whom I worked, he wrote down the poetry he collected from other poets' memories. I didn't have a written text from him, though, only recordings. This particular qasida is in the style called *rasma*. However, I am not sure we should say 'anonymous.' Some told me that this poem might be a version of a qasida by a mythical poet from the south, whose name would be Hammou Kerroum. (People told me the story of another qasida, which tells the story of the poet himself, on his deathbed, who is revived or at least capable of waiting for the arrival of the woman he loves—the 'Qasidat Agida.')"

Matoub Lounes (Taourirt Moussa, 1956–Tizi Ouzzou, 1998)

KENZA

Sky fades, flood rumbles, cloudburst washes the slabs,
rivers roar savagely.
The alluvial hearth crumbles into a torrent
in roaring pain a lament rises from the grave:
O my children!

If body rots
thoughts carry on
If passes are harsh to reach
we'll find a cure for exhaustion
they can wipe out many stars
but the sky itself cannot be wiped out

They have long sealed our fate
before these tragic days
the persecutors of knowledge
spread devastation on our land
they killed Rachid Tigziri
they didn't miss Smail
they also got Liabès & Flici
Boucebsi & so many others.

If only one remains
he will remember.
The wound will grow its scab.
We will rise among the other nations
our lineage will thrive
even in the midst of struggle

Kenza, my daughter,
bear mourning me
Sacrificed we died
for tomorrow's Algeria
Kenza, my daughter,
Don't cry

MY SOUL

I paid the mountain with my blood: the stain will remain
even if they've sworn to wipe it off
To those who are waiting for my death, who sully my name
At each pass: you will have to face me

Often I gave up my rights to find myself sullied
I gazed at my reputation—and found those who tarnished my honor
Strength has left my arms but
my voice still resounds and they will hear it!

Someone said: "The mountain trembled and you, you weren't there"
One human tells another: "It's New Year's Day"
The country's on fire, in Tizi the feast's going full blast.
Baroud guns go off in Bejaïa: victory! They broke the yoke of suffering

O my soul! O my soul! These are the mountains of my soul

I wish I were with you, just to grab a word.
The ordeals of my life became an asset.
Now that the Kabyles have united, misfortune will vanish
Why bother digging into words, why bother repeating
Tamazight is the origin, the roots of our lives
It's time that will sort it out

O my soul! O my soul! These are the mountains of my soul

I'm sorry I was not among you, but my hurt heart, brimful with aches
and pains, burst under its burden of sorrows:
let the wicked know and let them eat hay!
If that's how it is, then the wheat will separate from the chaff.
Alone and despised—yet he still speaks

O my soul! O my soul! These are the mountains of my soul

"Infamous rumblings wash off sins" say the ancients
Why pay attention to this nonsense,
Health will return, you'll hear the children sing the Berber lands
Da Mouloud's legacy is with us, loud and real as the thunder is.
Will you feel the raindrops?

O my soul! O my soul! These are the mountains of my soul!

Translations by Nicole Peyrafitte of French versions by Abdelfetah Chenni & A.B. from the original Kabyle

COMMENTARY

Matoub Lounes was a singer-songwriter-composer & poet from Kabylia known for his strong involvement in the struggle for Amazigh recognition. Born in 1956 in Taourirt Moussa, a village of the Aït Mahmoud in the *wilaya* of Tizi Ouzzou, he was assassinated on June 25, 1998, in Kabylia. Officially the assassination is attributed to the terrorists of the GIA (Armed Islamic Group), though his family & most Kabyles accuse the Algerian regime of having him killed. As the story has it, he built his first guitar from an empty car oil can at seven & composed his first songs as a teenager. The violent confrontations between the new Algerian central government & the people of Kabylia during the two years following independence (1963–64) brought him to the realization of his Kabyle identity. After the 1968 Arabization of the education system, he, like many young Kabyles, began skipping school & a few years later dropped out altogether. As he puts it: "We had to give up Berber and reject French. I said no! I played hooky in all my Arabic classes. Every class that I missed was an act of resistance, a slice of liberty conquered. My rejection was voluntary and purposeful." Influenced & helped by the great Kabyle singer Idir, Lounes recorded his first album, *Ay Izem* (The Lion), in 1978. After that album turned into a major success, he went on to record a further thirty-six.

FIFTH DIWAN

"Make It New": The Invention of Independence II

ALGERIA

After achieving independence in July 1962, Algeria embarked on a "road to socialism" that gave permission to the army, the only organized force in the country, to take power in the name of the people and the martyrs of the revolution. Progressively—though no official censorship mechanism was set up—the few reading committees of the SNED (National Company for Publishing and Distributing) became more and more timid, no longer daring to promote original or critical works. Despite a large budget and an official stance that claimed to favor the development of the literary and artistic sector, the Ministry of Information and Culture would never put a halt to the widely condemned "cultural emptiness" marked by limited and often mediocre publications and the absence of literary magazines, cultural imports, and sufficient distribution channels and bookshops.

Those writers who had made their name during the colonial era continued to publish in France, and new authors tried to find recognition outside the country (in France for the Francophones and in the Mashreq for the Arabophones).

After the urban riots of 1988 that marked the end of the single-party system and opened a period of uncertainty, and after the following period of Islamic terrorism (the "black decade")—with a death toll of about 150,000, including a number of intellectuals and writers, such as the poets Tahar Djaout (see p. 615) and Youcef Sebti (see p. 587)—new publishers started up and despite financial and bureaucratic difficulties could finally start publishing, as they continue to do, original works. Even before then, in 1989, several writers—including Sebti, Djaout, and the novelist Tahar Ouettar—created the cultural association Al-Djahidhiya, which organized public readings and literary colloquia that allowed Maghrebi and other Arab authors to express themselves. Their energies outlasted the Black Decade and still drive the risorgimento of a new literature that tries to avoid ideological strictures and make itself heard beyond the national borders.

How to present this literature?

Rigid categories lock authors into boxes unable to account for the dynamics of literary processes. Periodization in relation to political events (November '54, independence, the agrarian revolution, terrorism, etc.) occults the autonomy of the literary field and confuses the reception of the literary artifact by reducing it to the happenstance of historical circumstance and anecdote. Worse, setting up such airtight compartments blurs the visibility of the literary field.

One can, however, distinguish four generations up to the present. The first is that of the "founders" who started to publish right after World War II. All the great names of Algerian literature mentioned in other sections—such as Mouloud Feraoun, Mouloud Mammeri, Mohammed Dib, Kateb Yacine, Jean Sénac, Jean-Elmouhoub Amrouche, and Jean Pélégri—belong to it. For these authors the main difficulty was the absence of a national model in which to express themselves in an authentic writing. It is never easy to be at the beginning, because everything needs to be invented. Unable (and unwilling) to anchor themselves naturally in French literature, these Algerian writers nomadized through other literatures—American, Russian, Spanish, or ancient Greek, for example—to try to locate their voice(s) while also interrogating the oral Maghrebian tradition to find indigenous roots.

The writers who started to publish after independence could be called the generation of the predators, in that they challenged and disputed the practices of their predecessors. Iconoclasts rebelling against the sexual taboos and conformism of society, fully into the various formal innovations of the avant-garde, these authors—Rachid Boudjedra (see p. 580) and Nabile Farès (see p. 577) are exemplary—aimed at exploring the field of literature and inscribing their own selves upon it without having to answer for or to the tribe.

The third generation seems more pacified. It did not try to kill the father but rather wanted to get closer to the grandfather so as to project itself into the future. The war of liberation is a childhood memory for these authors. They have nothing to prove but want to relocate the formula that will rid the poem of the slag accumulated during the "years of lead." Rabah Belamri (see p. 590), Habib Tengour (see p. 593), and Tahar Djaout (see p. 615) are exemplary of this generation.

As for the fourth generation, born during the Black Decade, it is the generation of the tabula rasa. Without any illusions concerning society, it wants to live life to the full. Angry at the previous generation for having abandoned ship in the middle of the storm (though note that some were killed by the storm), skilled in the culture of the Internet, it puts everything into question and wants to find itself outside or beyond any national filiation. However, like Samira Negrouche (see p. 626) and Al-Mahdi Acherchour (see p. 623), it does not shy away from taking writing seriously.

A case of bad conscience in relation to its language of expression has long tormented Francophone Algerian writing. Early on this bad conscience could be located between two polar stances: Malek Haddad's absolute refusal of French, as it had been the colonizer's language, and thus his eventual, though logical, silence; and Kateb Yacine's claim that as Algeria had won the war, it could and had to keep French as the spoils of war. Today, half a century later, with the cultural and politico-economic situation much altered, this is clear: marginal in a society where mastery of French is weak and the book is expensive and badly distributed, given a lack of bookshops, how much (and what kind of) breathing space can Francophone literature hope for?

Algerian writers using Arabic—more and more numerous, given the country's massive efforts at schooling—feel themselves gaining legitimacy. But be the *writing* Arabo-graphic or Franco-graphic, the problem of its disconnection from the *spoken* mother tongues (whether vernacular Arabic or Amazigh) remains important. In fact, starting with the third generation, poets refused to be blocked by what they believe to be a false linguistic problem. They do not want to shut up "unhappy consciousnesses" in their own liberated lands. Burned by the fundamentalists' excesses, they have desacralized Arabic.

Though the 2009 Pan-African Arts festival did not have as powerful an impact as its original, 1969 version, for a few years now the emergence of some young, audacious publishers who promote their books at the International Book Fair of Algiers (SILA) every fall and the rebirth of public poetry events, foremost among them the "Printemps des Poètes," also in Algiers, have been creating places for exchanges beyond language divisions.

Mohammed Dib (Tlemcen, 1920–La Celle-Saint-Cloud, 2003)

from **FORMULAIRES**

I

language sovereign secret incompatible submerged in the universal wound let my life be lost there lived there without vindication wound let a thick wall of dark seal and deaf dumb let no medium be able to make it understood speech that hollows out an empty space

memory exchanged for night
disguising the night
a void that is infinitely radiant

and searches for
some out of the way forest
that will strike the morning
suddenly and blind

2

statue of shadow waits for you she waits she does not know she waits suspended in form and time she exists endures only through this pause in the abyss her visible decor the night which knows where to retreat battling with cries called by the ape of fire who spies does not return halt of dreams to rejoin the three phases of blood fill all the containers with spit and toss them to the wind its laugh its laugh to itself alone fills the high and the low

3

and unable to come back from the blandness dawning at the horizon the day recaptures its prey the spirit lays down its snares some orders of passage drive each tree back into its hole once again the fields begin to capsize merely for the illusion the rite dies some falling motions in the forest some falling shadows calling that crime why wait for the conflict why seek out the legs under the cactus hour of childbirth there's only an open road for this voyage the word that empties its wave only to surge up again in motion winding back into itself embraces the fertile chasm the circle of sacraments and the steps of Kore

4

to teach the singer how to sing again now that his voice is out of tune nothing is more a sacrament than a curse the anatomy's return is assured the breast will regard itself in the other breast questioning its identity and difference until it falls in love with its image which it will see of itself black and mortal if it is white to recognize this breast shelter it make it drink down to its very source carry it on your head stroll with it in broad daylight cum it into your glory

6

all the charitable images of the world lead me to you wondering how to thank them I followed your footsteps one by one in each I discovered signs of your passing wondering which way to turn which way preserves the voice so that all ways serve only as a path to you

7

count the links in the chain the ants in the ant-hill the stars in the sky there will always remain one link there will always remain one ant there will always remain one star and the word on the page will refuse to be entirely inscribed and you will start all over to recombine its letters in all of its meanings and out of this some secret words will be born that will make your knowledge fatten to the point of obesity and obesity will occupy the throne word of words out of which each changes into its neighbor rises up on the shoulders of its brother and builds you some towns makes up some lives for you offers to read you some books which begin at the end that you'll take back mix up throw on the soil so that it may speak to you through oracles

10

to the deceased who was passing the grass says relieve me of this post immobility drains me but what response could there be even the one that immobility would open its doors to wasn't left any less troubled yet one says the grass yet one that the misfortune of others hardly touches went by passing so smoothly one door gave way then another farther on then a third and from that moment on he will only meet doors swinging in an agitation of wings he fell asleep at the point of this incessant crossing of thresholds that rush from themselves to their meeting the fatigue of grass appears to him incomprehensible advancing without walking were it not for the highest form of joy at this moment he hears his own voice say relieve me of this post immobility drains me

Translation from French by Paul Vangelisti & Carol Lettieri

For commentary on Mohammed Dib, see p. 301.

Jean Sénac (Béni Saf, 1926–Algiers, 1973)

MAN OPEN

This man wore his childhood
on his face like a bestiary
he loved his friends, was loved
by nettle and ivy

This man had the truth
driven into his two joined hands
and he bled

To the mother who wished to take his knife away
to the daughter who wished to bathe his wound
he says, "do not stop my sun from marching"

This man was just like an open hand
we threw ourselves at him
to heal him to close him
but he only opened further
ushering the earth into him

When prevented from living
he became poem and kept mute

When we sought to make his portrait
he became tree and kept mute

When his branches were shorn
he became coal and kept mute

When we dug in his veins
he became flame and kept mute

Then his ashes in the town
testified to his defiance

This man was big; a hand open.

HELIOPOLIS

After Hell here is a season
Beautiful as the moon with her children.

.

Beautiful?

.

A town of thistles
Caught in the blue-green of daybreak.
One can only reach it after having a long time kept along
Ramparts of cacti
(The prickly flowers of barbarity are burnt to ashes, in you too).

Sly adolescents hone the insult on the doorstep
Pockets full of smiles.
(But who will force off their blue-jeans?)
In the suburbs an assailing fragrance
—Geraniums, tomatoes, piss—
Crowns the pimp players of dominos.
The women are behind the walls.

      •

And this town was nothing but despair's wish
To conjure your blood's prisons.
Glimpsed (like the bone beneath the wound). Imagined.
So that just one word can solder its future
To the next.
But what could we build upon lily pads?
Already the imperial mildew . . .

      •

Otherwise these triumphant beaches
A buttress of injuries,
But not
This base neighborhood of ulcers!
By just escaping
Our lips, the words are what escape, our sentences are what
aggress.
A few cold cigarette butts will be our bivouac.
Not magic not presence.
The vibrating
Knell that from one vertebra to the next
Plucks yet another name (the used carbon of a glance).

Sentences that were meant to give us
Vast expeditions from one nerve to the other, from one bone
To moon rock. Sentences
That only knew how to anchor us to exile,
To the perishable song, to the instrument
Of our abyss. Trivial
Seasons on the most monstrous wound.
Thrown to the stars.

You needed to leave so that the corpoème
Could recover the freshness of its burnt poppies
And again the word at our lips adjusts
Its secret slights, vertigo's underbrush.

So each was allowed to perish according to his joys.
The words no longer encumbered the vertebrae
Nor the marrow our horizon.
All hurdles abolished, you followed into the steps of those
who no longer expect the halt.
And they know what is stardust around our blood,
which is the paraphrase of nothingness.
God bellows in the disaster of your fingers.
"To wish" has disappeared,
All ceases, all is storm.
Sex—and only he exists more erect than your soul—
Has disappeared, the pulp of the poem
Isn't even a sperm's trace.
Alive, there was nothing left but to perish in the multitude of days.
(Beneath the fingernail, the frozen fruit and the spit of welcome.)
To each their own orgasm in the nothingness of God.

Words, transfigured vertebrae.

SONG OF THE MORTISE

For the bolt and the jack
For the tenon and the buffalo
For the pulley and the poppet
The mortise made itself beautiful.

For the thorn and the harpsichord
For the spinet and the hoe
For the sheaves and the wheels
The mortise made itself beautiful.

Did the poet?

I LIKE WHAT'S DIFFICULT, SAID YOU

Read
his poisonous spring
saw
his insistent desire
took
his vivid lead-filled dream
an impenetrable course
the naked foot the word the frond
and your invulnerable sex
magical mill of names.

THE LAST SONG

To laugh
So hard
That there is no more
Room in this body
For one word
For one death.

So hard
That the fold of your eyelids
Hides forever
The Mushroom.

That your jaw
And your temples—stuck—
Escape
To the mechanics of Pluto.

A laugh
More lathered than soap
To sign
And take off.

Goodbye dust.

Translations from French by Yolande Schutter

For commentary on Jean Sénac, see p. 318.

Kateb Yacine (Guelma, 1929–Grenoble, 1989)

from **LE POLYGONE ÉTOILÉ**

Not once was the return of the Banu Hilal expected. Always, however, they returned to upset the stelae and carry away the dead, jealous of their mystery, unknown and unrecognizable, among the founders.

Once upon a time they had adored the black stone. Now their idol had left the sanctuary, torn the curtain, and dispersed the priests. Since it had traveled through the great outside, its dark face had reddened, it had drunk the blood and dust of the battlefields, and they could no longer sequester it in a temple: "Will we bury it alive? Does it have to be sacrificed, or should it be left alive? It talks and we walk, it must be able to follow us, don't doubt it any longer, as it is what pushes as to walk on. Don't doubt *nanyang* longer! Here it is, accurate to its legend, after absurd persecutions, here it is, free, and yet we had thought it dead, as we had lost it during the war, lost, reconquered, and nothing threatens it more than the fervor of its own warriors; that's because we loved it too much and in relation to love we are ferocious . . . "

She could also remain anonymous, go back into obscurity like Osiris at the bottom of his grave, biding her time waiting for a new age or avatar; she was born there and elsewhere; how many peoples had left in black blood and red earth the signal and the regret of their turbulent childhood, without knowing what beauty, sand rose, dust flower, had kept the shape of their last breath, went to grow far from them, without them, against them, one day to throw off the veil of *pudeur* and offer herself to the last one among them, who would finally bring her back to her family, in a shroud or a palanquin, free or dead, torn from seclusion, profanation, slavery: hadn't they always doubted her birth? Had she lived? Since use had become conscious of a fate too rich, too loaded, it looked as if she was stuttering in the midst of a crisis of amnesia and disturbing the neighbors—quiet children or resigned elders—who still treated her as if her existence had been but a void, a hole, as if it wasn't enough to see her rise, in the five parts of the world, like a star of black blood.

Infested in her absence	Her distancing herself
	a happy foreboding
We practiced	In other times
fencing	
And gave up rivalry	She would have grown pale
As having failed	
stupefied.	Under the stars

Poured in the caves.   Let's draw closer
Of a port that distracts us   dangerously
   Salvation closed door
   Cover of another book
   Dropped on us
   The pages of the torn book
   Nedjma Nedjma open your door or window
   Or just trot through your corridor
   Or scream or scream or sing or weep
   Throw upon the lie owed to the faithful
   Or the bucket of water on the head of the mad
   Send us your dog or your cat
   Or one of the flies of your house
   Shake one of your old carpets out over us
   I can't stand this loneliness any longer!

Oh noble hypocrisy
Andalusian preterition
              And both composing
              The same poem, taciturn
Faced with the same disenchanting sojourn
   With phews
   Okay
   Ah
   Oh well
   That's life
   What
   So
   Oh
   Our
   That's the way it is

One single woman keeps us busy
And her absence unites us
And her presence divides us

   Dead tired, frantic, unshaven, they strode through the city, passed again and again before the door and the windows, passed again and again, every day, every day, every day.

   "Even when when we split up outside the village, we both had that disastrous pilgrimage in our minds, but we needed a break, back to back, like boxers, we couldn't bear the hand-to-hand any longer, clinched, ready to hit low and bang heads, so Rachid put an end to this friendly game, like a disgusted referee, and said, leaving us a clear field: I am going to Constantine. And I reacted like a son of a bitch by answering Rachid: I'll go with you until Bône. Yes, I already wanted to get ahead of Mustapha, while seeming to lower my guard, but by pronouncing the word *Bône,* the site of the championship, I had provoked him, pushed him back against the ropes, knowing he'd come back charging, that he was waiting for the end of the round to know if he had taken the beating well, let me have the upper hand and feigned giving up, hugged me, watched me follow with fist raised the steps of the referee— the spectators roaring deep down inside us, in a faraway rumbling from a disconcerted stand—without doubting getting back into the ring soon." And here now they met up again in the perfume of jasmine, in front of the lemon tree loaded to the hilt with fruit, the shutters closed, discolored.

Did she come into this room?
She came.
Disputed lover
Consoling musician
Coifed at the end of her trail
With the intimidating helmet of the warrior goddess
She was the veiled woman of the terrace
The unknown woman of the hospital
The libertine brought back to the Nadhor
The fake barmaid amidst the Pieds-Noirs
The unfindable amnesiac of the island of the lotus-eaters
And the Moorish woman sold by auction
With gunshots
And a fast and turbulent
And diabolic Algerio-Corsican argument
And the dust flower in the shadow of the fonduk
Finally the wild woman sacrificing her only son
And watching him in knife play
Wild?
Yes
Her native blackness had reappeared
Face hard smooth and cutting
We no longer manly enough for her
Somber silent dusty
Lip pallid lids inflamed
Eye barely open gaze lost
Beneath the thick fauve flame thrown back over her shoulders
Pants too big and rolled up at ankles

And a colt under the breast
With paperwork and burned galette

In our eyes growing uglier on principle
Rolled in the refusal of her colors
She was the ancestor's pricking handkerchief
Welcomed us fallen from on high
Like lice on maneuvers
The more her perfume of a flowering plebeian violated us
By its mixture disoriented
The more she threatened us
From the depths of her bruised transhumance
Picked or breathed in
She emptied on us
Her heart of vacant black rose
And we were nailed to her candid pride
While she took her flight petal after petal
Withered volcanic snow
Modest ash accumulating outrage
Exposed by herself to all relapses
Dilapidated to all four winds

Rarely, with a sigh, she would find the amber necklace she'd bite on rather or fingered, pensive, and brandishing the cracked lute of Prison Face, her last admirer, who pronounced her name from jail cell to jail cell, without speaking of Mourad and without speaking of the penal colony, without speaking of the blind one, someone named Mustapha, that her shadow pursued in another prison, he however had crossed the gates, but he didn't know he'd been freed.

We were then nothing but her litter
Shoved back into place by nips of her teeth
With distracted and quasi-maternal spite
She knew well
She
At each apparition of the Crescent
What it means to carry your wound in secret
She knew well
She
With her breasts stirring
What our raging hunger was

Could she
An already traced furrow
Not weep on edge skin deep
Over the sowing season?
Even at her rockery's gap
Could she ignore how torrents lose themselves
Chased from the springs of childhood
Prisoners of their dangerous overabundant origin
With neither love nor works?

   Fountain of blood, of milk, of tears, she knew by instinct, she did, how
they had been born, how they had fallen upon the earth, and how they'd
fall again, come into brutal consciousness, without parachute, exploded like
bombs, burned one against the other, grown cold in the ashes of the natal
pyre, without flame or heat, expatriated.

Translation from French by P.J.

   For commentary on Kateb Yacine, see p. 326.

Nadia Guendouz (Algiers, 1932–1992)

GREEN FRUIT

The sun ripens the fruit
But I am a man
Back home our sun is so fierce
It burns our soul
Before our flesh
But you, you don't know
   Algeria
You whose earth
Knows only rain
You think I'm still green
Green with hope yes
But hear me as I tell you
I am a man, not
   a piece of fruit
Our fruits are good
You have loved them

Gorged on sun on life
They resemble us
They are your foes
They dislike changing country
Despite your husbandry
When they land on your soil
They spoil
They love the sun
That kills them
On their earth
As your weapons do
Our own brothers
Neither our fruit nor our men
Are afraid of fire
Whether sent by man
Or sent by God
Fruit can remain green
A 10-year-old Algerian
Is not a child
He is ripe, he earns his living
He's a man, not a piece of fruit.

Paris, 1957

ON RUE DE LA LYRE

On Rue de la Lyre
There are gates
And piled up bodies
Against these gates, come
       nightfall
The baker's grates
The warm smell of bread
And these hungry bodies come
To warm themselves
Their belly cold
Their eyes burning
With fever with tears
Step over them, step over
And walk on by

Close your eyes
The small black hands
This is where they
        sleep
The whole day through
They've shone shoes
These kids' mouths
With no saliva
For having spat
Too much on shoes
Not for their feet
On Rue de la Lyre
You keep your bread
Keep your warm
        grates
Baker close
Your door
Damp your oven,
Useless now
Damp it, I tell you
Today
        I have a bed
Today
        I have bathed
Today
        I am Algerian
Today
        You hear me
I have a roof
Tomorrow I won't again extend
        a hand.
    Tomorrow my life will be sound

Tomorrow I will be
A man
Because too many
Are now dead
Because tomorrow
The sun has risen
Over Algeria.

Algiers, February 1963

1ST MAY 1963

On Independence Day
I wasn't there
I didn't march
My heart wasn't wrung with joy
With a joy that instills fear
With a joy that instills pain
My eyes drenched in tears
I saw alas not for real
But on TV
The image to which
I strive to devote myself
I saw the image for which
I will fight to the death
Algerians—Man and Woman
Hand in hand raised
Raised to the pride of freedom
But tomorrow this image
I will live it
I'll be the one to give
My brother my hand
He, though hesitant, will take it
I'll never let his go
Come what may. He will hold mine.
Yesterday I fought by his side
Today and tomorrow
Tomorrow most of all
I will labor to march
Among brothers
We help, we love one another
And so my brothers
Tomorrow's the First of May
And for us it truly is the first
Time we can shout
Sing, laugh, free
Free, free
Do you sense it
Tell me
Have you attained the joy
And the truth

The conscience of freedom
Yes!
So bring your sister
Not your neighbor's, yours
And take her by the hand
Tomorrow's our First of May
Teach her to read
Guide her hand
Come the First of May again
She will write
She will labor
Algeria needs her
As it needs you
And so
Tomorrow your heart
Tomorrow drunk with joy
Your conscience awakened
Then you may roar
Long live freedom
Long live Algeria
Long live our First of May.

Algiers, May 1963

Translations from French by Madeleine Campbell

COMMENTARY

Born on February 27, 1932, in downtown Algiers, Nadia Guendouz worked for the Fédération de France as a fund-raiser for the FLN (National Liberation Front) while pursuing nursing studies. She was arrested in 1959 and jailed in Skikda, where she returned after independence, becoming politically active in the National Union of Algerian Women. Though she published numerous poems in the Algerian press, only two collections—*Amel* (SNED, 1968) & *La Corde* (SNED, 1974)—came out during her lifetime. She died of a heart attack in 1992.

Assia Djebar (b. Cherchell, 1936)

POEM FOR A HAPPY ALGERIA

Snows in the Djurdjura
Lark traps in Tikjda
Plum tomatoes in the Ouadhias
I am being whipped in Azazga
A goat's kid gambols in the Hodna
Horses flee from Mechria
A camel dreams in Ghardaïa

And my sobs in Djemila
The cricket sings in Mansourah
A falcon flies over Mascara
Fire brands in Bou-Hanifia

No pardon for the Kelaa
Sycamores in Tipaza
A hyena comes out in Mazouna
The hangman sleeps in Miliana

Soon my death in Zemoura
A ewe in Nedroma
And a friend near Oudja
Night cries in Maghnia

My agony in Saida
The rope around the neck in Frenda
On the knees in Oued-Fodda
On the gravel of Djelfa

Prey of the wolves in M'sila
Beauty of jasmine in Kolea
Garden roses of Blida
On the road to Mouzaia

I'm dying of hunger in Medea
A dry river in Chellala
A dark curse in Medjana
A sip of water in Bou-Saada

And my tomb in the Sahara
Then the alarm sounds in Tebessa

Eyes without tears in Mila
What a racket in Ain-Sefra

They take up arms in Guelma
A shiny day in Khenchla
An assassination in Biskra
Soldiers in the Nementcha

Last battle in Batna
Snows on the Djurdjura
Lark traps in Tikjda
Plum tomatoes in the Ouadhias

A festive mood in the heart of El Djazira

Translation from French by P.J.

from *FANTASIA: AN ALGERIAN CAVALCADE*

Embraces

Lla Zohra, from Bou Semmam, is more than eighty. I cross the threshold of the house she lives in nowadays, just on the edge of the village of Ménacer. I walk up the path through her vegetable patch that she looks after herself, and under a walnut and an apricot tree that later she points out to me proudly.

I tap softly with the knocker on the second door and the hum of the sewing machine is suspended. The white-washed rooms open on to a modest patio; from there the slopes of the mountain are visible, Pic Marceau with its observation posts that are no longer in use.

A young woman, the one who was doing the sewing, comes out first. Then the old lady, my hostess. We embrace, we touch, we tell each other how well we look. I sit down. I talk of my grandmother's death, which occurred just after independence. I hadn't seen Lla Zohra since.

"We were cousins, your grandmother and I," she says. "It's true I'm closer to you through your mother's father; we belong to the same fraction of the same tribe. She was related to me through another marriage, through the female line!"

I listen as she unravels the genealogical skein; the threads pass from such and such a mountain to such and such a hill, winding through *zaouia* and hamlet, and then round the heart of the city. I drink my coffee. Finally I say, "I'm spending the night here! . . . We've plenty of time! . . . "

Her voice stirs the glowing embers of days past. The afternoon draws on, the mountainsides change color, the sewing machine resumes its monotonous humming-song at the far end of the patio. The old woman's adopted daughter has gone back to her sewing; she doesn't want to listen or be involved. Later, she asks me how she can get a job in the nearby town, in the post-office, or in a nursery school . . .

I agree to take you up to your farm, little mother, high in the mountains. After two hours' walk on thorny paths, we found the sanctuary, which you call "the refuge," using the French word, only slightly distorted: the walls are still standing among the rubble.

Their base is blackened with traces of extinct fires, lit by present-day vagrants. There, your voice took up your tale. The sun was still high. You let your veil fall around your waist and sat down among the gorse bushes and spring flowers. Your face, a network of fine wrinkles, was austere; you were lost for a moment in your own memories—I took a photograph of you among the poppies . . . The sun gradually sank low in the sky. We returned in the evening silence.

It is now my turn to tell a tale. To hand on words that were spoken, then written down. Words from more than a century ago, like those that we, two women from the same tribe, exchange today.

Shards of sounds which re-echo in the calm after the storm . . .

The oasis of Laghouat in the summer of 1853: the artist Eugène Fromentin has spent the preceding autumn and spring in the Sahel where peace has been restored, just as it has today, little mother.

Summer sets in. Giving way to a sudden impulse, he rushes southwards. Six months before, Laghouat had suffered a terrible siege. The oasis had been captured by the French, house by house. Traces of mass graves can still be seen under the palm trees, where Fromentin walks with a friend. And just as I listen to you unfold your tale during these few days, he hears his friend the lieutenant say, as he stops in front of a most wretched house, "Look!—Here's a miserable hut that I'd like to see razed to the ground!"

Fromentin continues: "And as we went along, he told me the following story in a few brief words, stamped with his sad reflections on the cruel hazards of war:

'In this house, which has changed hands since the capture of the city, lived two very pretty *Naylettes* . . . '"*

Fatma and Meriem, the *Naylettes,* earn their living in the oasis as dancers and prostitutes. They are twenty at the most. Fifteen years previously, the

*Eugène Fromentin, *Un été au Sahara* (A Summer in the Sahara).

Amir Abd al-Qadir had attacked El-Mahdi, near Laghouat, to try to subdue the lords of the south and unify resistance to the Christian . . . Had these women lost their father in this civil war, and some of their brothers? Let us suppose so; when we meet them in this digression into the past, they make a living out of their beauty which is in its prime . . .

If they were to live till they were forty, little mother, perhaps they would become like that woman, Khadija, with whom you kept company in the corridor of torture; wealthy sinners trying to make the pilgrimage "to win their pardon and give money to the Partisans!"

A few months or a few weeks before the siege of Laghouat, Fatma and Meriem secretly received two officers from a French column which patrols the district: not for betrayal, but simply for a night of love, "may God preserve us from sin!"

"After the street fighting of 4 and 5 December, the corpses were so numerous that they filled the well of the oasis!" I explained. "And Fatma? And Meriem?" Lla Zohra interrupted, catching herself following the story as if it were a legend recounted by a bard. "Where did you hear this story?" she went on, impatiently.

"I read it!" I replied. "An eye-witness told it to a friend who wrote it down."

The lieutenant, one of the officers who'd been received by the *Naylettes,* is a member of the first company which leads the attack. He fights throughout the day. "We fought our way right into the heart of the city," he explains. Suddenly he recognizes the district and goes with his sergeant to the dancers' house.

A soldier is just coming out, his bayonet dripping with blood. Two accomplices run out after him, their arms laden with women's jewellery.

"Too late!" the lieutenant thinks, as he enters the house which had previously welcomed him so warmly.

And night falls.

The lieutenant tells what he had seen and the artist writes it down: "Fatma was dead, Meriem was dying. The one lay on the paving-stones in the courtyard, the other had rolled down the stairs, head first, and lay at the bottom."

Two bodies of two young dancers lying half naked up to the waist, their thighs visible through the torn fabric of their clothes, without headdress or diadem, without earrings or anklets, without necklaces of coral or gold coins, without glass-beaded clasps . . . In the courtyard the stove is still burning; a dish of couscous has just been served. The spindle from the loom has been put down, still wound full of wool, never to be used; only the olive-wood chest lies overturned, rifled, its hinges wrenched off.

"As Meriem died in my arms, she dropped a button she had torn off the uniform of her murderer," sighed the lieutenant who had arrived too late.

Six months later, the officer gave his trophy to Fromentin, who kept it. Fromentin was never to paint the picture of the death of those dancers. Is it the feel of this object in his hand which transforms him from a painter of Algerian hunting scenes into the writer depicting death in words? . . . As if Fromentin's pen had taken precedence over his paint-brush, as if the story passed on to him could only find its final form in words . . .

Meriem's dying hand still holds out the button from the uniform: to the lover, to the friend of the lover who cannot now help but write. And time is abolished. I, your cousin, translate this story into our mother tongue, and tell it now to you, sitting beside you, little mother, in front of your vegetable patch. So I try my hand as temporary story-teller.

The nights I spent in Ménacer, I slept in your bed, just as long ago I slept as a child curled up against my father's mother. . . .

Soliloquy

I have been moving freely outside the harem since my adolescence, but every place I travel through is nothing but a wilderness. In cafés, in Paris or elsewhere, I am surrounded by murmuring strangers: I spend hours eavesdropping on faceless voices, catching snatches of dialogue, fragments of stories, an impenetrable mumble of sounds detached from the magma of faces, preserved from probing eyes.

The sharp ploughshare of my memory dig its furrows through the darkness behind me, while I tremble in broad daylight to find myself among women who mix with men, with impunity . . . They call me an exile. It is more than that: I have been banished from my homeland to listen and bring back some traces of liberty to the women of my family . . . I imagine I constitute the link, but I am only floundering in a murky bog.

My night stirs up French words, in spite of the resurrected dead . . . I thought when I grasped these words they would be doves of peace, in spite of the ravens hovering over the charnel houses, in spite of the snarling jackals tearing flesh to pieces. Cooing turtle-dove-words, chirruping robin-redbreasts like those that wait in opium-smokers' cages . . . The first strains of a dirge well up, penetrating the barriers of oblivion, at once a plaintive song and song of love in the first light of dawn. And every dawn is brighter because I write.

My fiction is this attempt at autobiography, weighed down under the oppressive burden of my heritage. Shall I sink beneath the weight? . . .

But the tribal legend criss-crosses the empty spaces, and the imagination crouches in the silence when loving words of the unwritten mother tongue remain unspoken—language conveyed like the inaudible babbling of a nameless, haggard mummer—crouches in this dark night like a woman begging in the streets . . .

I shelter again in the green shade of my cloistered companion's whispers. How shall I find the strength to tear off my veil, unless I have to use it to bandage the running sore nearby from which words exude?

Translation from French by Dorothy S. Blair

COMMENTARY

Born in 1936 in Cherchell, Assia Djebar—real name: Fatima-Zohra Imalayène—is the daughter of a schoolteacher. After high school in Blida & Algiers, she went to the École normale supérieure in Sèvres. She published her first novel, *La Soif*, with Editions Julliard in 1957. In 1958, after her second novel, *Les Impatients* (Editions Julliard), was published, she went to Rabat, Morocco, & studied history at the university there. After independence she returned to Algeria, where she continued her writing career (novels, plays, poetry, journalism) while teaching history at the University of Algiers. In 1977 she directed the feature film *La Nouba des femmes du Mont Chenoua*, awarded the Critics' Prize at the Venice Biennial in 1979. Her second film, *La Zerda ou les chants de l'oubli*, came out in 1982. In 1985 she began work on a large historical epic about Algeria, a trilogy that opens with *L'Amour, la fantasia* (published in English as *Fantasia: An Algerian Cavalcade* by Heinemann in 1993), followed by *Ombre sultane* (1987; published in English as *A Sister to Scheherazade*, translated by Dorothy Blair [Heinemann, 1987]) & *Loin de Médine* (1991; published in English in 1991 as *Far from Medina*, translated by Dorothy Blair). She has continued to publish many more novels & volumes of essays while living in Paris & New York, where she teaches at New York University. In 2005 she was the first Maghrebian woman to become a member of the Académie française.

Djebar's oeuvre is characterized by a series of in-betweens: Algeria-France, independence-colonization, Berber/Arabic/French language. Writes Beïda Chikhi: "A female writer who is a spokeswoman for sequestered women, a writer who is a witness for a historical era, a writer who stimulates the memories of the women ancestors and shakes up the archives, a writer who traverses her own body and surprises the couple, Assia Djebar is also the writer as architect testing the structures, constructing linguistic objects, and who, while remaining deeply anchored in an ideology of representation, is evolving toward a semiological quest and a reflection on the processes of creation."

Malek Alloula (b. Oran, 1937)

from **THE COLONIAL HAREM**

The Orient as Stereotype and Phantasm

Arrayed in the brilliant colors of exoticism and exuding a full-blown yet uncertain sensuality, the Orient, where unfathomable mysteries dwell and cruel and barbaric scenes are staged, has fascinated and disturbed Europe for a long time. It has been its glittering imaginary but also its mirage.

Orientalism, both pictorial and literary, has made its contribution to the definition of the variegated elements of the sweet dream in which the West has been wallowing for more than four centuries. It has set the stage for the deployment of phantasms.

There is no phantasm, though, without sex, and in this Orientalism, a confection of the best and of the worst—mostly the worst—a central figure emerges, the very embodiment of the obsession: the harem. A simple allusion to it is enough to open wide the floodgate of hallucination just as it is about to run dry.

For the Orient is no longer the dreamland. Since the middle of the nineteenth century, it has inched closer. Colonialism makes a grab for it, appropriates it by dint of war, binds it hand and foot with myriad bonds of exploitation, and hands it over to the devouring appetite of the great mother countries, ever hungry for raw materials.

Armies, among them the one that landed one fine 5 July 1830 a little to the east of Algiers, bring missionaries and scholars with their impedimenta as well as painters and photographers forever thirsty for exoticism, folklore, Orientalism. This fine company scatters all over the land, sets up camp around military messes, takes part in punitive expeditions (even Théophile Gautier is not exempt), and dreams of the Orient, its delights and its beauties.

What does it matter if the colonized Orient, the Algeria of the turn of the century, gives more than a glimpse of the other side of its scenery, as long as the phantasm of the harem persists, especially since it has become profitable? Orientalism leads to riches and respectability. Horace Vernet, whom Baudelaire justly called the Raphael of barracks and bivouacs, is the peerless exponent of this smug philistinism. He spawns imitators. Vulgarities and stereotypes draw upon the entire heritage of the older, precolonial Orientalism. They reveal all its presuppositions to the point of caricature.

It matters little if Orientalistic painting begins to run out of wind or falls into mediocrity. Photography steps in to take up the slack and reactivates the phantasm at its lowest level. The postcard does it one better; it becomes the poor man's phantasm: for a few pennies, display racks full of dreams. The postcard is everywhere, covering all the colonial space, immediately available to the tourist, the soldier, the colonist. It is at once their poetry and their glory captured for the ages; it is also their pseudoknowledge of the colony. It produces stereotypes in the manner of great seabirds producing guano. It is the fertilizer of the colonial vision.

The postcard is ubiquitous. It can be found not only at the scene of the crime it perpetrates but at a far remove as well. Travel is the essence of the postcard, and expedition is its mode. It is the fragmentary return to the mother country. It straddles two spaces: the one it represents and the one it will reach. It marks out the peregrinations of the tourist, the successive postings of the soldier, the territorial spread of the colonist. It sublimates the spirit of the stopover and the sense of place; it is an act of unrelenting aggression against sedentariness. In the postcard, there is the suggestion of a complete metaphysics of uprootedness.

It is also a seductive appeal to the spirit of adventure and pioneering. In short, the postcard would be a resounding defense of the colonial spirit in picture form. It is the comic strip of colonial morality.

But it is not merely that; it is more. It is the propagation of the phantasm of the harem by means of photography. It is the degraded, and degrading, revival of this phantasm.

The question arises, then, how are we to read today these postcards that have superimposed their grimacing mask upon the face of the colony and grown like a chancre or a horrible leprosy?

Today, nostalgic wonderment and tearful archeology (Oh! those colonial days!) are very much in vogue. But to give in to them is to forget a little too quickly the motivations and the effects of this vast operation of systematic distortion. It is also to lay the groundwork for its return in a new guise: a racism and a xenophobia titillated by the nostalgia of the colonial empire.

Beyond such barely veiled apologias that hide behind aesthetic rationalizations, another reading is possible: a symptomatic one.

To map out, from under the plethora of images, the obsessive scheme that regulates the totality of the output of this enterprise and endows it with meaning is to force the postcard to reveal what it holds back (the ideology of colonialism) and to expose what is represented in it (the sexual phantasm).

The Golden Age of the colonial postcard lies between 1900 and 1930. Although a latecomer to colonial apologetics, it will quickly make up for its belatedness and come to occupy a privileged place, which it owes to the infatuation it elicits, in the preparations for the centennial of the conquest, the apotheosis of the imperial epoch.

In this large inventory of images that History sweeps with broad strokes out of its way, and which shrewd merchants hoard for future collectors, one theme especially seems to have found favor with the photographers and to have been accorded privileged treatment: the *algérienne*.

History knows of no other society in which women have been photographed on such a large scale to be delivered to public view. This disturbing and paradoxical fact is problematic far beyond the capacity of rationalizations that impute its occurrence to ethnographic attempts at a census and visual documentation of human types.

Behind this image of Algerian women, probably reproduced in the millions, there is visible the broad outline of one of the figures of the colonial perception of the native. This figure can be essentially defined as the practice of a right of (over)sight that the colonizer arrogates to himself and that is the bearer of multiform violence. The postcard fully partakes in such violence; it extends its effects; it is its accomplished expression, no less efficient for being symbolic.

Moreover, its fixation upon the woman's body leads the postcard to paint this body up, ready it, and eroticize it in order to offer it up to any and all comers from a clientele moved by the unambiguous desire of possession.

To track, then, through the colonial representations of Algerian women—the figures of a phantasm—is to attempt a double operation: first, to uncover the nature and the meaning of the colonialist gaze; then, to subvert the stereotype that is so tenaciously attached to the bodies of women.

A reading of the sort that I propose to undertake would be entirely superfluous if there existed photographic traces of the gaze of the colonized upon the colonizer. In their absence, that is, in the absence of a confrontation of opposed gazes, I attempt here, lagging far behind History, to return this immense postcard to its sender.

What I read on these cards does not leave me indifferent. It demonstrates to me, were that still necessary, the desolate poverty of a gaze that I myself, as an Algerian, must have been the object of at some moment in my personal history. Among us, we believe in the nefarious effects of the evil eye (the evil gaze). We conjure them with our hand spread out like a fan. I close my hand back upon a pen to write *my* exorcism: *this text.*

Women from the Outside: Obstacle and Transparency

The reading of public photographs is always, at bottom,
a private reading.

    ROLAND BARTHES, *CAMERA LUCIDA*, 1981

The first thing the foreign eye catches about Algerian women is that they are concealed from sight.

No doubt this very obstacle to sight is a powerful prod to the photographer

Kabyle woman covering herself with the haik.

operating in urban environments. It also determines the obstinacy of the camera operator to force that which disappoints him by its escape.

The Algerian woman does not conceal herself, does not play at concealing herself. But the eye cannot catch hold of her. The opaque veil that covers her intimates clearly and simply to the photographer a refusal. Turned back upon himself, upon his own impotence in the situation, the photographer undergoes an *initial experience of disappointment and rejection*. Draped in the veil that cloaks her to her ankles, the Algerian woman discourages the *scopic desire* (the voyeurism) of the photographer. She is the concrete negation of this desire and thus brings to the photographer confirmation of a triple rejection: the rejection of his desire, of the practice of his "art," and of his place in a milieu that is not his own.

Algerian society, particularly the world of women, is forever forbidden to him. It counterposes to him a smooth and homogeneous surface free of any cracks through which he could slip his indiscreet lens.

The whiteness of the veil becomes the symbolic equivalent of blindness: a leukoma, a white speck on the eye of the photographer and on his viewfinder. *Whiteness is the absence of a photo, a veiled photograph, a whiteout, in technical terms.* From its background nothing emerges except some vague contours, anonymous in their repeated resemblance. Nothing distinguishes one veiled woman from another.

Translation from French by Myrna Godzich & Wlad Godzich

COMMENTARY

Born in Oran in 1937, Malek Alloula has lived & worked in Paris since 1968. He is the author of several volumes of poetry—*Villes et autres lieux* (Paris: Bourgois, 1979), *Rêveurs/Sépulture; suivi de L'exercice des sens* (Paris: Sindbad, 1982), *Mesures du vent* (Paris: Sindbad, 1984), *L'Accès au corps* (Lyons: Horlieu, 2003), & *Approchant du seuil ils dirent* (Al Manar, 2009)—& an important essay, illustrated by photographs, published in English as *The Colonial Harem* (University of Minnesota Press, 1986), extracted here.

Refined & demanding, the poetry invites us to undertake a journey through memory toward a point of arrival that remains to be (re)defined. Since the days of his collaboration with the magazine *Souffles* (see the commentary on Abdellatif Laâbi, p. 672), Alloula has not stopped questioning the routes & voices of poetry: "Why write in this night that surrounds us & in the middle of the greatest precariousness? A questioning that is vital to me but that in the long run must not propose any solution. Certainly a different voice from the one in 'Souffles' but, like that one, a voice that bears witness to an authentic experience" (*Souffles* 3 [1966]). & in an interview with Arezki Metref for *Soir d'Algérie* (February 19, 2009), Alloula said: "The furtive, clandestine side of writing troubles me a lot. At the same time, the image of burrowing excites me. We are, it seems, in the domain of an inviolable, unknowable intimacy. In poetry, where does that power of writing to create a void, to rarefy the air around the fingers that play on the keys or doodle over a sheet of paper, come from? It seems to me that, caught in the net of his writing, the poet essentially lives a sort of nonvirtual 'second life.'"

Mourad Bourboune (b. Jijel, 1938)

from *THE MUEZZIN*

They leave, return, leave each other, find each other again—I go up to the home place—I go down to France and in the caves, the attics, they pile up, fifteen, twenty. All day long they build, rebuild houses for the others, their own always threatens collapse. In the meantime. The construction site, the factory, the assembly line and the lovely life to come, later, and that will have to be lived. In the future. The salary that travels via money order, what remains of it on the counter of the owner of the café-bar-hotel-restaurant-cave. "I'm paying a week in advance and I'm offering you a drink." Better to make sure of the fetid friendship of the owner, who, someday, will give credit: in the future. They live one upon the other, the brain inhabited by the bosses; they never agree, for proof: they pay their contributions in contradiction. Unskilled laborer, skilled workman, foreman, number. "You can write me a letter: tell her I miss her a lot—*bezef.*"

Huge bag of quivering flesh under the spur of the tracts. Evenings, under the badly closing transom, sitting around the low table, they watch in a daze as the cards slide through the fingers of the dealer. In the corner the man from the south makes tea. Debris of dreams, cards put down on table, cigarette butt passed around, smoke. "I'm letting my mustache grow, I'll shave it on the great day, I swear." They found fatherlands from far away. They reside in the Elsewhere. They wait. Brahim speaks of the eternal value of the Qur'an while enjoying a glass of red and two franks: the violent faith of apostasy. "When it comes, the great day, let's hope there'll be a little of us left." The Muezzin said it. The Muezzin repeats himself, enough to lose his voice.

What about that tea? Ready?

If you're in a hurry, just go across the street to the café, answers the man from the south, disturbed in his ritual. I don't do vague imitations. It's either tea or it's nothing.

Belote. Do you really think he's returned?

Who?

The Muezzin, who else!

So what! Returned or not, what does it matter? You're all the same: always one prophet ahead.

I was just saying. Belote again.

Don't worry about it, he'll go get an armchair like all the others.

Not him, said the man from the south.

The tea hisses softly.

All the same.

Not him.

Even dead, come back, Muezzin. There'll always be victims. When you point a gun there's always some idiot that steps right up into the crosshairs.

I will not come back from Prague again with a bouquet of mimosas bought at Orly: "Look, Kittance, over there it's already spring." Bad. I'm a deep infidel. A deep sick man: the doctor said so. She could not understand that with this bouquet lyingly called Praguian, I no longer had the impression of returning from Czechoslovakia. I felt frustrated.

To sum up, said the dealer, before you believed too much and now not enough. What is it you really want.

I agree with you, said the man from the south, if the Muezzin comes back all will change.

You are in question, Muezzin, you'll have to exhaust all the verdicts. She said: "Of course you can do whatever you want, but it's not a life to always wait, wait, without knowing what for. And you who don't even know what you'll do tomorrow." We were making love cleanly. "Yes, tomorrow I'm off to the provinces." I woke up early, malcontent, packages, contacts, hideouts . . . And Rachid who said: "It's enough to drive you crazy . . . It will leave sequels." The asylum, puking oneself. "How do you live," said the doctor, "how do you do it, how do you live?" In the old days I had grand dreams, pure, milky, and waking up, I'd tell myself: someday . . . provided that . . . In crisis moments she'd lose herself in my nicknames, mix up my noms de guerre: Albert, Abdallah, Luc, Saïd, I'd see shadows parade by whose only support I was. I'd start doubting my own identity.

Twenty, thirty years of good and loyal services, helmet on head, digging up Paris asphalt, or straining backs on an assembly line, they return feet first (the Phrothers chip in to pay for the last journey) to the Promised Land.

You shouldn't leave, shouldn't return: but stay lying down in a perfect horizontal; sedimentary—strata. The earth would move for me. It would take charge of movement, no more things, no more room. To stay between the departure and the arrival, gaping hole I'd furnish with my ecstatic poses, while waiting for the irremissible dispossession. A seismic, vegetal season would split the earth with a solar indentation, the wadis would no longer be thirsty, and the four cardinal points would be dismantled. A disgusted Anti-Atlas would put down its load and say: "I'm fed up with minimum salary and with cooperation, I've had it with waiting in vain for the great break of the axis, your bankruptcy, your fears, and your kowtowing have exhausted my pagan patience." Reptation of the dunes toward the sea, sudden looming up of sandy spines between the fingers of the dead, the concrete that crumbles and the tribe that comes running, coming in for the kill to put an end to your reptilian swarming. You'll croak. The city too will croak and then the Great Book of Pains will come and it will write itself in epileptic ink.

To accept, wait, not leave, not endure, I will only endure the apocalypse and elementary truths.

The cemetery of El Alia will sputter under the greasy liquefaction of your bodies, a new avenue will grow there, digesting your solidified pukings, breaking down the dead-end lanes, and all around, the true city, the venomous city, will grow like a mushroom until the hour when the sea will come to wash it all.

I tell myself: I can no longer push back the struggle, the struggle against the city. My overseas city, pockmarked with casbahs, hooped with its watertight nationalism, dominated by its muezzins, who cast lubricious glances over the terraces where the Moorish women slump for a suntan in defiance of the harem. My city that starts on Place de la République, in Nanterre, where a brother wearing a tie asks me for direction toward the closest parimutuel betting office.

All this mass of fallen rocks . . . The City . . . The City . . . it harasses me.

I'm afraid of it, in one fell swoop my blood rushed back, I'm betrayed inside. No longer to push back the struggle. Let's redouble our vigilance, draw up a plan so as not to follow it. Beware of your left hand. The enemy: all, and all of me. Just as well not think it over and charge. I'll invent myself a traitor to be immolated before the prophecy. To the people I'll give ruin, which it will refuse, the Great Book, which it doesn't expect, a formidable compass: the anti-Qur'an. I'll announce the basement where, under the double horn of the Moorish crescent and the aegis of the Black Stone with the Saudi title, the semiliberations that bend the forehead to the earth and make the mosques land on their feet will be distilled. Later, after the crossing of the desert, we will pass the Hoggar through a fine sieve and the country will resurface, abrupt and pagan.

Enough already of fantasias, of *rahat-loukoum,* of the *aïd* sheep, the Berber rodeo, of couscous-*mechoui,* the assembly of village sages or of deep sociologists happening by and discovering their golden number, enough already of the veiled virgins and the amputation of foreskins. They should be given a head, two arms, two legs, a thing, and should stop passing through every color of their specific civil status. Let them invent themselves iguana-men, zebra-men, erg-men, not chameleon-men, not men who only change to resemble themselves all the more.

—Here begins the struggle against the City: the City, its avenues, its markets, its concrete, its metaled, vitrified, opaque walls, its crater-cafés from which you come out ejected, drunk, its minarets, its widows, its colonels, its *meddah*s, its *tahar*s, its Rachids, its Ramizes, its ulama, its RE-pulsionsvolutions, its sayyids, its gents, its secondhand goods and its whores, its sedition-submissions, its dissidences, its prefects, its suffetes, its consuls, all of it to be held at arm's length into a bag, to say: "Here's the City." And run to drown it like a litter of kittens in the wadi in November.

Its granites, its stuccos, its stones, its hothouse poppies. The City of everything except delirium—to cut it down.

For it I'll invent a delirium, I'll organize it so that the future City that will sprout in its place will bring the pubescent itch of freedom to come.

Translation from French by P.J.

COMMENTARY

Mourad Bourboune was born in 1938 in Jijel, Little Kabylia, studied in Constantine, & took part in the 1956 student strikes. At independence he played a role in the country's first government. After the coup d'état of 1965, he moved to Paris & worked as a journalist. His first novel, *Le Mont des genêts,* which depicts the explosion of the colonial world, was published by Editions Julliard in 1964. The volume of poems *Le pèlerinage païen,* also from 1964, investigates the past & questions the present in the search for a possible Algerian future. In 1968, Christian Bourgois Éditeur published a book often referred to as iconoclastic & unclassifiable, *Le Muezzin,* extracted above. This text—showing a powerful & intense poetic breath—throws a critical gaze on "the aborted revolution" ("a fetus between the fingers of the abortionists"), & after writing it, Bourboune abandoned all literary activities.

Nabile Farès (b. Collo, 1940)

OVER THERE, AFAR, LIGHTS

Gathering his few things, he says,
Good-bye, friends.

> FRANCESCO BIAMONTI,
> "WORDS IN THE NIGHT"

In the street, in the neighborhood, in the city,
people are afraid.

You can tell by the way they walk.

Even at the market, down by the arcades, though noisy,
they're just a crowd of silhouettes, dressed in all kinds of
costumes, but already gone—as if they were their own

shadows, or mine.
  Mannequins.

  The shadows whisper, despite the night.
  The night, where my words search for their accents.

  They say man lives by speech alone . . .

  But where is she?

So many cries surround me and then,
suddenly, silence—

The shadow made itself at home in my head.

Despite the darkness, I see little bursts of life there,
little lights of a lamp flickering just at the place I was heading
upside-down
in prayer
on the pillow of dreams
that I have
no longer—
I've lost the one I loved . . .

Have you heard?

I lost the one I loved . . .

On the threshold of her coming, life
took on a fragrance of almonds

I pulled her in
and then, after a while,
I began to talk about her

my jealousy so sweet
my words drank it in

her words touched
me to the quick

the forest didn't matter
nor the legends of its caves
with their ogres and ogresses
who gave birth to my fairies

The world has changed: I recross
the empty country:
nothing. No desert, no town,
no street, no neighborhood,
no countryside, not even rumor

I lie in wait,
over there,
oh my words
oh my legs
oh my steps
a light.

I hide, I like to hide.
I'm as small as a grain of sand—
    a shadow—sometimes it's hard to see me.
    This could be a game.
    I learned to make myself invisible, like Tania,
when she puts on her luminous cape,
    the one of sequined, light-blue silk:
when she flings this cape over her shoulders,
    it's as if she carried the starry sky upon her back,
    the Milky Way,
    over a country that has lost its dreams . . .

Translation from French by Barbara Ungar & Stuart Bartow

COMMENTARY

(1) Born in 1940 in Collo, Little Kabylia, to a prominent family (his grandfather was a notary & his father an important political figure), Nabile Farès took part in high school strikes in 1956 & then joined the FLN (National Liberation Front) & later the ALN (Armée de libération nationale). He moved to France in 1962, where he did graduate work in philosophy (MA, 1967), literature, & ethnology (PhD). He taught literature in Paris & Algiers & was a professor of comparative literature at the University of Grenoble. Presently he works as a psychoanalyst in Paris.

(2) A novelist & poet "known for his abstruse, poetic, and dreamlike style" (*Encyclopaedia Britannica*), Farès makes his mark from his earliest books on, with the themes of rebellion against established religious traditions & the newly formed conventions of Algeria since independence as the core of his work. In his first novel, *Yahia, pas de chance* (Yahia, No Chance), from 1970, Farès introduced a quest that was to haunt his later works: the search for the self takes him back to his childhood & further still, to the pre-Islamic voices of inspira-

tion tied to the earth. Farès's successive novels—*Un Passager de l'Occident* (A Passenger from the West, 1971—published in an English translation by Peter Thompson in 2010 by University of New Orleans Press, which also published Farès's *Hearing Your Story: Songs of History and Life for Sand Roses—A Trilingual Text for the Sahrawi People*) & the trilogy *La Découverte du nouveau monde* (The Discovery of the New World), including *Le Champ des oliviers* (The Field of Olive Trees, 1972), *Mémoire de l'absent* (Memory of the Absent, 1974), & *L'Exil et le désarroi* (Exile and Disorder, 1976)—carry forward the themes of lost innocence & delirium. Nourredine Saadi calls Farès's work "a polemical, polyphonic writing that violates narrative . . . [and] is never nihilistic, because open to humor, hope, and the possibilities of a *new world*."

Rachid Boudjedra (b. Aïn Beïda, Oum El Bouaghi province, 1941)

from **RAIN (DIARY OF AN INSOMNIAC)**

The Second Night

So I continued writing away under the spell of this musical sound like an effervescent drug. Sort of painlessness of fascinating images taking hold of my memory with their volubility, their din. Mental landscape apparently established once and for all. Volcanic mass of memories kind of tiresomely collated. Very quickly certain images deteriorated wore out and disappeared. Others came to the surface in the bowl of my pressurized skull like air bubbles bursting through the freezing field of solitude. They overflowed the boundaries of the small room in which I have buried my being, leaving it to die. They opened out onto the patios of childhood filled with playful rituals (water jousts. Repetitive signs coded ritually. Superstitiously. Memorable fits of the giggles. Unforgettable terrors. Hazy memories—my mother and her dresses my mother and her giggling fits) etc. Something like atmospherics flowed before my eyes like tiny quartz stones threaded in between the beads of an amber rosary. Or the sulfurous chips of mica. Or the splinters of phosphorescent light swarming under my eyelids as if I was suffering from trachoma or amaurosis. Unending. Visions of interlinked bundles of ganglions through the layers of smoke wafting from my cigarette. Feeling myself bobbing about in the matter of abstract night like a cork. Impression—because of insomnia and tiredness—of my head full of gravel and holes through which mournful dirges are playing. Impression—also—of hearing the sighs of bodies suspended above the evanescence of crumbling and madness. Such as that of my young neurotic aunt whose yellow flowers haunted my childhood. I had caught her in her bedroom with one of her friends. They were both naked, grappling in an interminable hold. With my aunt's genitals appearing now and again. Plucked. Smooth. Gray. Sort of peeled. Sort of ridiculous. With the red furrow. Damp. Like that of little girls when they urinate squatting. The lingua—kind of drain almost artificial sort of added on—swarthy like dripping from this indescribable crater. Panting. Moaning. Like a kind of death rattle. I was afraid one or other or both would breathe their last. Slightly neurotic, that particular aunt. Not really crazy. Strange. Already a spinster at twenty-five. Disappeared prematurely. Mysteriously, even! She had always terrorized men. Because she was herself terrorized—all her life long—by her horrible mother. That is to say, my grandmother. The one who was photographed—at her request—on her deathbed. Gelatinous glazed glassy eyes. Complexion blackened darkened through dying. Her bonnet rigid conical priestly, bright red velvet. Old maid then—my aunt—at twenty-five. Perhaps lesbian without even knowing it. With this passion for bouquets of yellow flowers, which she liked to arrange. And her friend that beautiful buxom woman with the fancy outfits musky perfumes carnival makeup who they said was married to a leading light in the medical faculty and who paid my aunt protracted visits. Locked in with her for whole afternoons. Whom I had surprised in the middle of. In the middle of what. Can't really say—even now—exactly what. A spinster at twenty-five. Yet very beautiful. Strange. But sumptuous. She had refused all offers of marriage, to the great dismay of my poor grandfather. Each time my aunt refused, for days on end, her mother's sneer became more pronounced. Then it seemed to me her bright red velvet conical bonnet was even more pointed than usual. One day they took a decision in my aunt's stead. She was labeled an old maid. Once and for all. Definitively. Her friend visited more and more frequently. She eventually came to the house almost every afternoon. They managed—the two women—to shut the black tomcat into the bedroom with them where they barricaded themselves for hours on end. But it was a difficult operation—even dangerous—since he—the cat—was proud. Fierce. Untouchable. Inflexible. Never wanted food. Then he suddenly bounded onto the table during the lavish meals and with a single lunge snapped up the best bits. Just a black streak with that blue stripe (the eyes) like a line across his face. Meat, fish, or chicken, of course. Hunched—the cat—both in his lightning mobility and in his lightning immobility! His lightning potential speed. His lightning and noble animality. That is to say this dense muscled powerful raw suppleness. Suddenly bounding up then among the plates cutlery glasses flowers and tablecloth woven à la Messaoudi. Tenth century of the Muslim era. Also à la Matisse. The tablecloth in embroidered silk, as I said. Here the black cat—there was always one in the house—stopped pretending. He so to speak raided the family, much to the fright of my grandmother, who—superstitiously—didn't dare curse swear or fix upon him that piercing awful gaze which pinned us to the spot and immobilized—especially—my grandfather, that slight loving crazy hesitant frantic man. So the two young women locked themselves in my neurotic aunt's bedroom and managed to corner the tomcat and keep him with them. That was—in our eyes—a truly prodigious sporting feat. Because we—the children—had never been able to approach him or catch hold of him, despite all our tricks and ambushes. Because to tell the truth we didn't really feel he was a cat but rather a feline abstraction: Indian ink with this Persian blue stripe across his face. In other words the terrifying materialization not of a cat's body such as you see everywhere but of the very idea of wildness primitiveness of bestiality violence movement and action. My aunt, as I was saying—an old maid already at twenty-five—had this habit of locking herself in with the doctor's wife. Striking. Untamable. Strange. But literally terrorized by her mother. Full of complexes. Often requesting a spell in the hospital, as if to escape her spiteful mother. And also her brother, one of my uncles—uncle Hussein— who never let go of the apron strings of this same terrifying horrible mother, saying, to stay in her good graces—that is to say, the good graces of his mother—repeating, deadly jealous, to flatter her, my poor sister, she never had any luck with men, nor my brother either, too naive with women, always gallivanting, makes your head spin, doesn't he, mother! Back to my neurotic aunt. Always busy arranging her ghastly yellow flowers. Or shutting herself in her bedroom with her friend. Or energetically rubbing her wretched brasses. Especially that wretched jug. Sort of crabbed, obstinate. Perhaps because of the spout on which she (the aunt) ruined her fingers trying to make it shine more than it should. More than it could. This spout whose disproportionate magnification at certain hours of the day made it look not like a spout disproportionately magnified but like a swollen bloated phallus not even lacking testicles which were merely the reflection of the bottom of the handle, rather more rounded than the rest of the tube gradually tapering away to the spout itself. On which (the spout) she slaved away as if it represented a substratum of what she most hated and perhaps also what she most wanted in the whole world. With dazzling speed lumps of imaginary strange schizophrenic sentences cross the frozen territory of my body. I am obsessed by sets of numbers and combination codes. Haunted by the whispers slipping into my deepest sleep. A storm of smashed up signs broken lines disintegrating features and distorted curves breaks loose inside my skull. Irruption—then—in my memory of narrow dead ends meandering medinas chanting voices and persistent whiffs of incense. Each time I think of my brother's body riddled with holes by still as yet unknown executioners I remember the skeletal corpses of the people living in the shanty towns where I did my practical training. I treated an endless succession of wounds burns and drownings. Feels like I'm squashing pinkish mollusks between my fingers. Black fat thick obese rubbery caterpillars. Exactly similar on all counts to those I pursued in the company of my younger brother (the pilot) around the mould-infested ponds when we were children. The prettily calligraphed amulets took on the shapes of sharp new scars. We made talismans out of them to please God. Wailings. Windows closed like hostile barricades. Women categorically forbidden to explore their bodies in depth. Deplorable attitudes. Narrow. Stuck somewhere. Impossible to know where . . .

Translation from French by Angela M. Brewer

COMMENTARY

Born in 1941 in Aïn Beïda, eastern Algeria, Rachid Boudjedra had a bilingual education, studying in Tunis & Paris, where he obtained a degree in philosophy at the Sorbonne. His first collection of poems, *Pour ne plus rêver,* came out in Algiers in 1965. But it is foremost his first novel, *La Répudiation,* published in 1969 in Paris, that marks a turning point in Francophone Maghrebian literature, both thematically & by the sophistication of his writing. During the 1970s he collaborated on several scenarios, most notably for *Chronique des années de braise,* a film that won the Palme d'Or at the Cannes Film Festival in 1975. A highly productive novelist, Boudjedra began publishing his books in Arabic & in his own French translations from the 1980s onward. Except for his two other poetry collections—*Extinction de voix* (Algiers: SNED, 1981) & *Greffe* (Paris: Denoel, 1984; a translation of his 1980 collection *Likah*)—his oeuvre's importance is anchored in his experimental prose, which is deeply concerned with reflections on writing, politics, & a Maghrebian sexuality that the tradition represses.

Abdelhamid Laghouati (b. Berrouaghia, 1943)

"TO EMBRACE"

TO EMBRACE
the stone
and
   reinvent
the tropics
hug

the rock
till it crumbles
redo
the desert
people it
with love
pick up
the stone
turn it
into the
plinth
of a
day.

INDICTMENT

You say,
you mumble in the sentences' funeral procession
   words of optimism
   indecent words
you say
that hopes dissipate in the eye
   of the vagabond ridge
   of the wall over there
   lost on the roadway of time
what do you know of the problems
that lie in wait in vain
in each alleyway
   in the shadow of the doorways
   of easy solutions
   the heart laid low behind the shutters
like a female hit by menopause
   suffering love
   and beautiful girls
what do you know of despair and reason to live
that lost themselves
in the smiles of the ephemeral
you say
and what do you know of the order
offal established chromes tarnished by man's

raggedy
shadow
hands stretched toward the city's handcuffs
you say and what do you know of this city sad
as a shroud without a corpse
and this laughter of the present
with its sickly and sad-sack old men
carrying each winter in their guts
the city is sad
its truth sucks on misery's maternal teats
gags on dawns reflecting themselves
in the daily noise of the record
what do you know of these open balconies able to harbor
hatred
and destruction
misery
and persecution
you say
you only speak
when duty is starved in rags
each morning taking the bus of indifference
what do you know
about all those faces tortured by a tiny patience

what do you know of these architects who barter
their personalities and creations
for a ridiculously small amount of power
what do you know of their stooges
defying all rules of honesty
distorted by bad faith
where have love and hope gone
   they have fled the city
   they have entered the sewer system
       to inhale silence
what do you know of this rain that expels water and instinct,
products of beauty,
and of smugness
on the indiscreet street
you say
that nature has drawn a bead on
      poets
       those large eczemas

to gun down the lie
accused of having glorified dirty reality
in the veins in the arteries of the urban sprawl
what do you know of the blood that runs on the held-out hands
    of the unskilled laborer
arms cut open by the too-skillful stones
    of his consciousness
you say
but . . .
what do you know of that coffee with milk that observes
your reaction
with the eyes of the beggar spying on your useless gestures
it's sad a city grown accustomed to luxury
and shantytowns
a city exhausted by trucks heavy
with consequences
it's sad a city laid waste
by these beings caged in a flood of swaying
rumps
of imagined pleasure
only
imagined
the city yields to indifference
inserting blindness into nicotine-fed
chests
you say
what do you know of those tongues untied
by the vapors of alcohol
mass-produced
what do you know of those blinkers
that circulate between the crosswalks
of their inaccessible dreams
what do you know of this butt that still smokes the thoughts
of some vagabond or other seeking refuge
in the filter yellowed by our disorders
how sad a city
when to love
becomes
an infirmity.

Translations from French by P.J.

Born in 1943 in Berrouaghia, a small town in the center of the country, to a modest family, Abdelhamid Laghouati saw his high school studies, started during the colonial period, quickly interrupted. After independence in 1962, he worked as a grade-school teacher & later for a governmental agency for housing. In 1999 he moved to the Grenoble region of France, where he began directing creative writing seminars. Like other poets of his generation, he was published in Jean Sénac's groundbreaking *Anthologie de la nouvelle poésie algérienne* (Editions Saint-Germain-des-Prés, 1970). Laghouati has also published a number of chapbooks in Algeria in collaboration with the painter Denis Martinez. A poet in revolt against the injustices of a corrupt society that flaunts those retrograde customs that keep women in scandalous bondage, he remains, however, someone who sings love & the desert with tenderness & depth.

Youcef Sebti (Boudious, 1943–Algiers, 1993)

THE FUTURE

Soon I don't know exactly when
a man will knock on your door
starved haggard moaning
with as only weapons a scream of pain
and a stolen stick.

sooner or later someone wounded
will drag himself toward you
will touch your hand or shoulder
and will demand help and shelter
from you.

sooner or later, I'll repeat it for you
someone will come from far far away
and will demand his share of happiness
and will accuse you of a calamity
of which you're the origin.

you
those like you
who sabotage the agrarian reform! . . .

HELL AND MADNESS

I was born in hell
I have lived in hell
& hell was born in me
& in hell
on hatred—that flaming compost—
flowers grew.
I felt them
I smelled them
I picked them
& inside me circulated
the bitterness
& bitterness
took hold of me.
Stop. Breath. Shadow.
Hope. Departure. New start.
Lost loves. Robbed loves. Possible loves.
On the path of a new start
on the path of a struggle
I have come to madness
I dove into madness
& I brought some algae back.
Hell goes on . . .
From the blazing inferno to the sea
from the sea to the blazing inferno
from combustion
to immersion
hell remains
& the insurgents
have madness as their fate . . .

Translations from French by P.J.

COMMENTARY

Born in 1943 in Boudious, Little Kabylia, into a modest rural family, Youcef Sebti attended grade school in el-Milia & the Franco-Muslim high school in Constantine from 1957 to 1963. He received degrees in agronomy & sociology in 1967. From 1969 to his assassination by fundamentalists in December 1993, he taught rural sociology at INA (National Institute of Agronomy). Sebti is the tortured rebel poet, traumatized by colonial injustices & the horrors of war. From his origins he always kept a love for the peasantry, who in his eyes represented oppressed people par excellence. This love did not, however, stop him from denouncing retrograde customs, the oppression of women, & the absence of freedom in an often dry, sometimes sarcastic, yet always tender style. His poetry—with no embellishments & no concession to rhetoric—shows traces of the hell he lived in (see, for example, "Hell and Madness" above). He patiently tore words from the solitude & reclusion that confined him in perpetual psychic torment.

Ismael Abdoun (b. Béchar, 1945)

"FAUN-EYE'D ICEBERG BURN"

Faun-eye'd iceberg burn
the scathing screams of the biting cord
in the heart of the lightning storm
poem push me
with little ant steps
into the maw
  of the furnace
  of a skeletal monster
my heart
's going it alone
eyes grew on its toes
I do
  not
  recognize
  it any
  longer

Translation from French by P.J.

COMMENTARY

Born in 1945 in Béchar, Ismael Abdoun is presently a professor of French literature at the University of Algiers. Even though he does not have a published volume of poems, Abdoun needs to be in this anthology, as he is one of those oral barfly poets, whose work fuses improvisationally over wine & talk with friends—underpinned by a truly encyclopedic knowledge of poetry & poetics. Rimbaudian from the start, he wrote an MA dissertation on Henri Michaux & a doctoral thesis on Kateb Yacine. In 1967, fired by experimental & avant-garde writing, he published "Palma," a text that mixes or collages poetry &

prose, in Abdellatif Laâbi's magazine *Souffles*. In those years when everything seemed possible, Abdoun circulated his manuscripts in samizdat fashion in the restricted milieu of the Algerian intelligentsia. Today he says that he has no time to give to poetic writing in a country that is collapsing under the weight of its problems. He now prefers to share the taste of poetry in his teachings & scholarly writings.

Rabah Belamri (Bougaa, 1946–Paris, 1995)

"HAVE WE EVER KNOWN"

have we ever known
though ardent at turning over darkness
which archangel weighs down on the gate of sleep
and if the lock were to break
would we have the strength to keep our eyes open

.

I

we enter into language armed with defiance
others have come before us
have ripened the battle where we'll bend the knee
we cross their dwellings barely surprised
eager to prove ourselves
to fill our gestures with oblivion

2

the house of my language is vast
so many pillars and shadows
so many praying so many recumbent figures
since the first letter
oblivion
spider at the center of its web
is sting of light

3

they come from all horizons
with the ardor of the hordes that sculpt
oblivion and legend
each one has seven mouths
to proclaim its birth
they separate our sleep
multiply the breaches in our eternity
the words
venom and delight

4

and in my throat
did you know anguish is throwing a party
with the gouge and the chisel
my prehistory can't stop writing itself.

5

the masks hollow us out
why lament over stainless mirrors
do we need only appearances

INVERSED JABBOK

to the memory of Jean Sénac

they met again
at night's third arch
not in the middle of the ford
like back then in Peniel
but under the arch
where the words came to sleep

the angel did not stand in the way
and the poet said:
I shall not pass
without having drunk
at the fit
of your hip

they wrestled
gestures of tenderness   laughter foils   moans
a ballet of seduction and rejection
before the angel granted
a drop of saliva

the poet held the taste
tight in his throat
blessed the angel and went away
with the words
that knew no more repose

it is since that night
—so they say—
that the angel weeps
at the foot of the tree of oblivion
the poet stole a syllable from its name

Translations from French by P.J.

COMMENTARY

Rabah Belamri, born in 1946 in Bougaa, near Sétif, lost his sight at sixteen &
had to stop his studies at the lycée in Sétif. He later got a high school diploma at
the Braille Institute in Algiers & then a BA in French literature in 1971. In 1972
he traveled to France to prepare an MA thesis on Louis Bertrand, an author of
the so-called School of Algiers, which he completed in 1977. Enthralled by the
oeuvre of Jean Sénac, he wrote a major essay on him, *Jean Sénac: entre désir et
douleur,* published in Algiers in 1989 by the Office of University Publications.
Belamri died in 1995 in Paris. He was primarily a poet, but his oeuvre also
includes novels, essays, & tales. Tahar Djaout wrote: "For Rabah Belamri, inde-
fatigable questioner of the world, poetry is no doubt only one means, which
participates with others in a quest for clarity and plenitude. A need for light as
if it were water refused him for a long time, but also a denunciation of every-
thing that burdens hope and dailiness: the alienated or negotiated women,
sequestered happiness."

Habib Tengour (b. Mostaganem, 1947)

from *GRAVITY OF THE ANGEL*

Memory's Raft

. . . taking a well-balanced oar, you must set forth
until you come to men
who do not know the sea
nor ships with purple prows
nor balanced oars
that are a ship's wings
and take no salt in their food.
. . . when another sojourner, having fallen in with you,
says that you carry a winnowing fan
on your illustrious shoulders,
then stick your balanced oar into the earth
and make a handsome offering to Lord Poseidon:
ram, bull, and wild boar that mounts sows . . .

ODYSSEY, BOOK XI—TRANSLATED
BY CHARLES STEIN

Shore
on the dampened sand you survey
light and salt   —drowsy

you smile
to what surrounds you older you present yourself
on the island in the silence

the sea proposes no complicity and you bathe
alone in an evocation said to be innocent

the long voyage faraway derisory
The art of accosting forgotten
all reference points muddled up

from shore to scar a gaze's intention slides

    •

Ulysses's palace the amnesiac isle
kids clusters of shellfish

chiseled coral
vendor with settled breath

far the school the gardens

it hurts

more than wounded salt
more than sea-obscure

you tell Ulysses's tale a kid
marveling a proffered sponge

a soul to be invested
what profits suggests the revived talk
insignificant
. . .

.

Lookout at the summit
and the sea sitting
suspension of a weft
the island desert since
black scorpions heavy with poisons vipers
brackish water bouncer of sailors
micaceous sand shimmers a murky blue-green

stones heaped in the north wind

the entrusted promise is there
heedful of the visitor's beating

.

She naked cleaving the water in nascent dawn
immobile mirror dilated
in exaltation recognition of the hours
spent sumptuous and transparent and blessed

a lie peacock ostrich
a weft weighed down with remorse
a fissure you observe growing wider
seizing your blood in plenary session

passion for patched up pieces
affable then numbed
lapidary hearth

the sea disgorged us of corrupt wisdom
on a shore of tarred algae naked as in a dream
and blue dawn of fog still lingers on our lips

·

A star a vase
and what is the string that hides the irradiated soul
jubilant passenger
—this fear of stumbling

on fire in sweat
audacity of a pause
keep me in the lamp
already the star hurls the first blade

meditating
a leaning to capture
aroma of a wave rich night coming undone

you grow pale god in the breeze and plumb me
idyl to become knife
morning clearing of rocks

·

Suddenly nothing and you reappear
and command to relive beyond

so many words draped in ermine
the taciturnity of a night bird
the garment torn by simple atavism

toward the isle by chance temporary accommodation
captive and the sailboard
to leave home nearly dead to die
alone
and go on
there on the island as if nothing had happened

you return to demand the ransom of a vision
to destroy a soul devastated by its journeys

you are my domain my link I settle in at home
and deliver you for I have learned to behave myself

.

On that day
we will raise up our lives wine unmixed united
in the crystal
a sign wakes up

For a long time
fixation of a timbre, any vanishing trace
sprayed
   —conjuration—
you said you were mourning me today

One threshold and it's exile
there's only easy temptation

                                too much! of a sob
a decision put off to later

                          overzealous preparations
flow into the vise you gasp for breath, at times.

. . .

You say you surprise me without knowing it halfway to a dream
to set traps for her who is delayed you in fact

What to do
as your ruses draw close

                         you induce the night to blush
a dusty turmoil

                   love me in the light

Our bodies wrangle our stranded lives sea urchin
shells

Inspire me, she says, now that I caught you.

Translation from French by P.J.

Habib Tengour, a coeditor of this anthology, poet, & anthropologist, born in 1947 in Mostaganem, lives & works between Constantine & Paris. Considered one of the Maghreb's most forceful & visionary poetic voices of the postcolonial era, Tengour, who authored a "Manifesto of Maghrebian Surrealism" in 1981, explores the Algerian, Maghrebian, &, more extensively, Mediterranean cultural spaces in all their ramifications—the oral & hagiographic traditions, the popular imagination & the founding myths, collective memory, *raï* music, & the lived experiences of exile—in some eight books of prose & twelve collections of poetry to date. Raised on the Arab & Berber voices of marketplace storytellers, taken to France by his parents as a pre-adolescent, Tengour incarnates &, in his writing, speaks to the nomadic & (post)colonial condition of his countrymen & -women. Jacqueline Arnaud, the great critic & holder of the first chair in Maghrebian studies at the University of Paris, called him "the major author of the second generation of Algerian immigrants." His work has the desire & intelligence to be epic, or at least to invent narrative possibilities beyond the strictures of the Western/French lyric tradition in which his colonial childhood schooled him. Core to it is the ongoing invention of a Maghrebi space for & of writing, the ongoing quest for the identification of such a space & self. For, as another Maghrebian, Jacques Derrida, put it: "Autobiographical anamnesis presupposes *identification*. And precisely not identity. No, an identity is never given, received, or attained; only the interminable and indefinitely phantasmatic process of identification endures."

Hamida Chellali (b. Algiers, 1948)

"IN THE DAYS"

In the days when things were magical there lived a man of power who, besides many other goods, owned a broken mirror that revealed the truth to him. When he became old, the man wanted to know his end. He questioned the mirror.

Man: Incoherent mirror, tell me the truth
Mirror: How can I, I am broken
Man: Tell me a part of it
Mirror: A part of the truth is not the truth
Man: I'll be satisfied with it
Mirror: Man of power, what do you want to know
       that you don't already know

```
Man:    I want to know my end
Mirror: Then let's go look for your end
        And when I see it you'll see it too
```

They looked for many days, but no end was reflected on the mirror, which didn't say a word during the whole journey. But one night it spoke.

```
Mirror: Man of power, I have finally seen your end, now you can see it
        too
```

Aghast, the man recognized the features of his face on those of a jackal pursued by peasants armed with sticks, stones, and pitchforks.

The mirror spoke again: Man of power, that is only a part of your end . . .

Knowing that the mirror always spoke the truth, the man became very afraid. He chased away his people and took refuge in an inaccessible room of his house with provisions to last him a full year. The year went by and the provisions came to an end. He questioned the mirror again.

```
Man:    Mirror, tell me the truth
Mirror: O, man of power
        throw yourself in a well
        that would be better for you
        for your end
        even a jackal wouldn't want it.
        Look at yourself.
```

The man of power looked at himself and screamed with terror. He threw himself and the broken mirror into the first well he came across.

One day during an exhausting trip in a lost landscape, a providential child offered me water. It was so fresh and sweet-tasting that I asked the child for the name of the well.

"They call it the well of the broken mirror."

It is for this child that I invented this legend.

from **THE OLD ONES**

If you meet her
at the entrance of Sidi-Abderahman
don't misjudge
if she raises a feverish glance toward you
she only believes she recognizes her children

don't misjudge
if the children of the hood bully her
that's surely because the adults when talking
of her say "Zouina the madwoman"
since then they sing
"Zouina the madwoman
fell into the well
who'll pull her out
I'll pay well"

Khalti Zouina
lives
in a famous alleyway
of the upper casbah
one room
very dark
very humid
and every night standing by a skylight
she spends hours
watching
thinking she recognizes
her son's step in each step

the neighbors however
murmur "those children will never come back"
Khalti Zouina
no longer loves her neighbors
she now knows
she knows
that they laugh behind her back
so she no longer offers her hot flat cakes
she invents at dawn
in her room
very dark
very humid
she offers them
to those who have nothing left
and who since pre-dawn
clutter the entrance of Sidi-Abderahman

Khalti Zouina
collects images
images of houses
houses in images she has many of
to dream evenings and for centuries
Every night, under the skylight's light
in her room
very dark
very humid
she chooses
the house she'll live in someday
with her children
the neighbors however
murmur "those children will never come back"
but Khalti Zouina
each night
with her images works furiously
away at building her house.

Khalti Zouina
feels her children's return to be closer and closer
and it is outside
in front of her room
very dark
very humid
that she's on the lookout
at night
seeing in each shadow
the shadow of her little ones.
And sensing the neighbors
laughing behind her back
she mumbles
laugh
laugh but when they return
they'll take me far away from this humid room
you'll see.

One morning
strangely enough
with her basket full of

hot flat cakes Khalti Zouina
hastily left her
very dark
very humid
room
ran down the casbah
yelling at the neighbors
you see
you see they have returned
they have returned by sea
they have returned in a white ship.
And the neighbors laughed
and the children sang
"Zouina the madwoman
fell into the well
who'll pull her out
I'll pay well"

The sea
but what does the sea matter.
The ships are so numerous
running from one dock to the other
dragging her basket full of hot flat cakes
Khalti Zouina
called her children
but her voice growing feebler and feebler
was soon covered by the siren of the white ship
that sailed away without a sign
for sweet Zouina.

But if you meet her
at the entrance of Sidi-Abderahman.

Translations from French by P.J.

COMMENTARY

Hamida Chellali is a painter & poet born in Algiers in 1948. A number of her paintings are in the museum of the Institut du Monde Arabe in Paris. Her poetry collection *Pieds nus au bord de l'eau* (Barefoot by the Water) was published by the SNED in 1982.

Hamid Skif (Oran, 1951–2011)

PEDAGOGICAL COUSCOUS SONG

PIM PAM POUM
Today's the wedding

PIM PAM POUM
Cadillacs
Mercedes
Villas.
Couscous with hot blood.

PIM PAM POUM
My hands clenched tightly
My lips sucked in
My sex ahead of me
I await my sister
My future wife.

PIM PAM POUM
A voice in the dark
The sister supplicating.

PIM PAM POUM
Couscous with hot sperm
PIM PAM POUM
The qadi wiping off
PIM PAM POUM
the RAPE's over

POEM FOR MY PRICK

Today they are burying my dog of a prick.
The imams surround it,
Those crows at all major feasts
Psalmodize
Its arrival in Paradise.

Earlier
They had a long discussion
All about
The possibility of embalming it.

HERE I AM

Here I am estranged and gone back
to the sources of the copper and the verses
I wear brambles, lightning flashes, cold light
sprung from the sword.

The words worn secure the fragile measure of my talk
the white she-camel drinks from the oblique shadow
of the palm tree
guides me along the voluptuous enigma of her track

I search for
the hill of ocher and gold
the falcon's eye
the remainder of a firebrand
the wind's bed
the voices of the deserted man

In Tipaza it is the hour of the olive trees
their leaves sing the psalms and
drape the open sepulchers

I walk clad in the breaths stolen from the tombs
in fragments of lost
stars
of petals found on the walls of time
I sing sweet cantilenas of freedom
I follow the traces of the knights of sand
the neighing of their mounts
the odor of their clotted blood
Every halt is my dwelling

I search for the inkwell of the centuries
the black rose of salt
a scream of fire
a tear of stone
wash your presence of its wounds.

Translations from French by P.J.

COMMENTARY

Mohammed Benmebkhout, who wrote under the nom de plume Hamid Skif, was born in 1951 in Oran, where he graduated from high school before working as a journalist for the APS (Algérie Presse Service) there & in Ouargla & Tipaza. In 1997, under threat from Islamic terrorists, he emigrated to Germany, where he died on March 18, 2011. Although primarily a poet, Skif also published several novels & short stories. His early poems were published on the cultural page of *République,* a newspaper of Oran. He became more widely known thanks to the inclusion in Jean Sénac's anthology of his breathtaking & rule-breaking poem "Pim Pam Poum," which denounced machismo & the taboo of virginity all-present in Algerian society. Skif's poetry promotes hope for a better life, in which "the citizens of beauty" can love & dream, expressing the hope of the 1970s & 1980s, when *les barbus* ("the bearded ones," the Islamic fundamentalists) had not yet gained the upper hand in the cities. His last volume of poems, *Ile-Espérance* (Hope Island), published in 2005, professes a certain serenity, tinted by melancholy: "It is time to sleep / this morning no one will come to speak to the ghosts / that live by my side."

Hamid Tibouchi (b. Tibane, 1951)

from *THE YOUNG TRAVELER AND THE OLD-FASHIONED GHOST*

for Kamel Yahiaoui
this serio-fantasy
in the style of his creations

I

there will be so much suffering
so much dying
there will be so many mirages
and so little courage
and inside—yes—lots of rage
beneath the riverbank there will be
so many shadows reflected
and—we must not forget—
lots of water on our little heads
it is so humid! oh these bones of mine!
oh my kidneys!
and you my heart, you mean little cur

little pig, you stupid little ass . . .
oh forget it,
little one,
just sleep.

2

is it the wind that is rattling my bones this way?
is it fear?
you rattling train, with cloudy windows,
landscapes like dirty watercolors,
where are you taking me?
toward which misfortunes and delights toward
which other griefs?
and now you stop
and drafty air flows inside you
through and through
and now you start to move again

3

many tunnels. Many
noises
and
    so little light
    so little air to breathe
and not even a glimpse of the sea
the merest trough or least bit
of warm sea spray or jot of lava
on which to stand
on which to rest
how fortunate are the larva the kelp
and the mineral salts, how miserable the cocoon
Life is funny, little friend, really funny
But *I* have never joked in my life, malodorous
old timer little guy cop dirty louse

4

what love? and what is love?
which Gorgon with its serpents mali(gni)ficently
lurking under the rug
atchoo!
cover yourself, little one, cover yourself

or you will catch cold
what a joke! oh that's a riot!
upon my word spelled with a small *w*
now that's a joke, I'd say!
   I DIDN'T DO IT IT'S MY SISTER
   WHO BROKE THE STEAM ENGINE
one always ends up laughing, little one,
one always ends up laughing like hell
but you see, frail old man,
miserable little runt, I am personally fed up
with your half-baked ideas.

5

so little peace and quiet around
that we might better see what's going on
behind each thing behind each
man behind the window pane what's going on
inside oneself
so little time   a lot
so little moss   of soot
so little potable water   many
under the moss   wells
and no beak alas   many
to gather   ·   years
the rare   many
drops   nights
of   much
dew   grief
many tormented nights and sharp
pebbles, tiny arrowheads,
prehistoric debris

6

What smile not hurt/hurtful?
What tenderness without thorns?
what soothing misfortune? what peace?
they have cut down all the trees around
the house. One can see it now: it is made of wood
the birds no longer have a place to roost
they are gone (where to?

any habitable lands left?
any trees still standing? still
verdant?)—Those that remain,
little frightened tufts of down,
are under the roof
and make terrible wing beats
an awful hell-bent din
when wharf rats visit them
what true happiness is there?
what life can possibly be left?
what comfortable situation?
indeed, what comfort?

7

The city. Black with ants. The rats
no longer dare come out of their holes
they find it difficult to get around
among these throngs of people!
they bring the plague
they cannot endure three days of fasting
and, desperate for food, devour each other
The beggars
my god! so many beggars!
they have replaced the trees
that once lined the sidewalks
my god, such faces!
ravaged by dint of expectation
frightening by virtue of their patience
I am afraid . . .
it's ridiculous, pal, ridiculous

8

I know
I too am a beggar
all along the way
and at every station
I have begged for a bit of love
a little hope and tenderness
a little courage
a little wine for the trip

a little of that damned mess
that makes men of us
I have reaped so little that is good in all of this
I promise you
they have lied to us you see
there's nothing
or at least almost nothing
and too many things that only exist
in one's head
grease and diesel fuel
all claiming to make the machine run
but in fact undermining it
throwing it out of whack—
what are we waiting for?
what party what trustworthy Scriptures?
what soul-saving rite?

9

The train has stopped.
"Snacks! Get your snack!" shouts
a child in rags, toting a plastic bag
stuffed with sandwiches
(a slice of soap posturing as
cheese in a loaf of bread),
distributing two here,
three there, surreptitiously,
and then vanishing *you gotta live that's for sure my friend*
an excellent purge for pampered stomachs

10

The train has stopped.
It is raining. For a long time now
movement, immobility: the same malaise
What do you say we have a drink, pal?
We have the time. And we could have
a cigarette? That should warm us up, my friend
Filthy old man, gaunt face,
you disgust me!
will you stop your damned smokestack, you
keep me from seeing the crows

I I

Those blessed delectable crows.
Rimbaud was one of them
a beautiful shiny black one
but the idiot got gangrene
and they cut off his leg
and his balls
but you must realize that he couldn't
do otherwise in this godforsaken world
it's too bad he didn't have the time
to complete his invention
of the atomic bomb
what a disaster!
that was unpardonable
and I told him so

(November 23, 1977—
aboard the Bejaïa–Algiers train)

Translation from French by Eric Sellin

COMMENTARY

Hamid Tibouchi was born in 1951 in Tibane, near Bejaïa, & after grade school in Bejaïa & high school in Algiers, he studied English literature at the École normale supérieure in Algiers (1971–76). He taught English in a high school near Algiers before moving to Paris in 1982, where he has followed a rich double career as a poet & a painter without worrying about the dictates of fashion. He published his first poems back in 1972, notably in the magazine *Alif,* founded in 1970 in Tunis by Lorand Gaspar & Salah Garmadi. Tibouchi is the author of a large number of chapbooks, often self-published. His writing is striking from the word go because of its corrosive humor, the freedom of its tone, & its subversiveness—& this always with a rare stylistic exigency. Tibouchi profoundly enjoys playing with & against all surrealist techniques of writing, & even though his painter's studio demands more & more of his time, the poetry keeps flowing.

Mohamed Sehaba (b. Tafraoui, 1952)

FAR FROM OUR ERG

Far from our saturated erg, we observed
that radiant creature, rising like joy
behind the sea, the sea cut off from all calls
exaggerated by tall waves, where our
memories are imperiled.

At first we greeted its mystery with
wan fervor, then we set up the expedition
of adoration and visionary sleep
(we wanted to climb our life).

After days and days of fighting with the
waves, you remarked as I did that
gradually, as we drew nearer
to it, the creature opened new roads of
foreboding in our voyage, then drew away
for endless days, changed moods,
and put on different faces.

THE BIRD NO LONGER SINGS

The bird no longer sings in our city;
The smell of life has retreated
From our dark climbing,
Full of wisdom,
Into the naive mysteries.

I sprout disorderly graves,
Of lapidary days,
To defend my solid heart,
To free the heart of the future,
And set up my silence
In pillars of truth.

I ache for speech,
In my livid journeys.
My hopes stuffed with returns
Make a desert of unseemly surfaces
Mingled with the refuse of shadows.

Full of broken dreams I cling
To the rags of childhood,
To my sweet need to endure intact,
Like the daggers of morning.

I cannot give the sea's response
To the tawny order,
Staggered over the seasons,
To the order that rends,
The freshness of my seeds
Into illicit divisions
Of likeness.

I MISS SOMETHING . . .

I miss something,
Like the purity of an ocean
Seen in happiness,
Like slumber
In the attentive arms
Of a private renunciation,
Like the taste of the unknown
That trembles in dreams,
Like a rediscovered place
That offers windows of tears
And roads to life.

I miss something,
Like the promise of oblivion,
Like a first light,
Like a love cleansed
Raised to a dune of delirium,
Like branches of water
That would excite my heart.

I miss something,
Like the road
Of a new beginning without remembrance,
Like the bland snow
To whiten the ships of illusions
And the impossible surf,
Like a tall forest
That would grow in the sweat of my skin,
In my denied seasons.

I miss something,
Like a man on the moon
Whom I would like to resemble,
Like a steady fire
that I would stoke higher,
Like an eternal smile on the horizon,
To melt my vacillations
To be escorted,
By the infinite face of life.

Translations from French by Jackie Michaud

COMMENTARY

Born in 1952 in Tafraoui (Oran region), the oldest son of a family of modest means, Mohamed Sehaba studied at the technical high school in Oran, then at the École Normale Supérieure Polytechnique. He taught industrial drawing for an Algerian industrial company, but after obtaining a BA in French in 1991, he started a career as a journalist & literary translator with *El-Ahram-Hebdo*, allowing him to live in exile in Cairo during the Black Decade. He now teaches French in Oran & writes on cultural matters for the local press.

Starting in 1986 with *Remparts* & continuing with *L'Aguellid* in 1988, Sehaba affirmed himself as a poet with an original voice characterized by an epic dimension, a finely honed lyrical breadth, & a rich but always precise lexical sweep. The collections *Erg* (1992) & *Hommage à l'errant* (2007) confirmed his originality & desire to explore the arcana of poems & cosmos in a *cante jondo* of incantatory dimensions, an uproar carefully channeled by an insistent questioning that aims for a soulful serenity at a far remove from mundane literary brouhahas.

Abdelmadjid Kaouah (b. Aïn-Taya, near Algiers, 1954)

NECK

Over there Algiers

behind fogs of images
& forests of salacious billboards
a little girl sews up
her mother's neck
before climbing back into
her crib.

MODERN BAR

to Larme

Forty-three years old
Place Bellecour
African drums
break the silence
Louis the Fourteenth
dances reggae

*When will you finally
shave off that beard*

Lyon, 21 June 1994

MAJESTIC

There in a hotel lobby
Listening to a bittersweet music
Barely different from the one
Supermarkets pipe in for ambience's sake.
How often haven't I sworn to myself not to break
the line again.
To write in a *dignified* prose. Having all the appearances of a writing
in prose, prosaic in fact. To the point of maintaining no link, no matter

how *confidential*, with poetry, that *incestuous sister*. Poetry, that heavily made-up *disrespectful* one.
To mask an age of no interest to any client. One takes out one's pen, it could be one's sex, one points to the margin, and one spreads one's shadow and the ink in between the lines. At the other end of the margin, the margin of the invisible, one goes limp, instantly, by *instinct*.
Ever since there is no more rime, one adds more grime to the makeup. / the makeup's more begrimed. / Poetry, one spreads it on any handy mattress with or without springs, no one gives a hoot. One will trust in some obscurity of the language to look poetic, lyrical, epic . . . , depending on the needs of a hypothetical market.

A few tics.
Interlaced with soundproof ticktocks. A few metaphors, or even ritornellos, and, presto, here are, made from odds and ends, vast semaphores to guide imaginary boats.

Toward nowhere.
When the poet himself amuses
He believes in muses, they're his excuses and vain ruses.

In *Barcelona,*
night's coming to rest, faster than the day, on simulacra. The sun hastens on its way between the Diagonal and the Passeig de Gracia, skirting the *Crayon.*
I write these lines without haste in the lobby of the Majestic, so far from Bab-el-Oued,
just to wait for the first metro
for *Fontana.*
The night servants pass the vacuum cleaner between two conferences on boredom punctuated by the languorous violins of a Strauss disguised as a groom.
I write this thick and heavy prose.
Will it pass for
a *poem?*

Barcelona, June 9, 1996

Translations from French by P.J.

Born in Aïn-Taya, near Algiers, in 1954, Abdelmadjid Kaouah is a journalist by profession. Forced into exile by the violence engulfing Algeria in the 1990s, he settled in the region of Toulouse, France, where he still lives & is actively engaged in work on Maghrebian cultural matters via his writing & other media, such as radio & television.

Tahar Djaout (Azeffoun, 1954–Algiers, 1993)

MARCH 15, 1962

how to curb their rage to dissolve the stars
and to birth eternal night
I challenge their iron
and the enraged ire with which they multiply the chains

in the blue smile
of the Admiralty open on the promises
today in long swallows I gulp
—sun thundering over Algiers—
the joys of a feasting
where resurrected dawns gambol
and yet I think on the holocausts
unleashed to make dawn break
I think of Feraoun
—smile frozen in the sun's circumcision

they are afraid of the truth
they are afraid of the straight pen
they are afraid of truly human humans
and you, Mouloud, you insisted and spoke
about wheat fields for the sons of the poor
and spoke of pulverizing all the barbed wire
that lacerated our horizons

they speak of you and say that you were too good
that you felt revolted
hearing shells greet each dawn
that you believed human beings to be born so as to be brothers
and though challenging all the orgies of horror
you were incapable of hatred

one day, Mouloud, goodness finally triumphed
and we could wear the sun's trident
and we could honor the memory of the dead
because
   with
        your hands, those gleaners of dawn's mysteries,
and your dreamy inveterate poet's face,
you have known how to fulfill our truths
written in sun scraps
on the breasts of all those who revolt

Translation from French by P.J.

COMMENTARY

After Tahar Djaout's assassination in 1993 by the Islamic terrorists who were waging a civil war in Algeria that was to cost close to 150,000 lives, one of us wrote: "Our eyes are fixed on the TV screen or the *New York Times* Op-Ed page, transfixed & horrified, emptied & blinded by what is happening in ex-Yugoslavia, in the ex–Soviet Union & its ex-satellites, that is, as usual, in ex-Europe & its ex-tensions. Blinded thus, we know little, if anything, about what is happening—*the horror, the horror,* to use a famous fictional European's dying words—in other parts of the world, & the media is certainly not going to deal with it unless it has some kind of marketable Euro-American angle. The quasi–civil war in Algeria, for example, is going largely unreported, except when a few weeks ago the ex-FIS (the outlawed fundamentalist Islamic party which, having more or less won the democratic elections a year ago, was sidelined by the FLN, the corrupt ex-revolutionary party that has been in power since independence in 1962, on which it has declared war) stated that to hasten its purification of the country it would kill all foreigners in Algeria. (Twenty-four were killed by the end of December.) Dozens of Algerians are being killed daily on both sides. The FIS's assassination strategy is simple: kill off the intelligentsia & anybody else able to voice any intelligent opposition—or at least enough of them as gorily as possible to make the rest shut up or leave the country for fear of dying. Among the many killed this past year were two poets: Tahar Djaout, who was shot May 26, & Youssef Sebti, knifed to death on December 28 as he was going to his job teaching sociology in a college of agronomy in the suburbs of Algiers. They were killed because they were, quietly & seriously, going about their business as writers & would not shut up, but kept writing & saying what needs to be said: that totalitarianism under any guise, religious or military, is the ultimate evil. In an eerie, prophetic mood, Tahar Djaout, more than twenty years ago, wrote the poem—*MARCH 15, 1962*—that celebrated the independence of his country, but that was simultaneously an elegy for the writer Mouloud Feraoun, who had been assassinated toward the end of the war of independence in not dissimilar circumstances & for not dissimilar reasons."

Amin Khan (b. Algiers, 1956)

VISION OF THE RETURN OF KHADIJA TO OPIUM

You run on the plains of death without fearing any obstacle black plough soft scents like traces of love on the skin of the beloved you gallop fluid without advancing a step conscience inundated with the smoke of blue herbs you escape from fear and enchantment brushing crimson shores and traps of light languages of love and the distress of meaning and the gold of the dagger thrusts in the burst of the cry and the sob

you stop breath weak lost body from you to yourself and in the virgin space of golden death by the hourly borders of the ultimate transparence you recognize in her the familiar dead the beloved of unhappiness so urgent to lament her her dead body laid softly returning gravely to love her dead eye of the sun caught in the pain of her dying body on the shore of the untouchable self

you are no more the sensitive prisoner rolling in the flight the rust the hair the bleached static of your body captive memory stopped in the silence of midday perfumes the odor of liberty white opacity that expands it's the death of you that touches me and brushes me with your fingers and pulls me toward your body of sadness neglecting

you silence me to myself injured body by chance blind tracing common aches tears births like light in the heart of the accident of the fatal rhythm of dazzling hooves gold fire error of the hand on the neck odor too ripe of the mane sweaty body of the lover the runaway frightened by the violence of the brassy hordes of chance

you sink the arm and the shoulder when lingers the regard of the disappointed lover too soft the skin of her hand on your body useless supplication of silence you sink an ancient light you're dying from feeling all the pain of the simulacra of the sleeping in the design of the lamp in your eye at night

you don't have the strength the desire you no longer recognize your actions and your lovers withdraw one after the other behind a drape thick red like blood you no longer recognize your country your people the servants of your fantasy stay clear and you remain the only captive of the absolute sadness of death

you knew the blue and the ocher unspoken and offered your veins to silence you confused numbers and people in the joy you confronted the deadline by sliding your language in hers you transformed yourself into seed of shadow in more than a memory you fractured the luminous trouble into essential stones lost in the confusion of a stony atmosphere you slept in the cruelty of absence

you are stopping me once again from coming to you even though you lightly touch me you rouse me lover extinguished dark forever you keep me at a distance for yourself useless for the hours for the fatal passengers of the immobile wreck useless you protect me with your gaze dead fixed dark excessive you welcome me with the extreme languor of your only certitude

you don't have any love any doubt any sensation for the servitude of those whom love devours you move among the fragile emerald lozenges of Hannibal's dusk you push your metal in the living flesh of those who hold onto the edge of another time fastening their bodies of ancient pain of infertile life prisoners erased from their fragile destiny who await you who go nowhere who take no path devoured by love innocent aching until the sudden instant of your encounter

you designate from afar traces of slavery of roads dusty with a false light that falls from a pale sky of barbarity you awake and appoint eternal journeys smoldering odors of the voyage of the unbelievers you play with their lucidity until the atrocious vomiting of ultimate truths you assassinate those who invoke another name another gesture of iron in the earth and in the loam you turn around and you fall sleep while the lover watches exhausts the precious light of a lying eye dead from imperious sun

you incise the painful signs of survivals in the atrocity of the trials of the race in the parched flesh and the bitter core in the most impoverished symbols of the enigma of the body that a blade's distance kills reflection of silver metal and bitter flame between the doomed bodies

you separate me from those whom I love from the world from matitudinal flights of blue birds in a sky of pale water you bring me back to the sad order of days that tearing rough silk wearied by so many hands sticky in the filth of morning earths the mist escapes like the dream that flees from us crepuscular smokers broken bits of the cortege of useless dreamers

you have no other empire than our bodies kneaded with lies than our lives separated by the knife of misfortune and doom than our will limed in the bad sleep of malediction slow malediction for the derisory tribe no more pity for you no more misery in the look when they see you chasing the shadows of the past oscillating like the memory of a white mule at noon lost among the rocks

you touch me with your scent you overcome me with the same slight perpetual feeling autumnal irrationality of my body that the pain of crippled loves imprison no honeyed light and space no tranquil domain of offered transparencies you tear off clothes of gold and pardon of courtesans fragile inlay of amber perspiration that pearls on your skin on mine you leave your scent you yield because the chronology of love is again absurd

you rip the veil of death perfumed by the softness of your shoulder time goes by in the clasped gardens of stone time tears courts of eroded turquoise staircases of blanched threatened jasmine time goes by we divine the port but no departure and in my heart no freedom

you are absent in the darkness of time in pale fractures of smoldering houses for the runaway you leave only the gathering of odors of ashed landscape let him walk let him return to the sad houses of illusion let him cross the black and the white let him smolder let him be hurt let him surrender himself to the sands of migrating sands and wind that halt neither will nor respiration

you pass in the distance of the plains of death unaccomplished body of obscure ardor you cross my conscience and the approach of your body burns me fan the weakened light you yourself free to cross body and soul free to burn the essences far and soft of the miserable dream pass in the distance you who shares me you that the griefs embellish and now stumble because I want you

Translation from French by Dawn-Michelle Baude

COMMENTARY

Amin Khan was born in Algiers during the Algerian war of independence, in 1956. He grew up in a revolutionary family, writing poetry & nurturing interests in philosophy & politics. Studies at the University of Algiers, the University of Oxford, & the Insitut d'Etudes Politiques in Paris followed. As a diplomat & international civil servant, he has held positions at the United Nations in New York, the World Bank in Washington, D.C., & the UN Educational, Scientific and Cultural Organization in Paris, where he now lives with his family. His books include *Les Mains de Fatma* (SNED, 1982), *Archipel Cobalt* (Editions MLD, 2010), & the forthcoming *Arabian Blues* (Editions MLD, 2012).

Mourad Djebel (b. Annaba, 1967)

SUMMER

It's how to suspend
Your breath
Total apnea
To force it into powerless
Observance
To fatten it all
It's how to join ends
Memory
Conjoining the shores of the wound
Repair patch, skin shreds and cauterize
So as to fill the sails, leave
You broke with nothing
In this estival disorder
And covering you offered the wait
From before the departures
Air, you said, maybe oxygen
And by it the ochers enrage
And by it the azure enflames
And by it return
The *bahri*s* and tramontanes
And at the nadir the crickets nidify
And at the zenith the sea
Inverses the horizon
I splashed myself with it and
Dispatched of scatterings
I saw you join as estuary
And your breath suggest
Foams that rise
And soap bubbles
Diffracting the light

Translation from French by P.J.

*Sea winds.

Born in 1967 in Annaba, Mourad Djebel studied architecture & urbanism at the university in Constantine, graduating with a degree in engineering. He left Algeria in 1994, & after spending time in western Africa, he moved to France, where he nomadized for a while before settling in Bordeaux. He has published two novels to date: *Les sens interdits* (2001) & *Cinq et une nuits de Shahrazède* (2005). He came out with a collection of poems, *Les Paludiques,* in 2006 & a translation/adaptation/re-creation of Algerian folktales in 2011. "To find my own words, my own phrasing, to tell the story, that, in a way, is to echo the women who told these tales," he said in an interview. Djebel is without a doubt the most demanding & the most promising of the poets of the "new literature" in Algeria, tough & without concessions.

Mustapha Benfodil (b. Relizane, 1968)

from *I CONNED MYSELF ON A LEVANTINE DAY*

Bad
Bad
Bad awakening

Algiers inside morning daylight
Day summer coffee TV
Levantine images crashing
Smoke
Smoke
Sm . . . stop !

I must have had ten thousand smokes

Bad
Bad
Bad awakening

I carried my sleep all night long
Like an Abrahamic tomb
My night . . .
My night was filled with deathly stars
Inlaid in my skin
My bed bristled with remorse

I must have lain on Lebanon

I entered via the Door of Tears
I saw the sea crying
Sea of lamentations
A sea of mothers of tears

I was looking for my friends in stripteased ruins
On sidewalks' solitude
And under crumbling shelters
I found one of them lying on his liver
Cannibal air force
A few yards away the arms and the watch around the port
One eye at Mar Elias, the other at the hospital
His last words were: *"Please, saw me back to my mother's uterus!"*

I was wandering through a field of dead consciences
Skeletons of goodwill
And rough drafts of epic blueprints
I collected fossil tears
Old 1948 awareness
A post-*Nekba* suicide cracking house walls
I panhandled an old lady
A little Arab dignity
She cursed my tribe

.

I ground my soul
I crushed my nights and turned them into grass
I added some tobacco from the south
And I rolled a reefer

I asked the hill for a light
It gave me a tank
Pulverized by a scream

I asked a fear peddler for a light
He handed me a poster
Bearing the effigy of Armageddon

Translation from French by Nicole Peyrafitte

Mustapha Benfodil, a novelist, poet, & journalist, was born in 1968 in Relizane, in the Oran region of Algeria. He is one of the important literary figures who emerged during the Black Decade of the civil war (1990s). To the question "Who are you?" he answers as follows: "My name is Mustapha Benfodil, and I am a young Algerian writer—well, a youth approaching its expiry date. My *benfothèque* contains three novels: *Zarta* (Algiers: Barzakh, 2000), *Les Bavardages du Seul* (Editions Barzakh, 2003; prize for "best Algerian novel"), & *Archéologie du Chaos amoureux* (Editions Barzakh, 2007). Latest published work: *Clandestinopolis*, a play (Paris: L'Avant-scène Théâtre, 2008). What else? Oh, a book about Iraq: *Les Six derniers jours de Baghdad* (Algiers: Liberté-Casbah, 2003). Oops, that's more than five hundred characters. I'll stop here."

Al-Mahdi Acherchour (b. Sidi-Aïch, 1973)

IN THE EMPTINESS

In what desert did you hear
The sermon come out of the unspeakable and itself?
No opening in your eyes,
They have not broken the light of their pane.
Not yet washed, the tender plates
Brimming with massacres.

In what place did you name the desert?
You already picked the wrong silhouette. With patience
You fed yourself in a hurry
To grow fat with the sob that doesn't come.
Re-chewed error, fluid error
Neither upriver nor downriver.

Nobody came.

RETURN TO THE MISSED TURN

like a beleaguered city
the madman's cell in the windows' ire
gives on a city freed from its metaphors

if the ceiling goes back to the night of times
time's no longer of the sun
that distributed insomnia's rewards

around the lamp full of itself
memory and this hour refresh themselves
for thinking of the turn that can't be circumvented

the road toward the one and only chance
has lost the errancy of a stone
tracked after each sculpting strike

before the majestic quest
a wall affected all the way to insolence
sways its hips under that many ants

the road needs a firm cane
so as to locate its massive need
at whose end greatness and lucky finds get mired

like a conquered country
in the helmet of a hero made insane
by the air he breathed from exile to exile

like a condemned man never naked
to clothe him outside the dreams
where hermetic freedom shines

to take him for a turn
through this city whose lights
go out at the slightest hasty advance

under the aggression of giant steps
to walk at the moon's edge
to take on the appearance of a tribe of signs

the new rite they celebrate
at the approach of the wind from yesteryear
is but a sign of agreement with the infinite

what has already been lived
what is lived every night
is the moon's hour removed from its face

to give and to not take anything
to turn unto death and come back safe and sound
in time to dig up the road for the immortals

at the horizon of any trace
it's still the same madness
believing to give up on creation

to see it closer up again
the turn rounds itself more beautifully
and farther away moves the bleeding eye

Translations from French by P.J.

COMMENTARY

(1) Born in Sidi-Aïch, near Bejaïa, in 1973, Al-Mahdi Acherchour was invited to come to the Netherlands by Stichting Amsterdam Vluchtstad (the Amsterdam City of Refuge Foundation) in 2005 & has made his home there ever since. He is the author of three collections of poetry—*L'œil de l'égaré* (Marso éditions, 1997), *Retour au Tour Manqué* (Propos2, 2003), & *Chemins des choses nocturnes* (Editions Barzakh, 2003)—& three novels. The Dutch translation of his second novel, *Pays d'aucun mal* (Editions Aden, 2008), appeared in 2009. His latest novel, *Moineau* (Editions Aden, 2010), was long-listed for the prestigious Prix Femina.

(2) In an interview with Saïd Khatibi for *Algérie News*, he said: "For me the word *aesthetic* is meaningless. I don't really know what it means, and worse, I don't even want to know. Erudition isn't my domain. . . . When I am in a writing situation, that word—*aesthetic*—never comes to mind. It would be better to speak of form, or better even, of the thing. . . . I much prefer to use the word *writing* rather than *literature*."

(3) He recently told one of us that he would henceforth concentrate on writing prose—a prose, we want to add, that is in no way less dense or tightly packed (as in dicht, thus dichten, Dichtung, as per Ezra Pound's definition "Dichtung = poetry").

Samira Negrouche (b. Algiers, 1980)

COFFEE WITHOUT SUGAR

The only liberty, the only state of liberty which I have
enjoyed without any restraint, has been in poetry, in
its tears and in the radiance of a few people who have
come to me from three remotenesses, that of love
multiplying me.

RENÉ CHAR, *ELOGE D'UNE SOUPÇONNÉE*

There are blank pages that run through you as night ends those which a publisher is not expecting and which point towards an imaginary book which you watch grow faint in step with time you prefer to think that it will be forever inside the computer's dead memory.

I like to drink coffee with a splash of synthetic cream I like coffee without anything without sugar I only like the misty cloud of dawn which I catch before sleep it slides fills silently the hills' hollows I like that trickle of cream I ride from breast to nipple.

She's served me murky water in an earth-coloured bowl she says I've written a novel but the floppy disc is defunct she says look at my field of olive trees I've always dreamed of having an orchard I descend the three steps I look in the distance at sun-scorched weeds a concreted lemon tree like a blind pillar I say your field of olive trees is beautiful change to a different make of floppy discs.

One two I count the drops falling from the sky onto the bit of insolent plastic left lying on the balcony three four all thoughts are fit to pursue when nothing comes not desire nor sleep I look for a cigarette furtively not that I even smoke.

Didouche Mourad Street 12.35 a.m. the two men move forward they say we're going to walk to the far end until you can hardly see us right to the 23rd century I say poets are mad and thankfully those two do exist we'll go they say on camelback into the desert meanwhile I must translate body forth some bends which aren't really mine Cats don't need us to talk to them right inside their ears they don't circle their bowls they remain patient then flat out on the jumbled desk skillfully they curl themselves around their centre of gravity at the optimum distance from the radiator you've scarcely even raised a foot and they already know if you're just changing position or leaving.

Still that trembling hand scarcely presses the vulgar biro to a crossword puzzle grid the piano lid stays dusty and closed the poet's a frightened shadow on a wrecked armchair facing the extinguished lamp of a sleeping mosque and dreams of the day that will dawn without him.

I say that to write the most obvious things you must first write about the birth from your mother your father love bodies of women of men of rapist and assassin and incest of doubt of night of hunger desert books jealousy suspicion sex ruins sea trees archaeology Greek and pagan gods stars I say all this is almost commonplace before and after writing.

The word mountain must be multiplied with sharp and hungry breathing retain what may resemble a blackout through lack of air like a frontier that can be drawn between mourning and resurrection.

Slide among the dead leaves of a winter that's late and let yourself roll dislocated knees rusty muscles deaf to all movement animal mineral scaling and tumbling amid a sensation of existing to embrace the horizon.

I like this Theatre Square where actors pour in and out of the no. 1 tram I sip a glass of some liquid which my hands have warmed and I await night I perform my theatre among the free and assured silhouettes I blame cultural shock and long to be insouciant just a touch.

Sometimes I think I should quickly slip the moorings take the first boat the first plane the first anything simply leave with dangling arms solitary heart with the sense that the world is immense I go the length of the port boulevard I hear the boat barking tempting distracting me I almost crush a pedestrian and tell myself Algiers is a whore I can't give up.

Yes I can believe the future will be nasty now that to cross the Mediterranean millimeter-measured photos are required taken against a crimson-tinged white background and an exercise bike to heel Achilles tendons before green spaces are aerated by leap-year rotations and the forests cleared by July's false fires.

I'm happy to encounter in the manner of Prevert the mysteries of New York and then the mysteries of Paris and why not make a lament out of my little demons and my big caprices.

Tomorrow's a day no one wants to think about so tomorrow goes through its hours and takes up position by the window without waiting for the moon to vanish.

The painter says written things are signs for me they're not graphics insects framed by my screen since I've taken my leave of Arab lettering I'm scared the mountain of books might become a wave of indecipherable signs.

She sets a writing task she says recount a day's events she says use the present tense and she constructs some little sentences I say my memory's jam packed too many things are happening or not enough in a day how to peel Günter Grass's onion how to press the alarm bell how to enter the day which relies on words that matter how to hold with your gaze the truth of that moment the birth or the death of language I as well would be happy to know what happened one day in the present live it all again but this day today I'm really tired

What sets up encounters are sometimes the four winds, homing in on an eagle's nest and the instant of a word of love, canceling out the forces of opposition.

There are times when sleep lifts from you something which seems like injustice or maybe madness.

Translation from French by Martin Sorrell

COMMENTARY

Samira Negrouche is a French-speaking Algerian poet & author living in Algiers. She is a medical doctor who also organizes literary & poetry events. She has authored several poetry collections, among others, *À l'ombre de Grenade* (Éditions A.P. l'étoile, 2003), *Iridienne* (Color Gang Édition, 2005), & *Cabinet Secret,* a book-work with Enan Burgos (Color Gang Édition, 2007). Negrouche also translates Arabic poetry into French & has worked on interdisciplinary projects with theater, video, photography, & plastic arts. Her last lecture/show, *sans précaution,* was presented with the Greek singer Angélique Ionatos at the Musée des Moulages in Lyon in October 2009. Her most recent publication is *Le Jazz des oliviers (avec 9 œuvres de Yves Olry),* published in 2010 by Tell in Algeria. She has two forthcoming works: *Instance/Depart,* from La passe du vent, & *Le dernier diabolo,* from Chèvre Feuille Etoilée.

MOROCCO

The current situation of literature in Morocco—especially in the domain of poetry—seems possessed of a dynamism that contrasts strongly with the marasmus the other Maghrebian countries have fallen into. After the difficult period of the reign of Hassan II, when every expression of free speech was immediately censored, the country seems to have gained a renewed confidence in its live forces and is allowing all voices and directions to express themselves. This becomes understandable if one realizes that Morocco did not suffer as profound and destructive an undermining of its society and culture as its neighbors did, due to the brevity and nature of the colonial occupation. Thus the Moroccan elites and intellectuals were in the main spared having to deal with the false problem of the question of identity, a problem that had catastrophic consequences in Algeria. There wasn't an absolute rupture between generations, and the transmission between Francophone and Arabophone elites could take place with relatively little animosity.

Paradoxically, the archaism of Hassan II's monarchic regime allowed the Moroccan intellectuals and artists, nourished by modernist, revolutionary, or humanist ideals, to evolve in the margins of the dominant political discourse, which did not have pretensions of modernity, unlike Habib Bourguiba in Tunisia or the populist nationalists of the FLN (Front de libération nationale) in Algeria. Many Moroccan writers founded and edited magazines important for their literary innovations but also for the essential cultural and political debates they foregrounded. The poetry magazine *Souffles* (Breaths), subtitled *A Cultural Arab Maghrebian Magazine,* created by Abdellatif Laâbi (see p. 668) in 1966, was a true poetic and political experimental laboratory for the first generation of postindependence writers, such as Mohammed Khaïr-Eddine (see p. 679), Mostafa Nissabouri (see p. 673), Malek Alloula (see p. 569), Daniel Boukman, Mohamed Aziza (see p. 401), and Abdelkebir Khatibi (see p. 654). Influential far beyond the borders of Morocco and even of the Maghreb, it was unhappily stopped just as it reached a wide readership, because the broth of ideas it contained made it suspect to an unenlightened monarchy. Laâbi was thrown into jail, where he remained for eight hard years.

The magazine *Al-Taqafa al-jadida* (The New Culture), founded by the poet Mohammed Bennis (see p. 692) in 1974, took up the gauntlet and gave a new breath to Arabophone poetry. The link that unites the poetic generations since independence in Morocco, and which is also found in the other Maghrebian countries, is modernity. Nearly all the poets have made Arthur Rimbaud's well-known directive theirs: "You have to be absolutely modern."

Not surprisingly, it was in Morocco, a few years ago, that the first edition of Stéphane Mallarmé's momentous poem *A Throw of the Dice* appeared for the first time in an Arabic translation, by Bennis, superbly produced and including the original poem for the first time with the exact layout its author had wanted when he wrote it more than a century earlier. This deep and careful concern with modernity and tradition—echoing Ezra Pound's dictum that "all ages are contemporaneous"—until recently spelled out in French and classical Arabic, is today also expressing itself in Amazigh and Darija, Moroccan vernacular Arabic.

Driss Chraïbi (El Jadida, 1926–Drôme, France, 2007)

from SEEN, READ, HEARD

I thank life. It has fulfilled me. Compared to it, everything else is literature, not to say loneliness. At my age—seventy-one already—with peaceful steps I retrace the road already traveled, without any sense of time or space. I turn toward my past. At least I try to. A lady of a certain age confessed to George Bernard Shaw, my regretted confrere from across the Channel, with cheeks reddening, that she was thirty. "Oh good," replied the sarcastic old gent, "but at what age were you born?" Relatively speaking, he could have asked me the same question. Not that I am a woman: you know me. But there remains a slight doubt concerning the date of my birth, a certain discrepancy between the oral and the written. One does not refute the written, especially when it is official. Concerning the oral . . .

   Let's consider the official version. I saw the light of day in Morocco, in El-Jadida (Mazagan in the days of the Protectorate), at the edge of the sea. The place of birth thus determined, there remains the question of the date. For us, the "natives," there was no registry office. And, as has often been written and affirmed since the Crusades, in the Arabo-Muslim world time does not count, despite the Moroccans' passion for high-precision watches. But we had to be "civilized," according to the French history schoolbook, the same one that praised my ancestors the Gauls. To enter the Lycée Lyautey in Casablanca, I had to have an ID card—and thus a legal age. Dressed in a white jellaba and accompanied by two trustworthy witnesses who owed him money, my father led me by the hand to the police station. It was a torrid afternoon, toward the beginning of World War Two. He gravely declared to the police commissioner that my name was Driss with two *s*'s, please, Idriss in Arabic, but the pronunciation is Driss, that I was indeed his son and that he was pleased with me, yes, sir, he's a good boy, obedient, studious . . .

"How old, did you say he was?"

"Oh, it was at harvest time that, with god's help, he was born."

"Which harvest?" asked the commissioner, who was sweating profusely. "Barley, oats, corn, wheat?"

"Wheat," said my father.

"Exactly," the two witnesses in one single voice tried to go one better, "we were with him."

"So it was July?"

"Indeed," said my father, "it was July."

"Exactly," said the witnesses, "in July."

"In the middle of July?" the commissioner proposed. (He wiped off his face and neck.) "The fifteenth?"

"Why not the fifteenth?" said my father.

The eyes of the policeman examined me from head to toe and from one shoulder to the other. If I've always been thin—let's say svelte—that day in the police station at first sight I must have measured one meter and sixty centimeters. After some quick calculations on a piece of blotting paper with a quartermaster's quill, I was provided with an official date of birth, certified and stamped by a police officer: 15 July 1926. Thus I am seventy-one at this moment as I begin to write down my memoirs. Mathematical proof is given by the fact that my brother Abdel Hak, who is four years younger than me, is seventy-five years old. I'm not sure if he went to the same police commissioner with the same trustworthy witnesses. He only ever frequented the alternative school of the streets, but he needed a driver's license. He is two meters tall. You are what you wear, and there is a humorous watch with hands that move backward, as, according to a tale by Mark Twain, height determines age—and paperwork, civilization. I know something about it: I am a writer.

Let's consider my mother's version (she is dead, the dear soul, but her words perdure): the bread dough had started to rise when she felt the first pangs, so it was between eight and ten in the morning; the lemon tree in the patio was flowering, so it was unquestionably spring: March, April, or May; her cousin Meryem was on a pilgrimage to Moulay Yacoub, she remembered with her emotional and associative memory. Thus I am supposedly born in May, April, or March 1930, '31, or '29, depending on the elastic concordance between the Christian and Hegirian eras, an algebraic equation with two unknowns, you could say. "But how long ago that was, my son!" my mother would say, breaking into laughter.

To conclude, let's attend to the official and peremptory declaration by the *Moroccan* civil service employee whom I had asked for a copy of my birth certificate in El-Jadida, my native city, and who had sweated blood and water for three days while digging through the archives:

"Nothing, my friend. Nothing of nothing. No trace whatsoever. You do not exist."

Which is the same as saying that I am a phantom/ghostwriter. Which resolves the problem.

I love my country. No matter how far away from it I may be, all I need to do is close my eyes to see and hear it, to feel it and feel its effects. Here it is called Morocco; on the other shore of the Mediterranean we call it Al Maghrib al aqsa, the Far West.

I am as curious as Inspector Ali, my favorite character. I have often asked a little question about identity to the citizens of the neighboring country. Among their answers: "I am Kabyle," "I am Arab," "Islamist," "From Oran," "Anti-Islamist," "Leave me alone, I don't do politics . . . " Ask a bourgeois from Fez, a peasant from the Doukkala, a mountain man from the Rif, a Jew like the writer Edmond Amran el-Maleh. They will answer without a nanosecond of hesitation: "I am Moroccan." Ask me. Morocco is my day-dream, my liver, my dwelling. You can give everything up, except childhood. The path that leads toward affective space meets the path of time.

Space. In the Middle Atlas, some distance from Khenifra, a steep, narrow road, in hairpin turns, leads to the mountain. Djebel Roumyat culminates at an altitude of about two thousand meters. But before you see it, two or three kilometers earlier, you hear the continuous, deafening, roar of thunder. And yet, there is not a cloud above your head. And what you'll see soon, what you'll hear cataracting more and more, what will sweep away your sight and intellect and bring you back instantly to the dawn of creation, is *this:* the naked limestone djebel, without tree or bush, except for a few rare boxwood bushes from which shoot, like projectiles, playful rock squirrels; from rock to rock the mouflons bound in love and arial jumps; on the left, beyond the ravine, a peak with just one white egg on top, as large as a Cavaillon melon, which in a few seasons will become a bearded vulture filling the sky with its spread wings; the golds and ochers, the amethysts and burnt siennas of the rising sun; and, at the bottom of the vertical rock face, the thousand-voiced abyss: from the loins of the mountain in rut, at full life's strength, shoots its seed, powerful and roaring: the forty springs of the Oum-Er-Bia. Here, no trace of pollution, no sign of ratiocination. You feel yourself being born again, being born, having shed the gangue of technocratic and dehuman-izing civilization. No gulf separates man and his instinct. This is, tangibly, the first dawn. It is all here—ready to be discovered, loved. And first of all, oneself. . . .

El-Jadida. It is at the hour of the milkman that I love my native city best, peopled exclusively and only for a few moments more by the of necessity industrious early risers: garbage men, fishermen, doughnut sellers, pious zealots, market gardeners, guardians of public ovens. One after the other they wish me a "day of light" while I wander through the streets and alleyways. Come with me, please, into the Portuguese city, where the past has been restored in its smallest details. Look: on this site, no larger than an esplanade, reside side by side a mosque, a church, and a synagogue.

Tangier, at the confluence of two seas, at the border of Africa and Europe. It is from this city that in 711 Tariq ibn Ziyad embarked, with a few hundred partisans, to go conquer Spain. He was Moroccan. He made his crazy dream come true for centuries: a multiethnic, multiconfessional Andalusia, an open society, with a flowering of arts and sciences, so much so that a majority of Muslims at present remember it in their collective memory as our golden age. I am a descendant of those Andalusians. From them I inherited my first culture. And one of my children, born in Vendée, is named Tariq. A question haunts me when I contemplate the whole of the Muslim world at this century's end: will we someday have another future than our past?

The Sahara. Do you know what the desert is? And who could ever tell you what the desert is? Have you heard it sing? It sings, truly, a few moments just before dawn, if you know how to listen. Myriads of grains of sand brought to white-hot heat through a full day in the furnace of the sun, then brutally refrigerated during the night. Intangible dust raised to the height of heaven and hesitating to fall down to earth. Drops of light falling thickly from the stars and transforming themselves into dewdrops. Congealing of the dew. Freezing of the stones. Roots of the date palms drawing from the liquid soul of the earth. Slow respiration of the earth, like that of a woman breast-feeding. Sap circulating from lacuna to lacuna along the trunks hardened by generations of droughts. Breath of ancient winds, fresh and blessed. Caravans, travelers who had crossed the desert and whose rumors had left behind them resonances of echoes: joys, sorrows, hopes. Meharis so loaded with experience that they couldn't say another word. Disappeared poets. Their live remembrance in memory, their words transmitted from mouth to mouth along the thread of generations. And the silence—this silence full of all the existences of time. Light and darkness, mineral, human, vegetal, past and present, languaged, each particle emits an infinitesimal note, an infinitesimal sign: the supreme future spread over the whole *oikoumene* of sand and reg. Have you heard the desert sing?

Translation from French by P.J.

My biography is very simple. I have always been crazy for light and water. Everything I have lived, written, or dreamed since I was born on the shores of the Oum-Er-Bia River can be explained by either the abundance or the lack of light and water.

D.C.

Driss Chraïbi, the elder statesman of the modern Moroccan—Maghrebian, really—novel, is the author of twenty-plus books, mainly novels, though also, late in life, of an essay/memoir, from which our selection is drawn. He startled & upset his country (while gaining immediate recognition in France) when, in 1954, just two years before Moroccan independence, he published his first novel, *Le Passé Simple* (Denoël), in Paris. This paradigmatic work, banned in Morocco until 1977, explores the epistemic break between the traditional, Arabo-Islamic & the modern, French-speaking Moroccan culture via a father/son opposition. Abdelfattah Kilito uses the expression *langue fourchue,* "forked tongue," in speaking of certain Maghrebian writers, & one of us has written at length on the complexity of Chraïbi's title, summing up as follows: "The poetics of Chraïbi's French title rehearse, while displacing, the initial and initiating Maghrebi wound of the forked tongue: here, rather than playing itself out between Arabic and French, the cut is (re)located in the other's language itself. The colonizer's language too is caught in an irresolvable double bind: no language is a house the writer can simply inhabit, the only home is to be found in the ever-shifting force field of the spaces of its internal contradictions—which it is the writer's job to bring to light."

Mohammed Sebbagh (b. Tétouan, 1929)

from *SEASHELL-TREE*

How often have I heard "vengeance" say, whip in hand: justice must be done!

A tomb is an island undiscovered and will remain forever so.

In her great wisdom Autumn said: when the time comes you may learn death from me.

When flowers wither in a vase, they become its burden.

Even sorrow dances, and sometimes it sings.

White ink cries out and calls for help when a black quill ruffles its surface.

Every newborn bears news our tired ears find hard to grasp.

The woodworker hums the same tune when making a rebec* or a coffin.

I don't know why a restless man should inspire more confidence in me than a quiet man.

Let him be, though you see him on the edge of a precipice, for he knows his path and purpose. Beware of sending rescuers. Tomorrow he'll return to you in triumph, bearing the dome of the precipice at arms' length.

Social justice: the words both ring false to my ears.

A Moroccan painter and disciple of the school of impressionism was pondering how to portray the face of modern-day Morocco. He settled for painting a beautiful woman, buried alive.

from **CANDLES ON THE ROAD**

Dust will soar and soar, yet ends up settling by itself.

Yes and no are two double-edged swords.

When Socrates swallowed the poison to convey his message, the poison took the glory.

I turned around before picking up the shards of a mirror. An old man stood behind me.

Descartes said: I think, therefore I am. I say: I love, therefore I am.

Within a tree trunk, water dwells in fire. The water doesn't run dry, nor does the fire die.

Every time I meet a pregnant woman, I hope she'll bring a poet or artist into this world.

Without mirages, many a thirsty man would die in despair.

Azure skies bid a warm welcome to the dove as to the crow.

*A type of medieval fiddle.

When the arrow seeks its prey, it says before wounding her: Forgive me, O sister, I cannot help it.

A man is only a man when he converts to humanity.

Dear God, in my life let me forever be as the fingers of an infant seeking its mother's breast.

Sometimes when I'm absorbed in writing, my pen will pause for a minute of silence. What's happened? Perhaps a poet has just passed away.

Many are the lamps that feel ashamed of what goes on around them. They look up at the ceiling.

I always feel imprisoned by the one who reaches out to me.

I find nothing offensive in what the truly inspired madman says or does, whether raving or dreaming. Give me a madman sincere in his madness, and I'll give up a country full of reasonable men.

Don Quixote's sword is brandished to this day by many a windmill-fighting hand. The sword isn't blunted, nor is the air refreshed.

When we are born, life opens the first door and holds the key to lock the final door behind us.

A BRIEF MOMENT

The past left on a wing
and said
—I've gone
The present crouched down
and said
—Present!
The future rose
and said
—Ready!
A brief moment had peaked
It took all three under its wing
and rushed toward the stream of Heraclitus.

THE MISSING READER

Don't look round
By your side
is a reader who reads what you're reading
When you read the word *bell*
he hears carillons
Even as you read the word *sea*
he's rocking on a sailboat
When you read the word *lamp*
It radiates light
Don't look round
There's a reader with you, in you
He reads what you read
He reads loud and clear
what you could not read
Now he's gone
and left you perplexed
Now you're gone
he must find you
Will you two ever meet?

MATERNAL INSTINCT

The shell
has learned by heart
all her daughters' names
She never gets it wrong
as she shells them out
                              Flux

IN SHACKLES

Some seed their dreams in winter
to flower in springtime
Some seed them in summer
to be born on the shore beneath the sun
As for me

I seed my dreams come autumn
among live embers
to pluck them
with my teeth
from the flames

IF I HAD A FRIEND

If I had a friend to gaze at me
and from my eyes to pluck the grape
If I had a friend to greet
and in the palm of his hands to quench my thirst
If I had a friend to lash out
yes to lash at me with dawn's tentacles
as the night embraces me . . .
I said this before I knew you
/before I knew roses suck in their nectar from the dead/
and pigeons drink from hollow skulls
and birds   they build their nests
from the earth's refuse
that the gardener sprays his tree
with sallow water
and then returns to pluck
their most luscious fruit
before I knew the blood of slaves
once flowed in free men's veins
and jewels were once
carbon and mire

Today I proclaim my hatred
Hatred of this air tainted by your breath
of this earth sullied by your step

The burning tree

Translations by Madeleine Campbell from Abdellatif Laâbi's French versions of the original Arabic

TWO POEMS

I

I want to think of nothing this morning, to write nothing,
   to be delivered of everything, of all encounters, of all greetings,
. . . To pluck the dreams of my very last night, place them in posies before
   me,
      offer them to a nameless woman . . .
To forget I exist, that my life began thirty years ago, is bound to meet with
   fate.
. . . I love how the fog sweeps over me, swallows
   the span of existence. No more distance,
      nor mass nor expanse.
. . . To give things other names,
mountain: catch a star,
sea: veil of snow,
butterfly: wind tattoo,
And to say to you: your fingers are buds of silk, or
   ember; beware of losing them in space. Harvest
      your jewel-encrusted garden: sun, dew, secret of the light,
         star and scent.

II

What do I see? An enormous droplet slithering down
a tree, then smashing, turning into a black egg
rolling over rocks. The egg cracks open, releasing a
rabbit with long claws, wide and fretful wings. It
enters the earth, soars to the brow of the sky, clasping
splinters of the sun. Bathes in a spring of ebbing waters,
tree branches with clashing colors. They stand
reflected in a moon mirror, behind a negro
woman painting a self-portrait. Little girls play naked
about her, prancing on threads of tears dangling
from my eyes.
   Help! Who is this mineral owl dancing to
the tears these chords have struck? He pierces my chest,
rips out my heart, flies to a pine tree. And erect,
an athletic lumberjack with chiseled features and an ax

strikes the tree trunk in the wake of my legs.

At the last blow I fall through the hollow mountains,
soaring on winged clouds.

Panting. And my breath shatters my teeth.

Dream. I wake: you are stalking my dream, Leïla!

Translations by Madeleine Campbell from Abdul Kader El Janabi's French versions of the original Arabic

COMMENTARY

Writes his translator Madeleine Campbell: "Mohammed Sebbagh was born in 1929 in Tétouan. After studying library science in Madrid, he took up his first library post in his native city before becoming the head of the Department for Arab Studies at the Centre universitaire de la recherche scientifique in Rabat & starting to work at the Ministry for Culture. All the while he has been writing & publishing work that has continuously been innovative in both form & style, & he was among the very first who, as far back as the fifties, introduced free verse & prose poems into Moroccan literature. Fluent in Spanish & nourished by this tongue's great literature, he is one of the first Moroccan intellectuals to have assumed the role of ferryman between cultures. This acknowledged father of modernism does not seem to age: his voice has never relinquished its sense of indignation, its lighthearted gravitas & almost childlike sparkle. The publication of his complete works in 2001 offered a timely opportunity to recognize the debt owed by Moroccan literature & culture to this master of learned elegance."

Mohamed Serghini (b. Fez, 1930)

POEM I

In the laboratories of the north, male and female genes torment their nuclei.
The leering vestige of their indecent quarrel flickers across their features.
Test tubes, glass and plastic, lead the white coats to stunt the development of any embryonic truth.
There are rebels who, like al-Antaki, suggest remedies to mortuary biologists, for a she-monkey's milk is what's required in the production of a gene.
As for Anatomy, it demands that the said female be vegetarian and adapted to inhaling the reproductive sap of fruit trees.

And since in total dark even the color-blind can sometimes almost see the white thread of dawn, it's natural that what a microscope can't see should be regarded as divine.

Nothing can elude this theological myelin.

No gene can alter sex or race when severed from its spinal nerve.

POEM III

Defiled on either side, a medal, a specter, and a ribbon decorate the cloak that Poetry offered a puppet who was concocted from terminology and verse. Every other century, generations bequeath their litany to literally contrived executioners.

Until now, the puppet was but a carousel, and when I startled her in her delirious homily, the image migrated to the frame in search of ecstasy.

I crossed her out like a tired phrase.

And like a hookah inspired by the sighs of glowing embers, a waiter's complicity, the stutter of tobacco, the stark persistence of a hard chair, and a nameless weariness, I am losing my way in this treacherous density.

I crown my glory with victory and countless defeats.

I grow accustomed to this slow rhythm of regret.

I return to the earth what's left of barley grain in my limbs.

Hideous garment.

The cloak is called upon to admit it has no guts.

Translations from French by Madeleine Campbell

from *ASSEMBLY OF DREAMS*

I

Four neighborhoods recount the soul of the city. Utopian melody in four/ four time; the birth cry of the disadvantaged, waking in an unattractive body. Reaction of libidinal chastity and the race of life's routine. Outside these four neighborhoods there are only nests of straw to shelter the old eagles at the summit of the mountains, only bramble reeds to nourish the stray goats in the plains. Evasion assures the survival of chaos. (No plenitude escapes emptiness.) What will the hanging gardens say when their rotations are paralyzed, when water no longer flows under the norias, and under the grindstones of the mills? Energy will be in a state of absolute grace. The wind yielding before the capricious pressure of the spheres. Blowing against the wishes of sailboats no longer.

II

The taste of the city is strange. A mix of kif, tobacco, and mint. Only these drugs can braid the strands of insomnia. Time passes inexplicably. The wax of candles illuminating only their own circles. Logics crack under the weight of heretical slander. The militias of grammarians, of lawyers and illustrious engineers sharpen their theoretical arms. Ancestors in intensive care (revived, we imagine, with cooking gas mixed with fish manure). . . .

III

At dawn the alleys and footpaths of the
Kingdom are deserted. The red of daybreak
No longer infects the ruins'
facades, receiving only a mute
Light from this red. (We fly over history
With red wings.) Taken with fire, a thief
Has taught the phoenix to fill
The attics with onions, garlic, coconut,
Dry figs, black pepper
And raisins. (This dosage an
Effective remedy for unrequited
Love.) Reviving the burnt
ashes, the same thief demands
that the genealogical tree blessed by the
City drug itself only with its own
Unripe fruits.
Who dares hope for the withering of this
Tree? Who dares refute the crime
Of its secular age.

From closed to open,
The shutters of the door
Reaffirm the nostalgia of two beings separated.

Reaffirm that return is nothing but union.
Reaffirm that leaving is nothing but divorce.
We carry our dreams to the next sleep
Where the bed, inert and shivering with cold,
Hides its insomnia under the sheets.

Translation from French by Deborah Kapchan

COMMENTARY

A translator (of Pablo Neruda, among others), a literary critic (writing on, among other subjects, the relations of poetry & painting), a novelist & prose writer, Mohamed Serghini is also the author of several collections, including *Wa Yakoun Ihraqou Asmaehi Alatiya* (And People Burn the Following Words, 1987), *The Sailor of Jabal Qaf* (1991), & *Al-Kaen Assibaey* (1992). Born in 1930 in Fez, he is an academic specializing in literature & a poet considered one of the pioneers of free verse in Morocco. His poems, says Abdul Kader El Janabi, "are gardens overtaken by words and images from past dreams." Or, as Deborah Kapchan writes in relation to *Assembly of Dreams:* "For Serghini, the city—its neighborhoods, its smells and tastes—comes to signify a home that is difficult to inhabit and yet provides one's only dwelling. It is a place of insomnia where ancestors are infirm and history itself is nourished only with fruits gathered before their time. There is a modernist tone of the wasteland here, the city both decrepit and seething, barren yet continuing."

Abdelkrim Tabbal (b. Chefchaouen, 1931)

TO THE HORSE

Oh you my horse
You give me life when you carry me away
like a dream
You scatter me rain on dry grass
You sow me voice in the rivers
You draw me on the wings of amorous butterflies
You restore me waves on the sea's bosom
and write my name on the mountain's gorges
The four winds traverse me
There remains only

Me the winds
The four seasons shatter me
There remains only
Me the seasons
O you my horse
If you stop
Death will carry me away.

HAPPINESS

How we laughed these past days
and we go on laughing and laughing
We don't know how we will weep
how funerals would be
in this country in tears
We laugh and we laugh
We walk in the street
and now the street is a coffin
We contemplate the trees immobilized in the street
the streets are gallows from which we hang dead
We look at the rains falling on the heart
the rains are the tears of all those killed
We laugh and we laugh
We scrutinize our faces that laugh into our faces
and we don't recognize them even in the future
We sit down around a table in the café
and suddenly the café is a tomb
We sip the small glass of coffee, the coffee is blood
We watch the waiter, he is a torturer
We look at the spoon stuck in the glass
the spoon is a mic

We laugh and laugh
until the head detaches itself from the body
until all our teeth fall out

our jaws rot
We laugh and laugh
until our eyes pour forth their full load of tears
until the tears become a sea
until the waves drag us down into its depths

THE SPEECH

In the final news bulletin of the night
the presenter with the marvelous voice and face said:
For you, dear audience of Radio Prophecy
here is the latest news: all is wonderful
The four seasons visit our country
We ask nobody for a passport
not even crazy summer
The sun enters each morning
before the caliph wakes up
The trees that inhabit the plains and the mountains
are exempt from taxes
we do not refuse entry
to the voice carried by the waves
we do not hide the earth
from the falling rain
We forbid nothing even to man
He can welcome the sun or the night as he pleases
smell perfume or stench
be hungry or sated
dress well or not have enough to
be healthy or sick
die or live
sleep by day or by night
drink water or tea
break his head against a wall
or break a wall over his head
We will simply keep him from dreaming during daytime
for daydreaming is always a folly
And now
for you, our dear dear audience of Radio Prophecy
here now the late-breaking news:
all is wonderful

ABSENT TIME

In the fifth bar
a love song rose all the way to fear
The red lantern was night's permanent sun
The rain that fell from the abandoned window's pupils
was the history of the creator of wine and the music of first love
The cupbearer knew all of wisdom
The glass, the snow calves, were genuine antiques
and the bar the whole world

In a corner, a stranger laughed all the way to fear
It was just decor
a representation
There was nothing here of love
nothing of wisdom
nothing of man
nothing of the world

Translations from French by P.J.

COMMENTARY

Born in 1931 in Chefchaouen in the mountains of northern Morocco, Abdelkrim Tabbal worked as a teacher until he retired, though he remains active on the literary scene of his hometown & beyond. Among his books are *The Road to Man* (1969), *The Diwan of Broken Things* (1974), *The Garden* (1983), *At Dusk* (1994), *The White Tree* (1995), *Watercolors* (1996), & *Capture the Water* (1997); his *Collected Poems* was published in 2000 in Rabat in two volumes. This selection does not allow us to show the breadth of a life's work consecrated exclusively to poetry. Tabbal's achievement sums up the development of Moroccan poetry during the second part of the twentieth century, & he remains one of the Maghreb's exemplary voices. He is indeed a "vigilant watchman of the human condition," as Abdellatif Laâbi has it.

Zaghloul Morsy (b. Marrakech, 1933)

from *FROM A RETICENT SUN*

1

From the tumult arises the fruit
took off the rose as auctioned
the gold of the bundles will fade
wings will shudder in the highest branches
the confused pack of cicadas
like a good-bye
melts with the sun

The madman of the mountains argues
halfway up the hill
with the sunset

To leave
if it isn't too late

2

You did not recognize the intruder in your reflection
When what was at stake was only a star given for
dead
It was a foregone conclusion, the mirror no longer had its immemorial
leprosy
. . .

Blind adventure
Come along in solitude
The road has drawn back like a sea's ebb
throwing a lacerated child up to the sun
. . .

Fugitive & umbilical road
A moment's mirage foiling all memory
Beyond the retreats & the forced marches
What will it be tomorrow, all gazes checked.

Translation from French by P.J.

Born in 1933 in Marrakech to an Egyptian father (who was a composer) & a Moroccan mother, Zaghloul Morsy is a Francophone Moroccan writer who now lives in Paris. After studies at the Muslim colleges of Marrakech & Rabat, he earned diplomas in modern languages & Arab studies from the Sorbonne. He directed the Department of Literature & French Civilization at the University of Rabat from 1960 to 1967, & after a brief stint as a diplomat, he worked for the United Nations Educational, Scientific and Cultural Organization from 1972 to 1993 as the editor & then the director of *Prospects,* a trimonthly magazine of comparative education. Best known for his writings on education—see *La Tolérance* (1976), an anthropological essay, & *The Challenge of Illiteracy* (1994)—he has also published two volumes of poetry (*D'un soleil réticent* [Grasset, 1969], much admired by Roland Barthes & Roger Caillois, followed by *Gués du temps* [L'Harmattan, 1985]) & the novel *Ishmaël ou l'exil* (La Différence, 2003).

Mohamed Choukri (Aït Chiker, 1935–2003)

from *THE PROPHET'S SLIPPERS*

More pleasure and fantasy. More money, more ways of getting hold of it. I was tired of enjoying myself, and yet I was not satisfied. Fatin walked toward me, white as snow in the blood-red light of the bar. She took one of my notebooks, looked at it, and grinned.

She muttered something unintelligible and moved away again, disappearing among those who were kicking the air. It was three o'clock in the morning, and I was bored and nervous. Om Kalsoum was singing: "Sleep never made life seem too long, nor long waiting shortened life."

A black man appeared, white on black. He took one of my books and began to read aloud: "This total liberty has its tragic and pessimistic side." He put it down. "What's that book about?" he demanded.

"It's about a man who doesn't understand this world," I said. "He hurts himself and everybody who comes near him."

He nodded, lifted his glass, and drank. When he had finished, he said: "You're crazy."

I saw Fatin writing in a notebook. Meanwhile I smoked, drank, and thought about the matter of the slippers. The lights went off. Women cried out. When they came on again, both men and women murmured. I bought another drink for Khemou, and she gave me a kiss that left a sweet taste in my mouth. Her brown tongue tickled. She was eating chocolate, and her laugh was red in the light from the bar. Khemou walked off and Fatin came up to me. She handed me a slip of blue paper. On it she had written: *Rachid. What do you know about love? You spend more time writing about love than you do making love. The one who has never studied love enjoys it more than the one who knows all about it. Love is not a science. Love is feeling, feeling, feeling.*

Miriam Makeba went into "Malaysia." She has a white voice. I began to write on the same piece of blue paper. *Fatin, you are my red bed, and I'm your black blanket. I'm beginning to see it that way.*

I looked around for Fatin. Her mouth was a wound in her face, and a foreign sailor was sucking on it. She had her right arm around him and was pouring her drink onto the floor with her left hand. Khemou came by and offered me her lips, like a mulberry. I bought her another drink. I was so pleased with the effect of her kiss that I began to think once more about selling the slippers. How much ought I to ask for them? A million francs, the Englishman ought to pay, if he wants the Prophet's slippers. He's an idiot in any case, or he couldn't be taken in by such a tale. But how can I tell just how stupid he is? It was he who first brought it up, the black-market story.

Fatin appeared, black, blonde, white. I handed her the slip of blue paper. She looked at me and smiled. I was thinking that girls like her only made trouble. Her little mouth now looked like a scar that had healed. I thought of the Indian poet Mirzah Asad Allah Ghalef:

*For those who are thirsty
I am the dry lip.*

She wants a kind of love that will make her unhappy. What I like about her is that she still believes the world ought to be changed.

Khemou and Latifa began to scream at each other like two cats fighting, while Miriam Makeba's white voice continued to sing. Khemou pulled Latifa's black hair, knocked her down, and kicked her face. Latifa screamed and the blood ran from her nose. The colors all came together in my head. Leaving the blue paper with me, Fatin ran to separate the two. I read on it: *You're right. I serve them my flesh, but I don't feel it when they eat me.*

Vigon is singing in his white voice. "Outside the Window." Vigon is singing, and I think of the almond trees in flower, and of snow, which I love.

Khemou and Latifa came out of the rest room. They had made up, like two little girls. They began to laugh and dance as if nothing had happened. I sat there smoking, while in my imagination I attacked each man in the bar whose face I didn't like. A kick for this one, a slap in the face for that one, a punch in the jaw for that one over there. Watching myself do as I pleased with them put me into a better frame of mind.

Tomorrow I'll sell the slippers. Fatin came past again, and I asked her why

Khemou and Latifa had been quarreling. She said it was because Khemou had told the man Latifa was drinking with that she had tuberculosis.

Is it true? I asked her.

Yes, she said. But she says she's cured now.

The Englishman and I were at my house, eating couscous. He turned to me and said: "This is the best couscous I've ever tasted."

From time to time he looked toward the corner where my grandmother sat, her head bent over. I told him the couscous had been sent from Mecca. "My aunt sends a lot of it each month."

He looked at me with amazement. "It's fantastic!"

So that he would get the idea, I added: "Everything in the house was brought from Mecca. Even that incense burning is sent each month."

We finished the couscous and started on another dish of meat baked with raisins and hot spices. "It's called *mrozeya,*" I told him.

He muttered a few words, and then said: "Ah, nice. Very nice." My grandmother's head was still bent over. I saw that the Englishman was looking at her, sitting there in her white robes. The incense and the silence in the room made her seem more impressive. She was playing her part very well. Our demure little servant brought the tea in a silver teapot. She too was dressed in immaculate white, and she too kept her face hidden. Her fingers were painted with elaborate designs in henna, and her black hair shone above her enormous earrings. She made no false moves. She greeted the Englishman without smiling, as I had instructed her to do. It became her to look grave. I had never seen her so pretty.

The mint tea with ambergris in it seemed to please the Englishman.

"Do you like the tea?" I asked him.

"Oh, yes! It's very good!"

There was silence for a while. I thought: The time has come to rub Aladdin's lamp. I got up and went to whisper in my grandmother's ear. I did not even form words; I merely made sounds. She nodded her head slowly, without looking up. Then I lifted the white cushion and removed the piece of gold-embroidered green silk that covered it.

The Englishman looked at the slippers, made colorless by age. His hand slowly advanced to touch the leather. Then he glanced at me, and understood that I did not want him to touch them.

"My God! They're marvelous!" . . .

I found him waiting for me in front of the hotel. He seemed nervous, and he looked wide-eyed at the bag I was carrying. I saw that he had a packet in his hand. Half a million, I thought. More pleasure, more time to think of other such tricks later. The colors in the bar.

I motioned to him to follow me, and stopped walking only when we were a good distance from the entrance to the hotel. We stood facing one another, and shook hands. He looked down at my bag, and I glanced at the packet he held in his hand.

I opened the bag, and he touched the slippers for a second. Then he took it out of my hands, and I took the packet from him. Pointing to a parked car, he said: "There's the car that's going to take me to the airport."

I thought to myself: And tonight I'll be at the Messalina Bar.

I sat down in the corner the same as always. I smoked, drank, and bought kisses without haggling over their price. I'm fed up with pleasure. Fed up, but not satisfied. One woman is not enough. "Khemou's in the hospital," Fatin told me. "And Latifa's at the police station. She got drunk and hit Khemou on the head with a bottle."

I asked Fatin who the girls were who were sitting in the corner opposite me. She said they were both from Dar el Beida. She picked up one of my notebooks and walked away with it. I waved at the younger of the two. She spoke for a while with her friend. And I drank and smoked and waited for the first kiss of a girl I had never yet touched.

She got up and came over, and I saw the small face relax. Her mouth was like a strawberry. She began to sip the drink I bought her. Her lips shone. Her mouth opened inside mine. A strawberry soaked in gin and tonic. Eve eating mulberries. Adam approaches her, but she puts the last berry into her mouth before he can get to her. Then he seizes the last berry from between her teeth. The mulberry showed Eve how to kiss. Adam knows all the names of things, but Eve had to teach him how to kiss.

Two men had begun to fight over one of the girls. The shorter of the two lost his balance. The other kicked until someone seized him from behind. Fatin put a piece of blue paper in front of me. I was drinking, smoking, and eating mulberries from the new small mouth. I read what was written on the piece of blue paper. *I'm not the same person I was yesterday. I know it but I can't say it clearly. You must try and understand me.*

The new face held up her empty glass. I looked again at the mulberries. The barman was busy drawing squares on a small piece of white paper. "Give her another drink," I told him. The friend who had been sitting with her came over. "Give her a drink too," I said.

I thought: More mulberries and human flesh. More tricks and money. I began to write on Fatin's slip of blue paper: *I must not try to understand you.*

Translation from Arabic by Paul Bowles

Mohamed Choukri (born July 15, 1935; died November 15, 2003) was raised in a very poor family in Aït Chiker in the Rif Mountains. He ran away from his tyrannical father & became a homeless child living in the poor neighborhoods of Tangier, surrounded by misery, prostitution, violence, & drug abuse. At the age of twenty he decided to learn how to read & write classical Arabic & later became a schoolteacher. A novelist & short story writer, Choukri is best known for the autobiographical book *For Bread Alone* (*Al-Khubz al-Hafi*), translated into English by Paul Bowles in 1973 & described by the American playwright Tennessee Williams as "a true document of human desperation, shattering in its impact." The book was censored in Morocco from 1983 until 2000 & adapted to cinema in 2004 by Rachid Benhadj in an Italian-French-Algerian production, which premiered at the first edition of the Festival of Casablanca, in 2005.

Ahmad al-Majjaty (Casablanca, 1936–1995)

ARRIVAL

That drunkard stumbled down over his lips and fell.
He shined the mirror's splinter of his sorrows and saw
His own funeral: lips chewing prayers
A star shouting and fading away.
Then slipped away from his hands a vine's dream, a rosary,
And a mother hanging linen on the roof.
Filled with barking, he closed his eyes, bit his tongue, and drew away.

DISAPPOINTMENT

We came. An illusion that set the square on fire kept us on the path.
We came from behind the rampart.
We shook off shadow, dust, sound, and shrouds
And then muttered: with God's help we start, O lamp!
Ink is your own, and you the oil, the Qur'an, and the Gospel.
An epoch elapsed and another, but we kept turning around.
Out of hunger, we killed the spiny-tailed lizard
And slept in the shade of wormwood.
The chords played only wind poems for our sake
Until we soared around.

Then passed the strewn one by our caravan
Chewing the bone of his she-camel, disappointed.
We were two people
Silence the third
And tears our fourth companion.

THE STUMBLING OF THE WIND

Snow and silence rest on the coast
The waves are motionless on the sand
And the wind—an unmanned boat.
Remnants of an oar
And a spider.
Who can ignite joy in my eyes?
Who can awaken the giant?
Who dies?
The smell of death in the garden
Mocks the seasons
And you, my girlfriend,
A choke and a tear in the virgin's eye.
Sounds of footsteps on the debris
Search for the truth
For a dagger, for a protective arm.
Deep down in my wounds
The eagle's feathers were
A voice and a silence
That yearn for the beats of drums
For a shower of rain
To water its palate,
And the (wrestling) ring
Is a soft cloud
That hovers around the horses' missteps.
Go back with my remains
My blood did not anticipate its course.
Who awaits the dawn and is impatient to arrive?
Who has clung to the rock of my speculations?
Who has stretched his beak out
Towards my eyes?
Oh robber of the torch
There is clamour in silence.

Pick up the daisies of light
In tenacious obscurity.
We sought silence in caves
For impurities cannot be purged by words
Let's dive beneath waves and rocks.
Surely there is a flicker of light at the bottom
Turn it into a spark
That rescues the wind
From the chains of silence
And teaches humanity how to die!

Translations from Arabic by Norddine Zouitni

COMMENTARY

Born 1936 in Casablanca, Ahmad al-Majjaty was one of the most powerful voices in modern Moroccan poetry. After completing graduate work in Damascus & getting a PhD in Arabic literature from Mohammed V University in Rabat, he taught Arabic literature at that university. He & Mohammed Bennis (see p. 692) are often considered *the* avant-garde poets who took the modernization of Moroccan poetry most seriously. Writes his translator Norddine Zouitni: "Al-Majjaty's poetry is characterized by its emphasis on pure Arabic diction and original syntactic formation. This is due to the poet's high respect for classical Arabic, a respect that amounts to an almost spiritual kind of veneration. This is perhaps the reason why, despite his great poetic skill and mastery of Arabic, he managed to publish only one book of poetry. In fact, the reader of his poems cannot but recognize a deep feeling of awe before language. . . . Al-Majjaty won the Ibn Zaydoun Award for poetry in Madrid in 1985, and the Morocco Award in 1986. He died in 1995."

Abdelkebir Khatibi (El Jadida, 1938–Rabat, 2009)

from *CLASS STRUGGLE IN THE TAOIST MANNER*

I

history is a word
ideology a word
the unconscious a word
words flutter
in ignorant mouths

for each sign is self-perpetuating
unchangingly new
don't get mixed up in your own speech
don't vanish in that of others

limit the life blood of your thought

because at your query
you will discover any ambiguous syllables
it is action that determines meaning
as the bow designs the arching arrow

2

orphaned
that's class struggle
sovereignly orphaned

What do we mean by "orphaned"?
all hierarchies rest on
a father a mother and an order
which is entirely political
a master a slave and an order

historical being is a disgrace
can you unmask the class enemy
without using his methods?
can you turn against
your own delusions?
everyone cherishes his identity
everyone looks for his origins
and me I teach orphaned knowledge

wander therefore along the paths
without getting lost in the grass

the song of the bird
will follow the tread of your foot in rain
your lips in rain
will reveal the sun's blisters

I teach irredeemable difference
and precise violence
this is what "orphaned" means

what do we mean by "sovereignly orphaned"?
the class fighter rarely reveals his weapons
he works from within
and destroys systematically
whoever does these things
is my orphaned comrade

this sovereignty burns
the class enemy
like a scarecrow

Translation from French by Abdallah Adady

from **LOVE IN TWO LANGUAGES**

Epigraph

(He left, he came back, he left again. He decided to leave for good. The story should stop here, the book close upon itself.)

Sentence that composed itself unaided. He jotted it down in his bedside notebook and reread it every night before going to sleep. When he was up, he was afraid. When he was in bed, he was distracted—more than ever—bewitched by this implacable sentence.

The sea had receded quietly, calmly. He was seated on the bed. All of a sudden, he had the extraordinary feeling that he was being written by the night. He shivered violently. Ah, he said to himself, every text should be final: he himself is final.

Was he sleeping at that very moment? The night watched him dozing, feeling him, taking his breath. The fear of being lost forever. Once again, he shivered. In waves, simultaneous dreams flooded into his mind. He nearly sobbed. The night came and went under the sound of the sea which, though far away, had suddenly surged up. He plugged his ears. It was then that the words fluttered in a parade in front of him, then they came crashing down on top of one another: language was mad.

Get up? He couldn't: instead of the fragments of a word, there was room for nothing visible: the sea itself had sunk in the night. And in French—his foreign language—the word for "word," *mot,* is close to the one for "death," *la mort;* only one letter is missing: the succinctness of the impression, a syllable, the ecstasy of a stifled sob. Why did he believe that language is more beautiful, more terrible, for a foreigner?

He calmed down instantly when an Arabic word, *kalma,* appeared, *kalma* and its scholarly equivalent, *kalima,* and the whole string of its diminutives, which had been the riddles of his childhood: *klima . . .* The diglossal *kal(i)ma* appeared again without *mot*'s having faded away or disappeared. Within him, both words were observing each other, preceding what had now become the rapid emergence of memories, fragments of words, onomatopoeias, garlands of phrases, intertwined to the death: undecipherable. The scene is still silent. And when he speaks, he will wear himself out in amnesia, dragged down by a prodigious weakness, forgetting even the words that are most often used in one or the other of his languages.

He thought of the sun and even in doing so its name, that of the moon, inverted itself—from feminine to masculine—in his double language. Inversion which makes words wheel with the constellations, making for a strange attraction of the universe. So saying, he believed he was explaining to himself his obsession with androgyny, attracted and repulsed by the same set of charms.

Impregnable love. At every moment, the foreign language, whose power is limitless, can draw back into itself, beyond any translation. He told himself, I am a midground between two languages: the closer I get to the middle, the further I am from it.

A foreigner, I must become attached to everything which exists on and under the earth. Language belongs to no one, it belongs to no one and I know nothing about anyone. In my mother tongue, didn't I grow up as an adopted child? From one adoption to another, I thought I was language's own child.

Bi-langue? My luck, my own individual abyss and my lovely amnesiac energy. An energy I don't experience as a deficiency, curiously enough. Rather, it's my third ear. Had I experienced some kind of breakdown, I liked to think I would have developed in the opposite direction, I would have grown up in the dissociation peculiar to any unique language. That's why I admire the gravity of the blind man's gestures and the desperate impossible love the deaf man has for language.

Yes, I spoke, I grew up around the Only One and the Name, and the Book of my invisible god should have ended within me. Extravagant second thought which stays with me always. This idea imposes itself as I write it: every language should be bilingual! The asymmetry of body and language, of speech and writing—at the threshold of the untranslatable.

From that moment, the scenario of the doubles was created. One word: now two: it's already a story. Speaking to you in your own language, I am yourself without really being you, fading away in the tracks you leave. Bilingual, I am henceforth free to be entirely so and on my own behalf. Freedom of a happiness which divides me in two, but in order to educate me in thoughts of nothingness. I know nothing and this nothing is twofold. I forget and that is already amnesia. When I lose my head, the madness collapses into its depths. This madness which denies as it affirms itself in a double foundation which is itself transitory keeps me in good health: truth and madness, both infinite.

(This beginning of a text seemed to consume the storyteller, who read it ceaselessly. Each time he approached this beginning, which excluded him: a story with no protagonist: or if there was one, it was the story itself, which heard itself utter the lone command: Start over.)

Translation from French by Richard Howard

COMMENTARY

history is a word / ideology a word / the unconscious a word / words flutter about / in the mouths of the ignorant / though each sign perpetuates itself / unavoidable freshness / don't fly away in your own words / don't fade away into those of the others / measure your thought's blood / because for your question / you'll find only moving targets / the act draws the word / as the bow consumes the crystalline arrow
A.K.

(1) Without a doubt one of the major intellectual figures—as an essayist, novelist, playwright, & poet—of the late twentieth century in the Maghreb & well beyond, Abdelkebir Khatibi was born in El Jadida (western Morocco) in 1938 & died in Rabat in 2009. (During the final stages of his illness, a measure of the high regard in which he was held was visible in the personal concern of King Mohammed VI, who directed his transfer to Morocco's premier medical facility, Sheikh Zayed Hospital.) He taught at Mohammed V University in Rabat, where he also directed the Institute for Sociology & the University Institute for Scientific Research. A member of the Moroccan Writers Union since 1976, he was the editor in chief of the *Bulletin économique et social du Maroc* while also directing the review *Signes du présent*. He authored more than twenty-five works, including *La Mémoire tatouée* (Denoël, 1971); *L'Art calligraphique de l'Islam* (Gallimard, 1976) (see p. 255); *Le Roman maghrébin* (Maspéro, 1968); *Le Livre du sang* (Gallimard, 1979); *Le lutteur de classes à la manière taoïste* (Sindbad, 1979), extracted above; *Amour bilingue* (Fata Morgana, 1983), also extracted above; *Figures de l'étranger dans la littérature française* (Denoël, 1987); *Un été à Stockholm* (Flammarion, 1990); *Penser le Maghreb* (Societe marocaine des editeurs reunis, 1993); *La civilisation marocaine,* coedited with Mohamed Sijelmassi (Actes Sud/Sindbad, 1996); *La langue de l'autre* (Les Mains secrètes, 1999); & *Quatuor poétique: Rilke, Goethe, Ekelof, Lundkvist* (Al Manar, 2006). La Différence in Paris is presently publishing his collected works.

(2) As he writes in *Quatuor poétique* concerning poetry & silence: "The paradox of language & of the poet obeys this feeling of magical disquiet. The poet feels that the language he speaks & that speaks him has been lent him, as if it would be withdrawn by extortion or by the weight of the silence that feeds, in moments of distress, his difficulty of living. The vow of silence—absolute or relative—he demands is what founds the man of solitude, that singular experience of the poet & his taciturn double."

Mohammed Khaïr-Eddine (Tafraout, 1941–Rabat, 1995)

HOROSCOPE

the wheel of the sky kills so many eagles save you
blue blood
who stray in this heart anointed with hyena brains
simple roadways—from mica derives a fresh childhood
and skinks my fingers of old nopal
as a star knotted peril into my belly buttons
old nopal
badly crowned by my wayless false adult dreams
the simoom does not deign revise my hatred
for whom I speak of transmutations in trance
for whom I erect a thunderbolt in early morning's gray wall

cadavers—that among the basil where I gorge myself
on the used oil of geological fears
opens up in an about-turn
the oblivion cell itches under my thumb's nail
the wheel of the sky and the cheap virgins
through the fetid bars of the cage of my throat
through my voice becomes swamp stealthily endorsing
a story of a pearly handle
through the bitter milk of peregrinations

I puncture you pygmy famines
in a rhythm in which the hands fall silent
I crush you
men-sleep-stiff-silos

you vomit our white teeth dirtying
the expensive china via my scared bloods
of a tiny noon from where rockets my populous knoll

earth under my tongue
earth
like the peasant's logic
silence sawing through the heads of moons falling
into my serpent caresses
and bite the custom officer's black lips full on
spurted from a bastard outside of corruptible vinestock
stay friend anyway
all time crook
of your tightenings of dilapidated algae
of your norms
of your sale of names having kept
a sparkle of the pure crystal of the names
of those dives full your twenty legs
of your moistness
leaves like a wing

for you Europe manufactures an asthma of sand
and drainpipes
Europe
with its fatal rat's tail
goes outside to hear winter's last act
the miracle does not bribe the wheel of the sky

INDICTMENT

when the poem shall be sated with the tarantulas' white honey and a bad
    star's albumen
hopelessly exploding under the coke of my diets
when the Berbers post-all fantasia
shall throw their calabashes into the nothingness of the carbines
a conspiracy of eagles hatched by the true cipher
of gratitude and joy
shall sign my humid fever like the milky
april of the almond and the torrent

when the widowers shall move the gray heart of the minaret
when the children shall embrace the scorpions on their spike
then the prose of exile will be sufficiently tempered
to cut my anguish's umbilical cord
and sever the paddles that beat my fatigue's backbone into delirium
I'll stretch you out
little world of nostalgias
on the wrecker gaze of the still hale and
fit dead
who at the chapter on heinous crimes read
the arachnids' indictment

from *I, BITTER*

He comes to terms with the devil. But he will no longer exist for us. The year went by between collective work and sanguine rumors. Everyone at my place. But I didn't feel alone enough. And yet I riveted them to my putrefied skin. I feed a guy who forgets spits fistulas at the good blood of heaven greener than gabbed. I erode crumbling into vast gluttonies and laughter, very studied. I strap them up mentally. I no longer listen to him; he clucks knowing that his caiman eggs have been sucked empty. The sour one plays with them in his belly. I issue a national death certificate and I make his seat crack.

Then he imagines himself dead laid out stiff in the process of sucking the soils that had never forgiven him. He was blistering under his skin. It was a much more wary laughter. He quartered us in his internal death. Not one word came out of him, not one. Maybe he was versifying while our heads baptized them Ax, Anthill, Nail. He waited for his coffin to be on our shoulders to see us sweat. *Voui z'il crottait.* Again, the dilettante earth! She ate me free of charge. They saw asthma rising. They gave themselves over to the most rancid copulation. Gutted time in a tree's nothingness. Thundered in the biliary gold of the rocks up front calling everything rat that crawled in the dust and at the foot of bars. The tumbler drowned even the water. Lukewarm my night crossed the boundary of being. But nothing resembled a festival. The lamps (there were none) would have given God's blood to spy on me. The next day I went to the cemetery to check if I was still there. I was neither in the entranceway's flagstone nor in the trees that were listening and distilling even the smallest of my movements. The birds had stopped to admonish the ground and the squares of grass. Everything was getting back to normal. Inside themselves things were railing against one another. He had done his book without warning me, but I knew that every second spent outside him was a life that didn't flow. He was fateless. The world of the roads, no matter its variety, tolerated him too much to permit him anything but an altercation. And yet he'd fold back upon himself and he screamed at himself, scratched his nerves and invented a decent death for himself. A real toad, half screech, half coo. How could that toad have cawed? Language, speech in fact, is treated as if it were the dish of daily grub. Everything's numbered, ciphered, my head included. So he'd reached his goal. What remained was to pierce the ears of the bushes. His country was traveling. His house? Nonexistent. Here and there a clamor rose that he had killed his gods and cut his mother's glottis. To honor his decrepitude, they had even erected ten new mosques bedecked the emptiness of his stature but he sent a pack of hyenas and the best tusks at his disposal to patiently gnaw away at the sacred stone. It had been said that he would not have any kind of ancestor.

Midnight. The alcoholic no one needs. She dragged him along to get his bone scraped and stuff a belly that spent its time watching television in a pool of piss and maybe picks his nose or dives head forward damning a heaven that I didn't know even though I had based my colic on it. She imagined him capable of building a paradise in his very ruins. A simple hearth with meadows to rip out your eye and ear while you're asleep. But he fell down stiff soon as she neighed. He burned up Africa in his kidneys and the blood chased from his heart. It was a seething of fermented fevers. Not a scream but a thunderclap or Hiroshima their damned glory. Not a star that smites you and modifies the lines of your hands. No, not even a man! That he had never been. They'd wanted to make him into one of those who asks only to stuff himself. He would have been incapable of dealing with that condition. An unqualifiable body that dispossessed itself continuously. A permanent torture or a scribe. A bird-man-stone whose movements atrophied everything that would have made it look like a human being. He had studied the concept of crime. For him crime was nothing less than a writing. A writing that couldn't be bothered with alphabetic signs. He didn't wage a guerrilla war either but a cyclone of sand-blast-God-get-your-feet-caught-in-the-trap. If he wrote, it was a tornado that stammered at you:

She sings only to displease me,
The gal who burps! A true statue
that had to be deciphered by a cannibal.
I dedicate that to those who can't,

those who don't tolerate being seen together.
And yet see you tomorrow in the great shebeen
where nobody ever enters.
This gent was laughing, forgetting himself.
Comrades who are waging war! You, guilty?

But while he was searching for the order which neither cement nor beaten earth could have erected, they slashed his arms, forcing him to devour himself. He had written that while discarnating himself, he, knocked out, Mister Useful-refusal-for-our-cause; we'll have to shoot him down sooner or later; we'll sleep on top of his debris of nightdog-incision-serpent-clock-that-bleats! When a man does as we do and does not find the means to change his body, he's an anarchist, you say! You worry yourself silly to know how to respond to what is not made out of your own matter. You'll be picked up by the street cleaners or the police. They'll detoxicate you with or without your consent. His burning body hit the road signs, the night of sweat and sperm and the red glowworms lighting up everything except the telephone poles! Her breast of earth of sap boiled impregnating her voice and her inaudible snore; she on the beach that I don't know, on a bed of tobacco leaves. No doubt we both mildewed there—and no other glue. This body dangling from my rhombi and feet swaying at the end of a rope that ate the lice of the nomad erasing darkness after ejaculation the lion's eyes breaking in the ground teeth broken by thirty reins and a few centuries of royalties that have never been in order with themselves. Twelve thousand prisoners who have their plasma burned. Often easily identified with rebels another title he claims. A few palaces bank accounts to avoid the ruin of the half-starved hillock. And his body what about his body. No one maybe has ever observed it closely enough. Write: His giving body given the epicenter opened the maw of the parricidal terrain And his snoring body in my body countering the ambushes The king finished his magotty toilet fed his bleaks the fishing hooks were rare a king doesn't get enamored easily of industries other than those that manufacture arms imported from Italy Let's not mention that prick! He doesn't even merit being called *surexistant* He knows his business all too well He strews too much feeling all over the carpet not to foreclose you and at the same time he is wary of stool pigeons, givers, donors They don't hesitate to cloister him Sabotaging the smallest pebble drinking the fraternal sperm of the public writers directly from their pricks directly from the belief in the unbelievable and during it all from the vermicular belt of a devil who hastens every end undermining the tree Let him enlighten himself! Not go anywhere except into the always absent silence! LET'S CUT HIM DOWN! He didn't want to hit the bull's-eye He doubted not only us but other wrecks as well that viciousness and rage will be but an unforeseeable tornado Listen you asses I bemoan the Blood-big-as-my-scepter Enormously the Adventure is so strong If you enter you will not leave again He writes caustically errs gives orders cuts up cracks without ever finishing himself off completely Oyez! Pour beer into his inkwell. Polish the shoes of his nothingness. Hasten your death. I want to remain alone my birds copulate on the rock finally locked and bolted. Where are you from? Dictate that they should rearm! That they fault the strophe low or the stone machine. In my palace only fresh breasts torn from the tree of science circulate. I have bought women and film directors without talent. Talent is in exile. All Africa won't put up with any. No one's on the heels of Mister Talent. He worries only the guinea pigs who drug themselves by themselves but we all admit that a people of talents doesn't suit the powers that be Talent leaves me cold but don't think that it preoccupies me Don't think that it makes uneasy cripples or kinglets me I'm exacerbated enough Let them simply forbid talent here It would grow in our clarity in the no-man's-land of our sun so beautifully situated and even cited in the prospectuses and by our real estate agents It is our soil & persistent phlegm It is also our desert nights that give it a place of honor above our heads Talent dies boorishly under our sun Let talent be born and grow in the cold and let's call our sun forbidden land

Translations from French by P.J.

COMMENTARY

All those who claim to be part of the avant-garde are fooling themselves. The avant-garde is everything that is being done in Africa.
M.K.-E.

The major Francophone poet of his generation, Mohammed Khaïr-Eddine was born in 1941 in Tafraout, southern Morocco, of Berber heritage. In 1961 he composed a major manifesto of contemporary Maghrebian literature, "Poésie Toute," that called for a "linguistic guerrilla" poetics, a program he was to stay faithful to all his life. One of the cofounders (with Abdellatif Laâbi) of the magazine *Anfas/Souffles* (Breaths), he lived in self-exile in France from 1965, returning to Morocco only in 1979. Khaïr-Eddine died in Rabat on November 18, 1995, Independence Day in Morocco. His core works (still untranslated into English, except for short extracts, & all published by Le Seuil) are *Nausée Noire* (1964), *Agadir* (1967), *Soleil Arachnide* (1969), *Moi, l'aigre* (1970), *Le Déterreur* (1973), *Une Odeur de mantèque* (1976), *Résurrection des fleurs sauvages* (1981), & *Légende et vie d'Agoun'chich* (1984). Strongly opposed to the regime of Hassan II, to religion, & to the cultural hegemony of Arabic, & an advocate for Berber culture, he quoted the Arabic historian Ibn Khaldun when asked about the cultural situation in the Maghreb: "When a habitation or a nation is Arabicized, it degenerates, and when it has degenerated, it is no longer inhabitable."

As one of us wrote in a memoir of M.K.-E., "What has remained with me . . . through all subsequent meetings with Khaïr-Eddine can be summed up in one word: intensity. A fierce intensity or an intense fierceness—it was often impossible to decide which it was. Here was someone totally gathered around, or rather, *in* a single point of focus, from inside out: a solar intensity radiating from somewhere deep inside, or better, gathering from *everywhere* inside (soul and skin, organs and bones, mind and blood) to radiate out through a gaze that concentrated the black sun of the interior, twin to the desert sun of his birthplace. Black suns may be more accurate, or as he put it in an early poem: 'My black blood contains a thousand suns.'"

Ali Sadki Azayku (Taroudant, 1942–2004)

NEIGHBOR TO LIFE

I am a neighbor to life
which hasn't spared me
but has grabbed me and
dunked me into the blood
of the living—
I drank little of it
but life still fires my heart
I desire and have nothing
my hand is far from Venus
I fight myself, get hold of myself again,
but, what shock?
I am the shadow of life,
a bramble bush in flames
there! the gift agitates me
the shackles fall away
and even if I'd braid
new ones
in resistant silk,
I'd still and always be this untamable
prey to tenacula!
that one who never finds himself

who can't quench his thirst
I am the wandering one
who sheds no tears
and if my laughter doesn't explode
it is because it has no true roots

THE SHADOWS

The stars bear witness to sidereal night
but it is rare for the moon
to bring light,
standing
at the gates of heaven.
Could god be absent? Could he have forgotten us?
I don't know. Earth
will breast-feed no one any more,
the heavens themselves reject us,
silence softens the field of our thirst . . .
But why don't my words come true?
We will not harvest on someone else's land . . .
Our spring does not dry up, we have found again
the old banner.
Where are the waters? The sorcerer
has bumped up against them for a long time.
The watchtower is cracking, men spy
on one another,
the cerastes that bites me dies.
For it is the poison of the soul that roots my life . . .
Have you ever seen a flower with no stem and no root?
Wherever the sun may appear, the pitfalls
encumber my path.
Buried under rocks, we don't even see the
light of dawn anymore . . .
But why don't my words come true?
So let us reap, let's take the harvest
from our field . . . it's been a long time
that we haven't plowed

Translations by P.J. of French versions by Mohammed Khaïr-Eddine from the original Berber

MOTHER TONGUE

Amazigh is my mother tongue
Understood by no one.
Pregnant with meaning,
Who can dance to its rhythms?
Alone, I struggle on.
My tongue is being slowly strangled
To death,
And yet lives on,
Speaks tirelessly to those who cover their ears
So as not to hear.
Thirst should be slaked
Amazigh is my mother tongue.
Rejected by everyone.
Some say that it is but a dream
And forsaking us, add
"One that will never come true."
Others mutter
"Your tongue has a painful and bitter past
and people do not want to share your sufferings"
Amazigh is my mother tongue
It longs to break the wall of silence
To set hearts ablaze
And make them flame like stars united
In the heavens above.

Rabat, April 1978

Translation from French by Wendy Ouali

COMMENTARY

(1)   Wrote Claude Lefébure in *Mediterraneans* 11, "Voices from Morocco" (Winter 1999–2000), translated from French by Wendy Ouali for Mondeberbere. com: "Ali Sadki, nicknamed 'Azayku' because his parents were members of a Berber-speaking tribe from the Izyuka (located between Agadir and Tiznit), was born in 1942. He first went to school in Tafingult, to the south of Tizi n Test, where his teachers were French. He then attended the nationalist Pasha School in Marrakech. At about eighteen years old, when he was at the Regional Primary Teachers Training College in the same town, he suddenly felt himself to be 'Berber,' as if he were coming out of a trance. At the beginning of the 1962 autumn school term, he was sent to teach in Imi n Tanut. . . . Azayku then [1970] went to Paris to attend Lionel Galand's Practical School for Further

Studies into, and the Teaching of, Berber at Langues O [Institut national des langues et civilisations orientales]. Returning to Rabat, he taught history at university and was an active member of the Moroccan Research and Cultural Exchange Association (AMREC), which rose from the ashes of the educational support programme. . . . In 1981, having left AMREC, Azayku founded, together with Mohammed Chafik of the Royal Academy, the Amazigh Cultural Organisation, run mostly by people from the Middle Atlas Mountains. The conference/debate on Berber civilisation, held in the presence of Léopold Sédar Senghor, Mahjoubi Aherdane, Minister of State, Chafik, Chaouki, Moatassime and so on, had undeniable repercussions. The short-lived Association published, in the space which should belong to the Berber language, the first part of a study by Azayku. The second part, published in April 1982 in Aherdane's magazine, was worth twelve months of prison for the historian-poet. . . . Ali Sadki Azayku published two volumes of poetry written in Arabic characters—*Timitar* (Tessaries or Tokens), a collection of 33 poems published in 1989, and *Izmulen* (Scars), published in 1995. . . . Around twenty of his poems have been set to music and performed by Ammouri Mbarek, the reviver of Moroccan Berber music. Ali Sadki Azayku passed away on the 10th of September, 2004 after a long illness."

(2) Mohammed Khaïr-Eddine called Azayku "an excellent Amazigh poet, but also a high-ranking Moroccan intellectual. . . . He lives in the ice rocks among the stars, in that dry and bare nature that links him to Mallarmé."

Abdellatif Laâbi (b. Fez, 1942)

I'm not the nomad
searches for the well
the sedentary has dug,
I drink little water
and walk
apart from the caravan.

LE SPLEEN DE
CASABLANCA, P. 14

THE PORTRAIT OF THE FATHER

The portrait of the father
has taken its place on the wall
behind me
I am alone
in my closed room

My wife has gone to work
Yet
a hand comes to caress my neck
gently
like a bird's feather
The taste of childhood
rises to my mouth

THE ANONYMOUS POET

Is it my voice
or that of an anonymous poet
come from the dark centuries
When did I live
On what earth
Which woman did I love
With what passion
But who can say
that it wasn't I who was a woman
and that I didn't know any man
because I was too ugly
or just not attracted
to men
Did I fight
for
against something
Did I have the faith
of children
Did I die young
not understood, miserable
or too old, surrounded, adulated
hero of a tribe preparing
to conquer the world
Did my works survive me
Did my language die
before being written down
But first off was I bard
or sluggard
priest

professional mourner
navigator
jinn or adamite
erudite oriental dancer
playing the lute in a harem
Maybe I was only
an obscure artisan a saddler
who had never ridden a horse
and who sang
laboring all day long
to soften the leather between his hands
and make for beautiful handiwork
the rich will bestride
So who was I
for my words to redouble
so that the evil double
that holds their reins
traps me
with this question that isn't one:
is it your voice
or that of an anonymous poet
come from the dark centuries?

LETTER TO FLORENCE AUBENAS

Walled in
Your heart goes on beating
Deep in the darkness
In your heart
An eye has opened
It sees what we no longer know how to see:
The executioner's snarl
That lies in wait in each of us
The face of innocence
Trampled underfoot by the horde
The spark of compassion that alone
Can illuminate us from the inside
The hand that opens
For tenderness to burst forth

Like a fresh spring
The sign of recognition
Before the melting of the human metals
In the prodigious act of love
The mouth without makeup
From which will flow
The words of truth so rare
The seven letters that more than speak
Of our sovereign liberty
Walled in
In their own darknesses
Your jailers camp outside time and the world
Of their humanity
They only have a vague remembrance
They have no other members
Than their weapons
No other head
Than the boiling cauldron of their hate
No other heart
Than the pumice stone used to sharpen their knives
Walled in
In their own darknesses
Your jailers don't know what they are doing
And we forget the nights
To count only the days
Spinning in the violently lit circus
Of our insipid liberties
We think of you Florence
While hoping that an eye will open in our heart
And reveal to us
What we no longer know how to see:
Our daily gestures of small predators
That rarely don't know themselves
The color of the lie
Spread over the whole palette of discourse
The irremediable crack in our planet
To better separate
The elected ones from the misfits
The solid web
Of the spider of indifference
That slowly encircles our faculties

The bars against which we hit our foreheads
Watching the caravan
Of our dreams go by in the distance
Walled in
Your heart continues to beat
In your heart
The eye that opened
Now sees into us
It rereads our history
Translating it into all the languages
Generous prince
It even corrects its mistakes
And cautions us
To write a new page
Inspired by the lesson of the darknesses
Finally enthroning reason and its lights
You see
Florence
It is you
Who come to rescue us!

Créteil, March 2005

Translations from French by P.J.

COMMENTARY

(1) In 1966 the young poet Abdellatif Laâbi (born in the city of Fez in 1942) called the magazine he founded with a few friends—Mohammed Khaïr-Eddine (see p. 659) & Mostafa Nissabouri (see p. 673) among them—*Souffles,* meaning "breaths." *Souffles* immediately became & remained the great North African avant-garde poetry magazine of the period. It took one's breath away & indicated changes that were being made in Maghrebian poetry & changes that needed to be made in the life of the people—that is, it could not but be a politically revolutionary magazine too. The absolute seriousness of Laâbi & his friends concerning this need for change did not escape the notice of the state, & the magazine was eventually censored & Laâbi thrown into jail in 1972, tortured, & submitted to all the humiliations a dictatorship will submit its opponents to. He survived & kept writing poems, letters, a continuous & courageous witness to his & his society's fate. In 1980 he was released, & in 1985 he moved to Paris, where he still lives—though in recent years he has been spending more time in Morocco—in that permanent exile that seems to be the lot of so many of the twentieth century's best poets & doers. (A poet, from the Greek *poesis,* "to make, to do," is or should be—& in Laâbi's case is indeed—

a doer, an activist.) Laâbi's oeuvre now comprises some fifty books: poems, novels, plays, memoirs, & more. City Lights published *The World's Embrace: Selected Poems* in 2003.

(2) Laâbi, without a doubt the major Francophone voice in Moroccan poetry today, writes with a quiet, unassuming elegance that holds & hides the violence any act of creation proposes. Every creation is of course a breaking apart, a making of fragments—making *is* breaking—something Laâbi states ab initio in his poem *Forgotten Creation:* "In the beginning was the cry / and already discord." And this poem—as does most of his vast oeuvre—follows the movements of this cry, tracing its starts & stops, circling its essential enigma, descrying all the false mysteries & hopes & fantasies it gives rise to, despite itself. Creating itself, the poem learns that "where nothing is born / nothing changes" & that eternity is but "an impenetrable jar / no magic will open." But the poem, Laâbi insists, will get us inside this act of imaginative creation.

Mostafa Nissabouri (b. Casablanca, 1943)

from *APPROACH TO THE DESERT SPACE*

I

Your country when it lingers on
in orphaned syllables
that country now belongs to a patrimony of absence
so elusive is it between musings
veiled at times by echoes from the plain
and a cypress stands on the slope of a hill
to keep the horizon in balance
and so that all around time
may be forever still

But you in the middle
standing in an affinity of tombs
you seem
the same anonymous traveler
the traveler long ready you claim
for the solemn observation of dunes
the one with a shadow seemingly revisited
in its profound texture
its essential prolongations
who has seen the restless latitude

the insistence of the desert space
where the body can no longer demand belonging
set out from this ambivalent structure
this fragmented perspective
this field of unknowing

Others have a shadow on the earth
in analogy with matter light and space
without being pursued to the limits
of all dissimilarities

Then you are taken with the desire to define right here
the ultimate metaphor in words that amalgamate
vaguely the position of the stars
with the stumbling points of denials
that approximately locate the axis
reserved for the occultation of its own matter
under a sky still linked to a telluric disorder
where each place has preserved
an unchanging moon incorporated
like a supreme incrustation
for an ineffable metrics of the desert

metaphor from the conifer and laurel rose
that together they may represent
the portico reserved for the study of the stars
from the trees producing on the bough side
an irruption of recollection
to the point of endowing memory at each step
with a conformity exuberant like the dunes
like the sermons of the past the confessions of atonement
mixed with an expectation of miracles
an incessant communion between notebooks of wandering
and incidentally a surrection of imperishable calligraphies
perpetuating through their romance
a sort of rhetoric of desire
hidden behind tufts of horehound
. . .

like a coincidence of foam with a country
that never stops catching up with itself
or getting lost starting over then getting lost again
inscribed each time in a decisive finality before

being devolved into words that have not been said
into fragments of words still clouded with their silence
into the gloss of sediment even in books
bound in dreams skin and blue with extinguished constellations

9

An approximate desert activated
in its primacy over any other expanse
until such time as my silence
may inaugurate it

the immensity to spare itself misunderstandings about
burial grounds
incarnations of cities
increasingly unrecognizable
as their inflated ruins are interpreted

about figurations of stone that completely absorb the entire site
haggard telluriums
sketched out by a nomadic and parcellary
oceanic system of the same words the same fragments
as gradual as the body I inhabit

. . .

it is the prolongation of the same raw territory
to the climax of deletions
dream punctuated by a thousand elsewheres
an alternative to a single night
enclosed in the vertebrae
with the feeling of this expectant measure
bound to the propagation of apocryphal lands
commingled with the eruption of the lentiscus
the forgetting of origins
and as an order of refutation in an arid sovereignty

itinerary free of otherwise more removable regions
major for its intermittences refractory for its roots
backcountry in the mobility of the preterit
should my speaking ever be articulated
through the angle of generic meandering
in a sustained persistence of fossilized archways
in which the permanently closed sky
sealed with terra-cotta wagers

dominated by its relationship with the other sky pursuing
a coercive blueness over the tops of the palm trees
and which lives on the fringe neither within nor without
disengaged from an auroral remainder but subordinate
to disruptions in the crossing
though all other realities have turned into
repetitive dunes
that it oscillates between the edges of writing
and the deeply established horizon of antithetical shorelines
attributing sight to graves
submerged in paradoxical night
. . .

dreams displacing thousands of tents
thousands of territories
and that our miracular sediments
could instantly radiate waking
provided they were overflown by its vibratile dimension
as if diffused from some deep recollection
refracted from the stellar bath at the source of wandering nebulae
and anchoring nowhere
is not organic complexity forging anterior seasons from a stationary body
or reclusion preoccupying evolution as each voyage ends
or which owing to antimony suggests
the pathos of a pure legendary face
only to reach us in spite of meridian suspensions
as the high place of syzygies as prerogative
of the hill-borne juniper
as perception of these geographies
simultaneously paramnesia and shadowed vagaries
withdrawn into a distant environment

ultimate compensation of stone attentive
in its atony
to some scattered divinity
and with it space devoted to the paradoxes of refusal
without the deambillations of the recent past
without all of these meditations
starting from the absence of citadels and the mental
coupé of its first water

A transitional vanity is given to him whose identity can barely contain
so many purely latent places; this multiplication of reference points is

marked by a seeming irreality, like a landscape increasingly chaotic in
relation to waking, a sky seemingly suffering from eccentricity in its
disparate molecules, a seemingly fragmented horizon, there aren't even
any travelers that we might postulate ourselves through regions otherwise
endowed with schizogenic virtues, regions so infinitely fertile that day
and night are unrecognizable; a seeming desire to declare the advent
of dissimilarities is initiated, a desire to reinvent for the consolidation
of signs a seeming hour of immanent apocalypse and an affection for
reviving transfigured forms of nostalgia for a new chain of appurtenances,
with the introduction of an ectoplasmic lesson for the metallic shadow
it will disclose over the legibility of despair, and for proof which, on the
imperious call of the desert, founds burning.
A pilgrimage can only be retrospective of processes combining cognitive
geographies and the shadowy environment which will immediately serve
to refute them;
like a place perceptible in its variations, this place a twilight word
divorced from its roots, with artificially hybrid travels, all the more
uncompromising in that it gradually dispels the entire specter of reality
which consolidates its patrimony—the putrid eye of the sun staring
fixedly at appropriated seas, a witness to the fossilization of all these
placental expanses whose interference has steeped the soul of my language
in laughter and blasphemy.
There are only stops, isolated perspectives in the recurrence of a single
approximation of the outside, there is only an equal space in which the
geometry of day displaces the same fascination with the arid in a memory
of things which no longer exists.
All is reverie, image, metamorphosis, a convulsion of clouds, a process of
dereliction with only silence to offer as pasture to wastelands;
this entire reiteration of moments at the very edge of experience, comparative
stopovers, contradictory dreams, all is derivation of a single, unique remark
placed as if each morning it were the fact of a new articulation of fevers
and not just the privileged place through which the moon and stars may be
evacuated, other suns may open like towering peonies;
all is monopolized by diffused lands, leaving no place for lost genealogies,
fundamental latitudes, or the country in its projection of a tree clouded
in a position to foster confidence as far as its drift very far as far as the
napping slum.
All is negation, charge taking of a now hypothetical crossing, contingent
chance, memory expulsion, amnesic sacrament, through a system of
manuring with native flowers, cinnabar and indigo flowers splashing the
woods with tall, ancient clocks like so many delirium-tapping machines,
and which until dawn pursue the activity of a story in which wild olive

trees and cyst-constellated underbrush are indecently profiled; all is
negation, simulacrum, underlying desert, exegesis of memory with no
other finality than memory itself, which encompasses Iram of the Columns
and the sanctuaries housing imputrescible bodies, the one exhibited for
the understanding of beings and things, the one that reaches its highest
point just as psycho-cosmic mountains erupt with a view to the dereality
of travel, seasons, and to act from the infinitely small to the infinitely large
by erasing all traces of evolution;
all is confined to the narrowness of a sigh, to a methodic ritual that
uniformly resumes fantasies, folk typologies, metaphors as a means
of making debris sacred, dolls adorned with tiny bells, embalmed,
subliminal duration with talismanic virtues, in a single, unique cycle of
tears and abandon;
all is obsessive fear of a thousand sessions devoted to these final chronicles
relating journeys cataloged as an illusory, agonizing repertoire, infinitely
listenable, like the noise of centuries running aground near my memory
in a succession of trawling topographies radiant with lost suns, faltering
stars, the sky a prolongation of a dream that refuses to end, spread out
over unsustainable expanses then carried ever farther on drifting dorsal
fins;
and the entire present would capsize, instantly losing some of its
consistency, its reassuring proximity; we me ourselves in a situation of
complete distortion with respect to our own existential experience; there
is no beginning no end no voyage as if the origin of every thing were
shrouded in a sort of mercurial night exuded by coastal borders
duration constantly renewed
by its network of ruptured sequences
plethora of dunes on the periphery of silence
which can only be inscribed
as the frontier zone of regions caught in identical images
in an impossible statement
which draws its resources
from its own displaced matter
from the same, always extreme place
bordering on that of roots

which is this nowhere whose desert
at my side is the shattered incidence
like an allegorical I
that never stops being multiple

Translation from French by Guy Bennett

Born in 1943, Mostafa Nissabouri is a core representative of contemporary Francophone Moroccan poetry, a cofounder—with Abdellatif Laâbi (see p. 668) & Mohammed Khaïr-Eddine (see p. 659)—of the magazine *Souffles* & later the editor of *Intégral*. Writes James Kirkup, who has translated some of his work: "His language, French, is both classical in its vocabulary and surreal in its style and in the play of its images. Mixed in among concrete and abstract terms, one finds specialized vocabularies belonging to botany, oceanography, geography and medicine. . . . The violent uprushes of his sonorous French remind me of the improvisations of the tellers of tales on the public squares of Fez and Marrakech." Nissabouri has published a number of volumes of poetry, most recently *Approche du désertique* (Al Manar, 1999) & earlier three major collections, *La mille et deuxième nuit, Rupture,* & *Aube.* He has said of his approach to writing: "I don't write *for,* I write *against.* . . . I remain strongly convinced that a true revolution is the result of the destruction of mental structures and consequently of those of language itself, the number one enemy of DESIRE."

Abdelmajid Benjelloun (b. Fez, 1944)

THE FLUTE OF ORIGINS, OR THE TACITURN DANCE

This image is dear to the Sufis: we must through love of God rise up to heaven in tandem with the Qur'an descending.

Listen to this beautiful phrase of a mystic: the believer must be proof of God.

Poetry is also the precise language of getting lost.

When I listen to enchanting music I shake my head as if telling all the pain of my life to my angels.

The raw flower of love.

All my loves are in danger of truth.

The woman suddenly beautiful.

What is happening to this woman is simply an aggravation of her smile.

We must from time to time order our freedom to drift, a question of religious hygiene.

If you want to know how Arabs love, watch them listening to Oum Koultoum.

ETERNITY COMES DOWN ON THE SIDE OF LOVE

I don't love myself although I am my closest neighbor.

The image of a man leaping on the Moon is no more extraordinary than the immobile stone.

This man is ill. His illness is social. His illness is called hate. He lives, but takes care of himself by hating others.

This comic copies someone who doesn't exist.

It's the barque shows the waves in the sea.

Peace is not for export, war is.

There are curtesies rendered for lack for nobleness.

She brings me a glass of thirst. She drinks it with me.

My hands complete, O wonder, the stone in her breasts!

Rock drawings await me at a young girl's. I must copy them onto my life. Whether she knows it or not.

Steps, sparks on the journey.

Silence, a side effect of the infinite.

Funny: the raindrop fallen on a tree keeps clinging to the branch before dropping to the ground.

A certain poet withdraws into the world.

What I love in this Flemish painter: he paints the inaudible.

A stone: feet planted in silence, head in immobility.

Inert, the stone can face the absolute.

Inertness rises from the stone like the very first dream.

For the stone, immobility is work.

A WOMAN TO LOVE AS ONE WOULD LOVE TO REVIVE AFTER DEATH

I'm only a sketch of myself. The finished work is with God.

The soul: a chaos of light.

God must have revealed himself to the first humans in dreams.

I am in the world and at the same time in myself: is there geometry more beautiful?

Every word is an amazement of truth.

In a quiet corner of the future we'll all die. Modestly.

To die, to be a little nap ahead of the others.

There are mysterious ties between a word and its sense. When the word is too strong it has almost no sense. Take for example *death*.

I've always regarded orgasm as a fantastic flight of birds toward a closed horizon.

Woman: love's windfall.

At moments, I catch myself thinking that the word incarnates its spirit.

What if the stars were just kisses lost among all the kisses of lovers?

In alleys, the scent of women turns inordinate because it resembles a scream.

I'll surely die still sleepy, as usual.

Very often truth triumphs only when not declared.

The perfect glance: things looking at us.

I'll not be famous or a doctor, no woman will die for love of me, no street bear my name, I'll not write books or be written about, will not be remembered, my life will be laughable, but at least I'll have my name on my tombstone.

O my riotous, elusive bridal guardian, when will we put wit in our wishes?

A young girl sleepwalks in a dance and already in a flood of caresses, and surely in a notch of a song. I would like to please her scent. I would like to assure her happiness. I would like her quick clay flower.

Translations from French by Rosmarie Waldrop

Born 1944 in Fez, Abdelmajid Benjelloun is a Francophone poet, a historian, & a painter who teaches law at the University of Rabat. Abdellatif Laâbi suggests that, influenced by surrealism in his beginnings, Benjelloun has developed a body of work exclusively using the form of the poetic aphorism. This trajectory only seems paradoxical, for with him the rigor of the aphorism comes accompanied by an excessive language bursting with bewildering images, all leading up to what one might be tempted to describe as philosophical humor. "My spontaneity is wrought," he says, which Salah Stétié caught so well when he introduced one of Benjelloun's collections: "In a few words he goes to the essential. He writes in scars. His sentences, like those of Rimbaud, sum up an experience, and, we might say, once this experience is accumulated, he risks it on a throw of dice."

Tahar Ben Jelloun (b. Fez, 1944)

from **HARROUDA**

Seeing a vagina was the main concern of our childhood. Not just any vagina—not a bald, innocent vagina, but a full-grown woman's vagina. One that had lived and endured, one that had grown tired. The one that haunted our first dreams and first dares. The vagina whose name you speak in a deserted street and outline in the palm of your hand. The one you invoke for insults. The one you dream of making and reinventing. The streets of our neighborhood know it well. The walls have tamed it and the sky has made a place for it. On the effigy of this sex we ejaculate words.

We caress the damp smell that we imagine. We learn our first lessons in pain and we baptize the blood in warm hands. Soon they celebrated our entrance to manhood. Real bleeding. Real pleasure of supersensitive skin. We cross the street with a new wound and we lie in wait for solitude, for new fantasies. We glue them onto a page of writing. Laughter. Only laughter to connect what we have dared. Nothing of that sort on our faces, just white innocence and the sweetness of agreed-upon escape. A return to our homes and then silence. Simulation.

But who dares?

Who dares speak to this woman?

Harrouda appears only in daytime. At night she disappears somewhere into a cave. Far from town. Far from our traps. She reestablishes her pact with the Ogre and gives herself to him. All to him. Without making him pay the slightest death rattle. We remain convinced that in the middle of the night she escapes him to haunt the cafés. She keeps watch over our sleep and presides over our dreams. Fear of meeting her manipulates our bartered desires.

We wait for daylight, stroking our nervous penises. Morning is amnesia. We wrap everything into flight and set off on illusory exile. But Harrouda emerges from the walls. Naked and ugly. Dirty and ironic. Intrigue under her armpits. She begins by letting down her hair in front and spinning in place. Makes the Ogre's soul come and pierces it with her fingers. Swallows his white blood and turns to us, smiling conspiratorially. She winks, squeezes her breasts between her hands, and invites us to drink wisdom from them. The craziest one of us is also the boldest. He buries his head in that wrinkled chest and disappears only to emerge with a star in his hand. Sometimes, some of us never reappear. They are swallowed by this flesh that never flinches. Others tickle her tattooed navel and run away. The hand drawn on her forehead bursts forth like lightning and brings them back. Sighing loudly, Harrouda squeezes children's heads between her thighs. Bones crack, dissolve. A whitish liquid trickles down Harrouda's legs. The children get up a little stunned but happy with this new baptism. They leave singing.

But the spectacle is elsewhere: when she lifts her dress. We just have time to believe our eyes before the curtain is lowered already. The rest has to be discovered in our sleepless nights.

Adults laugh, provoke her, bury their fists in her vagina, withdraw them bloody, and then leave. They make her cry. We at least give her oranges and sugar. She says we are all her children and can sleep between her legs.

During the months of Ramadan, Harrouda makes herself scarce. In the name of Virtue, she is no longer tolerated in the city of all Virtues. Sometimes she can be seen emerging from an oven. Alone and sad, a little ashamed. She puts on a black veil and speaks to no one. Discreetly, she crosses the city walking alongside the Boukhrareb wadi.

Fasting insinuates itself into our empty mornings, offers us a new nausea that will consume us just before sunrise. Our censored dreams are put on hold. Purified down to our blood, we prepare ourselves for the twenty-sixth evening so we can listen to the speeches of angels perched on our shoulders.

The day of the celebration, Harrouda reappears. She is at the end of the metamorphosis that she has undergone for thirty days. She returns in the limbo of difference. She returns in the body of an eighteen-year-old virgin. Beautiful and happy. She crosses the city in her transparency. Flies at street level. We scarcely look. She declares the pride of her new finery: a spotless memory. It is up to us to drink purity with an uncertain gaze. But who will initiate us into reading the whispered word? Who will speak the tattooed language to us? We abandon words for looking and waiting. At night Harrouda is already drunk. She has lived. She comes to spread her excrement in the dark streets. Countdown. Time plays against her. Every passing hour ages her five years. Around midnight Harrouda has completed all her ages. The young girl of the morning is nothing but a memory now. She throws off her underclothes, undoes her hair, puts down her spotless memory, retraces her wrinkles, and nonchalantly leaves to distribute fantasies. Her breasts hang heavy and pendulous. She dyes them blue, urinates standing up against the wall, and breathes in her body odor deeply. With all her strength she breathes in the smell of sweat, wine, and urine mingled. The other memory is reinaugurated in the form of bleeding. Memories quiver in disorder, they provoke chaos and delirium. Harrouda leaves to find her mistresses and ask the owl for amnesia or at least a cessation of the irruptions. Once she has reached the city's border, she expels night from her throat. Her laughter makes it rain in the cemetery. The dead shift position and are interrogated again by the angels. Harrouda stumbles from one grave to another. Her skin peels off and falls in a slow movement on to the stone. Her hair stays plastered to the back of her neck. A bitter liquid holds it down. The bones move and pile themselves up on the wet grass. She just has time to vomit up the last dream. It is blue. Like death, it is blue and transparent. It is red. Like the sky, limpid and censored. The images that troop across her forehead are poured into her open mouth. Spring in a body. Seaweed in the mouth. Paving stones on the chest. Sea in exchange. Song at dawn. Plural voice. Instant separated. Deed in color. Dying bird. Veins empty out. Only the head remains in place. It barely holds up. Eye open. Imprinted cry. Simulated decomposition. The moon will bear witness.

Harrouda gets up, gathers her limbs into a bag, and leaves to join the Ogre, who is getting ready for war. The war which will seep into all our fissures.

We waited a long time before seeing Harrouda again in our streets. It should be said that our parents locked us up. Doors sealed shut. With a double lock. Ever since foreigners descended upon the city, we have lost the right to cross the threshold of our houses. Fear. Fear of getting hit by a stray bullet. Fear of being trampled by demonstrators. Fear of being carried off by the Ogre's henchmen. The war is elsewhere. The adults remain glued to their radios, listening to Radio Cairo. War or resistance, the days are no less changed.

Harrouda has returned, wrapped in the flag. She has imprisoned the Ogre and freed the children. Upright and proud, she walks on the roofs. On her forehead a tattooed star. One day we followed her to the river. She was dragging her body along and spitting blood. We saw her fight against a shadow, then she disappeared into a whirlwind. We remained powerless in our wait. She did not reappear. She was carried away.

At night we slept without dreaming. Harrouda was no longer on the roofs. We were orphans already. Our first trembling ejaculation filled our hand. We poured the liquid into a little flask. The flask was not big enough. We took a bottle. The bottle was not big enough. We took a jar, until the day we decided to disappear into the jar.

Translation from French by Charlotte Mandell

COMMENTARY

Born in Fez to a shopkeeper & his wife in 1944, Tahar Ben Jelloun is probably the best-known (in Europe & America, at least) North African novelist at work today. At eighteen he moved from Fez to Tangier to attend a French high school before enrolling at the Université Mohammed V in Rabat in 1963. It was at the university that his writing career began. Exposed to the journal *Souffles* & one of its founding editors, the poet Abdellatif Laâbi (see p. 668), Ben Jelloun wrote his first poems, publishing his first collection, *Hommes sous Linceul de Silence* (Atlantes), in 1971. After completing his philosophy studies in Rabat, in 1971, he immigrated to France, attending the Université de Paris & receiving a PhD in psychiatric social work in 1975. Although he has moved more & more toward the novel—work that one could criticize as being too mainstream French & that has received every possible accolade, including the Prix Goncourt, France's most coveted literary prize—early on, besides writing poetry, he edited an excellent poetry anthology, *La Mémoire Future: Anthologie de la Nouvelle Poesie du Maroc* (Maspero, 1976), which promoted the work of many of the avant-garde poets of *Souffles*. His early prose has the power of a poem, in that it is in a rich, charged language that does not pull its punches—never more so than in his first novel, *Harrouda* (not available in a full English translation), the opening chapter of which we present above.

Mohamed Sibari (b. Ksar el Kebir, 1945)

from **VERY FAR AWAY . . .**

From far away,
very far away,
& in a hiding place . . .
I praised her with my eyes
most of all when she knelt
before God & bowed.

.

I, Sinbad,
daring captain
who every sea have crossed
many a giant swell
& tidal wave
have tamed
have received
whether or not
it was meant for me
the mad love
of every siren.

.

When the snow's cold
vanishes from
the cruel & necessary winter
you appear, sweet
brilliant budding Spring,
you, who engender birds
& their dear longed for song,
with their perfume plus flower fragrance,
change the entire world.

CONFESSION

Father,
Since the last
Trip we took
My brother
Has not been the same.
The man has changed
His way of being.
Locked himself up
He has in his study
Writing night
& day, going
To bed at dawn.

He barely eats at all;
Asks only for pad & pen,
Demands them.
Is it witchcraft?
Has he been led astray?
No, dear woman, he has not,
Replied the priest.
Larache . . . my daughter,
& God forgive me for saying so,
Inspires even the dead.

LADY NIGHT

In the evening, her gaze
Mesmerized me
With its siren's spell,
When I saw her, a tamed animal,
On the streets of La Medina
I followed her . . .
& she was followed by her shadow
That danced
Inside her white silk robe,
Her flirtatious colorful slippers
Radiated joy,
& blessed the sky
For having separated such
A beautiful body
From the soil,
As she finds herself facing a step,
With her hands of fingers slender
As supernatural crystal.
Her jellaba
She slightly raised,
Revealing her twins
Of saline white,
Toasted softly
Like a vin rosé,
Guarded by Achilles, & with imagination

Gave her invitation to ascend
The columns
Toward the silver-plated ceiling of the narrows.
The rough waters behind her
Salvation was in Troy
The black tail of his horse
His shoulders forward facing
As she sat up
Her beautiful face transparent behind the veil
& her neck of a gazelle outstretched
Split in two separate cushions
& the candle started to light.
Beneath an arch of ironwork
& infinite arabesques,
We crossed the courtyard
Where the "Lady Night,"
As if an accomplice,
As if really of day,
Her aroma
Immensely joyful
Bloomed even more
Strange music
& the distant babble
Of fountain water.
Our bodies entwined
Beneath a canopy of ceiling
Within mosquito nets
That covered everything on the bed.
As if the waters of the Atlantic
& the Mare Nostrum
Somewhere brutally converged
Into a stormy sea
At dawn
Our uncovered
Bodies
Formed a single being.

Translations from Spanish by Joseph Mulligan

Mohamed Sibari was born in the province of Larache, Morocco, in 1945. A prolific novelist & poet, he is one of the few Moroccan writers, with Dris Diuri & Mohamed Akalay, to prefer writing in Spanish over his native Arabic tongue. Sibari was awarded the Spanish National Cross of Merit in 2003 & the Pablo Neruda Prize for Poetry in 2004. His publications include *El caballo* (1993), *Cuentos de Larache* (1998), *Pinchitos y divorcios* (2002), *El babuchazo* (2005), *De Larache al cielo* (2006), & *Poemas del Lukus* (2007).

EDITORS' NOTE. Commentary by J.M.

Malika El Assimi (b. Marrakech, 1946)

THINGS HAVING NAMES

At moonset
I was born
Dawn leaned over the universe
and night's breast
in rage tore its tunic

The poor parents sat down
on the threshold of God's earth
That's when the birds of paradise sang
The eternal branch bent down
shadowed the earth
then covered itself
in silk
and sweetbriar

On the day of my birth
I was thunderstruck
Mount Tor appeared to me
and behind it the marvels of light
and the face of God
I heard the grandiose voice murmur:
O creature of the earth
go to the pond and the water
to the blue in the eye of the phoenix

and you will find the man bending
under the burden of earth
Don't get sad
In your right hand
there will be clouds
and in your left
the glebe
Don't be sparing with the water
for earth is in a state of neglect
God spoke to me
before sunrise
The branches broke down in tears
and the world still gave itself over to sin
"Pray, O daughter of the breeze and the storms
Your prayer will refresh those who suffer
the torments of Gehenna
will soothe the afflicted in this universe"
I prayed
calamity did not disappear
and His infinite mercy did not come down
upon this world of misfortune
Each time I want to pray
I have to fight those who seize the mihrab
and post watchmen in front of the mosques
My prayers have not purified the universe
but I keep praying

SMOKE

The evenings suffocate me
and through me grow light
I switch on my sun
and its clarity overwhelms me
I pursue the winds
so that they extinguish my fire
and reduce me
to a body
of smoke

MARIAM

O you who gathers me
on this rainy night
like a radiant cherry
on the humid branch
You who walk between the branches
and caress me
I collapse between your hands
and you discover the ecstasy
the just law of this universe
They said:
Shake, O Mariam, the palm frond
so that the dates will fall for the children
And Mariam shook her father's palm tree
Adam
O you who shudder
when the wind blows on eyelashes
and makes stars tremble
if you knew
what a heart holds

THE SNOUT

Poetry will be your dress
when you yield your soul
back to its maker
You'll strike down your enemies
through mortal silence
and the language assassinated
under your fingers
With it you'll tattoo
the snout of the good-for-nothings
and you'll bring down the sphinx a peg or two

Translations by P.J. from Abdellatif Laâbi's French versions of the original Arabic

Malika El Assimi, a poet, writer, & teacher actively involved in politics, has fought discrimination against women, especially in public service, all of her life. Though she lost her first electoral bid to represent her Marrakech district in the Moroccan Parliament, she won the seat on the second try. She founded & published the journal *Al-Ikhtiyar* (The Choice) in the early 1970s & has contributed to other journals, such as *Al-Thaqafa al-Maghribiyya* (Maghrebian Culture). Her poetry has always been strongly centered on empowering women in all aspects of their lives—socially, politically, & culturally. As Abdellatif Laâbi writes: "Malika al-Assimi has played the role of outrider for [Moroccan] women, when one realizes that before her, poetry was a quasi-male monopoly. Her contribution is all the more estimable as from the very start she took an offensive line. The stakes did not revolve around making a 'feminine voice' heard but were about inserting oneself naturally into the process of the poetic renaissance in progress. And to this process she brought something often lacking in the male voice: a different relation to the body, to the forces that manifest life or try to destroy it, including in the private sphere. In this rough male winter, it is through an interior sun that her poetry lights our way." Besides a number of volumes of poetry—including *Kitabat Kharij Aswar al-'Alam* (Writings Outside the Walls of the World, 1988) & *Aswat Hanjara Mayyita* (Voices from a Dead Throat, 1989)—she has published a book dealing with political issues regarding women, *Al-Mar'a wa Ishkaliyyat al-Dimuqratiyya* (Women and the Ambiguities of Democracy), & one on the history of Jam'i al-Fina, the famous square in Marrakech.

Mohammed Bennis (b. Fez, 1948)

from **THE BOOK OF LOVE**

For You

It is not morning, it is not evening. It is between morning and evening. A bit of morning, a bit of evening. Of the line, I see only the stammer of the clothes. The hand alone, and hanging. It sways with the terraces and their lime. I will smell the scent of the hand maybe, for it is close to the smell of the lime, and behind it I will smell the one who doesn't sleep in a bed. Nothing but a hand. I pour tea, and the proffered hand proffers the glass for fingers to touch fingers. The ring knots itself to my lips. And I fail to sit down in the silence. Why the hand, the ring, the glass? A path from hand to hand. An accident between hand and hand. The hand has abandoned the moon outside the room. I, I smell the scent of henna. A branch melts in my voice.

A bit of hand in my mouth or her mouth. I hand over the hand for it to be higher than my chest. The tea burns. The henna, the lime. Peaceful, my head on the ground. I pass the hand over the hand. The hand without a book because it is hand in hand. And tongue over skin. She suckles so as not to sleep. A bit of henna, a bit of moaning. The hand that proffered the glass has not yet handed it back. Entrancing game. The glass. When I stretched out on the ground, I grabbed a hand and the glass went up in flames. My hand on skin. Silence, tongue, loosening of organs. Chest bends down without seeming to bend. A tree turns around me. Marble pillars and we on a mat. Brown skin baring itself. Half sleep between two cities. A call from below. Intense upraising. From earth to earth. No thing abandons things. Leave themselves, meet themselves. In every sense. Role I had forgotten. On my hand or on hers. Violence, your tears. Loss of organs. A bit of morning, a bit of evening enters. The glass explodes. Scream. Master of silence and master of emptiness.

Letter to Ibn Hazm

Today there is no love
Man harassed
throws himself into the hole of his appointments
hangs on to his footsteps to defend
the rites of a beginning of being
And when he laughs the star fallen on his shoulders
is crushed and goes away

Woman goes astray in her enigma
Thinks about the hairdresser who will not wait
And when she opens her wardrobe
she forgets the one who tumbled her
murmuring
delight   your kiss   you are mine

Only the buses
and the elevators
exchange the meaning
of fugitive encounters

Kissed cheeks
good-bye's greetings
on the road a soul in tatters

Of an instant the blood's voice on fire manifests itself
This is the news of our new era
the era of our world
where nation kills nation
entrails of the innocents
on the screens of our generous television

news of blood of fire
hide dead lovers from us
or lovers about to die
in the name of the right
of the certainty
of a civilization condemns itself to expiate

Ibn Hazm
For us two al-Andalus is lost
A moment expressing neither a time nor a place
Al-Andalus was a state of soul
to you it taught friendship
to me it left only its desert
Granada lies abandoned on the side of snow
bared to visitors come from a disfigured memory
and Córdoba
repeats its delirium in the fortress of forgetting

Ibn Hazm
Is friendship of birth or of innocence?
This my time puts me into questions
at the end of a century when blood and disguised intentions
triumph

Will I speak to you of a people resisting exile and suffering?
Will I speak to you of a village where men women
children were exterminated?
Will I speak to you of the steel birds of prey that destroy
at will?
Will I speak to you of the ships of death?
Will I speak to you of my friends slaughtered one after the other?

What do you want me to tell you?
My time is the time of assassins
of Hatred
Treason
Kin knifes kin
Souls sick and soured
Hearts no longer warm themselves in the sun
sun of friendship protected and guided you through death and
disaster
rushing in

Ibn Hazm
My time is the time of an irresistible violence

And I, I search for a tree whose shade will be clement
I say
You, tree, my erring is yours

I know that you'll come
neither from the west
nor
from the east
and that you tremble in a book
But they, they burn the books
announce an image dies the moment it is
born
I, Ibn Hazm, in your friendship and love
I have accompanied you
Someone else walks beside us
I have no fear of a blessed solitude
as my last refuge
offering me lamp and gazelle
in this time of violence not
mine

Translations by P.J. from the author's French version of his original Arabic

SEVEN BIRDS

to Mahmoud Darwish

A White Bird

A breath condenses
Even density can be pleasant
Each wall widens its cracks

And retains the call

A height that remains a height
Springs that have gathered the winds of the fields

A Red Bird

It may have traveled the river in one night
The road may have guided it through the upper layers

I ponder the mystery of its redness
Then forget the sky
That has taken it

There

A Green Bird

There are sleeping feathers before me
Feathers that blast me with the fire of distance
And feathers without a body that bend
And collect
In a point

Between us speech is fluttering

A Blue Bird

So drunk in the evening it's almost unable to return
It would prefer that departure go on
Without departure

Reflections
Of light in the pool
Grow longer

A Black Bird

Each thing wants to emulate it
Water in the pots
Words on their birthdays
Caravans across borders
A girl not yet wet with dew

But the thrush
Emulates only
Itself

It stays on branches of joy

A Yellow Bird

That window remains open for it as they sit face to face
and the bird stays because of an approaching silence until
without even pecking the grains it soars just as its past did
just as its future will at dawn

A Colorless Bird

Elated it chirps on one of the nights of solitude
Before it flies
Where light unites with vibration
A draft that startles
Its visitor with a wing whose recurrent glitter
Is ever-changing and I can see it from a distance

It flies
So that what I see
Is this thing that resembles nothing distant

Translation from Arabic by Fady Joudah

COMMENTARY

Often mentioned in the same breath as the Syrian poet Adonis, the Iraqi Saadi
Youssef, or the Palestinian Mahmoud Darwish, Mohammed Bennis is without
a doubt one of the major poets writing in Arabic today. Born in Fez in 1948, he
started the avant-garde magazine *Al-Taqafa al-jadida* (The New Culture) in
1974. For the ten years it ran before being censored & killed off by the govern-
ment, this magazine was one of the essential centers for the development of the
new Moroccan poetics & a major platform for a dialogue between cultures &

for radical intellectual debate. In 1985 Bennis cofounded the publishing house Toubkal, still going strong today. In 1996 he was the founder of the House of Poetry in Morocco, one of whose achievements was to get the United Nations Educational, Scientific and Cultural Organization to make March 21 World Poetry Day. His achievement in poetry is to have brought a radically modern, & even postmodern, formal experimentation to Arab-language poetry, without, however, neglecting or belittling the poetic achievements of the heyday of Arab literature. Thus the extract here from his *Book of Love* is a writing-through of one of the core texts of Arabic love poetry & a dialogue with the great tenth-century al-Andalus Arab poet Ibn Hazm (see p. 67), as a necessary *No!* to the present situation, specifically the disaster of the wars in the Middle East.

Bennis's writings have been collected in a two-volume *Complete Works* published in Beirut in 2001. A range of his poetic work is available in French, translated by poets such as Bernard Noël, Abdelwahab Meddeb, & Mostafa Nissabouri.

Ahmed Lemsyeh (b. Sidi Ismail, 1950)

FRAGMENTS OF THE SOUL'S SHADOW

I saw Death hiding his face
Riding a horse
Tethering his horse to a palm tree
The horse becomes an ant
Goes into my body
My voice is an oven
Life for it is an onion
We are a truth for Death
Waiting to face Mecca
Every death renews our age
The wind is a soap singing
Trees are town criers without voices
Light has a henna
Speech doesn't sleep
Everyone tries to trick Death
But I live day by day
Whoever denies that Death exits
And wants to live forever
Can see his face in the clouds

Even as water splashes, some of it remains
The spirit goes, and leaves us watching
I say, Good-bye, my mind
The walls start to dance
Snow's sweat shines in the eyes of the dead
See you tomorrow
Life or death.

Translation from Arabic by Zakazia Lahlou & Pamela Nice

I MISS MY SELF

The words tug their brothers
Silence, a career
They didn't raze the borders
But built them tower-high
Light is handicapped and transformed
They did not let him go back
The beards all tangled together
Scrape the slopes of mountains
Comb the clouds
Make the oceans bald
The mirror pretends not to know them
For it saw them, and felt fear

.

His father, the waiter
Had promised him new shoes
All day he was on top of the world, then
He saw his father on TV
Swimming in his blood
Beside him, the shoes

.

Forget me so sorrow will forget you
You destroyed all that we recorded for each other
In those days
Wiped it from his memories

If all the threads come unpicked
Your words come first
Chop it, roll it, savor it
They say: Reap what you sow
If you adore him, heed him, follow him
Never deny him
Look at your shadow in the water, and talk to it

Translation from Arabic by Emma Hayward

COMMENTARY

Born 1950 in Sidi Ismail (in the province of El Jadida), Ahmed Lemsyeh has played a major role in bringing the spoken vernacular into contemporary Arabophone Moroccan poetry, as Abdellatif Laâbi notes, "due in part to his continuous poetic production & also to his stance: braving all prejudice, reticence, & even open hostility from the start but also breaking with a long tradition that always paired poetry & song, he has the merit of hopping the train of modernity & installing his preferred language there without qualms." Writes Deborah Kapchan: "Among the most vocal proponents of the movement for the canonization of *zajal* in the Moroccan literary realm is Ahmed Lemsyeh, a well-published poet (in classical and Moroccan Arabic), a long-time socialist, and a member of the Moroccan Writers Guild. . . . Lemsyeh posits an oedipal relation between classical Arabic and spoken dialect; he compares the dialect to a young bride who is ensorcelled and killed by her jealous cowives, only to turn into a dove that flies above them, making music high above their heads. . . . She is life, regenerating, transforming, allusive. For Lemsyeh, the mother tongue is a voice that translates 'the [acultural] being.' He asserts that he speaks neither in the name of the 'people,' nor the party, nor the nation, but rather for the rights of the individual." Despite this, his poetry overflows with allusions to popular culture in its use of proverbs, song lyrics, & history.

Rachida Madani (b. Tangier, 1951)

from *WALK THROUGH THE DEBRIS* . . .

Walk through the debris
which ruins us
and say to yourself that we are camping
in a scree of stones
even if no denunciation

is copied from the sand
to accumulate dune on dune storm on storm
until there is a fusion of sand and blood
at desert's end,
where the desert's dancing cadavers
cease stirring our sleep
cease pumping our mad blood of the damned
between two assassination attempts
two cells
two ambushes at the corner of a dark street
where we are storytellers of legends to come
weaving our discoveries in a network of obsessions
communicable by means of ruins' contagion.

We never drew up a pact with the desert
we set loose hostile camels there
near the outlines of false cities
constructed on mirages
where each person is buried in his metallic resonance
which serves as his compass
each person seeing his city according to its mirage.

Walk all the way to the sonorous end of the desert
that serves as a link
between errancy and the right to be human.
We are nomads to the point of attrition,
we have neither tents
    nor palm trees
    nor oases in the monstrous
    desert night.
We have neither language nor hope
nor anyone to listen to our voices
harsh like glass fragments
atop walls
    no dream to lose
    no throne to gain
scarcely a scarlet froth
after a long march.

I want you without hope
when you knock on my door
and when my door is a *flagrant délit*

of absence,
when all I can do is walk
through my obsession
when time only brings me time
and the sand only sand.
But in which divided fiber in me
in which excoriation should I place you
when I love you and when I walk
distanced from you
by too many wounds
by a shattered landscape where you persist to be
in the peripeties of erasures
alone
standing
thunderstruck
before the ruins.

Charred
uprooted
a knife held in your teeth
irrefutable under the stormy sky in your witness
against him who works us over with a razor
and the group that you love
beyond the infinite disaster.
. . .

Walk you know how mortal
love is.
I carry us wounded, dying
in the middle of the nightmare
in which I love you as I choose the group
erasing with my voice all the furrows
that block our march.
I love you.
It is a torn tendon
it is a shortness of breath
it is an eerie night
like a bursting vein
that I pick up in a sprain
that I have credited
to an imagination beyond the possible

and was not this blood itself
the exhibit
that acquits me of any imagination
of any sarcasm
and when I say blood
I am thinking of nothing if not of this land
that I locate nowhere
other than the place where I am arterial pressure
an omen boding
sure death
       running down
from my head to public squares.
In any event an intuition
that moves secretly
in my bone marrow
and spreads pestilence.
I love you and I am not singing about love
I am not interested in the encumbrance of song.
I do not know how to sing when it comes to
the ruins that wrack me.
I am howling a land that has cut right through me
from one end of my body to the other
that pulverizes me
slinging a desert in my face.

. . .

Walk you have never left me
you shall never leave me
as long as there is the semblance of a land
that we want to call our own at any cost
ready to end up unidentified
in the infernal infinity of the desert.
For you
for me
for all the plague-stricken in the world
love is a hallucinatory
       excrescence
           of the desert

Translation from French by Eric Sellin

Rachida Madani was born in Tangier in 1951 and still lives there, now retired from a career teaching French. A careful writer—who says, "I love to savor my words, especially when I find the one I need in the place it needs to be"— she has published three collections of poetry since 1981, when her first book, *Femme je suis* (Woman I Am; Inéditions barbares), came out. It was Mohamed Serifi, a high-profile political prisoner, who shared the poems with others in prison & encouraged Madani to publish them. "To shut up is not fair," says Madani, but also: "I am a passive militant. I don't know how to scream slogans or brandish banderoles. I militate with my words." When Abdellatif Laâbi was freed from prison, Madani asked him to write a preface for her book: "He told me that if he did that, the book would never be published. I insisted, and indeed it is because of his efforts that *Femme je suis* was published in France in 1981."

Mohammed al-Ashaari (b. Moulay Idriss Zerhoun, 1951)

from *A VAST SPACE . . . WHERE THERE'S NO ONE*

Sitting
On the edge of the bed
Where the sheets' flowers silently fall
The balcony sheds distant threads of light
While my hand strays on her waist
I stretch my body on clouds of sleep
How many words will we need
To hurl at the ceiling
Hesitating
Incomplete
Before we stumble on
The sentence that falls
Followed only by water, dust
And silent voices

Sitting
I hear two beats
Over her silence
I wipe her thin fingers
Her neck's skin
Her fresh chest
With dark silk

Eyelash by eyelash,
Alluring, soft,
As if one pulse

We lay our surprise on the bed
And we sleep, faces smooth
Hunt giant butterflies
In the jungles of our dreams
With our parasols
We nibble each other under their shade
While silent, distant rain knocks at our nap
Like a stranger asking for a wharf, hearing waves nearby
Unable to reach the wet jetty

As if with one gasp
An icy shadow passed across her kiss
He hears nothing but the anthem of the savanna
Now silence descends from an icebound cloud
The windows' glassy swallows flash past
Nervous, as though exile nears
Storms and between the words
The lamps light up her fingers
As if in a magic trick
She strews crystal dew from our fingers
Onto our bodies
Nothing will last
When she opens her eyes

The gusts of her tornado eyelashes lift everything
As the wind lifts dry leaves
But it's just my hand on her waist
She'll freeze
As if the hand were there before her form
Before the flapping that she heard
Near me
Uninterrupted
Panting
. . .

We will sit, like children with their toys
Destroy our bodies on the edges of mocking regret
Knowing that later we will be too tired
To celebrate the reconstruction of our scattered organs

Sitting on the edge of the bed
I hear the percussion of her breath
On the glass of my isolation
As if she had been
Here
As if the bed itself were nothing but a metaphor
That fell suddenly from the middle of the story
Like a dreamer born of wind
From her absent face
To the ceiling of a deserted room

Nothing remains of her heartbeat
But an old, sad echo.

. . .

Loss placed women and poems
Along my way
Goaded them into redoing my laces
Weaker than the world

She fixed my itinerary to end with a deaf headstone
Which befriends me
An infatuated shadow carries my bags
Guides me to good addresses
Along roads that nibble me
Distances drawn with steps
On water

Why don't I jump off the bed
And go
Leaving remnants of envy beside her
As light leaves bits of shimmer in the dark
Why don't I leave her a letter, many pages
To tell how I learned to watch so well
"The Prisoner of Love"
Why don't I add to this tale an age that wipes me off her map
Or a man to kill me
In an outburst of rage
Without taking the time to hate
I could add any move made of phrases I say to her
A river takes me
Carried away with joy

Takes her to the shores of distant longing
Sitting on the edge of the bed
I count our pulses
And outside the window, I see,
On the far side of the street
That faint light grow
While cold leaves fall, one by one, on the bed
From autumn's ghost

Translation from Arabic by Emma Hayward

COMMENTARY

(1) Writes Abdul Kader El Janabi in his anthology *Le poème arabe moderne* (Paris: Maisonneuve et Larose): "Before becoming Minister of Culture of Morocco [in 1998], Mohammed al-Ashaari was involved in a range of cultural activities. During the early eighties he was jailed for his political activities. A poet, novelist, and journalist, he has also been the president of the Moroccan Writers' Union for three terms and chief editor of the union's magazine *Afaq* (Horizons). He is the author of a number of books, most importantly *The Neighing of Wounded Horses* (1978), *Eyes as Large as the Dream* (1982), and *Biography of Rain* (1988). His latest collection, *A Bed for the Grain's Solitude* (1998), underlines his ambition to be modernist. The complexity of the images and extensive work on the language itself characterize a poetry marked by elegance and urbanity."

(2) His novel *The Arch and the Butterfly* was a cowinner (with the Saudi novelist Raja Alem's *The Dove's Necklace*) of the International Prize for Arabic Fiction—or, as it's popularly known, "the Arabic Booker"—in 2011.

Medhi Akhrif (b. Assilah, 1952)

from *THE TOMB OF HELEN*

Barefooted
Helen
Walks out of Suheil's paintings
And heads for Bab Al-Raml,
Prompting elegies with her silken rebec
Till the dusk that cleaves to the eyes of
The departing comer grows tired.

What mirror
Would disguise my mysterious face
That a pseudophrase may become transparent
In her silence,
Silence protected by
The last
Afterglow?

Helen
Is reborn
Whenever the waterwheels
Of thirsty indigo smolder
To ashes on a new line.

No, she returns
                    whenever
                    She strays.

Helen
Is a wine-rhyme
She is the ardor of the cupbearer
She is the one who stirs yearning for embers.
Helen is fading
And that millennial countenance
Unsheathes the hymn.

Helen
Stands at the edge of ink
Guiding errant journeys
To the gist of the ode.

Helen's absence is present,
Hers is the North Sea,
Here are the seasons of the impossible,
Here is her protective robe
And her harbor.

Helen
Dozes part of the year
Beneath the eyelid of an enchanted kitten
That belongs to the fairies of the black Jinn

Helen
Neither stayed nor departed.
. . . .
Where then
Is the poem?
Is it in the sea reefs,
Or in the obstinate dialect
Of limestone?
Or is it the storyteller who copied
                              the tale
                                        with his own
                                        spurious longing?

Wandering in memories
That left nothing but foam
And in the scattered fragments of renunciation
In the depths
Among paintings
Of seaweed
As they grow in amulets left over from
The epiphany of queens during Fassi carnivals
I would come near then run away
From your island
Which emerges in winter
To hide me deeply
                    in wine
                          skies.

O anise flower
On the Rilke cover
Do enter
The verse garden
And with the effervescence of metonymy
Daub the lips of Helen-the-poem
The poem ending (at the beginning)
The voice of Helen
    has not yet grown clear
    in my throat burnt
                        from calling!

Translation from Arabic by Hassan Hilmy

HALF A LINE

Half a line of poetry
is enough
for a lifetime
Edgar Poe spent the whole of his mad life
translating unsuccessfully
half a line of poetry
into incredible prose

The other half of the line
will come from another world
farther away than poetry
and the voyages
faster
than the sound of a rope

As far as you're concerned
it will be enough to prevaricate in the coming years
to be yourself
and to give yourself over to half a line of prose
that you have always skillfully missed
pretexting that we had gotten
to our appointment thirty years late
Let's add that to be standing up thus
on one single leg
like a heron
the voice turned toward your wet nurse the sea
(we wrote about the two of you
in *Low Ceiling*
—remember?)
enjoying in the here below and the beyond
only the sense of smell
is proof that the other half
of your line of poetry
was written well in advance
inside the bubbles
of this cold glass
foaming
empty

Translation by P.J. from Abdellatif Laâbi's French translation from the original Arabic

(1) Born in Assilah in 1952, Medhi Akhrif is a poet, writer, & translator (of Fernando Pessoa & Octavio Paz, among others, into Arabic). He is also a professor of Arabic literature, a member of the Union of Arab Writers, & a member of the Moroccan Maison de la Poésie. His major poetry collections are *First Love* (Cairo, 1979), *The Door of the Sea* (Beirut, 1983), *Low Ceiling* (Casablanca, 1989), *First Sun* (Rabat, 1995), *The Tomb of Helen* (Rabat, 1998), *Relatos* (Casablanca: Maison Toubkal, 2002), & *Whitenesses* (Casablanca: Maison Toubkal, 2002). In 2011 he shared the Tchicaya U Tam'si Prize for African poetry with the Senegalese poet Fama Diagne Sène. His work has been translated in French, Italian, Greek, Spanish, & English (see *Aufgabe* 5, which included a selection of Moroccan poets edited by Guy Bennett & Jalal El Hakmaoui).

(2) As Akhrif writes: "This page / trap / if it was white / white as when created / by the prodigious ink / in the silenced poems / the sea / would make me savor its rhymes / would permit me to master / the physics of the page."

Abdallah Zrika (b. Casablanca, 1953)

from *DROPS FROM BLACK CANDLES*

I

That's how I snuffed the candle
to light up the darkness

then I saw the sun
apart from the light

I saw doors
and no houses

Butterflies
coming out of the worms
swarming the corpses

I was afraid that my face
was another face
glued to mine

I was scared
when I saw my foot
on top of scorpions

And when I'd reached the water
I searched for a mouth in the earth

I only found an earth
looking like a turtle's carapace

I screamed
Hell's
all that's left
of paradise

Paradise annihilates itself
but the fire remains

When I left
only my hand
remained present

When I came back
my fingers had become
the tongues of flames

I said
Ah if you knew
how night cares more for me
than day

I exhaust myself
but the glass does not exhaust itself

I've sung
Foot oh my foot
O heel of voluptuousness

And when the woman appeared
I snuffed the candle

and yelled
Forget your language
and leave your tongue
chew by itself
another language

I thought of the sun
that had never
seen me naked

In the forest
I saw the wind
Not the flute

I wrote in the air
Don't sing with the wind

(And in the night
I saw birds
pecking only the tips
of the breasts)

I yelled at the ant
Don't go home
There's a jailer there
who waits for you
playing with his keys

In the water
I saw a serpent come out of my mouth

And in sleep
I saw a silence—
black
black!

from **SOME PROSE**

My Sister's Scream in Black and White

I always imagine photography as a room in which one washes a dead person.
This began the day my brother passed away at seventeen when I was five.
They were washing his body in a room when my sister let out a scream accus-
ing a man of having stolen the picture of my brother that was hanging on a
wall near a wardrobe. I still remember his shoes standing next to a ladder.
Since then, each time I pass in front of one of those photographers' "shops,"
I stop for a moment as if among the exhibited pictures I were searching for
the one of my brother robbed the day of his death. Many long years have
passed. One day I wanted to take pictures of people, but I could not do it.
As if their faces had lain with all their weight on my chest to the point of
keeping me from breathing. My brother's features have been nearly erased
from memory by now, but a few pictures still stick to my retina: the one of

his black shoes standing near a ladder; the one of rivulets of water escaping below the door of the small room where they were washing him; the one of a tiny sewing machine in a corner of the house. I always imagine this in black and white, maybe because the picture of my brother was black and white, maybe because of the color of death, which has tinted my memory. And then one day I found myself in the skin of a collector avidly cutting out everything that fell under his hand, to the point where my room was overflowing with cuttings from magazines and newspapers. One day a friend, noticing my "habit," gave me a camera. I never used it, though at times it happens that I touch or open it. Then one day I decided to make use of it. I took no one's portrait, but I took pictures of old photographs published in magazines, trying hard to inscribe them into compositions of my own making, next to various objects I found about the house. To this day I am incapable of taking someone's picture, as if I were afraid of causing the death of my "model." All the pictures I use belong to people with whom I have nothing to do whatsoever. I like to take pictures of inanimate objects, and especially of those things with which I share a sense of intimacy. The shadows peas make next to a jar, for instance, or the glimmer of a candle devouring darkness on a wall, or a naked foot set on the step of a staircase shaded in black. I found myself attached to everything that belongs to the world of darkness and shadows, because they embrace the earth. I mistrust faces because they remind me of death, and because they will be stolen the day they are washed. I still hear my sister's scream. But the one who stole my dead brother's picture did not think of stealing the ladder, the shoes, or the sewing machine. He put his hand on the picture of a dead man who was being washed in a room that was nearly dark. Before all, he put his hand on what was dearest to me: he stole from me the portrait of all living people by condemning me never to take the picture of anyone. But for me that has opened another world, which no one is dreaming of stealing from me, the world of things in all their solitude and which do not try to expose themselves to our gaze. That's why I too like to see myself as a used ladder hung on a wall, or as shoes that smell of indifference, or as a sewing machine that fills a corner with sweetness and calm. That's also why I refuse to be a portrait.

Translations by P.J. from author's French versions

Born in Casablanca in 1953, Abdallah Zrika grew up in the slums of Ben Msik. He wrote his first poems at age twelve & self-published his first book (*Dance of the Head and the Rose*) in 1977. In these so-called years of lead of political repression & student unrest, the book was an immediate popular success with the younger Moroccan generation—as were the many poetry readings he gave to audiences that often numbered in the thousands. In 1978 he was arrested & condemned to two years in jail for disturbing the public order & for supposed crimes against "the sacred values" of his country. Since his release in 1980 he has continued his career as a writer, becoming one of Morocco's major voices. Abdellatif Laâbi called the early work "brutal, disheveled, wild, blasphemous, one could be tempted to say that it is voluntarily ugly—the same way people found Picasso's paintings ugly," while he sees the more recent work as having "restructured itself to make room for the visionary" by becoming a "crucible in which human and historical matters are transmuted. . . . After having called for the destruction of the old world, he has now put his shoulder to the task of reinventing life." Of Zrika's ten or so books, three have been translated into French. The texts excerpted here come from the books *Bougies Noires* (Paris: La Différence, 1998) & *Petites Proses* (Bordeaux: L'Escampette, 1998), in Zrika's own French translation.

Mubarak Wassat (b. Mzinda, Safi region, 1955)

BALCONY

The resonance of the metallic muscles of the night, the din of the purulent days, the stray bullets of day and night, the ashes: that is what our mouths also know. I started out one day from that point, which now, rolls toward the neighboring point where a man, hunkered down beggarlike, releases a torrent of insults, seemingly not directed at anyone in particular. Drink a hymn of tears in a broken glass, weep under a balcony from which a woman has withdrawn, my lover of long ago, dance on hot coals, on the melodies of a flute and on shards of glass, while she watches the caravan of sighs that travels toward her vulva, and offers me, at wake up, a cup of wine and herbs extracted from the depths. . . . She repeats: "A cohort of wounds buzzes in my heart . . . "

"On the lips too, roses of blood open themselves to dawn," proclaims a skull raving in a bar. Behind its glasses, the mummy orders the empty bottles to go hang out in the trash can. Everything remains calm, until further notice.

INNOCENCE

The man who during long nights
advanced in the corners of the pale garden
did not steal the decorations of lavender
and is not the one who cut the nose
of the air

So why did they hunt him down

Now he hides in a cavern
that protects the clamor of the ants
leaves it only when forced to
and then he crisscrosses the desert
on which the dead make
trembling
shrouds
float

But nothing to fear for him
when he is hungry
he sits down at the table of the breeze
and if eagles pursue him
he can combine
with the foam

Nothing to fear for him
he has a tent
where the wind's apostles rest
when they are
tired

THE TIME OF THE ASSASSINS

for Tarafa

He enjoyed
singing
in his shoes
careful not to hurt a stone
unable to bear scoffing at
a flower
He felt emptied

of his being
and started to look like a bird
with fettered feet
The ambient air
suffocated him
and he no longer was able to stand
living among his kin
After he'd erred for a long time
in his thoracic cage
he drank until his shadow
became illuminated
and he left them busy opening
his veins

Translations by P.J. from French versions by Mohamed El Amraoui & Abdellatif Laâbi from the original Arabic

COMMENTARY

Mubarak Wassat was born in 1955 in Mzinda, a village in the region of Safi, Morocco. He teaches philosophy in Agadir, writes for various literary magazines, & translates from French into Arabic (Stéphane Mallarmé, Robert Desnos, Henri Michaux, & André Breton, among others). He started publishing poetry in 1974, & his work has been translated into French, Spanish, Macedonian, Swedish, & English (see *Aufgabe* 5, which has a selection of Moroccan poetry edited & translated by Guy Bennett & Jalal El Hakmaoui). His latest collection is *Un éclair dans la forêt* (Al Manar, 2010), with Arabic originals & facing translations into French by Mohamed El Amraoui (see p. 732), Abdellatif Laâbi (see p. 668), & others.

Hassan Najmi (b. Ben Ahmed, 1959)

THE WINDOW

Nothing remains:
only the wound of memory.
And the meeting place,
The smell of the paper of used books.

From the window:
a song about an ancient love.

As if to write the book of the dead,
night became his habit.

As if to entertain
a sadness that accompanies him
he dances alone at night.

COUPLETS

In the light of your eyes
no light can save me except the lamp of my body.

With which legs can I join your dance
while all my body's flutes are dumb?

Why did words pour?
And the pouring of silence . . .

how can I erase it from my body?
Everything in me is erased if I am erased.

Nothing remains after the body's erasure.
Except it: My body.

THE BLUENESS OF EVENING

I desire other places to see you
grass to rest on
and a thirsty tongue
to drink with and to name you.
I desire night.
I desire another settlement to my days.
And I desire you.

In the blueness of evening, how much I desire
and how much do I not desire . . .

Ah, and this shiver coming
with the cloud of night!

THE TRAIN YARD

A woman tourist in the station. A kiosk for newspapers, and tobacco. A depressing newspaper. A small corner in the bottom of the page for forgetting. Two hands with an extinguished cigarette. Blown nerves. Clouds in the faces. A closed shop. Police news bubbling in newspapers. Police that corrupt cities. A crime in the garden. Half bodies in the general's tapes. Two lovers on the right sidewalk. Bare legs. A maid pours a bucket of water by the entrance. A guard dozes off at the building gate. An advertising poster on the school gate. The remains of leaflets in the dirt beneath. A window without a curtain. An evening of nervousness. A nervousness hidden into the screens inside people's homes. Programmes for health awareness. A religious sermon. Chatter by the post office. A woman complains about her neighhour. A girl in the balcony in her nightgown. A silhouette walks to his bed. A dirty newspaper cut-out. An admirable rising. A striking-up of friendship. Solidarity in the grass. Emotions filling. Speeches by sycophants. Compensations for bribery. Immunities without immunity. The deviations of a time. Distortions without end. Silence seeping from human pores. Dead cities. Cities—Cemeteries . . .

> My cup and I
> I hoodwink my shadow
> In Ibn Batuta's café.
> Where are you?
> You didn't come?
> . . . .
> O how heavily night settles
> in my body

Translations from Arabic by Khaled Mattawa

COMMENTARY

A poet, journalist, ex-president of the Moroccan Writers' Union, & founding member of the Maison de la Poésie, Hassan Najmi (born in 1959 in Ben Ahmed) is also the main editor of the cultural pages of *Al-Itihad al-Ichtiraki*, a Moroccan Arab-language daily newspaper. He has published four collections of poetry, a novel, & a range of essays & portraits of poets (such as Philippe Jaccottet, Vladimir Mayakovsky, & Joyce Mansour). Abdul Kader El Janabi called Najmi's 1995 volume of poems, *Hayat Saghira* (Little Life; Casablanca: Touqbal Editions), "vibrant and chiseled writing fired by the sparks of dailiness that lights up feelings of friendship in the city, with blood and ether as ballast."

Waafa Lamrani (b. Ksar el Kebir, 1960)

ALPHABET FIRE

In the morning
at the hour when birds head in the direction of the ocean
disarray takes in me the form
of startled happiness

then the trace of a poem

in a glimmer is my lodge
to the sun it is hostage
the erring tongue is a star
punctuating the cosmos with a promise
   then receding
veering from me toward the light, astray
my bruises are the hearth of illusions
and love a coincidence with its exclusions
I have sung my time
Is history a die?
are events made of stones?
is there beyond this insanity any more
blood to be shed ?
A celestial body manifest in a panicked star
governing the intervals of its course
yet so great is the distance it holds
no power to betray

A SHADE OF PROBABILITY

I sprinkle the contours of my body with stars
communing with every sentient fiber, every cell:
what is the sense of name, verb, identity?
an interdict does not negate me,
nor does an imperative shape me,
nor does a name contain me.

Translations by Madeleine Campbell from French versions by Mostafa Nissabouri from the original Arabic

THE EIGHTH DAY

And he said to me: the day of death is the wedding day
and the day of solitude is the day of cheerfulness.

AL-NIFFARI

1. Root

I was born out of a sentiment that resembles neither love nor hatred; it
    often resembles pride.
They did not want me, but I came. By force did I emerge the moment I
    desired.
Before the beginning I identified with defiance
I announced that I together with the age were split on the edge of alienage,
That I together with time were forever two times . . .

2. Genesis

From insight do I initiate
My genesis
I extend along a space narrower than the eye of the needle,
I feign permeation into my own substance.
The wind of the hollow comes from neither Al-Sham nor Al-Maghreb.
Thus do I depart:
Departure could not carry me away,
Nor could transit escape me,
Nor even could arrival entomb me.

3. Body

Whenever the voice of the body waxes ecstatic
The femininity of wisdom blossoms
And with roses covers those of its own parts
That remain dreamy in their coyness.
I saddle the footsteps for craving . . .

4. Love

My free tender heart
I have posted on the highest summit of the Atlas Mountains,
For the stinking hyenas
Are accustomed to decadence
And heights usually make them feel

Dizzy and nauseous . . .
My heart is a flower mined with fragrance
But the picker is a chronic common cold!

5. Semiotica

I emerge out of the blast of a time
That cometh not,
I tame the leakage of seconds,
I spill them as signatures of a lifetime
Crammed with departures . . .

6. Bleeding

The loneliness of the evenings consumes me,
It nibbles at my passion
And then casts me off as a fragment
For the fugitive glow.

7. Pattern

If there were a meaning
If there were a colour
If there were a day
Not the Monday mail
Not the Tuesday train
Not the Wednesday laundry
Not the Thursday meeting
Not the Friday nausea
Not the Saturday loneliness
Not the Sunday ennui.
Oh, how weary is the Sunday afternoon . . .
If there were a face instead of a face,
A figure instead of a figure,
A lifetime instead of this lifetime,
A time instead of this time,
A sun instead of the sun,
An earth instead of the earth,
If there were an air that is really like air . . .
I am weary of what's around me, weary of parts me, weary of my entire
   self.

I am weary of being a muse for poets, weary of the earth that is not up to
    me, weary of the sky.
I am weary of my colleague, who backbites me, and of the street that
    molests me,
of my brother who bothers me and never cares for me.
I am weary of my dwelling and of my time.
I am weary of weariness and of myself,
I deny all conditions and am weary of even denial:
If there were a day,
A colour,
A meaning . . .

8. Coronet

What does the wisdom of the body say?
"Forlornness is pleasanter than weariness,
Gentler than rock."
This is why the eighth day is mine:
So that the letter may on that day impregnate me
And I give birth to twins
So that death may on that day utter me
And I thus get cured . . .

23 February 1992

Translation from French by Hassan Hilmy

COMMENTARY

A poet, a member of the Union des écrivains du Maroc, & the editor between
1993 & 1996 of its review *Afaq* (Horizons), Waafa Lamrani has passionately
promoted poetry from the Arab world. She runs a workshop titled "Poetic
Clearing" in the Faculty of Literature and Social Sciences at the University of
Mohammedia, where she lectures, & also takes part in many cultural events
& festivals across the Arab world & Europe. In 1999 she joined the General
Secretariat of the Maison de la Poésie du Maroc, where she continues to pro-
mote & foster writing. Her poetic output comprises four collections: *Toasts*
(Rabat, 1991), *The Wail of Heights* (Beirut, 1992), *The Magic of Extremes*
(Casablanca, 1997), & *For You I Have Prepared Myself* (1999).

Ahmed Barakat (Casablanca, 1960–1994)

AFTERWARDS

Why does a loud laugh burst out whenever the train passes by at
    mid-history
That glassy train whenever it would pass by inside the head of the woman
    struck by the impossible
Heading to where the shepherd knows not
The shepherd with the hat inhabited by swallows

Little by little the geometry of the heap clears up
A sharp stretch amidst white protuberances
The close one in his own closeness reaches not the distant one in his
    distance
A collective grave sealed with an old chain

In this narrow stretch how can a table be laid without prophets
A little while ago I looked about and viewed one single scene
A wallet
Besides it the remains of the glass smashed with love

Can the side-glance become so meaningless
As a mill in its owner's pocket

This is all what happened
Afterwards
Who among you knows not the number of the dead this morning
To my knowledge there are countless prisoners
This without mentioning the blind
And those with glasses
And those squatting on the electric rock
And those who love wolves

BLACK PAIN

Black is the waste matter of the daily blood
Black too is the special colour of the wound machines
And pain is black pleasure

Black is the stains on the ground
Of the burnt human oil

It is the oxide of thick fatigue on the eyes of cats
And pain is the broken mewing in the dark
In the chain of fire
In the ash of the aged fingers on the asphalt
In the child's decapitated head on the road

Black pain
Is also all this smoke
Which the wall breathes through iron lungs

THE TORN FLAG

Long live the general
Down with the general

The voices
were the same voices that were of old

Distributing their pain of longing
On reed grown in the wind

These loud voices
Are they her voices?

Long live the general
Down with the general

Is this the female inhabiting the holy lands
The owner of the old territory
And the guardian of jars full of names?
And the flag tattooed with the surprised blood
Is it her flag?

Blood is the only wanderer in the whole land
From desert to desert
And from the desert to the firmaments of Arabic

Long live the general
Down with the general

The wandering blood
Is the same blood left on the padlocks
Since very long

And on the keys
Hanging
In the void

And the door
Which is heavy
Like a corpse

Long live the general
Down with the general

Let the birds lay their eggs
In the mouth of the cannon

Translations from Arabic by Norddine Zouitni

COMMENTARY

(1) Ahmed Barakat was born in 1960 in Casablanca, where he grew up, studied, & worked as a journalist for the newspaper *Bayane Al Yawm*. His early death in 1994 at thirty-four was a major loss for Moroccan literature. As Norddine Zouitni (his translator) argues, "Barakat was a champion of the prose poem in Morocco, and is believed to be the writer of the first Moroccan manifesto defending and celebrating the Moroccan prose poem. This manifesto, titled 'We Are Diggers of Wells, or the Unsigned Manifesto,' was written on the night of March 18th, 1993, in Maamoura during the 5th poetry festival of Salé. Groundbreaking, it has subsequently become known as the Salé prose poem manifesto." (The Arab prose poem is a kind of free verse, unrhymed & with no fixed metrical scheme, & thus is not to be confused with the Occidental *poème en prose,* usually set up with the justified margins of regular prose.)

(2) Zouitni again: "The poetry of Ahmed Barakat, like that of Jalal El Hakmaoui and Abdel-ilah Salhi, reflects the urban cosmopolitan experience to the extent that one can say his poetry is one long interrupted eulogy to the city of Casablanca. He is also the first prose poem writer to succeed in transmitting the newness of the prose poem experience to a wider poetry audience. Indeed, his early poem 'abadan lan ussai'da azzilzal' ('Never will I sustain the schism'), first published in the Arab London magazine *Annakid,* was the spark that kindled the flame of the prose poem for many Moroccan readers of poetry afterwards."

Touria Majdouline (b. Settat, 1960)

A MINUTE'S SPEECH

to Oujda

The heart of Oujda is of stone,
Its hands a volcano and a wind,
And has no time for speech.

.

Here life passed me by
Here it passed
Leaving me in your weary arms
Striking the gates of silence,
O city of death,
Hoping that you open a door to dialogue
So can you spare some time for speech?

.

Your silence is exhausting
The choke became heavier
The bridge—to you—longer
So may I leave
Or can you spare
Some time
For speech?

.

You are a vertigo
With neither beginning
Nor end.
Come on stop a little while
I have a lot to say to you:
Air is all dust here
And life in you is like catching a cold.
So, could the world change tomorrow?
Could silence and gloom vanish?

.

you are a gate
opening onto another gate
A wall . . . a wall . . .
And a wall,
And I have for years
Been searching inside you
For a place
and for speech . . .

OUT OF CONTEXT

I gather my confusion and my things
My steps
And the remaining illusions
Of my body
I run beyond time
Beyond the vacant air
And space

.

Yesterday I drew my open space here
And dreamed a lot
I sowed shade, and fruit, and crops around
And with flames I wrote my poems . . .
Yesterday
I had plenty of time
To embroider space with words.
But today
I am left with nothing
But my dejection
And the crumbs of yesterdays gone by
Thus I gather my things
I wrap myself up in my own confusion
And I run
I run beyond time
I propagate into the distance
With neither shade
Nor sun.

Translations from Arabic by Norddine Zouitni & Abdellah Benlamine

(1) Touria Majdouline, born in 1960 in Settat, lives in Oujda, where she teaches Arabic. Poetry International Web characterizes her work as follows: "The peculiarity of her poetry resides in its unpretentious style, which thrives on simple but skillful representations of reality. Her tone is quiet and discreet, but hides a remarkable bravery and boldness underneath. The speakers in her poems display a certain weariness of being that is reminiscent in some ways of the poetry of reclusive American poet Emily Dickinson—although Majdouline's attitude to social life is very different. She is a highly active social [worker] and president of the important Albadil Alijtimai association ('the social alternative'), which promotes the integration of children and young people into Morocco's social and cultural milieu. She is also a member of the union of Moroccan writers, the House of Poetry in Morocco, and a founding member of the UNESCO association for creative women of the Mediterranean."

(2) She has published three books to date: *Uaraqu Arramad* (Leaves of Ashes; Rabat: Union of Moroccan Writers Publications, 1990), *Al-Mut'aboon* (The Weary; Oujda: Dar al Jusoor, 2000), & *Sama'un tushbihuni Qalilan* (A Heaven Which Somewhat Resembles Me, 2005).

Ahmed Assid (b. Taourmit, Taroudant province, 1961)

PRAYER

We all throw our verses into the sea
and live outside the words
outside the voice
outside of silence
If we walk
it is to mask our being stuck
Let's stop and weep
on the vestiges of remembrance
Now time stamps
its seal on our foreheads
and offers each new day
the dregs of an old dream

A CHAMBER THE COLOR OF DISGUST

The world is a thwarted dawn
Silence shows its claws
The dream
a thirst unfolded in my body
Heavy are the chains
heavy and getting heavier

The clock forgets
past time
the present
in the future
The future doesn't happen
The past hasn't been
The present is but drunkenness
The clock forgets
rings crazily
until it breaks down
The books have stupid eyes
the eyes of a lying story
written with hands
trembling in chains
Dust of the forgotten
Scars of memory
haunted by dawn and birth
The origin of the world is water
fire
grass
teats of a desperate god
who fell asleep smack in the middle of the racket
of genesis
and didn't wake up again
He failed the do-gooders
and the sinners
The origin of the world is fire, fire
and it will perish in fire.

SUNS

I know you have fingers
that create beauty
and a heart
with three suns
ripening at twilight
Silence gives you
a blank memory
and your words escape
the margins of the soul
You will as usual enjoy
the spectacle of dailiness
of a space that effaces all
without leaving scars
And now
your exquisite desert
spreading inside you, hiding
away to harden your gaze
and trigger in you that gypsy predilection
for travel.

Translations by P.J. from the French versions by Ahmed Assid & Abdellatif Laâbi from the original Amazigh

Translations by P.J. from the French versions by Ahmed Assid & Abdellatif Laâbi from the original Amazigh

COMMENTARY

A poet & activist for Amazigh/Berber language & culture, Ahmed Assid (born in Taourmit in 1961) is one of the most complex & energetic figures of Moroccan poetry since the 1980s. As a poet he works in two different modes in Amazigh—modes so different that he thinks of them as irreconcilable, as he said to one of us—namely a modern, writerly, open free verse form & a traditional, oral, & highly formal "jousting" form. After some youthful poems in Arabic, Assid switched to Amazigh in the early 1980s, when he also discovered his passion for & competence in *ahouache* by defeating some of the best traditional jousting poets in competition. As he put it: "I became confident in my abilities as a *raïs* [leader, chief] during the summer of 1983 after a verbal joust with Ajemaa, the greatest *ahouache* poet ever." A raïs's talent is measured by his ability to respond (in the same poetic measure) to the other party. Thus, a few years ago, when a raïs questioned the efficacy of the IRCAM (the Royal Moroccan Institute for Amazigh Studies, of which Assid has been a director since 2002) with the lines "You stand at the oven's door / they tell me they brought you dough / but we are still hungry," Assid answered: "To bake good bread / you need time / or you'll eat raw dough / which will make your stomach hurt." Asked to evaluate IRCAM, he said: "The institute's first achievement was to carry the Amazigh struggle from the streets into the establishment. For the first time in history, we have an official body gathering together great and renowned experts in the Amazigh field, enabling them to work collectively on comprehensive strategies. The institute has succeeded in introducing Amazigh-language programs into the education system on the grounds that the teaching of Amazigh, as a national language, should be available to every Moroccan. Work is also being done to gradually standardize the Amazigh language within educational establishments, promote the writing of Amazigh in its original tifinagh, and introduce the teaching of the language in all schools."

Mohamed El Amraoui (b. Fez, 1964)

EN QUELQUE

to Sylvie Germain

And thus, the infinite.

To meet infinity in some new sea, under a cliff dug into the night. Cliffs. Winters produced a singular loneliness.

Floating.

Neither good nor bad omens, but the coming of what's unexpected. A nakedness, for the first time, white, advancing

a dark disturbance in the water.

Thin fingers trace familiar air.

Then a knot ties and loosens in the chest and stomach, quick as a drum roll and no matter what it says—

Sliced stones. Blades.

Endlessly these lines, spaces and folds of meaning.
After, long after, on the edge of a cliff, and without bringing the question to the instant of death, sudden blood on breasts, neck straining slightly, whiteness even whiter and saved by a temporary heaven, Everything, by some strange trick, having spoken of the fragile passage between presence and savage absence.

Huge rats skulking around.

Clash of dream against dream, aggravated by a murmur of faith.

Above the forehead, great crackling—relentless, chronic as insomnia—
opens an unfinished chapter most likely defying the book

and striking the poem's gate.

The knot, the nakedness, a subtle gesture toward the infinitesimal and
a tremor—an alignment of unusual edges. Sounds, clashing sounds
abounding.

Heaven repairs each of these things. In brief intervals, what's pierced,
each by an eye—like that procession of leaders' comforts. An umber circle
surrounds the eye, the sea and the sky.

(And it's sky, not earth, which melted while looking at the earth.)

And letters to a leader were already
scattered, wrapped in a cold Sunday—say a cold Sunday in summer.

And tell me,

says the stranger to his best friend during breakfast, philosophical as
always:

Between one cliff and another, wasn't there a faint echo of the name
Tobias?

JERUSALEM

to Sappho

Two phases of the moon separated by a wire of blood, twisted around a
void.

Thus the void. Sheer. Even so, a spiral crawls up, like a gene.

(Think of the gaps in a DNA sketch.)

An old kinship turns pale green.

Left and right, the number 1, everywhere split and planted, raised from a
sort of cement or metal hat. Graves, remains, walls, skylights, invocations
filled with spirits. Forbidding signs. From time to time, the sky, no—a fog

strung along
with tanks and stone wings.

Stretched out in my bed, I see dry branches out the window—just the tops
of them, thin and bare.

Of course, there's a trunk, roots, hill behind—unless some artifice glued
them to my gazing sleep.

It doesn't matter.

There's what I see and what I don't see. But for some hours, a woman's
voice has made me friendly. A tune naked as the branches passing through
it, catchy, divine.

Outside,
a radio crackles and spits the usual news:
the whole city, west and east, has been stuffed into a missile.

Translations from French by Sam Ross

COMMENTARY

A native of Fez, Mohamed El Amraoui has lived in Lyon, France, since 1989
& writes in both French & Arabic. He has been an active presence on the spo-
ken word circuit, as both organizer & participant, often working with musi-
cians, in France, Morocco & beyond. He also collaborates with calligraphers,
painters, & photographers & has had installations in a number of galleries.
Since 1991 he has taught creative writing in a wide range of places, such as
grade schools, high schools, the Maisons de la Poésie cultural centers of Rhône-
Alps, Rennes, Nantes, & other places, & in prisons, psychiatric hospitals, &
hostels. Among his many publications are *La Lune, les divisions* (Éditions
Poésie-rencontres, 1997), *Collision,* with drawings by Jacky Essirard (Éditions
Atelier de Villmorges, 2003), *De ce côté-ci et alentour* (L'Idée bleue, 2006),
Monodie pour un deuil, with engravings by Nelly Buret (Éditions Dana, 2006),
& *Accouchement de choses* (Dumerchez, 2008). With Catherine Charruau he
edited *Anthologie de la poésie marocaine contemporaine* (Bacchanales/Maison
de la Poésie Rhône-Alps, 2006).

Mohammed Hmoudane (b. Maaziz, 1968)

from *INCANDESCENCE*

to my late father

Here a burning
Alphabet
Is the pact forever sealed
Between yourself and essential
Fire

Fire
Whose hearth
You would have been
Eternally . . .

.

From a secretive explosion
Of wings into ashes
You descend heralding
An already
Future fire . . .

.

Flames flare
Hardly do you dream of spreading
Your wings syllable by
Incendiary syllable

Flames flare
Strata by cleared-away strata
By beating wings that slice the air
By time weighted down
With blood and corpses . . .

Revolve tombs
Revolve carcasses
Stars and ashes
Dazzling bright . . .

Rise and fly from my hand
And beyond the immense lesion
Rise and fly off

Pour down
Upon the dark cities
The spectral fire that I feed . . .

•

With a hand seeming
To return from afar
From opaque evasions
Laden with emptiness
And blazing light
You sculpt from still
Glowing ashes
Myriad meteoric
Appearances

Of that ageless
Fire
Clutching at you
From within

•

From a tree-like hand
With flames for fingers
Tangled
Like candlestick branches,
A drop falls
Ripe fruit oozing ink,

Blood
Quintessenced by night

•

It is the dust of eternity
It is the shipwreck in the spyglass
In which mirror shall we cast anchor
In which image shall we die:
I am the creature grazing
In ashen deserts
I am the creature licking at
The hemorrhaging mirage
You are the branching star
The star blazing
In ink . . .

.

Dim as the most dazzling day
The day mirrors and sky are extinguished
I remove my skin and enter silence
Embracing embers

On tiptoe I enter
Through doors thick and shadowy
That fall and at each step
Raise nights
Irrigated with wine swords and ash
I enter as if in battle . . .

Translation from French by Guy Bennett

COMMENTARY

Writes his translator Guy Bennett: "Mohammed Hmoudane was born in
Maaziz in 1968 and immigrated to France in 1989. His work has appeared in
numerous magazines and anthologies, and he has authored five collections
of poetry to date, most recently *Blanche Mécanique* (White Mechanism; La
Différence, 2005). He also translates, and in 2003 he edited a special section of
Moroccan poetry in the French journal *Po&sie*. He lives and works in the Saint-
Denis suburb of Paris."

Ouidad Benmoussa (b. Kasr el Kebir, 1969)

RESTAURANT TUYETS

I love the morning of your heart
The night of your eyes
The cardinal points of your smile
. . .
. . .
. . .
The candle
Pricks up its ears to
Warmth
We could no longer offer
. . .
. . .
. . .
The candle awaits
The birth
Of a kiss . . .

THIS PLANET . . . OUR BED

This planet readied itself
For me to dwell in you
No ocean in my eyes
But waves
No spring in my hands but sound

I am created by a kiss
For me to dwell in you
Feeling my way along your shudders
As if we were sky and
Earth
. . .
. . .
This planet . . . our bed

ROAD OF CLOUDS

Until now your visions were unclear to me
Your horizon, too far to help
I follow your steps
Melt in your flawless crystal
Tell you the torment of my secrets
In
Passion
I name you:
My sister nomad
Oh cloud,
So distant

Translations from Arabic by Emma Hayward

COMMENTARY

Born in 1969 in Ksar el Kebir, in northwestern Morocco, the Arabophone poet Ouidad Benmoussa established herself as a poet to watch with her first collection, *Li jidrun filhawa* (I Have a Root in the Air), published in Rabat in 2001. Selected poems from her second collection, *Between Two Clouds* (Rabat: Marsam, 2006), appeared in *Banipal* 30 (Autumn–Winter 2007). Benmoussa is a member of the board of the House of Poetry in Morocco & writes for the country's *Al-Alam* newspaper. Abdellatif Laâbi's anthology *La Poésie marocaine de l'Indépendence à nos jours* (La Différence, 2005) includes French translations of some of her poems, while *Banipal* 35 has others translated into English by Ali Issa.

Omar Berrada (b. Casablanca, 1978)

SUBTLE BONDS OF THE ENCOUNTER

Alfred Jarry (1873–1907) / bpNichol (1944–1988) / Ibn Arabi (1165–1240)

What if metaphysics was a branch of cinéma fantastique? The playwright, like all artists, seeks the truth — of which there are many. Take a florid Helvetian (St. Gria). The idea that there could be other apples from other gardens, and consequently other towns, made him burst out laughing. His quill split in two and the symbol cymbal screeched. But let's leave aside that which causes acidity, and begin by turning the page. After all I'd almost prefer that it be fake, if it's futile: f + utile, beyond the utile. Facetiousness makes fun of function. Remedy: 'pataphysic unction. Ubiquitous e-xcess expressed ironic in the fifth-letter-of-the-first-word-of-the-first-act.

$$\frac{arrh}{art} = \frac{shite}{shit} : \text{the Marchand du sel's phynancial consideration of a letter in excress}$$

'Pataphysics beats science at its own game. It goes beyond physics and even metaphysics. Jarry studied Nietzsche in high school at Rennes before Nietzsche had been translated. As for Darwin, he is a tautologist: the survivor survived. Instead of expounding the law of falling bodies towards a center, why not the void's ascent toward a periphery? Evolution is a Sisyphean task. Not for the species but for the divinity which submits it to ever more difficult tests. And the object always triumphs. The lab rat conditions the researcher to feed him each time he carries off an experiment. "Programmed" by Penelope's waiting, Odysseus cannot not return. The target determines the arrow's path. The crystal ball takes its revenge on the will to know. To each her clinamen.

Doctor Faustroll was born in Circassia, in 1898 (the 20th century was [-2] years old), and at the age of 63. I know a poet born of excellent humour, in Paris, in April 1973, at the age of 33. So begins his bio-bibliography. In fact, and it's little known, he is the age of fire since there's a fire his age.

There's 'pataphysics and "pataphysics. The first has one inventor, the second has two. Jarry's 'pataphysics is the science of imaginary solutions. The "pataphysics of McCaffery and Nichol is the literature of all imaginary sciences. Doubling the elision opens a perpetual quote. "Pataphysics is the science of generalized inversion, the transcendental law of the "patadox, the non-art of the absent. For a long time in the land of maples it made prestigious institutions flourish *en masse:*

The Toronto Research Group, the Institute for Linguistic Ontogenetics, the "Pataphysical Hardware Company, the Institute for Creative Misunderstanding, the Institute for Applied Fiction, the non-College of Epistemological Myopia, Writers in Support of Alphabet Archaeology.

It's from within one of these that bpNichol measures the attributes of discourse (weight of a thought, circumference of words, square root of a sentence) in the half-scientific, half-kabbalistic tones of his *probable systems*. Letters have numerical equivalents and combine with each other to form words just like digits form numbers. Our 26-letter alphabet is nothing but a calculation base. The series of letters, like that of numbers, is infinite. Every letter beyond Z can be written as a combination of letters between A and Z. In a given base, a word is nothing but the complex expression of a simple letter situated a certain distance from A. bp shows, with supporting equations, that in base V the word sun is in fact the 124,645,213th letter after A. Armed with this discovery, he announces an unprecedented project: to calculate, in a base to be defined, the letter corresponding to the whole of Proust's *Recherche*. Death cut him down, alas, in front of his still-warm madeleine.

The alphabet is a narrative—a movement along the abc. Every written word is a displacement of this primary narrative, every sign the precarious site of a disarticulation. Every text deconstructs a given even as it writes out a new one.

P.S.

Plato	*post*
Socrates	*scriptum*

For bpNichol letters are tied to an image of childhood. "In Wildwood Park in Winnipeg the streets and/or sections were named after the letters of the alphabet. So in learning the alphabet, I was also learning my way home." In 1950 a natural catastrophe forced the Nichols to move (Saskatoon, then Calgary). "but something happened to me after that flood. when the water receded i had changed. i had become H obsessed." In the alphabetic section of Winnipeg, bp and his family lived in section H.

Nothing distinguishes memories from other moments. It's only later that they make themselves known, by their scars.

For bp letters are at the center of language's activity, which is sacred activity. While young, he came across the word "stranglehold." What he saw: st. ranglehold. From then, all words beginning ST are saints, and there are many saints. They live in Cloudville whose houses and streets change, dissolve and reform without end. bp frees words from their function. Who would dare to sit upon St. Rap-on?

bp is a consistent man. He marries Ellie, an ex-nun, and names his master work *The Martyrology* (9 volumes). A martyrology is a history of the lives of saints. *The Martyrology* is the history of an encounter with language.

Among other minor works, bp composes The Martyrology of Saint And, The Sorrows of Saint Orm, Saint Reat and the Four Winds of the World. *Le Petit Robert on CD-Rom, version 1.3 [1997], lists 448 St. words in French. One day someone will have to write* The Martyrs of Saint Alin, The Passion of Saint Akhanov, *or* Saint Ring and the Dance of the Seven Veils.

Konfessions of an Elizabethan Fan Dancer. bp confesses a curiosity in the Orient. Arabic and its calligraphic dances spark his unfulfilled desire for a comparative alphabetics. Islamic esoterism abounds in texts on the science of letters which Ibn Arabi, seal of the saints, named *the science of Jesus.* Semitic wisdom sees in letters a mediating principle (which joins in separating, separates in joining) between the creator and his creatures.

The production of the physical world and the production of language are one.

> Rotation of the spheres
> The primary Elements mingle
> Heat frigidity dryness humidity
> Engendering superior letters
> A being of limits   —   فرح
> Negation of all form
> of relation   (eternity)

Letters are the limit of the physical world.

No vocalization	=	inert body	أوْ
		unfigured breath	أوْ
		repose	أوْ
dead language			

Not signs of sounds but soundless signs.

I go beyond duality: I take off both sandals
I invent an order to match my infirmity
Strides forth the truthful foot
Archangel Israfel blows his trumpet

    a   u   i
open   purse   retract

Makes an image
position of the lips   shadings of the exhale
Three vowels in the world
of consonants among two
planes subtle bonds
of the encounter with djinn or angel
ascending   descending
               horizontal

The vowels حَرَكَات are the body's movement.

Within writing the solitary alif
aerial letter   vertical absolute
holds itself straight up
"Every thing attaches itself to it
and it attaches itself to nothing"
So the origin of all letters
is not one of them
"The alif supporting the hamza
is a half-letter
and the hamza the other half"
For that which joins also separates

Fusion without confusion is only show of science.

Translation from French by Stephen Ross

Omar Berrada is a writer, translator, & critic who grew up in Casablanca & lives in Paris. Between 2004 & 2007 he was a producer for French national radio & hosted *La nuit la poésie* & *Lumières d'août* on the France Culture channel. He curated the Tangier International Book Salon in 2008 & hosted talks & conferences at the Centre Pompidou in Paris between 2006 & 2009. He currently directs the library & translation center at Dar al-Ma'mûn in Marrakech. He is a member of Double Change, a French & American association devoted to poetry & translation, & the intercultural arts foundation Tamaas. He recently cotranslated Jalal Toufic's *The Withdrawal of Tradition Past a Surpassing Disaster* (Paris: Les Prairies ordinaires, 2011).

Permission for the inclusion in this gathering of the following material has been graciously granted by the publishers and individuals indicated below.

Texts

Nourredine Aba: *Le Chart Perdu au pays retrouvé/Lost Song of a Rediscovered Country* (Bilingual Edition) (Paris: L'Harmattan, 1999). Translation © 1999 by Cynthia Hahn. Used by permission of the translator.

Sidi Abderrahman el Mejdub: "Some Quatrains." Translation © 2012 by Abdelfetah Chenni. Used by permission of the translator.

Ismael Abdoun: "Faun-eye'd iceberg burn." From *Souffles* 10/11 (1968). © 1968 by Ismael Abdoun. Used by permission of the author.

Emir Abd El Kader: "I Am Love." Translation © 2012 by Sylvia Mae Gorelick and Miles Joris-Peyrafitte. Used by permission of the translators. "The Secrets of the Lam-Alif." From *The Spiritual Writings of Amir 'Abd al-Kader*, edited by Michel Chodkiewicz, translated by a team under the direction of James Chrestensen and Tom Manning. (SUNY Press, 1995). © 1995 by SUNY Press. Used by permission of SUNY Press.

Abraham Abulafia: *The Book of The Letter.* Translation © 2012 by Jack Hirschman. "How He Went as Messiah in the Name of Angel Raziel to Confront the Pope." Translation © by Harris Lenowitz. Used by permission of the translator. *Life of the World to Come:* "Circles." From Jerome Rothenberg and Harris Lenowitz, *Exiled in the Word: Poems & Other Visions of the Jews from Tribal Times to Present* (Port Townsend, WA: Copper Canyon Press: 1978). © 1978, 1989 by Jerome Rothenberg. Used by permission of Jerome Rothenberg.

Abu Hamid al-Gharnati: "Description of the Lighthouse of Alexandria." From *Tuhfat al-Albab.* Translation © 2012 by Peter Cockelbergh. Used by permission of the translator.

Abu Madyan Shu'ayb: "The Qasida in Ra" and "The Qasida in Mim." Translations © 2012 by Vincent J. Cornell. Used by permission of the translator. "You Will Be Served in Your Glass." Translation © 2012 by Sylvia Mae Gorelick and Miles Joris-Peyrafitte. Used by permission of the translators.

Al-Mahdi Acherchour: *Retour au Tour Manqué* (prspos2éditions, 2003). "In the Emptiness." © 2003 by Al-Mahdi Acherchour.

Ismaël Aït Djaafar: *Wail of the Arab Beggars of the Casbah.* Translation © 2012 by Jack Hirschman.

Al-Hani Ben Guenoun: "O Unfair Lady!" From *Ya Dhalma*. Translation © 2012 by Abdelfetah Chenni. Used by permission of the translator.

Abdelmajid Benjelloun: "Eternity Comes Down on the Side of Love," "The Flute of Origins, or the Taciturn Dance," and "A Woman to Love as One Would Love to Revive after Death." From *La poésie marocaine de l'Indépendance à nos jours*, edited by Abdellatif Laâbi. © 2005 by La Différence. Translations © 2012 by Rosmarie Waldrop.

Tahar Ben Jelloun: *Harrouda* © 2010 by Editions Gallimard. Translation © 2010 by Charlotte Mandell. © 2010 by Gallimard. Used by permission of the translator.

Ouidad Benmoussa: "Restaurant Tuyets," "Road of Clouds," and "This Planet . . . Our Bed." Translations © 2012 Emma Hayward, PhD candidate, University of Pennsylvania. Used by permission of the translator.

Sidi Mohammed Ben Msaieb: excerpt from *O Pigeon Messenger!* Translation © 2012 by Abdelfetah Chenni. Used by permission of the translator.

Mohammed Bennis: "For You" and "Letter to Ibn Hazm." From *The Book of Love*. "Seven Birds." Translation by Fady Joudah.

Boumediene Ben Sahla: "I Saw a Gazelle Today. . . . " From *Wahd al-Ghazal Rit al-Youm*. Translation © 2012 by Abdelfetah Chenni. Used by permission of the translator.

Midani Ben Salah: "Avec elles, dans le train." From *Ecrivains de Tunisie*, edited and translated by Taoufik Baccar and Salah Garmadi. © 1981 Actes Sud. Used by permission of Actes Sud.

Mohamed Ben Sghir: "Lafjar (Dawn)" and "Ya'l-Warchan (O Dove)." Translations © 2012 by Abdelfetah Chenni. Used by permission of the translator.

Ahmed Ben Triki: "My Pain Endures . . . " and "Burned to the Depths of My Soul!." From *Tal Nahbi* and *Sha'lat Niran Fi Kbadi*. Translations © 2012 by Abdelfetah Chenni. Used by permission of the translator.

Jacques Berque: *"Truth and Poetry" on the Seksawa Tribe*. Translation © 2012 by Peter Cockelbergh. Used by permission of the translator.

Omar Berrada: "Subtle Bonds of the Encounter." © 2011 by Omar Berrada. Translation by Stephen Ross. First published in Wave Composition: www.wavecomposition.com/2011/og/subtle-bonds-of-the-encounter/. Used by permission of the author.

Hafsa bint al-Hajj Arrakuniyya: "Eight Poems." Translation © 2012 by Abdullah al-Udhari. Used by permission of the translator.

Wallada bint al-Mustakfi: "Six Poems." Translations © 2012 by Abdullah al-Udhari. Used by permission of the translator.

Hafsa bint Hamdun: "Four Poems." Translations © 2012 by Abdullah al-Udhari. Used by permission of the translator.

Limam Boicha: "Boughs of Thirst," "Existence," and "The Roads of the South." Used by permission of the author.

Faraj Bou al-Isha: "Here I Am," "Sleep," "Wait," and "Where Does This Pain Come From?" Translations © 2012 by Khaled Mattawa. Used by permission of the translator.

Rachid Boudjedra: From *Rain (Diary of an Insomniac)*. Translation © 2012 Angela M. Brewer. Used by permission of the translator and the author. Originally published by Les Mains Secrètes (New York and Tunis, 2002).

Paul Bowles: "Africa Minor," excerpt from pp. 28–33. From *Their Heads Are Green and Their Hands Are Blue* by Paul Bowles. © 1957, 1963 by Paul Bowles. Used by permission of Harper Collins Publishers.

Callimachus: Translations © 2012 by George Economou. Used by permission.

Fadhila Chabbi: "The Blind Goddess" and "Engraving Twenty -Nine." From *The Poetry of Arab Women*, edited by Nathalie Handal (Brooklyn and Northhampton, MA: Interlink

Ahmed Ibn 'Ajiba: Maxims and qasida from *The Autobiography of a Moroccan Sufi, Ahmad Ibn Ajiba* (Fons Vitae Press, 1999), introduced and translated from the Arabic by Jean-Louis Michon. English translations © 1999 by David Streight. Used by permission of Fons Vitae.

Ibn Arabi: "'Gentle now, doves',", "I Wish I Knew if They Knew," "'O my two friends,'" and "Who is Here for a Braveheart." Translation by Michael Sells. © 2000 by Michael Sells. First appeared in *Stations of Desire: Love Elegies from Ibn Arabi and New Poems* (Jerusalem: Ibis Editions). Used by permission of Ibis Editions. "The Wisdom of Reality in the Words of Isaac." Translation by R. W. J. Austin. From *Ibn Al'Arabi, the Bezels of Wisdom*. © 1980 by the Paulist Press, London.

Ibn Baja/Avenpace: "Chapter XIII" from *The Governance of the Solitary*, translation by Lawrence Berman, in *Medieval Political Philosophy: A Sourcebook*, R. Lerner and M. Mahdi (eds.). © 1972 Cornell University Press. Reprinted by permission of Ralph Lerner.

Ibn Battuta: *Rihla* translated by H. A. R. Gibb as *Ibn Battuta: Travels in Asia and Africa 1325–1354* (London: Broadway House, 1929). Available in the "Internet Medieval Sourcebook," at www.fordham.edu/halsall/source/1354-ibnbattuta.html.

Ibn Darradj al-Qastalli: *Ode in Praise of Khairan al-'Amiri, Emir of Almería* and *Ode in Praise of al-Mansur al-'Amiri, Emir of Córdoba*. Translation © 2012 by Abdelfetah Chenni. Used by permission of the translator.

Abraham ibn Ezra: "'I have a garment'." Translation © 2012 by Robert Mezey. Used by permission of the translator.

Moses ibn Ezra: "Drinking Song" and "Song." From *The Collected Poems of Carl Rakosi* (Orono, ME: National Poetry Foundation, University of Maine, 1986). Translations by Carl Rakosi. Used by permission of The Estate of Carl Rakosi.

Salomon ibn Gabirol: "The 16-Year-Old Poet." From *The Crown of Kingdom*. From Jerome Rothenberg and Harris Lenowitz, *Exiled in the Word: Poems & Other Visions of the Jews from Tribal Times to Present* (Port Townsend, WA: Copper Canyon Press, 1989). © 1978, 1989 by Jerome Rothenberg. Used by permission of Jerome Rothenberg.

Ibn Hamdis: "He Said, Remembering Sicily and His Home, Syracuse." From *The Kingdom of Sicily, 1100–1250: A Literary History,* by Karla Mallette (University of Pennsylvania Press, 2005), pp. 134–137. © 2005 by the University of Pennsylvania Press. Used with permission of the University of Pennsylvania Press.

Ibn Hani al-Andalusi: "Al-Jilnar" and "Extinction is the Truth." Translations © 2012 by Abdelfetah Chenni. Used by permission of the translator.

Yusuf ibn Harun al-Ramadi: "Hugging Letters and Beauty Spots," "Silver Breast," "Gold Nails," "The Swallow," and "O Rose . . . " Translations © 2012 by Abdelfetah Chenni. Used by permission of the translator.

Ibn Hazm: *The Neck-Ring of the Dove*. Translations by A. J. Arberry. © 1953 by Luzac Oriental.

Ibn Jubayr: *The Travels of Ibn Jubayr*. Translated by R. J. C. Broadhurst. © 2008 by APH Publishing Corp.

Ibn Khafadja: "The River." From *Andalusian Poems* (Boston: David R. Godine, Publisher, 1993). Translation © 1993 Christopher Middleton and Leticia Garza-Falcón. Used by permission of the translators.

Ibn Khaldun: "The Craft of Poetry and the Way of Learning It" and "Poetry and Prose Work with Words, and Not With Ideas." From *The Muqaddimah*. © 2005 by Princeton University Press. Used by permission of Princeton University Press.

Ibn Labbana: "Al-Mu'tamid and His Family Go into Exile." Translated by Cola Franzen, from *Poems of Arab Andalusia*. © 1989 by Cola Franzen. Used by permission of City

Moncef Mezghanni: "A Duck's Speech" and "The Land of Narrow Dreams." Translations by Sinan Antoon.

Mbarka Mint al-Barra': "Poetry and I." Literal translation by Joel Mitchell, finalized translation by the Poetry Translation Workshop.

Aïcha Mint Chighaly: "Nostalgic Song about Life" and "Praise on the Site of Aftout." From Aïcha Mint Chighaly, *Azawan the Art of the Griots* (Paris: INEDIT/Maison des Cultures du Monde, 1996), compact disc. Translation of traditional songs by Sheikh Mohammed el-Arbi and J. Crews. Used by permission of INEDIT.

Si Mohand: *Si Mohand's Journey from Maison-Carrée to Michelet* and three other poems from *Les poèmes de Si Mohand* (Editions de Minuit, 1960). Translation by Mouloud Feraoun.

Zaghloul Morsy: "From a Reticent Sun." From *La poésie marocaine de l'indépendence à nos jours,* edited by Abdellatif Laâbi. © 2005 by La Différence.

Amel Moussa: "A Formal Poem" and "Love Me." Translations © 2012 by Khaled Mattawa. Used by permission of the translator.

Mohammed Mrabet: "Si Mokhtar." © 1974 by Mohamed Mrabet.

Musa ibn Maimon: *The Guide for the Perplexed*. Translation by Shlomo Pines. © 1974 University of Chicago Press. Used by permission of the University of Chicago Press.

Shams Nadir: *The Athanor* and "Echoes from Isla-Negra." © 2001 by Shams Nadir. Translation © 2012 by Patrick Williamson. Previously published in *The Parley Tree: Poets from French-Speaking Africa and the Arab World* (Arc Publications, 2012). Used by permission of the publisher.

Mririda N'aït Attik: "The Bad Lover," "The Brooch," and "What Do You Want?" Translations © 1974 by Daniel Halpern and Paula Paley.

Khaled Najjar: "Boxes," "Poems 1–5," and "Stone Castle." Translations © 2012 by Khaled Mattawa. Used by permission of the translator.

Hassan Najmi: "The Blueness of Evening," "Couplets," "The Train Yard," and "The Window." Translations © 2012 by Khaled Mattawa. Used by permission of the translator.

Samira Negrouche: "Coffee without Sugar." © 2010 by Samira Negrouche. Translation © 2012 by Martin Sorrell.

Laila Neihoum: "Melting Sun." Translation © 2012 by Laila Neihoum and Mohamed Hassan. Used by permission of the author.

Mostafa Nissabouri: *Approach to the Desert Space*. Translation © 2001 by Guy Bennett. © 2001 Mindmade Books. Used by permission of the translator.

Samia Ouederni: "For Tunisia." © 1998 by Samia Ouederni.

Cécile Oumhani: "Young Woman at the Terrace." © 2006 by Cécile Oumhani. Used by permission of the author.

Jean Pélégri: "Open the Pebble." Translation © 2012 by Kit Schluter. Used by permission of the translator.

Moncef Ouahibi: *Under Sargon Boulus's Umbrella*. Translation by Sinan Antoon.

Cheikha Rimitti: "The Girls of Bel Abbès," "He Crushes Me," and "The Worst of All Shelters." © 1993 by Marie Virolle-Souibès and Editions Karthala.

Emmanuel Roblès: *Mirror Suite* from *Cristal des jours, suivi de La Rose de l'énigme*. © 1990 Editions du Seuil. Used by permission of the publisher.

Abi Sharif al-Rundi: *Nuniyya* From *Translations of Eastern Poetry and Prose*. Translation by Reynold A. Nicholson. © 1987 by the Paulist Press, London. Used by permission of the publisher.

Abderrazak Sahli: "Clerare Drac." Used by permission of the Estate of Abderrazak Sahli.

Hamid Tibouchi: *The Young Traveler and the Old-Fashioned Ghost.* © 1977 by Hamid Tibouchi. Translation © 2012 by Eric Sellin. Used by permission of the translator.

Qasi Udifella: Four poems from *Poésie berbère et identité: Qasi Udifella héraut des At Sidi Braham*, edited by Tassadit Yacine. © 1987 by Maison des sciences de l'homme.

Al-Munsif al-Wahaybi: "Ceremony," "The Desert," and "In the Arab House." From *Modern Arabic Poetry*, edited by Salma Khadra Jayyusi and Naomi Shihab Nye. © 1991 by Columbia University Press. Used with permission of the publisher.

Mubarak Wassat: "Balcony," "Innocence," and "The Time of the Assassins." © 2010 by Mubarak Wassat. Used by permission of the author.

Kateb Yacine: *Nedjma.* Translation © 1961 by Richard Howard. Used by permission of the translator. *Le Polygone Étoilé.* © 1966, 1994 Editions du Seuil. Used by permission of the publisher.

Chejdan Mahmud Yazid: "Enough!," "The Expectorated Scream," and "Sirocco." Used by permission of the author.

Djibril Zakaria Sall: "To Nelson Mandela." Translation © 2012 by Sylvia Mae Gorelick and Miles Joris-Peyrafitte. Used by permission of the translators.

Abdallah Zrika: *Drops from Black Candles.* © 1998 by La Différence. Used by permission of the author. *Some Prose.* © 1998 by Abdallah Zrika. Used by permission of the author.

Figures

Abraham Abulafia: "Circles." From *Life of the World to Come* from *Exiled in the Word,* edited by J. Rothenberg and H. Lenowitz (Port Townsend, WA: Copper Canyon Press, 1989). Direct translation from one of several manuscripts of *Hayei ha-Olam ha-Ba* in the British Museum; the work is sometimes called *Sefer ha-Igulim,* "The Book of Circles."

Malek Alloula: Kabyle woman covering herself with the haik from *Le harem colonial* (Geneva and Paris: Editions Slatkine, 1981). © 1981 by Editions Slatkine.

Andalusian cursive script: From Abdelkebir Khatibi and Mohammed Sijelmassi, *The Splendor of Islamic Calligraphy* (New York: Thames and Hudson, 1996). Photo used by permission of the Estate of Mohammed Sijelmassi.

Archaic Kufic script: From Abdelkebir Khatibi and Mohammed Sijelmassi, *The Splendor of Islamic Calligraphy* (New York: Thames and Hudson, 1996). Photo used by permission of the Estate of Mohammed Sijelmassi.

Hawad: Transcribed poem from author's manuscript. Used by permission of the author.

Ibn al-Arabi: Manuscript page used from *Qantara* 28 (summer 1998), p. 41.

Maghrebian scripts: From Abdelkebir Khatibi and Mohammed Sijelmassi, *The Splendor of Islamic Calligraphy* (New York: Thames and Hudson, 1996). Photo used by permission of the Estate of Mohammed Sijelmassi.

Massinissa tablet and inscription: Used by permission of the Musée National du Bardo, Tunis.

Al-Qandusi: Bismillah and the word *Paradise* from Abdelkebir Khatibi and Mohammed Sijelmassi, *The Splendor of Islamic Calligraphy* (New York: Thames and Hudson, 1996). Photo used by permission of the Estate of Mohammed Sijelmassi.

Abderrazak Sahli: "Clerare Drac." From *Le Cahier du refuge* 31 (November 1993), pp. 12–13.

Shawia amulets: From Mathéa Gaudry, *La Femme Chaouia de l'aurès* (Paris: Chihab-Awal, 1998), p. 223.

Tassili cave painting: From Henri Lhote, *Vers d'Autres Tassilis* (Paris: Arthaud, 1976).

INDEX OF AUTHORS

Designer: Nola Burger
Text: Sabon
Display: Gill Sans
Compositor: BookMatters, Berkeley
Printer and binder: Maple Press